Financial Accounting and Reporting

Bill Collins and
John McKeith

London Boston Burr Ridge, IL Dubuque, IA Madison, WI New York San Francisco St. Louis
Bangkok Bogotá Caracas Kuala Lumpur Lisbon Madrid Mexico City Milan Montreal New Delhi
Santiago Seoul Singapore Sydney Taipei Toronto

Financial Accounting and Reporting
Bill Collins and John McKeith
ISBN-13 978-0-07-711452-7
ISBN-10 0-07-711452-3

Published by McGraw-Hill Education
Shoppenhangers Road
Maidenhead
Berkshire
SL6 2QL
Telephone: 44 (0) 1628 502 500
Fax: 44 (0) 1628 770 224
Website: www.mcgraw-hill.co.uk

British Library Cataloguing in Publication Data
A catalogue record for this book is available from the British Library

Library of Congress Cataloguing in Publication Data
The Library of Congress data for this book has been applied for from the Library of Congress

Senior Acquisitions Editor: Mark Kavanagh
Development Editor: Karen Harlow
Marketing Manager: Vanessa Boddington
Senior Production Editor: James Bishop

Text design by Hard Lines
Cover design by Adam Renvoize
Printed and bound in Great Britain by Ashford Colour Press

The **McGraw-Hill** Companies

Dedication

To my grandchildren, Chloe, Calum and Claudia.
Bill Collins

To my beautiful Flossie who sadly died before this book was finished.
John McKeith

Brief Table of Contents

Detailed Table of Contents

Preface

As business becomes more complex, accounting in its contribution to reporting financial information, does also. The importance of a solid understanding of the basic underpinnings of accounting has never been more important. Complicated accounting transactions have become the norm in many organisations, with the result that a top-down approach to learning is no longer possible. For the business student of today, such transactions, and their implications, can be fully understood only when the individual has a firm theoretical and practical understanding of the accounting issues involved.

Aim of the book

The aim of this textbook is to bridge the gap between introductory and so-called 'intermediate' textbooks. Many current intermediate texts fail in their attempts to get the main points across to students because they are too complex; examples used in such texts are usually too long and try to illustrate too many issues at one time. Often the organisation of material is complex and there is no clear structure to follow. This book's intention is to build on the basic knowledge gained by students from an introductory course and take them to a full level of understanding of the issues involved. Examples are used frequently throughout each chapter to deal with issues on a point-by-point basis, rather than trying to cover all points at once. Having acquired the basic knowledge and understanding, the book then leads the student to evaluate existing practice and, hence, encourages them to challenge it. This builds confidence in dealing with accounting issues, and provides a better way to acquire essential knowledge.

Unique section-by-section approach

This text is unique in its approach to achieving its aims: each chapter is divided into three sections – Basic Principles, Intermediate Issues and Advanced Aspects.

Section 1: Basic Principles

The basic, or introductory, sections set out the basic concepts and introduce the accounting issues involved so that the student is aware of the accounting problems relating to that particular topic. Many of the issues will already have been introduced at Level 1, so this is useful revision and also extremely helpful in ensuring that the student is actually aware of the reasons why certain accounting treatments are being adopted. This text does not encourage the adage 'that's what you do because that's what you do'. These introductory sections explain and explore principles rather than confusing the reader by making reference to accounting standards and legislation. Many examples illustrate accounting issues, however the authors are also very much of the opinion that practice makes perfect so each chapter has several Progress Points for students to test their understanding. Progress Points are a mixture of discussive and numerical questions, and are distributed throughout each chapter to give the student an opportunity to put into practice their earlier reading. Each Progress Point has a fully worked solution so the workings can be understood.

Section 2: Intermediate Issues

The intermediate sections allow students to build on the knowledge gained from the basic sections with references to accounting standards and legislation. Having acquired the 'tools' to do so in the introductory sections, the book encourages the student not simply to accept current practices but to evaluate and challenge them. Examples and Progress Points are used to consolidate learning. As is often the case in accountancy, a full understanding of a particular topic necessitates references to other concepts that, although essential to the understanding of the initial concept, have themselves not yet been explained. This book recognises this problem and ensures that there is a logical, step-by-step flow to each chapter.

Section 3: Advanced Aspects

The advanced aspects sections consider advanced accounting applications and situations as well as covering current issues relevant to the chapter topic. Each section within each chapter is a complete, self-contained unit. It is therefore not necessary to cover the whole of a chapter before moving on to the next chapter.

Theory and practice

This is a practical book, but one that does not shun the importance of theoretical underpinnings. What it does not do is prescribe a theoretical approach. Unlike other texts, a 'what if' approach is taken with the examples so that several permutations of a problem are dealt with to ensure a deeper level of understanding so that new problems encountered in academia, or indeed professional work, can be dealt with. Each chapter contains a critical appraisal of the existing treatment of particular accounting situations. The accounting practices and procedures prescribed by the standards are critically reviewed and their abilities to provide the user of the financial statements with their required information questioned. Accounting standards do not simply remain set in stone; they evolve as new issues arise and new complexities are introduced. By adopting an unbiased approach to explaining the accounting issues involved, and by using numerical examples to illustrate the principles, this book will stimulate students to challenge the theory behind the practice.

The audience for the text

Although the book is aimed at second-year accounting students at universities, the emphasis placed on explaining the accounting issues involved in the introductory sections of each chapter will also make it useful to students undergoing professional training who perhaps have no prior accountancy knowledge. The stepped approach will also make the book useful to those students undertaking professional examinations. Finally, the chapter summaries make this a useful text for accountants in practice by providing a quick reference for specific technical points, issues or problems.

The IASB Framework

It is generally accepted that the basic objective underlying the preparation of financial statements is to provide useful information for decision making. Frequent reference is made throughout the book to the IASB's Framework for the Preparation and Presentation of Financial Statements. This book follows the conclusion reached by the Framework that not all of the information needs of the various user groups can be met by financial statements. In doing so, the rationale is to strive for solutions. It is essential that the standard of reporting is continually improved if examples such as Enron are to be stopped from bringing this elegant discipline into disrepute. Throughout the text, emphasis is given to the usefulness and effectiveness of the information provided by adhering to accounting principles and standards.

Learning features

At undergraduate level, the study of accounting can often feel far removed from reality. The text overcomes this problem by including within some chapters coverage of the 'Position in practice'. These sections outline the problems the practising accountant faces in relation to the treatment of certain accounting situations, and explains how they are dealt with in practice.

Most texts refer to examples from plcs, which often bear no relation to the topic being explained and can be confusing. They overlook the most important issue in using real-life examples. The whole purpose of financial reporting is the presentation of financial information within sets of financial statements. The use of extract details from real-life accounts is the final product of the computations. Real-life examples are therefore used to illustrate disclosure requirements and are explained, linked and integrated with the text.

Please see the Guided Tour on page xv for a full summary of the learning features in the text.

Chapter content

- **Chapter 1**: the regulation of accounting is introduced where it complements the form and content of financial statements prescribed by IAS 1. The components of financial statements are outlined, and their preparation illustrated and demonstrated. Corporate governance issues arising as a result of previous accounting scandals are also dealt with. Conceptual frameworks are reviewed and a study made of the alternative measurement bases available to historical cost. Each of the main balance sheet items are then dealt with in turn. The book adopts a balance sheet approach, follows the balance sheet format as illustrated in IAS 1 And deals with each of the main balance sheet items in the same top-down order.

- **Chapters 2 and 3**: non-current assets are dealt with, and in particular the recognition and measurement issues arising as a result of following a historic cost basis of accounting. The quality of the information being presented by following generally accepted accounting principles is questioned.

- **Chapter 4**: this chapter looks at leasing and off balance sheet finance, again questioning the usefulness of the information provided by following the prescribed accounting standard treatment.

- **Chapter 5**: current assets and, in particular, inventories and construction contracts are covered. Here the emphasis is on the accounting for such items but with extensive coverage of the measurement issues arising.

- **Chapter 6**: this chapter looks at share capital and reserves and then, in relation to capital maintenance, the increase and reduction of share capital is examined in detail.

- **Chapter 7**: following a study of the Framework definition of a liability, this chapter considers in detail the importance of the distinction between those liabilities that are third-party liabilities and those liabilities that are due to the owners. Finally, the recognition and measurement problems associated with provisions are dealt with.

- **Chapter 8**: the accounting for taxation and in particular the concept of deferred tax is covered in this chapter. Emphasis is on the usefulness of the information given to users by adhering to the accounting standards in providing for deferred tax.

- **Chapter 9**: this chapter examines the preparation and usefulness of cash flow statements.

- **Chapter 10**: accounting for group structures and the preparation of consolidated financial statements is covered. Both practical issues and theoretical underpinnings of group accounting are considered in detail.

- **Chapter 11**: this chapter looks at foreign currency issues and covers the accounting treatment of single transactions through to the accounting requirements for a foreign-based subsidiary.

■ **Chapter 12**: having covered the component parts making up a set of financial statements, the final chapter analyses the information given within a traditional set of financial statements. It deals with the interpretation of financial statements and, while the calculation of key ratios is demonstrated, the emphasis is on the interpretation of these ratios, and how they can be used to explain what has happened and to predict what will happen.

Many texts fail to take account of the fact that their readers may be coming across issues for the first time and appear to take the view that, simply by reading chapters, students will automatically gain the required understanding. This text has been written with a strong emphasis on readability and understandability from the introductory sections through to the advanced aspects. It has been written with the student in mind.

Guided Tour

Learning Outcomes

These set out the knowledge and skills you should have acquired by the end of the chapter.

Sections

Each chapter is split into three sections – Basic Principles, Intermediate Issues and Advanced Aspects – to progress your learning in a step-by-step manner. Each section is a self-contained unit.

It is important to remember that this solution sh...
and not for publication. Financial statements for...

Section 2: Interm...

1.5 The regulatory framework...
financial statements

Company financial statements that are prepared for...
by law and by accounting standards in order to provi...
the information provided in company financial state...
In order for comparison to be meaningful, publish...

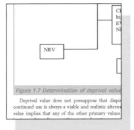

Figure 1.7 Determination of deprival value

Deprival value does not presuppose that dispo...
continued use is always a viable and realistic alterna...
value implies that any of the other primary values...

Figures and Tables

Figures and tables are distributed throughout chapters, as well as many boxed financial statements to help you apply theory to practice.

Examples

The text is bursting with fully worked examples to explain concepts, and real-life examples to illustrate disclosure requirements. Logica, a leading IT and business services company, is referred to throughout the chapters to demonstrate financial accounting in practice. All examples are explained, linked and integrated with the text.

situations where determining the cost of an a...

Example 1

A company buys a machine costing £20,000. T...
installed in the company's factory in Edinburg...
Edinburgh is estimated to be £500. In order...
company has to pay installation costs of £1,00...
Clearly the purchase price of £20,000 is pa...
are the costs of transport and installation to...
factory and then subsequently installed, it w...
transport and of installation are, therefore, n...
costs should be added to the cost of the asse...
benefit to the company at all.
In Example 1, above, while the purchase p...
concerned, the *cost* of the machine is £21...
installation costs).

Progress Points

These are a mixture of text and numerical questions, which give you an opportunity to put into practice your earlier learning. Each Progress Point has a fully worked solution so the workings can be understood.

Summaries

Each section concludes with a brief summary of the main issues covered. There is also a Chapter Summary that provides a brief synopsis of the main provisions of the accounting standards relevant to each topic. These offer you a further opportunity to consolidate and check your understanding of each topic.

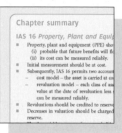

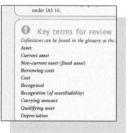

Key Terms for Review

These are highlighted throughout the text and cross-referenced at the ends of chapters. Definitions can be found in the Glossary at the end of the text.

End of Chapter Questions

Review questions allow you to check and assimilate the knowledge acquired from the chapter. Exercise questions offer an opportunity to test and demonstrate your learning. Questions range from foundation level through to a level found in most professional examinations.

Technology to enhance learning and teaching

Visit www.mcgraw-hill.co.uk/textbooks/collins **today**

Online Learning Centre (OLC)

After completing each chapter, log on to the supporting Online Learning Centre website. Take advantage of the study tools offered to reinforce the material you have read in the text, and to develop your knowledge of accounting in a fun and effective way.

Resources for students include:

- *Learning Outcomes*
- *Glossary by chapter*
- *Three sets of multiple choice questions per chapter at different levels*

Also available for lecturers:

- *Solutions Manual*
- *PowerPoint slides*
- *E2 Test Online test bank*

Test Bank available in McGraw-Hill EZ Test Online

A test bank of hundreds of questions is available to lecturers adopting this book for their module. A range of questions is provided for each chapter, including multiple-choice, true or false, and short answer or essay questions. The questions are identified by type, difficulty and topic to help you to select questions that best suit your needs, and are accessible through an easy-to-use online testing tool, **McGraw-Hill EZ Test Online**.

McGraw-Hill EZ Test Online is accessible to busy academics virtually anywhere – in their office, at home or while travelling – and eliminates the need for software installation. Lecturers can choose from question banks associated with their adopted textbook or easily create their own questions. They also have access to hundreds of banks and thousands of questions created for other McGraw-Hill titles. Multiple versions of tests can be saved for delivery on paper or online through WebCT, Blackboard and other course management systems. When created and delivered though EZ Test Online, students' tests can be marked immediately, saving lecturers time and providing prompt results to students.

To register for this FREE resource, visit www.eztestonline.com

Custom Publishing Solutions: Let us help make our **content** your **solution**

At McGraw-Hill Education our aim is to help lecturers to find the most suitable content for their needs delivered to their students in the most appropriate way. Our custom publishing solutions offer the ideal combination of content delivered in the way that best suits lecturers and students.

Our custom publishing programme offers lecturers the opportunity to select just the chapters or sections of material they wish to deliver to their students from a database called Primis at www.primisonline.com

Primis contains over two million pages of content from:

- textbooks
- professional books
- case books – Harvard Articles, Insead, Ivey, Darden, Thunderbird and BusinessWeek
- Taking Sides – debate materials.

Across the following imprints:

- McGraw-Hill Education
- Open University Press
- Harvard Business School Press
- US and European material.

There is also the option to include additional material authored by lecturers in the custom product – this does not necessarily have to be in English.

We will take care of everything from start to finish in the process of developing and delivering a custom product to ensure that lecturers and students receive exactly the material needed in the most suitable way.

With a Custom Publishing Solution, students enjoy the best selection of material deemed to be the most suitable for learning everything they need for their courses – something of real value to support their learning. Teachers are able to use exactly the material they want, in the way they want, to support their teaching on the course.

Please contact your local McGraw-Hill representative with any questions or alternatively contact Warren Eels e: warren_eels@mcgraw-hill.com.

Acknowledgements

Author acknowledgements

Accountancy is a brilliant subject. My interest originated at school following a talk by a local chartered accountant, John Keay at a careers evening. At University it was financial reporting that gripped my attention and my lecturers, Robin Limmack and my co-author Bill Collins taught the issues in such a manner that ultimately made me want to write a book on the subject. On graduating I gained a training contract to become a chartered accountant. During my contract I received great encouragement and advice from Gordon Beange, David Tait and Bill and the late Margaret Charles, all of whom were instrumental in me choosing my ultimate career path. Throughout all of this my parents Alastair and Isobel provided great support and guidance.

Working in general practice and teaching at Stirling University put me in a privileged position enabling me to bring theory to life by drawing upon my day-to-day experiences. It also made me realise that there were alternatives to presenting financial information. By this time writing a book was no longer just a vague ambition but a necessity. I could tell that my students struggled with their existing texts and that there was a need for a different approach.

In terms of the book itself, thanks must first of all go to Mark Kavanagh of McGraw-Hill for signing Bill and I up. My sincere thanks goes to my secretary, Brenda Soreide, who has done a superb job typing the majority of the manuscript and who managed to decipher my writing, abbreviations, arrows and boxes. Thanks also must go to Karen Harlow of McGraw-Hill who pushed when required and ensured that all deadlines were adhered to.

Finally, my biggest thanks is to my wife Evelyn who, without complaint, gave up her own evenings, many weekends and her dining room table over the last 3 years so that I could write this book. Without her support and understanding it would simply have remained an unfulfilled ambition.

John McKeith

I would like to thank Karen Harlow and Mark Kavanagh at McGraw-Hill for all the help and encouragement given during the darker moments of writing. I would also like to thank my wife, Janette, without whose support the project would not have been completed.

Bill Collins

Publisher acknowledgements

The publisher would like to thank the following reviewers for their comments at various stages in the text's development:

Roger Alderman, London Metropolitan University
Danny Chow, Birkbeck, University of London
Ken Delaney-Moore, University of Sheffield
Tony Hines, University of Portsmouth
Pik Liew, University of Essex
Kevin McMeeking, University of Exeter
Shaista Minhas, Canterbury Christchurch University
Brian Rutherford, University of Kent
Rasmus Sommer, Aarhus University
Dave Tyrall, City University
Jeffrey Unerman, Royal Holloway, University of London
Anne Marie Ward, University of Ulster
Mahbub Zaman, University of Manchester

The publisher would also like to thank Logica for granting permission for us to reprint the material on their company, International Accounting Standards Board for granting permission for Figure 7.1 and The Institute of Chartered Accountants of Scotland for question formats.

Chapter 1

The Preparation and Regulation of Company Financial Statements

LEARNING OUTCOMES

After studying this chapter you should be able to:

- ☑ explain the differences between the financial statements of an unincorporated business and a limited company
- ☑ identify and explain the features unique to company financial statements
- ☑ explain the need for accounting regulations and the main sources of regulations
- ☑ prepare financial statements of a company for internal use
- ☑ prepare profit and loss account and balance sheet of a company in accordance with IAS 1
- ☑ identify and explain the changes to company statements resulting from IAS 1
- ☑ prepare a statement of changes in equity
- ☑ identify and explain the respective roles of the directors, accountants and auditors in the preparation and publication of financial statements
- ☑ explain the term conceptual framework
- ☑ state the main purposes and explain the main sections of the IASB Framework
- ☑ explain the measurement bases that are identified in the Framework
- ☑ distinguish between alternative measurement systems.

Introduction

Financial accounting is concerned with the recording, classifying, summarising and reporting of those transactions undertaken by an entity, which are of a financial nature. It is also concerned with the construction of a theory of accounting, with identification of rules of measurement, and with regulation of the content of financial reports.

This first chapter outlines the main requirements in the preparation and presentation of financial statements for limited companies. It is assumed that a knowledge of the format of basic financial statements is possessed, for both sole traders and partnerships.

After an introductory section that examines the nature of limited companies and the regulatory requirements that have developed in order to safeguard financial statements users' interests, the following section examines how company financial statements are constructed. The chapter concludes with an overview of the conceptual framework within which accounting information is accumulated and reported, together with a study of measurement bases that could be used as an alternative to historic cost.

Section 1: Basic Principles

1.1 Types of business structure

There are many different ways in which a business can be structured. In broad terms, the type of structure can be divided into two categories: unincorporated and incorporated.

Unincorporated

An unincorporated business is one without a separate legal personality. This means that the business is conducted through the names of the persons behind it. The most common type of unincorporated business is a sole trader. A sole trader is a business run by an individual either in his own name or under a trade name (e.g. Robert Smith trading as RS Carpets). The basic characteristics of a sole-trader business are that the sole trader has personal liability for the debts and obligations of the business, owns personally the assets of the business, and is taxed personally on the profits and gains of the business.

A partnership is another common type of unincorporated business. A partnership is a business run by two or more persons in common with a view to profit. The basic characteristics of a partnership are that each partner has personal joint and several liability for the debts and obligations of himself and the other partners that are incurred in the ordinary course of partnership business, has the right to share in the profits and assets of the partnership business, and the right to take part in the management of the business.

Incorporated

An incorporated business is one with its own legal personality. This means that it has a legal identity that is distinct from that of its owners or managers. This provides many benefits but is accompanied by greater regulation.

Limited liability companies

A company limited by shares is the most common type of incorporated business structure. Such companies are owned by their shareholders but managed by their directors. The identifying feature of a company limited by shares is that the liability of the shareholders for the debts of the company is limited to the amount, if any, unpaid on the shares held by them. Since shareholders normally pay fully for their shares when they are issued, shareholders are rarely held liable for the company's debts.

A company limited by shares has a separate legal personality from its shareholders or directors. As such it can enter into contracts in its own name, it can sue and be sued, and it is liable to the tax authorities for tax on any profits earned. Because the company is a 'person' in its own right, the directors must manage it in the interests of the company, not themselves or individual shareholders.

Public and private companies

A company limited by shares can be a **private company** or a **public company**. A public company is one that is stated to be a public company, and is registered as such. A private company is defined in law as one that is not a public company.

The major features distinguishing a private company from a public company are that a private company is not allowed to offer shares in the company to the general public and a public company has minimum **share capital** requirements.

Public companies are subject to greater restrictions than private companies and, consequently, most companies limited by shares are private companies. Conversely, because of these restrictions, investors have greater confidence in public companies and therefore many large companies are public companies.

1.2 The need for regulation

Limited company financial statements, unlike those of sole traders and partnerships, are publicly available documents. As well as providing financial statements to their shareholders, limited companies are required to file accounts at Companies House, and these are available for all interested parties to see. The public availability of financial information about a company is a price that must be paid for the benefit of limited liability. With sole traders and partnerships, the owners of such a business can often glean considerable amounts of financial information from their day-to-day involvement in managing its affairs, and consequently do not depend solely on financial statements to provide them with this information. Indeed, many smaller businesses prepare accounts simply to satisfy the tax authorities and to determine their annual tax liabilities.

On the other hand, particularly with large limited companies where the shareholders have no direct involvement with the running of the business, the published financial statements will be all that such shareholders have with which to judge the performance of both the company and the directors. As a consequence of being publicly available, and to try to achieve uniformity so that meaningful comparison can be made, the form and content of these financial statements is subject to regulation by law, professional bodies and the stock exchange.

If the form and content of financial statements were not regulated it would be possible for dishonest or incompetent directors to provide shareholders and other users with misleading financial information.

Regulatory framework for financial accounting

The regulatory framework refers to the rules and regulations that apply to financial reporting. Accounting tends to be regulated in different ways in different countries; this is primarily due to the nature of the legal system prevailing in each country. This book deals with the position in the UK.

The system of accounting in the UK has been derived from statute, accounting standards and precedent. Collectively, these sources of reference give rise to the term 'Generally Accepted Accounting Practice' (GAAP), which is a widely used term that refers to rules that are followed in the preparation of financial statements. It is important to note that there are many different types of accounting entities and that the rules applying to each will differ. This book deals with financial reporting by companies however the international standards that are the subject of this book could be applied to any class of business entity. The regulatory framework that applies to financial reporting by companies consists of the following main components:

- legislation
- accounting standards
- stock exchange regulations.

Each of these is now considered in turn.

Legislation

The Companies Act 2006 contains rules and regulations relating to such matters as:

- record-keeping obligations
- the requirement to prepare annual accounts for each financial year
- the requirement that these accounts must show a 'true and fair' view
- the requirement that these accounts must be accompanied by a directors' report

- the requirement that the accounts must be prepared in accordance with either international standards or national standards
- the company's duty to circulate its accounts to shareholders and to make the accounts available for public inspection.

Some of these rules have arisen as a result of European Union (EU) Directives. For example, the European Commission adopted a regulation requiring all stock exchange-listed companies of EU member states to prepare their consolidated financial statements according to International Accounting Standards Board (IASB) standards.

Accounting standards

One of the most important principles in UK accounting is that the financial statements of a company must give a 'true and fair view' of its financial affairs. A similar principle applies in international accounting standards, which require 'fair presentation'. In most cases, compliance with accounting standards will ensure a true and fair view/fair presentation.

Accounting standards contain the detailed rules that govern the accounting treatment of transactions and other items shown in financial statements. Many countries have their own standard-setting bodies, which are responsible for devising and publishing accounting standards for use in the country concerned. In the UK this is the Accounting Standards Board (ASB), while the USA has the Financial Accounting Standards Board (FASB).

In recent years there has been a trend towards internationalisation of business and this has led to calls for the internationalisation of accounting rules to help both users and companies. The International Accounting Standards Board (IASB) has developed, and issues International Financial Reporting Standards (IFRS) (formerly International Accounting Standards, (IAS)). The IASB is currently working extensively with national standard setters to achieve global convergence and reflect international practice.

While in the UK the ASB's intention is to bring UK GAAP into line with IFRS, in practice there is likely to be a two-tier approach to financial reporting. The higher tier (of listed companies and publicly accountable bodies) will apply IFRS and the lower tier will continue to follow UK standards. Potentially and ideally, if the IASB's proposals on its SME (small and medium-sized entities) project are suitable for the UK's needs, then this would be adopted for all other companies.

This book deals mainly with the international standards, however comparisons are made in various chapters between UK and US standards in order to highlight the alternative accounting treatments available for transactions.

Stock exchange regulations

In addition to legislation and accounting standards, stock exchange listing rules also influence financial statements. These are regulations set out by the stock exchange, to which companies must adhere before their shares can be quoted on the stock exchange.

Progress Point 1.1

Explain the term 'regulatory framework' and why this framework is needed.

Solution

The term regulatory framework refers to the rules and regulations that govern financial reporting, and includes legislation, accounting standards and stock exchange regulations. This framework is needed so that shareholders and other users of financial statements can rely on their content.

1.3 Preparation of company annual accounts

The preparation of company annual accounts follows broadly the same principles as for sole traders and partnerships. The main differences are in relation to the presentation of figures and the inclusion of certain additional items that are not found in the accounts of sole traders and partnerships. The terminology used to refer to the financial statements also differs.

In relation to presentation, the income statement (profit and loss account) and balance sheet of limited companies are required to be in a particular format. The additional items are necessary as a result of a limited company's separate legal persona, while the terminologies differ as a consequence of adhering to international standards. The additional items are considered first.

Share capital

In the case of sole trader and partnership accounts, capital represents the owners' interest in the net assets of the business. That is, capital represents the residual claim on the net assets of the business once all its liabilities have been accounted for. When net assets increase, capital increases; and where there is a decrease in net assets there will be a corresponding decrease in capital.

With a limited company the ownership interest is split between the original investment and the subsequent changes in net assets made through profits. The original investment is usually made in return for shares in the company, and the subsequent profits and gains are known as reserves. Shares represent the basic units of ownership of a business and each share has a named value, which is called its nominal or par value. This nominal value is simply the value that is attached to the divided units of total share capital.

 Example

Suppose a company has share capital of £100,000. This could comprise:

- 100,000 shares of £1
- 200,000 shares of £0.50
- 400,000 shares of £0.25.

In companies, share capital is shown in an account that is kept separate from retained earnings and dividends. In sole traders, profits are usually added to the figure for capital and drawings are deducted from capital.

Ordinary shares and preference shares

Ordinary shares are sometimes referred to as 'equity shares' because each one represents an equal interest in the ownership of the company. A company might also issue preference shares, which entitle the holders to a dividend out of profits before the ordinary shareholders are entitled to them. This gives the preference shareholder some 'preferential' treatment. In general terms, the preference dividend is usually a fixed percentage each year. Once the preference dividend has been paid, the profit remaining belongs to the ordinary shareholders.

It would not be very prudent for directors to pay out all the remaining profits to shareholders, so it is likely that some profits will be retained in the business. These profits remaining after the company has paid the dividends are referred to as retained earnings. Any dividends paid by a company are based on the nominal value of the issued share capital.

 Example

A company has £100,000 ordinary share capital of £1 shares. The company pays a dividend of 10%. How much dividend will be paid?

The dividend to be paid is based on the nominal value of the share capital, in this case £100,000. So the dividend will be 10% of £100,000 = £10,000.

Reserves

Issued share capital is shown in the balance sheet. Any other amounts attributable to ordinary shareholders are shown as reserves. A company may have a number of different reserves, each for a different purpose. The main reserves include:

- retained earnings
- revaluation reserve
- general (or other) reserves.

Retained earnings

These are the profits after tax (less any losses), which the company keeps within the business. These profits have not been paid out by way of dividend, nor transferred to any other reserve. Each year the opening balance on retained earnings will be increased by the profit earned for the year, and reduced by any dividend payment and any other transfers to reserves. At the end of a period the amount remaining in the retained earnings of a company is the total (accumulated) profits (and losses) the company has built up over time. A company can choose to use some of these retained earnings to pay any future dividends.

Revaluation reserve

Some non-current (fixed) assets may have been purchased several years ago and have risen in value over time. This means that the amount shown in the balance sheet for such items is now out of date and no longer represents the current value of the asset. This is particularly true in the case of land and buildings. Land may have been purchased several years ago and may now be worth much more than was originally paid for it.

Certain non-current assets may therefore be revalued. If the asset value has increased then the company has made a revaluation gain. However, because such revaluation gains do not arise in the ordinary course of business they are not put into the income statement, but are taken directly to the revaluation reserve.

General reserve

A company may hold retained earnings that it has no intention of paying out to shareholders as a dividend in the future. In this case such earnings might be held in a general reserve, rather than in retained earnings.

Borrowing

A company may borrow directly from a bank, or it may borrow by issuing what is known as loan stock or debentures. The company is obliged to pay interest on this borrowing and will at some time in the future have to repay this loan. An interest payment due on this borrowing is shown as a finance cost in the income statement.

Taxation

A limited company is a separate legal entity and is liable for tax on its profits. As such, limited companies will show in the profit and loss account the amount of tax for the year and, in the balance

sheet, will record under current liabilities the tax due for the year. Taxation paid by sole traders or partners in a partnership is treated as a repayment of capital and is shown as a deduction in the capital account only.

Dividends

Shareholders receive a reward in the form of dividends for the capital they have invested. The equivalent payments to sole traders are called drawings.

Dividends on ordinary shares are accounted for only in the period in which they are declared as being payable by the directors. When directors declare that an ordinary dividend will be paid in respect of a particular accounting period, it is accounted for only at that time. Final ordinary dividends are usually declared only in the following period so they do not appear in the balance sheet as a liability on the balance sheet of the period to which they relate. Interim ordinary dividends are usually declared during the period to which they relate, and so are accounted for in the period to which they relate.

Dividends are not accounted for in the income statement but are treated as a reduction in retained earnings.

Shareholders' funds

In companies there is a heading for shareholders' funds, which can include a number of items such as share capital, share premium, revaluation reserve and retained earnings. In sole traders a single capital account usually includes all that the owners have invested in the business, capital and profits.

1.4 Preparing company financial statements for internal use

The preparation of the financial statements of limited companies does not present many new problems. Accruals, prepayments, provisions for bad and doubtful debts, and other similar adjustments are all prepared in the same way as for a sole trader, as is the income statement and balance sheet. However, once the profit is calculated, the amount of tax payable to the government has to be determined.

As far as the balance sheet is concerned, the main differences will be seen in the share capital and reserves section. The following simple example illustrates the financial statements of a company, prepared for internal use.

Example

The following trial balance is taken from the records of ST Ltd as at 31 December 2009.

	£000	£000
Ordinary share capital (£1 each)		300
Preference share capital (£1 each)		150
Share premium		25
Revaluation reserve		30
General reserve		20
Retained earnings at 1 January 2009		50
Long term loan (debentures)		80
Land and buildings	550	
Patents	50	
Motor vehicles	50	
Opening inventory	10	
Accounts receivable	80	
Accounts payable		45
Bank	75	
Electricity expense	8	
Wages expense	50	
Telephone expense	7	
Sales revenue		350
Purchases	150	
Loan interest	8	
Other expenses	12	
	1,050	1,050

Additional information

1. Closing inventory is £25,000
2. Amounts payable:

Ordinary dividend	£6,000
Preference dividend	£3,000
Taxation	£26,000

3. Authorised share capital is as follows:

Ordinary share capital	£350,000
Preference share capital	£200,000

The profit and loss account and the balance sheet will be similar to that for a sole trader. The only difference as was indicated above is in the capital and reserves section of the balance sheet.

Profit and loss account For the period ended 31 December 2009		
	£000	£000
Sales revenue		350
Less cost of sales		
Opening inventory	10	
Add purchases	150	
	160	
Less closing inventory	25	135
Gross profit		215
Less expenses:		
Electricity	8	
Wages	50	
Telephone	7	
Loan interest	8	
Other expenses	12	85
Profit before tax		130
Less taxation		26
Profit after tax		104
Less dividends:		
Ordinary	6	
Preference	3	9
Retained earnings		95

Balance sheet As at 31 December 2009			
Fixed assets			
Intangible assets			
Patents			50
Tangible assets			
Land and buildings			550
Motor vehicles			50
Total fixed assets			650
Current assets			
Inventory	25		
Accounts receivable	80		
Bank	75	180	
Current liabilities: amounts falling due within one year			
Accounts payable	45		
Tax payable	26		
Dividends payable	9	80	
Net current assets			100
Total assets less current liabilities			750
Amounts falling due after more than one year:			
Debenture loan			80
			670

	Authorised	Issued
Capital and reserves		
Share capital		
Ordinary share capital	350	300
Preference share capital	200	150
	550	450
Reserves		
Share premium	25	
Revaluation reserve	30	
General reserve	20	
Retained earnings (£50 + £95 (retained profit))	145	220
		670

It needs to be remembered that the above statements are prepared for *internal* use. However, these internal company accounts are not suitable for external users. In order to be suitable for external users, they need to be incorporated into the annual report of the company. The annual report of a company is governed by legal and professional requirements and has to be presented in a special way.

Progress Point 1.2

The following balances have been taken from the books of ABC Ltd at 31 December 2009.

	£	£
Share capital:		
900,000 ordinary shares of £1		900,000
450,000 6% preference shares		450,000
Share premium		255,000
Retained earnings		720,000
10% debenture loan		900,000
Accounts receivable	365,000	
Accounts payable		585,000
Cash	25,000	
Property (at cost)	2,400,000	
Plant and machinery (at cost)	2,850,000	
Inventory (at end)	450,000	
Provision against bad debts		30,000
Accumulated depreciation:		
Property		600,000
Machinery		1,050,000
Directors' remuneration	260,000	
Audit fee	15,000	
Administration expenses	400,000	
Selling expenses	525,000	
Debenture interest	90,000	
Sales		6,045,000
Cost of sales	4,155,000	
	11,535,000	11,535,000

The following information is to be taken into account.

1. Depreciation on plant and machinery is to be provided at 10% per annum on cost.
2. Provision for doubtful debts is to be adjusted to 2.5% of debtors.
3. Taxation on profit is estimated at £75,000. This amount will be paid next year.
4. The directors have decided to pay the preference dividend, payment to be made during 2010. In addition, the directors declare a dividend of 10p per share on the ordinary shares on 30 November. This was paid in January 2010.
5. At December 2009 the property was revalued at £3,000,000. This new value is to be brought into the balance sheet.
6. Depreciation of 5% per annum is to be provided on buildings that were valued at 2,000,000.

Required

Prepare a profit and loss account for the year ended 31 December 2009, together with a balance sheet at that date for internal use.

BASIC

INTERMEDIATE

ADVANCED

Solution

Profit and loss account for the year ended 31 December 2009		
Sales revenue (turnover)		£6,045,000
Cost of sales		4,155,000
Gross profit		1,890,000
Reduction in bad debt provision		20,875
		1,910,875
Directors' fees	260,000	
Audit fee	15,000	
Admin expenses	400,000	
Selling	525,000	
Depreciation: buildings	100,000	
Depreciation: plant	285,000	
Debenture interest	90,000	1,675,000
Profit before tax		235,875
Taxation		75,000
Profit after taxation		160,875
Dividends:		
Preference	27,000	
Ordinary	90,000	117,000
Profit for the year		43,875

Balance sheet As at 31 December 2009			
Fixed assets	Cost or valuation	Accumulated depreciation	
Land and buildings	£3,000,000	700,000	2,300,000
Plant	£2,850,000	1,335,000	1,515,000
	£5,850,000	2,035,000	3,815,000
Current assets			
Inventory		£450,000	
Accounts receivable	£365,000		
Less provision	£9,125	£355,875	
Cash		£25,000	
		£830,875	
Less current liabilities			
Accounts payable	£585,000		
Dividends payable	£117,000		
Tax payable	£75,000	£777,000	
Net current assets			£53,875
Total net assets			£3,868,875
Creditors: amounts falling due after more than one year:			
10% debentures			£900,000
			£2,968,875

Capital and reserves	
Share capital	
900,0000 ordinary shares of £1	£900,000
450,000 preference shares of £1	450,000
Share premium	255,000
Revaluation reserve	600,000
Retained earnings (£720,000 + £43,875)	763,875
	£2,968,875

Working notes:
Depreciation
Plant

Cost	£2,850,000	
Depreciation 10%	£285,000	
Depreciation for year		285,000
Accumulated to date		1,050,000
Total for balance sheet		1,335,000

Property

Total	2,400,000	
Buildings	2,000,000	
Therefore land	400,000	

Depreciation on buildings = 5% of £2,000,000 =	£100,000
Depreciation for year	£100,000
Accumulated depreciation	600,000
Balance sheet total	700,000

Bad debts provision

Accounts receivable (debtors)	£365,000
Provision 2.5% =	£9,125
Existing provision	30,000
Decrease in provision	£20,875

(Note: a decrease in provision is accounted for by increasing the profit, i.e. is a credit to the profit and loss account.)

Revaluation of asset
Property revalued upwards by £600,000 (£2,400,000 to £3,000,000)

Dividends

Preference 6% of £450,000 =	£27,000
Ordinary 10% of £900,000 =	90,000
	£117,000

It is important to remember that this solution shows the financial statements for *internal* use and not for publication. Financial statements for publication are dealt with in the next section.

BASIC

INTERMEDIATE

ADVANCED

Section 2: Intermediate Issues

1.5 The regulatory framework for company financial statements

Company financial statements that are prepared for external use and for publication are regulated both by law and by accounting standards in order to provide protection for investors. Investors in general use the information provided in company financial statements as a basis to compare different companies. In order for comparison to be meaningful, published financial statements need to be prepared on a similar basis by all companies.

Contents of annual accounts

While the preparation of company annual accounts follows the same principles as for sole traders and partnerships, as would be expected given the wider audience using the financial statements, the content of published annual accounts is significantly greater than for sole traders and partnerships. Users may be seeking more detailed explanation of what is revealed in the accounts, and they may be looking for information about future prospects and performance.

Consequently, as well as the formats of the financial statements being prescribed by law, the content of published financial statements is also prescribed by law.

In addition to a profit and loss account and balance sheet, companies are required to produce a directors' report that contains a great deal of fairly standardised formal information, including the following:

- principle activities of the company, and any changes
- business review of the activities during the year
- future developments
- research and development activities
- post-balance sheet events – any important changes since the balance sheet date
- value of land and buildings – significant differences between balance sheet values and market
- statement about employee involvement
- number of employees with disabilities
- donations to charities and to political parties, each disclosed separately
- purchase of own shares – number of shares purchased, amount paid and reasons for doing so
- information about directors – their names and the number of shares held by each at the beginning and end of the year
- creditor payment – the company's policy should be disclosed, and a calculation given of the average number of days taken to pay creditors.

Substantial information is also provided about director's remuneration and how it is determined, and about corporate governance and how the directors run the company. There will be an auditor's report and a statement of directors' responsibilities, confirming that the financial statements are the responsibility of the directors and not the auditors. Finally, the financial statements themselves are followed by substantial notes to the financial statements, which provide additional detail to the summarised figures in the profit and loss accounts and balance sheet.

Smaller companies

Disclosure requirements are significantly reduced for small and medium-sized companies. Because accounts have to be filed at Companies House it is not difficult to obtain them, however the amount of information that can be gleaned from them is extremely limited.

The purpose of financial statements

Financial statements are a structured representation of the financial position and financial performance of an entity. The objective of financial statements is to provide information about the financial position, the financial performance and cash flows of an entity. This information should be useful to a wide range of users in making economic decisions. Financial statements also show the results of how well the resources of the entity have been managed. In order to meet this objective, financial statements should provide information about an entity's:

- assets
- liabilities
- equity
- income and expenses, including gains and losses
- contributions by owners to the business
- payments to owners
- cash flows.

1.6 IAS 1 *Presentation of Financial Statements*

This standard sets out the structure and content of financial statements. According to IAS 1, financial statements should consist of:

- a statement of financial position (formerly called a balance sheet)
- a statement of comprehensive income (formerly called an income statement or profit and loss account)
- statement of changes in equity
- statement of cash flows
- notes, comprising a summary of the significant accounting policies and other explanatory information.

   This chapter will concern itself with the first three. Statements of cash flow will be considered in more detail in Chapter 9.

Statement of financial position (formerly the balance sheet)

IAS 1 does not prescribe the specific format this statement should follow, but does set out the minimum information that should be presented on the face of the statement. This information includes:

- non-current assets
- current assets
- assets held for sale
- non-current liabilities
- current liabilities
- equity.

   Assets can be presented current, then non-current, or vice versa. Liabilities and equity can be presented current then non-current then equity, or vice versa. A net asset presentation (assets less

liabilities is allowed). The long-term financing approach used in the UK and elsewhere is also acceptable, i.e. fixed assets + current assets – short-term liabilities = long-term debt + equity.

In addition, details of share capital, such as the number of shares and their par value must also be shown. To avoid cluttering up the balance sheet this additional information may be shown in the notes.

Current and non-current assets

An asset is classified as current if it satisfies *any* of the following criteria:

- it is expected to be realised, or is intended for sale or consumption, in the normal operating cycle of the business
- it is held primarily for the purpose of being traded
- it is expected to be realised within 12 months after the balance sheet date
- it is cash, or a cash equivalent (e.g. receivables).

All other assets are non-current. Such assets will include tangible, intangible and financial assets.

Current and non-current liabilities

A liability is classified as current if it satisfies *any* of the following criteria:

- it is expected to be settled in the normal operating cycle of the business
- it is held primarily for the purpose of being traded
- it is due to be settled within 12 months after the balance sheet date
- the business does not have a right to defer settlement of the liability for at least 12 months after the balance sheet date.

Equity

This includes share capital and reserves.

Summary and content

As a minimum the following information should be presented in the statement of financial position:

- property, plant and equipment
- investment property
- intangible assets
- financial assets
- investments in associates and joint ventures
- inventories
- trade and other receivables
- cash and cash equivalents
- trade and other payables
- provisions
- financial liabilities
- deferred tax
- minority interest presented within equity
- issued capital and reserves attributable to equity holders of the parent.

In addition, a separate line item is required for:

- total assets classified as held for resale
- total liabilities classified as held for resale.

Additional line items, headings and subtotals should be presented on the face of the balance sheet when such presentation is relevant to the understanding of the financial position of the business.

It is important to note that some of the line items given above can contain a variety of different items and it may be useful to users to be aware of the make-up of such items. IAS 1 has a general requirement that, either on the face of the balance sheet or in the notes, further sub-classifications should be provided as appropriate. Some sub-classifications are required by accounting standards, others are a matter of judgement. Examples given include:

- property, plant and equipment analysed into major classes (as required by IAS 16)
- receivables, analysed into, for example, trade receivables, prepayments and other amounts, receivables from other customers
- inventories analysed as required by IAS 2
- provisions analysed into provisions for employee benefits and others as required by IAS 37
- equity, analysed into share capital, share premium, and revaluation reserve.

BASIC

INTERMEDIATE

ADVANCED

Figure 1.1 is an illustrative presentation of a statement of financial position in accordance with IAS 1.

XYZ Group Statement of Financial Position as at 31 December 2009	
ASSETS	
Non-current assets	£
Property, plant and equipment	350,700
Goodwill	80,800
Other intangible assets	227,470
Investment in associates	100,150
Available for sale financial assets	142,500
	901,620
Current assets	
Inventories	135,230
Trade receivables	91,600
Other current assets	25,650
Cash and cash equivalents	312,400
	564,880
Total assets	1,466,500
EQUITY AND LIABILITIES	
Equity attributable to owners of the parent	
Share capital	650,000
Revaluation reserve	240,000
Retained earnings	83,750
Total equity	973,750
Non-current liabilities	
Bank loans	100,000
Long term borrowings	40,000
Deferred taxation	20,000
Obligations under a finance lease	10,000
Provisions	7,650
Total non-current liabilities	177,650
Current liabilities	
Trade and other payables	115,100
Bank overdrafts and loans	150,000
Current tax	45,000
Provisions	5,000
Total current liabilities	315,100
Total liabilities	492,750
Total equity and liabilities	1,466,500

Figure 1.1 Statement of financial position in accordance with IAS 1

Statement of comprehensive income

IAS 1 sets out the minimum information to be presented on the face of the income statement. The statement will include all items of income and expense recognised in a period. The information may be presented in:

■ a single statement
■ two statements: a statement displaying the components of profit or loss (i.e. a separate income statement) and a second statement beginning with the profit or loss, and showing other comprehensive income in a separate statement (statement of comprehensive income).

Information to be presented in the statement of comprehensive income includes the following minimum information requirements:

■ revenue
■ finance costs
■ Share of profit (or loss) of associate and joint ventures (see Chapter 10)
■ tax
■ a single amount comprising
  – the post-tax profit (or loss) on discontinued operations
  – the post-tax profit (or loss) on discontinued operations and the post-tax gain (or loss) on adjustment of fair value
■ profit or loss
■ each component of other comprehensive income
■ share of other comprehensive income of associates and joint ventures
■ total comprehensive income.

In addition to this information, the following items should be disclosed on the face of the income statement as allocations of profit or loss for the period:

■ profit (or loss) attributable to non-controlling interests (minority interest) (see Chapter 10)
■ profit (or loss) attributable to owners of the parent (see Chapter 10).

Also total comprehensive income for the period attributable to:

■ non-controlling interests, and
■ owners of the parent.

A non-controlling interest is the proportion of a company that is owned by outside interests. This is often referred to as the minority interest. This is dealt with more fully in Chapter 10.

Profit or loss for the period

An entity shall recognise all items of income and expense in a period in profit or loss. In addition, the amount of taxation relating to each component of other comprehensive income needs to be disclosed. The components of other comprehensive income may be disclosed either net of taxation, or before taxation with one amount shown for the total amount of taxation relating to those components.

Information to be presented in the statement of comprehensive income or in the notes

When items of income or expense are material, an entity needs to disclose these separately. There are a number of circumstances that will give rise to separate disclosure of such items. These include:

■ write-down of inventories to net realisable value
■ restructuring of a business

- write-down of property, plant and equipment to recoverable amount
- disposals of items of property, plant and equipment
- disposals of investments
- discontinued operations
- legal settlements.

How are expenses to be shown?

Expenses should be analysed either by *nature* (e.g. raw materials, staffing costs, depreciation) or by *function* (e.g. cost of sales, administration, finance). The information must be shown either on the face of the income statement or in the notes. If a business classifies expenses by function, then additional information on the nature of expenses, such as depreciation and staff costs, must be disclosed.

 ## *Example 1*

Analysis of expenses by nature of expense

Income statement	£000
Revenue	25,000
Other income	700
Changes in inventories of finished goods and work in progress	(1,000)
Raw materials used	(10,200)
Employee benefit costs	(5,600)
Depreciation	(1,300)
Other expenses	(900)
Operating profit	6,700
Finance costs	(1,500)
Profit before tax	5,200
Taxation	(1,800)
Profit for the period	3,400

 ## *Example 2*

Analysis of expenses by function of expense

Income statement	£000
Revenue	25,000
Cost of sales	(14,800)
Gross profit	10,200
Other income	700
Distribution costs	(1,900)
Administration costs	(1,400)
Other expenses	(900)
Operating profit	6,700
Finance costs	(1,500)
Profit before tax	5,200
Taxation	(1,800)
Profit for the period	3,400

BASIC   INTERMEDIATE   ADVANCED

Both statements in the examples produce the same profit figure. The only difference is how the expenses are analysed. Companies that analyse expenses by function must disclose this information in the notes. This must include information on the nature of expenses, including depreciation and employee benefit expenses.

There is no definitive list of items that should appear under the functional headings. The following is a suggested list.

(a) *Cost of sales*

This relates to the cost of production or provision of goods, and services and will include:

- ■ direct costs of production (raw materials, labour, components, direct expenses)
- ■ production overheads – overheads should be classified by function and can include costs that vary with time as well as with output; depreciation, rent and costs associated with production would be included; the costs of general management as opposed to functional management would not be included as these are not related to current production.

(b) *Distribution costs*

This deals with the cost of the distribution of goods to customers. A delivery charge is part of the cost of obtaining the goods and so would be included in cost of sales. Distribution costs can include wages and salaries, freight charges, fuel and road tax. Distribution overheads can include depreciation of vehicles used in distribution.

(c) *Administrative expenses*

These deal with the general costs of running the business, such as salaries and related costs of general management. This would include administrative overheads.

Figure 1.2(a) is an illustration of comprehensive income presented in one statement with expenses classified within profit by *function*.

XYZ Statement of comprehensive income for the year ended 31 December 2009	
Revenue	390,000
Cost of sales	(245,000)
Gross profit	145,000
Other income	20,667
Distribution costs	(9,000)
Administrative expenses	(20,000)
Other expenses	(2,100)
Finance costs	(8,000)
Share of profit of associate	35,100
Profit before tax	161,667
Taxation	(40,417)
Profit for the year	121,250
Other comprehensive income	
Exchange differences on foreign operations	5,000
Gains on property revaluation	50,000
Other comprehensive income for the year	55,000
Total comprehensive income for the year	176,250
Profit for the year attributable to: Note 1	
Owners of the parent	97,000
Non-controlling interests	24,250
	121,250
Total comprehensive income attributable to: Note 2	
Owners of the parent	141,000
Non-controlling interests	35,250
	176,250
Earnings per share	0.46

Note 1
The assumption made is that the non-controlling interest is 20%. This means that, out of the profit of £121,250 for the year, 20% of this, (£121,250 x 20%) = £24,250, is the non-controlling interest (i.e. the minority interest).

Note 2
In this case the non-controlling interest is 20% of £176,250 = £35,250. This means that there will be a non-controlling interest in both the exchange difference of foreign operations and in the gain on property revaluations. This would be represented as follows:

	Total	Owners	Non-controlling
Exchange difference	£5,000	£4,000	£1,000
Property revaluations	£50,000	£40,000	£10,000

Figure 1.2(a) Comprehensive income in one statement

Alternatively this information could be presented in two statements as shown in Figures 1.2(b) and (c).

XYZ Income statement for the year ended 31 December 2009	
	£
Revenue	390,000
Cost of sales	(245,000)
Gross profit	145,000
Other income	20,667
Distribution costs	(9,000)
Administrative expenses	(20,000)
Other expenses	(2,100)
Finance costs	(8,000)
Share of profit of associate	35,100
Profit before tax	161,667
Taxation	(40,417)
Profit for the year	121,250
Profit for the year attributable to:	
Owners of the parent	97,000
Non-controlling interests	24,250
	121,250
Earnings per share	0.46

Figure 1.2(b) Comprehensive income statement in two parts: income statement

Statement of comprehensive income for the year ended 31 December 2009	
	£
Profit for the year	121,250
Other comprehensive income	
Exchange differences on foreign operations	5,000
Gains on property revaluation	50,000
Other comprehensive income for the year	55,000
Total comprehensive income for the year	176,250
Total comprehensive income attributable to:	
Owners of the parent	141,000
Non-controlling interests	35,250
	176,250
Earnings per share	0.46

Figure 1.2(c) Comprehensive income statement in two parts: other comprehensive income

Any taxation relating to each component of comprehensive income should be disclosed in the notes to the accounts.

In addition to the statement of comprehensive income (income statement) and statement of financial position (balance sheet), IAS 1 requires an additional primary financial statement: *statement of changes in equity*.

Progress Point 1.3

The following is an extract from the trial balance of H plc as at 30 November 2009

	£	£
Purchase of raw materials	2,100,000	
Sales revenue		9,300,000
Wages and salaries	1,850,000	
Stock at 1 December 2008	325,000	
Depreciation:		
Plant and machinery	185,000	
Motor vehicles	26,000	
Office equipment	10,400	
Buildings	28,000	
Employer's national insurance	190,000	
Rent received		12,500
Other external charges	2,620,000	
Company contribution to pension	160,000	

Additional information

1. Stock at 30 November 2009 has been valued at £348,000. Stock comprises the following:

	31.11.09	30.11.08
Raw materials	£65,000	£60,000
Work in progress	£34,000	£38,000
Finished goods	£249,000	£227,000
	£348,000	£325,000

2. It is estimated that employment costs and other external charges can be allocated as follows:

	%
Cost of sales	72
Distribution	18
Administration	10

3. Plant and machinery, motor vehicles and office equipment relate to cost of sales, distribution costs and administrative expenses, respectively. Buildings depreciation is 60% to cost of sales; 20% to distribution and 20% to administration.

Required

As far as the information given permits, prepare the income statement of H plc in accordance with IAS 1, using:

(a) analysis by function
(b) analysis by nature.

Solution

(a) Classification of expenses by function:

Income statement For the year ended 30 November 2009	
Revenue	£9,300,000
Cost of sales	(5,749,200)
Gross profit	3,550,800
Other income	12,500
Distribution costs	(899,200)
Administrative expenses	(498,000)
Operating profit	2,166,100

Working notes

	Cost of sales	Distribution	Administration
	£	£	£
Opening inventory	325,000	–	–
Purchases	2,100,000	–	–
Wages and salaries	1,332,000	333,000	185,000
Employer's NI	136,800	34,200	19,000
Pension contributions	115,200	28,800	16,000
Other charges	1,886,400	471,600	262,000
Depreciation			
P&M	185,000	–	–
Motor vehicles	–	26,000	–
Office equipment	–	–	10,400
Buildings	16,800	5,600	5,600
Closing inventory	(348,000)	–	–
	5,749,200	899,200	498,000

Each expense is allocated to the appropriate function, either directly or apportioned according to the information given.

(b) Classification by nature:

Income statement For the year ended 30 November 2009	
Revenue	£9,300,000
Other income	12,500
Change in inventories of finished goods and work in progress	18,000
Raw materials and consumables used	(2,095,000)
Employee benefits	(2,200,000)
Depreciation	(249,400)
Other expenses	(2,620,000)
Operating profit	£2,166,100

Working notes

Change in inventory	£
Finished goods and work in progress at 30.11.09 (£34,000 + £249,000)	283,000
Finished goods and work in progress at 30.11.08 (£38,000 + £227,000)	265,000
Increase	18,000

An increase in closing inventory will have the effect of reducing the cost of sales and so will increase profit. It will be a credit in the income statement. The converse would be true of a reduction in closing inventory.

Raw materials	£
Opening inventory	60,000
Purchases	2,100,000
Less closing inventory	(65,000)
	2,095,000
Employee benefits	
Wages and salaries	1,850,000
Employer's NI	190,000
Pension contributions	160,000
	2,200,000
Depreciation	
Plant and machinery	185,000
Motor vehicles	26,000
Office equipment	10,400
Buildings	28,000
	249,400

Statement of changes in equity

IAS 1 requires a company to present a statement of changes in equity as a separate component of the financial statement. The statement reconciles the capital and reserves at the beginning of the period with those at the end.

A statement of changes in equity will show:

(a) total comprehensive income for the period, showing separately the total amount attributable to owners of the parent company and to non-controlling interests

(b) for each component of equity, a reconciliation between the carrying amount at the beginning and end of the period; changes resulting from the following should be disclosed separately

- profit or loss
- each item of other comprehensive income
- transactions with owners, e.g.
  - Contributions by owners
  - Distributions to owners (dividends).

Figure 1.3 is an illustration of the statement of changes in equity. The information used is taken from both the examples of a statement of comprehensive income and the statement of financial position given above.

Statement of changes in equity					
	Share capital	Retained earnings	Foreign currency	Revaluation surplus	Non-controlling interests	Total
	£	£	£	£	£	£
Balance at start	650,000	1,750	0	200,000	64,750	916,500
Total comp. income		97,000	4,000	40,000	35,250	176,250
Dividends		(15,000)				(15,000)
Balance at end	650,000	83,750	4,000	240,000	100,000	973,750

Figure 1.3 Statement of changes in equity

BASIC

INTERMEDIATE

ADVANCED

Progress Point 1.4

The following are the extracts from the accounts of ABC Ltd.

Balance sheet extract		
Year ended	31 Dec	31 Dec
	2008	2009
Capital and reserves	£000	£000
Share capital	8,000	7,000
Share premium	890	600
Revaluation reserve	870	400
Retained earnings	3,380	2,600
	13,140	10,600

Income statement extract	
For the year ended	31 Dec
	2008
	£000
Profit before tax	1,100
Taxation	(300)
Profit for the year	800

Additional information

1. The company issued 1 million ordinary shares of £1 at £1.29 per share. The issue was made during the year ended 31 December 2008.
2. Property revaluation at the year end gave a surplus of £350,000 and there was a revaluation gain of £250,000 on investments.
3. Additional depreciation on previous revalued assets was £40,000.
4. An asset previously revalued in 2003 was sold. The balance in the revaluation reserve relating to this asset at the date of disposal was £90,000.
5. Dividend payments of £150,000 were made during the year.

Required

Prepare the following for inclusion in the financial statements of ABC plc for the year ended 31 December 2008 in, accordance with IAS 1:

(a)   statement of comprehensive income
(b)   statement of changes in equity.

Solution

(a)

Statement of comprehensive income	£000
Profit for the year	£800
Other comprehensive income	
Gain on revaluation of investments	250
Gain on property revaluation	350
Other comprehensive income for the year	600
Total comprehensive income for the year	£1,400

(b)

Statement of changes in equity					
	Ordinary share capital	Share premium	Revaluation reserve	Retained profits	Total
	£000	£000	£000	£000	£000
At 31.12.07	7,000	600	400	2,600	10,600
Profit for the year				800	800
Dividends				(150)	(150)
Revaluation surplus			600		600
Revaluation gain realised			(90)	90	
Additional depreciation			(40)	40	
Issue of shares	1,000	290	–	–	1,290
At 31.12.08	8,000	890	870	3,380	13,140

Progress Point 1.5

The following trial balance is taken from the books of Krystal, a publicly listed company.

Trial balance At 31 March 2009		
	£000	£000
Land and buildings at cost	270,000	
Plant and machinery at cost	156,000	
Investment properties at valuation	90,000	
Purchases	78,200	
Operating expenses	39,500	
Dividends paid	15,000	
Inventory at 1 April 2008	37,800	
Trade receivables	53,200	
Revenue		278,400
Income from investment property		4,500
Equity shares of £1 each		150,000
Retained earnings at 1 April 2008		119,500
Long-term loan (8%)		50,000
Accumulated depreciation at 1 April 2008		
Buildings		60,000
Plant and machinery		26,000
Trade payables		33,400
Deferred taxation		12,500
Bank		5,400
	739,700	739,700

The following notes are relevant.

1. The land and buildings were purchased on 1 April 1993. The cost of the land was £70 million. No land and building have been purchased since that date. On 1 April 2008 the company had its land and buildings professionally valued at £80 million and buildings valued at £175 million. The estimated life of the buildings was originally 50 years and the remaining life has not changed as a result of the valuation.

2. Plant is depreciated at 15% per annum using the reducing balance method. Depreciation on buildings and plant is charged to the cost of sales.
3. The long-term loan was raised on 1 April 2008. At year end, interest had not yet been paid.
4. The provision for taxation for the year to 31 March 2009 has been estimated at £28.3 million.
5. Inventory at 31 March 2009 was valued at £43.2 million.

Required

Prepare the following financial statements for the year ended 31 March 2009 in accordance with IAS 1:

(a) statement of comprehensive income
(b) statement of changes in equity
(c) statement of financial position.

Solution

Working notes

Cost of sales:

Opening inventory	£37,800
Purchases	78,200
	116,000
Closing inventory	43,200
	72,800
Depreciation: plant	19,500
Depreciation: buildings	5,000
	£97,300

Depreciation:

Plant at cost:	£156,000
Accumulated depreciation	26,000
Net book value	130,000
Depreciation rate	15%
Depreciation =	£19,500

Land and buildings			
	Land	Buildings	Total
	£000	£000	£000
Cost	70,000	200,000	270,000
Depreciation	0	60,000	60,000
Carrying amount	70,000	140,000	210,000
Revaluation	10,000	35,000	45,000
Carrying amount	80,000	175,000	255,000

Buildings have been depreciated from 1993 to 2008, a period of 15 years. Therefore, £60m represents depreciation of £4m each year. New carrying amount = £175m; remaining life = 35 years, therefore new depreciation = £5,000 per annum.

Carrying amounts for property, plant and equipment

Plant	Cost	Depreciation	Net book value
	£000	£000	£000
Costs	156,000	26,000	130,000
Depreciation for the year	–	19,500	–
	156,000	45,500	110,500
Property (land and buildings)			
Carrying amount	255,000	5,000	250,000
Total			£360,500

(a) Statement of comprehensive income

	£000
Revenue	278,400
Cost of sales	(97,300)
Gross profit	181,100
Other income	4,500
Operating expenses	(39,500)
Finance costs	(4,000)
Profit before tax	142,100
Taxation	28,300
Profit for the year	113,800
Other comprehensive income	
Gains on property revaluation	45,000
Other comprehensive income for the year	45,000
Total comprehensive income for the year	158,800

If there was a minority share in the company, then both the profit for the year and total comprehensive income would be split into that portion which was attributable to the parent company and that which was attributable to the minority (non-controlling) interest.

(b) Statement of changes in equity

	Share capital	Revaluation reserve	Retained profits	Total
	£000	£000	£000	£000
At 1.04.2008	150,000	–	119,500	269,500
Profit for the year			113,800	113,800
Revaluation of property	–	45,000		45,000
Dividend paid	–	–	(15,000)	(15,000)
At 1.04.2009	150,000	45,000	218,300	413,300

(c) Statement of financial position as at 31 March 2009

Assets	
Non-current assets	£000
Property, plant and equipment	360,500
Investment property	90,000
	450,000
Current assets	
Inventory	43,200
Trade receivables	53,200
	96,400
Total assets	546,900
Equity and liabilities	
Equity attributable to owners	
Share capital	150,000
Retained earnings	218,300
Revaluation reserve	45,000
Total equity	413,300
Non-current liabilities	
Long-term borrowing	50,000
Deferred taxation	12,500
Total non-current liabilities	62,500
Current liabilities	
Trade payables	33,400
Accrued interest	4,000
Taxation	28,300
Bank overdraft	5,400
Total current liabilities	71,100
Total equity and liabilities	546,900

Disclosure in practice

Companies are required to meet the specific disclosure requirements as laid down by legislation. Logica, which controls a number of companies, discloses information for Logica, the company, and for combined information of Logica and all the other companies it controls. This is referred to as the 'consolidated financial statements of the group'. This is covered in detail in Chapter 10, on business combinations.

The company balance sheet is given in Figure 1.4. Note that information is given for the current and the previous year.

Company balance sheet 31 December 2009			
	Note	2009 £'m	2008 £'m
Fixed assets			
Investments	V	1,416.3	1,486.0
Current assets			
Debtors: amounts due within one year	VI	376.3	388.6
Cash at bank and in hand		4.2	2.5
		380.5	391.1
Creditors – amounts falling due within one year	VII	(295.4)	(284.7)
Net current assets		85.1	106.4
Total assets less current liabilities		1,501.4	1,592.4
Creditors – amounts falling due after more than one year	VIII	–	(175.1)
Net assets		1,501.4	1,417.3
Capital and reserves			
Called-up equity share capital	X	145.8	153.6
Share premium account	XI	1,098.9	1,097.0
Profit and loss account	XI	225.0	143.4
Capital redemption reserve	XI	8.4	
Other reserves	XI	23.3	23.3
Equity shareholders' funds	XII	1,501.4	

Figure 1.4 Logica: company balance sheet

The term 'comprehensive income' is not used by Logica at present. Instead it shows a statement of recognised income and expense. This in essence follows the same principles as outlined in the chapter, but the terminology is different. Had there been any gains on revaluation of assets, they too would have been shown in Figure 1.5.

Consolidated statement of recognised income and expense For the year ended 31 December 2009	2009 £'m	2008 £'m
Exchange differences on translation of foreign operations	97.4	(4.1)
Exchange differences recycled on disposal of foreign operations	5.1	–
Cash flow hedges transferred to income statement on settlement	–	(2.0)
Actuarial gains on defined benefit plans	3.6	17.5
Tax on items taken directly to equity	–	(3.9)
Net income recognised directly in equity	106.1	7.5
Profit for the year	168.1	89.1
Total recognised income and expense for the year	274.2	96.6
ATTRIBUTABLE TO:		
Equity holders of the parent	274.0	89.4
Minority interests	0.2	7.2
	27	

Figure 1.5 Logica: consolidated statement of recognised income and expense

In terms of changes in equity, Logica show this in the notes to the accounts as part of the note on other reserves. This appears as shown in Figure 1.6.

Other reserves							
	Retained earnings	Treasury shares	Translation reserve	Capital redemption reserve	Merger reserve	Other	Total
	£'m	£'m	£'m	£'m	£'m	£'m	£'m
At 1 January 2008	(344.0)	(35.9)	0.6	–	–	(0.8)	(380.1)
Net profit for the year	82.0	–	–	–	–	–	82.0
Dividends paid	(61.1)	–	–	–	–	–	(61.1)
Share-based payment, net of tax	9.1	–	–	–	–	–	9.1
Actuarial gains	17.5	–	–	–	–	–	17.5
Acquisition of WM-data	–	–	–	–	617.1	–	617.1
Cash flow hedges – transferred to income statement	(2.0)	–	–	–	–	–	(2.0)
Tax on items taken to equity	(3.9)	–	–	–	–	–	(3.9)
Other	(0.1)	–	–	–	–	–	(0.1)
Exchange differences	–	–	(6.8)	–	–	2.7	(4.1)
At 1 January 2009	(302.5)	(35.9)	(6.2)	–	617.1	1.9	274.4
Net profit for the year	169.9	–	–	–	–	–	169.9
Dividends paid	(85.9)	–	–	–	–	–	(85.9)
Share-based payment, net of tax	9.5	–	–	–	–	–	9.5
Shares purchased and cancelled	(130.8)	–	–	8.4	–	–	(122.4)
Actuarial gains	3.6	–	–	–	–	–	3.6
Recycled on disposal of foreign operations	–	–	5.1	–	–	–	5.1
Other	–	0.8	–	–	1.9	–	2.7
Exchange differences	–	–	95.0	–	–	0.4	95.4
At 31 December 2009	(336.2)	(35.1)	93.9	8.4	61		

Figure 1.6 Logica: other reserves

1.7 The annual audit

It is generally accepted that compliance with accounting standards will ensure that financial statements will present a true and fair view. Another key protection for investors and other users of financial statements is the annual audit requirement. In an external audit, independent auditors examine the financial statements of an entity and express an opinion on them.

The annual accounts of all companies (with the exception of small companies) must be independently audited. An audit involves obtaining evidence about the amounts and disclosures in the financial statements sufficient to give reasonable assurance that the financial statements are free from material misstatement, whether caused by fraud or error. This includes an assessment of: whether the accounting policies are appropriate to the company's circumstances and have been consistently applied and adequately disclosed; the reasonableness of significant accounting estimates made by the directors; and the overall presentation of the financial statements.

It is worth pausing at this stage to consider the roles of the directors, accountants and auditors in the financial reporting process, and to clarify the responsibilities of each.

The directors

A company's financial statements are the responsibility of the directors. Directors are responsible for the preparation and fair presentation of these financial statements in accordance with International Financial Reporting Standards. This responsibility includes: designing, implementing and maintaining internal controls relevant to the preparation and fair presentation of financial statements that are free from material misstatement, whether due to fraud or error; selecting and applying appropriate accounting policies; and making accounting estimates that are reasonable in the circumstances.

The accountant

The role of the accountant very much depends upon the size of the entity. While the financial statements may well be the responsibility of the directors, in many small limited companies, the directors themselves may not have the appropriate accounting and technical knowledge to prepare the financial statements, and consequently will employ accountants to carry out this work. The financial statements will remain the responsibility of the directors, even though they may not have prepared them.

In larger organisations, particularly plcs, it is likely that these will have their own 'in-house' accounting departments that will undertake to prepare the entity's accounts and ensure compliance with the appropriate rules and standards. Again, even though most of the directors may have little accounting expertise, nevertheless the directors will continue to remain responsible for the financial statements.

The auditor

Auditors are professionally qualified persons from the accounting field who are appointed by the company. They are responsible for expressing an opinion on the financial statements. Auditors are required to report to the members whether, in their opinion, the financial statements give a true and fair view, and that the financial statements have been properly prepared in accordance with the Companies Act 2006 and International Financial Reporting Standards.

It is important to note that the auditor may also be the preparer of the financial statements. As noted above, in the case of large plcs, it is likely that there will be an in-house accounting department. In such instances, the role of the auditor will be to examine the financial statements that have been prepared by the company. In many smaller businesses that require an audit, it may well be the case that the auditor will prepare the accounts and then audit them. There is, therefore, a potential conflict of interest. It is not difficult to imagine that pressure could be placed upon auditors/accountants by directors in order

to present information in a particular manner. It is for reasons such as this that auditors are subject to extensive and rigorous regulation to ensure their independence, and to ensure that users of financial statements may rely on the reported figures.

The audit report

The annual audit requirement is a further regulation that helps to ensure that publicly available financial statement information can be relied upon. Ultimately, however, the financial statements are the responsibility of the directors and therefore the quality of the reported information is very much dependent on them producing reliable accounting information. Clearly, there may be unscrupulous and dishonest directors who will seek to present misleading information, however this ought to be identified at the audit stage and brought to the members' attention by means of the annual audit report.

Unqualified opinion

Where an auditor is satisfied of the correctness of the financial statements, an 'unqualified' audit opinion will be given, which states that:

> the accounts give a true and fair view of the state of affairs of the company and that they have been properly prepared in accordance with all the relevant legislation and accounting standards.

Qualified opinion

An opinion is referred to as 'qualified' when the directors state that, in their opinion, the accounts give a true and fair view except for certain material matters on which the auditors have reservations. A reservation is material if its omission or misstatement would reasonably influence the decisions of a user of the financial statements. The reservations must be fully explained either in the audit opinion or by reference to a note to the accounts.

Adverse opinion

An adverse opinion is issued when the effect of a disagreement between the auditor and the directors about the treatment or disclosure of a matter in the financial statements is so material and pervasive that the auditor feels that the financial statements are seriously misleading. In this instance, they are required to express the opinion that the 'financial statements do not give a true and fair view'.

Disclaimer of opinion

A disclaimer of opinion is expressed when there has been a limitation on the scope of the auditor's work, and the possible effect of that limitation is so material and pervasive that the auditor has 'not been able to obtain sufficient evidence to form an opinion'. The nature of the limitation should be explained in the audit report together with the fact that the auditor is unable to express an opinion on the financial statements.

Summary

Legislation governs the contents and presentation of financial statements; accounting standards provide mandatory guidance on the accounting treatment of items within the financial statements; directors are responsible for the financial statements; and auditors are responsible for expressing an opinion on the financial statements. Collectively, there is a system in place to ensure the publication of high-quality accounting information by companies. This system, by which companies are directed and controlled, is

known as corporate governance. The next section looks in detail at corporate governance requirements and how such requirements have shaped the content of company financial statements.

1.8 Corporate governance

Introduction

In general terms, corporate governance refers to the way in which an organisation is administered or controlled. This is usually done by means of a set of processes, policies, laws and institutions. Corporate governance also refers to the ways in which stakeholders in the company, such as shareholders, company management and the board of directors, interact with each other. One important theme of corporate governance is to ensure accountability. Since 2001 there has been a renewed interest in corporate governance practices mainly due to high-profile company failures, such as Enron Corporation and Worldcom, in the USA. Following these company failures, the US Federal Government passed the Sarbanes-Oxley Act, with the intention of restoring public confidence in corporate governance.

Both the US and UK capital markets have widely dispersed share ownership. This is in contrast to the concentrated shareholdings predominant in Europe and in many developing countries. In general terms, ownership patterns influence the way in which corporate governance is approached by policy makers, and how the potential conflicts of interest between ownership and control are managed. This potential conflict of interest between ownership and control is often referred to as the 'principal/agency' problem. The principals are the owners of the company (the shareholders) and the agents are the boards of directors who have effective control over the company. In countries with widely dispersed shareholdings, the conflict of interest arises between these two groups, in that the agents may allow self-interest to influence decision making.

In contrast, countries that have more concentrated ownership structures often have majority shareholders who have a significant influence on the board of directors. So, in this context a potential conflict can arise between the controlling 'majority' shareholders who may gain additional benefits at the expense of 'minority' owners.

The aim of corporate governance is to protect shareholder rights, improve disclosure of information, help provide an efficient legal framework, and help the board of directors to function more effectively. The principal/agency problem is addressed through a mixture of company law, stock exchange requirements and self-regulatory codes.

It should be noted that there is no single approach to corporate governance and it is unlikely that 'one size will fit all'. Some countries in continental Europe have adopted an inclusive 'stakeholder' approach where companies are considered to have a wider remit than being accountable to shareholders. In these countries companies are considered to be 'social institutions' and as such are accountable, not just to shareholders, but to the wider community in general. This is in contrast to the US and UK approaches, where the emphasis is on wealth creation for shareholders.

Principles of good corporate governance

While the approaches to corporate governance may differ it would be fair to say that most would adhere to the Organisation for Economic Co-operation and Development (OECD's) generic corporate governance principles of responsibility, accountability, transparency and fairness:

- responsibility of directors, who take strategic decisions and who employ, monitor and reward management
- accountability of the board of directors to the shareholders, who have a right to receive information on the financial stewardship of their investment
- transparency of information, which is clear and from which some analysis of the company can be made
- fairness, so that all shareholders are treated equally.

Key elements of good corporate governance include honesty, trust, integrity, accountability and commitment to the organisation. Senior executives of a company should be seen to be conducting themselves both honestly and ethically in terms of managing a potential conflict of interest and in disclosure of information in financial reports. Commonly accepted principles of corporate governance include those discussed below.

Equitable treatment of shareholders

Organisations should respect the rights of shareholders and also help shareholders exercise those rights though effective means of communication. This implies that information that is communicated to shareholders is both understandable and accessible. Shareholders should also be encouraged to participate in the annual general meeting of the company.

Other stakeholders

Other stakeholders include, suppliers, customers, employees, creditors and the community at large. Organisations should recognise they have obligations, both legal and otherwise, to all such stakeholders.

Board of directors

In order to deal with the various business issues that arise, the board of directors needs to have a range of skills and abilities. In addition, the board needs to have the ability to review and challenge management performance. The board therefore needs to be of sufficient size and have an appropriate level of commitment to fulfil its responsibilities and duties. The mix of executive and non-executive directors needs to be carefully considered. The key roles of chairperson of the board and chief executive officer (CEO) should not be carried out by the same person.

Ethical behaviour

Organisations need to develop a code of conduct that promotes ethical and responsible decision making by the directors.

Disclosure

Organisations should disclose the roles and responsibilities of the board of directors, and of management, so as to provide shareholders with a degree of accountability. Any material matters concerning the organisation should be disclosed in good time so as to ensure that all investors have access to factual information, which is clear.

Specific issues involving corporate governance principles include:

- preparation of financial statements
- independence of auditors
- internal controls
- review of compensation arrangements for chief executive
- management of risk
- how individuals are appointed to the board of directors
- dividend policy.

Role of the accountant

For a corporate governance system to function effectively, financial reporting is very important. Accountants and auditors are in essence, the main providers of information that helps investors and potential investors with their decision making. The directors of a company are entitled to expect that the management of a company conforms with both statutory and regulatory obligations when preparing financial statements.

Under current accounting standards, a degree of choice of method of accounting is possible. This may lead to management selecting an accounting choice to maximise reported profit. This is sometimes referred to as 'creative accounting' and, in extreme cases, this can lead to the non-disclosure of information.

Sometimes an accounting firm acts as both management consultant to an organisation and as independent auditor. This may give rise to a conflict of interest in that, if an accounting firm is acting both as consultant and as auditor, there may be some pressure put upon the client to follow the wishes of management. It is also within the power of management to appoint and dismiss the auditors. This conflict of interest was addressed by the US Government, after the collapse of Enron, through the Sarbanes-Oxley Act, which prohibits accounting firms from providing both auditing and management consulting services.

Corporate governance models

The corporate governance models that exist around the world tend to differ according to the variety of capitalism in which they are embedded. The model that is common in Anglo-American countries, often referred to as the 'liberal model', tends to give priority to the interests of shareholders. On the other hand, the model common in continental Europe and Japan, the 'coordinated' model, gives recognition to the interests of workers, managers, customers, suppliers and the community. The liberal model of corporate governance encourages radical innovation and cost competition, whereas the coordinated model favours step-by-step innovation and quality competition. However, that said, there are important differences between the USA and the UK in recent approaches to governance.

Codes and guidelines

Corporate governance principles and codes have been developed in different countries and issued from stock exchanges, companies and, institutional investors with the support of governments. In general, compliance with such codes is not a legal requirement, although if a company does not follow stock exchange requirements then it will fail to get a listing. For example, companies quoted on the London Stock Exchange (and Toronto Stock Exchange) need not formally follow the recommendations of the national corporate governance codes. However, if they do not do so, explanations must be provided as to where adherence to the code is not undertaken and reasons why should be given. Such disclosure requirements do put significant pressure on listed companies to comply with the recommendations of the codes.

One of the most influential guidelines has been the OECD Principles of Corporate Governance, published in 1999. This code was revised in 2004 and remains a major focus for corporate governance principles throughout the world. Building on the work of the OECD, other international organisations and national corporate governance codes, the United Nations Intergovernmental Working Group of Experts on International Standards of Accounting and Reporting (ISAR) has produced a voluntary Guidance on Good Practices in Corporate Governance Disclosure. This internationally agreed benchmark consists of more than 50 distinct disclosure items across five broad categories. These categories are identified as:

1. board and management structure and process
2. ownership structure and exercise of control rights
3. financial transparency and information disclosure
4. auditing
5. corporate responsibility and compliance.

Corporate governance in the UK

Corporate governance developments in the UK began in the late 1980s and early 1990s in the wake of company scandals such as Polly Peck and Maxwell. Polly Peck reported very healthy profits one year while the following year filed for bankruptcy. The Maxwell group of companies had entered into a series of high-risk acquisitions, which resulted in a high level of debt being financed by diverting resources from the companies pension funds. It emerged that one of Maxwell's companies (the Mirror Group) had debts greater than its level of assets, and £440 million was 'missing' from the pension fund.

It was such scandals that led to the formation of the Financial Aspects of Corporate Governance Committee, chaired by Adrian Cadbury. The report published by this committee in 1992 (the Cadbury Report) outlined a number of recommendations around the separation of the role of the chief executive and chairman, balanced composition of the board of directors, selection process for non-executive directors, transparency of financial reporting and the need for good internal controls.

The Cadbury Report included a Code of Best Practice, and its recommendations were incorporated into the listing requirements of the London Stock Exchange. The report's recommendations have been adopted in varying degrees by the European Union, the USA, the World Bank and others.

Following on from Cadbury, a Working Group on Internal Control was established. The remit of this group was to provide guidance to companies on how to comply with 'reporting on the effectiveness of the company's system of internal control', one of the principles of the Cadbury Report. The outcome of this was the publication in 1994 of the Rutteman Report on 'Internal Control and Financial Reporting'.

Following concerns about the level of directors' pay and share options, the Greenbury Report was published in 1995. Greenbury recommended extensive disclosure in annual reports on the remuneration of directors. The report called for the establishment of a remuneration committee comprising non-executive directors. The stock exchange listing rules were amended to incorporate the majority of the recommendations.

The extent to which the Cadbury and Greenbury Reports had been implemented and whether the objectives of these reports had been met was reviewed by the Hampel Committee. The report from this committee, the Hampel Report published in 1998, found there was no need for a revolution in the UK system of corporate governance. The Hampel Report led to the publication of the Combined Code of Corporate Governance.

Part of the Combined Code requires that companies provide a statement in their annual report on how they have applied the provisions of the code relating to internal control. The need for guidance led to the establishment of the Turnbull Committee in 1998 by the Institute of Chartered Accountants in England and Wales (ICAEW), which resulted in the publication of 'Internal Control: Guidance for Directors on the Combined Code'.

In 2001 the relationship between institutional investors and companies was addressed by the Myners Review, commissioned by the government. The resulting report, 'Institutional Investment in the UK', included suggestions for the improvement of communication between investors and companies, and encouraged institutional investors to consider their responsibilities as owners and how they should exercise their rights on behalf of beneficiaries.

The 'Directors' Remuneration Report Regulations' were introduced in 2002. These regulations were to further strengthen the powers of shareholders in relation to directors' pay. The regulations increased the amount of information shareholders are given on directors' remuneration.

A review of the Combined Code was carried out in 2002 at the request of the Department of Trade and Industry (DTI) and the Treasury. This resulted in the publication of the Higgs Report on 'The Role and Effectiveness of Non-Executive Directors', in 2003. The Higgs Report made a number of recommendations, including the definition of 'independence', and the proportion of non-executive directors on the board and its committees. The role of the senior independent director was to be expanded to provide an alternative channel to shareholders and to lead evaluations on the performance of the chairman. There was also to be added emphasis on the process of nominations to the board of directors through a process that was to be both transparent and rigorous. The performance of the board, its committees and of individual directors was to be evaluated. Higgs strongly backed the existing non-prescriptive approach to corporate governance, yet advocated more provisions with more

stringent criteria for board composition and evaluation of independent directors. Higgs wanted to remove some of the discretion of the Combined Code.

Around this time, the Financial Reporting Council published the Smith Report, 'Guidance on Audit Committees'. The UK Government was concerned with the independence of auditors in the wake of the collapse of Arthur Andersen and the Enron scandal in the USA in 2002. The Higgs Report was substantially influenced by the views taken by the EU Commission. One important point was that an individual auditor should look at whether a company's corporate governance structure provides safeguards to preserve that individual's independence. The Higgs and Smith Reports were published in 2003, and were followed by the publication of the Tyson Report on the recruitment and development of non-executive directors (NEDs). The Tyson Report was commissioned by the DTI.

Recommendations from the Higgs and Smith Reports led to changes in the Combined Code of Corporate Governance, published in 2003.

The revised code was in sections, covering the following elements.

- Directors:
  this section sets out the requirements for non-executive directors; the appointments committee should be run by NEDs and the independence needs to be assured.
- Directors' remuneration:
  this section sets out guidance for the committee that determines directors' remuneration; its focus is that of performance-related pay; the remuneration committee is meant to be composed of NEDs.
- Accountability and audit:
  in this section rules are discussed about the audit committee. The audit committee is meant to be composed only of NEDs; in the wake of the Enron scandal, more emphasis has been placed on high standards of integrity.
- Relations with institutional shareholders:
  this section sets out the best practice of maintaining good relationships with shareholders and keeping them well informed on company affairs.
- Responsibilities of institutional shareholders:
  these provisions deal with a unique part of UK financial market structure, which tends to have a high level of involvement and influence of institutional investors.

The Turnbull Review Group was established in 2004 by the Financial Reporting Council (FRC). The group was to consider the impact of 'Internal Control: Guidance for Directors on the Combined Code', and to determine the extent to which guidance needed to be updated. Revised guidance was published in 2005.

In 2005, following a Company Law Review, the statutory requirement to produce an Operating and Financial Review (OFR) was removed. At the beginning of 2008, the ASB issued a notice reminding companies of the need to follow the enhanced business review reporting requirements contained in the Companies Act 2006.

The European Union also significantly influences corporate governance in the UK. The European Commission's 'Corporate Governance and Company Law Action Plan (May 2003)' proposes a mix of legislative and regulatory measures that will affect all member states. Such measures relate to:

- disclosure requirements
- exercise of voting rights
- cross-border voting
- disclosure by institutional investors
- responsibilities of board members.

The UK has pioneered a flexible model of regulation of corporate governance, known as the 'comply or explain' code of governance. This is a principle-based code that lists a number of recommended practices, as indicated above.

Publicly listed companies in the UK have to either apply such principles or, if they choose not to, to explain in a designated part of their annual reports why they have decided not to comply. The shareholders are then in a position to monitor and judge such explanations. The tenet of the code is that one size does not fit all in matters of corporate governance. Some flexibility needs to be left to companies themselves to make choices appropriate to their particular circumstances. If companies have a good reason not to comply with a particular aspect, then they should be able to explain this to shareholders.

Disclosure in practice

Companies are taking this aspect of reporting very seriously. Consequently, a large part of company reports is devoted to corporate governance aspects. The following sections are given by Logica.

Corporate governance aspects

> The Board endorses and supports the best practice guidelines contained in the 2006 Financial Reporting Council's Combined Code (the Combined Code) through its commitment to the highest standards of corporate governance. Apart from a few limited exceptions as described below, the Board believes that the Group has fully complied with the Combined Code throughout 2007; where it has not, an explanation has been provided.

Note the reference by Logica to the Combined Code.

Non-executive directors' independence

In terms of non-executive directors, and their independence, Logica makes the following disclosures.

> The Board recognises the valuable contribution independent Directors can make. During 2007 the Board considered the independence of the Non-Executive Directors and concluded that each of the Non-Executive Directors were independent in character and judgement.
>
> The Company believes that all Non-Executive Directors bring relevant experience to the Board and make valuable contributions to achieving its objectives. They do not act with self-interest and their primary aims are to maximise shareholder wealth and develop the Company in line with its strategic goals.
>
> During the year, the Company believes that none of the Non-Executive Directors held significant commitments outside the Company which would interfere with their ability to execute their responsibilities effectively.

Logica also take its responsibility regarding shareholders very seriously. Shareholders views are sought, and the company claims these views are listened to. The company indicates that shareholders are welcome to attend the AGM, and provides information about the company on its website. Disclosure is given as outlined below.

Communication with shareholders

> The Board gives a high priority to communication with shareholders and takes the opportunities afforded by the AGM and meetings with institutional investors to ensure a mutual understanding of the Company's objectives and performance. During the year, members of the Board have listened to a number of key investors in order to understand their views fully. These exchanges led to the Nominations Committee and the Board reconsidering the size and structure of the Board, and led to its restructuring during 2007.
>
> All shareholders are welcomed to the AGM where developments in the business are explained and shareholders have the opportunity to ask questions of any of the Directors.

BASIC

INTERMEDIATE

ADVANCED

The Company's website www.logica.com provides access for all shareholders to information about the Company, including results presentations and all press releases. Financial reporting is presented in such a way as to provide a balanced and understandable assessment of the Company's position and prospects.

The board is made aware of shareholders' views through feedback from face-to-face meetings and presentations with institutional shareholders.

As required by the codes, separation of the role of chairman and chief executive is followed by Logica.

Chairman and chief executive officer

There is a clear division of responsibility between the running of the Board by the Chairman, and the Chief Executive Officer's responsibility for running the business. The Chairman is responsible for ensuring the effectiveness of the Board and is Chairman of the Nominations Committee. He also liaises with the Chief Executive Officer on strategic issues. The Chief Executive Officer is responsible for the overall management of the Company and for leading the Executive Directors and the Executive Committee.

Again, in accordance with the Combined Code requirements and those of Smith, an audit committee has been established. Note the list of some of the matters considered by the audit committee. Some of this information is disclosed by Logica, as follows.

Audit committee

The composition of the Company's Audit Committee and its terms of reference reflect the Combined Code and the Smith Guidance.

The Committee is authorised by the Board to investigate any activity within its terms of reference and to seek any information that it requires from any employee of the Company and its subsidiaries. All employees are directed to cooperate with any request made by the Committee. The Committee has the right to consult the Company's professional advisers or, if it is not satisfied with the advice received, seek further independent professional advice at the Company's expense in the furtherance of its duties. The Committee believes that the skills, qualifications and commercial experience of its members are appropriate for them to perform their duties in accordance with the terms of reference laid down by the Board.

During the year, the Committee specifically considered, among other things, the following matters:

- the appropriateness of the Company's accounting policies were also reviewed and approved
- the review of the 2006 full-year preliminary and 2007 interim announcements
- the review of the Company's 2006 annual report and accounts, in particular the financial overview, report of the Directors, financial statements (including notes to the accounts) and relevant sections of the Corporate Governance report. These were recommended for approval to the Board
- the internal audit and quality assurance plans for 2007 were reviewed and approved. These reports and updates additionally covered the Company's management of its internal controls
- the review of the financial position of the Company's defined benefit pension schemes
- an extensive goodwill evaluation covering the Group's activities which supported the carrying value thereof with no impairment deemed necessary.

As required by the Combined Code, a remuneration committee is also necessary.

Remuneration committee

The Company's Remuneration Committee is comprised of at least three independent Non-Executive Directors in accordance with the recommendations of the Combined Code.

The Committee is authorised by the Board to investigate any activity within its terms of reference. The Committee has the right to appoint independent advisers and, if it is not satisfied with the advice received, seek further independent professional advice at the Company's expense in the furtherance of its duties. For the year reported, Kepler Associates were the principal independent advisers to the Committee. The Committee's key role is to determine the Company's senior executive remuneration policy and levels of remuneration for the Company's Executive Committee, the higher paid senior management, Company Secretary and Head of Internal Audit. The Committee takes into consideration the pay and conditions of employment for employees when considering Executives' remuneration.

Summary

Limited company financial statements are publicly available documents. As such, their presentation and content is standardised and is prescribed by law. In addition, various regulatory bodies govern the content and the rules to be followed in the preparation of published financial statements. There are various stakeholders who may have an interest in financial statements, but the primary users are taken to be investors. As well as an income statement and balance sheet, financial statements comprise additional narrative information to assist the user in the decision-making process.

This intermediate section has focused on the preparation and presentation of company financial statements. Basic understanding of how to prepare a set of financial statements was extended by introducing the requirements of company law and accounting standards. This knowledge was then applied in order to prepare financial statements that would be published and made available to shareholders and other users.

Company financial statements follow the same accounting principles as those applied to other types of business organisation. However, in the case of companies, the differences arise in terms of financing and in ownership. Companies are financed by issuing shares, to shareholders, and sometimes by long-term borrowing (debentures). Shareholders are rewarded by being paid a dividend, while debenture holders will receive an interest payment.

Company financial statements, as well as being required to show minimum amounts of information, must be presented in a specific way. The rules governing the presentation and preparation of company financial statements are specified in the law and in the accounting standards.

The law requires that companies, or more specifically those running the company, the directors:

- maintain proper accounting records
- prepare annual financial statements
- give a report on their (i.e. the directors') activities
- make sure the reports are available.

The regulations governing how the statements should be prepared are contained in the International Financial Reporting Standards, or IFRS. These were formally known as International Accounting Standards, or IAS. Specifically, the standard that applies to company financial statements is IAS 1 *Presentation of Financial Statements*. This standard sets out the structure and content of financial statements. Financial statements should comprise:

- a balance sheet, now to be called a statement of financial position
- a profit and loss account, sometimes called an income statement, now to be called a statement of comprehensive income
- statement of changes in equity
- statement of cash flows
- notes containing a summary of the main accounting policies of the company and other information.

The annual audit requirement is a further regulatory function that helps to ensure the publication of high-quality accounting information by companies.

The section concludes with an overview of corporate governance. Corporate governance refers to the way in which a company is administered and controlled. It is becoming increasingly important for companies not only to act ethically, but be seen to be so doing. The principles of good corporate governance are outlined by the OECD as:

- responsibility
- accountability
- transparency
- fairness.

Common accepted principles of corporate governance tend to differ, depending on the variety of capitalism in which they are embedded. The two general models are the 'liberal' model, which gives priority to the interests of shareholders, and the 'coordinated' model, which gives priority to the interests of workers, managers, customers, suppliers and the wider community.

Codes and guidelines have been developed worldwide, the most influential coming from the OECD.

As far as the UK is concerned, corporate governance came into being with the formation of the Financial Aspects of Corporate Governance, leading to the publication of the Cadbury Report. Over time, various other reports and recommendations were issued, resulting in the Combined Code being published. This code has subsequently been updated.

Clearly corporate governance is seen to be a very important aspect of company reporting. In matters of corporate governance it is recognised that one specific set of rules will not necessarily work for every company. So, while there is no strict legal requirement to comply with the provisions of corporate governance codes, should a company choose not to, an explanation must be given as to the reasons for non-compliance. Shareholders and other users are then in a position to monitor and judge for themselves such explanations.

Section 3: Advanced Aspects

1.9 Conceptual framework

Introduction

As the previous sections of this chapter have illustrated, financial reports are constructed in accordance with generally accepted accounting principles. In reality, there is potentially an almost unlimited number of ways in which financial transactions could be recorded and accumulated to produce financial reports. Without any rules or guidelines as to how these reports should be prepared, accountants would be faced with an impossible task in preparation, and users would have little confidence in their content. The guidelines that govern financial reporting have evolved over time as being those that help in the achievement of overall objectives. Consequently, the overall objectives of financial reporting first need to be identified before the rules and guidelines can be formulated.

For a number of years, attempts have been made to develop an agreed conceptual framework for financial accounting and reporting. A conceptual framework consists of a set of agreed fundamental principles that underpin financial accounting, and consequently provide a sound theoretical basis for developing new financial reporting practices and for assessing existing ones. A conceptual framework addresses such issues as:

- what a set of financial statements should include
- which events should be included in a set of financial statements

- how these events should be measured
- how these events should be communicated to users.

The development of such a conceptual framework is not an easy task; as business becomes more and more complex, so too do the accounting transactions that serve as the monetary audit trail evidencing complicated contracts and events. Moreover, as the objectives of financial reporting may change over time, it is possible that the guidelines that helped the achievement of objectives in one time period will no longer be relevant in later time periods. In this sense, accountancy can be seen to be a continually evolving discipline. It is perhaps an indication of the complexity of the task that there is no currently agreed conceptual framework. Work began in the 1970s in both the UK and the USA to devise such a framework and, while both the UK and the USA have their own frameworks, the UK has its Statement of Principles and the USA its Statements of Financial Accounting Concepts; there is not one common conceptual framework.

1.10 The IASB Framework

The IASB conceptual framework is termed the 'Framework for the Preparation and Presentation of Financial Statements' (the 'Framework'). The Framework itself is not an accounting standard and does not override any standards. Indeed, the Framework specifically states in paragraph 3 that, where there is a conflict between the Framework and an International Accounting Standard, 'the requirements of the IAS will prevail over those of the Framework'.

Purposes of the IASB Framework

The main purposes of the IASB Framework are stated in paragraph 1 as being to:
(a) assist in the development of future international standards and in the review of existing standards
(b) assist in the harmonisation of regulations, accounting standards and procedures by providing a basis for reducing the number of alternative treatments permitted by international standards
(c) assist national standard-setting bodies in developing national standards
(d) assist preparers of financial statements in applying international standards and in dealing with topics that have yet to form the subject of an international standard
(e) assist auditors in forming an opinion as to whether financial statements conform with international standards
(f) assist users of financial statements in interpreting the information contained in financial statements prepared in accordance with international standards
(g) provide information about the formulation of international standards.

Scope

The Framework deals with:
(a) the objective of financial statements
(b) the qualitative characteristics that determine the usefulness of information in financial statements
(c) the definition, recognition and measurement of the elements from which financial statements are constructed, and
(d) concepts of capital and capital maintenance.

The Framework is concerned with general-purpose financial statements (including consolidated financial statements) that an enterprise prepares and presents at least annually and that are directed towards the common information needs of a wide range of users. Special-purpose reports, such as prospectuses and computations prepared for tax purposes, are outside the scope of the Framework. The Framework states that a complete set of financial statements normally includes a balance sheet, an income statement and a cash flow statement, and those notes and other statements and explanatory

BASIC

INTERMEDIATE

ADVANCED

material that form an integral part of the financial statements. Financial statements do not, however, include certain other items, such as reports by directors or statements by the chairman. The Framework applies to the financial statements of all commercial, industrial and business reporting entities. A reporting entity is an entity for which there are users who rely on the financial statements as their major source of financial information about the entity.

Users and their information needs

The main users of financial statements are identified as follows.

■ *Investors* need information to:
   – assess the stewardship of management, e.g. in safeguarding the entity's resources and using them properly, efficiently and profitably
   – take decisions about management, e.g. assessing the need for new management
   – take decisions about their investment or potential investment, e.g. deciding whether to hold, buy or sell shares, and assessing the ability to pay dividends.

■ *Lenders* need information to:
   – determine whether their loans and interest will be paid on time
   – decide whether to lend and on what terms.

■ *Suppliers* need information to:
   – decide whether to sell to the entity
   – determine whether they will be paid on time
   – determine longer-term stability if the company is a major customer.

■ *Employees* need information to:
   – assess the stability and profitability of the company
   – assess the ability to provide remuneration, retirement benefits and employment opportunities.

■ *Customers* need information to:
   – assess the probability of the continued existence of the company, taking account of their own degree of dependence on the company, e.g. for future provision of specialised replacement parts and servicing product warranties.

■ *Government and other agencies* need information to:
   – be aware of the commercial activities of the company
   – regulate these activities
   – raise revenue
   – produce national statistics.

■ *Public.* Members of the public need information to:
   – determine the effect on the local economy of the company's activities, e.g. employment opportunities, use of local suppliers
   – assess recent developments in the company's prosperity and changes in its activities.

The Framework recognises that financial statements cannot provide all the information that users may need to make economic decisions, but states that there are needs that are common to all users, and that the provision of financial statements that meet the needs of investors will also meet most of the general information needs of other users. This statement is open to contradiction.

1.11 Responsibility for financial statements

The Framework states that the management of an enterprise has the primary responsibility for preparing and presenting an entity's financial statements.

The main sections of the IASB Framework are as follows:

(a) the objective of financial statements
(b) underlying assumptions
(c) qualitative characteristics of financial statements
(d) the elements of financial statements
(e) recognition of the elements of financial statements
(f) measurement of the elements of financial statements
(g) concepts of capital and capital maintenance.

Each of these is dealt with below.

Objective of financial statements

The objective of financial statements is to provide information about the financial position of an enterprise that is useful to a wide range of users in making economic decisions (para. 12). The Framework states in paragraph 19 that:

- information about financial position is primarily provided in a balance sheet
- information about performance is primarily provided in an income statement
- information about changes in financial position is provided in the financial statements by means of a separate statement (usually a cash flow statement).

The financial statements also contain notes and supplementary schedules, and other information that:

- explains items in the balance sheet and income statement
- discloses the risks and uncertainties affecting the enterprise, and
- explains any resources and obligations not recognised in the balance sheet.

The Framework recognises that financial statements do not provide all the information that users may need to make economic decisions since they largely portray the financial effects of past events and do not necessarily provide non-financial information.

The Framework includes two underlying assumptions: that the financial statements are prepared on the accruals basis and that the business is a going concern.

Accruals basis

Under the accruals basis, the effects of transactions and other events are recognised when they occur (and not when cash is received or paid), and are recorded in the financial statements of the periods to which they relate. Consequently, financial statements include obligations to pay cash in the future (e.g. creditors) and resources that represent cash to be received in the future (e.g. debtors).

Going concern

The financial statements are normally prepared on the assumption that the business is a going concern and will continue in operation for the foreseeable future. Under this assumption fixed assets, for example, are depreciated over their estimated useful life as it is assumed that the business will continue and use the asset in the future. If the company is not a going concern it would be more relevant to value the assets on a sales basis.

BASIC

INTERMEDIATE

ADVANCED

Qualitative characteristics of financial statements

These characteristics are the attributes that make the information in financial statements useful to users. The Framework identifies four principal qualitative characteristics:

1.   understandability
2.   relevance
3.   reliability
4.   comparability.

Each of these characteristics is explained below.

Understandability

An essential quality of the information provided in the financial statements is that it is readily understandable by users. There is a problem in that different users will have differing levels of accounting knowledge. The Framework suggests that 'users are assumed to have a reasonable knowledge of business and economic activities and accounting and a willingness to study the information with reasonable diligence'. It is also stated that relevant information should not be excluded merely on the grounds that it may be too difficult for certain users to understand.

Relevance

To be useful, information must be relevant to the decision-making needs of users. Information in financial statements is relevant when it influences the economic decisions of users by helping them evaluate past, present or future events, or confirming or correcting their past evaluations.

Materiality is a component of relevance. Information is material if its omission or misstatement could influence the economic decisions of users.

Reliability

Information in financial statements is reliable if it is free from material error and bias, and can be depended upon by users to represent events and transactions faithfully. Information is not reliable when it is purposely designed to influence users' decisions in a particular direction. There are various aspects in relation to reliability, as discussed below.

■   *Faithful representation:* to be reliable, information must represent faithfully the transactions and other events it purports to represent or could reasonably be expected to represent. However, there may be inherent difficulties either in identifying the transactions and other events to be measured or in devising and applying measurement and preparation techniques that can convey messages that correspond with those transactions and events. Consequently, the measurement of an item could be so uncertain that an entity would not recognise the item in the financial statements at all. The Framework cites the example of internally generated goodwill as being difficult to identify or measure reliably. In other cases, however, it may be relevant to recognise items but then disclose the risk of error surrounding their recognition and measurement.

■   *Substance over form:* this requires that transactions and other events are accounted for and presented in accordance with their substance and economic reality and not merely their legal form. The substance of transactions may be very different from their legal or contrived form. For example, an entity may dispose of an asset to another party in such a way that legal ownership of the asset is transferred but (in actual fact) the entity continues to enjoy the economic benefits associated with the asset. In such circumstances, the reporting of a sale would not faithfully represent the reality of the situation.

- *Neutrality:* to be reliable, the information contained in financial statements must be neutral (i.e. free from bias). Financial statements are not neutral if they are prepared so as to achieve a predetermined result.
- *Prudence:* prudence is the inclusion of a degree of caution in the exercise of the judgements needed in making the estimates required under conditions of uncertainty, such that assets or income are not overstated, and liabilities or expenses are not understated. However, prudence does not justify the deliberate overstatement of liabilities or expenses, or the deliberate understatement of assets or income, because the financial statements would not be neutral and, therefore, would not have the quality of reliability.
- *Completeness:* to be reliable, the information in financial statements must be complete within the bounds of materiality and cost. An omission can cause information to be false or misleading, and thus unreliable and deficient in terms of its relevance. This aspect is another reminder of the dilemma facing any search for reporting objectives. Sufficient disclosure to meet the needs of one group of users may be considered excessive disclosure, and thereby harmful by another group of users.

Comparability

Users must be able to compare the financial statements of an entity over time so that they can identify trends in its financial position and performance. Users must also be able to compare the financial statements of different entities. Comparability will be improved if entities adopt accounting policies that are consistent over time as well as consistent with the accounting policies adopted by other entities. In addition, users need to be informed of the accounting policies employed in the preparation of the financial statements, any changes in those policies and the effects of such changes. Finally, it is important that the financial statements show corresponding information for preceding periods.

Compliance with international standards helps to achieve comparability. The Framework does note, however, that the need for comparability should not be allowed to become an impediment to the introduction of improved accounting standards. It would be inappropriate for an entity to leave its accounting policies unchanged when more relevant and reliable alternatives exist.

Constraints on relevant and reliable information

The Framework identifies three constraints that may prevent the information provided in financial statements from being completely relevant and reliable.

1. *Timeliness:* to be useful, information must be provided to users within the time period in which it is most likely to bear on their decisions. Consequently, while highly reliable information may be obtained by delaying the reporting of an event, if users have had to make decisions in the interim, the information may be of little use. It is, therefore, necessary to achieve a balance between relevance and reliability to best satisfy the economic decision-making needs of users.
2. *Balance between benefit and cost:* the benefits derived from information should exceed the cost of providing it. The evaluation of benefits and costs is, however, a judgemental process and it is therefore difficult to apply a cost–benefit analysis in practice.
3. *Balance between qualitative characteristics:* in practice a trade-off between qualitative characteristics is often necessary. Generally, the aim is to achieve an appropriate balance among the characteristics in order to meet the objectives of financial statements. The relative importance of the characteristics in different cases is a matter of professional judgement.

The elements of financial statements

Financial statements portray the financial effects of transactions and other events by grouping them into broad classes according to their economic characteristics. These broad classes are termed the elements of financial statements, and the Framework distinguishes between those elements that are

BASIC

INTERMEDIATE

ADVANCED

directly related to the measurement of financial position in the balance sheet and those that are directly related to the measurement of performance in the income statement.

Financial position

The elements directly related to the measurement of financial position are assets, liabilities and equity. These are defined as follows.

- *Assets:* an asset is a resource controlled by the entity as a result of past events and from which future economic benefits are expected to flow to the entity. In Chapter 2, this definition is examined in detail.
- *Liabilities:* a liability is a present obligation of the entity arising from past events, the settlement of which is expected to result in an outflow from the entity of resources embodying economic benefits. This definition is examined in detail in Chapter 7.
- *Equity:* equity is the residual interest in the assets of the entity after deducting all its liabilities. This is examined in detail in Chapter 6.

Performance

The Framework states that profit is frequently used as a measure of performance and that the elements directly related to the measurement of profit are income and expenses. These are defined as follows.

- *Income:* income is increases in economic benefits during the accounting period in the form of inflows or enhancements of assets or decreases of liabilities that result in increases in equity, other than those relating to contributions from equity participants. The definition of income encompasses both revenue and gains. Revenue arises in the course of the ordinary activities of an entity (e.g. sales, fees, interest, dividends, royalties and rent). Gains represent other items that meet the definition of income, and may or may not arise in the course of the ordinary activities of an entity (e.g. gains arising on the disposal of fixed assets).
- *Expenses:* expenses are decreases in economic benefits during the accounting period in the form of outflows or depletions of assets or incurrence of liabilities that result in decreases in equity, other than those relating to distributions to equity participants. The definition of expenses encompasses losses as well as those expenses that arise in the course of the ordinary activities of the entity. Expenses that arise in the course of the ordinary activities of the entity include, for example, cost of sales, wages and depreciation. They usually take the form of an outflow or depletion of assets such as cash, inventory, plant and equipment. Losses represent other items that meet the definition of expenses, and may or may not arise in the course of the ordinary activities of the entity. Losses represent decreases in economic benefits and as such they are no different in nature from other expenses. The fact that income and expenses are defined in terms of increases or decreases in net assets has led to the suggestion that the IASB Framework takes a 'balance sheet approach' to defining the elements of financial statements.

Recognition of the elements of financial statements

Not all the items that meet the above definitions will be recognised in the financial statements. Recognition is the process of incorporating in the balance sheet or income statement an item that meets the definition of an element and satisfies the following criteria for recognition:

- it is probable that any future economic benefit associated with the item will flow to or from the entity, and
- the item has a cost or value that can be measured with reliability.

These criteria apply principally to the recognition of assets and liabilities, since equity is defined as the difference between an entity's total assets and total liabilities, and the other elements of the financial statements (income and expenses) are defined in terms of changes in the entity's assets and liabilities.

That is, the recognition criteria for an asset, for example, automatically requires the recognition of another element, for example, income or a liability.

The probability of future economic benefit

The use of the word probable in the recognition criteria is simply to reflect the environment in which the entity operates. There will always be a degree of uncertainty surrounding particular transactions – no one, for example, can say for certain that a debtor will pay. However, if it is probable that the amount will be received then the recognition of this amount as an asset (and related revenue) will be justifiable.

Reliability of measurement

In some instances, it may not be possible to obtain a precise cost or value and therefore an estimate must be used. The Framework acknowledges that the use of estimates is an essential part of the preparation of financial statements and that this does not undermine their reliability. When, however, a reasonable estimate cannot be made the item is not recognised in the balance sheet or income statement.

An item that possesses the essential characteristics of an element but fails to meet the recognition criteria may instead warrant disclosure in the notes to the financial statements.

Based on these general recognition criteria:

- an *asset* is recognised in the balance sheet when it is probable that the future economic benefits will flow to the entity and the asset has a cost or value that can be measured reliably
- a *liability* is recognised in the balance sheet when it is probable that an outflow of resources embodying economic benefits will result from the settlement of a present obligation and the amount at which the settlement will take place can be measured reliably
- *income* is recognised in the income statement when an increase in future economic benefits related to an increase in an asset or a decrease of a liability has arisen that can be measured reliably; this means, in effect, that recognition of income occurs simultaneously with the recognition of increases in assets or decreases in liabilities
- *expenses* are recognised when a decrease in future economic benefits related to a decrease in an asset or an increase of a liability has arisen that can be measured reliably; this means, in effect, that recognition of expenses occurs simultaneously with the recognition of an increase in liabilities or a decrease in assets.

Measurement of the elements of financial statements

Measurement is the process of determining the monetary amounts at which the elements of the financial statements are to be recognised and reported.

The Framework acknowledges that a variety of measurement bases are used today to different degrees and in varying combinations in financial statements. They include the following.

- *Historical cost:* assets are recorded at the amount paid to acquire them. Liabilities are recorded at the amount of proceeds received in exchange for the obligation, or in some circumstances (e.g. income taxes) at the amount expected to be paid to satisfy the liability in the normal course of business.
- *Current cost:* assets are carried at the amount that would have to be paid to acquire an asset currently (replacement cost). Liabilities are carried at the undiscounted amount that would be required to settle the obligation currently.
- *Realisable (settlement) value:* assets are carried at the amount that could currently be obtained by selling the asset in an orderly disposal. Liabilities are carried at the undiscounted amount expected to be paid to satisfy the obligation in the normal course of business.

BASIC

INTERMEDIATE

ADVANCED

■ *Present value*: assets are carried at the present discounted value of the future cash inflows that the item is expected to generate in the normal course of business. Liabilities are carried at the present discounted value of the future net cash outflows that are expected to be required to settle the liabilities in the normal course of business.

The Framework states that the measurement basis most commonly used is historical cost, but that it is usually combined with other measurement bases. For example, inventories are usually carried at the lower of cost and net realisable value. The Framework also states that some entities use the current cost basis to deal with the effects of changing prices of non-monetary assets (e.g. inflationary pressures on property). A particular criticism of the Framework is that it does not include concepts or principles for selecting which measurement basis should be used for particular elements of financial statements or in particular circumstances. A conceptual framework ought to prescribe such measurement bases rather than simply describing the bases that tend to be adopted in practice. The qualitative characteristics noted earlier do, however, provide some guidance.

The concept of capital and capital maintenance

The final section of the Framework is concerned with the concept of capital and capital maintenance. The Framework states that a financial concept of capital is adopted by most entities in preparing their financial statements. Under a financial concept of capital, capital is synonymous with the net assets or equity of the entity. The Framework offers an alternative view of capital, however: that of physical capital. Under a physical concept of capital, capital is regarded as the productive capacity of the entity based on, for example, units of output per day.

The selection of the appropriate concept of capital by an entity should be based on the needs of the users of its financial statements. The concept chosen indicates the goal to be attained in determining profit. For example, if the users of the financial statements are primarily concerned with the maintenance of invested capital then a financial concept of capital should be adopted. If, however, the main concern of users is with the operating capability of the entity, a physical concept of capital should be used.

The Framework distinguishes between these two ways of comparing an entity's capital at the beginning and the end of the accounting period, and so determining the profit, as follows.

1. *Financial capital maintenance*: under this concept a profit is earned only if the financial amount of the net assets at the end of the period exceeds the financial amount of net assets at the beginning of the period after adjusting for any amounts distributed to or contributed by the owners during the period. Financial capital maintenance can be measured in either nominal monetary units or units of constant purchasing power, i.e. where purchasing power is determined in accordance with changes in an index of general prices.

2. *Physical capital maintenance*: under this concept a profit is earned only if the physical operating capability of the entity at the end of the period is greater than its physical operating capability at the start of the period after adjusting for any amounts distributed to or contributed by the owners during the period.

The Framework states that the selection of measurement bases and concept of capital maintenance will determine the accounting model used in the preparation of the financial statements. The Framework does not, however, prescribe a particular model other than in exceptional circumstances, such as those entities reporting in the currency of a hyperinflationary economy. Instead, the Framework merely points out that different accounting models exhibit different degrees of relevance and reliability, and states that an entity's management must seek a balance between relevance and reliability when choosing an appropriate model.

In the introduction to this section it was suggested that accountancy could be seen as a 'continually evolving' discipline. The final sentence of the Framework concurs with this suggestion by concluding. 'This intention [to prescribe a particular model] will, however, be reviewed in light of world developments.' The implications this would have are considered in more detail in the following section.

1.12 Income, value and capital

Income

Introduction

In financial statements, the measurement of income is a basic requirement. Income is generally used as a basis for determining the tax to be paid, as a basis for paying dividends and also, in some contexts, as a basis for decision making. The income statement is an important part of the stewardship function of accounting reports, in that it provides information to shareholders on how well or how badly the company is performing.

The main problem with the income statement stems from the fact that there is not one universally agreed concept of 'income'. There are many ways in which net income can be derived. In addition, there are different viewpoints on how income should be measured, especially in times of price level changes. Income statements are of little use in short-term decision making, nor do they provide any physical or behavioural information that would have the potential to increase the usefulness of income statements.

Generally speaking, income can be defined in one of two ways.

1. *Operationally:* some theorists have argued that the only way of measuring income is to apply a set of measurement rules and so calculate income this way.
2. *Conceptually:* this is perhaps a more satisfactory way to define income. Individuals need to have some mental 'picture' of what income means to them. If this is not possible, then the calculation of income must be open to different interpretations. In its broadest sense, income is a concept of being 'better off'.

Value

At its more theoretical, and possibly in its most relevant sense, value is a totally *subjective* and individualistic concept, but may have a meaning as an *objective* concept.

Subjective vs objective notions of value

Consider the situation where there are two individuals. Individual A, who owns a boat, and Individual B, who owns a car. Individual A exchanges the boat for Individual B's car. Are the car and the boat of equal value?

In a *subjective* sense (i.e. directly involved sense) the car and the boat are not of equal value, since if the two objects were of equal value in all senses, why would individuals go to the bother of exchanging the items?

In an *objective* sense (third party looking in), the two objects must be of equal value since no further consideration was required by either party. So, the boat and the car can be said to be of 'equivalent value in exchange'.

From a theoretical point of view, subjective value is the most relevant since it is this value that motivates economic activity. This economic activity is what accountants report on, and it is to the directly involved individuals that accountants report to.

Concepts of value

Economic value (present value) of individuals

In an ideal sense, the value to be measured and reported would be related to individuals, and would be the present value of the future cash flows to be derived from individual investment. These cash flows would be discounted at a rate that would reflect individual time preferences for cash. Because this concept of value represents the 'ideal' situation, it gives rise to certain problems.

- It would require the preparation of reports for each individual.
- It would be necessary to establish individual tastes and preferences to establish the appropriate discount rate.
- It would require the projection of future cash flows, in terms of when these would occur and how much they would be.

This measure of income tends therefore to be rather subjective and impractical. A more practical method would be to measure from the point of view of a firm, since some kind of investment value of the firm could be determined.

Economic value (*present value*) of firms (*EV*)

This measure of value gives the closest approximation to the 'ideal' situation. Value in this context is what the existing asset will be worth to the business over the rest of its useful life. It is measured as the present value of the future cash flows associated with the net assets of firms, discounted at the firms' cost of capital. It is objective in the sense that it is market determined (investment market) but is still subjective in that it rests on expectations regarding future cash flows and continued use of assets.

In this sense, value measured from this perspective is more realistic than the individualist 'ideal' concept of economic value, and is more objective as a possible basis for accounting measurement. Direct measurement, however, still entails considerable problems.

Current entry value (*replacement cost*) (*NRC*)

Entry value is the current cost to replace an asset (or its services) and represents an input market value. It is a measure of what it would cost to replace the asset (net of depreciation on a fixed asset). Entry value is a more objective measure of value than economic value, but is still subjective in the sense that it is based on future expectations, that of replacing like with like.

Current exit value (*net realisable value*) (*NRV*)

Exit value represents what the asset could be sold for (net of any disposal costs). Exit value is objective in the sense that it is a function of market price, but there is still an element of subjectivity since it is based upon future expectations – not in the sense of disposal, but in the sense of 'opportunity cost'-based decision making.

Each of the above concepts of value seeks to be objective, since each concept relates to:

- market prices relevant to the firm
- the activities of the firm
- decision making
- the cost of investment capital for the acquisition and/or the disposal of resources.

Each concept taken on its own as the proper valuation method for all resources for all firms under all circumstances is likely to present problems.

Deprival value (*value in use*)

Deprival value has been defined as follows:

> The value of a property to its owners is identical in amount with the adverse value of the entire loss, direct or indirect, that the owner might expect to suffer if he were to be deprived of the property.

In other words, this is a concept based on 'value to the business'. This is the extra funds that would be required to maintain the operating capability of the business if it suddenly lost (was deprived of) the asset.

Deprival value avoids the implicit assumptions of a 'single value' approach applied across all resources since it does not presuppose the superiority of the firm's production process in the future – in other words, that replacement is a viable and realistic alternative. Nor does it presuppose that disposal is always a realistic alternative.

What deprival value does imply is that one of the other three 'primary' measures of value – EV, NRV or NRC – might be the value to the business depending on the specific circumstances a firm might face. Deprival value therefore raises the possibility of different alternative measures of value in difference circumstances. Table 1.1 elaborates on these circumstances.

	Ranking	Explanation
1	NRV>EV>NRC	This ranking implies that the firm holds its assets for resale. Since NRV is greater than EV the firm would expect to sell the asset rather than use it. But since NRV>NRC the firm could get more from selling the asset than it would cost to replace. The firm would be induced to sell and replace the asset. Deprival value would therefore be NRC.
2	NRV>NRC>EV	A similar argument applies here as in (1) above, so deprival value is again NRC.
3	EV>NRC>NRV	In this situation, since EV is greater than NRV the asset would be held for use rather than for resale. However, since EV>NRC the firm would replace the asset, so the deprival value would be NRC.
4	EV>NRV>NRC	A similar argument applies here as in (3) above. The maximum loss the company would suffer, i.e. deprival value would be NRC.
5	NRC>EV>NRV	In this situation since EV is greater than NRV the firm would hold the asset for use, rather than sell. Since NRC is greater than EV (value in use) if the firm were deprived of the asset it would not replace it. Deprival value in this case is EV.
6	NRC>NRV>EV	Since NRV is greater than EV the firm would hold the asset for resale rather that for use. However, NRC is greater than NRV, which means that the firm would not sell the asset, so is deprived of selling the asset. Deprival value in this case is NRV.

Table 1.1 Alternative ranking of value measures

In all but two of the above cases, deprival value is the same as NRC. In only one case is deprival value the same as NRV, and there is one case where deprival value is the same as EV. The following rule may be applied to determine deprival value:

Deprival value is the lower of replacement cost (NRC) and the higher of economic value (EV) and net realisable value (NRV). In other words, a comparison is made between EV and NRV, and the higher figure is chosen. This figure is compared with NRC and the lower figure is chosen (see Figure 1.7).

Figure 1.7 Determination of deprival value

Deprival value does not presuppose that disposal is a viable and realistic alternative, nor that continued use is always a viable and realistic alternative with any particular resource. Instead deprival value implies that any of the other primary values – EV, NRV or NRC – might be the value to the business depending on the particular circumstances. Deprival value therefore allows alternative measures of value.

Capital

Capital may be thought of as a mirror image of net assets of a firm. For any set of assets there will be a set of individuals who have a beneficial interest in those assets. These individuals could be, for example, shareholders or lenders. In this context, capital is a concept of an investment interest, money at risk looking for a return. The major interest is that of the owners, therefore 'capital' is often used to refer to owners' equity:

Capital = Owners' equity

Capital may also be thought of as the investment by the firm in productive assets. These assets are the resource base of the firm. In this context:

Capital = Total assets

These two concepts of capital lead to two concepts of return on capital: return on investment and return on assets.

1. *Return on investment:* in this case, capital is defined as owners' equity. If this is measured, then from the point of view of the shareholders there will be some efficiency measure, e.g. earnings per share. Capital in this context is based on proprietary theory.
2. *Return on assets:* in this case, capital is defined as the resources of the firm. If these resources are measured, then there will be an efficiency measure from the point of view of the firm. An example of such an efficiency measure is return on assets (profit/total assets). In this context capital is based on entity theory.

These two concepts of capital and return on capital lead to two concepts of capital maintenance: maintaining the value of the owners' investment and the capacity of that investment to generate future cash flows; alternatively, maintaining the value of the productive capacity of the firm to generate positive cash flows in the future. This could be done by replacing assets actually used, maintaining assets needed to produce the same volume or sales value of output.

The concepts of capital maintenance identified above relate to the maintaining of 'value'. However, it should be noted that 'value' is measurable in money, the purchasing power of which can vary over time. In an accounting measurement sense, over a specific time period the measured value of assets can change.

The measured gain (loss) can therefore be determined by comparing the change in the net assets with the change in owners' equity. The total gain measured will depend on the measurement rules and the various accounting principles applied. Recognition of a major gain (loss) is a distinguishing feature of alternative theories and measurement systems.

It is important to measure separately and report any gains (losses), since there is a presumption that information about the past is useful in the formulation of expectations regarding the future and, as such, is a useful aid to decision making. The total gain (loss) recognised by any system can contain only two types of gain (loss), mainly because firms can do only one of two things with assets:

1. keep (hold) them, so if there is a price change during the holding period the firm can be said to have made a *holding gain* (incurred a holding loss)
2. do something with them – the firm can add/combine to produce new assets or provide services, and in doing so firm can be said to have made an *operating gain* (incurred an operating loss).

Two further distinctions can be drawn. Holding and operating gains (losses) may be incurred, but be either:

1. *realised* – this is associated with the actual sale or disposal of the asset or liability
2. *unrealised* – this is a gain or loss associated with an asset or liability still retained by the firm.

Accounting reporting methods may be classified according to the asset valuation method used and the capital maintenance concept employed. The asset valuation method determines the 'value' of assets in the balance sheet and the amount of operating cost to be included in the income statement.

The capital maintenance concept determines how much income is required to be set aside to maintain the 'value' of invested capital. As indicated in the previous section, assets may be valued using a number of different bases.

1.13 Concepts of income

Accounting concept of income

Accounting income is defined in an operational sense as the difference between realised revenues that arise from transactions in a particular time period and the costs associated with earning those revenues. From this perspective, accounting income is based on the actual transactions entered into by the firm.

Accounting income is also based on a specific time period and refers to the financial performance of the firm during this time period. The test for recognition of revenue is the realisation principle. Measurement of expenses is done in terms of historic cost. An asset is accounted for at the cost of acquisition, so from this point of view expenses are expired assets or expired acquisition costs. Accounting income is based on the matching principle in that it requires that realised revenues are related to the corresponding costs associated with earning these revenues.

Advantages and disadvantages of accounting income

■   It has survived the test of time. Most users of accounting information believe that accounting income is useful.
■   It is based on actual transactions, and therefore measured and reported objectively. It is basically verifiable.
■   It is 'conservative' in that it relies on the realisation principle for the recognition of revenue.
■   It is considered useful for control purposes, especially in the context of reporting on stewardship of resources.

BASIC

INTERMEDIATE

ADVANCED

However, accounting income has also been criticised on the following grounds.

- It fails to recognise unrealised increases in the values of assets held. This prevents useful information from being disclosed.
- It makes comparability difficult given the many different ways of computing 'cost' and the many different ways of cost allocation.
- It relies on the realisation principle, historic cost principle and conservatism principle, and so may result in the production of data that is misunderstood by or is irrelevant to users.
- The reliance on the historic cost principle may give the impression that the balance sheet gives some approximation of 'value' rather than just representing the unallocated costs.

Economic concept of income

A new perspective on the nature of the economic concept of income came from the writings of Fisher, Lindhal and Hicks. Fisher defined economic income as a series of events that corresponds to different states.

- *Psychic income:* this is the actual personal consumption of goods and services that produces the satisfaction of wants and so produces psychic enjoyment. It is a psychological concept and as such cannot be measured directly, but it can be approximated by real income.
- *Real income:* this is the expression of events that give rise to psychic enjoyment, and is best measured by living costs. In other words, the satisfaction created by the psychic enjoyment of profit is measured by the amount paid in order to buy goods and services.
- *Money income:* this represents all the money received and intended to be used for consumption to meet living costs.

The economist's view is that an individual will be motivated into generating income because of a need to satisfy some personal 'wants', usually manifested through the consumption of goods and services.

Lindhal introduced the concept of income as *interest*, referring to the continuous appreciation of capital over time. The difference between the interest and the consumption anticipated for a given period are savings This led to the basic idea of economic income being measured as consumption plus savings expected to take place during a certain period, savings being equal to changes in economic capital. Economic income is expressed as follows:

$$Y_e = C + (K_t - K_{(t-1)})$$

Y_e = economic income

C = consumption

K_t = capital (now)

$K_{(t-1)}$ = capital at previous period

Hicks used the concepts of income introduced by Fisher and Lindhal, and developed a more generally accepted theory of economic income. Hicks introduced savings as part of this model and also introduced the notion of 'well offness'. Income was the amount an individual could consume during a period of time and still be left with the original capital stock. This view recognises the changes in economic wealth over time and the need to maintain closing capital at the prescribed opening level before income can be recognised. A good example of this is given by Lee (1985), as follows.

Example

S buys shares (invests) in AB plc on 31 December Year 0. The amount of dividends received is as follows:

31 December Year 1	£1,000
31 December Year 2	£2,500
31 December Year 3	£3,700
31 December Year 4 shares are sold for £7,000	

Economic income is the amount an individual, S, could consume and still be as well off – in other words, still have the same capital stock at the end of the period as in the beginning. Economic income recognises the need to maintain closing capital at the same level as opening capital, before determining income.

Economic		Realised		(Closing		Opening)
Income	=	Cash Flow	+	(Capital	–	Capital)
Y_e	=	C	+	$(K_t$	–	$K_{t-1})$

In order to determine the income figure, economic capital needs to be valued. How is this to be done? Capital is measured as the present value (PV) of future cash flows. Assuming a rate of return of 7% the PV of cash flows would be:

	31.12.00	31.12.01	31.12.02	31.12.03	31.12.04
Future cash flow		£1,000	£2,500	£3,700	£7,000
PV factor (7%)	0	(1.07)	$(1.07)^2$	$(1.07)^3$	$(1.07)^4$
PV		£935	£2,184	£3,020	£5,340

Capital at 31.12.00 = £935 + £2,184 + £3,020 + £5,340 = £11,479

	31.12.00	31.12.01	31.12.02	31.12.03	31.12.04
Future cash flow		0	£2,500	£3,700	£7,000
PV factor (7%)		0	(1.07)	$(1.07)^2$	$(1.07)^3$
PV			£2,336	£3,232	£5,714

Capital at 31.12.01 = £2,336 + £3,232 + £5,714 = £11,282

	31.12.00	31.12.01	31.12.02	31.12.03	31.12.04
Future cash flow		0	0	£3,700	£7,000
PV factor			0	(1.07)	$(1.07)^2$
PV				3,458	6,114

Capital at 31.12.02 = £3,458 + £6,114 = £9,572

	31.12.00	31.12.01	31.12.02	31.12.03	31.12.04
Future cash flow		0	0	0	£7,000
PV factor				0	(1.07)
PV					£6,542

Capital at 31.12.03 = £6.542 = £6,542
Capital at 31.12.04 = £0
Economic income is calculated, as follows: $Y_e = C + (K_t – K_{(t-1)})$

Time period	C	$K_t - K_{(t-1)}$	Y_e
31.12.00 – 01	£1,000	(£11,282 – £11,479)	£803
31.12.01 – 02	£2,500	(£9,572 – £11,282)	£790
31.12.02 – 03	£3,700	(£6,542 – £9,572)	£670
31.12.03 – 04	£7,000	(£0 – £6,542)	£458
Total	**£14,200**		**£2,721**

Out of the total benefits of £14,200 received, £11,479 (£14,200 – £2,721) should have been re-invested (assuming an interest rate of 7%):

(£1,000 – £803)	=	£197
(£2,500 – £790)	=	£1,710
(£3,700 – £670)	=	£3,030
(£7,000 – £458)	=	£6,542
		£11,479

There is a danger that if the periodic change in capital is not recognised then there will be overconsumption. The return from re-investment is as follows:

Re-investment	Return (7%)
£197	£13
£197 + £1,710	£133
£197 + £1,710 + £3,030	£345
£197 + £1,710 + £3,030 + £6,542	£803

Time period	Y_e	Income from re-investment	Total Y_e
31.12.00 – 31.12.01	£803	0	£803
31.12.01 – 31.12.02	£790	£13	£803
31.12.02 – 31.12.03	£670	£133	£803
31.12.03 – 31.12.04	£458	£345	£803
31.12.04	£0	£803	£803

This measure of income is called *ideal income* since it is measured under conditions of certainty, that is with perfect knowledge of the future.

Measurement of economic income under conditions of uncertainty

Under conditions of uncertainty, economic income can be measured either at the beginning of the period to which it relates, by looking forward, or at the end of the period to which it relates.

Income measured at the beginning of the period is called *income ex-ante* and income measured at the end of the period is called *income ex-post*. Again, good examples of such measures of income are given by Lee (1985).

Income ex-ante

As indicated above, from this perspective income is measured at the beginning of the period to which it relates. Expected income of the period is measured as a proportion of the anticipated realisations for that same period. Cash flow over the period 1 January (t – 1) to 31 December (t) is anticipated at 1 January (t – 1), while the closing capital at 31 December (t) is measured at 1 January (t – 1). Income is measured before the event. This means that the individual has some idea of how much can be consumed during the period and how much needs to be re-invested.

Example

S buys shares (invests) in AB plc on 31 December Year 0 (t_0) for £11,479. At this point, t_0 S anticipates dividends as follows:

31 December Year 1 (t_1)	£1,000
31 December Year 2 (t_2)	£2,500
31 December Year 3 (t_3)	£3,700

31 December Year 4 (t_4) shares are sold for £7,000. This sale is anticipated at 31 December Year 0 (t_0).

However, on 31 December Year 2 (t_2) S's original sales proceeds prediction changes. Instead of anticipating £7,000, this changes to £8,000. At 31 December Year 4 (t_4) the actual amount realised is £8,500. (All the other predictions are realised in full.)

As before, the original investment is assumed to be the present value of the future cash flows anticipated at t_0.

	31.12.00	31.12.01	31.12.02	31.12.03	31.12.04
Future cash flow		£1,000	£2,500	£3,700	£7,000
PV factor	0	(1.07)	$(1.07)^2$	$(1.07)^3$	$(1.07)^4$
PV		£935	£2,184	£3,020	£5,340

Capital at 31.12.00 = £935 + £2,184 + £3,020 + £5,340 = £11,479

	31.12.00	31.12.01	31.12.02	31.12.03	31.12.04
Future cash flow		0	£2,500	£3,700	£7,000
PV factor		0	(1.07)	$(1.07)^2$	$(1.07)^3$
PV			£2,336	£3,232	£5,714

Capital at 31.12.01 = £2,336 + £3,232 + £6,530 = £11,282

	31.12.00	31.12.01	31.12.02	31.12.03	31.12.04
Future cash flow		0	0	£3,700	£7,000
PV factor			0	(1.07)	$(1.07)^2$
PV				£3,458	£6,114

Capital at 31.12.02 = £3,458 + £6,114 = £9,572

At this point the prediction of sales proceeds changes to £8,000 so opening capital must be adjusted since there is a change in expectations.

	31.12.00	31.12.01	31.12.02	31.12.03	31.12.04
Future cash flow		0	0	£3,700	£8,000
PV factor			0	(1.07)	$(1.07)^2$
PV				£3,458	£6,987

Capital at 31.12.02 will now be £3,458 + £6987 = £10,445

This adjustment results in 'windfall' gains (or losses). In this example there is a windfall gain of £873 (£10,445 − £9,572).

	31.12.00	31.12.01	31.12.02	31.12.03	31.12.04
Future cash flow		0	0	0	£8,000
PV factor				0	(1.07)
PV					£7,477

Capital at 31.12.03 = £7,477
Capital at 31.12.04 = £0

Economic income (ex-ante) can now be shown in full as follows:

Time period	C	$K_t - K_{(t-1)}$	Y_e ex-ante	Windfall gain	Total Y_e
31.12.00 – 01	£1,000	(£11,282 – £11,479)	£803		£803
31.12.01 – 02	£2,500	(£9,572 – £11,282)	£790		£790
31.12.02 – 03	£3,700	(£7,477 – £10,445)	£732	£873	£1,605
31.12.03 – 04	£8,000	(£0 – £7,477)	£523		£523
Total	£15,200		£2,848	£873	£3,721

The windfall gain is an increase in the capital value arising because expectations of future cash flows differ from those actually received. The windfall gain of £873 in this example arises at t_2 because expectations of the sales proceeds at t_4 change from £7,000 to £8,000. This change in anticipated future cash flows, which amounts to £1,000 at t_4 has a value of £873 at t_2 if it is discounted over two years at 7% [£1,000 / $(1.07)^2$]. This windfall gain is unrealised.

There is also a realised windfall gain at t_4 of £500, which arises when £8,500 is received instead of £8,000.

So, total economic income (ex-ante) including all windfall gains would be £4,221 (£3,721 + £500).

In order to avoid overconsumption, re-investment will be required as before. Out of the total benefits of £15,200 received, £11,479 (£15,200 – £3,721) needs to be re-invested.

Income ex-post

This is an alternative economic income model, which measures economic income at the end rather than at the beginning of each period. It is similar to income ex-ante in that it requires cash flows to be predicted in order to value opening and closing capital. It differs from the ex-ante model in that any adjustments required can be made to past as well as future capital values.

✿ *Example*

S buys shares (invests) in AB plc on 31 December Year (t_0) for £11,479. At this point, t_0, S anticipates dividends as follows:

31 December Year 1 (t_1)	£1,000
31 December Year 2 (t_2)	£2,500
31 December Year 3 (t_3)	£3,700
31 December Year 4 (t_4) shares are sold for £7,000. This sale is anticipated at 31 December Year 0 (t_0).	

However, on 31 December Year 2 (t_2), S's original sales proceeds prediction changes. Instead of anticipating £7,000, this changes to £8,000. At 31 December Year 4 (t_4) the actual amount realised is £8,500. (All the other predictions are realised in full.)

The calculation in income ex-post makes adjustments to the past as well as to the future capital values. Closing capital is measured at the end of the period, as is opening capital. Opening capital will include any revisions resulting from changes in expectations.

As before, the original investment is assumed to be the present value of the future cash flows anticipated at t_0.

	31.12.00	31.12.01	31.12.02	31.12.03	31.12.04
Future cash flow		£1,000	£2,500	£3,700	£7,000
PV factor	0	(1.07)	$(1.07)^2$	$(1.07)^3$	$(1.07)^4$
PV		£935	£2,184	£3,020	£5,340

Capital at 31.12.00 = £935 + £2,184 + £3,020 + £5,340 = £11,479

	31.12.00	31.12.01	31.12.02	31.12.03	31.12.04
Future cash flow		0	£2,500	£3,700	£7,000
PV factor		0	(1.07)	$(1.07)^2$	$(1.07)^3$
PV			£2,336	£3,232	£5,714

Capital at 31.12.01 = £2,336 + £3,232 + £5,714 = £11,282

However at 31.12.02 expectations change. In accordance with the ex-post model this is related back to the start of the period. Therefore capital at the start will no longer be £11,282 but will be recalculated as follows:

	31.12.00	31.12.01	31.12.02	31.12.03	31.12.04
Future cash flow		0	£2,500	£3,700	£8,000
PV factor		0	(1.07)	$(1.07)^2$	$(1.07)^3$
PV			£2,336	£3,232	£6,530

Capital at 31.12.01 = £2,336 + £3,232 + £6,530 = £12,098

This results in a windfall gain of £816 (£12,098 – £11,282).

Capital at 31.12.02 will be calculated as follows:

	31.12.00	31.12.01	31.12.02	31.12.03	31.12.04
Future cash flow		0	0	£3,700	£8,000
PV factor			0	(1.07)	$(1.07)^2$
PV				£3,458	£6,987

Capital at 31.12.02 will now be £3,458 + £6987 = £10,445

And capital at 31.12.03 is:

	31.12.00	31.12.01	31.12.02	31.12.03	31.12.04
Future cash flow		0	0	0	£8,000
PV factor				0	(1.07)
PV					£7,477

Capital at 31.12.03 = £7,477 = £7,477

At this point £8,500 is realised and, in accordance with the ex-post model, opening capital is adjusted retrospectively:

	31.12.00	31.12.01	31.12.02	31.12.03	31.12.04
Future cash flow		0	0	0	£8,500
PV factor				0	(1.07)
PV					£7,944

This results in another windfall gain, this time £467 (£7,944 – £7,477)

Economic income (ex-post) can now be shown in full, as follows:

Time period	C	$K_t - K_{(t-1)}$	Y_e ex-post	Windfall gain	Total Y_e
31.12.00 – 01	£1,000	(£11,282 – £11,479)	£803	0	£803
31.12.01 – 02	£2,500	(£10,445 – £12,098	£847	£16	£1,663
31.12.02 – 03	£3,700	(£7,477 – £10,445)	£732	0	£732
31.12.03 – 04	£8,500	(£0 – £7,944)	£556	£467	£1,023
Total	£15,700		£2,938	£1,283	£4,221

In order to avoid overconsumption, re-investment will be required as before. Out of the total benefits of £15,700 received, £11,479 (£15,700 – £4,221) needs to be re-invested.

BASIC

INTERMEDIATE

ADVANCED

Evaluation of the economic income model

The economic income model contains some fundamental assumptions that tend to be a bit impractical. First of all, it is necessary to predict future cash flows. This means that these cash flows are the subject of a great deal of uncertainty, not only in their prediction, but in their timing. In practice, therefore, the economic income model is extremely subjective, which leaves the accuracy of the income measure in some doubt. The second assumption lies in the choice of the discount factor used in computing the present value of the opening and closing capital figures. The choice of rate would have to be related to the preferences of the individual. Again this is very subjective and leaves the income figure based on these assumptions suspect.

Another problem results from the concept of capital maintenance. There is a need to maintain the value of capital before recognising income. Any returns on capital included in the realised cash flow must be re-invested at the same rate of interest used as a discount factor, if capital and future income is to be maintained. This assumes interest rates remain constant.

1.14 Current entry values

As indicated above, current entry value represents the amount of cash or other consideration that would be required to obtain the same asset or its equivalent. Current entry value stems from the work of Edwards and Bell, and has been interpreted as follows.

- *Replacement cost – used:* this is equal to the amount of cash or other consideration that would be needed to obtain an equivalent asset on the second-hand market having the same remaining useful life.
- *Reproduction cost:* this is equal to the amount of cash or other consideration that would be needed to obtain an identical asset to the existing asset.
- *Replacement cost – new:* this emphasises the replacement of the productive capacity of the assets. Replacement cost – new is equal to the amount of cash or other consideration needed to replace or reproduce the productive capacity of an asset with a new asset that reflects changes in technology.

The common characteristic of the three notions of current entry value is that they all relate to the costs of replacing or reproducing an asset held. What is not clear is how current entry values are to be measured. The three most popular methods are:

1. quoted market prices
2. specific price indices
3. management estimates.

The valuation of assets and liabilities at current entry prices gives rise to holding gains or losses.

⬡ *Example*

A company bought an item of inventory on 1 January Year 0 for £1,000. At 31 December Year 0, if the company were to buy this inventory now, it would cost £1,500. On 31 December Year 1 the inventory was sold for £2,000. To replace the inventory on 31 December Year 1 it would now cost £1,800.

Traditional viewpoint

From a traditional accounting viewpoint, income would be recognised and measured when the sale took place, which was at the end of Year 1.

So, profit for period ending 31 December Year 0 = £0 (no sale had taken place).

Profit for period ending 31 December Year 1 = £1,000 (£2,000 – £1,000).

Under the traditional accounting model, income is recognised on 31 December Year 1 when the sale is made (on realisation).

However, the measure of accounting income may be broken down as follows.

- There is a gain that can be measured at the time of the sale by comparing the selling price with what it would cost to replace the asset at this time. This is a measure of the *realised operating gain*. Realised operating gain = £2,000 – £1,800 = £200
- There is a gain that can be measured prior to the sale by comparing the increase in replacement cost over the period. This would be a holding gain and would be measured as follows.

Replacement cost at 31 December Year 1	£1,800
Cost at 31 December Year 0	£1,000
Holding gain	£800

This holding gain of £800 can be split into two parts as follows:

(i)	Prior period (£1,000 – £1,500)	£500
(ii)	Current period (£1,500 – £1,800)	£300
		£800

So, accounting income may be defined as:

Current operating profit	+	Realised holding gains (current period)	+	Realised holding gains (prior period)
£200	+	£300	+	£500

Current entry values

On the other hand, income based on current entry values would recognise both the operating and holding gains for current and prior periods whether realised or not. Income under the current entry value model would be recognised as follows.

For the period ending 31st December Year 0:

Income = £1,500 – £1,000 = £500. This income is a holding gain, which is unrealised but may still be recognised as income.

For the period ending 31 December Year 1:

Income = £2,000 – £1,500 = £500

This £500 income can be divided into:

  (i) current operating gain (£2,000 – £1,800) = £200

(ii) realised holding gain (£1,800 – £1,500) = £300

All this income is realised since the asset was sold during the period.

The above example shows that the valuation of assets and liabilities at current entry prices gives rise to holding gains and losses. This is because entry prices change during a period of time when they are held or owned. As was seen, holding gains and losses may be divided into two elements:

1. realised holding gains and losses that relate to items sold or to the liabilities discharged
2. unrealised holding gains and losses that relate to items still held or to liabilities still owed at the end of the reporting period.

These holding gains and losses may be classified as income when capital maintenance is viewed solely in money terms. However, because they measure the additional income that must be retained to maintain the existing productive capacity, such holding gains may also be classified as adjustments to capital.

Those who support the capital adjustment approach view income based on the preservation of physical capital. Such an approach would define the profit of an entity for a given period as the maximum amount that could be distributed and still maintain the operating capability of the business at the level that existed at the beginning of the period. Changes in replacement cost cannot be distributed therefore without impairing the operating capability of the entity so this approach classifies replacement cost changes as capital adjustments. This argument is generally regarded as a valid one and it is generally agreed that the central profit figure under a current entry value system should consist of operating profit alone.

The depreciation problem

Under the current entry value system assets are shown at their replacement cost. This means that depreciation has to be based on this replacement cost. As the replacement cost of assets increases over time, then the depreciation expense will need an adjustment to make it 'catch up'.

 *Example*

ABC purchases a fixed asset on 1 January Year 0 for £100. The asset is to be depreciated at the rate of 25% per annum. The replacement cost of a new asset increases by £20 each year. The company's financial year ends on 31 December each year.

At 31 December Year 0		
Historic cost depreciation	= 25% of £100 =	£25
Replacement cost depreciation	= 25% of £120 =	£30

At 31 December Year 1		
Historic cost depreciation	= 25% of £100 =	£25
Replacement cost depreciation	= 25% of £140 =	£35

In the replacement cost balance sheet at 31 December Year 1 the fixed asset would appear as follows:

Asset at replacement cost	£140
Accumulated depreciation (£30 + £35)	£65
Net replacement cost	£75

But, total depreciation for the two years ought to be 25% of £140 = £70.

This means that depreciation has not kept pace with the changing replacement cost. There is a shortfall of £5 (£70 − £65). This shortfall is referred to as *backlog depreciation* and is usually deducted from the total amount of holding gains.

Example: replacement cost techniques

The following are the financial statements of XYZ plc on 31 December Year 1, after one year's trading.

XYZ Balance sheet as at 31 December Year 1			
Fixed assets	Cost	Depreciation	NBV
Land	£110,000	–	£110,000
Equipment	40,000	4,000	36,000
	£150,000	£4,000	£146,000
Current assets			
Inventory		£90,000	
Accounts receivable		£90,000	
		£180,000	
Current liabilities			
Accounts payable	£50,000		
Loan	£50,000	£100,000	£80,000
			£226,000
Capital and reserves			
Share capital (£1 ordinary shares)			£200,000
Retained profit			£26,000
			£226,000

Profit and loss account for year ending 31 December Year 1		
Sales		£156,000
Cost of sales		
Opening inventory	£60,000	
Purchases	£130,000	
	£190,000	
Closing inventory	£90,000	£100,000
		£56,000
Expenses		
Administration	£26,000	
Depreciation	£4,000	£30,000
Profit		£26,000

Additional information

1. Land was valued at £135,000 on 31 December Year 1
2. Replacement costs are as follows:
   - (i) opening inventory   £79,000
   - (ii) closing inventory   £101,740
   - (iii) equipment   £44,000
3. Depreciation is charged on equipment at 10% p.a.

Determination of holding gains is as follows.

1.	Cost of sales		
		HC	RC
	Opening inventory	£60,000	£79,000
	Purchases	£130,000	£130,000
		£190,000	£209,000
	Closing inventory	£90,000	£101,740
		£100,000	£107,260
	Cost of sales historic cost		£100,000
	Cost of sales replacement cost		£107,260
	Realised holding gain		£7,260

2.	Closing inventory historic cost	£90,000
	Closing inventory replacement cost	£101,740
	Unrealised holding gain	£11,740

3.	Fixed assets	
	Land at historic cost	£110,000
	Land at replacement cost	£135,000
	Unrealised holding gain	£25,000

Equipment				
			Depreciation	
Historic cost	£40,000		£4,000	£36,000
Replacement cost	£44,000		£4,400	£39,600
	£4,000		£400	£3,600
Total holding gain	£4,000			
Realised	£400	(depreciation)		
Unrealised	£3,600			

Income statement (replacement cost) for year ending 31 December Year 1		
Sales		£156,000
Cost of sales		
Opening inventory	£79,000	
Purchases	£130,000	
	£209,000	
Closing inventory	£101,740	£107,260
		£48,740
Expenses		
Administration	£26,000	
Depreciation	£4,400	£30,400
Profit		£18,340

Summary of holding gains

Realised holding gains:

Cost of sales	£7,260	
Depreciation	£400	£7,660

Unrealised holding gains:

Closing inventory	£11,740	
Equipment	£3,600	
Land	£25,000	£40,340
		£48,000

XYZ
Balance sheet as at 31 December Year 1

Fixed assets	Replacement cost	Depreciation	Net replacement cost
Land	£135,000	–	£135,000
Equipment	£44,000	£4,400	£39,600
	£179,000	£4,400	£174,000
Current assets			
Inventory		£101,740	
Accounts receivable		£90,000	
		£191,740	
Current liabilities			
Accounts payable	£50,000		
Loan	£50,000	£100,000	£91,740
			£266,340
Capital and reserves			
Share capital (£1 ordinary shares)			£200,000
Retained profit			£18,340
Holding gains			£48,000
			£266,340

Evaluation of current entry based accounting

The following *advantages* are claimed.

- Current entry based accounting provides more information in that it splits total profit into holding gains and operating gains. This permits a better appraisal of earlier actions and provides more useful data for decision-making purposes.
- By allowing holding gains to be excluded from reported profit, operating capacity can be properly maintained.
- The balance sheet is based on current values.
- It is consistent with the going concern, accruals, consistency and prudence principles; and, if holding gains are excluded from reported profit, current entry based accounting is more prudent than historic cost.
- Holding gains are recognised and reported as they occur.

The following *disadvantages* are claimed.

- Replacement cost figures are required for assets the firm does not intend or perhaps could not replace.
- It gives no indication of the current market value of most assets, nor of the business as a whole.

BASIC

INTERMEDIATE

ADVANCED

- It fails to take account of general price rises or of changes in the purchasing power of money.
- There may be problems in determining which replacement cost is to be applied: that which relates to an identical resource or to an 'equivalent' resource. It may be that a particular asset is 'unique' in some way.

1.15 Current exit values (net realisable value)

This is the alternative to entry values, and was first advocated in 1939 by MacNeal. It has since been developed and extended by writers such as Chambers and Sterling. The concept of realisable income is concerned with the periodic change in the realisable value of capital.

There are different measures of realisable value that could be used. These include:

- realisable values arising on an assumed liquidation, as in bankruptcy
- realisable values arising on an orderly liquidation as in the normal course of business
- realisable values of resources in their existing state
- realisable values of resources in their finished state, adjusted for future costs.

While it is recognised that there can be different measures of realisable values, it is generally agreed that exit values should refer to assets in their existing state on the assumption these assets are sold in an orderly manner in the normal course of business.

The exit value capital at any particular time shows the amount of money that the business could obtain from its assets. This implies that the exit value model is based on the economic concept of opportunity cost. The value expressed is in terms of what the owner of the resources is sacrificing by holding them in their existing form rather than in the next best alternative. In other words, exit value is the amount of cash the business could obtain if it did not keep the asset.

Such a sacrifice is often expressed in terms of the firm's command over goods, in other words, what the firm could acquire with the cash by realising its existing resources.

According to the current exit value approach, all assets and liabilities are revalued at their net realisable values. Net realisable values are generally obtained from market quotations adjusted for estimated selling costs. The main feature of current exit price systems is that they completely abandon the principle of realisation for recognising revenues. When all non-monetary assets are valued at current exit prices this means that all gains are immediately recognised. Operating gains are recognised at the time of production, whereas holding gains and losses are recognised at the time of purchase, and consequently when prices change, rather than at the time of sale.

On assets held for resale, for example, inventory, there will be operating gains that can be realised or unrealised. On assets held for use, there will be non-operating gains that can be realised or unrealised. Since the opening and closing balance sheets are now value based and not cost based, the income statement will also be value based. Depreciation is no longer a process of cost allocation under the matching principle, it simply becomes the loss in value of the asset over the period.

Holding gains as income

The realisable income model includes non-operational gains as income, similar to the replacement cost model. The argument for doing so rests on the fact that capital in the realisable income model is an expression of the command over goods a firm has. Any increase in this expression of wealth could be described as income. The reason for this is that it is not the intention of the realisable value model to maintain capital in terms of physical operating capacity. If the potential realisable proceeds of the existing resources of a firm have increased over a period, then it has potentially more available to invest and so has increased its wealth. Income may be said to exist because if the value change was consumed by way of dividend, then capital in terms of command over goods and services would still be maintained.

Example: exit value techniques

ABC plc starts in business on 1 January Year 1 with capital in cash of £15,000, and buys a fixed asset for £10,000. The following information is given for the periods ended 31 December Year 1 and Year 2. (Assume depreciation is the same under historic cost and current exit value.)

	Year 1	Year 2
Fixed assets at net realizable value	£6,000	£4,000
Sales revenue	£20,000	£25,000
Cost of sales	£11,000	£12,000
Closing inventory (at cost)	£2,000	£3,000
Closing inventory (at net realisable value)	£2,500	£3,800

Prepare the financial statements on an exit value basis at the end of Year 1 and Year 2.
Some preliminary working notes are needed, as follows.

1. Calculation of opening cash balance:

Capital (all cash)	£15,000
Less fixed asset bought	£10,000
Cash at start	£5,000

2. Opening and closing inventory

	Year 1		Year 2	
	Cost	NRV	Cost	NRV
Opening inventory	0	0	£2,000	£2,500
Purchases (note 1)	13,000	13,000	13,000	13,000
	13,000	13,000	15,000	15,500
Closing inventory	2,000	2,500	3,000	3,800
Cost of sales	11,000	11,500	12,000	11,700

Note 1: the purchases amount is the balancing figure, given that opening and closing inventory is known together with cost of sales.

3. From the above information, the cash account can be constructed.

Opening cash	£5,000	£12,000
Sales	20,000	25,000
	25,000	37,000
Purchases	(13,000)	(13,000)
Closing cash	£12,000	£24,000

4. Depreciation   (£10,000 − £6,000) = £4000   (£6,000 − £4,000) = £2,000

5. Asset held for sale is inventory so this will give rise to a realised operating gain.
Closing inventory at the end of each year will result in an unrealised operating gain.

Year 1	(£2,500 − £2,000) = £500
Year 2	(£3,800 − £3,000) = £800

Income statement (current exit values) period ending 31 December Year 1		
	HC	NRV
Sales	£20,000	£20,000
Cost of sales	11,000	10,500
	9,000	9,500
Depreciation	4,000	4,000
	5,000	5,500

The difference between the HC profit and the NRV profit is the unrealised operating gain of £500.

Income statement (current exit values) period ending 31 December Year 2		
	HC	NRV
Sales	£25,000	£25,000
Cost of sales	12,000	11,700
	13,000	13,300
Depreciation	2,000	2,000
	11,000	11,300

The difference between the HC profit and the NRV profit is the unrealised operating gain of £300. The total unrealised operating gain in Year 2 is £800, of which £500 was recognised in Year 1. This £500 is carried into Year 2 as part of the opening inventory and so needs to be eliminated.

Balance sheet (current exit values) as at 31 December				
	Year 1			Year 2
Fixed assets	£6,000			£4,000
Inventory	2,500			3,800
Cash	12,000			24,000
	£20,500			£31,800
Capital	15,000			15,000
Profit retained	5,500		£5,500	
			11,300	16,800
	£20,500			£31,800

Evaluation of current exit price based accounting

This model presents advantages and disadvantages. The *advantages* have been identified as follows.

- The fact that current exit price and capitalised value of an asset provided different measures of opportunity cost means that both values are relevant in making decisions as to whether or not a firm should continue to use or to sell assets already in use, and whether or not a firm should remain a going concern. Opportunity cost in this context is either the cash value from the sale of the asset or the present value of the benefits from using the asset.
- Current exit price provides information on which to evaluate the financial adaptability and liquidity of a firm.
- Because it reflects current sacrifices and alternative choices, current exit price provides a good guide for the evaluation of managers.
- It avoids the need for arbitrary cost allocation in terms of estimating depreciation. Depreciation expense is the difference between current exit price at the beginning and end of the period.
- Exit values are already being used in current accounting practice – for example, money assets and inventories (lower of cost and net realisable value).

The *disadvantages* have been identified as follows:

- The current exit price based system is relevant only for assets that are expected to be sold for a specific market price. Assets that are unique and have no alternative use cannot easily be valued.
- This system is not relevant for assets the firm intends to use. The amount of cash a firm could get for such an asset by selling it and moving out of the industry is not likely to be relevant to any user who is interested in the profitability of the firm.
- The problem of valuing certain assets, such as intangibles, has not yet been resolved. It is not clear either how liabilities should be valued: at their contractual amount or at the amounts required to fund the liability?
- The abandonment of the realisation principle and the assumption of the liquidation of the resources of the firm contradict the going concern assumption.

1.16 Accounting for changes in the purchasing power of money

The value measures indicated so far have been expressed in money terms. However, money by itself has no intrinsic value. The value of money is related to what it can buy. When prices are rising, then less and less will be obtained with any given number of pounds sterling. If under any particular valuation basis, as indicated above, capital has been maintained in pounds sterling, it does not necessarily follow that capital has been maintained in terms of purchasing power of those pounds.

Current purchasing power accounting

Current purchasing power (CPP) is a general purchasing power concept. The concern is with general price rises, which is usually expressed in terms of the average rise in the cost of living, measured by a general price index.

For example, if inflation over the last year was 10% then £100 last year has the same general (average) purchasing power as £110 this year. All pounds sterling have to be 'dated' since pounds at different dates can no longer be regarded as the same. In order to have a common measuring unit, it is necessary to convert pounds sterling from the purchasing power at one point in time to the purchasing power at another point in time.

 ## *Example: purchasing power*

Consider a situation where a business makes purchases of two assets as follows:

1.   first purchase on 1 January Year 1 for £200 cash
2.   second purchase on 31 December Year 1 for £350 cash.

From a traditional accounting viewpoint the total cost of the purchases would be £550. However, each purchase is being measured against the scale of money values at its transaction date. In other words, two different measurement scales are being used. By using general price indices, each individual purchase can be measured at a specific point in time.

If financial statements were to be prepared at 31 December Year 2, then by using the general price index each individual purchase can be restated in terms of purchasing power at that date. Assume that the general price index was as follows:

	General price index
1 January Year 1	100
31 December Year 1	105
31 December Year 2	112

In order to restate in CPP terms:

£HC X	Index at balance sheet date
	General price level index at the date of the original transaction

Date of purchase	£HC	Index	CPP at 31 December Year 2
1 Jan Year 1	£200	112/100	£224
31 Dec Year 2	£350	112/105	£373
			£597

Monetary items

It is important to make a distinction between monetary and non-monetary items. Monetary items are those items fixed in terms of number of pounds sterling regardless of changes in the purchasing power of money. Examples of monetary items include, cash, accounts receivable, bank overdraft, accounts payable and loan capital. Non-monetary items are all items not so fixed in terms of number of pounds – for example, land, machinery and inventory.

Holders of monetary assets will lose general purchasing power in times of rising prices, whereas holders of monetary liabilities will gain.

 ## *Example*

Company A purchases an item costing £1,000 from Company B on credit at a time when the general price level index is 100. This item is paid for later when the general price level index is 110. In order to compensate Company B for the price level rise, Company A should pay:

£1,000 X 110/100 =	£1,100
Debt is fixed at	£1,000
Gain to Company A in terms of purchasing power	£100

This implies that Company B has lost £100 in purchasing power terms.

The above example is oversimplified in that it is based on one single monetary item. In practice, the monetary position of a company will fluctuate on a daily basis. The gain or loss on holding net monetary items is one of the more important features of CPP accounting in that CPP accounts attempt to show the financial position of the company from the point of view of the equity shareholders.

Treatment of general price level gain or loss

There is no general agreement on how such a gain or loss is to be treated. Early accounting studies suggested that any general price level gain or loss should be included in current income, and this position has been supported over the years by various accounting bodies.

Example: current purchasing power techniques

This is the same example that was used for replacement cost (see p. 67).

The following are the financial statements of XYZ plc on 31 December Year 1, after one year's trading.

XYZ Balance sheet as at 31 December Year 1			
Fixed assets	Cost	Depreciation	NBV
Land	£110,000	–	£110,000
Equipment	£40,000	£4,000	£36,000
	£150,000	£4,000	£146,000
Current assets			
Inventory		£90,000	
Accounts receivable		£90,000	
		£180,000	
Current liabilities			
Accounts payable	£50,000		
Loan	£50,000	£100,000	£80,000
			£226,000
Capital and reserves			
Share capital (£1 ordinary shares)			£200,000
Retained profit			£26,000
			£226,000

Profit and loss account for year ending 31 December Year 1		
Sales		£156,000
Cost of sales		
Opening inventory	£60,000	
Purchases	£130,000	
	£190,000	
Closing inventory	£90,000	£100,000
		£56,000
Expenses		
Administration	£26,000	
Depreciation	£4,000	£30,000
Profit		£26,000

Additional information
1. The capital and loan had been contributed in cash, and the land and equipment and inventory of £60,000 had been purchased on 1 January Year 1.
2. General price indices were as follows:

1 January	100
30 June	110
31 December	120

3. Depreciation is charged on equipment at 10% p.a.

Before preparing the CPP financial statement the following working notes are necessary.

1.   Compute the cash at 1 January.

Capital (contributed in cash)	£200	
Loan (contributed in cash)	£50	
	£250	
Cash paid:		
Equipment	£40	
Land	£110	
Inventory	£60	£210
Opening cash		£40

Other cash transactions:

Account receivables	
Accounts receivable at start	£0
Sales during the year	£156,000
Accounts receivable at end	£90,000
Cash received	£66,000
Account payables	
Accounts payable at start	£0
Purchases during the year	£130,000
Accounts receivable at end	£50,000
Cash paid	£80,000
Expenses paid	£26,000

Cash balance at 31 December:

Opening cash	£40,000
Cash from accounts receivable	£66,000
Cash paid to accounts payable	(£80,000)
Expenses paid	(£26,000)
Closing cash	£0

2. Determine gain or loss from holding monetary items.

	HC	Index	CPP at 31 December
Opening			
Cash	£40,000	120/100	£48,000
Loan	(£50,000)	120/100	(£60,000)
	(£10,000)		(£12,000)
Sales	£156,000	120/110 (midpoint taken)	£170,182
	£146,000		£158,182
Purchases	(£130,000)	120/110	(£141,819)
Expenses	(£26,000)	120/110	£28,363)
	(£10,000)		(£12,000)
Closing			
Accounts receivable	£90,000		
Accounts payable	(£50,000)		
Loan	(£50,000)		
Net monetary liabilities	(£10,000)		(£12,000)

Gain from holding net monetary liabilities = £2,000 (£10,000 − £12,000).

Income statement (current purchasing power)			
Sales		£170,182	
Cost of sales			
Opening inventory (120/100)		£72,000	
Purchases		£141,818	
		£213,818	
Closing inventory (120/120)		£90,000	£123,818
			£46,364
Expenses		£28,364	
Depreciation (10% of £48,000)		£4,800	£33,164
			£13,200
Gain from holding net monetary liabilities			£2,000
			£15,200

Balance sheet (current purchasing power)			
Fixed assets	Cost	Depreciation	Net book value
Land (120/100)	£132,000	0	£132,000
Equipment (120/100)	£48,000	£4,800	£43,200
	£180,000	£4,800	£175,200
Current assets			
Inventory		£90,000	
Accounts receivable (monetary item)		£90,000	
		£180,000	
Current liabilities			
Accounts payable (monetary item)		(£50,000)	
Loan (monetary item)		(£50,000)	£80,000
			£255,200
Capital (120/100)			£240,000
Retained profit			£15,200
			£255,200

Evaluation of current purchasing power accounting

The following *advantages* have been claimed.

- Since CPP statements are expressed in terms of a common measuring unit, comparisons between firms are made easier.
- It makes a distinction between gains or losses on the net monetary items.
- It requires only a simple adjustment to the historic cost accounts.

The following *disadvantages* have been claimed.

- When CPP is applied to the original historic based account, all the disadvantages of such accounts will be incorporated into the CPP adjusted accounting information.
- It fails to give any meaningful 'value' to the balance sheet items, although it gives the impression to non-accountants that it has done so.
- General purchasing power has no direct relevance to a specific person or situation.

It is of course possible to apply CPP thinking to any valuation basis, not just historic cost. This means, for example, current entry (replacement cost) or exit (net realisable) value systems could be adjusted for purchasing power gains or losses. This would have the effect of converting *current* value systems to *real* value systems. The best known of such systems is the real value selling price system, known as Continuously Contemporary Accounting (CoCoA).

Example: price level adjusted replacement cost

Assume the historic cost of an item is £10 and the replacement cost of the same item a year later is £13, then there would be a holding gain of £3.

However, if during the period there was a general price level increase of 10% then the holding gain would need to be adjusted as follows:

£10 (historic cost) × 110/100 = £11 in closing rate pounds

Replacement cost at end = £13

Real holding gain = £2

1.17 Overview of income and value measurement

As has been shown, income measurement is a very important issue in financial reporting. However, the measurement of income has not been resolved, as yet, by IASB. The reasons for this have been articulated above, and mainly stem from the fact that financial reporting has been based on historic cost, whereas current values have only been adopted more recently in certain areas of financial reporting.

For example, the current standard on financial instruments, IAS 39, uses current market values since these are seen to be more reliable and more relevant. It is possible to use current market values in this context because markets in financial instruments are well developed. Thus, some current financial reporting standards contain a mixture of current and historic measures. As markets develop and financial reporting evolves to meet the needs of users, then current value measures will become more important. However, there is no agreement as to how current value should be defined and measured. The two main contenders in this debate are deprival value and fair value.

Emergence of fair value

Fair value is a recent concept and has emerged as a term used in the standards of the IASB during the past 20 years or so. Demands that financial statements show current values have started to re-emerge, particularly where current values can be measured with some degree of reliability. The form of current value adopted has been described as *fair value*. The essential idea of fair value is that it is an 'arm's length' market price.

Within a mixed measurement system, fair value has been used as a basis for measurement, along with historic cost, historic cost measurement usually being kept for those items considered to be more costly or more unreliable to measure in fair value terms. A good example of this mixed measurement system can be seen in IAS 39 *Financial Instruments: Recognition and Measurement,* and in IFRS 3 *Business Combinations.* What is happening is that fair value is being used in certain accounting standards as a response to needs rather than as a result of an amendment to the conceptual framework.

Initially, fair value had been defined by the IASB as the amount for which an asset could be exchanged between knowledgeable, willing parties in an arm's length transaction. While this definition is consistent with either an entry or exit value system, it omits the issue of transaction costs. A new definition of fair value has emerged from the IASB discussion paper, which now defines fair value as the price that would be received to sell an asset or paid to transfer a liability in an orderly transaction between market participants at the measurement date.

Chapter summary

IAS 1: *Presentation of Financial Statements*

- Financial statements should comprise:
  - a balance sheet, now to be called a statement of financial position
  - an income statement (profit and loss account), now to be called a statement of comprehensive income
  - a statement of changes in equity
  - a statement of cash flows
  - notes containing a summary of the main accounting policies of the company and other information.
- Current and non-current assets and current and non-current liabilities should be shown separately on the face of the balance sheet.

The Framework for the preparation and presentation of financial statements

- The Framework is not an accounting standard.
- It provides fundamental principles and definitions that underpin the preparation of financial statements.
- The objective of financial statements is to provide financial information that is useful to a wide range of users.
- The users of financial statements include investors, employees, lenders, suppliers, customers, the government and the public.
- The financial statements are prepared on the accruals basis and the going concern basis.
- The four principal qualitative characteristics of financial statement information are relevance, reliability, comparability and understandability.
- The main elements of financial statements are assets, liabilities, equity income and expenses.
- An element is recognised in the financial statements when it is probable that any economic benefits associated with the element will flow to or from the entity, and that element has a cost or value that can be reliably measured.
- A number of measurement bases exist, including historical cost, current cost, realisable value and current value.
- Profits and losses can be measured in terms of financial or physical capital.

🔑 *Key terms for review*

Definitions can be found in the glossary at the end of the book.

Private company	*Reserves*
Public company	*Share premium*
Share capital	*Revaluation reserve*
Shareholders	*Retained earnings*
Dividend	*Statement of comprehensive income*
Ordinary shares	*Statement of changes in equity*
Preference shares	

Review questions

1. What different types of business structure exist, and how are the preparation and presentation of their financial statements affected by that structure?
2. Explain the term 'generally accepted accounting practice' (GAAP).
3. (a) State the objectives of financial statements.
   (b) Identify the main users of financial statements and explain why each user group might be interested in the information provided in these statements.
4. What are the qualitative characteristics of information and what use are they?
5. What criticisms can be levelled at the conceptual framework?
6. Explain what is meant by income 'ex-ante' and income 'ex-post', and outline the limitations of each measure of income.
7. How is capital defined in the historic cost accounting model?
8. Describe the differences between an 'entity' approach and a 'proprietary' approach to defining capital.
9. What do the terms 'entry value' and 'exit value' mean?
10. Explain the difference between the entity view and the proprietary view of the entity, and identify which view the CPP model adopts.
11. How is capital defined in the CPP model?
12. What is a *monetary* and a *non-monetary* item, and why is the distinction important under CPP.
13. Explain how monetary gains and losses arise.
14. What are the arguments for and against the CPP model?
15. How is capital defined in the replacement cost model?
16. Explain the difference between operating gains and holding gains.
17. What are the major criticisms of the replacement cost model?
18. Define deprival value and explain why it could be seen as an improvement on the replacement cost model.
19. In what circumstances would deprival value be something other than replacement cost?

 Exercises

1. Level II

The following trial balance is taken from the books of Krystal, a publicly listed company:

Trial balance At 31 March 2009		
	£000	£000
Land and buildings at cost	270,000	
Plant and machinery at cost	156,000	
Investment properties at valuation	90,000	
Purchases	78,200	
Operating expenses	39,500	
Dividends paid	15,000	
Inventory at 1 April 2008	37,800	
Trade receivables	53,200	
Revenue		278,400
Income from investment property		4,500
Equity shares of £1 each		150,000
Retained earnings at 1 April 2008		119,500
Long-term loan (8%)		50,000
Accumulated depreciation at 1 April 2008		
Buildings		60,000
Plant and machinery		26,000
Trade payables		33,400
Deferred taxation		12,500
Bank		5,400
	739,700	739,700

The following notes are relevant.

1. The land and buildings were purchased on 1 April 1993. The cost of the land was £70 million. No land and buildings have been purchased since that date. On 1 April 2008 the company had its land and buildings professionally valued at £80 million and buildings valued at £175 million. The estimated life of the buildings was originally 50 years and the remaining life has not changed as a result of the valuation.
2. Plant is depreciated at 15% per annum using the reducing balance method. Depreciation on buildings and plant is charged to the cost of sales.
3. The long-term loan was raised on 1 April 2008. At the year end, interest had not yet been paid.
4. The provision for taxation for the year to 31 March 2009 has been estimated at £28.3 million.
5. Inventory at 31 March 2009 was valued at £43.2 million.

Required

Prepare the following financial statements for the year ended 31 March 2009 in accordance with IAS 1:

(a) statement of comprehensive income
(b) statement of changes in equity
(c) statement of financial position.

2. Level II

Flofoam plc is a manufacturer and supplier of specialist seat padding for passenger aircraft. The following trial balance has been extracted from the financial records of Flofoam plc at 31 March 2009.

	Dr £000	Cr £000
Bank	14	
Trade creditors		62
Other creditors		77
Trade debtors	300	
Chairman's salary	50	
Electricity (factory)	33	
Insurance	17	
Workshop building at cost	200	
Machinery	420	
Accumulated depreciation (machinery)		152
Office expenses	25	
Share capital (£0.50 shares)		300
Profit and loss account at 1 April 2008		132
Provision for bad debt and doubtful debts		8
Purchases	1,314	
Rent of distribution depot	28	
Workshop rates	40	
Sales		2,350
Stock at 1 April 2008	156	
Vehicles at cost	96	
Accumulated depreciation (vehicles)		56
Wages and salaries	448	
Royalties received		4
	3,141	3,141

Additional information:

1. Stock at 31 March 2009 valued at cost amounted to £164,000.
2. Depreciation is to be provided on machinery and vehicles at rates of 25% and 20%, respectively. Flofoam plc has adopted the reducing balance method of providing for depreciation. Machinery is used entirely for production and vehicles are used 75% in distribution and 25% in administration.
3. The audit fee for the year to 31 March 2009 is estimated to be £12,000 and should be accrued in the 2009 financial statements.
4. Insurance paid in advance at 31 March 2009 amounted to £3,000.

    Insurance should be allocated as follows:

    Production – 50%
    Administration – 50%

5. The provision for bad debts is to be set to 5% of the outstanding trade debtors at 31 March 2009.
6. Corporation tax of £80,000 has been estimated in respect of the profit for the year.
7. An ordinary dividend of 10p per share is declared.
8. The salaries expense can be analysed as follows:

Sales directors' salary	48
Production staff wages	150
Distribution depot staff	80
Administration wages	170
	448

Required

Prepare the following financial statements for the year ended 31 March 2009 in accordance with IAS 1:

(a) statement of comprehensive income
(b) statement of changes in equity
(c) statement of financial position.

3.   Level II

Burnfoot Brickworks plc is a manufacturer and supplier of bricks to the construction industry. The following trial balance has been extracted from the financial records at 31 March 2009.

	£000	£000
Accumulated depreciation – buildings		80
Accumulated depreciation – plant and machinery		160
Advertising	112	
Bank	214	
Bank interest received		17
Debenture loans – 10% (repayable 2016)		200
Electricity	80	
General administration expenses	128	
Insurance	93	
Interest paid on debentures	20	
Land and buildings	600	
Plant and machinery	840	
Purchases	1,427	
Purchases returns		35
Rents receivable		100
Sales		3,480
Sales returns	60	
Share capital (£1 ordinary shares)		600
Stock at 1 April 2008	211	
Telephone	456	
Trade creditors		296
Trade debtors	584	
Wages and salaries	740	
Retained earnings b/f		597
	5,565	5,565

Additional information:

1.   Depreciation for the year is to be calculated as follows:

Buildings (cost £400,000) – 2% straight line

Plant and machinery – 20% reducing balance

Depreciation should be allocated as follows:

Production	50%
Distribution	25%
Administration	25%

2.   Audit fees of £18,000 should be accrued for the year to 31 March 2009.
3.   Closing stock was valued at cost on 31 March 2009 at £223,000.
4.   A dividend of 10p per share is declared.
5.   Insurance prepaid at 31 March 2009 amounted to £3,000. The insurance expense should be allocated as follows:

Production	$33\frac{1}{3}$%
Distribution	$33\frac{1}{3}$%
Administration	$33\frac{1}{3}$%

6.   An electricity bill of £14,000 for the final quarter did not arrive until mid-April 2009. This should be accrued in full in the year to 31 March 2009.

Electricity and telephone should be allocated as follows:

Production	20%
Distribution	50%
Administration	30%

7.   Corporation tax on the profits for the year is estimated at £105,000.

8.   The wages and salaries expense can be analysed as follows:

Factory salaries	150
Salesmen's salaries	370
Office staff	220
	740

Required

Prepare the following financial statements for the year ended 31 March 2009 in accordance with IAS 1:

(a)   statement of comprehensive income

(b)   statement of changes in equity

(c)   statement of financial position.

4.   Level II

Orangejuice plc is a manufacturer of soft drinks. At 30 June, 2009, the following list of balances was extracted from the company's accounting records.

	£000
Warehouse rates	10
Wages and salaries	400
Cash and bank	275
Production costs	630
Vehicle repairs and petrol	125
General expenses	450
Trade creditors	105
Trade debtors	210
Land and buildings at cost	2,000
Plant and machinery at cost	850
Fixtures and fittings at cost	340
Accumulated depreciation:	
Land and buildings	180
Plant and machinery	120
Fixtures and fittings	136
Share capital (£1 ordinary shares)	1,000
Loan stock (10%)	500
Heat and light	125
Sales	2,600
Closure costs	187
Other creditors including taxation	355
Retained profit at 1 July 2008	606

Notes:

1.   Depreciation for the year is to be calculated as follows:

Buildings (cost £500,000) – 2% straight line

Plant and machinery 20% – reducing balance

Fixtures and fittings 10% – straight line

Depreciation should be allocated as follows:

Production – 30%

Distribution – 40%

Administration – 30%

2.   Closing stock on 30 June 2009 was £150,000. Opening stock has already been accounted for.

3.   The company has declared a dividend of 5p per share. Interest payable to debenture holders is still outstanding.

4.   The invoice for the audit fee arrived in the post on 2 July 2009. The amount was £35,000.

5. Corporation tax on the profits for the year has been estimated at £110,000.
6. Wages and salaries expense should be allocated on the same basis as depreciation.
7. Vehicle repairs and petrol costs relate 100% to delivery lorries and sales representatives' cars.
8. Heat and light costs are to be allocated as follows:

Production – 50%
Distribution – 20%
Administration – 30%

9. One of the factories was closed during the year as part of a restructuring programme, incurring closure costs of £187,000. In relation to this, closure turnover was £185,000 and the operating loss was £2,000.

Required

Prepare the following financial statements for the year ended 31 March 2009 in accordance with IAS 1:

(a) statement of comprehensive income
(b) statement of changes in equity
(c) statement of financial position.

5. Level II

Oakwood plc manufactures kitchen furniture. The following trial balance has been extracted from Oakwood's accounting records at 31 March 2009.

	£000	£000
Accumulated depreciation:		
Land and buildings		720
Plant and machinery		480
Fixtures and fittings		544
Warehouse rates	40	
Wages and salaries	1,600	
Cash and bank	1,100	
Production costs	2,520	
Vehicle repairs and petrol	500	
General expenses	920	
Trade creditors		420
Trade debtors	840	
Land and buildings at cost	8,000	
Plant and machinery at cost	3,400	
Fixtures and fittings at cost	1,360	
Share capital (£1 ordinary shares)		4,000
10% debenture loan stock		2,000
Corporation tax	880	
Heat and light	360	
Auditors fees	140	
Sales		10,400
Closure costs	748	
Other creditors including taxation		1,420
Retained profit at 1 April 2008		2,424
	22,408	22,408

Notes:

1. Depreciation for the year is to be calculated as follows:

    Buildings (cost £1,500,000)– 2% straight line
    Plant and machinery – 20% reducing balance
    Fixtures and fittings– 10% straight line
    Depreciation should be allocated as follows:
    Production – 40%
    Distribution – 30%
    Administration – 30%

2. Wages and salaries expense should be allocated on the same basis as depreciation.
3. Vehicle repairs and petrol costs relate 100% to delivery lorries and sales representatives' cars.
4. Heat and light costs should be allocated as follows:
    Production – 50%
    Distribution – 20%
    Administration – 30%

5. Closing stock on 31 March 2009 was £150,000. Opening stock has been accounted for in the trial balance.
6. A dividend of 5p per share is declared. Interest to debenture holders is outstanding.

Required

Prepare the following financial statements for the year ended 31 March 2009 in accordance with IAS 1:

(a)   statement of comprehensive income
(b)   statement of changes in equity
(c)   statement of financial position.

6. Level II

The following is the trial balance of Cooper plc as at 31 March 2009.

	Debit £	Credit £
Share capital: authorised and issued		
150,000 ordinary shares of £1 each		125,000
25,000 7% preference shares of £1 each		25,000
Property (at valuation)	140,000	
Plant and machinery	66,900	
(cost £80,000)		
Goodwill	30,000	
Vehicles (cost £25,000)	19,100	
Wages and salaries	25,000	
Stock	9,400	
Debtors/creditors	11,200	8,300
Bank overdraft		7,800
Purchases/sales	49,700	160,250
Directors' salaries	22,000	
Rates	4,650	
Light and heat	3,830	
Interest on debentures	1,200	
Repairs	1,270	
10% debentures		24,000
Provision for bad debts		910
Share premium		25,000
Profit and loss account		2,580
General reserve		10,200
Interim dividend on	3,250	
ordinary shares		
Audit fees	3,350	
Revaluation reserve		9,860
Bad debts	700	
Listed investments	8,000	
Investment income		650
	399,550	399,550

The following additional information is available:

1. Stock at 31 March 2009 is valued at £13,480.
2. Rates include a payment of £2,300 for the six months from 1 January 2009.
3. Depreciation is to be applied as follows:
    Plant and machinery – 15% per annum on cost
    Vehicles – 10% on cost.
    Depreciation is to be allocated: 50% cost of sales, 25% administration and 25% selling and distribution.
4. Wages and salaries expense should be allocated on the same basis as depreciation. Vehicle repair costs relate to delivery lorries and sales representatives' cars.
5. Heat and light costs should be allocated as follows:
    Cost of sales – £2,000
    Distribution – £1,500
    Administration – £330
6. The provision for bad debts is to be adjusted to 10% of the debtors at the end of the year.
7. The preference share dividends are outstanding at the end of the year and the last half year's interest on debentures has not been paid.
8. Corporation tax on this year's profit is £6,370.

9.   The directors declare a final dividend on the ordinary shares of 5p per share.

10.   The balance on the revaluation reserve relates to the company's property and arose as follows:

Balance at 1 April 2008	£2,860
Revaluation during the year to 31 March 2009	£7,000
	£9,860

Required

Prepare the following financial statements for the year ended 31 March 2009 in accordance with IAS 1:

(a)   statement of comprehensive income

(b)   statement of changes in equity

(c)   statement of financial position.

Further reading

Companies Act 1985

Companies Act 2006

Framework for the Presentation and Preparation of Financial Statements. IASB, 1989

IAS 1 *Presentation of Financial Statements*. IASB, revised 2004

IAS 1 *Presentation of Financial Statements*. IASB, revised 2007

Statement of Principles for Financial Reporting. ASB, 1995

Alexander, D., Britton, A. and Jorissen, A. (2007) *International Financial Reporting and Analysis*. Thomson Learning.

Bedford, N.M. and McKeown, J.C. (1972) Net realizable value and replacement cost. *Accounting Review*, April, 333–8.

Belkaoui, A. (2000) *Accounting Theory* (4th edn). Thomson Learning.

Berry, A. (1999) *Financial Accounting: An Introduction*. Cengage Learning.

Black, G. (2003) *Students' Guide to Accounting and Financial Reporting Standards* (9th edn). FT/PrenticeHall.

Chambers, R.J. (1975) *Accounting for Inflation: Methods and Problems*. University of Sydney, August.

Edwards, E.O. and Bell, P.W. (1961) *The Theory and Measurement of Business Income*. University of California Press.

Elliott, B. and Elliott, J. (2007) *Financial Accounting and Reporting*. FT/PrenticeHall.

FASB (1974) *Conceptual Framework for Accounting and Reporting: Consideration of the Report of the Study Group on the Objectives of Financial Statements*. FASB.

Fisher, I. (1930) *The Theory of Interest*. Macmillan.

Hicks, J. (1946) *Value and Capital*. Clarendon Press.

Lee, T.A. (1985) *Income and Value Measurement* (3rd edn). Van Nostrand Reinhold.

Lewis, R. and Pendrill, D. (2004) *Advanced Financial Accounting* (7th edn). FT/PrenticeHall.

Limmack, R.J. (1985) *Financial Accounting & Reporting*. Macmillan.

Lindhal, E. (1933) *The Concept of Income. Economic Essays in Honour of Gustav Cassel*. Allen & Unwin.

MacNeal, K. (1970 reprint) *Truth in Accounting*. Scholars Book Co.

Mason, P. (1956) Price-level Changes and Financial Statements: Basic Concepts and Methods. AAA.

Miller, E.L. (1978) What's wrong with price-level accounting? *Harvard Business Review*, November/December, 87–95.

Objectives of Financial Reporting by Business Enterprises, Statement of Financial Accounting Concepts no. 1, 1978.

Objectives of Financial Statements, Report of the Study Group on the Objectives of Financial Statements. AICPA, 1973.

Parker, R.H. and Harcourt, G.C. (eds) (1969) *Readings in the Concept and Measurement of Income.* Cambridge University Press.

Rosenfield, P. (1975) Current replacement value accounting: a dead end. *Journal of Accountancy*, September, 63–73.

Sterling, R.R. (1970) *Theory and Measurement of Enterprise Income.* University of Kansas Press.

Sutton. T. (2004) *Corporate Financial Accounting and Reporting.* FT/PrenticeHall.

Van Zijl, T. and Whittington, G. (2006) Deprival value and fair value: a reinterpretation and a reconciliation. *Accounting and Business Research*, 36, 2, 121–30.

Weetman, P. (2006) *Financial and Management Accounting* (4th edn). Pitman.

Whittington, G. (1983) *Inflation Accounting: An Introduction to the Debate.* Cambridge University Press.

Wilson, A., Davies, M., Curtis, M. and Wilkinson-Riddle, G. (2001) *UK and International GAAP* (7th edn). Ernst & Young, Butterworths Tolley.

Non-current (Fixed) Assets

LEARNING OUTCOMES

After studying this chapter you should be able to:

- ☑ define a non-current (fixed) asset
- ☑ explain under what conditions non-current assets are recognised
- ☑ explain the nature of depreciation
- ☑ explain the requirements of IAS 20 on how government grants are treated
- ☑ explain how borrowing costs are treated under IAS 23 relating to borrowing costs
- ☑ explain and apply the principles of IAS 16 *Property, Plant and Equipment*
- ☑ evaluate the alternative treatments for investment properties
- ☑ explain and evaluate the requirements of IAS 40 relating to investment properties.

Introduction

This chapter considers the nature of tangible fixed assets – that is, those assets that can be seen and touched. It is worth noting at this stage that the IASB uses the term 'non-current assets' rather than fixed assets. This chapter will use both terms interchangeably.

Section 1: Basic Principles

2.1 What are fixed assets?

Of all the items contained on a company's balance sheet, fixed assets are probably considered by many to be the most straightforward and understandable of figures. Tangible fixed assets are the 'resources' a company uses to generate revenue. The 'value' of those assets in the balance sheet is often seen as a reflection of the financial strength of a company, and also the extent to which a company can offer security to lenders and investors.

Unfortunately, tangible fixed assets can also be the most misinterpreted and contentious items within a company's balance sheet. Although the term 'fixed asset' is used frequently in accounting literature, there is no precise definition of what constitutes a fixed asset. In order to recognise an asset as a fixed asset several features have to be identified. The asset will:

- be retained for several accounting periods
- give service during those periods
- eventually be disposed of.

A fixed asset can be defined as an item that is held by a company for use in the production and supply of goods or services, for rental to others, or for administrative purposes, and is expected to be used during more than one period.

In this context, while a motor trader will classify cars for resale as a current asset (stock), a furniture dealer will treat cars as a non-current (fixed) asset. In other words, motor cars will be classified according to the use to which they will be put, and according to how long they will be in the business.

2.2 The accounting issue involved: depreciation

When a company acquires a fixed asset it will be shown in the balance sheet and recorded initially at cost. However, since fixed assets are 'acquired for use within the business' this means that these fixed assets will be used in generating revenue for the business.

Revenue generation is important in that revenues generated contribute to the measure of profit. In order to measure profit it is necessary to match the revenue generated with the costs associated with this revenue generation. So in using fixed assets to generate revenue the company will have to identify the cost of the fixed assets associated with it. How is the company to measure the cost of the fixed assets used up in generating revenue? The cost of the fixed assets used up in generating revenue, in accounting terms, is known as depreciation.

What is depreciation?

Depreciation is an estimate of how much of an asset has been used up in generating revenue. If the matching concept is adhered to, it follows that the measure of the amount of asset used up should be based on the pattern of benefits expected to be derived from using the particular asset. In order to calculate the depreciation the following information is required:

- cost of the asset
- residue value, i.e. the value at the end of the asset's life
- useful life of the asset.

Given that depreciation is an estimate of the cost of an asset used up in generating revenue, this depreciation charge will be shown in the profit and loss account as an expense, and so will be matched against the revenues generated for the period.

There are a number of ways of calculating this depreciation charge, the most common ones are:

- straight line method
- reducing balance method.

Straight line method of depreciation

This method of depreciation allocates an equal amount of depreciation over the life of the asset. It is calculated by dividing the net cost of the asset by its useful life. Net cost is the cost of the asset less the scrap value. This net cost is also knows as 'depreciable amount' and is the cost of an asset less its residual value.

Example

A company buys an asset costing £7,000 that is expected to last for three years. At the end of the three-year period the scrap value is estimated to be £1,000. The depreciation charge can be calculated as follows:

$$\text{Depreciation charge} \quad = \quad \frac{\text{cost} - \text{residual value}}{\text{useful life}}$$

$$= \quad \frac{£7,000 - £1,000}{3}$$

$$= \quad \underline{\underline{£2,000}}$$

This means that the net cost of the asset, £6,000, is spread over the life of the asset. The depreciation charge is recorded in the profit and loss account in each of the three years at £2,000 each year.

Profit and loss account (for Year 1)	
Depreciation	£2,000
Balance sheet (for Year 1)	
Fixed asset	£7,000
Less depreciation	£2,000
Net book value	£5,000

The profit and loss account shows the charge for depreciation, while the balance sheet shows the cost of the asset minus the total depreciation allocated to the asset.

In Year 2, the financial statements will show:

Profit and loss account (for Year 2)	
Depreciation	£2,000
Balance sheet (for Year 2)	
Fixed asset (cost)	£7,000
Less total depreciation	£4,000 (for two years)
Net book value	£3,000
And in Year 3	
Profit and loss account (for Year 3)	
Depreciation	£2,000
Balance sheet (for Year 3)	
Fixed asset (cost)	£7,000
Less total depreciation	£6,000 (for three years)
Net book value	£1,000

This shows that the asset is now reduced to its scrap value at the end of the three-year period.

It is worth pausing at this stage to look more closely at the above figures in the preceding example.

The profit and loss account entries are readily understandable. This shows that the asset is expected to make an even contribution to revenues over the three years. The cost of the asset used up in generating these revenues is £2,000 each year.

The information disclosed by the balance sheet entries is perhaps less obvious. In Year 1 the original cost of £7,000 and the first allocation of depreciation of £2,000 is deducted from that cost to give what accountants call 'net book value'. The net book value is £5,000.

What does the term 'net book value' mean?

This term is rather unfortunate, since the figure of £5,000 has nothing to do with value. It does not represent what the company could sell the asset for – that is, its market value – nor is it the amount the company would have to pay to replace the asset – that is, its replacement cost. As was noted in the introduction to this chapter, fixed assets can be the most misinterpreted and contentious items within a company's balance sheet. This example clearly illustrates why. Far from being a market value, all net book value represents is the cost of that asset, which has still to be allocated. A better description of the £5,000 net book value, would be 'unallocated cost'.

Progress Point 2.1

What does depreciation do and why is it necessary?

Solution

Depreciation spreads the cost of an asset over its useful life in appropriate proportion to the benefit gained from its use.

It is necessary to adhere to the matching principle – allocating expense against corresponding benefit, as part of the profit calculation.

Reducing balance method

This method of depreciation applies a higher depreciation charge in the earlier years of an asset's life and a lower charge in the later years. The same three basic pieces of information are used: asset cost, scrap value and asset life. The reducing balance method calculates a rate of depreciation that will reduce the cost of the asset to the scrap value over the life of the asset.

As with the straight line method of depreciation, part of the asset's cost is allocated to the profit and loss account each year, while the balance sheet entries show the unallocated cost of the asset.

It could be argued that the reducing balance method reflects the efficiency and maintenance costs of the asset. When it is new, the asset will be operating at maximum efficiency with few repair costs, especially if under guarantee. As the asset gets older, repair costs are more likely to occur and these will tend to offset the lower depreciation charge.

The formula for calculating the appropriate percentage to make the net book value equal to the residual value is as follows:

$$r = 1 - \sqrt[n]{} \text{ (scrap value/cost)}$$

Where:

r is the required rate and n is the number of years.

In practice, this formula is rarely used and instead a standard 'round' figure is usually taken as a satisfactory rate for the type of asset under consideration (e.g. motor vehicles 25%). This formula will not work if the residual value is zero. In this case residual value has to be imputed as 1.

✦ Example

An asset with an initial cost of £10,000 is expected to be used for three years and to have a residual value at the end of the three years of £7,290.

Depreciation rate	=	$1 - \sqrt[3]{}$ (7,290/10,000)
	=	$1 - \sqrt[3]{}$ (0.729)
	=	1 – 0.9
	=	0.1 or 10%

BASIC

INTERMEDIATE

ADVANCED

The depreciation would be calculated as follows:

Asset cost	£10,000
Depreciation in Year 1 (10% of £10,000)	£1,000
Net book value	£9,000
Depreciation in Year 2 (10% of £9,000)	£900
Net book value	£8,100
Depreciation in Year 3 (10% of £8,100)	£810
Net book value	£7,290

This means that the cost of the asset has been reduced to its residual value of £7,290 at the end of three years. The accounting entries are identical to those given for the straight line method, except of course the amount of depreciation is different.

Profit and loss account (for Year 1)	
Depreciation	£1,000
Balance sheet (for Year 1)	
Fixed asset	£10,000
Less depreciation	£1,000
Net book value	£9,000

As before, the profit and loss account shows the charge for depreciation, while the balance sheet shows the cost of the asset minus the total depreciation allocated to the asset.

In Year 2 the financial statements will show:

Profit and loss account (for Year 2)		
Depreciation	£900	
Balance sheet (for Year 2)		
Fixed asset (cost)	£10,000	
Less total depreciation	£1,900	(for two years)
Net book value	£8,100	

And in Year 3:

Profit and loss account (for Year 3)		
Depreciation	£810	
Balance sheet (for Year 3)		
Fixed asset (cost)	£10,000	
Less total depreciation	£2,710	(for three years)
Net book value	£7,290	

BASIC

INTERMEDIATE

ADVANCED

Progress Point 2.2

Explain how the straight line and reducing balance methods of depreciation work. What different assumptions does each method make?

Solution

The straight line method charges a constant percentage of the cost of the asset each year as depreciation; the reducing balance method charges a constant percentage of the net book value (i.e. cost less accumulated depreciation brought forward), as depreciation each year.

The straight line method therefore results in a constant charge, while the reducing balance method has a charge reducing each year of the asset's life. The two methods, therefore, make different assumptions about the usefulness, the trend or pattern of benefits of the fixed asset concerned.

The straight line method assumes that the asset will give a constant return over its useful life, while the reducing balance method assumes that the benefits will be higher in the early years and diminish as the asset tends towards the end of its useful life.

Other methods of calculating depreciation

In addition to the methods of calculating depreciation indicated above, there are another two methods, which are described below.

Sum of the digits method

This method, while popular in the USA, is not all that common in the UK. Under this method, the depreciation rate is calculated by relating the remaining life of an asset to its initial expected life. The asset's initial expected life is expressed in digits and the digits are then summed.

 ### Example

An asset costing £12,000 has an estimated useful life of four years and a residual value at the end of Year 4 of £2,000.

$$\text{Depreciation rate} = \frac{\text{No. of remaining years of asset's life}}{\text{Asset's initial expected life, expressed in digits and summed}}$$

Depreciation charge in Year t = Depreciable amount x depreciable rate in Year t

Charge: – Year 1 $= \dfrac{4}{(4+3+2+1)}$ x (£12,000 – £2,000) = £4,000

Charge – Year 2 $= \dfrac{3}{10}$ x £10,000 = £3,000

Charge – Year 3 $= \dfrac{2}{10}$ x £10,000 = £2,000

Charge – Year 4 $= \dfrac{1}{10}$ x £10,000 = £1,000

The sum of the digits method has the advantage that, unlike the reducing balance method, it can use a residual value of zero. In addition, the pattern of depreciation is similar to that of the reducing balance method, giving a higher depreciation charge in the earlier years of an asset's life.

Output or usage method

The depreciation rate is the ratio of the asset's output or usage in a period to its total expected output or usage.

$$\text{Depreciation rate in the year} = \frac{\text{Output or usage in the year}}{\text{Total expected output or usage}}$$

Depreciation charge = Depreciable amount x Depreciation rate in year

This method of depreciation results in a depreciation charge that fluctuates with the output or asset's use. This method is commonly employed in the aviation industry, where aircraft are depreciated on the basis of flying hours.

As far as the accounting is concerned, in each case the profit and loss account will show the annual charge for depreciation. This will be recorded as an expense and so will reduce the profit for the year. In the balance sheet the fixed asset will be recorded at cost less the total (accumulated) depreciation to date.

Progress Point 2.3

The Pizza Company has just opened a pizza restaurant in Glasgow. The restaurant contains a new pizza oven that cost £110,000 to buy and install. The oven has an expected life of ten years with a residual value of zero. The total expected output of the oven over ten years is 600,000 standard-size pizzas. The forecast output for Years 1 to 5 is as follows:

Year 1	30,000 pizzas
Year 2	48,000 pizzas
Year 3	66,000 pizzas
Year 4	78,000 pizzas
Year 5	84,000 pizzas

(a) Calculate the depreciation charge in each of the five years using:
   (i) the straight line method
   (ii) the reducing balance method (assume a rate of 15%)
   (iii) sum of years digits
   (iv) units of production.
(b) Show the net book value of the oven at the end of each of Years 1 to 5.

Solution

(a)
   (i) Straight line method of depreciation:

$$\text{Depreciation charge} = \frac{\text{cost} - \text{residual value}}{\text{life}}$$

$$= \frac{£110,000 - £0}{10}$$

$$= £11,000 \text{ per annum for each of Years 1 to 5}$$

BASIC

INTERMEDIATE

ADVANCED

(ii) Reducing balance:

Cost of asset	£110,000
Depreciation Year 1 (15%)	£16,500
	£93,500
Depreciation Year 2	£14,025
	£79,475
Depreciation Year 3	£11,921
	£67,554
Depreciation Year 4	£10,133
	£57,421
Depreciation Year 5	£8,613
	£48,808

(iii) Sum of years digits:

Digits = 1 + 2 + 3 + 4 + 5 + 6 + 7 + 8 + 9 + 10 = 55

Cost	£110,000
Depreciation Year 1 = 10/55	£20,000
	£90,000
Depreciation Year 2 = 9/55	£18,000
	£72,000
Depreciation Year 3 = 8/55	£16,000
	£56,000
Depreciation Year 4 = 7/55	£14,000
	£42,000
Depreciation Year 5 = 6/55	£12,000
	£30,000

BASIC

INTERMEDIATE

ADVANCED

(iv) Units of production:

> Depreciation rate is calculated as follows:
>
> | | | |
> |---|---|---|
> | Year 1 | (30,000/600,000) = | 5% |
> | Year 2 | (48,000/600,000) = | 8% |
> | Year 3 | (66,000/600,000) = | 11% |
> | Year 4 | (78,000/600,000) = | 13% |
> | Year 5 | (84,000/600,000) = | 14% |
>
> | | |
> |---|---|
> | Cost | £110,000 |
> | Depreciation | £5,500 |
> | Year 1 (5%) | |
> | | £104,500 |
> | Depreciation | £8,800 |
> | Year 2 (8%) | |
> | | £95,700 |
> | Depreciation | £12,100 |
> | Year 3 (11%) | |
> | | £83,600 |
> | Depreciation | £14,300 |
> | Year 4 (13%) | |
> | | £69,300 |
> | Depreciation | £15,400 |
> | Year 5 (14%) | |
> | | £53,900 |

(b) Net book values of assets:

Year	Straight line	Reducing balance	Sum of years digits	Units of production
	£	£	£	£
1	89,000	93,500	90,000	104,500
2	78,000	79,475	72,000	95,700
3	67,000	67,554	56,000	83,600
4	56,000	57,421	42,000	69,300
5	45,000	48,808	30,000	53,900

Regardless of the method chosen, the issue with respect to depreciation is that the cost of using the asset is being allocated to the profit and loss account as an expense over the period the asset is being used. This allocation process is matching the cost of using the asset with the benefits being derived from the asset.

An alternative way of describing an asset's value is as an unallocated cost. This cost will be allocated, that is – spread over the life of the asset in the form of a depreciation expense in the profit and loss account. So what has been described at the 'net book value' of an asset has, in reality, nothing to do with the 'value' of the asset, but is the cost of the asset that has still to be allocated over the life of the asset.

2.3 Asset cost

As was noted earlier, in order to calculate the depreciation charge, the cost of the asset has to be determined. On the face of it, this would seem to be a straightforward figure to identify. Surely the cost of an asset is the amount paid for it (i.e. its invoice cost)? While in some cases this is true, there are situations where determining the cost of an asset is less clear. Consider the following example.

Example 1

A company buys a machine costing £20,000. This machine is in a warehouse in London and has to be installed in the company's factory in Edinburgh. The cost of transporting the machine from London to Edinburgh is estimated to be £500. In order to get the machine operational and ready for use, the company has to pay installation costs of £1,000. What is the cost of the machine?

Clearly the purchase price of £20,000 is part of the cost of the asset. The question is, however, how are the costs of transport and installation to be treated? Without the machine being delivered to the factory and then subsequently installed, it would not be able to be used. The additional costs of transport and of installation are, therefore, necessary. It could be argued, then, that these additional costs should be added to the cost of the asset. Indeed, without them, the machine would be of no benefit to the company at all.

In Example 1, above, while the purchase price of the machine is £20,000, as far as the company is concerned, the *cost* of the machine is £21,500 (i.e. the purchase price, plus transportation and installation costs).

Example 2

Instead of buying a new machine, suppose the company buys a second-hand machine for £10,000. Transportation costs and installation costs remain the same at £500 and £1,000 respectively. When the machine was installed it was found that it was not working properly and had to be repaired at a cost of £800. After two months' production the machine broke down again and was repaired at a cost of £300.

As before, the purchase price of the machine is £10,000. In addition, the transportation and installation costs will also form part of the cost of the machine. However, before the machine could be used, further repairs were necessary. Without those further repairs the machine would not work properly. It could be argued therefore that this cost, too, should be added to the cost of the asset. Indeed, without these essential repairs, the machine would not be of any benefit to the company.

The accounting treatment of the other repairs that were carried out after two months' production is less clear cut.

It could be argued that these repairs are simply due to normal wear and tear, and consequently should be treated as simply being the cost of running the machine. This is similar to the cost of car repairs, which can be viewed as part of a maintenance programme to keep the car working properly.

The above examples illustrate that there can often be problems in determining the cost of an asset. Each case needs to be judged on its merits, but, as a general rule, the cost of an asset will include all the costs incurred in bringing the asset to its location and making it ready for use. Such costs would include acquisition cost, delivery costs and installation costs. A feature of such costs is that they are generally non-recurring.

Problems can arise with repair costs, however, but again, as a general rule, if the cost is necessary in order to bring the asset into use for the first time it should be capitalised; if it is being incurred after the asset is brought into use and is simply maintaining the asset at its current operating levels, then it should be treated as an expense.

BASIC

INTERMEDIATE

ADVANCED

Progress Point 2.4

A German engineering company decides to replace an older machine with a new one because of efficiency concerns and higher quality requirements. The machine was bought in Canada and transported by plane to Germany. This new machine replaces an old one, which was dismantled.

Which of the following items of expenditure will be included in the initial cost of the new machine?

1. Air transportation costs
2. 7% trade discount on the purchase price
3. Production losses in the start-up phase of operations
4. Installation costs paid to installing company
5. Personnel costs of employees involved with testing the machine before bringing it into production
6. Training costs of the personnel required to operate the machine
7. Insurance cost of transport from Canada to Germany

Solution

The items to be included in the initial cost of the machine are: 1, 2, 4, 5 and 7.

2.4 Residual value

The residual value is the amount received by a business for the sale of an asset at the end of its expected useful life. This is highly subjective and usually involves estimating the future disposal value. It is not an easy task to estimate a residual value. Estimating a residual value involves an attempt at forecasting what might be expected from the sale of an asset at some point in the future. Such an estimate involves many variables. Such variables include:

*   when the asset will be disposed of
*   the expected condition of the asset at the end of its useful life
*   the possible technological advances that may have occurred over the years
*   the amount that the company would currently obtain from selling the asset (assuming the asset was already of the age and condition expected at the end of its useful life).

Estimated useful life

The useful life of an asset is its economic life and not its physical life. Many assets become less efficient, both economically and technologically, as they grow older. While careful maintenance can extend the economic life of an asset, it is likely that the effects of technological progress, the cost and availability of replacements and repair costs, will render the economic life of an asset much shorter than the working life – for example, a computer may have a physical life of eight years and an economic life of only three years.

In addition to estimating the length of the useful life, an estimate needs to be made of the expected pattern of benefit or usefulness to be derived from the asset – all highly subjective.

Disposal of assets

The calculation of a depreciation charge involves an estimate of the expected useful life, the pattern of the expected benefits and the expected residual value.

The depreciation charge is a positive calculation (i.e. it needs to be calculated). It cannot be found by comparing balance sheet values from one accounting period to the next. At the outset, however, the charge can only ever be at best an estimate. There is subjectivity involved in this calculation and, consequently, at the end of the asset's useful economic life, a company may realise more or less for the asset than it had anticipated.

If a company sells an asset for more than the net book value, it will have made a gain on disposal. The converse is also true: if a company sells an asset for less than the net book value, there will be a loss on disposal.

Example

A company buys an asset costing £10,000 with an estimated useful life of four years and no anticipated residual value. It expects a constant flow of benefits from the asset and adopts the straight line method to calculate its depreciation charge. At the end of Year 2, however, the company decides to sell the asset and receives £6,500.

At the end of Year 2 the asset will have a net book value of:

£10,000 – 2 x (10,000/4)	=	£5,000
Cost of asset		£10,000
Net book value after two years		£5,000
Selling price		£6,500
The company will have made a gain on disposal of £6,500 – £5,000 =		£1,500

The accounting issue involved

The accounting issue involved is what the gain (or loss) on disposal actually represents. The gain (or loss) on disposal is calculated by comparing the sales proceeds with the net book value. The net book value of an asset is the amount of the original cost of an asset not yet allocated to the income statement – that is, the opening carrying value less the accumulated depreciation. It follows therefore that a gain or loss on disposal arises because of an 'incorrect' depreciation charge in earlier years. In other words, had the company known that it would keep the asset for only two years and be able to sell it for £6,500, it would have depreciated the asset as follows:

Year 1	=	$\dfrac{(10,000 - 6,500)}{2}$	=	£1,750
Year 2	=	$\dfrac{(10,000 - 6,500)}{2}$	=	£1,750
Total depreciation charged				£3,500

These facts were not, however, available at the outset and consequently the depreciation was calculated as shown below.

Year 1	=	$\dfrac{(10,000 - 0)}{4}$	=	£2,500
Year 2	=	$\dfrac{(10,000 - 0)}{4}$	=	£2,500
Gain on disposal				(£1,500)
Total depreciation/gain on disposal				£3,500

Note that, overall, the total amount charged to the income statement in respect of the use of the asset is still the same: £3,500. It is the pattern of the charges that differs.

BASIC

INTERMEDIATE

ADVANCED

Note also that it is the depreciation expense that is being positively calculated and not the reduction in the asset figure. It is only when the asset is ultimately disposed of that the net book value is used to positively calculate any gain or loss on disposal. At that point the exact amount of the asset used in generating economic benefits is determined.

Land

So far in this chapter the analysis has been concerned with assets whose useful economic life is limited. Moreover the contention that assets held on a company's balance sheet are simply costs yet to be allocated to the company's income statement further emphasises the limited life span of the assets and their ultimate usage in generating income. Whichever valuation base is placed on such fixed assets, there can be no doubt that the 'value' of such assets will reduce over time as the asset is used.

The position regarding land is somewhat different. Land itself will tend to have an infinite life unless it is held for the extraction of minerals (e.g. a diamond mine). As such, land will not tend to be 'used up' in the course of generating income, and consequently it does not require to be depreciated.

2.5 Revaluation of fixed assets

As noted above, land that is not held for the extraction of minerals does not require to be depreciated. In reality, the price of land tends to increase virtually every year and, its inclusion in the balance sheet at historic cost is likely to seriously understate its value, particularly if looked at over a long period of time.

In order to remove such distortions, a company may choose to bring the asset value up to date, and so may choose to revalue the asset.

In order to account for an increase in value, the asset account is increased by the amount of the revaluation and this is put into a revaluation reserve. In other words, the asset account will be debited and the corresponding credit entry is made to a revaluation reserve.

An increase in value of an asset is not shown in the profit and loss account since the gain is not realised. The gain is being **recognised**, however, and this recognised gain will be included in the 'statement of recognised income and expense' (see Chapter 1).

 ### *Example*

A business has its land valued at £100,000. The directors wish this value to be reflected in the accounts. The balance sheet before the revaluation showed land at cost of £70,000.

The revaluation will be recorded as follows:

Dr	Fixed assets – land	£30,000	
	Cr Revaluation reserve		£30,000
Being revalutaion of land.			

Extract balance sheet entries will show:

Fixed assets	
Land	£70,000
Revaluation	£30,000
At valuation	£100,000
Financed by:	
Revaluation reserve	£30,000

Summary

This chapter started with the widely held perception that fixed assets are one of the most reliable, robust figures in a company's balance sheet. However, the determination of the cost of an asset can be difficult to measure and may involve subjective judgement. Moreover, the subsequent depreciation calculation based on that cost figure involves even more uncertainty and subjectivity.

In addition, the chapter shows that the fixed asset value in the balance sheet represents the cost of that asset which has still to be allocated – that is, the unallocated cost. A company can also show fixed assets at their up-to-date value by revaluing them.

Section 2: Intermediate Issues

This section extends and develops some of the ideas from Section 1. In particular it will focus on the International Accounting Standards (IAS) Framework in terms of how it defines assets, and identify the detailed reporting requirements of the international standards.

2.6 Definition of assets

An asset is defined as:

> a resource controlled by the entity as a result of past events and from which future economic benefits are expected to flow to the entity. (Framework, para. 49a)

This definition is deliberately wide so that it encompasses all possible assets and not simply the more obvious tangible assets.

To understand this definition fully, each phrase must be considered separately.

- *Controlled by the entity*: control can either be used in the positive sense in that the company has access to the economic benefits derived from using an asset, but it can also be used in the negative sense of preventing others from accessing such benefits. From this perspective, an asset such as skilled employees cannot be included on the balance sheet. While there is no doubt that having a skilled workforce will benefit a company, there is no way a company could exercise control over the workforce. It is important to note that the definition does not make any reference to ownership. While ownership is likely to be the strongest form of control available to a company, the right to use an item may, in practice, be very similar to the right of ownership. Such rights may be conferred by legal arrangements such as an agreement to lease or rent a resource, or a licence allowing exclusive use of a resource.

- *A result of past events*: A resource cannot simply appear and be recognised. Something must have happened for a resource to have been identified and there must be objective evidence to prove that the entity has some entitlement to the resource. A past event provides objective evidence that an entity has done something to create a resource or has purchased it. The evidence provided by a past transaction is, therefore, an objective starting point. A transaction is an agreement between two parties, which usually involves exchanging goods or services for cash or a future right to cash. Sometimes, however, there may be no transaction as such but there is an event that is sufficient to give this objective evidence. The event could be the performance of a service that, once completed, gives the right to demand payment.

- *Future economic benefits*: An entity may use up many resources in the expectation that they will provide future cash. Some resources generate cash more quickly than others. For example, stocks of goods purchased for resale carry a future economic benefit in terms of the expectation of sale. Such a benefit comes to the entity relatively quickly. The entity may also own a warehouse where goods are stored before being sold. The warehouse also provides future economic benefits since it helps create the cash flow from the sale of goods (by having them available for sale).

In addition, the warehouse itself could be sold at some point in the future, which again would generate cash.

It is important to note that the future economic benefits may be direct, as in the case of stocks purchased for resale, or indirect, as in the case of the warehouse that assists in the generation of those directly identifiable benefits.

In addition, there may be uncertainty surrounding the amount of future economic benefits. Stock purchased for resale may or may not be sold at a profit; stocks sold on credit to a customer may or may not be paid for, i.e. bad debts. This uncertainty does not prevent the resource being recognised as an asset, but it may impact on how the asset is measured in money terms.

Table 2.1 gives examples of assets commonly found in company balance sheets and illustrates the test aspects of the definition being satisfied.

Asset	Controlled by the entity by means of	Past event	Future economic benefits
Land and buildings owned by the company	Outright ownership	Signing the contract as evidence of purchase of land and buildings	Used in continuing operations of the business; possible future sale of items
Plant and machinery owned by the company	Outright ownership	The receiving of the goods and a supplier's invoice	Used in continuing operations of the business
Equipment used under a finance lease	Contract for exclusive use	Signing lease agreeing rental terms	Used in continuing operations of the business
Goods purchased for resale	Ownership	The receiving of the goods and a supplier's invoice	Expectation of sale
Amounts due from customers (trade receivables)	Contract for payment	Delivery of goods to customer; issue of sales invoice and creation of obligation to pay for goods at future date	Expectation that the customer will settle the obligation and pay cash
Work in progress (partly finished goods)	Ownership	Costs incurred to date and evaluation of the state of completion of works as evidenced by work records	Expectation of completion and sale
Prepaid insurance premiums	Contract for insurance cover for a specific period	Paying insurance premiums in advance; cheque payment	Expectation of continuing insurance cover

Table 2.1 How test aspects of the definition of assets are met

It is conventional practice to divide assets into current assets and fixed (non-current) assets.

An asset should be classified as a current asset when it:

- is expected to be realised in, or is held for sale or consumption in, the normal course of the entity's operating cycle
- is held primarily for trading purposes or for the short term, and expected to be realised within 12 months of the balance sheet date, or
- is cash or a cash equivalent asset that is not restricted in its use.

All other assets should be classified as fixed (non-current) assets.

The classification between current and non-current is the intention to which the asset is to be put, and not the length of the life of the asset. If the intention is to use the asset over an extended period then it will be classified as a non-current asset. In contrast, if the asset is likely to undergo some transaction within 12 months, then it should be classified as current.

2.7 Recognition and non-recognition of assets

Recognition

Although an item may have satisfied the criteria to be defined as an asset, this in itself does not qualify the item as an asset for inclusion in the balance sheet. There are further tests of recognition that must be met.

Recognition means reporting an item by means of words and amounts within the main financial statements in such a way that the item is included in the arithmetic totals. An item that is reported in the notes to the accounts is said to be disclosed but not recognised.

An asset is recognised in the balance sheet when:

- it is probable that future economic benefits associated with the item will flow to the entity, and
- the cost of the item to the entity can be measured reliably.

In order to satisfy the first criterion for recognition, an entity needs evidence that the future benefit will flow to it – proof of ownership (e.g. vehicle registration documents, title deeds of property, invoices from suppliers of machinery). Existence of such evidence suggests that an entity can be reasonably certain that it will receive the rewards attaching to the asset.

The second criterion is usually satisfied by the exchange transaction that gave rise to the expenditure in the first instance (i.e. the purchase of the asset identified its cost). As we discovered in the first section of this chapter, the purchase price of the asset will not always necessarily be equal to the assets cost and, indeed, as we will see later on in this section, there are other factors that may affect the calculation of an asset's cost.

Non-recognition

It is worth pausing to consider the following items that pass the definition tests of assets but fail the recognition tests:

- a skilled workforce
- a quality product
- a strong customer base.

All the above meet the conditions of rights or other access to future economic benefits, control (to an extent) and a past transaction or event.

In addition, however, they all have some degree of uncertainty attached to them and, as a result, fail one or both of the recognition tests.

A skilled workforce may, as a result of unforeseen circumstances, become unreliable or problematic; a product may have a reputation for quality but as fashions and tastes change, that reputation may not carry the value it once did; customers may well be loyal but they could change their allegiance at a moment's notice.

These items, then, cannot be recognised in the financial statements. Should they, however, be disclosed in the notes to the financial statements?

The answer is that because of the level of uncertainty attaching to the future benefits, the prudent approach is to avoid being over-optimistic and consequently not to disclose such items as assets in the notes.

2.8 More on cost

In the first section of this chapter the cost of an asset was shown to include all the costs incurred in bringing the asset to its present location and in a condition ready for use. Cost therefore can include cost of acquisition, delivery and handling costs, installation costs and professional fees.

Accounting policies in relation to government grants receivable and to capitalisation of borrowing costs may also have a bearing on the calculation of the capitalised cost figure. Both are subjects of separate international standards and it is helpful to look briefly at their requirements before moving on to examine the requirements of IAS 16 *Property, Plant and Equipment* in detail.

Government grants

Government grants are broadly defined as assistance in the form of cash to a company in return for past or future compliance with certain conditions relating to the operations of the enterprise.

Government grants may be either revenue-based grants or capital-based grants. Revenue-based grants, as their name suggests, are intended to be a contribution towards revenue expenditure, and capital-based grants are a contribution towards capital expenditure.

Common to both types of grant, however, is the accruals concept, which requires the matching of cost and revenue so as to recognise both in the income statements of the periods to which they relate. This treatment should, of course, also take account of any potential claw-backs of the grants. Prudence requires that revenue is not anticipated and, consequently, credit should never be taken until the receipt of the grant is relatively certain. Indeed, failure to comply with the grant covenants may mean that the grant has to be repaid.

IAS 20 *Accounting for Government Grants and Disclosure of Government Assistance* sets out two acceptable methods of dealing with grants relating to assets in the balance sheet.

The first is to set up the grant as a deferred credit in the balance sheet and to release a portion of it annually to revenue over the useful life of the asset.

 ## Example

A government grant is paid to an enterprise under the strict condition that the enterprise purchases a piece of manufacturing equipment.

The relevant figures are:

Purchase price	£60,000
Expected useful life	4 years
Expected residual value	NIL
Grant received	£20,000

This 'deferred income method' would give the following income statement and balance sheet extracts for the four years.

Income statement	Year 1	Year 2	Year 3	Year 4
	£	£	£	£
Depreciation	(15,000)	(15,000)	(15,000)	(15,000)
Grant released	5,000	5,000	5,000	5,000
Net effect on profit	(10,000)	(10,000)	(10,000)	(10,000)

Balance sheet extracts				
Assets	Year 1	Year 2	Year 3	Year 4
	£	£	£	£
Fixed assets at cost	60,000	60,000	60,000	60,000
Accumulated depreciation	15,000	30,000	45,000	60,000
Net book value	45,000	30,000	15,000	0
Liabilities				
	£	£	£	£
Deferred credit	20,000	15,000	10,000	5,000
Less: grant released	5,000	5,000	5,000	5,000
	15,000	10,000	5,000	0
Net effect on net assets	30,000	20,000	10,000	0

There would be an initial carrying amount for the asset of £60,000 and a deferred income credit of £20,000. In the first year of use there would be a straight line depreciation charge of £15,000 (£60,000/4). A similar rate of release will be applied to the grant in order to recognise both in the income statement of the period to which it relates, i.e. £5,000 (£20,000/4).

The net charge to the income statement in Year 1 would therefore be £10,000 (£15,000 – £5,000) and, as a straight line policy for the depreciation charge and grant release has been adopted, there would be a net £10,000 charge in Years 2 through to Year 4.

The balance sheet extracts show the asset being depreciated down to its residual value of NIL and the grant being reduced to nil as it is released to income over the four years.

The second method deducts the grant in arriving at the carrying amount of the relevant asset. This 'netting method' would give the following income statement and balance sheet extracts using our example figures above.

 Example

Income statement	Year 1	Year 2	Year 3	Year 4
	£	£	£	£
Depreciation	(10,000)	(10,000)	(10,000)	(10,000)
Net effect on profit	(10,000)	(10,000)	(10,000)	(10,000)
Balance sheet				
Fixed asset at net cost	40,000	40,000	40,000	40,000
Accumulated depreciation	10,000	20,000	30,000	40,000
Net book value	30,000	20,000	10,000	0
Net effect on net assets	30,000	20,000	10,000	0

Using this 'netting method' there would be an initial carrying amount of the asset at its net cost after deducting the grant of £40,000 (£60,000 – £20,000). The straight line depreciation charge for each of the four years would be £10,000 (£40,000/4). As can be seen from the above, the net effects on profit and net assets are exactly the same for each of the years using both methods. The only difference is in balance sheet presentation.

Progress Point 2.5

A government grant is paid to an enterprise under the strict condition that purchases a piece of manufacturing equipment.

The relevant figures are:

Purchase price	£90,000
Expected useful life	3 years
Expected residual value	NIL
Grant received	£30,000

(a) Show the income statement for each of the Years 1 to 3 using:
   (i) deferred income method
   (ii) netting method.
(b) Show the balance sheet extracts for each of the years 1 to 3.

Solution

Deferred income method			
Income statement	**Year 1**	**Year 2**	**Year 3**
	£	£	£
Depreciation	(30,000)	(30,000)	(30,000)
Grant released	10,000	10,000	10,000
Net effect on profit	(20,000)	(20,000)	(20,000)

Balance sheet extracts:

Assets	Year 1	Year 2	Year 3
	£	£	£
Fixed assets at cost	90,000	90,000	90,000
Accumulated depreciation	30,000	60,000	90,000
Net book value	60,000	30,000	nil
Liabilities			
Deferred credit	30,000	20,000	10,000
Less: grant released	10,000	10,000	10,000
	20,000	10,000	nil
Net effect on net assets	40,000	20,000	nil

There would be an initial carrying amount for the asset of £90,000 and a deferred income credit of £30,000. In the first year of use there would be a straight line depreciation charge of £30,000 (£90,000/3). A similar rate of release will be applied to the grant in order to recognise both in the income statement of the period to which it relates, i.e. £10,000 (£30,000/3).

The net charge to the income statement in Year 1 would therefore be £20,000 (£30,000 – £10,000) and, as a straight line policy for the depreciation charge and grant release has been adopted, there would be a net £20,000 charge in Years 2 and 3.

The balance sheet extracts show the asset being depreciated down to its residual value of NIL and the grant being reduced to nil as it is released to income over the four years.

BASIC

INTERMEDIATE

ADVANCED

▶

Netting method

Income statement	Year 1	Year 2	Year 3
	£	£	£
Depreciation	(20,000)	(20,000)	(20,000)
Net effect on profit	(20,000)	(20,000)	(20,000)

Balance sheet			
Fixed asset at net cost	90,000	90,000	90,000
Accumulated depreciation	30,000	60,000	90,000
Net book value	60,000	30,000	nil
Net effect on net assets	40,000	20,000	nil

Using this 'netting method' there would be an initial carrying amount of the asset at its net cost of £60,000 after deducting the grant (£90,000 – £30,000). The straight line depreciation charge for each of the four years would be £30,000 (£90,000/3). As can be seen from the above, the net effects on profit and net assets are exactly the same for each of the years using both methods.

Asset disposal

In a situation where the company disposes of an asset on which a deferred income balance remains, and where the grant has to be repaid, this should be accounted for by first reducing the balance on the deferred income account, with any additional charge being direct to the income statement.

Where the grant itself does not need to be repaid, then the balance on the deferred income account should be considered in calculating the profit or loss on disposal.

Borrowing costs

Borrowing costs are another expense that may have an impact on the cost of an asset. If cost is to include *all* the costs incurred in bringing the asset to its location and in a position to make it ready for use then under the accruals basis of accounting it could be argued that such costs should be included in that asset's cost.

This would be particularly relevant to an asset that takes a substantial period of time to get ready for its intended use or sale (for example, the construction of a cruise ship).

There are convincing arguments for and against capitalisation of finance costs.

Arguments for capitalisation

1. If finance costs are incurred as a result of a decision to acquire an asset, then these costs are no different from other costs that are commonly capitalised, e.g. transportation or installation costs. Moreover, if the asset takes a substantial period of time to bring it to the condition and location necessary for its intended use, the finance costs incurred during that period as a result of expenditures on the asset are a part of the cost of acquiring the asset.
2. This treatment better adheres to the matching principle in that the interest incurred with a view to future benefit (i.e. the asset) is carried forward to be expensed in the periods expected to benefit; if, on the other hand, the interest is immediately expensed, this will reduce current earnings and distort reported profits – all as a consequence of the acquisition of assets.
3. This method allows better comparison between companies constructing assets and other companies buying similar completed assets. This is because the purchase price of completed assets

acquired will normally include interest as the seller will require to take account of all his costs, including interest, in pricing the asset. By treating the interest cost as an expense, this could artificially reduce the cost of the self-constructed asset and result in an incorrect make or buy decision.

Arguments against capitalisation

1. The treatment of the interest expense should be consistent. It does not make sense to treat finance costs as a period expense in normal circumstances, then to treat them as a direct cost of an asset during its period of construction, and then to revert to treating them as a period expense once the asset is complete. The nature of the interest cost does not change because of the use to which the funds are put. Interest cost is a period cost incurred in financing the business and its treatment should not change merely as a result of the completion of a fixed asset.
2. Because finance costs are incurred for the whole of the activities of the entity, it can be difficult to identify specific borrowings with specific projects. Where funds are raised centrally, any attempt to allocate finance costs with a particular asset will necessarily be arbitrary.
3. It is inappropriate that the same type of asset would have a different carrying amount depending on whether its construction was financed by borrowings or by equity. By limiting capitalised interest to interest on borrowings this would preclude the equity – funded enterprise from capitalising interest – even though it incurs an economic cost of the same order as an enterprise that has borrowed funds. It is inconsistent to allow debt-funded entities to include interest costs in the cost of an asset while prohibiting equity funded entities from reflecting similarly the cost of capital in the cost of an asset.

IAS 23 *Borrowing Costs* sets out the prescribed accounting treatment for borrowing costs.

Borrowing costs that are directly attributable to the acquisition, construction and production of a qualifying asset should be treated as part of the cost of that asset.

A qualifying asset is an asset that takes a substantial period of time to get ready for its intended use (e.g. ships, aircraft, long-term construction contracts, wine and spirits being aged).

The foregoing reflects revisions to IAS 23 adopted by the IASB in March 2007, which prohibit immediate expensing of borrowing costs. Prior to the revision, the previous version of IAS 23 permitted, as an accounting option, the 'immediate expensing model'. Under that model, all borrowing costs could be expensed in the period in which they were incurred.

The IASB believes that application of the revised standard will improve financial reporting in three ways. First, the cost of an asset will include all costs incurred in getting it ready for use or sale. Second, comparability is enhanced because one of the two accounting treatments that previously existed for those borrowing costs is removed. Third, the revision to IAS 23 achieves convergence in principle with US GAAP.

Where funds are borrowed specifically for obtaining a qualifying asset, the amount of borrowing costs eligible for capitalisation as part of the cost of that asset is the actual costs incurred less any income earned on the temporary investment of such borrowings.

Where funds are borrowed generally and used for the purpose of obtaining a qualifying asset, then the enterprise should use a capitalisation rate to determine the borrowing costs that may be capitalised. The capitalisation rate will be the weighted average of the borrowing costs applicable to the enterprise.

Capitalisation should commence when:

- expenditures for the asset are being incurred
- borrowing costs are being incurred
- activities that are necessary to prepare the asset for its intended use or sale are in progress.

Capitalisation should cease when:

- substantially all of the activities necessary to prepare the asset for its intended use or sale are complete.

An enterprise should disclose in its financial statements:

- the accounting policy adopted
- the amount of borrowing cost capitalised during the accounting period
- the capitalisation rate used.

 ## Example

On 1 April 2010 a company engages in the development of a property that is expected to take five years to complete, at a cost of £6,000,000. The balance sheets of the company at 31 December 2009 and 31 December 2010, prior to capitalisation of interest, are as follows:

Balance sheets as at	31/12/09	31/12/10
	£	£
Development property		1,200,000
Other assets	6,000,000	6,800,000
	6,000,000	8,000,000
Loans:		
8% debenture stock	2,500,000	2,500,000
Bank loan (10% per annum)		2,000,000
Bank loan (12% per annum)	1,000,000	1,000,000
	3,500,000	5,500,000
Shareholders' equity	2,500,000	2,500,000

The bank loan at 10% was taken out on 31 March 2010 and the total interest charge for the year ended 31 December 2010 was as follows:

	£	
Debenture stock £2,500,000 x 8%	200,000	
Bank loan £2,000,000 x 10% x 9/12	150,000	(9 months only)
Bank loan £1,000,000 x 12%	120,000	
	£470,000	

Expenditure was incurred on the development as follows:

	£
1 April 2010	600,000
1 July 2010	400,000
1 October 2010	200,000
	£1,200,000

(i)   If the bank loan at 10% p.a. is a new borrowing taken out specifically to finance the development, then the amount of interest to be capitalised is as follows:

	£
£600,000 x 10% x 9/12 =	45,000
£400,000 x 10% x 6/12 =	20,000
£200,000 x 10% x 3/12 =	5,000
	70,000

That is, the amount of the loan interest that can be specifically attached to the project expenditure as it progresses can be capitalised.

(ii)   If all the borrowings would have been avoided but for the development then the amount of interest to be capitalised would be found as follows.

(a)   First, determine the weighted average of the borrowing costs applicable to the company.

i.e. $\dfrac{\text{Total interest expense}}{\text{Weighted average total borrowings}} \times 100\%$

$\dfrac{470{,}000}{(3{,}500{,}000 + (2{,}000{,}000 \times 9/12))} = 9.4\%$

(b)   Next, apply the capitalisation rate to the expenditure as incurred.

		£
i.e.	£600,000 x 9.4% x 9/12 =	42,300
	£400,000 x 9.4% x 6/12 =	18,800
	£200,000 x 9.4% x 3/12 =	4,700
		65,800

Note that had the 8% debenture stock been irredeemable, then as the borrowings could not have been avoided, the calculation would be done using the figures for the bank loans and their related interest costs only. The debenture interest and debenture itself would not form part of the calculation.

2.9 IAS 16 *Property, Plant and Equipment*

The objective of IAS 16 is to prescribe the accounting treatment for property, plant and equipment. The principal issues are the timing of recognition of assets, the determination of their carrying amounts, and the depreciation charges to be recognised in relation to them.

Scope

IAS 16 notes that the general definition and recognition criteria for an asset given in the Framework for the Preparation and Presentation of Financial Statements must be satisfied before IAS 16 applies. While IAS 16 does not apply to biological assets related to agricultural activity (IAS 41), or mineral rights and mineral reserves such as oil, natural gas and similar non-regenerative resources, it does apply to property, plant and equipment used to develop or maintain such assets.

Definition

IAS 16 defines property, plant and equipment as tangible items that:

- are held for use in the production or supply of goods or services, for rental to others, or for administrative purposes, and
- are expected to be used during more than one period.

Recognition

Items of property, plant and equipment should be recognised as assets when it is probable that (IAS 16.7):

(i)   the future economic benefits associated with the asset will flow to the enterprise, and

(ii)   the cost of the asset can be measured reliably.

The recognition principle is applied to all property, plant and equipment costs at the time they are incurred. These costs include costs incurred initially to acquire or construct an item of property, plant and equipment and costs incurred subsequently to add to, replace part of, or service it.

The normal point of recognition is delivery to the company. It is not usual to recognise the item on order as the company does not control the item at this point, does not have access to most of the future benefits and is not exposed to most of the risks.

Cost can usually be measured reliably as it is normally evidenced by purchases from third parties. This also applies to self-constructed assets where purchase of materials, labour, etc., will indicate the cost.

IAS 16 does not prescribe the unit of measure for recognition of what constitutes an item of property, plant and equipment.

Judgement is required in applying the recognition criteria to an entity's specific circumstances – that is, what may be recognised as an asset by one entity may not necessarily be recognised as an asset by another.

IAS 16 allows for the aggregation of items that may, individually, be insignificant (e.g. moulds, tools, dies). The aggregation is then treated as an asset if the recognition criteria are met.

Conversely, although an asset may initially be acquired as a whole, each part of the asset with a cost that is significant in relation to the total cost of the asset should be accounted for and depreciated separately. The standard cites an aircraft and its engines as a likely example. This separation allows the depreciation figures to more accurately reflect the different consumption patterns of the various components (e.g. the aircraft body will probably last significantly longer than its engines).

Fixed assets acquired for safety or environmental reasons should be capitalised even though they do not directly generate benefits in themselves. Indirectly they allow the entity to secure benefits from its other assets.

Subsequent costs

Note that the recognition principle applies to costs incurred subsequently to add to, replace part of, or service an item of property, plant and equipment.

Ongoing maintenance costs – often described as 'repairs and maintenance' – are revenue expenses and not additions to costs. Such expenses, as we have covered earlier in this chapter, simply maintain an asset at its current operating level.

IAS 16 recognises, however, that major parts of some items of property, plant and equipment may require replacement at regular intervals, e.g. the seats and galleys of an aircraft may require replacement several times during the life of the airframe.

Under the recognition principle, an entity will include the cost of replacing the part of such an item in the carrying amount of the item. The carrying amount of those parts that are replaced is derecognised in accordance with the derecognition provisions of the standard.

Note that, in order to facilitate this, the component parts of the original example need to have been accounted for separately in the first place.

 ## Example

An aircraft is purchased for £15,000,000. Past experience has shown that the useful life of the seats is five years and that the cost of replacing these is £2,000,000.

The carrying amount of the aircraft would be recorded in the financial statements as follows:

Airframe	£13,000,000
Seats	£2,000,000
Total	£15,000,000

In a similar vein, the continued operation of an item of property, plant and equipment may require regular major inspections for faults regardless of whether parts of the item are replaced.

When each major inspection is performed, its cost is recognised in the carrying amount of the item of property, plant and equipment as a replacement if the recognition criteria are satisfied. Any

remaining carrying amount of the cost of the previous inspection (as distinct from the physical parts) is derecognised. This occurs regardless of whether the cost of the previous inspection was identified in the transaction in which the item was acquired or constructed.

If necessary, the estimated cost of a future similar inspection may be used as an indication of what the cost of the existing inspection component was when the item was acquired or constructed.

Example

A company buys a new helicopter for £750,000. The helicopter requires a major inspection every two years at a cost of £100,000. Two years after purchase the helicopter undergoes its first major inspection.

The costs of the inspection amount to £110,000.

The original carrying amount would have been allocated as follows:

Helicopter	£650,000
Inspection cost	£100,000
	£750,000

The original inspection costs will be derecognised and the new inspection costs will be recognised in the carrying amount of the asset.

Helicopter	£650,000
Inspection costs (original)	(£100,000)
Inspection costs (new)	£110,000
Carrying value	£760,000

That is, the new inspection costs are accounted for as an asset addition and the original inspection costs accounted for as an asset disposal.

Once the criteria for recognition have been met, the next issue to be considered is that of measurement. IAS 16 deals with this in two stages: initial measurement and measurement subsequent to initial recognition.

Initial measurement

An item that qualifies for recognition as an asset should be initially recorded at cost.

Cost includes all costs necessary to bring the asset to working condition for its intended use. These can include:

(a) purchase price (including import duties, stamp duty, etc., after deducting any trade discounts and rebates, but not early settlement discounts)
(b) directly attributable costs in bringing the asset to the location and condition necessary for its intended use, including
- cost of site preparation
- delivery and handling
- installation
- professional fees for architects and engineers
- costs of testing whether the asset is functioning properly after deducting the net proceeds from selling any items while bringing the asset to that location and condition
- dismantling and removing the asset and restoring the site.

Example

Pecant Ltd completed construction of a chemical plant at a cost of £25m in early 2008. As part of the planning permission, Pecant Ltd agreed to dismantle the plant at the end of its useful life. The present value of dismantling is £2m.

Pecant Ltd should capitalise the construction costs of £25m as well as the estimated costs of dismantling of £2m as it has an obligation under the terms of the planning permission.

The journal entries to record this would be as follows:

Dr	Plant	£25m	
	Cr Bank		£25m
Being purchase of plant.			
Dr	Plant	£2m	
	Cr Provision for dismantling		£2m
Being provision for dismantling costs.			

The standard also identifies items of expenditure that would not be included in the cost:

(a) costs of opening a new facility
(b) costs of introducing a new product or service (including costs of advertising and promotional activities)
(c) costs of conducting a new business in a new location (including staff training costs), and
(d) administration and other general overhead costs.

Where payment for an item of property, plant and equipment is deferred, the defined or imputed interest must be removed from the total of the payments, thus reducing the cost to the cash purchase price equivalent.

If an asset is acquired in exchange for another asset, the cost will be measured at the fair value unless:

■ the exchange transaction lacks commercial substance, or
■ the fair value of neither the asset received nor the asset given up is reliably measurable.

If the acquired item is not measured at fair value, its cost is measured at the carrying amount of the asset given up.

The recognition of costs in the carrying amount of an item ceases when the item is in the location and condition necessary for it to be capable of operating in the manner intended by management.

 Example

Portelux buys a new fixed asset and makes the following payments in relation to it:

	£	£
Cost – as per brochure	15,000	
Less: discount received	2,000	13,000
Delivery charge		200
Erection charge		100
Maintenance charge		300
Replacement parts		150
Additional components to increase capacity		400

The costs that Portelux should recognise in relation to the fixed asset are as follows:

		£
(i)	The purchase price of the asset	13,000
(ii)	Delivery charge	200
(iii)	Erection charge	100
(iv)	Additional components	400
		13,700

Costs (i), (ii) and (iii) are all incurred in bringing the asset to working condition for its intended use. The additional component (iv) is included in the cost of the machine as it enhances the revenue-earning capacity of the asset.

The maintenance costs and replacement parts are a cost of usage and are not included in the cost. These items will be expensed as incurred through the income statement.

Progress Point 2.6

Morkirk Ltd purchased an asset from abroad at invoice price £450,000. Import duties were an additional £25,000. Installation costs totalled £28,000. The company was granted a discount of £10,000 by the supplier for early payment. Testing the asset cost £40,000 but goods produced during testing were sold for a net profit of £15,000.

Calculate the cost of the asset to be recognised in the financial statements of Morkirk Ltd.

Solution

Cost comprises all costs necessary to bring the asset to working condition for its intended use:

	£
Invoice price	450,000
Installation costs	28,000
Import duties	25,000
Testing (£40,000 – £15,000)	25,000
	£528,000

The discount for early settlement should not be deducted as it relates to financial settlement rather than the purchase of the asset.

Measurement subsequent to initial recognition

Choice of models

IAS 16 permits two accounting models – the cost model or the revaluation model – and an entity decides which model to choose as its accounting policy for an entire class of property, plant and equipment. A class of property, plant and equipment is a grouping of assets of a similar nature (e.g. land, machinery).

Cost model

The cost model (which is the most common) results in an asset being carried at cost less accumulated depreciation and any accumulated impairment losses.

Revaluation model

Under the revaluation model the asset is carried at a revalued amount, being its fair value at the date of revaluation less subsequent accumulated depreciation and subsequent accumulated impairment losses.

The fair value of an asset is defined in IAS 16 as 'the amount for which an asset could be exchanged between knowledgeable and willing parties in an arm's length transaction' – in effect, the asset's market value.

If a market value is unavailable because of the specialised nature of the plant and equipment, and because these items are rarely sold, then IAS 16 requires that the revaluation be based on depreciated replacement cost.

 ## Example: revaluation model – no fair value

A company purchased an item of plant for £12,000 on 1 January 2008. The estimated useful life of the plant was six years and the straight line basis of depreciation was adopted. On 1 January 2010, management took the decision to revalue its plant.

There was no fair value available for the item of plant which had cost £12,000 on 1 January 2008 however the replacement cost of the plant at 1 January 2010 was £21,000.

The carrying value of the plant immediately before the revaluation would have been:

Cost		£12,000		
Annual depreciation charge	=	$\dfrac{£12,000}{6}$	=	£2,000
Written down value	=	£12,000	–	(£2,000 x 2)
	=	£8,000		

Under the principles of IAS 16, the revaluation would be based on depreciated replacement cost. The revalued amount would therefore be:

Replacement cost		£21,000		
Annual depreciation charge	=	$\dfrac{£21,000}{6}$	=	£3,500
Written down value	=	£21,000	–	(£3,500 x 2)
	=	£14,000		

Accumulated depreciation

IAS 16 (paragraph 35) discusses the treatment of accumulated depreciation, as follows.

When an item of property, plant and equipment is revalued, any accumulated depreciation at the date of revaluation is treated in one of the following ways:

(i) restated proportionately with the change in the gross carrying amount of the asset so that the carrying amount of the asset equals its revalued amount; this method is often used when an asset is revalued by means of an index to its depreciated replacement cost, or

(ii) eliminated against the gross carrying amount of the asset and the net amount restated to the revalued amount of the asset; this method is often used for buildings.

Example: treatment of accumulated depreciation

Continuing with our example – revaluation model, no fair value – this would give the following results.

(a)   Restated proportionately:

Fixed assets	
	£
Cost	12,000
Change after valuation	9,000
Revised value	21,000

Accumulated depreciations	
	£
At 1 January 2010	4,000
Change on revaluation	3,000
	7,000
Net book value	14,000

i.e.   the gross figure and the accumulated depreciation would both be restated by the proportionate increase in replacement cost:

$$\text{Valuation} = £12,000 \times \frac{21,000}{12,000} = £21,000$$

$$\text{Accumulated depreciation} = £4,000 \times \frac{21,000}{12,000} = £7,000$$

(b)   Revised gross figure:

Fixed assets	
	£
Cost	12,000
Change after valuation	2,000
Revised value	14,000

Accumulated depreciation	£
At 1 January 2010	4,000
Written back on revaluation	(4,000)
	–
Net book value	14,000

i.e.   the gross figure is revised to £14,000 and the accumulated depreciation charged to date is reversed out so as to give a carrying value at £14,000.

Requirements regarding revaluations

Under the revaluation model, revaluations should be carried out regularly, so that the carrying amount of an asset does not differ materially from its fair value of the balance sheet date.

If an item is revalued, the entire class of assets to which that asset belongs should be revalued. Examples would include:

■   land
■   land and buildings
■   machinery.

This provision is important because it prevents companies from 'cherry picking' their best assets for revaluation.

Revalued assets are depreciated in the same way as under the cost model (see below).

If a revaluation results in an increase in value, it should be credited directly to equity under the heading 'revaluation surplus'. The only exception is where it represents the reversal of a revaluation decrease of the same asset previously recognised as an expense, in which case it should be recognised as income.

A decrease arising as a result of a revaluation should be recognised as an expense to the extent that it exceeds any amount previously credited to the revaluation surplus relating to the same asset.

When a revalued asset is disposed of, any revaluation surplus may be transferred directly to retained earnings, or it may be left in equity under the heading revaluation surplus. Note that the transfer to retained earnings should not be made through the income statement (that is, no 'recycling' through the profit and loss account).

Accounting for revaluations

The adjustments that require to be made to the revaluation reserve and accumulated depreciation will now be illustrated for the following scenarios:

1. a first revaluation gain after initial recognition
2. a first revaluation decrease after initial recognition
3. revaluation gain followed by revaluation loss
4. revaluation loss followed by revaluation gain
5. sale of revalued asset and the transfer of any revaluation surplus to realised reserves.
6. sale of revalued asset – proceeds greater than revalued amount.

Example 1: revaluation gain after initial recognition

An entity has a tangible fixed asset that cost £15,000 at the start of Year 1; it has a useful economic life of ten years, a residual value of £3,000 and is being depreciated on a straight line basis. At the end of Year 1, the asset was revalued upwards to £17,500.

Accounting treatment: Year 1	
	£
Cost of asset	15,000
Residual value	3,000
Useful life	10 years

Annual depreciation charge $\dfrac{£15,000 - 3,000}{10} = £1,200$ per annum

		£
∴	Cost of asset	15,000
	Depreciation charge	1,200
	Adjusted book amount	13,800
	Gain on revaluation	3,700
	Closing book amount	17,500

Notes

(a)   The initial depreciation charge is charged to the income statement:

Dr Depreciation	1,200	
Cr Accumulated depreciation		1,200
Being depreciation charge.		

(b)   The gain on revaluation of £3,700 should be credited to reserves.

(c)   The corresponding debit entries are as follows:

    (1)   the initial depreciation charge that was credited to accumulated depreciation – fixed assets will be removed, i.e:

Dr Accumulated depreciation	1,200	
Cr Revaluation reserve		1,200
Being removal of accumulated depreciation on revaluation.		

    (2)   The balance (3,700 – 1,200) will be dealt with as follows:

Dr Fixed assets	2,500	
Cr Revaluation reserve		2,500
Being revaluation of fixed assets.		

(d)   The asset will be depreciated over its remaining useful life:

i.e. $$\frac{17{,}500 - 3{,}000}{9}$$

$$= \ £1{,}611 \text{ per annum}$$

The relevant income statement and balance sheet extracts are as follows:

Income statement Expenses	£
Depreciation	1,200

Balance sheet				
Fixed assets:		Revaluation reserve		
Cost or valuation	£			£
At beginning	15,000	At beginning		0
Surplus on revaluation	2,500	Surplus on revaluation		3,700
At end of year	17,500	At end of year		3,700
Depreciation	£			
Charge for year	1,200			
Written back on revaluation	1,200			
	0			
Net book value	17,500			

Note that the closing value under 'Cost or valuation' is the revalued amount.

Example 2: revaluation decrease after initial recognition

An asset has a cost of £1,000,000 and a life of ten years. At the end of Year 3, the asset is revalued downwards to £350,000.

Accounting treatment: Years 1 and 2	
Cost of asset	£1,000,000
Residual value	0
Useful life	10 years

Annual depreciation charge $\dfrac{1,000,000 - 0}{10 \text{ years}} = £100,000$ p.a.

	Year 1	Year 2
	£	£
Opening book amount	1,000,000	900,000
Depreciation	100,000	100,000
Closing book amount	900,000	800,000
Accounting treatment: Year 3		
Opening book amount	800,000	
Depreciation	100,000	
Adjusted book amount	700,000	
Loss on revaluation	350,000	
Closing book amount	350,000	

Notes

(1)   The depreciation charge for Years 1, 2 and 3 is £100,000, charged to the income statement as follows:

Dr	Depreciation		100,000	
	Cr	Accumulated depreciation		100,000
Being depreciation charge.				

(2)   The loss on revaluation is charged to the income statement:

Dr	Loss on revaluation		350,000	
	CR	Fixed assets – revaluation deficit		350,000
Being loss on revaluation.				

(3)   A transfer between accumulated depreciation and fixed assets is required in order to reflect the new valuation for the asset:

Dr	Accumulated depn – write back on revaluation		300,000	
	Cr	Fixed assets – deficit on revaluation		300,000
Being write back of depreciation on revaluation.				

(4)   The asset will be depreciated over its remaining useful life at:

$\dfrac{350,000}{7 \text{ years}} = £50,000$ per annum.

The relevant income statement and balance sheet extracts for Year 3 are as follows:

Income statement Expenses	£
Depreciation	100,000
Loss on revaluation	350,000

Balance sheet Fixed assets: Cost or valuation	£	
At beginning	1,000,000	
Deficit on revaluation	650,000	(350,000 + 300,000)
At end	350,000	
Accumulated depreciation	£	
At beginning	(200,000)	
Charge for year	(100,000)	
Written back on revaluation	300,000	
	0	
Net book value	350,000	

Note that the closing value under cost or revaluation is the revalued amount.

Example 3: revaluation gain followed by revaluation loss

A company buys freehold land for £100,000 in Year 1. The land is revalued to £150,000 in Year 3 and £90,000 in Year 5. The land is not depreciated.

In Year 3, a surplus of £50,000 (£150,000 − £100,000) is credited to equity under revaluation surplus. The relevant balance sheet extracts are as follows:

Balance sheet Year 3 Fixed asset Cost or valuation:	£	Revaluation reserve	£
At beginning	100,000	At beginning	0
Surplus on revaluation	50,000	Surplus on revaluation	50,000
At end	150,000	At end	50,000

In Year 5 a deficit arises of £60,000 (£90,000 − £150,000) on the second revaluation. This deficit is dealt with as follows:

- the amount previously credited to reserves is reduced, i.e. £50,000
- the excess, i.e. £60,000 − £50,000 = £10,000, is recognised as an expense.

The relevant income statement and balance sheet extracts are as follows:

Income statement Year 5	
Expenses	
Loss on revaluation	£10,000

Balance sheet Year 5				
Fixed assets				
Cost or valuation:		Revaluation reserve		
	£			£
At beginning	150,000	At beginning		50,000
Deficit on revaluation	60,000	Deficit on revaluation		50,000
At end	90,000			0

Note that the only effect on the income statement is when the carrying amount of the land falls below its original cost. That is, the £10,000 is the amount by which the Year 5 carrying amount is lower than the cost of the land (£100,000 – £90,000 = £10,000).

Example 4: revaluation loss followed by revaluation gain

An asset costs £15,000 at the start of Year 1; it has a useful economic life of ten years, a residual value of £3,000 and is being depreciated on a straight line basis. At the end of Year 1 the asset was revalued downwards to £10,500. At the end of Year 2 the asset is revalued upwards to £17,500.

Accounting treatment: Year 1

$$\text{Depreciation charge} = \frac{15,000 - 3,000}{10 \text{ yrs}} = £1,200 \text{ per annum}$$

		£
∴	Cost of asset	15,000
	Depreciation charge	1,200
	Adjusted book amount	13,800
	Loss on revaluation	3,300
	Closing book amount	10,500

Notes

(1)   The initial depreciation charge is charged to the income statement:

Dr	Depreciation	1,200	
	Cr Accumulated depreciation		1,200
Being depreciation charge.			

(2)   The revaluation loss of £3,300 should be charged to the income statement because it represents the fall in value below depreciated historical cost (i.e. that depreciated historical cost that would have arisen had no revaluation taken place):

Dr	Loss on revaluation	3,300	
	Cr Fixed assets – deficit on revaluation		3,300
Being deficit on revaluation.			

(3)   Finally a transfer between accumulated depreciation and fixed assets is required to reflect the new valuation for the asset.

Dr	Accumulated depreciation – write back on revaluation	1,200	
	Cr Fixed assets – deficit on revaluation		1,200
Being write back of accumulated depreciation on revaluation.			

The relevant income statement and balance sheet extracts are as follows:

Income statement	
Expenses	£
Depreciation	1,200
Loss on revaluation	3,300

Balance sheet		
Fixed assets:		
Cost or valuation	£	
At beginning	15,000	
Deficit on revaluation	4,500	(3,300 + 1,200)
At end	10,500	

Depreciation	£
At beginning	–
Charge for year	(1,200)
Write back on revaluation	1,200
At end	0
Net book value	10,500

At the end of Year 2, the asset is revalued upwards to £17,500.

Accounting treatment: Year 2

$$\text{Depreciation charge} = \frac{10,500 - 3,000}{9} = £833$$

		£
∴	Valuation b/f	10,500
	Depreciation charge	833
	Adjusted book amount	9,667
	Gain on revaluation	7,833
	Closing book amount	17,500

Notes

(1)   The depreciation charge (Year 2) is charged to the income statement:

Dr	Depreciation	833	
	Cr Accumulated depreciation		833
Being depreciation charge.			

(2)   The revaluation gain of £7,833 should be accounted for as follows.

First, a portion of the loss on revaluation made in Year 1 can be reversed. The amount that can be reversed is the amount of the loss less that sum that, had the original downward revaluation not been carried out, would have been charged as additional depreciation.

Had the downward revaluation not been made, then the depreciation charge in Year 2 would have been £1,200. As a result of the downward revaluation to £10,500, the actual depreciation charge was only £833 (i.e. it was reduced by £367). The standard allows us to reverse out the previously posted loss, but net of the amount of depreciation that would have been charged had the loss not been recognised, i.e. £3,300 − £367 = £2,933.

The balance of £4,900 (£7,833 – 2,933) should be credited to reserves:

Dr	Fixed assets	7,833	
	Cr Income statement		2,933
	Cr Revaluation reserve		4,900
Being revaluation of asset.			

(3)   Finally, a transfer between accumulated depreciation and fixed assets is required to reflect, in cost or valuation, the new valuation for the asset:

i.e.	Dr Accumulated depreciation – write back on revaluation	833	
	Cr Fixed assets – surplus on revaluation		833
Being write back of accumulated depreciation on revaluation.			

Note: the credit entry to fixed assets is required to reduce the carrying amount for cost or valuation to £17,500.

The relevant income statement and balance sheet extracts are as follows:

Income statement	
Expenses	£
Depreciation	833
Revaluation loss reversal	(2,933)

Balance sheet		
Fixed assets		
Cost or valuation	£	
At beginning	10,500	
Surplus on revaluation	7,000	(7,833 – 833)
At end	17,500	

Depreciation	£
At beginning	0
Charge for year	(833)
Write back on revaluation	833
At end	0
Net book value	17,500

Revaluation reserve	£
At beginning	0
Surplus on revaluation	4,900
At end	4,900

Note that the asset would now be depreciated as follows:

$$\frac{17,500 - 3,000}{8 \text{ yrs}} = £1,813 \text{ p.a.}$$

✺ Example 5: sale of revalued asset and the transfer of any revaluation surplus to realised reserves

An asset is purchased for £12,000 on 1 January 2006. It was depreciated on a straight line basis over its useful economic life, which was estimated at six years. On 1 January 2008 the asset was revalued at £14,000. The asset was finally sold on 1 January 2010 for £5,000.

BASIC

INTERMEDIATE

ADVANCED

Accounting treatment: Year 1 and Year 2

Cost of asset   £12,000

Useful life   6 years

Annual depreciation charge: $\dfrac{£12,000}{6 \text{ yrs}}$ = £2,000 per annum

	Year 1 £	Year 2 £
Opening book amount	12,000	10,000
Depreciation	2,000	2,000
Closing book amount	10,000	8,000

On 1 January 2008 the asset is revalued to £14,000. The revaluation surplus of £6,000 will be credited to a revaluation reserve; the accumulated depreciation of £4,000 reversed out and the gross carrying value increased by £2,000 to give a carrying value of £14,000.

Accounting treatment: Year 3 and Year 4

Revised carrying amount   £14,000

Useful life   4 years (remaining useful life)

Annual depreciation charge: $\dfrac{£14,000}{4 \text{ yrs}}$ = £3,500 per annum

	Year 3	Year 4
Opening book amount	14,000	10,500
Depreciation	3,500	3,500
Closing book amount	10,500	7,000

On 1 January 2010, the asset is sold for £5,000.

i.e.	Book amount	£7,000
	Sales proceeds	£5,000
	Loss on sale	£2,000

The loss on sale would be taken to the income statement and the revaluation surplus would be transferred to realised reserves.

It is worth summarising the above to see the effects on the income statement and reserves.

The total charges to the income statement were:

		£
Year 1	Depn	2,000
Year 2	Depn	2,000
Year 3	Depn	3,500
Year 4	Depn	3,500
Year 5	Loss	2,000
		£13,000

On the disposal of the asset a transfer from the revaluation reserve to realised reserves was made of £6,000. The net effect on realised reserves was £13,000 − £6,000 = charge £7,000. Note that this equals the original cost less the sales proceeds, i.e. £12,000 − £5,000 = £7,000.

It is important to note, however, that the revaluation surplus was transferred directly to realised reserves; it was not credited to the income statement and, consequently, as a result of the revaluation –

and the increased depreciation charges – the actual amounts charged to the income statement are significantly greater than if no revaluation had been made.

Had the revaluation not taken place then the charges to the income statement would have been as follows:

		£	
Year 1	Depn	2,000	
Year 2	Depn	2,000	
Year 3	Depn	2,000	
Year 4	Depn	2,000	
Year 5	Gain on sale	(1,000)	(NBV £4,000 – proceeds £5,000)
		£7,000	

i.e.   £13,000 compared with £7,000 if no revaluation. The end result on realised reserves is the same – it is just that profits have been reduced in the income statement up to the point of disposal.

Alternative treatment

IAS 16 allows for the revaluation surplus to be transferred to realised reserves as the asset is depreciated.

Continuing with our example, the annual depreciation charge increased from £2,000 to £3,500 following the revaluation; IAS 16 allows an amount equivalent to the 'excess depreciation' to be transferred from the revaluation surplus to realised reserves as the asset is depreciated. This would lead to a transfer of £1,500 (£3,500 – £2,000) to be made in Years 3 and 4. In Year 5, the remaining revaluation surplus of £3,000 (£6,000 – (2 × £1,500)) would be transferred to realised reserves.

Note that there is no effect on the income statement either with this alternative treatment. The income statement will be charged in full with the increased depreciation expense.

 Example 6: sale of revalued asset – proceeds greater than revaluation

Teranga acquired freehold premises in 2007 for £120,000. These premises were revalued in 2009 at £150,000, recognising a gain of £30,000. In 2010 the freehold premises were sold for £225,000. Teranga does not depreciate freehold premises.

Accounting treatment: 2009
The initial revaluation of £30,000 will be credited to the revaluation reserve:

i.e.	Dr	Freehold premises – revaluation	30,000	
	Cr	Revaluation reserve		30,000
Being revaluation of freehold premises.				

The freehold premises will then be carried at their revalued amount of £150,000.

Accounting treatment: 2010
The freehold premises are sold for £225,000.

The gain on disposal is calculated as follows:

Sales proceeds		225,000
Less:	Carrying value	150,000
Gain on disposal		75,000

The gain on disposal of £75,000 will be recognised in the income statement.

The original revaluation gain of £30,000, which was recognised in the revaluation reserve, will be transferred directly to retained earnings (i.e. not through the income statement).

The overall gain between the original cost of £120,000 and the sales proceeds of £225,000, i.e. £105,000, has been dealt with as follows.

(1)   £30,000 of the gain was recognised on the first revaluation. It was not a realised gain and therefore was recognised in the revaluation reserve.

(2)   On disposal, the remaining gain of £75,000 was realised and was recognised in the income statement. The earlier recognised gain was transferred directly to retained earnings.

(3)   The realised gain is therefore the difference between the sales proceeds and the original cost less any previous recognised gains. In this example the total gain made was £105,000 (£225,000 – £120,000), however as £30,000 had previously been recognised then only £75,000 was recorded as a realised gain.

Effect of revised version of IAS 1

The revised version of IAS 1, which takes effect for accounting periods that begin on or after 1 January 2009, requires that revaluation gains and losses that would previously have been shown in the statement of equity should instead be recognised in 'other comprehensive income' and shown under that heading in the statement of comprehensive income.

Depreciation

IAS 16 defines depreciation as the systematic allocation of the depreciable amount of an asset over its useful life. The depreciable amount is the cost of an asset, or other amount substituted for cost, less its residual value.

✪ Example

Mallit buys plant and machinery for £1,800,000. It has an estimated useful life of ten years, no residual value and company policy is to depreciate such assets on the straight line basis. A full year's depreciation is charged in the year of purchase.

At the beginning of its fourth year of using the plant and machinery, Mallit decides to report the plant and machinery at open market value, which is £1,960,000. Company policy when dealing with revaluations is to show the revalued amount at cost/revaluation and to reverse out the accumulated depreciation charges.

When the plant and machinery are purchased the initial depreciation charge will be:

$$\frac{1,800,000}{10 \text{ yrs}} = 180,000 \text{ p.a.}$$

Following the revaluation, the depreciation charge will be based on the revalued amount and depreciated over the remaining useful life:

Revalued amount   =   1,960,000
Remaining useful life   =   10 – 3 = 7 yrs

$$\therefore \text{ Revised depreciation charge} = \frac{1,960,000}{7 \text{ yrs}} = 280,000 \text{ per annum}$$

IAS 16 requires that the residual value and the useful life of an asset should be reviewed at least at each financial year end and, if expectations differ from previous estimates, any change is accounted for as a change in accounting estimate under IAS 8 *Accounting Policies, Changes in Accounting Estimates and Errors*.

The depreciation method used should reflect the pattern in which the asset's economic benefits are consumed by the enterprise. The standard mentions three depreciation methods by name – straight line, reducing (diminishing) balance and the units of production method – although this list is neither exhaustive nor in order of preference. Once the method has been chosen, it should be applied consistently from period to period.

The depreciation method should be reviewed at least annually and, if the pattern of consumption of benefits has changed, the depreciation method should be changed and accounted for as a change in estimate under IAS 8.

Depreciation should be charged to the income statement as an expense, unless it is included in the carrying amount of another asset.

Depreciation begins when the asset is available for use, and continues until the asset is derecognised (derecognition is covered in the next section of this chapter), even if it is idle.

Depreciation is recognised even if the fair value of the asset exceeds its carrying amount, as long as the asset's residual value does not exceed its carrying amount.

This requirement is designed to forestall the arguments that some companies have made in the past to justify non-depreciation of certain properties. It is sometimes argued, in the case of licensed premises, that depreciation of the building is not necessary, on the grounds that the fair value is being maintained by incurring maintenance costs that are being charged as expenses. Such premises require to be maintained to high standards in order to attract and maintain custom, and it is argued that to charge depreciation as well would appear to be double counting.

Repair and maintenance of an asset does not, however, negate the need to depreciate. The basic requirement of IAS 16 is that the depreciable amount should be allocated over the useful life of an asset using a method that reflects as fairly as possible the pattern in which its economic benefits are being consumed. This is done in order to charge the income statement with the consumption of the asset, i.e. the treatment has an income statement objective, not a balance sheet one, and depreciation must be charged whether or not the asset has declined in value in the period.

Furthermore, the depreciable amount of an asset is determined after deducting its residual value. In practice, the residual value of an asset is likely to be insignificant and therefore immaterial in the calculation of the depreciable amount. In the case of licensed premises, however, the residual value may well increase to an amount equal to or greater than the asset's carrying amount. In such circumstances, the asset's depreciation charge is nil unless and until its residual value subsequently decreases to an amount below the asset's carrying amount.

It is worth pausing at this point to consider the implications of this.

IAS 16 recognises and confirms that while a depreciation charge is required for all items of property, plant and equipment, the correctly calculated charge may well be zero.

Land and buildings are separable assets with different accounting characteristics and should be considered separately, even if acquired as a single purchase. Freehold land is considered to have an infinite life, unless it is held simply for the extraction of minerals, etc., and is not therefore depreciated. Note, however, that IAS 16 stresses that an increase in the value of the land on which the building stands does not affect the determination of the depreciable amount of the building.

Recoverability of the carrying amount

It is necessary to determine whether or not an item of property, plant and equipment has become impaired. An asset is said to be impaired when its recoverable amount falls below its carrying amount. Recoverable amount is the higher of net selling price or value in use, with value in use being the present value of estimated future cash flows generated by the asset. Impairment is covered by IAS 36 *Impairment of Assets* and is covered in detail here in Chapter 3. For the purposes of this section, however, if there is an indication that impairment may have occurred then non-current assets will be required to be reviewed for impairment (e.g. slump in property market or expected future losses).

The objective of IAS 36 is to ensure that relevant assets are recorded at no more than their recoverable amount.

This objective may impact on the depreciation charge, and paragraph 17 of IAS 36 states:

> If there is an indication that an asset may be impaired this may indicate that the remaining useful life, the depreciation method or the residual value for the asset need to be reviewed and adjusted under the IAS applicable to the asset, even if no impairment loss is recognised for the asset.

Example

Ion is a machinery company producing specialist automotive engine parts for high-performance cars. A change in technology means that one of its machinery tools, which was being depreciated over five years, will become obsolete in two years.

Ion, faced with this indication of impairment, would revise its depreciation method to take account of the revised estimated useful life, and depreciate the machine over its remaining useful life of two years.

Where there is evidence of impairment and that level of impairment has been quantified, the impairment loss should be recognised immediately as an expense in the income statement and the carrying amount of the related asset reduced to its recoverable amount.

Example

Hambald plc has a piece of very sensitive laboratory equipment costing £35,000. It has a useful life of five years and is being depreciated at £7,000 per annum. The residual value is expected to be zero.

At the beginning of its third year of operations, a technician accidentally spills a cup of coffee over the equipment. Although the equipment can still be used, it is estimated that its value has been impaired by £3,000.

The effect this has on the financial statements and on the annual depreciation charge is as follows.

At the beginning of Year 3, the asset will have been written down as follows.

$35,000 - (2 \times 7,000) = 21,000$

Following the impairment the asset will be further written down:

	£
Carrying value	21,000
Less impairment	3,000
Revised carrying value	18,000

The depreciation charge for Years 3 to 5 will now be based on the asset's written-down value, i.e. $18,000 \div 3$ years = £6,000 per annum.

The impairment loss of £3,000 will be charged in the income statement for Year 3 as an expense.

Any claim for compensation from third parties for impairment is included in profit or loss when the claim becomes receivable.

The cost of items of property, plant and equipment restored, purchased or constructed as replacements is determined in accordance with IAS 16.

Derecognition (retirements and disposals)

An asset should be removed from the balance sheet on disposal or when it is withdrawn from use and no future economic benefits are expected from its disposal.

The gain or loss arising from the derecognition of an item of property, plant and equipment is the difference between the net disposal proceeds, if any, and the carrying amount of the item, and should be recognised in the income statement. Gains shall not be classified as revenue and any element of revaluation reserve relating to the item will not pass through the income statement (i.e. it will transfer directly to retained earnings).

Disclosure

For each class of property, plant and equipment the following should be disclosed:

■ basis for measuring carrying amount

- depreciation method(s) used
- useful lives or depreciation rates
- gross carrying amount, and accumulated depreciation and impairment losses
- reconciliation of the carrying amount at the beginning and the end of the period, showing
  - additions
  - disposals
  - acquisitions through business combinations
  - revaluation increases
  - impairment losses
  - reversals of impairment losses
  - depreciation
  - net foreign exchange differences on translation
  - other movements.

In addition, disclosure should be made of:

- restrictions on title
- the existence and amounts of property, plant and equipment pledged as security for liabilities
- expenditures to construct property, plant and equipment during the period
- commitments to acquire property, plant and equipment
- compensation from third parties for items of property, plant and equipment that were impaired, lost or given up that is included in profit or loss.

If property, plant and equipment is stated at revalued amounts, certain additional disclosures are required:

- the effective date of the revaluation
- whether an independent valuer was involved
- the methods and significant assumptions used in estimating fair values
- the carrying amount that would have been recognised had the assets been carried under the cost model
- the revaluation surplus, including changes during the period and distribution restrictions.

2.10 Disclosure in practice

In practice, the required disclosures of IAS 16 *Property, Plant and Equipment* are given in distinct sections. The accounting policies note is normally used to disclose the entity's policy on measurement bases and depreciation rates while, the balance sheet discloses the total figure for PPE and the note to the balance sheet provides the detail.

Property, plant and equipment

Property, plant and equipment are stated at cost less accumulated depreciation and any accumulated impairment losses. The cost of an item of property, plant and equipment comprises its purchase price and any costs directly attributable to bringing the asset into use.

Depreciation is calculated on a straight-line basis to write down the assets to their estimated residual value over their useful economic lives at the following annual rates [shown in Table 2.2].

BASIC

INTERMEDIATE

ADVANCED

Furniture	10–20%
Computer equipment	25–33%
Partitions and office equipment	10–20%
Motor vehicles	25%
Freehold property	2%
Leasehold equipment and plant	Life of lease

Table 2.2 Logica: property, plant and equipment depreciation rates

The residual values and useful economic lives of property, plant and equipment are reviewed annually. Freehold land and properties under construction are not depreciated. Borrowing costs related to the purchase of fixed assets are not capitalised.

Logica's policy note on PPE shows the measurement base used, together with the rates of depreciation used to depreciate its various classes of PPE. The note also states that residual values and useful economic lives are reviewed annually. It is interesting to note Logica's policy on capitalising borrowing costs. This treatment was permitted prior to the revision of IAS 23 in 2008.

	Note	Current year £m	Previous year £m
Non-current assets			
Goodwill	17	1,604.0	1,552.1
Other intangible assets	18	358.0	415.1
Property, plant and equipment	19	132.1	136.6
Investments in associates	20	2.4	6.0
Financial assets	21	11.0	10.1
Retirement benefit assets	38	12.0	18.7
Deferred tax assets	28	54.5	50.6
		2,174.0	2,189.2

Figure 2.1 Logica: carrying values of property, plant and equipment

The extract from Logica's balance sheet in Figure 2.1 shows property, plant and equipment in the non-current assets section as expected. The current year carrying value of £132.1 million and comparative balance of £136.6 million are detailed further in Note 19 to the financial statements.

	Freehold land and buildings £m	Leasehold property and improvements £m	Equipment and plant £m	Total £m
Cost				
At 1 January 2006	19.3	55.9	203.4	278.6
Additions	–	4.4	29.7	34.1
Acquisition of subsidiary	5.3	–	30.9	36.2
Disposals	(0.5)	(0.6)	(22.5)	(23.6)
Exchange differences	(0.1)	(0.7)	(4.0)	(4.8)
At 1 January 2007	24.0	59.0	237.5	320.5
Additions	0.1	3.1	36.8	40.0
Acquisition of subsidiaries	–	–	3.9	3.9
Disposals of subsidiaries/businesses	(0.1)	(1.5)	(46.5)	(48.1)
Disposals	(1.8)	(4.8)	(32.5)	(39.1)
Exchange differences	1.0	1.9	16.3	19.2
At 31 December 2007	**23.2**	**57.7**	**215.5**	**296.4**
Accumulated amortisation				
At 1 January 2006	0.7	24.6	150.8	176.1
Charge for the year	0.1	5.1	27.5	32.7
Disposals	(0.2)	(0.3)	(21.0)	(21.5)
Exchange differences	–	(0.3)	(3.1)	(3.4)
At 1 January 2007	0.6	29.1	154.2	183.9
Charge for the year	0.7	5.8	33.6	40.1
Disposals of subsidiaries/businesses	–	(1.7)	(38.2)	(39.9)
Disposals	(0.1)	(4.1)	(30.1)	(34.3)
Impairment	2.6	–	–	2.6
Exchange differences	0.2	1.0	10.7	11.9
At 31 December 2007	**4.0**	**30.1**	**130.2**	**164.3**
Net carrying amount				
At 31 December 2007	**19.2**	**27.6**	**85.3**	**132.1**
At 31 December 2006	23.4	29.9	83.3	136.6

Figure 2.2 Logica: summary of property, plant and equipment

The impairment of £2.6 million in the table above [Figure 2.2] related to buildings previously occupied by the graphic services business in Portugal prior to the disposal of this business. The disposals are described further in Note 35.

Equipment and plant included assets held under finance leases with a net book value of £3.4 million (2006: £5.2 million). Additions to equipment and plant during the year amounting to £4.7 million (2006: £3.1 million) were financed by new finance leases.

The note to the balance sheet discloses the movements in cost and accumulated depreciation over the year for the classes of fixed assets identified within the accounting policies note. Logica has grouped together all classes of fixed assets with the exception of freehold land and buildings, and leasehold property and improvements. Note the way that Logica deals with disclosing comparative balances. It adopts a columnar approach beginning at 1 January 2006 and shows vertically the various movements in cost, accumulated depreciation and, ultimately, net carrying amount (net book value).

Summary

This section has considered in detail the IAS definition of an asset. The definition clearly indicates that it is not the physical existence of the asset itself which qualifies it to be classified as an asset, but rather the rights to income which are embodied within the asset. Indeed a company may well own a piece of equipment but if it is not, or can not, be used in generating future benefits then it would not be included as an asset on that company's balance sheet.

The recognition criteria of assets has been explained. While an item may pass the definition tests of an asset, in order for it to be included as an asset within a balance sheet, it also has to satisfy strict recognition tests.

Finally, the accounting policies adopted by a company, particularly with respect to government grants and borrowing costs, may have a bearing on the calculation of the capitalised cost figure.

Progress Point 2.7

Pathfoot Estates is a property company. It earns revenues from renting out the properties it owns. Traditionally the company has shown its properties at cost. Starting in Year 4, it decides to revalue them annually and record any surplus (over cost) in a revaluation reserve. Any gains made are considered distributable only when realised. It will continue its policy of not charging depreciation on the properties.

Summary accounts for Year 3 are shown below:

Income statement	£m
Rental revenues	30
Operating expenses	18
Profit	12

Balance sheet	
Properties	100
Share capital	100
Retained profit	0
	100

Pathfoot Estates undertakes the following.

1. A revaluation of properties in Year 4. External valuers estimate their value at £150 at the end of Year 4.
2. In Year 5 a property is sold for £37. This property originally cost £26 and was valued at £39 at the end of Year 4. A new property is bought for £37 during the year. There is no further adjustment to property values as a result of the end of Year 5 valuation.
3. Property prices fell sharply in Year 6. The valuers estimate the end Year 6 market value of the Year 5 properties is £28 and that of the remaining properties is £90.

Required

Draw up summary profit statements and balance sheets for the three years, 4, 5 and 6. Assume the following:

- annual rental revenues and operating expenses remain at Year 3
- non-property assets are zero
- all transactions are in cash
- the company pays a dividend of £12 in each year.
- ignore taxation.

Solution

Summary profit statements

	Year 3	Year 4		Year 5		Year 6
	£	£		£		£
Revenues	30	30		30		30
Expenses	18	18		18		18
Profit	12	12		12		12
Dividend	(12)	(12)		(12)		(12)
			Loss on sale of asset		Revaluation deficit	
				(2)		(9)
	0	0		(2)		(9)

Summary balance sheets

	Year 3		Year 4		Year 5		Year 6
Properties	100	+50	150	+37 – 39	148	21 – 9	118
Capital	100		100		100		100
Profit reserve	0		0	+ 13 – 2	11	– 9	2
Revaluation reserve	0		50	– 13	37	– 21	16
	100		150		148		118

Working notes

1. Property revalued to £150 at end of Year 3. This has the effect of increasing the asset of properties and also the revaluation reserve would increase by £50 in Year 4.

2. In Year 5 a property is sold for £37. This property originally cost £26 and had been revalued at £39 (this £39 is part of the previous revaluation of £50). The gain on sale of the property is measured by comparing the carrying value (i.e. the revalued amount) with the selling price. Revalued amount is £39, selling price is £37, so there is a loss on disposal of £2. This loss is shown in the profit and loss account as a deduction from profit (i.e. an expense). Also the fact that a property has been sold, the total properties figure of £150 will have to be reduced by £39.

   This property sold originally cost £26 and was revalued at £39, so there is a revaluation increase of £13, which would be part of the original £50 and will be in the revaluation reserve. When the property is sold, this revaluation reserve amount of £13 will be transferred to the profit reserve, i.e. will be a movement on reserves. There will also be a cash movement. Cash will increase by £37 when the property is sold and reduce by £37 when the new property is bought. The net effect on cash is nil.

3. In Year 6 there is a fall in property values. The properties shown in the balance sheet in Year 5 of £148 can be analysed as follows:

	Year 5 properties £37	Other properties £111	Total properties £148
Valuation in Year 6	28	90	
Fall in value	(9)	(21)	

BASIC

INTERMEDIATE

ADVANCED

▶

The treatment of the fall in value depends on whether it is permanent or temporary. Assuming the fall in value is permanent, the decrease will be removed from the revaluation reserve to the extent that there is already an existing revaluation reserve for the asset. In this case there is already a revaluation reserve for other assets of £37. So, the revaluation deficit of £21 will be deducted from the revaluation reserve and from the fixed assets. Nothing has been put in the revaluation reserve for the asset bought in Year 5. This means that no adjustment can be made to the revaluation reserve; instead this fall in value will be deducted from profit (i.e. will be an expense in the profit and loss account) and deducted from the fixed assets. If the fall in value is temporary, it may be possible to deduct the fall in value of £9 from the revaluation reserve in the expectation that this would be reversed in the very near future. Doing this may result in negative reserves in the short term.

Section 3: Advanced Aspects

This section considers problems faced by the accountant in practice, and the accounting treatment required where properties are purchased not for use within the business, but for investment purposes. Finally, the section concludes with a critical appraisal of IAS 16 and once more considers the implications of reporting property, plant and equipment in accordance with IAS 16 for the user of the financial statements.

2.11 Problems in practice

Notwithstanding the definitions and guidance given in the Framework and IAS 16, in practice there can be some difficulty in deciding when an item should be classified as a non-current asset. For example, a kit of hand tools may well be shown as property, plant and equipment in the financial statements of a self-employed carpenter, while, in the financial statements of a large company, a similar kit of tools will generally be written off as an expense.

In practice, items of expenditure may not always be so obvious and often there may be as much compelling evidence to treat the expenditure as revenue as there is to treat it as capital. Each case must be judged on its own merits with consideration given to both the Framework definition and the IAS recognition criteria. What would almost certainly be classified as a non-current asset in one enterprise may not necessarily be classified as such in another.

Materiality is another useful indicator of recognition. An item is said to be material if it is likely to influence decisions or provide useful information to decision makers. Accordingly, many firms treat smaller items as an expense even although they fulfil all the theoretical requirements of fixed assets. This is done because it is easier and because the amounts involved are not material.

The issue of taxation is another problem faced by the reporting accountant in practice. Expenditure on non-current assets tends to attract tax relief over a number of accounting periods, whereas revenue expenditure normally attracts tax relief in the accounting period in which it is incurred. An item of expenditure that falls into the 'middle ground' may well be written off for tax purposes while meeting all the theoretical requirements to be treated as a fixed asset.

Having decided to treat an item of expenditure as a non-current asset, the next problem faced by the accountant in practice is how, and over what period, that asset should be depreciated. Accountants understand that the inclusion of depreciation in the profit statement is designed to show a fair charge for the use of assets. This means the statement will show a true and fair view. Many company directors, particularly those in owner-managed businesses, leave the choice of depreciation method up to the accountant.

Assets are conventionally grouped into classes or categories. A class of property, plant and equipment is a grouping of assets of a similar nature and use in an enterprise's operations, e.g. land and buildings, machinery, motor vehicles. Depreciation is normally calculated on the class of assets as a whole with reference taken from the rates used for similar types of assets used in similar businesses. However, this is not necessarily appropriate as the level of activity demanded by different users may vary. For example, consider two motor cars owned by a business: one is used by the national sales manager covering 100,000 miles per annum visiting clients; the other is used by the finance director to drive from home to work and covering perhaps 10,000 miles per annum.

Self-constructed assets

Occasionally, an enterprise may construct, rather than purchase, an item of property, plant and equipment. The cost of a self-constructed asset is determined using the same principles as for a bought asset. The cost is the total of all costs incurred in bringing the asset to its location and in a condition for use. If the constructed asset is one the enterprise would construct in the normal course of business then the cost of the asset is usually the same as the cost of producing the asset for sale, it would be determined under the principles of IAS 2 *Inventories*.

Note that the normal profit the enterprise would make if the asset were sold to a third party is not recognised in cost. This means that identical assets may be carried at different values depending on whether they were self-constructed or purchased.

 ## Example

Buildwell plc, a construction company, began construction of an asset for its own use in April 2009 and this is scheduled to be complete in August 2010. Payments for materials were:

	£
30 September 2009	200,000
31 December 2009	214,500
28 February 2010	210,000

A further £75,100 was outstanding at the year end. A firm of architects was paid £51,000 at the end of January 2010 and consulting engineers were paid £67,900 at the end of November 2009.

The company's own staff were used to clear and prepare the site at an additional direct cost of £96,000. Buildwell plc would normally expect to charge £288,000 for this labour. Based on this figure, an additional allocation of general overheads of £36,200 has been calculated.

What is the cost of the asset as at 31 March 2010?

			£
Materials costs	–	paid	624,500
	–	accrued	75,100
Professional fees	–	architects	51,000
	–	engineers	67,900
Own staff			96,000
Total cost			£914,500

The normal profit that Buildwell would make on the labour is not recognised in cost. The general overhead allocation is not directly attributable to the construction and should be excluded.

Non-current assets held for sale

It may be that an enterprise decides to cease a particular area of operations and dispose of the constituent components making up the operation. IFRS 5 deals with *Non-current Assets Held for Sale and Discontinued Operations.*

IFRS 5 classifies a non-current asset as 'held for sale' if its carrying amount will be recovered principally through a sale transaction rather than through continuing use.

The IFRS requires that assets 'held for sale' should:

- be measured at the lower of carrying amount and fair value less costs to sell
- not continue to be depreciated, and
- be presented separately on the face of the balance sheet.

In addition, disclosure needs to be made of the circumstances surrounding the sale, including the expected manner and timing of the sale and the gain or loss if not separately presented on the face of the income statement.

Renewals accounting

Infrastructure assets of certain public utilities (e.g. water companies) require special consideration. It has been argued, in a manner similar to the arguments put forward by hoteliers and brewers, that the amount spent on maintenance removes the necessity to depreciate.

Renewals accounting is a solution to this problem. Under renewals accounting, the level of the annual expenditure required to maintain an infrastructure asset is deemed to be the depreciation charge. This amount is charged to the income statement and deducted from the carrying value. The *actual* expenditure on maintaining the system is capitalised as part of the cost of the asset and added to the carrying value. The carrying value of that part of the infrastructure asset that is replaced or restored by the subsequent expenditure should be eliminated.

Example

A water company spends £5,000,000 maintaining its infrastructure in the year to 31 March 2009. The balance sheet extract for the company is as follows:

	Infrastructure assets £m
Cost	
Balance b/f	10,000
Additions	5
Disposals	(5)
	10,000
Accumulated depreciation	
Balance b/f	0
Charge for year	5
On disposals	(5)
	0
Net book value	10,000

The journal entries help to explain the treatment

Dr	Asset additions	£5,000,000	
	Cr Bank		£5,000,000
Being annual expenditure on maintenance.			

Dr	Depreciation	£5,000,000	
	Cr Accumulated depreciation		£5,000,000
Being notional depreciation charge based on annual maintenance expenditure.			

Dr	Accumulated depreciation	£5,000,000	
	Cr Asset disposals		£5,000,000
Being carrying value of restored asset eliminated.			

2.12 Accounting for investment properties

An **investment property** is property, land or a building, or part of a building, or both, held by the owner (or by the lessee under a finance lease) to earn rentals or for capital appreciation, or both.

The accounting issues involved

As we have seen from IAS 16, the purpose of the annual depreciation charge is to reflect the general wearing out of assets used in generating revenues. Such assets are necessary to support the day-to-day operations of the business, and are used in production, distribution and administration. They are an integral part of the enterprise's activities, and the depreciation charge recognises and reflects the systematic allocation of these assets' costs over their useful lives.

Investments, on the other hand, are not an integral part of an enterprise's activities. An investment is held to earn positive returns in the form of interest, dividends or rent, or through capital appreciation. Moreover an investment is not normally 'consumed' while delivering its returns; the main issue is the investment's positive or negative changes in value. Depreciation, therefore, would not appear to be appropriate or indeed necessary.

The accounting issue involved is that where a property is held for its investment potential, should the provisions of IAS 16 apply and the property be subject to an annual depreciation charge; or is there some other means of accounting for such a property, which gives a more accurate reflection of its purpose and value?

2.13 IAS 40 *Investment Property*

Accounting for investment properties is dealt with in IAS 40 *Investment Property*. The need for a standard arises from the specific problem with properties in that they can be held for either usage or investment purposes or for both purposes, at different times. Moreover, given the tendency over time for property prices to rise significantly, then the distinction in practice is correspondingly significant.

It follows from the definition of an investment property that it will generate cash flows 'largely independently' of other assets held by an enterprise. It is this that distinguishes investment property from owner-occupied property – the latter only generating cash flows in conjunction with other operating assets necessary for the production or supply process.

Examples of investment property include:

- land held for long-term capital appreciation
- land held for undecided future use
- building leased out under an operating lease
- vacant building held to be leased out under an operating lease.

The following are not investment properties and, therefore, are outside the scope of IAS 40:

- property held for use in the production or supply of goods or services, or for administrative purposes – normal IAS 16 treatment would apply
- property held for sale in the ordinary course of business, or in the process of construction or development for such sale – dealt with by IAS 2 *Inventories*
- property being constructed or developed on behalf of third parties – dealt with by IAS 11 *Construction Contracts*
- owner-occupied property, i.e. held by the owner or by the lessee under a finance lease for use in the production or supply of goods or services, or for administrative purposes
- property held for future use as owner-occupied property
- property held for future development and subsequent use as owner-occupied property
- property occupied by employees
- owner-occupied property awaiting disposal
- property that is being constructed or developed for use as an investment property – in such cases, IAS 16 applies until construction or development is complete.
- property leased to another entity under a finance lease.

In some cases, judgement may be required in distinguishing investment properties from owner-occupied properties.

Partial own use

It may be that part of a property is used by the owner and part let out to earn rentals or for capital appreciation. If the portions can be sold or leased out separately, they are accounted for separately. The part that is rented out is investment property. If the portions cannot be sold or leased out separately, the property can be classified as investment property only if the owner-occupied portion is insignificant.

Ancillary services

The level of ancillary services provided to the occupants of a property held by an enterprise will also help determine the appropriateness of classification as investment property. If the ancillary services provided are a relatively insignificant component of the arrangement as a whole, then the enterprise may treat the property as investment property. For example, the building owner supplies security and maintenance services to the lessees. If, however, the services provided are more significant – for example, in the case of an owner-managed hotel – the property should be classified as owner-occupied.

Note, however, that the owner of a building that is managed as a hotel by a third party is deemed to be holding an investment. That is, the cash flows arising from the rental are 'largely independent' from the cash flows arising from the hotel operation.

Intracompany rentals

Property that is rented to a parent, subsidiary or fellow subsidiary is not investment property in the consolidated financial statements that include both the lessor and the lessee. This is because, from a group perspective, the property is owner (group) occupied. Note, however, that the property could qualify as investment property in the separate financial statements of the lessor if the definition of investment property is otherwise met.

Property held under an operating lease

A property interest that is held by a lessee under an operating lease may be classified and accounted for as an investment property provided that:

- the rest of the definition of an investment property is met (i.e. held for rentals)
- the operating lease is accounted for as if it were a finance lease in accordance with IAS 17 *Leases*, and
- the lessee uses the fair value model (see below) set out in IAS 40 for the asset recognised.

IAS 40 allows this classification to be made on a property-by-property basis. If, however, this classification alternative is selected for one such property held under an operating lease, *all* property classified as investment property should be accounted for using the fair value model. This is because, if adopted, the fair value model applies to all investment property whether owned outright or leased, as in the case above. Note, however, that this is an option, not a requirement, and it would therefore be possible to treat the operating lease payments as operating lease payments and expense them, and not account for them as if they were a finance lease. In this case, the fair value model would not require to be adopted and consequently the remaining investment properties could be accounted for using the cost model or fair value model.

Recognition

An investment property within the definition should be recognised as an asset when, and only when:

- it is probable that the future economic benefits that are associated with the property will flow to the enterprise, and
- the cost of the investment property can reliably be measured.

Initial measurement

Investment property is initially measured at cost including any directly attributable expenditure such as professional fees for legal services and property transfer taxes.

Measurement subsequent to initial recognition

IAS 40 permits enterprises to choose between either:

- a fair value model, or
- a cost model.

An enterprise must apply the model chosen for all of its investment property. A change from one model to the other is permitted only if this will result in a more appropriate presentation, however IAS 40 notes that this is highly unlikely to be the case for a change from the fair value model to the cost model.

Fair value model

Under the fair value model, investment property should be measured at fair value, and changes in fair value, should be recognised in the income statement. The standard makes it absolutely explicit that changes in fair value are to be taken directly to earnings and not taken to or from reserves.

Fair value is the amount for which the property could be exchanged between knowledgeable, willing parties in an arm's length transaction. Fair value should reflect the actual market state and circumstances as of the balance sheet date – not as of either a past or future date.

The best evidence of fair value is normally given by current prices on an active market for similar property in the same location and condition, and subject to similar lease and other contracts. In the absence of current prices on an active market, the entity may consider current prices for properties of a different nature or subject to different conditions, recent prices on less active markets with adjustments to reflect changes in economic conditions, and discounted cash flow projections based on reliable estimates of future cash flows.

There is a rebuttable presumption that an enterprise will be able to determine the fair value of an investment property reliably on a continuing basis. However, in the rare situations in which fair value measurement proves impossible for a particular property, the property should be accounted for in accordance with the benchmark treatment in IAS 16 (i.e. using the cost model). The residual value of the investment property should be assumed to be zero and IAS 16 should be applied until the disposal of the investment property.

Where a property has previously been measured at fair value, it should continue to be measured at fair value until disposal, even if comparable market transactions become less frequent or market prices become less readily available.

Although not specifically mentioned in the standard, a consequence of the fair value model is that no depreciation is charged.

Cost model

After initial recognition, an enterprise that chooses the cost model should measure all its investment property using the benchmark treatment in IAS 16 – that is, at cost less accumulated depreciation and less accumulated impairment losses.

It should be noted, however, that IAS 40 requires an enterprise that has chosen the cost model to disclose the fair value of its investment properties in the notes to the accounts. Fair value, therefore, has to be determined in *all* cases.

Subsequent expenditure

When an investment property has already been recognised, subsequent expenditure on that property should be recognised as an expense when it is incurred unless it is probable that this expenditure will enable the asset to generate future economic benefits in excess of its originally assessed standard of performance, and the expenditure can be measured and attributed to the asset reliably.

✪ Example

A company has three properties at 31 December 2009.

Property A

This has been an investment property for a number of years. It had a fair value of £7.5m at 31 December 2008 and £8.7m at 31 December 2009. Maintenance of the property cost £200,000 during 2009.

Property B

This was bought for £5.1m on 1 August 2009. Legal fees and stamp duty amounted to £300,000. The property was rented to a third party from 1 August 2009 and had a fair value of £5.9m at 31 December 2009.

Property C

This is in the process of being constructed by the company. At 31 December 2009 a total of £7.9m had been spent. The property is expected to be completed in early 2010. A tenant has already been found and the level of rent indicates the property will have a market value of £9.0m.

The policy of the company is to value investment properties at fair value, and property, plant and equipment at cost.

Required

Explain how each of the properties should be treated in the accounts of the company for the year to 31 December 2009.

Property A

Property A should be stated in the balance sheet at £8.7m. The gain in value of £1.2m in the year should be credited to the profit and loss account.

The maintenance expenditure should be written off as an expense to the profit and loss account as it does not improve the property.

Property B

The initial cost of the property, which would be recorded when it was purchased, is £5.4m (i.e. purchase price plus legal fees on acquisition). It would immediately be classified as an investment property on 1 August 2009. At 31 December 2009, the property would be stated at market value of £5.9m with the gain over the initial cost, £0.5m (£5.9m – £5.4m) being credited to the profit and loss account.

Property C

At 31 December 2009 the property is in the course of construction and should be accounted for under IAS 16. The property would be included at cost of £7.9m.

Property held under a finance lease

The initial cost of an investment property held under a finance lease shall be as prescribed for a finance lease by paragraph 20 of IAS 17. That is, the asset shall be recognised at the lower of the fair value of the property and the present value of the minimum lease payments. A corresponding amount shall be recognised as a liability in accordance with that same paragraph.

Transfers and disposals

Almost inevitably, an enterprise may decide to change the use to which its properties are being put, resulting in a transfer to or from investment property classification to owner-occupied classification. Under IAS 40, transfers to or from investment property should be made only when there is a change in use, evidenced by:

- commencement of owner occupation, i.e. a transfer from investment property to owner-occupied property
- commencement of development with a view to sale, i.e. a transfer from investment property to inventories
- end of owner occupation, i.e. a transfer from owner-occupied property to investment property
- commencement of an operating lease to another party, i.e. a transfer from inventories to investment property
- end of construction or development, i.e. transfer from property in the course of construction/ development to investment property.

Note that when an enterprise decides to sell an investment property without development, the property is not reclassified but is dealt with as investment property until it is disposed of.

Accounting for transfers between categories

When an enterprise uses the cost model for investment property, transfers between investment property, owner-occupied property and inventories do not change the carrying amount of the property transferred, and they do not change the cost of the property for measurement or disclosure purposes. It should be remembered, however, that the fair value of investment properties accounted for using the cost model needs to be disclosed in the notes to the accounts. No such requirement exists in respect of properties held as owner occupied or inventories.

A transfer to or from investment properties that are being carried at fair value has the potential to have very significant effects on the measurement process and the carrying amount of an asset.

The following rules apply for accounting for transfers between categories:

- for a transfer from investment property being carried at fair value to:
    - (i) owner-occupied property, or
    - (ii) inventories

BASIC

INTERMEDIATE

ADVANCED

the fair value at the date of the change of use is the 'cost' of the property under its new classification

■   for a transfer from owner-occupied property to investment property carried at fair value, IAS 16 should be applied up to the date of reclassification; any difference arising between the carrying amount under IAS 16 at that date and the fair value is dealt with in the same way as a revaluation under IAS 16; that is, if the fair value is greater than the carrying amount, the increase will be taken to revaluation reserve; note that, once classified as an investment property, subsequent changes in fair value will be dealt with through the income statement

■   for a transfer from inventories to investment property at fair value, any difference between the fair value at the date of transfer and its previous carrying amount should be recognised as part of the net profit or loss for the period; that is the treatment is consistent with that of a sale of inventory under IAS 2

■   when an entity completes construction/development of an investment property that will be carried at fair value, any difference between the fair value at the date of transfer and the previous (cost-based) carrying amount should be recognised as part of the net profit or loss for the period; again, the treatment is consistent with that of a sale of inventory under IAS 2.

It is worth pausing at this point to consider the implications of the last two requirements under IAS 40, i.e. the transfers from inventory and self-constructed property to investment property carried at fair value.

This requirement to recognise as income – what is effectively an unrealised gain – would appear to contradict the requirements in IAS 1 and the underlying concept in the IAS Framework to be prudent. What we have is an entity 'selling' an item to itself and recognising a gain.

This is, however, the whole point of the fair value concept. Because there is reliable evidence to determine fair value by reference to current prices in active markets, it follows logically and consistently with what is in effect a true sale, i.e. that a gain relating to operating processes has been 'made'. It is as if the property has been sold at fair value and immediately reacquired at that same value. Those who argue against fair value accounting are of the view that only a completed transaction provides adequate evidence of fair value.

Disposal

An investment property should be derecognised on disposal or when the investment property is permanently withdrawn from use and no future economic benefits are expected from its disposal.

The gain or loss on disposal should be calculated as the difference between the net disposal proceeds and the carrying amount of the asset, and should be recognised as income or expense in the income statement. This treatment is, of course, consistent with the treatment of annual changes in fair value of a retained investment property, which are likewise taken directly to the income statement.

Disclosure

The disclosure requirements of IAS 40 are extensive and detailed, and the standard itself should be consulted for a full description. In general, full details and reconciliations of movements concerning additions, disposals, depreciation, impairments, fair value adjustments, and transfers to and from inventories and owner-occupied property, and other changes are required.

Given the potential for significant effects in reported figures, the standard requires that disclosure be made of the methods and assumptions applied in determining the fair value of investment property and the extent to which the fair value is based on a valuation by a qualified independent valuer; if there has been no such valuation, that fact must be disclosed. Crucially, the point to note is that if the cost model is being used, then disclosure by way of note is still required of the fair values.

International divergence

In the UK, the accounting treatment of investment properties is governed by SSAP 19. This requires investment property be carried at open market value (fair value). The standard specifically prohibits,

however, the recognition at depreciated historical cost and in this respect is very different from IAS 40. Furthermore, there is a major difference between the UK and IAS when it comes to the treatment of gains or losses.

SSAP 19 requires that changes in the market value of investment properties should be taken to the statement of total recognised gains and losses (being a movement on an investment revaluation reserve) unless a deficit (or its reversal) on an individual property is expected to be permanent, in which case it should be charged (or credited) in the profit and loss account of the period. This is in marked contrast to the IAS 40 requirements, which require such changes in market value to be taken directly to annual reported earnings in the income statement. The UK requirements are, therefore, significantly more prudent than the requirements of the fair value alternative in IAS 40.

US GAAP, under ARB 43 and APB 6, currently requires that investment properties be treated in the same way as any other properties; US GAAP is, therefore, totally inconsistent with the original IAS E64 proposals for recognition at fair value, and the UK proposals which do not permit the depreciation of investment properties.

 ## Example

Roget plc has the following details regarding the investment property it purchased on 1 January 2006.

Purchase price (01/01/06)	£400,000
Expected useful life	25 yrs
Residual value	£150,000
Open market (fair) value (01/01/09)	£600,000
Open market (fair) value (31/12/09)	£680,000

Roget plc adopts the straight line method for providing for depreciation.

The major differences that would arise between applying UK GAAP, US GAAP and IAS 40 are as follows.

UK GAAP

Under SSAP 19, investment properties are carried at open market (fair) value and must not be depreciated. Changes in open market value between one balance sheet date and the next are taken directly to revaluation reserve.

US GAAP

Under US GAAP, the investment property would be treated the same as any property and would be carried at depreciated historical cost.

IAS 40 Cost Model

Using the cost model under IAS 40, the property would be carried at depreciated historical cost and the fair value would be disclosed in a note to the accounts.

IAS 40 Fair Value Model

Using the fair value model under IAS 40, the property would be carried at fair value and changes in fair value, between one balance sheet date and the next would be dealt with in the income statement.

The balance sheet and income statement extracts shown in Figures 2.3(a) and (b) show the position at 31 December 2009 under each of the four different sets of rules.

Balance sheet				
	UK GAAP	US GAAP	IAS 40 Cost Model	IAS 40 Fair Value Model
Investment properties: Cost or valuation	£	£	£	£
At 01/01/09	600,000	400,000	400,000	600,000
Revaluation	80,000	–	–	80,000
At 31/12/09	680,000	400,000	400,000	680,000
Depreciation				
At 01/01/09	N/A	30,000	30,000	N/A
Charge for period	N/A	(i) 10,000	(i) 10,000	N/A
At 31/12/09	N/A	40,000	40,000	N/A
NET BOOK VALUE	680,000	360,000	360,000	680,000
Fair value disclosure	N/A	N/A	680,000	N/A
Revaluation reserve				
At 01/01/09	200,000	N/A	N/A	N/A
Surplus	80,000	N/A	N/A	N/A
At 31/12/09	280,000	N/A	N/A	N/A

Figure 2.3(a) Balance sheet

Income statement				
Depreciation	N/A	(£10,000)	(£10,000)	N/A
Surplus on revaluation	N/A			£80,000

(i) Depreciation = $\dfrac{400,000 - 150,000}{25\ \text{years}}$ = £10,000 p.a.

Figure 2.3(b) Income statement

As can be seen, under UK GAAP and the IAS 40 *Fair Value* model, the net book values of the property are the same. Note, however, that the revaluation surplus in the year of £80,000 is taken directly to the balance sheet under UK GAAP, while IAS 40 deals with this through the income statement.

Under IAS 40, if the cost model is used then the position is very similar to the US GAAP situation – the main difference being that, under IAS 40, the fair value needs to be disclosed.

It goes without saying that, overall, there are very significant differences.

2.14 Property, plant and equipment: a critical appraisal

At the beginning of this chapter it was suggested that, far from being the most straightforward and understandable of figures, tangible fixed assets were possibly the most misunderstood and contentious items within an enterprise's balance sheet.

This becomes all the more apparent when the effects of the accounting policy adopted for property, plant and equipment are considered when interpreting financial statements.

Although the provisions of IAS 16 go some way towards making accounting information more consistent and comparable, i.e. by requiring companies to provide for depreciation, and, where a policy of revaluation exists, to keep such valuations current and applied to all assets within a class, nevertheless different management policies on the method of depreciation can have a major impact on the profit for the year. Moreover, the very nature of the depreciation calculation itself is fraught with difficulties. The amount of depreciation charged depends on the estimate of the economic life of assets, which is affected not only by internal factors such as the workload to which the asset is subjected, but also by external factors outwith the control of management. Technological, commercial and economic factors may all have a bearing on an asset's useful economic life and, hence, the depreciation charged on that asset.

This means that the interpreter of the accounts must pay particular attention to the depreciation policies of an enterprise, and pay attention also to the market in which the enterprise operates.

The effects of inflation are also a limiting factor in terms of ensuring comparability both between companies and with the same company over time.

Two companies following the historical cost convention may own identical assets, but, as they were purchased at different times, may well appear as dramatically different figures in the accounts. This problem is particularly relevant in respect of purchases of land and buildings. While IAS 16 allows revaluation of assets it is not compulsory and consequently the depreciation charged on non-revalued assets may well be significantly less than on revalued assets. IAS 16 is concerned to ensure that the earnings of an enterprise reflect a fair charge for the use of the assets by the enterprise. Unless revaluations are made to reflect increases in asset values, depreciation will be based on historic cost. A further issue arising from this is the calculation of the return on capital employed. To make a fair assessment of return on capital it is essential to know the current replacement cost of the underlying assets. It is only the provisions of IAS 40 in relation to investment properties that require such up-to-date valuations.

At a more simplistic level, perhaps the biggest difficulty facing the user of accounting information is the multitude of valuation bases used on a balance sheet. The net book value of fixed assets is the, as yet, unallocated cost or valuation. Net book value is not intended to be (although many non-accountants assume it is) an estimate of the value of the underlying assets.

Monetary current assets are valued at current values; non-monetary current assets at the lower of cost or net realisable value. With such a variety of valuation methods, it would take a particularly skilled investor to establish the valuation of a business from a balance sheet.

Finally, consider whether the objectives of IAS 16 meet the needs of the user. For the business owner, the supplier, the creditor, the unsophisticated investor, it is likely that IAS 16 adds little to their understanding of fixed assets. Unless specifically studied, it is unrealistic to expect such users to know that net book values have no relevance to current values; nor to know that the depreciation charge is a subjective, arithmetical calculation that will not wholly provide the finance to replace assets or ensure maintenance of the business's operational base.

Indeed, even for sophisticated users, fund managers, directors, accountants, these problems still exist. To deal with the effects of lost purchasing power through inflation, to compensate and adjust for the effect of changes in supply and demand on replacement prices, and external factors such as technological change and competition, requires not only a very high level of skill, but also far more information than is available in a set of financial statements.

One further point, which indicates clearly at which user groups the standard setters are aiming with IAS 16, is that property, plant and equipment deals with non-current assets. This assumes that users will know what current assets are. It would seem that the level of complexity now inherent in both the definitions and the standard itself has effectively determined its intended audience. IAS 16 is a standard by accountants for accountants.

Chapter summary

IAS 16 *Property, Plant and Equipment*

■ Property, plant and equipment (PPE) should be recognised when it is:
   (i) probable that future benefits will flow from it, and
   (ii) its cost can be measured reliably.
■ Initial measurement should be at cost.
■ Subsequently, IAS 16 permits two accounting models:
   – cost model – the asset is carried at cost less accumulated depreciation and impairment
   – revaluation model – each class of asset is carried at a revalued amount, being its fair value at the date of revaluation less subsequent depreciation provided that fair value can be measured reliably.
■ Revaluations should be credited to reserves unless reversing a previous charge to income.
■ Decreases in valuation should be charged to income unless reversing a previous credit to reserve.
■ The depreciable amount of an asset shall be allocated on a systematic basis over its useful life.
■ The depreciation method used shall reflect the pattern in which the asset's future economic benefits are expected to be consumed by the entity.
■ Depreciation begins when the asset is available for use and continues until the asset is derecognised, even if it is idle.
■ Gains or losses on retirement or disposal of an asset should be calculated by reference to the carrying amount.

IAS 20 *Government Grants*

■ Grants related to assets should be deducted from the cost or treated as deferred income.

IAS 23 *Borrowing Costs*

■ Borrowing costs in relation to the acquisition, construction and production of a qualifying asset form part of the cost of that asset and, therefore, should be capitalised.
■ Other borrowing costs should be recognised as an expense.
■ Where funds are specifically borrowed, the borrowing costs should be calculated after any investment income on temporary investment of the borrowings. If funds are borrowed generally, then a capitalisation rate should be used based on the weighted average of borrowing costs for general borrowings outstanding during the period.
■ Capitalisation should commence when expenditures and borrowing costs are being incurred and activities are in progress to prepare the asset for use or sale.
■ Suspension should occur when active development is suspended for extended periods.
■ Cessation of capitalisation should occur when all activities are substantially complete.

IAS 40 *Investment Property*

■ Investment property is held to earn rentals or for capital appreciation, rather than being owner occupied.
■ Initial measurement should be at cost, and there should be subsequent capitalisation of expenditure that improves the originally assessed standard of performance.
■ Subsequently, IAS 40 permits an enterprise-wide choice between:
   – the fair value model, and
   – the cost model.
■ Under the fair value model, gains and losses are taken to income. If fair value is not determinable at the beginning then cost should be used.

- Under the cost model, investment property is accounted for in accordance with the cost model as set out in IAS 16 *Property, Plant and Equipment* – cost less accumulated depreciation and less accumulated impairment losses.
- Under the cost model, fair value should be disclosed.
- Transfers to owner-occupied property or inventory should take place at fair value.
- Transfers to investment property should treat the initial change to fair value as a revaluation under IAS 16.

 Key terms for review

Definitions can be found in the glossary at the end of the book.

Asset

Current asset

Non-current (fixed) asset

Cost

Recognised

Recognition (of asset/liability)

Borrowing costs

Carrying amount

Qualifying asset

Depreciation

Depreciable amount

Useful life

Residual value

Impairment loss

Recoverable amount

Fair value

Property, plant and equipment

Investment property

Grants related to assets

Review questions

1. What is the definition of a non-current (fixed) asset?
2. Define the term 'property, plant and equipment'.
3. When should an item of property, plant and equipment be recognised in the financial statements?
4. Define cost in relation to property, plant and equipment.
5. 'Depreciation is a process of allocation not of valuation.' Say whether you agree with this statement, and explain why, or why not.
6. What factors need to be taken into account in determining the useful life of an asset?
7. How should grants received towards the cost of buying property, plant and equipment be treated?
8. Outline general guidelines for determining whether expenditure on repairs should be treated as capital rather than revenue expenditure.
9. Define the term 'borrowing costs' and explain the required accounting treatment of the revised standard IAS 23.
10. Define an investment property and explain the required accounting treatment of IAS 40.

 # Exercises

1. Level I

Silver Tours plc buys a motor vehicle with a useful economic life of five years, costing £25,000 and with a residual value of £5,000.

Required

(a) Calculate the depreciation charge in each of the five years using the following methods of providing for depreciation:
   (i) straight line
   (ii) reducing balance (assuming a rate of 27.5% per annum)
   (iii) sum of years digits.

(b) Show the net book value of the vehicle at the end of each of the Years 1 to 5 under each of the above methods.

2. Level II

(a) Thomson plc has acquired a new piece of specialised, very sensitive laboratory equipment. Its invoice price was £26,000. Installation costs amounted to £8,000, of which £4,000 related to the cost of labour supplied by Thomson's own staff. The equipment's residual value is expected to be £2,500. Its useful life was estimated as being three years, however immediately on installation one of Thomson's experienced technicians made changes to the equipment, at a cost of £4,000, which will extend its life by a further two years. Thomson adopts the straight line method of providing for depreciation.

    (i) At what cost will Thomson plc recognise the equipment in its financial statements? Explain your answer.

    (ii) Calculate the annual depreciation expense. Explain your answer.

(b) At the beginning of Year 3 of operations, a technician accidentally spills a cup of coffee over the equipment, causing £5,800 of damage.

    (i) How should the costs to restore the equipment be accounted for? Explain your answer.

(c) Assuming the equipment cannot be restored and its value has been impaired by £5,800, what is the effect on the carrying value and on the annual depreciation charge?

3. Level II

The financial statements for Leith plc for the year ending 31 March 2009 are currently being drafted. Below is information relating to the fixed asset table, which is to appear in the notes to the financial statements.

Tangible fixed assets (£)				
	Land and buildings	Plant and equipment	Motor vehicles	Total
Cost or valuation				
Cost as at 01/04/08	684,200	447,900	123,400	1,255,500
Additions during year				
Disposals during year				
Cost as at 31/03/09				
Accumulated depreciation				
Acc. depn as at 01/04/08	161,500	268,300	85,000	514,800
Provided in year				
Disposals				
Acc. depn as at 31/03/09				
Net book value				
NBV as at 01/04/08	522,700	179,600	38,400	740,700
NBV as at 31/03/09				

Further information: additions during the year, at cost, were land and buildings, £46,700; plant and equipment, £34,500; motor vehicles, £66,800.

The company's policy is to provide a full year's depreciation in the year of acquisition and none in the year of disposal. The depreciation charge for the year for buildings is £5,800. Land is not depreciated. Depreciation for plant and equipment is calculated on a straight line basis at 10% (residual value is assumed to be negligible). Motor vehicles are depreciated at 25% reducing (declining) balance.

The only disposal during the year was a building that had cost £90,000. Leith plc received £120,000 cash for this building. The gain on disposal was £34,600.

Required

(i) Complete the fixed asset table.
(ii) What is the total for tangible fixed assets to appear on the face of the balance sheet?

4. Level II

At 1 January 2009, the fixed asset balances of Sunnyside Greenhouse Supplies plc, comprised the following:

	Original cost	Accumulated depreciation
	£	£
Freehold land and buildings	1,165,000	119,000
Leasehold improvements	890,000	89,000
Plant and equipment	456,000	101,000

The company's policy is to charge depreciation at the following rates:

Buildings: 2% straight line

Plant and equipment: 15% reducing (declining) balance

The leasehold taken on the property and to which improvements had been made in 2007 was 20 years, and company policy is to depreciate such improvements over the period of the lease. A full year's depreciation is charged in the year of acquisition for all assets, however no depreciation is charged in the year of sale. The following additional information is relevant to the calculation of depreciation for the year to 31 December 2009.

 (i) The amount of the original cost relating to buildings is £850,000, and these were purchased in June 2002.

(ii) The company traded in a forklift during the year and acquired a new one costing £50,000. A cheque for £25,000 was written by the finance director of Sunnyside Greenhouse Supplies plc, being the balance due for the new forklift. The forklift traded in had originally cost £40,000 in May 2007 and had a net book value of £28,900 at 1 January 2009.

(iii) Additional leasehold improvements were carried out during the year, costing £190,000. Legal and architect's fees in relation to the improvements were also incurred, amounting to £8,000.

(iv) A second-hand loader was purchased during the year for £30,000. Sunnyside Greenhouse Supplies incurred additional expenditure on the loader amounting to £5,000 without which it could not have been used. Mr Burleigh, the workshop foreman declared the machine to be 'like new'.

Required

(a) Prepare a schedule of fixed assets for inclusion in the company's notes to the financial statements for the year to 31 December 2009.
(b) Show all the relevant profit and loss account entries that would result.
(c) Briefly explain the differences between the straight line and the reducing (declining) balance methods of depreciation, outlining the different assumptions the use of each method makes.

5. Level II

Mawrill plc buys an asset for £100,000. It receives an investment grant of 30% towards the cost of purchase. The asset is depreciated on a straight line basis over ten years, assuming no residual value.

Required

(a) Calculate the income statement charges/credits for each year using:
     (i) the deferred income method

(ii) the netting method.

(b)   Show the balance sheet extracts for Years 1 to 3 under both methods.

6.   Level II

Park Transport Ltd sells for £8,000 an asset originally purchased for £45,000. Depreciation of £30,000 has been charged on the asset, which had an estimated useful life of 15 years. Park Transport Ltd was awarded a government grant of £22,500 to help fund the purchase and adopted the deferred income method to release the grant over the useful life of the asset (15 years). The asset was subsequently sold after Year 10 and Park Transport was not required to repay the outstanding grant.

Required

Calculate the gain or loss on disposal of the asset.

7.   Level III

Denlar plc acquired a hotel on 1 January 2002 for £12m. Depreciation is charged at 2% per annum straight line. The estimated residual value was £4m.

   Denlar Plc incorporated the following revaluations relating to the hotel into its financial statements:

31/12/06   £14m
31/12/08   £9m

The estimated useful life and estimated residual value have remained the same throughout. Denlar plc makes transfers between revaluation reserve and profit and loss reserve equivalent to the difference in depreciation on the historical cost and revalued amount of the asset.

Required

Show extracts from the income statements and statement of recognised income and expenses for the years from 31 December 2005 to 31 December 2009.

8.   Level III

Invercraft plc purchased freehold property costing £440,000 on 1 February 2005. The property is depreciated on a straight line basis over 50 years, in accordance with the company's accounting policy. Company policy is to charge a full year's depreciation in the year of purchase and none in the year of sale.

   At 30 June 2008, the company's year end, the property was valued at £520,000. The property was estimated to have a remaining useful life of 46 years as of that date. Invercraft has a policy of eliminating accumulated depreciation on revaluations. In addition, it is company policy to transfer an amount from revaluation reserve to profit and loss reserve each year equal to the difference between depreciation on the revalued carrying amount and the asset's original cost. The property was sold in August 2009 for £596,000.

Required

 (i)   Record the revaluation of the property as at 30 June 2008.
 (ii) Record the depreciation charge and movements on reserves for the year ended 30 June 2009.
(iii) Prepare the journal entries to incorporate the sale of the property in August 2009.

9.   Level II

DialM plc undertook a major construction project during the year to build a new petrochemical processing plant for its own use. Work started on 1 July 2008 and the plant is scheduled to be ready for operation by early 2010.

   You are preparing the accounts for the year to 31 March 2009. The following information relates to the project.

(a) **Analysis of payments made in the year to 31 March 2009:**

Date	Details	Amount
		£
01/08/08	Purchase of land and site clearance costs	3,800,000
01/10/08	First payment to construction company	4,000,000
01/12/08	Second payment to construction company	4,500,000
01/01/09	Professional fees – surveyor	200,000
01/02/09	Purchase of chemical distillation machinery	1,300,000

(b) **Year end accruals**

At 31 March 2009, DialM plc owed £2,400,000 to the construction company and the architects have advised that their fee will amount to £700,000.

(c) **Financing arrangements**

DialM plc arranged a loan facility of £25m to cover the payments to the construction company. Appropriate amounts were drawn down when the payments were made. Interest is charged at 7% per annum from the date of draw down.

All other costs are being financed by the company's overdraft facility. The average overdraft interest rate was 8.5% for the year to 31 March 2009.

(d) **Accounting policy**

The policy of the company is to capitalise borrowing costs.

Required

Calculate the cost of the plant as at 31 March 2009.

10. Level III

Marros plc has a policy of depreciating assets using the straight line method, with the following average estimated useful lives:

> Buildings   20–50 years
> Plant   6–10 years
> Vehicles   4–8 years

Marros charges a full year's depreciation in the year of acquisition and none in the year of disposal.

The accountant of Marros plc, Mr Walker, would like advice relating to depreciation on the following transactions and events in the year to 30 June 2009.

(a) A factory building that cost £5m in July 1999 and was being depreciated over 40 years has had its total estimated life reduced to 25 years.

(b) A piece of equipment was purchased in January 2007 for £120,000 and is being depreciated over six years with an estimated residual value of £30,000. Recent information indicates that a revised residual value of £20,000 as at 1 July 2008 is more appropriate.

(c) Office buildings with a cost of £10m, a net book value of £8m at 1 July 2008 and total estimated useful life of 50 years, were revalued on 1 July 2008 to £20m. The total estimated useful life is still 50 years and the residual value is now estimated to be £4m.

(d) A production line was refurbished during the year at a cost of £2.6m. It had originally cost £1.8m in December 2003 and was depreciated to zero over five years. The refurbishment has led to the restoration of the asset's productive capacity, and the production line is expected to be useful for another four years and then have an immaterial scrap value.

(e) The company spent £250,000 on the maintenance of its fleet of vehicles.

Required

Draft a letter to Mr Walker, the accountant of Marros plc, explaining how the above matters should be treated in the accounts of Marros plc for the year to 30 June 2009 so far as they affect depreciation.

11.   Level III

Bilmont Properties plc has a number of investment properties at 31 January 2009. Details of certain properties are as follows.

Property A

Acquired for £4.5m in December 2008. Stamp duty and legal fees on acquisition totalled £250,000. The fair value of the property at 31 January 2009 was £4.9m. The estimated useful life is 25 years.

Property B

Acquired in 2001 for £2.6m (with an estimated useful life of 40 years) and included at fair value of £6.3m as at 31 January 2008. The fair value at 31 January 2009 is estimated to be £6.1m.

Property C

Acquired in 2003 for £3.4m and included at fair value of £5.1m as at 31 January 2008. During the year to 31 January 2009, £3.1m was spent upgrading and refurbishing the property. This has led to increases in the rent for the property and, as a result, its estimated fair value at 31 January 2009 is £9.4m. Had the additional expenditure not been incurred it is estimated that the value of the property would have been £5.2m. The property has an estimated useful life of 35 years.

Property D

Purchased on 1 June 2008 for £4.2m with an estimated useful life of 40 years. The property is specialised and the directors are of the opinion that it will not be possible to obtain reliable fair values on a continuing basis.

Property E

Held under an operating lease commencing on 1 March 2008. Annual rentals of £1.6m are payable. The fair value of the property on 1 March 2008 is estimated at £20m. The present value of the minimum lease payments is £22m. The fair value at 31 January 2009 is estimated at £21.2m.

Accounting policy

(a)   Investment properties, including those held under operating leases, are measured at fair value.

(b)   Where no reliable fair values can be obtained on a continuing basis, properties are carried at cost and amortised over their estimated useful life on a monthly basis.

Required

Explain how the properties should be dealt with in the accounts of Bilmont Properties plc for the year to 31 January 2009.

12.   Level III

Archfield plc has a number of investment properties, which it carries at fair value. Other assets are held at cost. The following information is relevant.

 (i) At 31 December 2008 investment properties had a fair value of £100m.

 (ii) During the year to 31 December 2009, four new investment properties were bought from another company for a total of £17m. Legal fees and other acquisition costs amounted to an additional £0.4m.

(iii) On 1 August 2009, Archfield occupied for its own use a property that up until then had been rented out as an investment property. Its fair value at 1 August 2009 was £5.2m (£5.1m at 31 December 2008). The property had an estimated remaining useful life of 20 years. Archfield's policy is to depreciate buildings straight line on a monthly basis. The land element of the property is £1.2m at 1 August 2009.

(iv) On 1 December 2009, Archfield decided that two investment properties should be sold as soon as possible.

   Property A (fair value of £3m at 31/12/08 and £2.8m at 01/12/09) is to be sold after redevelopment. Redevelopment work started on 1 December 2009.

   Property B (fair value of £4m at 31/12/08 and £4.1m at 01/12/09) is to be sold without redevelopment.

(v) The fair value of investment properties, which were investment properties as at 31 December 2009, equals £125m.

Required

(a) Explain how the situations in notes (ii) to (iv) should be dealt with in the financial statements of Archfield for the year to 31 December 2009.

(b) Calculate the credit/charge to be taken to the profit and loss account of Archfield for the year to 31 December 2009 in respect of investment properties.

Further reading

FAS 58 *Capitalisation of Interest Cost in Financial Statements.* FASB

Framework for the Presentation and Preparation of Financial Statements. IASB, 1989

IAS 1 *Presentation of Financial Statements.* IASB, revised 2004

IAS 1 *Presentation of Financial Statements.* IASB, revised 2007

IAS 11 *Construction Contracts.* IASB, 1993

IAS 16 *Property, Plant and Equipment.* IASB, revised 2004

IAS 20 *Accounting for Government Grants and Disclosure of Government Assistance.* IASB, 1983

IAS 23 *Borrowing Costs.* IASB, revised 2004

IAS 40 *Investment Property.* IASB, 2004

IAS 8 *Accounting Policies, Changes in Accounting Estimates and Errors.* IASB

Logica plc: www.logica.co.uk

SSAP 19 *Accounting for Investment Properties.* ASB, July 1994

3

Intangible Assets and Impairment of Assets

LEARNING OUTCOMES

After studying this chapter you should be able to:

- ☑ define and distinguish intangible assets and goodwill
- ☑ explain and apply the recognition requirements of IAS 38 to intangible assets
- ☑ explain and appraise alternative treatments for purchased goodwill
- ☑ explain and apply the recognition requirements of IFRS 3 relating to purchased goodwill
- ☑ explain and apply the requirements of IAS 36 relating to impairment of assets
- ☑ critically appraise the effectiveness of IAS 38, IAS 36 and IFRS 3 in achieving their stated objectives.

Introduction

This chapter will outline the key characteristics of intangible assets. Intangible assets are those long-term assets that lack physical substance. However, these assets are important to a company since they represent the right to future economic benefits. After introducing the main characteristics of intangible assets, this chapter will examine the reporting requirements of the international accounting standards relating to intangible assets.

Section 1: Basic Principles

When considering what constitutes an asset, the tendency is to think of physical, tangible items such as land and buildings, machinery, vehicles, and other such readily identifiable and definable items. These items are normally classified as tangible fixed assets – that is, assets of a business having a physical substance that are expected to benefit accounting periods extending more than one year.

However, in terms of the definition of what constitutes an asset, then an asset need not necessarily be physical or tangible. Indeed, as was covered in Chapter 2, an asset is defined as a resource, controlled by an enterprise, as a result of past events, from which future benefits are expected to flow to the enterprise. There is no reference to the asset having physical substance.

This section examines the non-physical resources that satisfy the accounting criteria for classification as an asset, together with related accounting issues. Such non-physical resources are commonly referred to as intangible assets.

3.1 The accounting issue involved

Accounting standards and procedures have developed to help convey to the user of the financial statements a clearer picture of the economic reality surrounding a particular business. The problem of how to account for intangible assets is perhaps one of the best examples, which demonstrates how accounting information can be shown in dramatically different forms, with each form claiming to be the economic reality.

A number of intangible assets will be dealt with. However, at this stage, the two main ones outlined are research and development expenditure, and goodwill.

Research and development expenditure

This is expenditure undertaken by a company to develop a new product or process – for example, developing a new piece of computer software. As noted above, the traditional view of what constitutes an asset tends to involve the asset having physical substance. Consider the example of a company undertaking expansion and constructing a new factory. The costs of the factory will be readily identifiable, and there will be little argument that such costs should be capitalised and shown as fixed assets. The factory building will be the new asset that will give benefit to the company in future accounting periods.

A problem arises, however, when a company spends money with a view to obtaining a future economic benefit – not, on physical assets, but on intangible assets. This problem is best explained using a simple example.

 Example

A computer software company currently manufactures and sells its software product. The profit statement relating to the company for the year is as follows:

Profit statement		
Sales		£200,000
Wages and salaries	£200,000	
Direct overheads	£100,000	
		£300,000
Loss for period		(£100,000)

The company is now developing a new product: a new piece of software. A team of specialist software engineers is being employed to write and develop the new software and, in order to have the product finished at an early stage, all available resources are being utilised to ensure speedy completion. Of the overall costs, approximately £150,000 of the wages and salaries costs and £90,000 of the direct overheads relate entirely to the development of the new product. The approximate costs relating to the development of the company's existing product are wages and salaries £50,000 and direct overheads £10,000.

While the cost information shows all the revenues and expenses for the period, the figures do not show the underlying reality of the situation.

The company is developing a new product – an asset – which in essence will be the same as any other asset yielding future economic benefits. The only difference will be that this asset does not have physical substance. Unless some adjustment or reclassification is made to the figures, it would appear that no asset exists.

If, however, the definition of an asset is considered in terms of its constituent parts, it becomes apparent that an asset, albeit intangible, could be created from the expenditure incurred by the company.

That is:

■   the product is expected to yield future benefits
■   it is controlled by the company
■   the company has spent large sums by way of wages and other overhead expenses (the result of a past transaction).

By applying the above criteria to the expenditure, it becomes possible to restate the profit statement as follows:

Profit statement (restated)		
Sales (old product)		£200,000
Wages and salaries (old product)	£50,000	
Direct overheads (old product)	£10,000	
		£60,000
Profit for period		£140,000

The balance sheet would show:

Balance sheet	
Intangible assets	
Software	£240,000

The costs relating to the development of the new product, wages and salaries of £150,000 and direct overheads of £90,000 have been reclassified as intangible assets, and reallocated from the profit and loss account to the balance sheet. Moreover, the profit and loss account once more adheres to the matching principle whereby the expenditure relating to sales of the old product is matched with the revenue generated from sales of that product.

This example illustrates clearly the accounting issue involved. The picture being portrayed by simply classifying the expenditure as expenses is that a substantial loss is being made. The economic reality is that a new asset is being developed.

3.2 The position in practice

The problem of how to account for research and development expenditure is perhaps one of the best examples of how accounting information can be shown in two dramatically different forms, with each purporting to be the economic reality.

A real-life example will illustrate the problem.

 ### *Example*

As a newly qualified accountant, I was sent to do the audit of a software development company. In my earlier years as a trainee I had often assisted the audit senior with the job and in that time had established that this was a particularly profitable company.

On my arrival at the firm's premises, however, I found the MD to be in a particularly sad state.

'I don't know what to do,' he said. 'We have been developing new software, which I know will sell, but because of the decision to concentrate on the new product, sales of our old software have fallen dramatically. Our existing customers will buy the new product but only if we can keep going long enough to complete it. Our accounts are showing a substantial loss, the bank is threatening to foreclose and my family fear that we will lose our house. I would give the company away if I could.'

Taking all that the MD said on board, I asked to see the latest management accounts. They looked exactly as he had portrayed – a substantial loss caused by falling sales and large wages costs paid to the software developers:

Sales		£100,000
Wages and salaries	£100,000	
Other overheads	£50,000	
		£150,000
Loss for period		£50,000

I quizzed the MD about the future potential of the new software and, although despondent about the current situation, he felt that it would be a better seller than the existing software had been at the peak of its popularity. It would be very profitable.

I then asked him roughly what percentage of the overhead expenses related to the development of the new software. He advised that it was approximately 75%.

I quickly took the figures and reworked them as follows:

Sales	£100,000
Expenses	£25,000
Net profit	£75,000

'How would you feel if these figures were presented to you?' I asked. 'I'd be delighted,' he said. 'Indeed – that's roughly the profit I would expect to make on the remaining sales of the old software. How did you manage that?'

The principle issue here was that the company was developing a new product – an asset – no different from any other income-generating asset, other than that it had no physical substance. The problem was that, on the face of it, no assets actually existed but rather all the costs were expenses and had been classified as such.

If the definition of an asset is considered in terms of its constituent parts, however, it becomes apparent that an asset could be created from the expenditure incurred by the firm.

An asset is defined as 'an economic resource expected to yield future benefits, which is controlled by the firm and acquired as a result of a past transaction'.

(i)   A probable future benefit exists:
   ■   the MD was in no doubt the new software would sell.
(ii) Controlled by the firm:
   ■   the company had applied for licences to limit usage of the software to licence holders only.
(iii) Past transaction:
   ■   the company had paid large sums by way of wages and other overhead expenses.

By applying the above criteria to the expenditure it became possible to reclassify it as an asset and therefore reallocate it from the profit and loss account where it was causing a substantial loss, to the balance sheet where it would increase net assets and, in the case of this company, return it to a solvent position. The reality of the picture portrayed by simply looking at the expenses incurred for the year was that a loss had been made. The economic reality was that a new asset was being developed. When the accounts were eventually finalised they did show a completely different picture from the management accounts shown to me. The bank suddenly became supportive and the MD regained the enthusiasm he had always shown in the past. The project was eventually completed and this proved to be extremely successful – so successful, in fact, that the MD received an offer for the sale of his company, which he accepted.

3.3 Goodwill

Another example of an intangible asset is goodwill. Goodwill is the excess of purchase price of a business acquired over the fair value of the net assets. Purchased goodwill is the additional sum paid for a business than would normally be expected for a similar business with equivalent net assets. The additional sum is therefore related to the expected stream of additional income, and its inherent definition effectively qualifies purchased goodwill as an asset.

Goodwill can also be generated internally. This non-purchased goodwill can arise when the reputation of the business, or its skilled workforce or management team, enables the business to achieve a greater income than would be obtainable without the goodwill.

If a company with non-purchased goodwill were to be sold, the amount of the non-purchased goodwill would be determined and recognised by the acquiring company. The actual price paid would reflect the additional earning potential of the business over and above the fair value of the net assets. That premium would then become purchased goodwill.

Why it matters

Two types of intangible asset have been considered: research and development expenditure, and goodwill. Both satisfy the accounting definition of an asset. Why, then, should these intangible assets be treated any differently from tangible fixed assets?

The first reason is that a greater uncertainty surrounds the likely stream of future benefits obtainable from intangible assets. For example, the computer software example given above may not reach its expected sales level; with the goodwill example, the skilled workforce may resent a change in owners. Consequently, because of this uncertainty, the allocation of the intangibles cost to accounting periods can be problematic. Prudence would suggest an immediate write-off.

The second reason is that, in addition to the uncertainty surrounding the likelihood of future benefits, a further element of uncertainty is the actual cost of acquisition. This is particularly true in the case of research and development expenditure, where the cost of a product not only includes direct costs but also an allocation of overheads from other areas of the business.

Concepts in conflict

As a result of this, a conflict arises between the prudence concept, which holds that all such expenditure should be written off, and the matching concept, which holds that expenditure should be matched against the income that it has generated.

Progress Point 3.1

A pharmaceutical company spends £500,000 on labour costs developing a new drug to combat hair loss.

Explain, with reference to the prudence and matching concepts, how this expenditure could be treated. Why would it be necessary to have an accounting standard governing the accounting treatment of such expenditure?

Solution

Labour costs are traditionally period expenses and, as such, are expensed in the income statement in the period in which they are incurred. In this instance, there are labour costs that have been incurred developing a new product that, if successful, could yield future economic benefits. The prudence concept would dictate that the costs should be expensed as incurred as, unless there was reasonable certainty of future economic benefits, it would be imprudent to defer the expenditure to a future accounting period. This would, however, result in expenses being £500,000 greater than they would have been had the development not taken place. The matching concept, on the other hand, would suggest that the expenditure should be deferred and then written off in the accounting periods in which the new drug generated sales revenues. This treatment would more accurately reflect the company's intention in incurring the expenditure in the first instance (i.e. to develop a new drug). This would result in an intangible asset being created, of £500,000.

An accounting standard is necessary to govern the accounting treatment of such expenditure as a result of the significant differences in reported earnings between the two methods. Moreover, given these differences, companies could, if not adequately regulated, argue the case for capitalisation/non-capitalisation of such expenditure to manipulate reported earnings to suit their needs (i.e. to reduce profits or to boost profits).

Summary

Assets can be classified as tangible or intangible. Intangible assets are created, as in the case of research and development, when costs that are normally expensed in the profit and loss account are reclassified and capitalised as assets. Goodwill is another intangible asset, which can be purchased or internally generated.

The rationale for carrying such items as assets comes from the supposition that they will provide positive cash flows to the business in future accounting periods. The accounting problems arise in measuring the amount of the expenses to be capitalised and taking care not to overstate the future economic benefits expected to be derived from the asset.

It can be demonstrated, however, that to ignore the fact that the expenditure satisfies the criteria for classification as an asset can result in a misleading presentation of reported figures with understated profits and understated net assets.

Section 2: Intermediate Issues

This section looks in more detail at the measurement and classification issues faced in accounting for intangible assets, the problems surrounding internally generated intangible assets and, in particular, the important distinction and differences between capitalised research and development expenditure and internally generated goodwill.

3.4 Internally generated intangible assets

Many businesses will have ongoing staff development programmes. Depending on the type of business, this may involve staff training to ensure that individuals' knowledge is kept up to date, or performance is kept at a particular level. There may be ongoing product testing and evaluation, or research into new products or production methods.

BASIC

INTERMEDIATE

ADVANCED

The accounting issues arise when development goes beyond maintaining performance at a particular level, to a situation where there is enhancement of performance. In this way a business effectively creates the ability to earn future cash flows above their current levels. In such cases, it may be that a new asset has been created. Unless additional accounting information relating to this expenditure on this development is disclosed, then valuable information on the performance of the company may not be disclosed.

When might an asset be created?

As noted above, many businesses will have some type of ongoing development programme, not necessarily causing any accounting problems. Consider, for example, a travel agency. Travel agencies provide personal service, and it is likely that staff training will be extensive and continuous. The importance placed on good customer relations will be at the forefront of the travel agency's training aims, and will ensure that customers' enquiries are dealt with courteously, efficiently and knowledge-ably.

The question arises whether such staff training costs constitute the creation of an asset and so require disclosure in the financial statements of the travel agency. There is no doubt that such qualities in a workforce create goodwill – the problem is how to quantify it.

One way of dealing with these training costs is to capitalise them as goodwill. However, this would result in an ever increasing goodwill figure. Moreover, the reality is that the expenditure is more than likely to maintain good customer relations and hence maintain goodwill at its current level. Is it possible therefore to measure the level of goodwill?

If the goodwill has been purchased as part of a business acquisition then the answer is undoubtedly yes. The goodwill will be the excess of the price paid over the fair value of the net assets of the business acquired. If no such purchase has taken place then the valuation of goodwill becomes more problematic. It may be possible to have an external valuation made of the business, however such valuations tend to be very subjective. Moreover, if the desirable characteristics of accounting informa-tion are considered, then objectivity and reliability cast doubt on the acceptance of such a proposal.

Because non-purchased goodwill has been created but has not arisen as a result of a past transaction it is not recorded in the books of account. Consequently according to the accounting records it has zero value. It may, however, have a very real value to the business itself.

Now consider a company in the pharmaceutical industry employing scientists to research alternative drug therapies. The work carried out by the scientists could be on a variety of levels. For example, it may involve continuous testing of drugs currently on sale and monitoring any adverse reactions to them. Such tests and trials are an essential part of any ongoing analysis and it will be generally agreed that the costs associated with drug testing should be expensed.

The work may involve the creation of a new drug. At the initial stages of such a project, there may be a high level of uncertainty as to its outcome. Any costs incurred at this early stage ought, according to the prudence concept, to be written off. As the research continues, the project may reach the point where the outcome becomes more certain and the likelihood of a marketable, income-generating final product arises.

It is at this point that any costs incurred could be considered as creating an intangible asset – development expenditure, and consequently capitalised. Note, however, that an element of uncertainty may still exist. It would only be once all the clinical trials of the new drug had been carried out successfully, that there would be any certainty of income. Note also that the certainty of income does not necessarily mean the certainty of profits.

3.5 Internally generated goodwill vs internally generated intangible assets

The above analysis has demonstrated that goodwill is something that is attached to a business, inherently present and subject to many variables. It may have arisen through a determined course of

action by management or simply by the determined efforts of staff to provide a quality service. One thing that is clear, however, is that the inherent goodwill of a business could not in itself be sold. Goodwill cannot therefore be separately identified. It is this difficulty in identifying and therefore valuing goodwill that sets it apart from other internally generated intangible assets.

Compare and contrast this with the illustration of a development programme within a pharmaceutical company. The expenditure relating to the development of a product will have been part of a conscious management decision, and it will be identifiable and capable of measurement. It may also, on completion, be possible to sell the product or even the rights to sell the product.

It is this distinction between the two that determines the appropriate accounting treatment of intangible assets.

Intangible assets are dealt with by IAS 38 *Intangible Assets*. The next part of this chapter examines the IAS definition of intangible assets and goodwill, and looks in detail at the conditions that must be satisfied before expenditure can be capitalised and intangible assets created. The chapter also considers the subsequent treatment of intangible assets following their initial recognition.

3.6 IAS 38 *Intangible Assets*

Objective

The objective of IAS 38 is to prescribe the accounting treatment for intangible assets that are not dealt with specifically in another IAS. The standard requires an enterprise to recognise an intangible asset if, and only if, certain criteria are met. The standard also specifies how to measure the carrying amount of intangible assets and requires certain disclosures regarding intangible assets.

IAS 38 applies to all intangible assets other than:

- financial assets
- mineral rights, and exploration and development costs incurred by mining and oil and gas companies
- intangible assets arising from insurance contracts issued by insurance companies
- intangible assets covered by another IAS, such as intangibles held for sale, deferred tax assets, lease assets, assets arising from employee benefits, and goodwill (goodwill is covered by IFRS 3).

IAS 38 defines an intangible asset as: 'an identifiable non-monetary asset without physical substance'.

An asset is a resource that is controlled by the enterprise as a result of past events and from which future economic benefits are expected. Note that the past events need not necessarily relate to an actual purchase – self-creation is possible, and the future economic benefits can be reduced future costs as well as revenues. The importance of the IAS definition of intangible assets is the word 'identifiable'. An intangible asset is identifiable when it:

- is separable, i.e. it is capable of being separated and sold, transferred, licensed, rented or exchanged, either individually or as part of a package, or
- arises from contracted or other legal rights, regardless of whether those rights are transferable or separable from the entity or from other rights and obligations.

It is important to note that this definition of intangible assets *excludes* goodwill. Goodwill is the difference between the value of a business as a whole and the aggregate of the fair values of its separable net assets.

Example

Purchase price	£1,000,000
Fair value of net assets acquired	£800,000
Goodwill	£200,000

The goodwill figure as calculated above is the amount that is left over after applying valuation rules to the *identifiable* assets and liabilities. The goodwill figure is a residual amount and cannot be identified separately. That is, the fair value of the net assets can be identified; the purchase price can be identified; the goodwill, however, cannot be identified in the absence of the purchase price and the net fair value. Goodwill can be calculated only once the other two components of the calculation are known. Consequently, the provisions of IAS 38 do not extend to goodwill. Goodwill is covered instead by IFRS 3. Note, however, that goodwill is still an intangible asset. It is just that it is dealt with in a different manner from other intangible assets.

Examples of possible intangible assets include:

- computer software
- patents
- copyrights
- motion picture films
- customer lists
- licences
- import quotas
- franchises
- marketing rights
- trade marks
- costs of research and development.

The purpose of IAS 38 is to distinguish between those items that qualify as assets and those that do not. For example, IAS 38 mentions items of expenditure that it refers to as intangible resources and that do not meet its asset recognition criteria. Such items of expenditure include:

- internally generated goodwill
- start-up costs
- training costs
- advertising costs.

Where such items are reflected in the cost of acquiring a business, they should be included in the amount of goodwill on acquisition.

Intangible assets can be acquired in several ways:

- by separate purchase
- as part of a business combination
- by a government grant
- by an exchange of assets
- by self-creation (internal generation).

Recognition under IAS 38

The three critical attributes that apply in the recognition of an intangible asset are as follows.

1. *Identifiability*: this is necessary to distinguish an intangible asset from goodwill.
2. *Control*: control is exercised by an enterprise over an asset if the enterprise:
   (a) has the power to obtain the future economic benefits flowing from the underlying resource
   (b) can restrict the access of others to such benefits; this generally results from legal rights.
3. *Reliable measurement* : an intangible asset should be recognised only if its cost can be measured reliably. The asset should then be recorded at that cost.

IAS 38 requires an enterprise to recognise an intangible asset, whether purchased or self-created (at cost) if, and only if:

- it is probable that the future economic benefits that are attributable to the asset will flow to the enterprise, and
- the cost of the asset can be measured reliably.

This requirement applies whether an intangible asset is acquired externally (i.e. through purchase) or generated internally. Additional recognition criteria apply to internally generated intangible assets, and this is covered later in this section.

The probability that future economic benefits will flow to the enterprise must be based on reasonable and supportable assumptions about conditions that will exist over the life of the asset. Where a company acquires an intangible asset, whether separately or through a business combination, this usually means that future economic benefits will flow to the enterprise.

In other words, where intangible assets have been paid for by an enterprise, it is assumed that these intangible assets will give future economic benefits. The rationale behind this is that such assets would be acquired only if they were going to provide future economic benefits.

Recognition criteria not met

If an intangible item does not meet *both* the definition of *and* the criteria for recognition as an intangible asset, IAS 38 requires the expenditure on this item to be recognised as an expense in the period in which it is incurred.

 ## *Example*

Probelt Ltd is a long-established supplier of specialist seat belts to the aviation industry. Elqual Ltd, a manufacturer of oxygen masks, has developed a product for use in aircraft in emergency situations and requires contact in the aviation industry in order to market its new product. Probelt Ltd has agreed to sell its customer list to Elqual for £100,000. Will the purchase of the customer list qualify as an asset in the books of Elqual?

In order to answer this question, the constituent elements of the definition of and criteria for recognition as an intangible asset need to be considered.

The purchase of the customer list by Elqual Ltd is:

- identifiable – a distinct item has been purchased
- measurable – an amount of money, £100,000, has been paid
- likely to result in future economic benefits – IAS 38 considers the probability recognition criteria to be satisfied for intangible assets that are acquired separately
- as a result of a past transaction – the customer list has been purchased by Elqual, not self-created.

The final recognition criterion to be satisfied that would enable Elqual to recognise the customer list as an asset is control. As Elqual will have purchased the list then it will have control of as well as access to the customer base in order to derive benefits from it. The customer list will therefore be recognised as an intangible asset at cost £100,000.

Progress Point 3.2

The accountant of Antar Holdings plc, a transport company, is considering whether the following meet the definition of an intangible asset.

1. Recruitment and training of the workforce: Antar Holdings has been using television advertising to recruit new employees and has spent considerable amounts on training.
2. Bus licence: the licence gives Antar Holdings the right to operate a bus route in the south-east of England. The licence was granted by the government to Antar Holdings after satisfying rigorous safety and reliability tests. The licence is not transferable.
3. Domain name: the company registered ' imyourbus.com' as its domain name.
4. Advertising: Antar Holdings plc advertises heavily to promote its services.
5. Brand 'Country-wide Cruisers': this was purchased from a competitor.

6.   Investment: Antar Holdings plc owns the entire share capital of Kyles & Isles plc.

Required

Explain to the accountant whether the above meet the definition of an intangible asset.

Solution

1.   Recruitment and training: in order for an item to be recognised as an intangible asset, a company must be able to exercise control over the asset. It is unlikely that Antar Holdings has sufficient control over the workforce to give access to future economic benefits. The staff could leave. This, therefore, does not meet the definition of an intangible asset.

2.   Bus licence: although the licence is not transferable, it confers a legal right to access the future economic benefits and therefore meets the definition of an intangible asset. It may or may not be separable, but that is not relevant due to the existence of legal rights.

3.   Domain name: the domain name is registered and therefore Antar Holdings has the legal rights to it. It may or may not be separable from Antar Holdings itself. Nevertheless, it meets the definition of an intangible asset.

4.   Advertising: although it would be expected that advertising would yield future economic benefits (i.e. sales), there is insufficient control to give rise to an asset. Even if there was, advertising would fail the identifiability test as it is neither separable nor does it arise from contractual or other legal rights.

5.   Brand: as this brand was purchased it is separable and meets the definition of an asset. It can, therefore, be regarded as an intangible asset.

6.   Investment: this meets the definition of an asset, albeit a financial asset. Financial assets are outwith the scope of IAS 38.

IAS 38 and internally generated intangible assets

Inherent goodwill and research and development costs are the most common internally generated intangible resources. Inherent goodwill, as has already been explained, does not meet the IAS 38 criteria of an intangible asset and so cannot be capitalised. There are no such restrictions on research and development expenditure, which can, if certain criteria are met, be capitalised.

Before considering in detail the IAS requirements, it is worth revisiting the accounting issue involved.

If a company undertakes research and development expenditure, if no adjustments are made, there will be charges to the income statement in respect of such expenditure. These charges will reduce profits and reduce the net assets in the balance sheet. This may be advantageous for some companies since low profits may reduce shareholder pressure for dividends and make the company less attractive to a potential takeover bid.

If, on the other hand, the directors are being put under pressure by the shareholders or other financiers to show profits then the directors will wish to show a profitable income statement and strong net asset position. This impact could be achieved by capitalising some or all of this research and development expenditure. As has been seen, the decision whether or not to capitalise research and development expenditure can have a dramatic effect on the financial statements, and unscrupulous directors may attempt to mislead users by adopting a policy of capitalising expenditure to suit their own ends.

IAS 38 attempts to remove these ambiguities by setting out a methodology to assess whether or not an internally generated intangible resource meets the criteria for recognition as an asset.

Research and development costs

IAS 38 requires any internal project resulting in the generation of a resource to the business to be classified into two phases:

1.   a research phase, and
2.   a development phase.

   If the distinction cannot be made, then the entire project should be considered as a research phase and all research costs charged as expenses.

Research defined

Research is original and planned investigation undertaken with the prospect of gaining new scientific or technical knowledge and understanding. It is highly speculative and, at this early stage, there is no certainty that any benefits will flow to the enterprise. Given this inability to demonstrate future benefits, IAS 38 takes a prudent approach and requires that such research expenditure be charged as an expense when incurred and not capitalised.
   Examples of research activities include:

■   activities aimed at obtaining new knowledge
■   the search for, evaluation and final selection of, applications of research findings or other knowledge
■   the search for alternatives for materials, devices, products, processes, systems and services
■   the formulation, design, evaluation and final selection of possible alternatives for new or improved materials, devices, products, processes, systems or services.

Development defined

Development is the application of research findings to a plan or design for the production of new or substantially improved materials, devices, products, processes, systems or services before the start of commercial production or use.
   Examples of development activities include:

■   the design, construction and testing of preproduction and pre-use prototyping and models
■   the design of tools, jigs, moulds and dies involving new technology
■   the design, construction and operation of a pilot plant that is not of a scale economically feasible for commercial production
■   the design, construction and testing of a chosen alternative for new or improved materials, devices, products, processes, systems or services.

   Development expenditure is less speculative than research expenditure and, as the production and sale of the product comes nearer, it becomes more predictable to forecast its future outcome. As such, the matching concept argues that such development expenditure should be capitalised and then expensed at some future date against the resulting benefits.
   IAS 38 requires (note the compulsion of the standard) that an intangible asset be recognised in respect of such development expenditure if the enterprise can demonstrate *all* of the following:

■   the technical feasibility of completing the intangible asset so that it will be available for use or sale
■   its intention to complete the intangible asset and use or sell it
■   how the intangible asset will generate probable future economic benefits, i.e. the existence of a market for the intangible asset or, if it is to be used internally, its usefulness to the enterprise
■   the availability of adequate technical, financial and other resources to complete the development and to use or sell the intangible asset; this may be demonstrated by the use of a business plan

BASIC

INTERMEDIATE

ADVANCED

■   the enterprise's ability to measure reliably the expenditure attributable to the intangible asset through its development, e.g. by means of its costing system.

If all the above conditions are met then IAS 38 *requires* that the development costs be capitalised.

The costs that are capitalised are the sum of the expenditure incurred from the date when the intangible asset first meets the recognition criteria.

Cost includes all expenditure that is either directly attributable to generating the asset or that has been allocated, on a reasonable basis, to the activity that gave rise to it. Expenditure that is not part of the cost includes expenditure on selling, administration and training staff to operate the asset.

Expenditure on an intangible resource that was initially recognised as an expense in previous financial statements (i.e. expenditure during the 'research' phase) should not be recognised as part of the cost at a later date.

Finally, any expenditure that is not part of the cost of an intangible asset is to be recognised as an expense when incurred. These points can be illustrated as follows.

 ## Example

Bizant is a computer software developer. As part of the company's research into ways of improving software, the directors have identified a product that, they believe, will dramatically improve computer processing times and, consequently, will generate significant sales and profits for the company.

Bizant maintains a detailed costing system, which indicates that expenditure incurred on the project to date is £200,000. The directors have decided that the new product is both technically feasible and commercially viable, and that Bizant can finance the development through to the product's launch.

From this point up to the launch date, development costs can be capitalised as the relevant tests have been met. The £200,000 expenditure on development costs prior to this point should have been expensed and IAS 38 does not allow the reinstatement and capitalisation of such costs.

Internally generated brands, mastheads, titles and lists

Brands, mastheads, publishing titles, customer lists and items similar in substance that are internally generated should not be recognised as assets.

Subsequent expenditure

Expenditure incurred after the initial recognition of a purchased intangible asset or after the completion of an internally generated intangible asset should be recognised as an expense, except in the rare cases where:

■   it can be demonstrated that probable enhancement of the economic benefits will flow from the asset

■   the expenditure can be measured and attributed to the asset reliably.

Measurement subsequent to initial recognition

An intangible asset should be carried at cost less any accumulated depreciation and (if any) accumulated impairment losses (the concept of impairment will be dealt with more fully later in this chapter). Generally speaking, an asset is impaired when an entity cannot recover the balance sheet carrying value of the asset, either through using it or selling it.

Progress Point 3.3

Cornton plc entered into the following transactions in the year ending 31st December Year 6

1. The company had developed a new invention and has now applied for a patent. Development work incurred a cost of £400,000 and the application for the patent cost £20,000. At the present time the invention has no commercial market, but the company is hopeful of finding one.
2. The company bought a patented design for a product. The patent cost £300,000.
3. A new company was acquired for £6 million. This new company has a special brand, but the directors of Cornton were unable to place a value on it.
4. Staff training costs amounted to £120,000.
5. Cornton spent £2 million developing a new brand.

Explain how each of the above should be treated in the accounts of Cornton for the year ended 31 December Year 6.

Solution

1. Invention and patent. This is an internally developed intangible. As no market has been identified it fails at least one of the criteria for recognition as an intangible. This expenditure should be written off to the profit and loss account.
2. This is a purchased intangible. Cost is known and therefore can be measured reliably. By paying £300,000 it is assumed that benefits will be generated by the asset.
3. No reliable value can be placed on the brand so it should not be separately recognised.
4. Staff training does not meet the definition of an intangible asset. There is insufficient control, and such expenditure is specifically required to be written off to the profit and loss account.
5. Internal brand being developed. The standard prohibits internally generated brands from being recognised.

Progress Point 3.4

During the year to 31 December Year 4, a company spent £400,000 researching and developing a new product. At 31 December Year 4 not all the criteria were met for recognising an intangible asset. During Year 5 all the intangible asset recognition criteria were met and a further £620,000 was spent on the product by the end of the year.

How should the expenditure be treated in the accounts for the year ended December Year 4 and Year 5?

Solution

December Year 4

The expenditure should be written off to the profit and loss account as the criteria has not been met.

December Year 5

The expenditure of £620,000 should be capitalised as the criteria are now met. The £400,000 written off in Year 4 remains written off, and is not credited from the profit and loss account and added to the cost of the intangible asset.

Revaluation model

IAS 38 allows a revaluation model to be adopted and to carry the intangible asset at a revalued amount based on fair value less any subsequent amortisation and impairment losses. This revaluation model cannot apply to initial recognition, which should be at cost; it can apply only after initial recognition, (i.e. all the relevant conditions for classification as an intangible asset must have been fulfilled).

If an intangible asset is revalued, a revaluation of all the other assets in the same class should also be carried out, except for those assets for which there is no active market. In this case these intangibles for which there is no active market should be shown at cost less accumulated amortisation and impairment losses.

Fair value should be determined by reference to an active market. Revaluations should be made regularly so that the carrying amount of the asset does not diverge materially from the fair value of the asset at the balance sheet date. Such active markets are, however, expected to be uncommon for intangible assets, although there may be exceptions to this generalisation. For example, milk quotas, taxi licences, and airport take-off and landing slots are exceptions. If an active market is not available, the revaluation model cannot be used.

Recognition of revaluation gains and losses

Revaluation gains (i.e. increases in an intangible asset's carrying amount) should be credited directly to 'revaluation surplus' within equity, except to the extent that this gain reverses a revaluation decrease previously recognised in the profit and loss statement. In this case the amount of the reversal is recognised as income and as such is credited to the income statement.

Decreases in value are recognised as expenses and are charged against the profit for the year. However, if the decrease in value is a reversal of a previous revaluation gain, the amount of the reversal should be offset against the revaluation surplus.

The cumulative revaluation surplus may be transferred directly to retained earnings when the surplus is realised. Realisation may occur through retirement or disposal of the asset or through the process of using up the asset. Note, however, that the transfer is made directly in the balance sheet. The transfer does not affect reported earnings in the year the transfer is made.

Effect of revised version of IAS 1

The revised version of IAS 1, which took effect for accounting periods that began on or after 1 January 2009, requires that revaluation gains and losses that would previously have been shown in the statement of equity should instead be recognised in 'other comprehensive income' and shown under that heading in the statement of comprehensive income.

Measurement: a critical appraisal

The standard sets out rigorous tests that require to be satisfied before intangible resources can be classified as intangible assets. The standard also prohibits the inclusion as intangible assets of internally generated brands, customer lists, publishing titles and other items similar in substance. It does, however, allow the revaluation of intangible assets to fair value if an active market exists.

On the face of it, this seems to be reasonable. It would be imprudent and perhaps misleading to have items disclosed as assets that did not yield any future benefits to the company. It would also seem reasonable to reflect the fair value of intangible assets within the balance sheet so as to convey the true value of those intangible assets to the user of financial statements. The standard's prohibition on capitalising certain items as intangibles can, however, give rise to some problems. Consider the following example.

Example

JAR Ltd has been trading for a number of years and, over that time, has accumulated a substantial customer list of businesses to which it sells its product. JAR Ltd has been approached by a company, Brinley Ltd, which has a product that will complement that which JAR Ltd currently sells. JAR Ltd has followed the requirements of IAS 38 and has not capitalised the value of its customer lists. Brinley Ltd, however, is prepared to pay JAR Ltd £50,000 for its customer lists.

Two questions arise from this:

1.   If JAR Ltd accepts the £50,000 from Brinley Ltd, how should this income be classified?
2.   Given that the customer list has a 'value', should JAR not be allowed to capitalise it?

There is no asset in JAR Ltd's records so there is no asset disposal. Nor can it be classified as sales revenue. The 'sale' must therefore be classified as either sundry income or as gain on disposal of an asset with no value!

The strict application of the standard may prevent a true picture being presented. By adhering to the standard, JAR Ltd has an unrecognised intangible asset, which means its 'value' is unrecognised. The exclusion of this intangible asset from the balance sheet results in a substantial asset being omitted from the balance sheet, and so results in the loss of valuable information about the business.

While the requirements of the standard in relation to what items may or may not be capitalised are effective in deterring inappropriate expenditure from being classified as intangible assets, strict adherence to the standard in certain self-created intangibles can, it seems, be counter-productive.

Amortisation and depreciation

The main argument for the creation of intangible assets is that, although lacking physical substance, they share all the same characteristics of tangible assets. As such, intangible assets are expected to yield future benefits to the enterprise over the period of their useful lives. Consequently, the net carrying amount of an intangible asset requires to be allocated to the profit and loss account in a systematic way over the useful life of the asset. Such an allocation is known as amortisation. The residual value should be assumed to be zero unless:

- there is a commitment by a third party to purchase the asset at the end of its estimated useful life, or
- there is an active market for the asset such that the asset's residual value can be determined by reference to that market.

Useful life

Intangible assets are classified as having either an indefinite life or a finite life, and the accounting treatment is applied accordingly.

An intangible asset with an indefinite life (i.e. no foreseeable limit to the period over which the asset is expected to generate net cash in flows for the entity) should not be amortised.

An intangible asset with a finite life (i.e. a limited period of benefit to the entity) should be amortised.

Intangible assets with finite lives

The cost less residual value of such an intangible asset should be amortised over the life of the asset.

The amortisation should start when the asset first becomes available for use – that is, when it is in the location and condition necessary for it to be capable of operating in the manner intended by management.

The amortisation method chosen should reflect the pattern of benefits derived from using the asset, however if the pattern of benefits cannot be determined reliably then the straight line method must be used.

The amortisation charge for each period is recognised in the profit or loss account as an expense (unless another standard requires that it be included in the cost of another asset).

The amortisation shall cease at the earlier of the date that the asset is classified as held for sale and the date that the asset is derecognised.

An intangible asset shall cease to be recognised:

- on disposal, or
- when no future economic benefits are expected from its use.

The amortisation period and method should be reviewed at least annually. If the expected useful life of the asset is significantly different from previous estimates, then the amortisation period should be changed accordingly. If the expected time pattern of economic benefits has changed, then the amortisation method, too, should be changed.

In addition to all the above, the requirements of IAS 36 *Impairment of Assets* (covered later in this chapter) will apply.

 ## Example

A manufacturing company acquires a patent with a remaining legal life of ten years for the manufacture of a particular product. Technological advances suggest that the product is likely to become obsolete in five years.

The patent would be amortised over its five-year estimated useful life. The patent would also be reviewed for impairment in accordance with IAS 36 by assessing at each reporting date whether there is any indication that it may be impaired.

Intangible assets with indefinite useful lives

Note that the term indefinite does not mean infinite. An infinite life would imply that, once purchased or self-created, the intangible asset would yield economic benefits continuously. The term indefinite is intended to reflect the fact, that providing the asset is properly maintained, then it will continue to yield economic benefits.

However, the asset should not be classified as having an indefinite life if planned future expenditure is greater than that required to maintain the asset at its standard of performance at the time of estimating its useful life. In other words, if the intangible asset will require to be 'improved' with subsequent expenditure, then it should not be classified as having an indefinite life.

An intangible asset with an indefinite useful life should not be amortised.

Instead, a review of the asset's useful life should be carried out annually. If the findings do not support an indefinite useful life assessment for the asset then the change in the useful life assessment from indefinite to finite should be accounted for as a change in an accounting estimate.

In addition, an impairment test should be carried out annually and whenever there is an indication that the intangible asset may be impaired. If the findings suggest impairment then this will lead to reductions in carrying value to the recoverable amount at the date of the impairment test.

Example

A radio station acquires a broadcasting licence, renewable every five years. The licence is renewed at little cost as long as the radio station provides at least an average level of service to its customers and complies with the relevant legislative requirements. The licence has been renewed twice before the most recent acquisition. The radio station intends to renew the licence indefinitely and evidence supports its ability to do so. Historically, there has been no challenge to the licence renewal and the technology used in broadcasting is not expected to be superseded in the foreseeable future. The licence is, therefore, expected to contribute to the radio station's net cash inflows indefinitely.

The broadcasting licence would be treated as having an indefinite useful life because it is expected to contribute to the radio station's net cash inflows indefinitely. Therefore, the licence would not be amortised until its useful life is determined to be finite. The licence would be tested for impairment in accordance with IAS 36 annually and whenever there is an indication that it may be impaired.

Derecognition

Retirements and disposals

The gain or loss arising from the derecognition of an intangible asset should be the difference between the net disposal proceeds (if any) and the carrying amount of the asset. This gain or loss should be transferred to the profit and loss account when the asset is derecognised.

3.7 Disclosure

The disclosure requirements in IAS 38 are long and detailed, and require full information in relation to balances, useful lives, amortisation rates and methods, any changes over the year, and any revaluations or impairment losses.

Disclosure in practice

The required disclosures of IAS 38 Intangible Assets are usually contained in the accounting policies note, the balance sheet and the notes to the balance sheet.

Intangible assets
All intangible assets, except goodwill, are stated at cost less accumulated amortisation and any accumulated impairment losses. Goodwill is not amortised and is stated at cost less any accumulated impairment losses.

Goodwill
Goodwill represents the excess of the cost of acquisition over the fair value of the Group's interest in the identifiable assets, liabilities and contingent liabilities acquired in a business combination and the excess of the consideration paid for an increase in stake in an existing subsidiary over the share of the carrying value of net assets acquired.

Development costs
Expenditure incurred in the development of software products or enhancements, and their related intellectual property rights, is capitalised as an intangible asset only when the future economic benefits expected to arise are deemed probable and the costs can be reliably measured. Development costs not meeting these criteria, and all research costs, are expensed in the income statement as incurred. Capitalised development costs are amortised on a straight-line basis over their useful economic lives once the related software product or enhancement is available for use.

Other intangible assets
Intangible assets purchased separately, such as software licences that do not form an integral part of related hardware, are capitalised at cost and amortised over their useful economic life. Intangible assets acquired through a business combination are initially measured at fair value and amortised over their useful economic lives.

The useful economic lives of the other intangible assets are as follows:

Brand names	3–5 years
Purchased computer software	3 years
Software products recognised on acquisition	3–7 years

Customer contracts and relationships are amortised over their useful economic life which are between five and eight years, except for one contract in the international category which has a useful life of 10 years.

This extract from Logica's accounting policies note discloses the measurement base adopted for intangible assets together with the types of intangible assets contained within the financial statements and the amortisation period adopted for each of the classes identified.

Consolidated balance sheet 31 December 2007			
	Note	2007 £m	2008 £m
Non-current assets			
Goodwill	17	**1,604.0**	1,552.1
Other intangible assets	18	**358.0**	415.1
Property, plant and equipment	19	**132.1**	136.6
Investments in associates	20	**2.4**	6.0
Financial assets	21	**11.0**	10.1
Retirement benefit assets	38	**12.0**	18.7
Deferred tax assets	28	**54.5**	50.6
		2,174.0	2,189.2

Figure 3.1 Logica: consolidated balance sheet

Intangible assets are contained within the non-current assets section of Logica's balance sheet (Figure 3.1). The carrying value at 2007 is £358 miillion with a comparative 2006 balance amounting to £415.1 million. Analysis of both these balances is given in note 18 to the financial statement.

Other intangible assets					
	Purchased computer software £m	Develop- ment costs £m	Brand names £m	Customer contracts/ relationships £m	Software products £m	Total £m
Cost						
At 1 January 2006	21.9	17.7	4.0	6.1	–	49.7
Additions	8.3	11.3	–	–	–	19.6
Acquisition of subsidiary	3.3	1.5	100.0	278.4	31.9	415.1
Disposals	(5.0)	(0.8)	–	–	–	(5.8)
Exchange differences	(0.4)	(0.4)	0.8	2.4	0.4	2.8
At 1 January 2007	28.1	29.3	104.8	286.9	32.3	481.4
Additions	9.6	6.7	–	–	–	16.3
Acquisition of subsidaries/businesses	–	–	–	1.9	–	1.9
Disposals of subsidiaries/businesses	(3.0)	(15.6)	(4.0)	(6.6)	–	(29.2)
Disposals	(1.1)	(0.2)	–	–	–	(1.3)
Exchange differences	3.0	0.8	7.0	19.2	2.4	32.4
At 31 December 2007	**36.6**	**21.0**	**107.8**	**301.4**	**34.7**	**501.5**
Accumulated amortisation						
At 1 January 2006	13.4	10.0	0.5	0.5	–	24.4
Charge for the year	5.8	2.6	13.1	22.9	1.6	46.0
Disposals	(3.2)	(0.5)	–	–	–	(3.7)
Exchange differences	(0.2)	(0.1)	–	(0.1)	–	(0.4)
At 1 January 2007	15.8	12.0	13.6	23.3	1.6	66.3
Charge for the year	6.4	3.0	28.6	39.8	6.3	84.1
Disposals of subsidiaries/businesses	(2.7)	(11.4)	(0.8)	(0.4)	–	(15.3)
Disposals	(0.9)	(0.2)	–	–	–	(1.1)
Exchange differences	1.6	0.3	2.8	4.2	0.6	9.5
At 1 December 2007	**20.2**	**3.7**	**44.2**	**66.9**	**8.5**	**143.5**
Net carrying amount						
At 31 December 2007	**16.4**	**17.3**	**63.6**	**234.5**	**26.2**	**358.0**
At 31 December 2006	12.3	17.3	91.2	263.6	30.7	415.1

Purchased computer software represented assets bought from third parties, while development costs represented internally generated intangible assets. Brand names, customer contracts/relationships and software products represented assets recognised as part of a business combination.

The net book values of individually material intangible assets and their remaining useful life at 31 December 2007 were as follows:

	Carrying value £m	Remaining useful life Years
WM-data brand name	36.7	1.8
Unilog brand name	25.7	2.3

Figure 3.2 Logica: other intangible assets

This note to Logica's balance sheet discloses the movements in the various classes of intangible assets held at each balance sheet date (Figure 3.2). A columnar approach is used to assist in the disclosure of comparative balances beginning at 1 January 2006 and showing vertically the various additions, disposals and exchange differences in cost, accumulated amortisation and net carrying amount (net book value).

International differences

The UK position

Research and development expenditure is regulated by SSAP 13. This standard is very similar to IAS 38 but does not require that expenditure be capitalised if all criteria are met. Instead, it states that the expenditure may be capitalised.

The US position

With the exception of certain software development costs, which are required to be capitalised in accordance with FAS 86, US GAAP (FAS 2) requires all research and development costs to be immediately expensed. In addition, while International GAAP permits the reinstatement of intangible assets to their fair values where an active market for that type of asset exists, this treatment is not permitted by US GAAP. US GAAP permits useful lives of identified intangibles to have a duration of up to 40 years.

3.8 Goodwill

Goodwill can be self-generated or purchased. IAS 38 *Intangible Assets* deals with self-generated goodwill and prohibits its recognition as an intangible asset within the financial statements.

The reason for this is the potential to alter reported figures. If companies were permitted to include self-generated goodwill in their financial statements they could:

- boost assets and produce a stronger balance sheet (e.g. by reducing gearing)
- if the credit entry was to the profit and loss account reserve or a capital reserve in the balance sheet, there would be no effect on reported profits, but
- if the credit entry was to the income statement, this would boost the profit for the year, which would allow the manipulation of reported profit.

IFRS 3 *Business Combinations* deals with purchased goodwill. As already noted, goodwill is a residual amount and is defined as: 'future economic benefits arising from assets that are not capable of being individually identified and separately recognised'.

Goodwill is the amount remaining after applying valuation rules to the *identifiable* assets and liabilities.

 ## Example

	£
Purchase price	1,000,000
Net fair value of assets acquired	800,000
Goodwill	200,000

Goodwill is not therefore an identifiable asset in itself, but is instead a residual amount.

Why does goodwill arise?

As noted earlier in this chapter, goodwill can arise when a skilled workforce, an efficient production process or an established customer base results in an enterprise returning greater profits than could be generated by another company utilising the same net assets. The cost of this self-generated goodwill is the cost of the training, production reviews and advertising incurred in developing the business to this particular level.

Purchased goodwill arises when one company acquires another company in a business combination and the purchase price paid reflects the ability of the acquiring company to earn these future super-profits.

From the acquiring company's point of view, this excess amount paid over the fair value of the net assets acquired is expected to yield future benefits. The anticipation of expected future benefits effectively constitutes goodwill as an asset in the same way as any other tangible asset that would be expected to yield future benefits.

It is important to remember that in arriving at the purchase price of an acquisition in a business combination, the value placed on the net assets will be the fair values and the excess is likely to have been based upon an estimate of the future maintainable earnings of the acquiring company.

Accounting treatment of purchased goodwill: the options

There are a number of possible approaches to accounting for purchased goodwill.

(i) *Carry the purchased goodwill as an asset and amortise it over its estimated useful life through the profit and loss account.* It could be argued, however, that to charge amortisation of the goodwill figure is effectively a double charge to the profit and loss account if the goodwill itself is being 'maintained' by other revenue expenditure (i.e. training, advertising, quality controls).

(ii) *Carry the purchased goodwill as an asset and amortise it over its estimated useful life by writing off directly against reserves.* The problem here is that, as amortisation is an expense, it ought to be treated as such and charged to the profit and loss account, not against reserves.

(iii) *Eliminate purchased goodwill against reserves immediately on acquisition.* This would effectively treat purchased goodwill in the same way as non-purchased goodwill (i.e. it solves the problem as if the goodwill had never existed in the first place).

(iv) *Retain purchased goodwill in the accounts indefinitely unless a permanent reduction in its value becomes evident.* This is acceptable if the view is taken that goodwill can be maintained, as, for example, a building can. The costs of maintaining the goodwill are being expended as they occur and to charge amortisation as well would be double counting. As we have seen, however, goodwill is a variable figure and it could be argued that, over time, the purchased goodwill is being replaced by self-generated non-purchased goodwill.

(v) *Charge purchased goodwill as an expense against profits in the period when it is acquired.* This seems to suggest that the goodwill on acquisition will have suffered an immediate reduction in value. This is clearly not the case as a loss in value, if at all, will take place over a longer period of time. Moreover, the write-off is not related to the results of the year in which the acquisition was made.

(vi) *Show purchased goodwill as a deduction from shareholders' equity (and either amortise it or carry it indefinitely).* This 'moves' the goodwill down the balance sheet, reducing both net assets and, correspondingly, shareholders' funds. The figure is shown as a debit but not on the net asset side. Instead it is shown as a deduction from shareholders' equity. It is the same as writing off purchased goodwill against reserves while implying that the goodwill remains available as a form of asset. Ultimately, however, this treatment can be rejected as it represents the offset of a liability against an asset, which, under certain countries' legislation, is not permitted.

(vii) *Revalue it annually to incorporate later non-purchased goodwill.* This would be consistent with the trend towards fair value, but is highly subjective. Moreover, if self-generated (i.e. non-purchased) goodwill is not recognised as an asset, this treatment would, it could be argued, be inconsistent with the international accounting standard, particularly if, over time, purchased goodwill is replaced by non-purchased goodwill. This treatment would also be particularly susceptible to manipulation.

Goodwill and IFRS 3

The excess of purchase cost over the fair value of the identified net assets is the goodwill on acquisition figure. This is positive goodwill.

Positive goodwill should be:

- recognised in a business combination as an asset
- initially measured as the excess of the cost of the business combination over the proportion of the fair value of the identifiable net assets acquired.

Goodwill acquired in a business combination should not be amortised. Instead it should be tested annually for impairment. The impairment test may be applied more frequently in accordance with IAS 36 if events or circumstances indicate that the asset might be impaired. Note that this treatment is exactly consistent with the requirements for identifiable intangible assets with indefinite lives.

Negative goodwill

So far the examples given have all assumed that the calculated goodwill is a positive figure. In other words, that the payment made is greater than the fair value of the net assets acquired. It is, of course, possible for the goodwill figure to be negative. This could happen if the price paid by the acquiring company was less than the fair value of the tangible net assets acquired.

How can this happen?

In order to determine the purchase price, accountants will restate the individual assets and liabilities at their fair values. These new values will then become the historical cost to the new owners of the individual assets and liabilities recognised at the date of acquisition. Consequently, negative goodwill or, to put another it way, a 'bargain' purchase, should not be possible if correct valuation procedures have been followed. This is certainly the case if one is concerned only with the cost of the investment. The cost of the individually identified assets and liabilities cannot exceed the cost of the business purchased.

If, however, in the assessment of the purchase price, *future* reorganisation costs are anticipated, then this can give rise to the negative goodwill phenomenon. Why might it be that these future liabilities have not been taken into account in the net fair value calculation? The reason for this is that, although clearly quantifiable, they do not satisfy the criteria for recognition as provisions at the date of acquisition and consequently cannot be included in the net fair value calculation. They can, however, be included in the calculation of what the acquirer is prepared to pay for the investment.

Accounting treatment of negative goodwill: the options

In the same way that there are several methods of dealing with positive goodwill, negative goodwill can also be accounted for in a number of different ways.

(i) If the negative goodwill arises as a result of the future expectation of losses and expenses identified by the acquirer in the assessment of the value of the acquisition, and can be measured reliably, then the negative goodwill could be included as income in the periods when the future losses and expenses are identified. This would certainly adhere to the matching principle, however the measurement of future losses is likely to be problematic.

(ii) If negative goodwill arises, the acquirer could reassess the identification and measurement of the acquiree's identifiable assets, liabilities and contingent liabilities, and the measurement of the cost of the combination. In this assessment there will be two types of assets and liabilities; these will be monetary and non-monetary. Monetary assets and liabilities are those assets and liabilities whose amounts are contractually fixed and as such can be excluded from the computation. This is because, in any reassessment, these values will, by definition, be fixed. Any negative goodwill and hence any uncertainty must therefore relate to the non-monetary items.

A possible method of dealing with the negative goodwill could be to recognise it in the profit and loss account in the periods over which the non-monetary assets are recovered, either through depreciation or disposal. Any negative goodwill in excess of fair values of the non-monetary assets acquired could be recognised in the profit and loss account for the period expected to benefit.

Example

Lanbell plc acquired its investment in Prion plc in the year ended 31 December 2009. The goodwill on acquisition was calculated as follows:

	£000	£000
Cost of investment		250
Fair value of net non-monetary assets		
(remaining useful life 4 years)	400	
Stock (non-monetary asset)	50	
Net monetary assets	100	
		550
Negative goodwill		300

The negative goodwill could be accounted for as follows.

Allocated, first, against the non-monetary assets recognised through the profit and loss account for the year ended 31 December 2009:

	£000
Stock (on the assumption it is all sold)	50
Depreciation (£400,000/4 years)	100
	150
Total non-monetary assets at acquisition (400,000 + 50,000)	450
Proportion recognised in year to 31 December 2009 is $\frac{150}{450}$ i.e. $\frac{1}{3}$	
Credit to profit and loss account is $\frac{1}{3}$ x £300,000 =	£100,000

The balance sheet will show negative goodwill of £300,000 – £100,000 = £200,000.

This negative goodwill will be released to the profit and loss account over the remainder of the net assets' useful lives, i.e. 3 years (4 years – 1 year):

$= \frac{1}{3}$ x £200,000 = £66,667

If the negative goodwill had been greater than the fair values of the non-monetary assets acquired (£450,000) this could have been written off over the periods expected to benefit.

(iii) Any negative goodwill arising could be credited to the profit and loss account immediately.

(iv) A combination of (i), (ii) and (iii).

There are a number of ways that negative goodwill could be accounted for, each with its own merits and problems.

IFRS 3 and negative goodwill

IFRS 3 requires that negative goodwill should be recognised immediately in the income statement as a gain.

However, before concluding that 'negative goodwill' has arisen, IFRS 3 requires that the acquirer reassess the identification and measurement of the identifiable assets, liabilities and contingent liabilities, and the measurement of the cost of the combination of the company acquired.

BASIC

INTERMEDIATE

ADVANCED

Example

Horatio plc acquires its investment in Denlon plc in the year ended 31 December 2009. The goodwill on acquisition was calculated as follows:

	£000
Cost of investment	700
Fair value of net assets	900
Negative goodwill	(200)

The negative goodwill figure of £200,000 is shown in the income statement for the year ended 31 December 2009 as a gain.

International differences

The UK position

Goodwill and intangible assets are regulated by FRS 10. FRS 10 does not allow the inclusion of internally generated goodwill in accounting statements. FRS 10 permits the non-amortisation of goodwill if it is expected to be maintained indefinitely. If the goodwill is not amortised, then FRS 10 requires that an annual impairment review be carried out. Where positive purchased goodwill is not expected to be maintained indefinitely it should be amortised over a period not exceeding 20 years.

Negative goodwill up to the fair value of the non-monetary assets acquired should be recognised in the profit and loss account for the periods in which the non-monetary assets are recovered, either by depreciation or disposal. Any negative goodwill should be recognised in the profit and loss account for the period expected to benefit.

The US position

US GAAP now requires annual impairment reviews and prohibits amortisation.

3.9 IAS 36 *Impairment of Assets*

Reference to impairment of assets has been made in this and earlier chapters.

If an asset is regarded as being an unallocated expense (or deferred charge) then the principle of deferring charges to future periods means that such deferred charges appear as assets in balance sheets. The going concern convention assumes that there will be future accounting periods in which such assets can be allocated to the income statement as expenses. At an intermediate stage in this allocation process, assets will have a carrying amount equal to the unallocated cost. This unallocated cost is more usually referred to as the 'book value' and, in accounting terms, represents the value of the non-monetary benefit yet to be derived from the asset.

If, however, the carrying amount of an asset is greater than the amount that will be gained from the asset's use or from its sale, then to continue carrying the asset at its book value would be imprudent. Where the carrying amount of an asset is greater than this recoverable amount (i.e. the value in use or the asset's net selling price), the asset is said to be impaired. If such a situation arises, and if no action is taken, then this would conflict with the prudence convention and could be potentially misleading to users of the accounting statements.

IAS 36 *Impairment of Assets* deals with this issue. The objective of IAS 36 is to ensure that assets are carried at no more than their recoverable amount. Where the recoverable amount is lower than the carrying value, an impairment loss must be recognised immediately.

Scope of IAS 36

IAS 36 applies to all assets except those that are covered in detail by other international accounting standards. The scope of IAS 36 includes land, buildings, machinery and equipment, investment property carried at cost, intangible assets, goodwill, investments in subsidiaries, associates and joint ventures, and assets carried at revalued amounts under IAS 16 and IAS 38.

IAS 36 does not apply to inventories (IAS 2), assets arising from construction contracts (IAS 11), deferred tax assets (IAS 12), assets arising from employee benefits (IAS 19), financial assets (IAS 39), investment property carried at fair value (IAS 40), certain agricultural assets carried at fair value (IAS 41), insurance contracts assets (IFRS 4) and assets held for resale (IFRS 5).

Key definitions

IAS 36 gives a number of key definitions – many of them inter related and contained within the definition of other key terms.

 (i) *Impairment*: an asset is impaired when its carrying amount exceeds its recoverable amount.
 (ii) *Carrying amount:* the amount at which an asset is recognised in the balance sheet after deducting accumulated depreciation (amortisation) and accumulated impairment losses.
(iii) *Recoverable amount:* the higher of an asset's fair value less costs to sell (sometimes called net selling price) and its value in use.
(iv) *Fair value:* the amount obtainable from the sale of an asset in an arm's length transaction between knowledgeable, willing parties.
 (v) *Value in use:* the discounted present value of estimated future cash flows expected to arise from the continuing use of an asset and from its disposal at the end of its useful life.

Identifying an asset that may be impaired

A review of all assets should be made at each balance sheet date to look for any indication that an asset may be impaired. This does not mean that the recoverable amount must be determined annually in order to test for impairment. IAS 36 has a list of external and internal indicators of impairment. If there is an indication that an asset may be impaired, the recoverable amount of the asset must be calculated. This is done using a two-stage process:

1.   assess at each balance sheet date (annually) whether there is any *indication* that an asset may be impaired
2.   estimate the recoverable amount of the asset if any such indication exists.

Notwithstanding, the recoverable amounts of the following types of intangible asset should be measured annually whether or not there is any indication that they may be impaired:

■   an intangible asset with an indefinite useful life
■   an intangible asset not yet available for use
■   goodwill acquired in a business combination.

Progress Point 3.5

Describe what is meant by impairment. When would an impairment review be carried out?

Solution

Impairment refers to the loss of value of an asset below its book value (i.e. generally, its depreciated cost). It is found by comparing the book value with the recoverable amount. The recoverable amount is the higher of an asset's net selling price and its value in use.

An impairment review would be carried out when there is an indication that assets might be impaired. If there are no such indications, there may be no reason to suspect that assets might be impaired.

Indications of impairment (stage 1)

IAS 36 suggests that when assessing whether or not there is any indication that an asset may be impaired, as a *minimum* the following indications should be considered.

External sources

- Where the market value of an asset has declined significantly more than would be expected as a result of either the passage of time or of normal use.
- Where significant technological, market, economic or legal changes have occurred, having an adverse effect on the entity.
- Where market interest rate increases have a bearing on the discount rate used in calculating the value in use of an asset, thereby decreasing its recoverable amount.
- Where the company's stock price is lower than the book value of the net assets.

Internal sources

- Evidence of obsolescence or physical damage of an asset.
- The asset is part of a restructuring or held for disposal.
- Evidence that the economic performance of an asset will be worse than expected.

If any indication of impairment exists then the second stage in process happens. Note that the move to the second stage is necessary only *if* an indication of likely impairment exists.

Determining recoverable amount (stage 2)

The 'recoverable amount' of an asset is the higher of net selling price or value in use. It follows that *if either* net selling price or value in use is greater than the asset's carrying amount, the asset is not impaired.

Also, if the net selling price is not obtainable because there is no active market for the asset, then the recoverable amount can be taken as equal to value in use. Conversely, the recoverable amount may be taken as the net selling price if the value in use is unlikely to differ materially from the net selling price. It is necessary to calculate value in use only if the carrying amount is greater than net selling price.

Net selling price

The net selling price is defined as being fair value less any incremental costs directly attributable to the disposal of the asset. If there is a binding sale agreement, the price under that agreement less costs of disposal should be used as net selling price.

If there is an active market for the asset, the market price should be used less costs of disposal. If there is no active market, the best estimate of the asset's selling price less costs of disposal should be used.

Costs of disposal are the direct added costs only. Examples of such costs are legal costs, stamp duty and costs of removing the asset.

Value in use

The **value in use** of an asset is defined as the present value of estimated future cash flows expected to arise from the continuing use of an asset and from its disposal at the end of its useful life.

The calculation of value in use is therefore likely to be more difficult. However, a detailed calculation of value in use will not be necessary if:

- the net selling price is greater than the carrying amount, or
- a simple estimate is sufficient to show that value in use is higher than the carrying amount, or
- value in use is lower than net selling price, in which case impairment is measured by reference to selling price.

If value in use does have to be calculated, that calculation should reflect the following elements:

- an estimate of the future cash flows the entity expects to derive from the asset in an arm's length transaction
- expectations about possible variations in the amount or timing of those future cash flows
- the time value of money, represented by the current market risk-free rate of interest
- the price for bearing the uncertainty inherent in the asset, and
- other factors, such as illiquidity, that market participants would reflect in pricing the future cash flows the entity expects to derive from the asset.

Cash flow projections should be based on reasonable and supportable assumptions, and should include projections of cash inflows from the continuing use of the asset, net of projections of cash outflows that are necessarily incurred to generate the cash inflows and that can be directly attributed to the asset. The net cash flows, if any, to be received for the asset at the end of its useful life should also be included. The most recent budgets and forecasts should be used but they must not go beyond five years.

Cash flow projections should relate to the asset in its current condition – future restructurings to which the entity is not committed and expenditure to improve or enhance the asset's performance should not be anticipated.

Discount rate

The discount rate should be the pre-tax rate that reflects current market assessments of the time value of money and the risks specific to the asset.

The discount rate should not reflect risks for which future cash flows have been adjusted, as this would involve double counting.

For impairment of an individual asset or portfolio of assets, the discount rate is the rate the company would pay in a current market transaction to borrow money to buy that specific asset or portfolio.

If a market-determined asset-specific rate is not available, a surrogate must be used that reflects the time value of money over the asset's life as well as country risk, currency risk, price risk and cash flow risk. The following would normally be considered:

- the enterprise's own weighted average cost of capital
- the enterprise's incremental borrowing rate, and
- other market borrowing rates.

The effect of all of the above considerations means that the appropriate discount rate may be different for different types of asset or different circumstances within the same entity.

Example

KPA is carrying out an impairment review of a piece of production machinery at 31 December 2009. Budgeted information concerning net cash flows for the next three years has been provided by the marketing department as follows:

2010	£35,000
2011	£30,000
2012	£15,000

The production director has estimated that the scrap value of the machinery would be £10,000 in 2012. KPA currently borrows at a rate of 10%.

Value in use is calculated as follows:

	2010	2011	2012	Total
	£	£	£	£
Net cash inflows	35,000	30,000	15,000	
Scrap proceeds	–	–	10,000	
Cash flows	35,000	30,000	25,000	
Discount rate[1]	0.909	0.826	0.751	
Present value	31,815	24,780	18,775	£75,370

[1]   From tables: present value of £1

i.e. the value in use of the production machinery is £75,370.

Recognition and measurement of impairment losses

After all the complexities of the previous section it is perhaps worth remembering at this point what the objectives of IAS 36 are. They are to ensure that assets are carried at no more than their recoverable amount. In the event the recoverable amount of an asset is less than its carrying amount, the carrying amount of the asset should be reduced to its recoverable amount. That reduction is an impairment loss.

When impairment occurs, a revised carrying amount is calculated as shown in Figure 3.3.

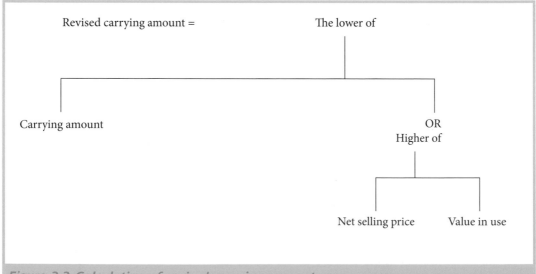

Figure 3.3 Calculation of revised carrying amount

 BASIC

 INTERMEDIATE

 ADVANCED

Example 1

As part of the annual review for impairment, a company identifies a machine that, as a result of technological advances, gives concern as to possible impairment. The machine is currently held in the financial statements at £80,000. It is estimated that the machine could be sold for scrap for £50,000. Its value in use has been calculated at £110,000. What value should the asset be carried at in the financial statements?

Impairment occurs when the recoverable amount is less than the carrying amount.

The recoverable amount is the higher of an asset's net selling price and its value in use. In this illustration the recoverable amount is £110,000, (i.e. the higher of value in use and net selling price).

The recoverable amount is greater than the carrying amount of £80,000 and therefore no impairment has arisen. The asset will continue to be carried in the financial statements at £80,000.

Example 2

Suppose the asset in Example 1 had a value in use of £40,000. What value should the asset be carried at now in the financial statements?

The recoverable amount is now £50,000 – that is the higher of net selling price (£50,000) and value in use (£40,000).

The recoverable amount is now less than the carrying amount and consequently the carrying amount requires to be reduced to the recoverable amount:

	£
Carrying amount	80,000
Recoverable amount	50,000
Impairment loss	30,000

The new carrying amount of the asset will be £50,000 (£80,000 – 30,000).

Progress Point 3.6

Sherton plc purchased a non-current asset for £200,000 in January 2007. Sherton depreciates non-current assets at 15% using the straight line method with a nil residual value. A full year's depreciation is charged in the year of acquisition. At 31 December 2009 the net selling price of the asset is £98,000 and the value in use is estimated at £85,000.

Required

Has an impairment occurred and, if so, how much?

Solution

The net book value (carrying amount) of the asset at 31 December 2009 is:

Cost		£200,000
Less: accumulated depn		
Y/e 31/12/07 (15% x £200,000)	£30,000	
Y/e 31/12/08 (15% x £200,000)	30,000	
Y/e 31/12/09 (15% x £200,000)	30,000	
		£90,000
Net book value at 31/12/09		£110,000

BASIC

INTERMEDIATE

ADVANCED

Recoverable amount is higher of:

Net selling price	£98,000	
and		
Value in use	£85,000	
i.e. Net selling price		£98,000

Revised carrying amount is lower of:

Carrying amount	£110,000	
and		
Recoverable amount	£98,000	
i.e. Recoverable amount		£98,000

As the recoverable amount is £98,000, there has been an impairment of £12,000 (i.e. carrying amount of £110,000 less £98,000).

Accounting for an impairment loss

An impairment loss should be recognised immediately as an expense in the income statement unless it relates to a revalued asset where the value changes are recognised as a revaluation decrease.

If the impaired asset has been revalued, the impairment loss should be treated as a new revaluation. If the asset is at cost the impairment loss is additional depreciation.

The corresponding credit entries depend on how the amount at which the asset is carried is determined. If the asset is carried on a historical cost basis, the impairment loss should be included within accumulated depreciation. If the asset is carried at market value, the impairment loss should be included within the revalued carrying amount.

After an impairment loss has been recognised, the depreciation charge for the asset should be adjusted to allocate the revised carrying amount, net of any expected residual value, over its remaining useful life.

Cash generating units

Wherever possible, individual non-current assets should be tested for impairment. In practice, however, it is rare to be able to identify cash flows arising from a single asset. Often, several assets are interrelated in their usage in a way that makes it impossible to attribute cash inflows to each individual asset. In such cases, cash flows can be seen to be attributable to a collection of assets. Such a collection of assets is called a cash generating unit (CGU) and is defined as being the smallest identifiable group of assets that generates cash inflows that are largely independent of the cash inflows from other assets or groups of assets.

An example will help to illustrate CGUs.

Example

A company has a three-stage production process:

1. acquisition of raw materials
2. conversion of materials into components
3. assembly of components into finished products.

The company also sells raw materials, but there is no market for components.

The first stage (acquisition of raw materials) is independent of the second and third stages. Moreover, there is an external market for the raw materials and this price can be used for the internal transfers. It is therefore a CGU.

The second stage is dependent upon the products being sold at the third stage because there is no market for the components. The second- and third-stage processes should therefore be combined into a single CGU.

The company has two CGUs: stage 1, and stages 2 and 3 combined. Once the CGU has been identified, the recoverable amount should be calculated and compared with the carrying amount.

Allocation of impairment losses

Where an impairment loss arises, the loss should ideally be set against the specific asset to which it relates. Where the loss cannot be identified as relating to a specific asset, it should be apportioned within the CGU to reduce the most subjective assets first, as follows:

- first, to reduce any goodwill within the CGU
- then, to the other assets of the unit on a prorata basis based on the carrying amount of each asset in the unit
- however, no individual asset should be reduced below the higher of
  - its net selling price
  - its value in use
  - zero.

The amount of impairment loss that would otherwise have been allocated to the asset should be allocated to the other assets of the unit on a pro rata basis. The effect of this is to:

- eliminate goodwill, but
- to ensure that the carrying amount of any individual asset is not reduced to the extent that it produces an amount not economically relevant to that asset.

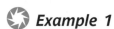 ## *Example 1*

An impairment review has revealed that a CGU has a value in use of £25 million and a net realisable value of £23 million.

The carrying values of the net assets comprising the CGU are as follows:

	£000
Goodwill	5,000
Property, plant and equipment	18,000
Net current assets	4,000
	27,000

The review also indicated that an item of plant (included within the figure of £18 million) with a carrying value of £1 million had been severely damaged and was virtually worthless. There was no other evidence of obvious impairment to specific assets.

Calculate the impairment loss and show how it should be dealt with in the accounts.

The impairment loss is the difference between the recoverable amount and the carrying amount.

The recoverable amount is the higher of the net selling price and value in use:

Value in use (£25 million) > net selling price (£23 million)
∴ recoverable amount is (value in use) £25 million

The recoverable amount (£25 million) is less than the carrying amount (£27 million), therefore impairment exists:

	£000
Carrying value	27,000
Recoverable amount	25,000
Impairment loss	2,000

The impairment loss should be allocated as follows:

- first, against the item of plant specifically identified as being worthless, which has a carrying value of £1 million
- then against the goodwill.

	Carrying value £000	Impairment £000	Revised carrying value £000
Goodwill	5,000	(1,000)	4,000
Property, plant and equipment	18,000	(1,000)	17,000
Net current assets	4,000		4,000
	27,000	(2,000)	25,000

 ## Example 2

A CGU has a carrying value of £190 million. An impairment review shows that the recoverable amount is £130 million and that the intangible assets have a net realisable value of £20 million.

The assets making up the CGU are as follows:

	£m
Goodwill	25
Intangible assets	45
Tangible assets	120
	190

Calculate the impairment loss and show how this would be allocated.

	£m
Carrying value	190
Recoverable amount	130
Impairment loss	60

	Carrying value £m	Impairment £m	Revised carrying value £m
Goodwill	25	(25)	–
Intangible asset	45	(9.5)	35.5
Tangible assets	120	(25.5)	94.5
	190	(60)	130

The impairment loss of £60m is allocated:

- first to goodwill – £25m
- then to the other assets of the unit on a pro rata basis, based on the carrying amount of each asset in the unit.

Intangible assets $\dfrac{45}{(120 + 45)} \times (60 - 25) = 9.5m$

Tangible assets $\dfrac{120}{(120 + 45)} \times 35 = 25.5m$

International perspective

The requirements of the UK's FRS 11 are very similar to those of IAS 36, and compliance with the FRS will ensure conformity with IAS 36 in all material respects. However, under FRS 11 an impairment loss is written off in the order:

- first to goodwill
- then to intangible assets, and
- finally to tangible fixed assets.

In IAS 36, intangible and tangible assets are grouped together.

Under FRS 11, which aims to write down the assets with the most subjective valuations first, no intangible asset with a readily ascertainable market value should be written down below its net realisable value.

Continuing with Example 2, this gives:

	Carrying value £m	Impairment £m	Revised carrying value £m
Goodwill	25	(25)	–
Intangible asset	45	(25)	20
Tangible assets	120	(10)	110
	190	(60)	130

The impairment loss of £60m is allocated:

- first to goodwill
- then to intangible assets – but only so as to reduce them to their net realisable value
- then the remainder to the tangible fixed assets.

That is, the most subjective valuation first, then the next subjective, then, finally, the tangible fixed assets.

Impairment of goodwill

Goodwill is the amount that is left over after applying valuation rules to identifiable assets and liabilities, and comparing this value with the acquisition cost. Goodwill cannot be identified separately so, by definition, does not generate cash flows independently from other assets or groups of assets. It follows that the recoverable amount of goodwill cannot be determined. Consequently, if there is an indication that goodwill may be impaired, the recoverable amount is determined for the cash generating unit (CGU) to which the goodwill belongs. This recoverable amount is then compared to the carrying amount of this CGU and any impairment loss is recognised.

The allocation of goodwill to CGUs

As the preceding paragraph explains, goodwill is not separately identifiable but instead forms an integral part of CGUs.

IAS 36 requires that the goodwill on acquisition should be allocated to each of the acquirer's CGUs, or group of CGUs, that are expected to benefit from the synergies of the business combination, irrespective of whether other assets of liabilities of the acquiree are assigned to those units or groups of units.

Each unit or group of units to which the goodwill is allocated should:

(a) represent the lowest level within an entity at which the goodwill is monitored for internal management purposes

(b) not be larger than a segment based on either the entity's primary or the entity's secondary reporting format determined in accordance with IAS 14 *Segment Reporting*.

Where goodwill cannot be allocated to individual CGUs:

- calculate any impairment of the assets (excluding goodwill) of individual CGUs
- identify the smallest group or groups of CGUs (which may be the whole company) to which goodwill can be allocated on a reasonable basis (the 'larger' CGU), and
- then compare the recoverable amount of the larger CGU to its carrying amount (including the carrying amount of allocated goodwill) and recognise any impairment loss.

Example

Robren pays £1,000,000 for the net assets of Henon, which at acquisition has a fair value of £900,000. Henon has two identifiable CGUs and their relative net asset values are £500,000 for CGU A and £400,000 for CGU B. The relative benefits expected from the CGUs are assumed to be in proportion to their net asset values.

The goodwill of £100,000 (£1,000,000 – £900,000) would be allocated as follows:

CGU A $\frac{500,000}{900,000}$ ×   £100,000   =   55,555

CGU B $\frac{400,000}{900,000}$ ×   £100,000   =   44,445

The carrying values of the two CGU's would therefore be the net asset value together with the appropriate allocation of the goodwill on acquisition. That is:

CGU A   £500,000   +   £55,555   =   £555,555
CGU B   £400,000   +   £44,445   =   £444,445

Progress Point 3.7

Malafed plc operates three department stores, which it purchased from a competitor several years ago when goodwill of £2m arose. Each department store is a separate cash generating unit (CGU).

As part of the company's annual impairment review process, the following information at 31 March 2009 is available.

	Store 1 £m	Store 2 £m	Store 3 £m
Carrying amount	4.1	5.6	3.8
Net selling price	3.8	6.0	2.9
Value in use	4.3	5.8	3.2

It has not been possible to allocate goodwill to individual stores. The three stores form the smallest CGU to which the goodwill can be allocated and management monitors goodwill at this combined level.

The recoverable amount of the three stores together is estimated at £13.8m.

Required

What impairments arise?

Solution

As the goodwill cannot be directly allocated, impairment of each individual store (CGU) is calculated excluding goodwill.

	Store 1 £m	Store 2 £m	Store 3 £m
Carrying amount	4.1	5.6	3.8
Recoverable amount	4.3	6.0	3.2
(Higher of net selling price and value-in-use)			
Impairment	–	–	(0.6)

The smallest group of CGUs to which goodwill can be allocated on a reasonable basis is the three stores combined (i.e. the larger CGU).

	£m
Carrying amount (£4.1m + £5.6m + £3.8m)	13.5
Less: impairment	(0.6)
Add: goodwill	2.0
Total carrying amount	14.9
Recoverable amount of three stores combined	13.8
Impairment	1.1

Consequently, goodwill should be reduced by £1.1m (i.e. to £0.9m).

Testing for impairment

IAS 36 requires that goodwill be tested for impairment annually. A cash generating unit to which goodwill has been allocated shall be tested for impairment at least annually by comparing the carrying amount of the unit, including the goodwill, with the recoverable amount of the unit.

If the recoverable amount of the unit exceeds the carrying amount of the unit, the unit and the goodwill allocated to that unit is not impaired.

If the carrying amount of the unit exceeds the recoverable amount of the unit, the entity must recognise an impairment loss.

The impairment loss should be allocated to reduce the carrying amount of the assets of the unit in the following order: -

- first, to goodwill allocated to cash generating unit
- then to the other assets of the unit on a pro rata basis, based on the carrying amount of each asset in the unit.

The carrying amount of an asset should not be reduced below the *highest* of:

- its **fair value less costs** to sell (if determinable)
- its value in use (if determinable)
- zero.

The amount of the impairment loss that would otherwise have been allocated to the asset should be allocated to the other assets of the unit on a pro rata basis. The effect of this is to initially eliminate

BASIC

INTERMEDIATE

ADVANCED

goodwill, but then to ensure that the carrying amount of any individual asset is not reduced to the extent that any amount arrived at is not economically relevant to that asset.

✪ Example

Dupover has identified an indication of impairment and is conducting an impairment review.
Its summarised balance sheet is:

	£000
Goodwill	600
Property	820
Plant	730
Net current assets	265
	2,415
Share capital and reserves	2,415

The whole of the company is considered to be a cash generating unit.
The present value of the future cash flows is estimated at £1.2 million.
Assuming that the net current assets are at the lower of cost and net realisable value, and that the net realisable value of the property is £900,000, calculate the impairment loss and prepare a revised balance sheet for Dupover.

Carrying value	£2,415,000
Recoverable amount (present values)	£1,200,000
Impairment loss	£1,215,000

The impairment loss is allocated as follows:

	Carrying value £000	Impairment £000	Revised carrying value £000
Goodwill	600	(600)	–
Property	820	–	820
Plant	730	(615)	115
Net current assets	265	–	265
	2,415	(1,215)	1,200

The allocation of the loss has been made:

- first to goodwill – £600,000
- then the balance to plant – £615,000.

No allocation of the loss has been made against the property as it has a net realisable value higher than its carrying value.
Similarly, no allocation of the loss has been made against the net current assets as these are already being carried at the lower of cost and net realisable value.

Progress Point 3.8

Jackson Ltd acquired 100% of the ordinary share capital of James Ltd for £10 million on 1st January Year 1. This figure included £960,000 for goodwill. Jackson Ltd is preparing group accounts for the year to 31 December Year 5 and, due to a decline in the market conditions, has decided to carry out an impairment review of the fixed assets and goodwill of James Ltd.

James operates in two distinct business areas, which are largely independent, one is services to the oil industry and the other is the operation of a rail franchise. The following assets have been attributed to these activities as follows:

	Oil services £000	Rail franchise £000
Fixed assets:		
Tangible	10,000	6,900
Intangible	0	1,200

All assets are held at depreciated cost. The following items have still to be allocated:

- head office property with a net book value of £3,200,000; it is estimated that this can be split 60:40 between oil and rail
- goodwill – it is estimated that 75% of this relates to the rail franchise and the remainder to oil.

The directors estimate that the rail franchise has a net sales value of £7,500,000 and oil services a net sales value of £9,600,000.

The intangible asset in the rail franchise relates to the net book value of the operating licence associated with the franchise. The following pre-tax cash flows have been estimated for each CGU:

Year	Oil services £000	Rail franchise £000
6	3,000	4,200
7	2,800	3,400
8	2,800	3,400^
9	4,800*	

*   The rail franchise expires at the end of Year 9 and the oil services division will be wound up in Year 9. The pre-tax market rate of return for oil services is estimated at 15% and 20% for the rail franchise.

Required

 (i) Calculate the total net assets for each CGU.
 (ii) Calculate the value in use for each CGU.
 (iii) Calculate the impairment (if any) for each CGU.

▶

Solution

(i)   Total net assets:

	Oil services £000	Rail franchise £000
As allocated	10,000	8,100
Head office (60:40)	1,920	1,280
Goodwill (25:75)	240	720
Total net assets	12,160	10,100

(ii)   Value in use:

Workings

Oil services	Discount factor (15%)	Cash flow £000	PV £000
Year 6	0.870	3,000	2,610
Year 7	0.756	2,800	2,117
Year 8	0.658	2,800	1,842
Year 9	0.572	4,800	2,746
			9,315

Rail franchise	Discount factor (20%)	Cash flow £000	PV £000
Year 6	0.833	4,200	3,499
Year 7	0.694	3,400	2,360
Year 8	0.579	3,400	1,969
			7,828

(iii)   Impairment:

	Oil services £000	Rail franchise £000
Carrying amount of net assets	12,160	10,100
Net sales value	9,600	7,500
Value in use	9,315	7,828
Impairment (£12,160 – £9,600)	2,560	
Impairment (£10,100 – £7,828)		2,272

Progress Point 3.9

Using the same information as in Progress Point 3.8, show how the impairment of the assets would be recorded at 31 December Year 5.

Solution

There is no indication that any specific assets are impaired. The assets are held at cost, therefore losses go to the profit and loss account. The write-down should be treated as additional depreciation.

Oil services

The impairment loss of £2,560,000 would first be allocated to the goodwill (£240,000) and the balance to tangible fixed assets £2,320,000. Each tangible fixed asset would be written down by 19.46% (2,320/(10,000 + 1,920)):

	£000	£000
Dr Profit and loss account	2,560	
Cr Goodwill		240
Cr Tangible fixed assets: accum. depreciation		2,320
Being recognition of impairment loss.		

Rail franchise

The impairment should first be allocated to goodwill, then to the other assets. No distinction is made between intangible and tangible assets.

Dr Profit and loss account	2,272	
Cr Goodwill		720
Cr Intangible assets		199
Cr Tangible fixed assets: accum. depreciation		1,353
Being recognition of impairment loss.		

Working notes

Total impairment loss to be allocated:	£2,272,000
Less: allocated to goodwill	720,000
Remaining loss	1,552,000

Remaining loss allocated on a pro rata basis based on the carrying amount of each asset in the unit.

Carrying amount of:

Tangible fixed assets	
As given	6,900
Head office allocation	1,280
	8,180
Intangible fixed assets	1,200

Loss allocated as follows:

	NBV	%	Remaining loss allocated
Tangible fixed assets	8,180	87.2	1,353
Intangible fixed assets	1,200	12.8	199
	9,380	100.0	1,552

Reversal of an impairment loss

The objective of testing for impairment is to ensure that assets are carried at no more than their recoverable amount in the financial statements. It may be the case, however, that the indicators that gave cause for the original impairment tests – and subsequent impairment losses – now indicate that

Property, plant and equipment			
	Freehold land and buildings £m	Leashold property and improvements £m	Equipment and plant £m	Total £m
Cost				
At 1 January 2006	19.3	55.9	203.4	278.6
Additions	–	4.4	29.7	34.1
Acquisition of subsidiary	5.3	–	30.9	36.2
Disposals	(0.5)	(0.6)	(22.5)	(23.6)
Exchange differences	(0.1)	(0.7)	(4.0)	(4.8)
At 1 January 2007	24.0	59.0	237.5	320.5
Additions	0.1	3.1	36.8	40.0
Acquisition of subsidiaries	–	–	3.9	3.9
Disposals of subsidiaries/businesses	(0.1)	(1.5)	(46.5)	(48.1)
Disposals	(1.8)	(4.8)	(32.5)	(39.1)
Exchange differences	1.0	1.9	16.3	19.2
At 31 December 2007	**23.2**	**57.7**	**215.5**	**296.4**
Accumulated amortisation				
At 1 January 2006	0.7	24.6	150.8	176.1
Charge for the year	0.1	5.1	27.5	32.7
Disposals	(0.2)	(0.3)	(21.0)	(21.5)
Exchange differences	–	(0.3)	(3.1)	(3.4)
At 1 January 2007	0.6	29.1	154.2	183.9
Charge for the year	0.7	5.8	33.6	40.1
Disposals of subsidiaries/businesses	–	(1.7)	(38.2)	(39.9)
Disposals	(0.1)	(4.1)	(30.1)	(34.3)
Impairment	2.6	–	–	2.6
Exchange differences	0.2	1.0	10.7	11.9
At 31 December 2007	**4.0**	**30.1**	**130.2**	**164.3**
Net carrying amount				
At 31 December 2007	**19.2**	**27.6**	**85.3**	**132.1**
At 31 December 2006	23.4	29.9	83.3	136.6

The impairment of £2.6 million in the table above related to buildings previously occupied by the graphic services business in Portugal prior to the disposal of this business. The disposals are described further in Note 35.

Equipment and plant included assets held under finance leases with a net book value of £3.4 million (2006: £5.2 million). Additions to equipment and plant during the year amounting to £4.7 million (2006: £3.1 million) were financed by new finance leases.

Figure 3.4 Logica: property, plant and equipment

As this extract from Logica's property, plant and equipment disclosure note shows (Figure 3.4), there was an impairment of £2.6 million in the year to 31 December 2007. Details are given with the PPE note as well as a further explanation in note 35.

Summary

As with other assets, intangible assets are expected to bring future benefits to the enterprise. Internally generated intangible assets such as employee skills and product design can bring such benefits to the enterprise. The difficulties in quantifying the future benefits – and indeed claiming rights to the benefits – however, prevents them from being classified as fixed assets under the Framework's definition. Research expenditure must be written off as incurred, however under certain circumstances, internally generated development expenditure must be capitalised as an intangible asset.

The IAS 38 definition of intangible assets excludes goodwill. Intangible assets are classified as having indefinite lives or finite lives. Intangible assets with finite lives should be amortised over that life. Intangible assets with indefinite lives should not be amortised but should be assessed for impairment in accordance with IAS 36.

Internally generated goodwill should not be capitalised. Purchased goodwill should be capitalised and not amortised. Instead it should be tested for impairment at least annually in accordance with IAS 36.

The objective of IAS 36 *Impairment of Assets* is to ensure that assets are carried at no more than their recoverable amount. The recoverable amount of an asset is the higher of the net selling price or the asset's value in use.

The accounting treatment of goodwill and intangibles has been – and continues to be – the subject of great debate. The next section considers what problems practitioners come up against in practice and some of the other accounting methodologies put forward for dealing with these issues over the years.

Section 3: Advanced Aspects

This section looks in more detail at the measurement and classification issues faced in accounting for intangible assets, the problems surrounding internally generated intangible assets and, in particular, the important distinction and differences between capitalised research and development expenditure, and internally generated goodwill. It will examine in more detail some of the accounting issues and dilemmas arising from intangible assets and goodwill.

3.10 Research and development: problems in practice

In an ideal world it would theoretically be possible to clearly distinguish between the research and development stages of particular projects; to accurately quantify the costs attributable to each stage and therefore the amounts to be capitalised; to accurately determine the future benefits; and to accurately forecast the related pattern of benefits expected to flow from the capitalised expenditure.

The reality of the situation could not be more different.

In practice, the first hurdle of uncertainty to overcome is in respect of the viability of the project itself. Inventors, developers and researchers tend to be notoriously optimistic about their ideas. By their very nature, these individuals are enthusiastic about their projects and often have no real idea as to what the ultimate development costs are likely to be. They are not accountants nor do they understand fully the information that accountants require. Furthermore, accountants are not inventors and consequently have to rely on inventors' assertions for estimates, timescales and future expected benefits. There is therefore the potential for a gulf to develop between the quality of information required by accountants to prepare meaningful figures, and the quality of the information provided by the developers.

Whenever an accountant is faced with uncertainties, a prudent approach needs to be adopted. This can result in those costs attributable to and classified as research costs being expensed for longer into the project than the benefit of hindsight would more accurately determine. This means that the development project will probably be approaching completion before future development costs can be estimated reliably.

Once the development project has been completed, the next problem is in determining whether sales of the product will be profitable. In many cases, the product is likely to be highly innovative and consequently there will not be a great deal of market data available to assess its profitability. In addition, it is possible that similar products have been developed at the same time, spelling potential competition in the market. As the development in computers has demonstrated, high-technology products command a high price for only a relatively short period of time, as competitive firms develop their own technology and drive the market price down.

Given these uncertainties, the unambiguous, prudent approach would be to write off all research and development expenditure as it occurred. This would remove all doubt as to its accuracy and correctness of classification within the financial statements. This approach could also be potentially very misleading. As has been pointed out, such development expenditure can meet the Framework's definition of an asset and therefore to not be classified as an asset can be very misleading indeed.

The difference between expensing such costs and capitalising them may mean the difference between losses and profits, and an insolvent balance sheet and a solvent balance sheet. This potential to vary reported figures adds a further problem for the reporting accountant. As noted above, the accountant may have to rely very heavily on the representations made by the developers of products in his assessment of the appropriate accounting treatment to be adopted. Desperate times may result in desperate measures and, unfortunately, projects may be credited with greater probabilities of success than they should be.

Do the requirements of the standard in relation to research and development expenditure satisfy user needs? As ever, the answer to this depends on the user. The detailed disclosure requirements of IAS 38 in relation to R&D are comprehensive and if adequate detail is provided then there ought to be sufficient information to enable a wide range of users to make economic decisions. From an enterprise's perspective, however, it perhaps, more importantly, allows it to present a more accurate statement of affairs – and a more realistic reflection of its activities.

3.11 Internally generated goodwill vs purchased goodwill: a critical appraisal

IAS 38 prohibits the recognition of internally generated goodwill. Purchased goodwill is dealt with under IFRS 3, which states that it must not be amortised but instead requires to be subject to an annual impairment review.

It is worth considering what purchased goodwill actually represents. IFRS 3 defines goodwill as 'future economic benefits arising from assets that are not capable of being individually identified and separately recognised'. Purchased goodwill is therefore the amount paid for these future economic benefits.

As far as the acquiring company is concerned, it will be acquiring, and indeed disclosing as an intangible asset, the purchased goodwill. As far as the acquiree company is concerned, this 'goodwill' is not something that has simply arisen as a result of its sale. The goodwill may have been in existence for a long time, the terms of the accounting standards prohibiting its recognition. What this gives rise to is effectively the same asset, but because of the terms of the IAS, the asset is unrecognised in one set of financial statements yet recognised in the other.

There is, as a consequence, an inconsistent treatment for the same 'asset' (i.e. the goodwill). While the reasons for not allowing the recognition of internally generated goodwill are numerous, nevertheless its non-recognition is undoubtedly leaving a very important asset off many companies' balance sheets – an asset that will be recognised only when a business combination occurs.

If the internally generated goodwill cannot be capitalised, in order to achieve consistency, any purchased goodwill could be written off immediately. By doing this, however, we are in exactly the same situation. Valuable information will not be being disclosed.

The IFRS 3 requirement not to amortise goodwill also makes the treatment of goodwill inconsistent with the treatment of other assets. Under IFRS 3, a charge is made to the income statement only when the goodwill becomes impaired. This 'balance sheet' approach concurs with the Framework's assertion that 'Expenses are recognised in the income statement when a decrease in future economic benefits related to a decrease in an asset has arisen.'

This balance sheet approach can itself be open to criticism. An income statement approach would suggest that the goodwill be written off over the period it is expected to produce benefits (i.e. it would be depreciated). Adopting a balance sheet approach to fixed assets would mean that, instead of depreciation being charged, the assets would be written off immediately after they come into use down to their residual values.

Adopting a balance sheet approach – and the IFRS 3 requirement not to amortise goodwill – means that the timing of any charge to the income statement will be incorrect. A charge to the income statement will be made when the goodwill becomes impaired (i.e. when its recoverable amount falls below its original cost). This effectively means that when profits are being generated, and the recoverable amount exceeds the carrying amount, no element of the original cost will be charged to the income statement. Conversely, as soon as the goodwill, having been tested for impairment, falls below the carrying amount, a charge will be made to the income statement to reflect the level of impairment. This treatment results in a charge being made not when profits are being made (and the goodwill being consumed) but instead when profits are not being made (and the goodwill has been consumed). The treatment is therefore in conflict with the matching principle.

Is there a solution?

From what appears to be, on first consideration, an impossible task, the solution to the problems of the inconsistency of treatment between internally generated goodwill, and purchased goodwill, and the subsequent problem of measurement after initial recognition, may actually be quite simple.

In arriving at the solution, the objectives of financial statements need to be considered. The objectives of financial statements are to provide information about a firm that is useful to a wide range of people making economic decisions. 'Useful information' is information on a company's financial position, performance and liquidity.

The constraints imposed by the standards on what information is presented within traditional financial statements results in the problems detailed above. What is required therefore is an extension to traditional financial statements to allow additional information to be presented in a manner that will remove the lack of comparability caused by the prohibition of capitalising internally generated goodwill and the subjective problem of its subsequent write-off.

A possible solution

Given the difficulty – indeed the impossibility – of arriving at a meaningful figure for goodwill in the traditional financial statements (i.e. profit and loss account and balance sheet), all goodwill should be written off immediately. Then, in a new separate statement, companies could summarise the current values of the individual assets and liabilities recognised in the balance sheet and, in addition, provide an estimate of the valuation of the business as a whole – perhaps based on its market capitalisation. In other words, companies could use the IFRS 3 definition of goodwill to actually try to disclose it – that goodwill figure being the difference between the market capitalisation and the current values of net assets.

The benefits of such an approach are numerous and varied. It removes the problem of distinguishing between purchased and self-generated goodwill, particularly over time. If an efficient market exists then a company's share price will reflect all information relevant to it. This will effectively discount the total goodwill. The fact that no distinction is made between purchased and self-generated goodwill is arguably not relevant. Indeed, a year-on-year comparison would show any changes and deeper investigation made at that point. This treatment also addresses the fungible nature of goodwill – that is, it is not a constant, the constituent 'parts' will vary and the level of purchased/self-generated goodwill will fluctuate over time.

More importantly, however, it addresses many of the issues arising in respect of providing useful information. At the moment there are two extremes: companies with inherent goodwill that is not being disclosed and companies with purchased goodwill that may or may not be carried at the correct amount. This treatment allows a greater level of analysis to be made and arguably discloses a greater wealth of information about a company. For example, if using market capitalisation as a benchmark results in a company displaying a high level of goodwill, this could be an indicator of high efficiency.

BASIC

INTERMEDIATE

ADVANCED

Changes over time could indicate improvements or highlight potential problems. Conversely, low levels of goodwill could be indicators of poor efficiency and under-utilisation of resources.

This is not a perfect solution to the goodwill issue. Depending on the size of the company, market capitalisation data may not be available. Indeed, for smaller companies whose shares are not actively traded, there will be no such data at all. The method of calculation would, however, be apparent and the resulting information presented would be no more misleading than that which is currently being disclosed by following existing standards' requirements.

3.12 Brand accounting

A brand is the registered trade mark of a particular product. Some examples of companies whose names are brands are Mercedes-Benz, Coca-Cola and Microsoft. Brand accounting refers to the practice of including, as separate fixed assets, the amount attributable to brands and including them with the fair values of other identifiable assets acquired.

Prior to IAS 38, brand accounting emerged for two main reasons.

First, if brand values were included with the fair values of other identifiable assets acquired, this would mean that the amount of the purchase price attributable to goodwill (i.e. the premium over the fair value of net assets) would be reduced:

Goodwill = purchase price – fair value of net assets acquired including brands

Reducing the goodwill figure had a two-fold effect:

1.   it reduced the charge to the income statement in respect of the amortisation of the goodwill, and
2.   there was no income statement charge in respect of the brand, as brands were not usually amortised.

Second, non-acquisitive companies that created self-generated brands argued that their balance sheets would be strengthened if they were permitted to include a valuation of these brands.

The IAS 38 treatment of brands is, however, very clear:

■   internally generated brands are not to be recognised as assets
■   brands acquired in a business combination are not considered to be separately identifiable assets, and are thus part of goodwill.

Conclusion

The current requirements of IAS 38 and IFRS 3 can result in valuable information being omitted from company balance sheets. The failure to recognise internally generated goodwill and other intangible assets means that the value of those assets is excluded from the traditional financial statements.

A solution to this problem has been put forward in the form of an extension to the traditional accounting statements to include an attempt at an objective goodwill calculation with reference to market capitalisation and valuations of current net assets in the balance sheet.

The provision of useful information to a wide range of users, to enable economic decisions to be made, is not being achieved by following the current standards' requirements. As historical analysis shows, over the years firms have been aware of the values of their intangible assets. Brand accounting developed as a mechanism to detach the value of brands from goodwill, and hence strengthen balance sheets and reduce charges to the income statement. Expect further revision to these standards.

Chapter summary

IAS 38 *Intangible Assets*

- Intangible assets should be recognised where it is:
  - (i) probable that future economic benefits will flow to the enterprise, and
  - (ii) cost can be measured reliably.
- All research costs should be charged as expenses.
- Development costs are capitalised only after the technical and commercial feasibility of the asset for sale or use has been established.
- Costs treated as expenses cannot subsequently be capitalised.
- Brands, mastheads, publishing titles, customer lists and items similar in substance that are internally generated should not be recognised as assets.
- Internally generated goodwill must not be capitalised.
- Initial measurement should be at cost.
- Subsequently, IAS 38 permits two accounting models:
  - cost model – intangible assets should be carried at cost less any amortisation and impairment losses
  - revaluation model – intangible assets for which there is an active market can be carried at fair value.
- Revaluation increases are credited directly to reserves unless reversing a previous charge to income.
- Decreases in valuation should be charged to income unless reversing a previous credit to reserves.
- Intangible assets are classified as having a:
  - (i) finite life – a limited period of benefit to the entity, or an
  - (ii) indefinite life – no foreseeable limit to the period over which the asset is expected to generate net cash inflows for the entity.
- Intangible assets with finite lives should be amortised over the life of the asset.
  - the amortisation period and amortisation method should be reviewed at least annually
  - the asset should also be assessed for impairment in accordance with IAS 36.
- An intangible asset with an indefinite useful life should not be amortised:
  - a review of the asset's useful life should be carried out annually
  - the asset should also be assessed for impairment in accordance with IAS 36.

IAS 36 *Impairment of Assets*

- Enterprises are required to check at each balance sheet date whether there are any indications of impairment.
- If an indication, external or internal, of impairment exists, the assets recoverable amount must be calculated.
- The recoverable amounts of the following types of intangible assets should be measured annually:
  - an intangible asset with an indefinite useful life
  - an intangible asset not yet available for use
  - goodwill acquired in a business combination.
- The recoverable amount should be determined for the individual asset if possible.
- If it is not possible to determine the recoverable amount for the individual asset, the recoverable amount for the asset's cash generating unit (CGU) should be determined.
- An impairment loss should be recognised whenever recoverable amount is below carrying amount.

- The impairment loss should be recognised immediately as an expense in the income statement unless it relates to a revalued asset where the value changes are recognised as a revaluation decrease.
- Where an impairment loss arises, the loss should ideally be set against the specific asset to which it relates.
- Where the loss cannot be identified as relating to a specific asset, it should be allocated to reduce the carrying amount of the assets of the CGU in the following order:
  - first to reduce any goodwill within the CGU
  - then, to the other assets of the unit on a pro rata basis, based on the carrying amount of each asset in the unit.
- The carrying amount of an asset should not be reduced below the highest of:
  - its fair value less costs to sell
  - its value in use
  - zero.
- If the preceding rule is applied, further allocation of the impairment loss is made pro rata to the other assets of the unit.
- Impairment losses should be reversed under certain circumstances. Enterprises should assess at each balance sheet date whether there is an indication that an impairment loss may have decreased. If so, the recoverable amount should be calculated.
- The increased carrying amount due to reversal should not be more than the depreciated historical cost would have been had the impairment not been recognised.
- Reversal of an impairment loss is recognised as income in the income statement unless the asset is carried at a revalued amount, in which case it should be treated as a revaluation increase.
- Reversal of an impairment loss for goodwill is prohibited.

🔑 Key terms for review

Definitions can be found in the glossary at the end of the book.

Asset	*Carrying amount*
Intangible asset	*Costs of disposal*
Research	*Value in use*
Development	*Impairment loss*
Cost	*Recoverable amount*
Fair value (*of an asset*)	*Cash generating unit*
Amortisation	*Fair value less costs to sell*
Useful life	

❓ Review questions

1. In connection with IAS 38 *Intangible Assets*:
   (a) distinguish between *research* expenditure and *development* expenditure
   (b) explain the accounting treatment required by IAS 38 in relation to each of these types of expenditure.
2. Give some examples of intangible assets that are unlikely to be included in financial statements, and the reason for their exclusion.
3. What is goodwill, and how does it arise?
4. Explain the requirements of IFRS 3 in relation to goodwill.
5. Define the term *impairment loss*.
6. List the main indications which would suggest that an asset might be impaired.

7. Which assets must always be tested for impairment even though there are no indications that impairment has occurred?

8. What is the *recoverable amount* of an asset?

 # Exercises

1. Level II

The following information relates to Entrepreneurial Enterprises plc.

(i) Purchased a brand in 1992 for £2 million. The directors believe the brand is now worth £7 million.

(ii) Acquired a patent in January 2004, with ten years left to run, for £350,000.

(iii) Bought a fishing quota to catch 1,000 tonnes of fish for £1,000 per tonne on 1 January 2009. The market value for the quota, for which there is an active market, was £1,400 per tonne on 31 December 2009.

(iv) Acquired a bus operating licence on 30 June 2009 to operate routes for the next eight years. The initial price paid was £480,000. A further £120,000 is payable on 1 January 2010. In addition, the company directors and senior management spent time (costed at £80,000) in developing the bid.

(v) A major advertising campaign was carried out in the autumn of 2009. The directors believe the main benefits of this will arise in 2010.

(vi) The accounting policy of the company in respect of intangible assets is as follows.

    (a) Amortisation:

        On a straight line basis over:

Quota	20 years
Brands	20 years
Patents, licences, etc.	remaining legal life when acquired

    (b) Valuation:

        Intangible assets for which there is an active market are revalued annually.

Required

Explain how each of the above items should be dealt with in the accounts of Entrepreneurial Enterprises plc for the year to 31 December 2009, and prepare the journal entries to show the adjustments for each of the items in preparing the accounts to 31 December 2009.

2. Level II

During the course of a year Venture Forth Ltd incurred expenditure on many research and development activities. Details of two of them are given below.

Project 3

To develop a new compound in view of the anticipated shortage of raw material currently being used in one of the company's processes. Sufficient progress has been made to suggest that the new company can be produced at a cost comparable to that of the existing raw material.

Project 4

To improve the yield of an important manufacturing operation of the company. At present, material input with a cost of £100,000 p.a. becomes contaminated in the operation and half is wasted. Sufficient progress has been made for the scientists to predict an improvement so that only 20% will be wasted.

The directors of Venture Forth Ltd consider that both projects will be successful. In addition, the company has enough finances to complete both projects and enough capacity to see both projects through to a successful conclusion.

Costs incurred during the year were:

Project	3	4
	£	£
Staff salaries	5,000	10,000
Overheads (direct)	6,000	12,000
Plant at cost (life 10 years)	10,000	20,000

Required

In relation to IAS 38 *Intangible Assets*,

(a)   define
   (i)   research, and
   (ii)   development
(b)   say under what circumstances it would be appropriate to defer development expenditure to future periods
(c)   show how the expenditure on Projects 3 and 4 would be dealt with in the balance sheet and profit and loss account in accordance with IAS 38 *Intangible Assets*.

3.   Level II

Wyse Associates Limited has recently embarked on several projects designed to expand its business in the future. During the year to 30 June 2009, the following information is available regarding two of the projects.

Project A

Cost of £80,000 was incurred in substantially improving an existing product with a view to making it safer and with fewer side effects. Tests were still ongoing at 30 June, but it was hoped to market the product in time for Christmas 2009. In addition to the above £80,000, a special analysis machine has been purchased costing £50,000, which has a useful life of four years with a residual value of £10,000. This will be used to carry out a range of research activities over its useful life.

Project B

The company has spent £60,000 investigating possible alternative raw materials with similar properties that it could use instead of asbestos. It also purchased a machine to assist in analysing the properties of various alternative materials, for £30,000. It is the company's intention to spend another two years researching into this field. At the end of this time, if the search for an alternative to asbestos has not proved fruitful, it will research into making asbestos safer to use.

Required

Discuss how the expenditure on Projects A and B would be dealt with in the company's accounts for the year to 30 June 2009, and justify your decisions.

4. Level II

Montezemolo Engineering produces highly sensitive thermostatic switchgear for use in aeronautic and satellite production. As chief accountant at Montezemolo, you have been given the following information by the director of research in respect of the year ended 30 September 2009.

Project F550

This project commenced on 1 October 2008. By December 2008, the viability of the project was confirmed and it was agreed that the final product would be produced for sale. Costs incurred to 30 September 2009 amounted to £200,000, of which 25% relate to research expenditure and 75% to development expenditure.

   Additional further costs to complete the development are £350,000 and these will be incurred in the year to 30 September 2010. The first sales are expected on 1 October 2010.

It was necessary to purchase a highly specialised electronic analyser, which was to be used initially to test production prototypes, then, when production commences, the analyser will be used to ensure the correct operation of the completed thermostatic switchgear. Given the highly specialist nature of the analyser it would be used only on Project F550. The analyser was purchased on 1 January 2009 at a cost of £2,500,000, has an estimated useful life of six years and a forecast residual value of £100,000. Montezemolo Engineering charges a full year's depreciation in the year of purchase.

The board of directors considers that this project will be similar to the other projects the company undertakes and is confident of a successful outcome. Sales forecasts have been prepared following completion as shown:

	£000
Year to 30 September 2011	1,000
Year to 30 September 2012	1,000
Year to 30 September 2013	1,000
Year to 30 September 2014	1,000

It is estimated that the final product would have a sales life of four years.

The company has sufficient finance to complete the development and enough capacity to produce the new product.

Required

Show how the expenditure on Project F550 would be dealt with in the profit and loss account and balance sheet of Montezemolo Engineering for each of the years ending 30 September 2009 to 30 September 2014 inclusive. Extract entries only are required.

5. Level II

Main Enterprises Ltd ('Main') is a farm management company operating in central Scotland. An innovative management approach by the directors has seen the diversification of the business into a number of new areas.

The following information is available in respect of the year ended 31 December 2009.

1. Main purchased a suckler cow quota for 100 cows for £250 per cow on 1 January 2009. There is an active market for suckler cow quotas, which must be owned to enable an application for subsidy income to be made. On 31 December 2009, the market value of the quota was £300 per cow.
2. On 1 April 2006, Main acquired an operator's licence for a fleet of 20 heavy goods vehicles to set up a haulage division. Main had rented out several of its farm sheds to manufacturing companies and it had identified a further source of revenue by offering a haulage service to the tenants. The price paid for the licence, which is for five years, was £3,000 per vehicle. In addition to the initial price, Main spends £4,000 each year advertising the haulage division. Main received the invoice for the year ended 31 December 2009 from the advertising agency in January 2010.
3. On 1 July 2007, Main purchased for £28,000 shooting rights which entitle the company to seven years' shooting on a nearby estate. The managing director uses this primarily for corporate entertaining. The rights are non-transferable during the seven-year period and therefore there is no active market.
4. During the year to 31 December 2009, Main began the development of a new type of organic crop spray. The costs incurred on this project in the year amounted to £40,000. The book-keeper, who was unsure how to classify this expenditure, has posted it to a suspense account. The research manager believes that the product will be both technically feasible and commercially viable. However, the product is still at an early stage and it is not certain how long it will be before it can be marketed.

    The accounting policy of the company in respect of intangible assets is:
    - intangible assets with an active market are revalued on an annual basis
    - intangible assets are amortised on a straight line basis over 20 years or their estimated useful lives, whichever is the lower, on a monthly basis.

Required

(a) Explain how each of the items 1 to 4 should be dealt with in the accounts of Main for the year ended 31 December 2009, and prepare the journal entries required.

(b) Prepare the disclosure note in respect of 'intangible assets' for inclusion in Main's financial statements for the year ended 31 December 2009.

6. Level II

Bartpart plc has 800 hectares of agricultural land among its fixed assets at cost of £4,400,000 as at 30 June 2009.

Due to the general downturn in the agricultural sector, the directors have carried out an impairment review.

The land has been rented out at an annual rent of £400 per hectare with five yearly rental reviews. The rent has recently been renegotiated for the five years commencing 1 July 2009 at an annual rent of £350 per hectare.

Agricultural valuers have estimated that the land would realise £4,000 per hectare on a sale at 1 July 2009.

The required rate of return for Bartpart plc is 7%.

Required

Advise the directors if an impairment has occurred and, if so, provide the accounting entry required to reflect the impairment in the accounts for the year to 30 June 2009.

Note: land is assumed to have an indefinite life. The rental income should also be indefinite.

7. Level III

CMG Exporting Ltd revalued a tangible fixed asset from net book value £1m (cost £2m, depreciation £1m) to £2.5m on 31 December 2006. The asset's remaining useful life is ten years from the date of revaluation. It is company policy to make reserve transfers annually in respect of the difference between the depreciation charge on revalued and historical cost amounts. Due to a downturn in economic conditions, the asset suffered an impairment loss of £1.15m at 31 December 2009.

Required

How should the above be treated in the accounts for the four years from 31 December 2006 to 31 December 2009?

8. Level III

Elimax plc has recently been acquired by a new owner, who has installed a new management team. Elimax has faced difficult trading activities in the past few years and the new finance director has doubts about the value of some of the assets on the balance sheet. Elimax consists of two divisions, which currently employ the following net assets:

	Estate agency division £000	Public relations division £000
Fixed assets		
Tangible	16,750	15,900
Intangible	400	–
Goodwill	–	620
	17,150	16,520

In addition the company has central tangible fixed assets of £4,500,000. These are estimated to be equally related to the two divisions. None of the assets has been revalued in the past.

The intangible asset of the estate agency division relates to the cost of a trade mark acquired from a competitor several years ago. It is estimated that the trade mark has a net selling price of £380,000.

Both divisions have suffered from under-investment in recent years.

The net fair value of the estate agency division is estimated to be £13,500,000, and £12,000,000 for the public relations division.

Budgeted pre-tax cash flows for the next four years are as follows:

	Estate agency £000	Public relations £000
Year 1	3,800	4,700
Year 2	3,900	4,750
Year 3	5,500	5,300
Year 4	5,200	6,000

The required rate of return is 14% for both divisions. The significant increases in cash flow will arise from the impact of the new management team. There will be no significant cash flows from the assets employed in each division after Year 4.

Required

(a) Calculate the extent of any impairment in either division.
(b) Prepare a schedule of adjustments to the net assets of each division.

Discount factors at 14% are:

Year	Factor
1	0.877
2	0.769
3	0.675
4	0.592

9. Level II

Ernon plc has identified an indicated of impairment and is conducting an impairment review. Its summarised balance sheet at 31 March 2009 is as follows:

	£000
Goodwill	600
Property	820
Plant and equipment	730
Net current assets	265
	£2,415
Share capital and reserves	£2,415

The whole of the company is considered to be a single cash generating unit (CGU). The net current assets have been valued at the lower of cost and net realisable value, and the net realisable value of the property is £900,000. The plant and equipment is estimated to have a sale value of £115,000. The value in use is estimated to be £1.4 million.

Required

Calculate whether an impairment loss has occurred and, if so, prepare a revised balance sheet for Ernon plc 31 March 2009. Explain your workings fully.

10. Level II

Shankers Ltd has carried out an impairment review of its telecommunications division. The assets allocated to the division were as follows:

	£000
Property, plant and equipment	15,100
Intangible assets	2,300
Goodwill	1,100
	£18,500

The net selling price has been estimated at £14m and value in use calculated at £14.4m.

Required

Compare the allocation of any impairment loss in the telecommunications division of Shankers Ltd under IAS 36 with that under FRS 11.

11. Level II

JAJ Industries plc operates a number of businesses. Evidence suggests that one of these may have impaired assets. The following information has been obtained:

CGU	Construction £m	Haulage £m	Maintenance £m
Carrying amount	3.1	2.6	1.8
Net selling price	2.5	2.1	2.0
Value in use	2.7	1.7	1.9

In addition to the carrying amount of the assets allocated to the above cash generating units there is goodwill of £2.3m. The goodwill relates to construction and haulage, but it is not possible to allocate it between the two. It is estimated that the combined recoverable amount of construction and haulage is £5.0m.

None of the assets has previously been revalued.

Required

Calculate, and prepare journal entries, for any impairment of:

(a) the individual cash generating units, and

(b) the goodwill relating to construction and haulage.

Further reading

FAS 86 *Accounting for the Costs of Computer Software to be Sold, Leased or Otherwise Marketed.* FASB Framework for the Presentation and Preparation of Financial Statements. IASB, 1989

IAS 36 *Impairment of Assets. IASB, 2009*

IAS 38 *Intangible Assets.* IASB, 2009

IFRS 3 *Business Combinations.* IASB, 2008

Logica plc: www.logica.co.uk

Leases

LEARNING OUTCOMES

After studying this chapter you should be able to:

- ☑ identify the main characteristics of leases and identify the different types of leases
- ☑ explain the advantages of capitalising leased assets
- ☑ identify the accounting issues involved in leasing assets
- ☑ demonstrate the accounting entries required in the books of the lessee
- ☑ demonstrate the accounting entries in the books of the lessor.

Introduction

The decision by companies to invest in new equipment can often be very complex. Once a company has identified a need for a particular asset there are a number of options open to the company on how to acquire the asset.

If the company has enough cash available then the asset could be bought for cash. If not, the company may obtain a bank loan to finance the purchase of the asset, or perhaps buy it on hire purchase. Another alternative is for the company to rent the asset for a period of time. Such rentals are commonly known as leases.

Section 1: Basic Principles

A lease is a contract between two parties: a *lessor* and a *lessee*. The lessor is the legal owner of the asset and the lessee rents the asset from the lessor. The lessor keeps the ownership of the asset and agrees to rent the asset to the lessee for an agreed period of time in return for a rental payment. Examples of assets that can be the subject of a lease agreement include motor vehicles, aeroplanes, ships, machines and computer equipment.

4.1 Why might a company choose to lease an asset?

There are several reasons why a company may choose to lease a particular asset rather than buy it and these include those discussed below.

It permits flexibility

An asset may be leased for a specific period of time. A company that needs a particular asset for a specific time period can lease the asset for that specific time period. This avoids the company having to buy the asset and then having to sell it at the end of its period of use. By tailoring the lease agreement to its specific needs, a company can have the use of the asset for the optimum length of time.

It avoids obsolescence

Many assets become obsolete in relatively short time periods. This problem is particularly relevant to computers and computer equipment. By leasing computer equipment rather than buying it, companies will have up-to-date equipment and can avoid the problem of outdated technology.

It gives tax advantages

Certain tax advantages are available when assets are leased rather than purchased. In the UK, for example, tax allowances granted in the year of purchase are 50% of the asset's cost and 25% per annum (on a reducing balance basis) thereafter. Lease rentals can attract 100% relief of payments made against tax.

It improves cash flow

Although a company may buy an asset for cash, such a decision very often would put a strain on the company's cash resources. Many companies would not have sufficient cash reserves to finance asset purchases this way. Indeed even if the purchase of the asset was financed by borrowing, there is usually a deposit to be paid. Leasing avoids the need for companies to find relatively large sums of cash either to buy the asset outright or for deposits, and so helps the cash position of the company.

> ## Progress Point 4.1
>
> Outline four different ways in which a business may obtain the use of an asset.
>
> ### Solution
>
> A business may obtain the use of an asset by: (i) outright purchase if it has cash funds available; (ii) purchase using a bank loan; (iii) hire purchase; or (iv) entering into a lease agreement whereby the asset is rented for a specific period of time.

4.2 The accounting issues involved

Where a company acquires assets outright, or through bank loans or hire purchase arrangements, then the assets belong to the company and are therefore disclosed on that company's balance sheet. Where assets are leased, then these assets belong to the lessor and their use is simply being granted to the lessee in return for a rental payment.

The accounting problems that arise with leases are in the definition of assets and what is disclosed in a company's financial statements.

As noted above, a lease is a rental and, as such, rental payments are expensed through the income statement. If, however, the terms of the lease agreement are of sufficient length and obligation such that it permits the lessee to use the item as if it had bought the item, then the financial statements will omit valuable information if the lease payments are simply expensed through the income statement.

The financial statements will not show that the company is using the particular asset, nor will they show that the company has an obligation to make future lease payments.

 Example:

Company A and Company B are firms producing the same manufactured product. The policy of Company A is to buy equipment, whereas the policy of Company B is to lease equipment. Company A borrows £50,000 from its bank to finance the purchase of a machine, while Company B leases the identical machine on a long-term lease.

The balance sheet of Company A will be as follows:

Company A Balance sheet			
Fixed assets: machine	£50,000	Loan	£50,000

Company B, because it is leasing the asset, and because the ownership of the asset will remain with Company A (the lessor), will not record any information regarding the leased asset on its balance sheet. There will be no evidence that Company B is using this particular asset, other than the fact that lease rentals are shown in the profit and loss account.

It could be argued that in order to provide users with information to help them make correct and meaningful decisions, Company B should disclose on its balance sheet the facts that:

- it is using this particular machine, and
- it has an obligation to make lease payments in the future.

If so, then a more informative balance sheet for Company B could be produced as follows:

Company B Balance sheet			
Leased assets	£50,000	Lease creditor	£50,000

By adopting this treatment a fairer comparison can be made between Company A and Company B. Indeed, unless such a treatment is adopted, any comparison between Company A and Company B using financial ratios – for example, return on capital employed (ROCE) – will be distorted. In addition, the liabilities of a company leasing the equipment will be understated.

4.3 Accounting for leases

We have seen in Chapter 2 that fixed assets have been defined as those assets that are intended for use by a company on a continuing basis, have a physical substance, and are held to be used in the production or supply of goods and services. Note that there is no reference to ownership.

It follows from this, that where a lease agreement allows the lessee company to use the item for most of its useful life, requires the lessee company to pay the full cost (possibly more than the purchase price of the item) and to look after the item as though it had been purchased by the lessee, then in terms of the *substance* of the transaction, it is clear that the lessee company would be in the same position in terms of deriving benefit from the usage of the asset, as if it actually *owned* the asset.

Moreover, the requirement to make lease payments greater than the normal purchase price of the asset means that the lessee company is effectively in the same economic position *as if* it had taken out a loan to purchase the asset at an agreed rate of interest.

In such circumstances, the economic substance of the transaction is that the lessee company has both:

- an asset, *and*
- a liability to make future payments.

However, the legal ownership, by virtue of the legal form of the lease agreement, remains with the lessor.

In order to take account of the substance of the leasing arrangement, rather than the legal form, it could be argued that the lessee company ought to record both the leased asset and the obligation to pay in its balance sheet. The lessor company will record the asset as sales revenue and as a debtor in its balance sheet.

This treatment will allow greater comparability between companies who purchase assets and those companies leasing identical assets. The balance sheets will show:

- the underlying assets in use by the lessee company (whether owned or not), and
- the liabilities associated with such leasing contracts.

The 'value' of the leased asset can be measured. The purchase price of the asset will be available and the lease payments will be quantified by reference to the lease agreement. Any lease payments made in excess of the purchase price of the asset will represent the cost of leasing the asset. This cost is effectively the same charge as a bank or other lender would impose in lending to finance the purchase of an asset – in other words, interest.

Given that such information is available within the financial statements, it seems reasonable to proceed on the basis that where a lease agreement essentially conveys all the risks and rewards of ownership of an asset to the lessee company, then from an accounting point of view, the asset should be treated as a 'legal purchase'. This would imply that the leased item would be included on the balance sheet of the lessee company as an asset, while the obligation to pay the lease rental would be recorded as a liability.

Progress Point 4.2

Explain why the substance of a leasing transaction rather than its legal form should determine the accounting treatment used to record it in the financial statements.

Solution

If the terms of a lease are such that the lessee has effective ownership of the asset then although outright ownership does not transfer, it is as if the lessee has acquired the asset. In such circumstances, by following the substance of the transaction it could be argued that valuable information is being disclosed by showing the leased item as an asset with a corresponding lease creditor (i.e. the financial statements will disclose the assets in use by the business together with details of its current and future lease obligations). If the legal form were adopted then no such asset would be shown and therefore it could be argued that valuable information is being omitted from the financial statements with regard to assets in use and future lease obligations.

Example

A machine is leased for a period of four years at a rate of £1,000 per year payable in advance. The machine could have been purchased outright for £3,486.

The machine is recorded in the financial statements as:

■   an asset (at cost) – £3,486
■   an obligation to pay – £3,486.

Over the period of the lease, the total lease payments will amount to £4,000 (4 × £1,000). The difference between these total lease payments (£4,000) and the cost of the machine (£3,486) is the interest charge of £514. This interest charge is essentially a charge for the deferred credit being extended by the company.

Each lease payment of £1,000 would consist of two elements:

1.   a capital element that will go towards reducing the lease obligation, and
2.   an interest element, charged to the profit and loss account, reflecting the finance charge payable on the outstanding lease obligation.

Allocating the interest

Having calculated the interest charge, this amount now requires to be allocated to the profit and loss account according to the matching principle. This would allocate the interest charge over the period being financed. One method of doing this is by the straight line method.

Straight line method

Continuing with the above example, the annual interest charge to the profit and loss account would be calculated as follows:

$$\frac{£514}{3 \text{ years}} = £171 \text{ per year}$$

Note that because the first lease payment is in advance then the number of periods being financed is only three, (i.e. the final lease payment will fall just after the end of the third period). Had payments been made in arrears then the number of periods financed would have equalled the number of payments.

The annual rentals would be apportioned as follows:

Period	Total rental £	Finance charge £	Capital repayment £
1	1,000	171	829
2	1,000	171	829
3	1,000	172	828
4	1,000	–	1,000
	4,000	514	3,486

Note that the total capital repayment corresponds to the originating lease obligation. The above transactions would be reflected in the financial statements as follows:

Profit and loss account	
Period	Finance charge £
1	171
2	171
3	172
4	–

Balance sheet		
Period	Lease obligation £	
1	2,657	(3,486 – 829) i.e. originating creditor less capital repayment
2	1,828	(2,657 – 829) b/f creditor less capital repayment
3	1,000	(1,828 – 828) b/f creditor less capital repayment
4	–	(1,000 – 1,000) b/f creditor less capital repayment

Sum of digits method

This is an alternative method of allocating the interest. The annual allocation of the interest charge is calculated by relating the remaining number of periods being financed to the total number of periods being financed.

As before, the number of periods being financed is three and the sum of the digits is therefore 6, i.e. (3 + 2 + 1).

The following formula can be used to establish the sum of the digits.

$$S = \frac{n\,(n + 1)}{2}$$

Where n = number of periods being financed.

The finance charge is found by applying the 'relevant digit' to the finance charge.

In this example the allocation would be:

Period	Relevant digit	Finance charge £	Workings
1	3/6	257	(3/6 x 514)
2	2/6	171	(2/6 x 514)
3	1/6	86	(1/6 x 514)
4	–	–	

Using the sum of digits method, the annual rentals of £1,000 would be apportioned as follows:

Period	Total rental £	Finance charge £	Capital repayment £
1	1,000	257	743
2	1,000	171	829
3	1,000	86	914
4	1,000	–	1,000
	4,000	514	3,486

Note again that the total capital repayment corresponds to the originating lease obligation, and these would be reflected in the financial statements as follows:

Profit and loss account	
Period	Finance charge £
1	257
2	171
3	86
4	–

Balance sheet		
Period	Lease obligation £	
1	2,743	(3,486 – 743) i.e. originating creditor less capital repayment
2	1,914	(2,743 – 829) b/f creditor less capital repayment
3	1,000	(1,914 – 914) b/f creditor less capital repayment
4	–	

Actuarial method

Another alternative allocation method that could be used is the actuarial method. The actuarial method allocates the interest charge to the accounting periods so as to produce a constant periodic rate of charge on the remaining balance of the lease obligation.

Continuing with the example:

 (i)   the cash price of our asset is £3,486
 (ii) this represents the present value at an implied interest rate of four annual rentals payable in advance, of £1,000
 (iii) the present value of the first rental is £1,000 (i.e. it is payable now)
 (iv) it follows that £2,486 (£3,486 – £1,000) = the present value at implied interest rate of three rentals of £1,000
 (v)   therefore 2,486/1,000 = 0.248 = present value at implied interest rate of three rentals of £1.00
 (vi) using present value of annuity of £1 tables, the interest rate is 10%.

The total interest charge of £514 will be allocated as follows:

Period	Capital sum at start of period £	Rental £	Capital sum during period £	Finance charge (10%) £	Capital sum at end of period £
1	3,486	1,000	2,486	249	2,735
2	2,735	1,000	1,735	174	1,909
3	1,909	1,000	909	91	1,000
4	1,000	1,000	–	–	–
				514	

The annual rentals can now be apportioned between a capital repayment and a finance charge, as follows:

Period	Total rental £	Finance charge £	Capital repayment £	
1	1,000	249	751	(£1,000 – £249)
2	1,000	174	826	(£1,000 – £174)
3	1,000	91	909	(£1,000 – £91)
4	1,000	–	1000	
	4,000	514	3,486	

Note that the total capital repayment corresponds to the originating lease obligation.

Profit and loss account	
Period	Finance charge
	£
1	249
2	174
3	91
4	Nil
	514

Balance sheet				
	Obligations under finance leases at start of year	– Capital repayment	=	Obligations under finance leases outstanding at end
	£	£		£
1	3,486	751		2,735
2	2,735	826		1,909
3	1,909	909		1,000
4	1,000	1,000		–

Discounting and present value

It is perhaps worth pausing at this point to consider further what is meant by present value. The IASB refers to discounting and present value in a number of standards, and therefore an understanding of present value calculations is necessary to fully understand the requirement of those standards.

The concept of present value is concerned with the fact that money has a 'time value'. In other words, an amount of money received today will be worth more than the same amount of money in, for example, a year's time. This is because it is possible to invest money and it will therefore grow. For example, if money can be invested at 10% p.a., each £1 invested will grow to become £1.10 in one year's time. If the money is invested for a further year, then it will become £1.21 in two year's time, and so on [£1.10 + (£1.10 × 10%)]. It can be said, therefore, that in present value terms, £1.21 to be received two years from now is worth £1.00 in today's terms (assuming a rate of interest of 10%).

The process of determining the present value of an amount to be received (or paid) in the future is known as 'discounting' and involves multiplying the amount concerned by a discount factor. Discount factors can either be calculated or found within present value tables.

Comparison of leasing methods

The interest/capital split is different under each method because different assumptions have been made about how interest is incurred (see Table 4.1). Both the actuarial method and sum of digits method allocate the interest in relation to the capital amount outstanding during the period. As this is in effect how a bank would charge interest on a loan then these methods would seem to be the preferred methods. The straight line method, although simpler to use, does not make any reference to the capital amount outstanding and therefore does not produce as comparable a result.

Depreciating a leased asset

In addition to the interest cost, the other item that requires to be recorded in the financial statements is depreciation. As the asset in the example is being leased over four years, if a straight line depreciation policy is adopted the annual charge will be:

$$\frac{£3,486}{4 \text{ years}} = £871 \text{ p.a.}$$

Comparison of profit and loss account charges

	Actuarial			Sum of digits			Straight line		
Period	Depn	Finance	Total charge	Depn	Finance	Total charge	Depn	Finance	Total charge
	£	£	£	£	£	£	£	£	£
1	871	249	1,120	871	257	1,128	871	171	1,042
2	871	174	1,045	871	171	1,042	871	171	1,042
3	871	91	962	871	86	957	871	172	1,043
4	873	–	873	873	–	873	873	–	873
	3,486	514	4,000	3,486	514	4,000	3,486	514	4,000

Table 4.1 Comparison of profit and loss account charges under each method

Note that the total lease payments (£4,000 i.e. 4 × £1,000) regardless of the method used have been charged to the profit and loss accounts in a combination of depreciation (reflecting the usage of the asset) and the finance charge (reflecting the interest payable on the outstanding lease obligation).

4.4 The accounting issue revisited

It is worth recapping the reasons for adopting the substance over form treatment of leases – that is, capitalising the leased assets and including as liabilities the obligations to make future lease payments. Comparing the total profit and loss account charges (depreciation and interest charges under the actuarial method with the actual lease payments made) gives the following result:

Period	Depreciation + finance charge	Lease payment	Difference
	£	£	£
1	1,120	1,000	+ 120
2	1,045	1,000	+ 45
3	962	1,000	- 38
4	873	1,000	- 127
	4,000	4,000	0

The differences are not significant although the higher depreciation and finance charges compared to the lease payments in the earlier periods tend to concur with the concept of the asset, providing a greater benefit to the company when the asset is new and that benefit diminishing as the asset ages.

It is the balance sheet, however, that provides the user with the otherwise 'hidden' information. From an informational point of view the user can now see the assets the company is using to generate income. If accounting ratios are to be calculated using total assets then it is clear that, without capitalising leased assets, comparison with similar companies that purchase assets would not be possible. Similarly, without adopting the substance over form approach, the obligations to make such lease payments would not be disclosed either. It should also be noted that the amounts disclosed as lease obligations are not the actual amounts payable but rather the present value of the future amounts payable, discounted at the interest rate implicit in the lease. In the actuarial example given above, the obligations under finance leases at the end of period 1 are £2,735. The actual payments still to be made at that point are £3,000 (three payments of £1,000).

So why the fuss?

The informational value of capitalising leases is clear: both assets in use and future obligations to pay are disclosed. Such informational value is not, however, always welcomed. A traditional attraction of leasing assets and indeed one of the perceived benefits, is that of off balance sheet financing. Off balance sheet financing is the use of assets and related obligations not being disclosed within the financial statements.

The analysis thus far has been based upon the lease agreement conveying benefits to the lessee to such an extent that it is as if the lessee actually owns the asset. Clearly not all leases convey the risks and rewards to such an extent. Where this is not the case it may be that an alternative accounting treatment is required.

In such cases, it may be appropriate to treat the rental payments as costs, and charge them in the profit and loss account. The problem is identifying at which particular point the lease ought to be capitalised rather than expensed. If such a point is made too prescriptive then companies may well attempt to 'push the boundaries' to be able to disclose lease obligations in such a way as to provide maximum benefit for the company. This issue is considered at length in the next section.

Progress Point 4.3

A company enters into a lease on 1 January 2007. The following information is available regarding the lease and the asset that is the subject of the lease. Show the effect of this lease on the financial statements.

Company's year end	31 December
Date of lease	1 January 2007
Value of leased asset if purchased	£12,500
Term of lease	3 years
Rentals half-yearly in advance	£2,500
Implied interest rate (given)	7.93%
Depreciation policy	straight line

(a) Identify the capital value.
(b) Calculate the total rentals.
(c) Calculate the total finance charge.
(d) Calculate the periodic finance charge.
(e) Show the rentals apportioned between capital and revenue.
(f) Calculate the depreciation.
(g) Show the effect on the profit and loss account, and balance sheet.

Solution

(a) Capital value in this case is the fair value: £12,500.
(b) Total rentals are £2,500 × 6 = £15,000.
(c) Total finance charge is total rentals, £15,000, less capital value: £12,500 = £2,500.

(d)   Periodic finance charge is calculated as follows:

Period	Capital sum at start	Rental paid	Capital sum during period	Finance charge (7.93%)	Capital sum at end of period
£	£	£	£	£	£
1/1/07	12,500	2,500	10,000	793	10,793
1/7/07	10,793	2,500	8,293	658	8,951
				1,451	
1/1/08	8,951	2,500	6,451	511	6,962
1/7/08	6,962	2,500	4,462	354	4,816
				865	
1/1/09	4,816	2,500	2,316	184	2,500
1/7/09	2,500	2,500	–	–	–
				184	
				2,500	

Note that, in this example, the rentals are paid in advance.

(e)   Rentals are apportioned between capital and interest (finance charge) as follows:

	Capital	Interest	Total
	£	£	£
2007	3,549	1,451	5,000
2008	4,135	865	5,000
2009	4,816	184	5,000

(f)   Depreciation is calculated as follows:

Lease term 3 years
Annual depreciation (straight line) $\frac{12,500}{3}$ = £4,167 p.a

(g)   Effect on reported figures in annual accounts:

Profit and loss account

	Depreciation	Finance charge
	£	£
Y/e 31/12/07	4,167	1,451
Y/e 31/12/08	4,167	865
Y/e 31/12/09	4,166	184

Balance sheet

Fixed assets	Cost	Accumulated depreciation	NBV
	£	£	£
Y/e 31/12/07	12,500	4,167	8,333
Y/e 31/12/08	12,500	8,334	4,166
Y/e 31/12/09	12,500	12,500	–

Obligations under leases

	£
Y/e 31/12/07	8,951
Y/e 31/12/08	4,816
Y/e 31/12/09	nil

Summary

The issue of accounting for leases can be summarised very simply. If a lease agreement essentially conveys all the risks and rewards of ownership to the lessee then the accounting treatment proceeds as if it were an actual 'legal' purchase. This ensures that the assets in use by a company are disclosed and that the associated obligations inherent within leasing agreements are also adequately disclosed.

Section 2: Intermediate Issues

This section develops some of the ideas from Section 1. In particular it examines how leases may be classified. The section also explains the requirements of IAS 17 *Leases*. The section concludes with an overview of the treatment of leases, and examines the distinction of operating and finance leases from the point of view of the IASB.

4.5 Classification of leases

When leases are disclosed as assets together with the corresponding liability to pay the obligations under a lease, such information is of more value to a user of financial statements. Such leases are referred to as finance leases. Leases that do not convey such ownership rights, and are therefore not disclosed as assets in the balance sheet, are referred to as operating leases. In the case of operating leases, payments made for lease rentals are expensed in the profit and loss account.

 Example

AWF plc is a manufacturing company that prepares accounts to 31 December each year. The company negotiates a lease to begin on 1 January 2010 with the following terms:

Terms of lease	4 years
Annual payments	£4,000
Useful life of machine	10 years
Age of machine on 1 January 2010	3 years
Purchase price of new machine	£35,000

In this example the lease applies to only part of the asset's useful life. Such a lease is classed as an operating lease. The lessor will be able to lease the asset again at the end of the lease term agreed with AWF plc.

The profit and loss account entry for AWF plc is as follows:

Profit and loss account	
Operating lease rentals	£4,000

Operating lease rentals should be charged to the profit and loss account on a straight line basis over the term of the lease unless another systematic basis is more representative of the time pattern of the user's benefit. If the charge for the period does not equal the payments made, accruals and prepayments can arise.

No asset or lease obligation will be recorded in the balance sheet. This is an example of off balance sheet financing. In this case there is a debt that is not shown as a liability on the face of the balance sheet.

Progress Point 4.4

Explain how the accounting treatment for operating leases differs from the accounting treatment for finance leases.

Solution

The accounting treatment of leases classified as finance leases results in an asset being capitalised in the financial statements with a corresponding lease creditor.

In the case of a lease that is classified as an operating lease, the payments made for the lease rentals will be expensed in the profit and loss account, and no asset or liability will be recognised.

In practice all leases transfer some of the risks and rewards of ownership to the lessee, and the distinction between a finance lease and an operating lease is essentially one of degree.

The question that must now be considered is where exactly the dividing line is between a finance lease and an operating lease. Unfortunately, the dividing line is not always clear cut. The key test, which is applied in practice, is whether or not the lessee faces the same risks and rewards as an owner. If the answer is yes, the lease is judged to be a finance lease.

4.6 IAS 17 *Leases*

Definitions

From an accounting perspective the distinction between operating and finance leases is particularly important. Under international accounting rules the two types of lease are accounted for very differently. IAS 17 deals with leases, and some of the main points are dealt with in this section. Appendix 1, at the end of this chapter, contains detailed provisions from IAS 17:

- a finance lease is a lease that transfers *substantially all* the risks and rewards incidental to ownership of an asset; title may or may not be transferred
- an operating lease is a lease other than a finance lease.

The IAS 17 definitions are based on an ownership concept. The risks of ownership can be identified as:

- asset breakdown
- repairs
- theft.

The rewards of ownership are those benefits derived from the asset while in use by the lessee.

Unfortunately, IAS 17 does not define 'substantially all', however it does give a number of situations that 'would normally' point to a lease being classified as a finance lease:

(i) ownership of asset transferred to lessee by end of lease
(ii) bargain purchase option at end of lease

(iii) lease term is a major part of economic life of asset
(iv) present value of the minimum lease payments amounts to substantially all of asset fair value (see below)
(v) leased asset of a specialised nature (specific to lessee).

IAS 17 also provides situations that 'could' point to a lease being classified as a finance lease:

(i) if lessee cancels lease, lessee bears lessor's losses associated with cancellation
(ii) gains/losses in residual value fall to lessee
(iii) lessee can continue lease for secondary period at low rent (bargain rental option).

It is worth noting that some national GAAPs take a more numerical approach. For instance, the USA and Germany require that at the inception (start) of the lease, the present value of the minimum lease payments must be 90% or more of the fair value of the asset. The UK suggests that 90% or more gives the 'presumption' of a finance lease but that the determining factor is 'substantially all' and not 90%.

The attractions of a numerical approach are clear. It is an objective benchmark and one that auditors can calculate exactly. Unfortunately, a cleverly worded lease could be drawn up such that the present value of the minimum lease payments falls just short of the benchmark and a company could argue that the lease did not therefore require to be capitalised.

It is for reasons like this that a definition based on an ownership concept is perhaps more beneficial.

Finance leases: minimum lease payments

One of the major criteria for deciding whether or not a lease is a finance lease is the total minimum amounts payable under the lease contract. In the substance over form approach, a contractual requirement to make payments greater than the cost of the leased asset effectively places the lessee in the same economic position as if the asset had been acquired at arm's length through a loan under agreed repayment and interest terms. This 'arm's length' value is known as the 'fair value' and the excess paid over the fair value is the interest.

There are instances, however, where the minimum lease payments are less than the fair value of the asset and, as has been noted, some national GAAPs take a numerical approach to lease classification.

An example of such a situation would be where a lessor company has, by virtue of perhaps bulk ordering, been able to negotiate substantial discounts on the purchase of assets and some of this discount is being passed on to the lessee by way of a favourable lease rental.

Another example may be where the lessor, at the end of the lease, has a market for the asset and effectively 'discounts' the lease for the future sales proceeds.

Progress Point 4.5

(a) Explain the difference between a finance lease and an operating lease?
(b) Petter acquires three identical pieces of machinery for use in his factory on the same day.
   (i) Machine 1 is rented from Busco at a cost of £250 per month payable in advance and terminable at any time by either party.
   (ii) Machine 2 is rented from CB Dobco at a cost of eight half-yearly payments in advance of £1,500.
   (iii) Machine 3 is rented from Adenco at a cost of six half-yearly payments in advance of £1,200.

The cash price of this type of machine is £8,000 and its estimated life is four years.

Explain how the leases would be classified?

▶

Solution

(a) A finance lease is a lease that transfers substantially all the risks and rewards of ownership of an asset to the lessee. Such a transfer is normally assumed to have taken place when at the inception of the lease the present value of the minimum lease payments amounts to substantially all (90% or more) of the fair value of the leased asset. Present value is computed using the interest rate implicit in the lease. This assumption may be refuted by other evidence. An operating lease is any lease other than a finance lease (i.e. one that fails to meet the above conditions).

(b) (i)   Machine 1 is held on an operating lease – the contract is terminable at any time and so there is no transfer of the risks or rewards of ownership.

   (ii)   Machine 2 involves total lease payments of £12,000. Although we have not been given details of the interest rate implicit in the lease, the present value of the lease payments will almost certainly be more than the £8,000 fair value of the asset. Machine 2 is therefore held on a finance lease.

   (iii)   Machine 3 involves a total payment of £7,200. Again, although we have not been given details of the interest rate, the present value will be significantly lower than £8,000 and certainly less than 90% of the fair value (i.e. £8,000 × 90% = £7,200). This would mean that Machine 3 is held on an operating lease.

What value should be recognised?

IAS 17 requires that lessees should recognise finance leases as assets and liabilities in their balance sheets at amounts equal at the inception of the lease to:

- the fair value of the leased property or, if lower
- at the present value of the minimum lease payments.

Fair value is a general term indicating the arm's length market value of an asset today. In calculating the present value of the minimum lease payments, the discount rate is the interest rate implicit in the lease.

 Example

A machine is leased for four years at a rental of £1,000 per year payable in advance. The fair value (i.e. cash price) of the machine is £3,828. The interest rate implicit in the lease is 10%.

Fair value = £3,828

Present value of minimum lease payments (£1,000 + (1,000 × 2.486)) = £3,486 (from present value tables)

The machine would be capitalised in the financial statements at the lower of the two values (i.e. £3,486).

Implicit interest rate

It may be the case that the implicit interest rate is not practicable to determine, in which case the lessee's incremental borrowing rate should be used.

This situation is not uncommon. Remember that the interest rate is determined by the lessor and not the lessee. Moreover, the terms that are set by the lessor will be determined by many factors, including the lessor's own tax position, the price the lessor paid for the asset, the expected residual value of the asset and the lessor's own expected profits on the transaction.

Any initial direct costs of the lessee should also be added to the amount of the asset. Initial direct costs are incremental costs that are directly attributable to negotiating and arranging a lease, and include costs such as legal costs and professional fees.

BASIC

INTERMEDIATE

ADVANCED

Depreciating a finance lease asset

A leased asset, if capitalised, requires to be depreciated.

The period over which the asset should be depreciated will depend upon the expected useful life of the asset and the terms of the lease itself. For example, if an asset has an expected useful life of five years but is being leased for only four years, then it would not be appropriate to depreciate the asset over the longer term. This would understate the depreciation charge reflecting the usage of the asset.

The length of term of the lease can, in practice, be more complicated to determine. Many leases consist of two distinct parts:

1.   the primary term, which is usually non-cancellable, and
2.   the secondary term for which the lessee has the option to continue to lease the asset with or without payment.

When calculating the length of term of the lease at the outset, a company will require to make a judgement as to what its intentions are likely to be at the end of the primary term. Unless it is reasonably certain that the option to continue leasing the asset beyond the primary term will be exercised then the secondary period should be ignored.

As a general rule the asset should be depreciated over the shorter of the lease term and the asset's useful life.

 ## *Example*

(i)   A company enters into a finance lease for a machine with a useful life of five years. The primary term of the lease is three years and the company expects to return the asset at the end of that primary term.

    The company should depreciate the asset over three years (i.e. the shorter of the lease term and the asset's useful life).

(ii)   Suppose at the outset of the lease the company had the option to continue leasing the asset for a further two years after the primary term and thought it highly likely that it would do so.

    The company would depreciate the asset over five years (i.e. in this instance the lease term and the useful life are the same and so the capitalised cost would be written off over the longer term). To be prudent the secondary term should be included only when it is reasonably certain that it will be taken up.

(iii)   Suppose that at the outset of the lease the company planned to take full advantage of the secondary term and lease the asset for an indefinite period until the asset wears out.

    The company would depreciate the asset over five years. Although the secondary term is indefinite, the asset's useful life is five years. The asset is expected to be used, therefore, for five years.

Note from the above example that the useful life relates to the expected situation for the lessee. The useful life can exceed the lease term. This is because the current lessee may or may not be the only user.

Residual values

It is not uncommon at the end of a lease for the lessor to sell the leased asset, and to pass back to the lessee some or all of the sales proceeds. This is known as the lessee having an interest in the residual value and can vary between 0% and 100%. Where a lessee has a 100% interest in the residual value, this means that it will receive back from the lessor 100% of the sales proceeds of the asset.

At the outset of a lease therefore, where it is anticipated that the lessee will return the asset to the lessor and will share in the sales proceeds, the depreciation charge should reflect this in the same way as if the lessee company were disposing of an owned asset (i.e. it would take account of any expected residual values at disposal).

Example

Cost of asset	£50,000
Primary lease term	8 years
Expected residual value at end of primary term	£2,000
Lessee's interest in residual value	100%
Secondary lease term	indefinite
Residual value at end of secondary term	nil
Estimated useful life of asset	10 years

Situation 1

At the outset of the lease the lessee intends to use the asset for the period of the primary lease term only.

The depreciation will be calculated as follows:

$$\frac{£50,000 - £2,000}{8 \text{ years}} = £6,000 \text{ per annum}$$

Situation 2

The lessee intends to use the asset for an indefinite period until the asset wears out. The secondary term is indefinite but the useful life is ten years. The asset is expected to be used therefore for ten years. The depreciation charge would be:

$$\frac{£50,000 - £0}{10 \text{ years}} = £5,000 \text{ per annum}$$

Remember that the secondary term is included only when at the commencement of the lease it is reasonably certain that it will be taken up; and remember also that the asset will be depreciated over the *shorter* of the lease term and the asset's useful life.

Progress Point 4.6

Statco acquires a loader with a fair value of £45,000 on a finance lease from Demenco, a specialist supplier of lifting machinery. Lease payments are £10,000 per annum for five years payable in advance (i.e. the first payment is made on taking delivery of the asset). The interest rate implicit in the lease is 10%. Demenco, being a specialist supplier, is able to obtain bulk discounts on machinery and its policy is to pass such discounts on to the lessee. In addition, at the end of the lease, the loader is expected to have a residual value of £2,500, which will be passed to the lessee as a refund of rentals.

At what value should Statco capitalise the loader in its financial statements, and what will be the depreciable amount?

Solution

IAS 17 requires that lessees should capitalise leased assets at the lower of

- the fair value of the leased asset, or
- the present value of the minimum lease payments.

The present value of the minimum lease payments discounted at 10% can be calculated using the present value of £1 in n years' time.

BASIC

INTERMEDIATE

ADVANCED

Payment date	Present value of £1	Present value of £10,000 payment
On delivery	1.000	£10,000
In 1 year	0.909	£9,090
In 2 years	0.826	£8,260
In 3 years	0.751	£7,510
In 4 years	0.683	£6,830
Present value of minimum lease payments		£41,690

The fair value of the loader is £45,000. The present value of the minimum lease payments is £41,690. Statco requires to capitalise the loader at the lower of these amounts (i.e. £41,690).

The depreciable amount is calculated as being the capitalised cost less residual value (i.e. £41,690 − £2,500 = £39,190).

Note that the expected residual of £2,500 does not affect the value at which the asset is capitalised. The expected residual affects the depreciation policy of the lessee only as regards the capitalised asset. Statco will depreciate the loader to an expected residual of £2,500, and any difference between this net book value figure and the amount received by the lessee will give rise to a gain or loss on disposal of the asset.

Classification of land and buildings

Land and buildings can be the subject of leases and are classified as operating and finance leases in the same way as other leased assets. This means that, depending upon the terms of the lease, land and buildings could be shown as assets on a company's balance sheet.

Under the terms of a 'true' lease, ownership never passes to the lessee although many lease arrangements are such that the title of the asset subject to the lease is transferred to the lessee at the end of the lease term. This is likely to be the case when the present value of the minimum lease payments has effectively 'paid' the lessor for the asset and satisfied the lessor's profit objective. Moreover, the useful life of the leased asset at the end of the lease term is likely to be very limited and perhaps may even have expired.

A characteristic of land, however, is that it normally has an indefinite economic useful life. Therefore, if legal title is not due to pass to the lessee by the end of the lease term, then substantially all of the risks and rewards of ownership have not been transferred. The lease of land would therefore be classified as an operating lease.

This means, therefore, that where a lessee enters into a land and buildings lease, and title is not due to pass to the lessee the lease should be classified into two leases: a land lease, which is an operating lease, and a buildings lease, which could be an operating or finance lease.

Where the lease of land is classified as an operating lease and the lease of buildings as a finance lease, the minimum lease payments should be allocated between land and buildings in proportion to the fair values of each at the inception of the lease.

Land and buildings: from a user's perspective

Of all the assets a company may disclose on its balance sheet, none provides more information to a user than land and buildings. They are the most tangible of assets, usually the greatest value and, from the point of view of a user of financial statements, the assets that indicate the wealth of a business.

It has been suggested that incorporating leased assets on a company's balance sheet adds to the informational value provided by the financial statements. This is undoubtedly true when plant and equipment, vehicles and machinery are concerned – such capitalisation is essential when comparison

BASIC

INTERMEDIATE

ADVANCED

between companies that lease and companies that buy assets is attempted. Moreover, the disclosure of the related lease obligations is invaluable information to the user of the financial statements whether the user is an investor, a supplier or a lender.

The distinction made, therefore, between land and buildings, and the subsequent classification between operating leases and finance leases is extremely important. When reviewing sets of accounts – and in particular the balance sheet – the fixed asset note is often the schedule on which time is spent.

If accurate classification has not been made, nor adequate disclosure in the notes is given that clearly emphasises the legal form of the transaction, then the information provided, regardless of whether it conforms to the substance of the transaction or not, could be very misleading. The distinction has to be made very clear between a company using land and buildings and a company *owning* land and buildings.

4.7 The impact of capitalisation

Prior to IAS 17, one of the major attractions of leasing was the off balance sheet nature of the transaction. A company could have the use of – and generate income from – an asset that was not disclosed on its balance sheet. Moreover the related lease obligations – which could be substantial – were also not disclosed.

The capitalisation of finance leases effectively means that key accounting ratios such as gearing, return on assets and return on investment are substantially affected.

 ***Example***

Satnav Logistics, a delivery company, currently leases its fleet of delivery vehicles. Cleverly worded lease agreements have ensured that the leases all qualify as operating leases and all lease payments have been treated as revenue expenditure. The managing director asks you to show the impact of capitalising the leases on the financial statements and on key ratios.

The annual lease payments are £120,000 per annum.

The fair value of the leased vehicles is £309,250, and you have calculated that in the current year the depreciation charge on the vehicles would be £103,083 and that, if capitalised, the leases would give rise to a finance interest charge of £24,740. At the end of the year the obligations under leases were £102,881 due within one year, and £111,109 due after one year.

The financial statements before and after capitalisation are as follows:

BEFORE		AFTER	
		Profit and loss account	
	£		£
Turnover	3,000,000	Turnover	3,000,000
Operating profit	100,000	Operating profit	100,000
Interest charge	5,000	Add: lease rentals[1]	120,000
	95,000		220,000
		Less: extra depn[2]	103,083
		Adjusted operating profit	116,917
		Interest charge	5,000
		Lease interest[3]	24,740
			87,177
Taxation	17,000	Taxation	17,000
Retained profit	78,000		70,177

Balance sheet				
	£			£
Fixed assets	200,000	Fixed assets		200,000
		Leased assets (309,250 – 103,083)[4]		206,167
				406,167
Net current assets	220,000	Net current assets		220,000
		Lease due < 1 year[5]		102,881
	420,000			523,286
Long-term loans	100,000	Long-term loans		100,000
		Leases due > 1 year		111,109
	320,000			312,177
Share capital	100,000	Share capital		100,000
Profit and loss a/c	220,000	Profit and loss a/c		220,000
		Change in p&l a/c (78,000 – 70,177)		(7,823)
	320,000			312,177

Notes

1. The annual lease payments of £120,000 will have been deducted in arriving at the operating profit of £100,000. This lease payment requires to be added back as it will instead be going to (a) partly reduce the lease creditor and (b) lease interest.
2. The depreciation on the leased assets will require to be deducted in arriving at the adjusted operating profit.
3. The lease interest will be shown as a finance charge.
4. The balance sheet will include the leased asset at net book value.
5. The lease obligations will be included and disclosed as appropriate between amounts falling due less than and greater than one year.

The difference in retained profit is relatively small. Note, however, that the operating profit has increased under capitalisation. This is due to the lease rental payments of £120,000 being substituted with the lower depreciation charge of £103,083.

The ratio of operating profit/sales is therefore 3.33% before capitalisation and 3.89% after.

It is the balance sheet that shows a dramatic difference following lease capitalisation.

If the return on capital employed is considered, the following changes demonstrate this point:

$$\text{Before} \quad \frac{£100,000}{£200,000} = 50\% \qquad \text{After} \quad \frac{£116,917}{£311,109} = 37.5\%$$

This is because the leased asset now forms part of the capital employed.

Of even greater significance is the worsening in reported gearing:

$$\text{Gearing} = \frac{\text{Long-term debt}}{\text{Shareholders' funds}}$$

$$\text{Before} = \frac{£100,000}{£320,000} = 31.25\% \qquad \text{After} \quad \frac{£211,109}{£312,177} = 67.6\%$$

This is because the commitment to long-term lease rentals has been recognised in the financial statements.

Operating leases are not required to be capitalised, and they remain therefore a form of off balance sheet financing. Consequently they remain popular with lessees, and many leasing agreements are structured specifically to be classified as operating leases.

Progress Point 4.7

(a) Summarise the effect on the financial statements of a lessee treating a lease as an operating lease as opposed to a finance lease; and explain the importance of the categorisation of the lease transactions into operating lease or finance lease decisions when carrying out financial ratio analysis. What ratios are particularly affected?

(b) Midson plc, a haulage company leases a truck on 1 January 2009 under the following terms:

   - annual rental of £10,000 for four years, first payment on 31 December 2009
   - cash price of truck is £28,550
   - Midson plc adopts the straight line method of providing for depreciation.

   (i) Calculate and state the charges to income for 2009 if the lease is treated as an operating lease.

   (ii) Calculate and state the charges to income for 2009 if the lease is treated as a finance lease and capitalised using the sum of digits method for the finance charges.

   (iii) Show how the truck would be incorporated in the balance sheet at 31 December 2009 if capitalised.

   (iv) Comment on your findings.

Solution

(a) The accounting treatment for the lessee of an operating lease is that the income statement is simply charged with the periodic rentals and there is no effect on the balance sheet. By contrast, the accounting treatment for a finance lease takes a substance over form approach – as if the lessee had taken out a loan to purchase an asset. This means that both the asset and the obligations under the lease are shown on the balance sheet.

The impact on the income statement of treating a finance lease as an operating lease is minimal; over the lifetime of the lease, substantially the same amount of depreciation and interest (finance lease) will be charged to income as would operating lease rentals.

The impact on the balance sheet is more dramatic and highlights the importance of the correct categorisation between operating lease and finance lease. Treatment as an operating lease means that neither the asset nor the liability is included on the lessee's balance sheet. This will hide the true level of assets employed in the business and will result in an artificially high return on capital employed figure.

The absence of the lease obligation from the balance sheet will also mask the true level of gearing (i.e. the level of interest bearing liabilities to shareholders' funds).

(b) Midson plc:

(i) Income statement extract:

Year Ended 31 December 2009	
	2009
	£
Operating lease	10,000

As an operating lease each annual payment is simply rent.

BASIC

INTERMEDIATE

ADVANCED

▶

(ii)   Working notes: finance lease treatment

Total lease payments = 4 × £10,000 =	£40,000
Cash price	£28,550
Finance charge	£11,450

Period of lease = 4 years
Sum of the digits = 4 + 3 + 2 + 1 = 10
∴ Charge to 2009 = 4/10 × 11,450 = £4,580

Depreciation charge = 28,550 ÷ 4 = £7,138 p.a.

Income statement extract:

Year to 31 December 2009	
	£
Finance charge	4,580
Depreciation	7,138
	11,718

(iii) Working notes

Lease creditor: At 1 January 2009	£28,550
Less: payment	10,000
	18,550
Add: finance charge	4,580
Lease creditor at 31 December 2009	23,130

Balance sheet extract:

As at 31 December 2009			
	Cost	Acc. depn	NBV
Fixed assets	£	£	£
Leased truck	28,550	7,138	21,412
Creditors			
Leases			23,130

(iv)   The income statement is not greatly affected by treating a finance lease as an operating lease, however the effect of capitalising the lease on the balance sheet more realistically states the assets employed by Midson plc. In addition, the lease obligations are shown on the face of the balance sheet.

4.8 Disclosure requirements

The disclosure requirements of IAS 17 are considerable and aim to highlight to users of financial statements the various risks faced by companies that lease assets. The main disclosures are in paragraph 31 for finance leases and paragraph 35 for operating leases.

Finance leases and hire purchase contracts

Fixed assets

IAS 17 requires the net carrying amount of assets leased through a finance lease to be identified within the fixed asset note to the accounts. This should be disclosed for each class of asset held.

Creditors

A reconciliation between the total of minimum lease payments at the balance sheet date, and their present value. In addition, disclosure must be made of the total minimum lease payments at the balance sheet date, and their present value for each of the following periods:

- not later than one year
- later than one year and not later than five years
- later than five years.

Total minimum lease payments are the minimum payments that the lessee is obliged to make to the lessor over the remaining part of the lease term.

This means, therefore, that at the balance sheet date a reconciliation is required between the lessee's future payments in total and that recognised as the lease liability in the balance sheet. Usually the only reconciling item is unallocated interest (i.e. interest to be charged in future income statements).

 ## *Example*

Finance lease creditor	Minimum lease payments £	Present value of minimum lease payments £
Due within 1 year	10,000	6,756
Due in 2 to 5 years	40,000	32,998
Due in more than 5 years	10,000	10,000
	60,000	49,754
Less: finance charges allocated to future periods	(10,246)	
Present value of minimum lease payments	49,754	

Income statement

Any contingent rent payments that have been made during the year must be separately disclosed in the notes to the financial statements. A contingent rent payment is not fixed in amount and occurs when the lessee has been charged on a basis other than the passage of time (e.g. charge per mile for a leased car).

IAS 32 *Financial Instruments: Disclosure and Presentation* requires that a company should disclose the total interest expense for the year. This will include finance lease interest.

Significant leasing arrangements

A general description of the significant leasing arrangements that have been entered into should be disclosed. This should include detail of any renewal or purchase options, any escalation clauses and the basis on which contingent rent payments are calculated.

If any restrictions have been imposed on the lessee by the finance lease agreement then these should be disclosed. These restrictions include limits on dividend payments, any further debt and any other lease obligations.

Operating leases

Income statement

IAS 17 requires that the total operating lease rentals included in the income statement be disclosed, analysed between amounts relating to contingent rents and minimum lease payments.

Commitments

In respect of operating leases, the lessee should disclose the total future minimum lease payments the business is committed to make under operating leases for each of the following periods:

- not later than one year
- later than one year and not later than five years
- later than five years.

   This disclosure allows users of the accounts to anticipate future cash outflows that are not reflected anywhere else in the accounts. With operating leases, although they are normally non-cancellable, there is no liability reflected in the balance sheet. This is, therefore, a very important disclosure and is made in the notes to the accounts.

Significant leasing arrangements

A general description of the significant leasing arrangements that have been entered into should be disclosed. This should include detail of any renewal or purchase options, any escalation clauses and the basis on which contingent rent payments are calculated.

   If any restrictions have been imposed on the lessee by the lease agreement then these should be disclosed. These restrictions include limits on dividend payments, any further debt and any other lease obligations.

Disclosure in practice

As noted earlier, the disclosure requirements of IAS 17 are considerable, and the relevant disclosures can be found within the accounting policies, income statement and balance sheet, and notes to the accounts.

Leases

Leases are classified as finance leases whenever the terms of the lease transfer substantially all the risks and rewards of ownership to the lessee. All other leases are classified as operating leases.

   Assets held under finance leases are initially recognised as property, plant and equipment at an amount equal to the fair value of the leased assets or, if lower, the present value of minimum lease payments at the inception of the lease, and then depreciated over their useful economic lives. Lease payments are apportioned between repayment of capital and interest. The capital element of future lease payments is included in the balance sheet as a liability. Interest is charged to the income statement so as to achieve a constant rate of interest on the remaining balance of the liability.

Rentals payable under operating leases are charged to the income statement on a straight-line basis over the lease term. Operating lease incentives are recognised as a reduction in the rental expense over the lease term.

Logica's policy note on leases echoes the requirements of IAS 17 in relation to initial measurement and measurement subsequent to initial recognition: the policy note also discloses that Logica uses the actuarial method to allocate finance charges (i.e. interest is charged so as to achieve a constant rate of interest on the remaining lease liability balance).

Property, plant and equipment

	Freehold land and buildings £m	Leasehold property and improvements £m	Equipment and plant £m	Total £m
Cost				
At 1 January 2006	19.3	55.9	203.4	278.6
Additions	–	4.4	29.7	34.1
Acquisition of subsidiary	5.3	–	30.9	36.2
Disposals	(0.5)	(0.6)	(22.5)	(23.6)
Exchange differences	(0.1)	(0.7)	(4.0)	(4.8)
At 1 January 2007	24.0	59.0	237.5	320.5
Additions	0.1	3.1	36.8	40.0
Acquisition of subsidiaries	–	–	3.9	3.9
Disposals of subsidiaries/businesses	(0.1)	(1.5)	(46.5)	(48.1)
Disposals	(1.8)	(4.8)	(32.5)	(39.1)
Exchange differences	1.0	1.9	16.3	19.2
At 31 December 2007	**23.2**	**57.7**	**215.5**	**296.4**
Accumulated amortisation				
At 1 January 2006	0.7	24.6	150.8	176.1
Charge for the year	0.1	5.1	27.5	32.7
Disposals	(0.2)	(0.3)	(21.0)	(21.5)
Exchange differences	–	(0.3)	(3.1)	(3.4)
At 1 January 2007	0.6	29.1	154.2	183.9
Charge for the year	0.7	5.8	33.6	40.1
Disposals of subsidiaries/businesses	–	(1.7)	(38.2)	(39.9)
Disposals	(0.1)	(4.1)	(30.1)	(34.3)
Impairment	2.6	–	–	2.6
Exchange differences	0.2	1.0	10.7	11.9
At 31 December 2007	**4.0**	**30.1**	**130.2**	**164.3**
Net carrying amount				
At 31 December 2007	**19.2**	**27.6**	**85.3**	**132.1**
At 31 December 2006	23.4	29.9	83.3	136.6

Figure 4.1 Logica: property, plant and equipment (showing leased assets)

The following extract from Logica's note to the financial statements on property, plant and equipment discloses the net book value of assets held under finance leases of £3.4 million included within the overall net book value of assets in use of £132.1 million:

The impairment of £2.6 million in Figure 4.1 related to buildings previously occupied by the graphic services business in Portugal prior to the disposal of this business. The disposals are described further in Note 35. Equipment and plant included assets held under finance leases with a net book value of £3.4 million (2006: £5.2 million). Additions to equipment and plant during the year amounting to £4.7 million (2006: £3.1 million) were financed by new finance leases.

This disclosure allows the user to determine the return on all the assets in use by the company and not simply those that are owned. This disclosure also aids the user in determining the financial strength of the company by providing important information about those assets that are used but not owned, and that would not be available for distribution in, for example, a winding up.

Borrowings

	2007 £m	2006 £m
Current		
Bank overdrafts	9.1	26.4
Bank loans	84.8	1.6
2.875% 2008 convertible bonds	220.0	202.4
Finance lease obligations	2.4	4.1
Other borrowings	0.9	1.0
	317.2	235.5
PRESENTED AS:		
Convertible debt	220.0	202.4
Other borrowings	97.2	33.1
	317.2	235.5
Non-current		
Bank loans	269.9	496.4
Finance lease obligations	4.8	2.4
Other borrowings	–	0.1
	274.7	498.9

Figure 4.2 Logica: borrowings showing finance lease obligations

Operating lease commitments

At 31 December, the Group had commitments under non-cancellable operating leases, principally for offices and computer equipment, as [shown in Figure 4.3].

	2007		2006	
	Land and buildings £m	**Other** **£m**	Land and buildings £m	Other £m
Future minimum lease payments payable				
Within one year	**78.6**	**54.1**	78.6	59.5
Between two and five years	**246.4**	**55.4**	217.5	71.1
After five years	**173.0**	**–**	196.0	–
	498.0	**109.5**	492.1	130.6

Figure 4.3 Logica: operating lease commitments

The expense recognised in the income statement for payments under non-cancellable operating leases for the year ended 31 December 2007 was £139.4 million including a Telecoms Products charge of £3.0 million (2006: £108.9 million including a Telecoms Products charge of £6.4 million). At 31 December 2007, the total future minimum sub-lease payments expected to be received under non-cancellable sub-leases were £23.0 million (2006: £29.6 million).

	2007		2006	
	Group £m	**Associates** **£m**	Group £m	Associates £m
Contracted at the balance sheet date	**0.8**	**–**	0.1	–

Figure 4.4 Logica: capital expenditure commitments

In accordance with the requirements of the standard, Logica discloses its obligations under both finance lease and operating lease arrangements. In addition, disclosure is made of the lessor's security over finance lease assets and, in respect of operating leases, that these are principally for offices and computer equipment.

4.9 Change in accounting focus

Capitalisation of finance leases has for a long time been mandatory in countries with an Anglo-Saxon accounting tradition (e.g. the UK, USA and Commonwealth countries). In countries with a continental European accounting tradition, the distinction between operating and finance leases is relatively new. Until recently, all leases in these countries were treated as rentals.

An international group has questioned this distinction between finance and operating leases. Standard Setters from the UK, Australia, Canada, New Zealand, the USA and the IASC issued a Special Report, *Accounting For Leases – A New Approach*, which concluded that non-cancellable operating leases should be treated in the same way as finance leases. Regardless of the length of the lease, the lessee has:

- an asset – the lessee can *control* the future economic benefits embodied within the leased asset for the period of the lease term
- a liability – the lease contract establishes an obligation on the lessee to make future lease payments.

This approach firmly addresses the problems with the current approach and removes the ambiguity that can exist between finance leases and operating leases. Moreover, it removes the potential for creatively manipulating a finance lease as an operating lease to avoid having to capitalise the leased asset on the lessee's balance sheet.

A further position paper was issued by the G4+1 group in 1999.

This paper followed on in a similar vein to the previous report, and further argued the reasons for capitalising all operating leases.

It was argued that capitalisation would result in 'fair value' balance sheet disclosure – that is, the assets and liabilities resulting from the capitalisation of operating leases would be reported at the fair value of the rights and obligations in the lease (e.g. where a lease is only for a small part of an asset's economic life, only that part would be reflected in the lessee's balance sheet).

Moreover, assuming that in an arm's length transaction, the present value of the lease payments will correspond to the fair value of the asset, then the assets and liabilities referred to in the proposals appear to be able to be calculated. A further possibility would, however, be to include the leased asset at its full value, in which case the liability would be the present value of the minimum lease payments plus the obligation to return the asset at the end of the rental period.

However, the question arises whether it is correct to capitalise a particular asset at only a fraction of its 'true' fair value (i.e. at a fraction of its market value). One of the arguments for capitalising leases was to facilitate comparison between companies that leased assets and companies that bought assets. It is questionable whether following such an approach will enhance comparability, or indeed result in accountants and finance companies devising more ingenious schemes to creatively manipulate the figures to best advantage.

4.10 The accounting issues revisited: a critical appraisal

So far in this chapter the positive aspects of capitalising leases have been clearly demonstrated. Comparison between companies is made easier, the underlying assets in use by a company are disclosed and the associated obligations related to leased assets are also disclosed. Indeed the current view is that all leases – whether they be finance or operating – should be capitalised to show the assets in use by companies and the related lease obligations.

Care must be taken, however, with the extent to which the substance over form approach is taken. That there are advantages to capitalising leases is not being disputed. There are unfortunately disadvantages, however, and some of these are considered below.

Disadvantages

Sophistication of the user

The informational benefit of capitalising leases will depend upon the sophistication of the user. A professional accountant will appreciate the need to look at the financial statements as a whole and will be able to put figures in context. The accountant will look at a fixed asset schedule knowing that the notes pertaining to the schedule contain relevant information, and will be able to identify the associated obligations relating to any leased assets within the liabilities section of the balance sheet.

Contrast this, however, with an unsophisticated user – for example, a potential supplier to a company who has no accounting background. As far as the supplier is concerned, an asset is an asset. The supplier will have no concept of the accountant's definition of an asset being 'a right to future economic benefits embodied within the leased asset' and may not fully appreciate the information provided in the notes to the accounts, or even realise that it is relevant.

The danger is that some users may look at the figures in isolation when forming their opinion of a particular company. As has been noted earlier, many users focus on the fixed assets on a balance sheet when determining that company's wealth, and unless adequate disclosure is made and sufficient information given to draw the user's attention to the fact that the assets may not be assets as such, then capitalising leases could be very misleading indeed.

Company financial statements can run to several pages and it must be questioned whether it is reasonable to expect users to be able to refer to all the relevant sections.

Reliance on the notes

As noted above, the extent to which the benefit of capitalising leases is appreciated by the user depends upon the sophistication of the particular user. There is only a benefit where the financial statements are read as a whole and constituent parts not looked at in isolation. It could perhaps be suggested therefore that the legal form of the transaction should take precedent and all the information regarding the leases be given in the notes to the financial statements instead. No leased 'assets' would be in the balance sheet, however the payments due under the leases would be shown in the notes. While comparability between companies would suffer, the sophisticated user could – if sufficient information was given in the notes – be able to make appropriate adjustments to the figures to make comparison possible. The unsophisticated user would have the benefit of not being misled.

To what extent should future liabilities be disclosed?

A further issue worthy of consideration is the position regarding the associated costs of leasing particular assets. Land and buildings provides a useful illustration of this particular point. Where a lease is taken on land and buildings then it depends on whether the lease on the buildings element is determined as being a finance lease or an operating lease whether the building is capitalised and the corresponding lease creditor shown, or treated as revenue expenditure and the future lease obligations disclosed in the notes to the accounts.

There will also be associated costs of leasing the building, however, such as rates, insurance and upkeep, and these will continue for as long as the lease is in place. Should disclosure of the likely future

payments due on these expenses be noted also? After all, they will most certainly become due, and if the aim of the financial statements is to disclose information to enable decisions about future performance to be made then this could be argued to be very relevant also.

Summary

The use of a substance over form approach ensures that important omissions in respect of leased assets do not occur. Care must be taken, however, to ensure that information is presented in such a way so that leased assets are easily identifiable and not mistaken for assets actually owned by a company.

Section 3: Advanced Aspects

This section identifies some of the more advanced aspects of leasing. In particular it addresses sale and leaseback agreements, under both operating and finance leases. It concludes by examining leases from the point of view of the lessor.

4.11 Sale and leaseback agreements

It is not uncommon for companies to enter into sale and leaseback agreements whereby a company (the owner) sells an asset and immediately reacquires the right to use the asset by entering into a lease with the purchaser.

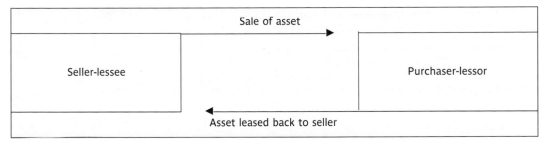

Figure 4.5 Illustration of sale and leaseback agreement

Such arrangements can involve the sale of a major asset and are often done as a way of raising funds while retaining use of the asset.

IAS 17 deals with the accounting treatment of sale and leaseback transactions in paragraphs 58 to 66. In order to determine the correct accounting treatment for such transactions, it must be established whether the leaseback is a finance lease or an operating lease.

Leaseback under a finance lease

If the lessee is still the economic owner of the asset then the leaseback is judged to be a finance lease and the seller-lessee has, in effect, borrowed funds against the asset. The position before and after the transaction is relatively unchanged: the seller may have disposed of the legal title of the asset but has not disposed of the ownership interest in the asset.

Further, when the substance of the transaction is considered, it is as if there has been no sale at all, the substance of the transaction being to raise finance and not to dispose of an asset. It would not be appropriate, therefore, to recognise a gain or loss on disposal as, in substance, there has been no disposal. The lease is effectively a mechanism for raising a loan with the asset as security.

If the sale proceeds exceed the carrying amount then the 'gain' needs to be treated as deferred income and released to the profit and loss account over the period of the lease. The asset is retained in the balance sheet but at its fair value at the date the lease is entered into, with the corresponding sale proceeds treated as the initial lease creditor. The asset will be depreciated over the shorter of the remaining useful life and the term of the lease, and the lease payments will be treated partly as a repayment of the lease creditor and partly as a finance charge to the profit and loss account.

Example

A company has a building with a net book value of £5m at 1 January 2009. The remaining useful economic life is 28 years. On 1 January 2009, the company enters into a sale and leaseback transaction with a finance house and sells the building at its market value of £8.5m. The building is immediately leased back for 25 years at an annual lease payment of £1m payable in arrears.

A lease creditor of £8.5m would be set on 1 January 2009 and the accounting entries would be as follows:

			£	£
Dr	Bank		8.5m	
	Cr	Finance lease creditor		8.5m
Being proceeds from sale and leaseback of asset.				

The excess of the fair value (sale proceeds) over the carrying amount (£5m) would be recorded as deferred income and amortised over the lease term.

			£	£
Dr	Fixed asset		3.5m	
	Cr	Deferred income		3.5m
Being deferred income recognised at start of lease.				

The rental payable on 31 December 2009 would be split between capital and interest based on the rate of interest implicit in the lease or the sum of the digits method.

The building would be depreciated over 25 years (the shorter of lease term and useful economic life).

If the fair value at the time of the sale and leaseback transaction is less than the carrying amount of the asset then the apparent loss should not be taken to the profit and loss account – again, because in substance there has been no sale. However, such a difference might indicate an impairment and may require an immediate write-down in the profit and loss account.

Example

A company has a property with a net book value of £13m on 1 January 2009. On that date it enters into a sale and leaseback arrangement for £9m. The property is immediately leased back for £0.8m per annum.

In this instance, a lease creditor would be set up on 1 January 2009 as follows:

			£	£
Dr	Bank		9m	
	Cr	Finance lease creditor		9m
Being proceeds from sale and leaseback of asset.				

The property would continue to be carried in the financial statements at £13m and depreciated over the shorter of the lease term and the useful economic life. The difference between the fair value (sales

proceeds) and carrying value would give an indication that an impairment review would be required and, if impairment was necessary, any impairment loss would be recognised immediately in the profit and loss account.

Leaseback under an operating lease

If the leaseback is an operating lease, and the lease payments and sale price are established at fair value, the seller has in fact disposed of substantially all the risks and rewards of ownership. There has been a normal sale transaction and any profit or loss on sale can be recognised immediately. Consequently, if the fair value is less than the carrying amount of the asset a loss equal to the amount of the difference between the carrying amount and fair value should be recognised immediately. A gain would be recognised immediately where the fair value is greater than the carrying amount.

It may be the case, however, that the sale price is less than the fair value and the seller will be compensated by future lease payments at below market price. In this case, the loss as calculated between the difference of the carrying value and fair value should be recognised immediately, and the additional loss as calculated between the fair value and sales value should be deferred and written off over the period for which the asset is to be used.

❂ *Example*

RJL Ltd enters into a sale and leaseback transaction with a finance house in respect of a ship. The carrying value in the financial statements of RJL Ltd is £5m and the fair value of the ship is £4m. RJL Ltd agrees to sell the ship for £3.5m following an agreement with the finance house to lease back the ship for a period of five years at £0.5m per year. A fair market rental for such a lease would normally be £0.6m.

RJL Ltd will record in its financial statements the disposal of the ship as follows:

$$\text{Loss on disposal of ship} = \text{carrying value} - \text{fair value}$$
$$= \text{£5m} - \text{£4m} = \text{£1m}$$

The additional 'loss' on disposal between the fair value and the sale price (i.e. £4m – £3.5m = £0.5m) will be deferred and written off to the profit and loss account over the period for which the asset is expected to be used (i.e. five years). The additional loss will therefore be charged to the profit and loss account at £0.1m per annum.

The effect of this treatment is that the total charges going through the profit and loss account in respect of this leasing transaction (i.e. the operating lease payments and the deferred additional loss), should equate to a fair market value lease payment for a similar asset had the leasing payments not been artificially lowered by the sale of the asset at less than fair value.

There are a number of possibilities where the transaction is not based on the fair value of the asset. The following schedule identifies the various permutations that may arise and explains the appropriate accounting treatment. The following amounts are used.

1. CV = carrying value of the asset prior to its sale by the seller/lessee.
2. SV = sales value at which the asset is sold to the buyer/lessor.
3. FV = fair value of the asset (i.e. value if a sale at arm's length).

Possible permutations

1. SV < CV < FV: loss (CV – SV) recognised immediately unless lease rentals are below normal levels, when it should be deferred and amortised.
2. SV < FV < CV: loss based on fair value (CV – FV) recognised immediately. Balance (FV – SV) should also be recognised immediately unless lease rentals are below normal levels, when it should be deferred and amortised.
3. CV < SV < FV: gain (SV – CV) recognised immediately.

BASIC

INTERMEDIATE

ADVANCED

4. CV < FV < SV: profit based on fair value (FV – CV) recognised immediately. Balance (SV – FV) deferred and amortised.
5. FV < CV < SV: loss based on fair value (CV – FV) recognised immediately. Profit (SV – FV) deferred and amortised.
6. FV < SV < CV: loss based on fair value (CV – FV) recognised immediately. Profit (SV – FV) deferred and amortised.

The rationale behind the above treatments is that if the sales value is not based on fair values then it is likely that the normal market rents would have been adjusted to compensate. The effect of the treatment is to record the transaction as if it had been based on fair values.

It should be noted, however, that fair disclosure will not always result. For example, where the fair value is greater than the carrying value, the seller may arrange to have the sale value anywhere within that range and report a gain in the year of sale based on that sales value. Any compensation that the seller/lessee obtains by way of reduced rentals will be reflected in later years.

However, there may also be perfectly legitimate reasons why the sale value is less than the fair value. If the seller has had to raise cash quickly (i.e. a forced sale) then the sale value may be less than the fair value. In these cases, though, as the rentals are unlikely to have been reduced to compensate, the profit or loss should be based on the sales value.

4.12 Operating leases: incentives to customers

Many leasing companies offer incentives to attract potential customers and to encourage existing customers to renew leases, and these include rent-free periods and cash-back offers. IAS 17 does not deal specifically with such matters, but the Standing Interpretations Committee has clarified the position in SIC 15 *Incentives in an Operating Lease*. Such incentives should be recognised by the lessee as a reduction of the rental expense over the lease term on a straight line basis unless another systematic basis is more representative of the time pattern in which benefit is derived from the leased asset.

Rent-free periods

As noted earlier in the chapter, operating lease rentals should be charged to the profit and loss account on a straight line (or other systematic) basis, irrespective of the timing of the payments. Incentives also require to be recognised on the same basis.

✦ *Example*

Obelisk leases a second-hand machine for a five year period on 1 January 2009. Annual rentals of £4,000 are payable from 1 January 2010 to 2013. Obelisk was given the first year's rental free of charge as an incentive to take out the lease. What entries are required in Obelisk's financial statements assuming a 31 December year end?

Although Obelisk has not paid anything to the leasing company in the year to 31 December 2009, nevertheless it has had the use of the leased asset to generate income. In order to match the appropriate expense with the benefits generated we need to:

1. establish the total amount of lease payments made i.e. $4 \times £5,000 = £20,000$
2. allocate the total over the period of the lease on a straight line basis
    (i.e. £20,000/5 = £4,000 per annum).

£4,000 will therefore be charged to each accounting period in respect of the operating lease.
Note that the lease charge does not correspond with the relevant cash payments.

In the year to 31 December 2009, there will need to be an accrual to record the lease charge for that year, which will be reduced in subsequent years. That is:

Year 1			
Dr	Operating lease rentals (p&l a/c)	£4,000	
	Cr Accrual		£4,000
Being recording of lease charges.			

Years 2 – 5			
Dr	Operating lease rentals (p&l a/c)	£4,000	
	Accrual	£1,000	
	Cr Bank		£5,000
Being payment and recording of lease charges.			

Cash-back incentives

A similar approach is adopted where a company is offered cash back or reverse premium deals. These are treated as being a reduction of the rental expense over the lease term, and are recognised in the profit and loss account on a straight line (or other systematic) basis. The initial receipt of cash back is treated as deferred income and subsequently released to the profit and loss account.

 ## *Example*

Carpetbag leases a machine for five years and under the terms of the lease is required to make payments of £4,000 at the end of each year. As an incentive to take out the lease, Carpetbag was given an immediate cash back of £2,000 on signing the lease agreement.

In this example, the cash back is effectively a reduction in the net cost of the lease. The total lease payments are therefore:

(5 years × £4,000 per year) – cash back £2,000 = £18,000

As the lease is over 5 years, the annual charge to the profit and loss account will be £18,000/5 = £3,600.

In order to achieve this charge in the profit and loss account, the following entries will be recorded:

Year 1

Dr Bank	£2,000	
Cr Deferred income		£2,000
Being cash back received.		

This £2,000 will be released to the profit and loss account over the lease term at (£2,000/5) = £400 per annum.

The annual adjustments will therefore be:

Dr Operating lease charges (p&l a/c)	£4,000	
Cr Bank		£4,000
Being lease payments made.		

Dr Deferred income	£400	
Cr Operating lease charges (p&l a/c)		£400
Being annual release of cash back.		

The effect of the adjustments is that the annual charge in the profit and loss account in respect of operating lease charges is £3,600 (i.e. £4,000 – £400).

The profit and loss account extracts will be as follows:

	Yr 1 £	Yr 2 £	Yr 3 £	Yr 4 £
Lease income	4,000	4,000	4,000	4,000
Depreciation	3,500	3,500	3,500	3,500

The balance sheet would contain the net book value of the machine. Assuming the machine was purchased at the start of Year 1, the balance sheet entries would show the following:

	Yr 1 £	Yr 2 £	Yr 3 £	Yr 4 £
Fixed assets	31,500	28,000	24,500	21,000

Summary

The accounting provisions for some of the more common leasing arrangements have been set out from both the lessee's and the lessor's perspective. The main arguments for capitalising leases and the substance over form approach have also been put forward. It is now perhaps worth looking again at what adoption of IAS 17 prescribed accounting treatment achieves and whether this does meet the needs of the user.

This question instantly reverts to one of not whether a particular accounting treatment meets the needs of the user, but rather, what *are* the needs of the user. Moreover, are not the needs of the user determined by that user's expectations and what information is available to meet those expectations?

The question has perhaps therefore altered to one of identifying the user's expectations.

Accounting practices have evolved differently in different countries according to the cultural, economic, legal and political environments prevailing in those countries. Accordingly, if a legal bias is an overriding condition of 'fair view' reporting, then adoption of IAS 17 and capitalisation of leases will not meet the needs of those users. Such users expect to receive accounting information detailing total lease payments made in a year, not manipulated reconstructions of non-existent purchase agreements.

In such environments, IAS 17 will not meet its objectives. Consequently while IAS 17 fulfils expectations of reporting for many cultures, it should be remembered that it fulfils those expectations only because the users *have* those expectations of what accounting information should provide. That is, in these cultures and environments, the prerequisite expectation is a true and fair view, and the disclosure of the relevant information to provide that – for example, a substance over form approach allowing users to determine the assets in use by a reporting entity.

Equally convincing arguments could be put forward that show such treatments to be misleading. The values at which companies carry fixed assets are often a cause for criticism (i.e. historic cost). The capitalising of assets subject to lease agreements, it could be argued, simply adds to users' confusion as to what those values actually represent.

The final question must be therefore whether or not capitalising leases is desirable.

The answer to this is a resounding 'it depends': it depends on the user's needs, expectations, culture and legal background. In other words, 'yes' and 'no'.

BASIC

INTERMEDIATE

ADVANCED

Chapter summary

IAS 17 *Leases*

In the books of the lessee:

- accounting treatment depends on whether an operating or finance lease
- a finance lease is a lease that is, in substance, the purchase of an asset with debt
- an operating lease is any lease other than a finance lease; such a lease is treated as a rental transaction for accounting purposes
- finance leases should initially be recorded as an asset and a liability at the lower of the fair value of the asset and the present value of the minimum lease payments (discounted at the interest rate implicit in the lease)
- finance lease payments should be apportioned between the finance charge and the reduction of the outstanding liability (the finance charge to be allocated so as to produce a constant periodic rate of interest on the remaining balance of the liability)
- the asset should be depreciated over the shorter of the lease term and its useful life
- for operating leases, the lease payments should be recognised as an expense in the income statement over the lease term on a straight line basis.

In the books of the lessor:

- accounting treatment depends on whether an operating or finance lease
- finance leases should initially be recorded in the balance sheet as a receivable at an amount equal to the net investment in the lease
- finance income should be recognised in the income statement based on a pattern reflecting a constant periodic rate of return on the lessor's net investment outstanding in respect of the finance lease
- assets held for operating leases should be shown as assets and depreciated
- lease income from operating leases should be recognised in the income statement over the lease term on a straight line basis.

 Key terms for review

Definitions can be found in a glossary at the end of the book.

Lease	*Minimum lease payments*
Finance lease	*Net investment (in the lease)*
Operating lease	*Gross investment (in the lease)*
Lease term	*Interest rate implicit in the lease*
Lease payments (operating lease)	*Initial recognition (of finance lease)*
Fair value	

Review questions

1. Explain why a company might choose to lease an asset.
2. Explain the difference between a finance lease and an operating lease.
3. What are the advantages of capitalising leases in financial statements?
4. Explain the accounting treatment of a finance lease in the books of a lessee under IAS 17.
5. Explain the accounting treatment of an operating lease in the books of a lessee under IAS 17.
6. At the inception of a lease, at what value should lessees recognise finance leases as assets in their balance sheets?
7. Explain how an asset held under a finance lease should be depreciated.
8. Explain the accounting treatment of a finance lease in the books of a lessor under IAS 17.
9. Explain whether the legal form of all leases should take precedence over their substance.

 Exercises

1. Level I

On 1 January 2009, Ofbal Ltd took delivery of a new machine from Equipment Solutions Ltd on a finance lease. The terms of the lease are as follows:

Fair value of leased asset	£31,700
Primary period of lease	4 years
Rentals payable annually in arrears	£10,000
First payment	31/12/09
Implied interest rate	10%

The estimated useful life of the machine is five years, with a nil residual value.

At the end of the primary lease term the expected residual value is £5,000 and Ofbal Ltd can retain all of these proceeds.

Ofbal Ltd provides for depreciation on a straight line basis.

Required

Show the effect of this lease on the income statements and balance sheets of Ofbal Ltd for the four years to 31 December 2012, under the following headings:

 (i) lease creditor
 (ii) finance charge
(iii) depreciation charge, and
(iv) net book value of assets.

2. Level I

On 1 January 2009, Main Contractors Ltd leased a new machine from the Solvitol Finance Company. The following details were obtained from the lease agreement.

The capital cost of the machine at 1 January 2009 was £50,000.

Six half-yearly payments of £11,000 each are payable in advance, commencing 1 January 2009 in the primary term.

Three annual payments of £100 are payable in the secondary term. Main Contractors Ltd has not yet decided if it will take advantage of the secondary term.

The estimated useful life of the machine is five years, with a nil residual value. The estimated residual value after three years is £10,000 and, of this, 95% is accountable to Main Contractors Ltd. It is the policy of Main Contractors Ltd to use the straight line method of providing for depreciation.

Required

Calculate the effect of this rental on the annual accounts of Main Contractors Ltd to 31 December for the relevant years using the sum of the digits method to allocate finance charges under the following headings:

- (i) lease creditor
- (ii) finance charge
- (iii) depreciation, and
- (iv) net book value of asset.

3. Level I

Easygrow Ltd has leased an asset from the Lendalot Finance Co. Details are as follows:

- (i) Easygrow is responsible for insurance and maintenance, and is required to make five annual payments of £3,000, all payable in advance beginning on 1 January 2009, the date of commencement of the lease.
- (ii) After the primary lease period, Easygrow Ltd has the right to continue leasing the asset for an indefinite period for a nominal rental, which may be ignored.
- (iii) The asset may be bought outright for £10,620, which, it can be assumed, provides an acceptable approximation to the present value of the minimum lease payments discounted at the rate of interest implicit in the lease of 21%.
- (iv) Residual values may be ignored. The anticipated useful life of the asset is ten years and Easygrow intends to use the asset for this period. Easygrow uses the straight line method of providing for depreciation.

Required

Show the effect of this lease on the annual accounts of Easygrow Ltd for the years 2009 to 2013 under the following headings:

- (i) lease creditor
- (ii) finance charge
- (iii) depreciation charge, and
- (iv) net book value of assets.

4. Level II

On 1 January 2009, Osprey Fish Processing Company Ltd took delivery of a new fish filleting machine from the JLA finance company, on a finance lease.

The terms of the lease are as follows:

Primary period of lease	3 years
Frequency of rental payments	6 monthly in arrears
Amount of each rental	£5,000
First payment	30 June 2009

The cost of the machine was £25,379, which is thought to be fair value. The implied rate of interest applied half yearly is 5%.

The estimated useful life of the machine is three years, with a nil residual value.

It is the policy of the Osprey Fish Processing Company to depreciate assets on the straight line basis.

Required

- (a) Show the effect of this lease on the profit and loss accounts and balance sheets of Osprey Fish Processing Company Ltd for each of the three years to 31 December 2011.
- (b) Discuss the arguments for and against the capitalisation of finance leases in the accounts of the lessee.

5. Level II

In November 2009, the directors of Shockers Ltd, a manufacturer of electrical generators, were successful in their tender for a contract to supply generators to an international mining operator. An additional machine is now required to cope with the increased production levels resulting from the new contract and the directors have decided to lease, rather than buy the required machine. On 1 January 2010, the company took delivery of the new machine, which was leased through the Phoenix Finance Co Ltd. The terms of this lease are as follows:

Primary period of lease	4 years
Frequency of rental payments	Annually in advance
Amount of each rental	£10,000
First payment	1 January 2010

The cost to buy the machine is £34,868. The rate of interest implicit in the lease is 10% per annum. The estimated useful life of the machine is four years and Shockers Ltd provides for depreciation on the straight line basis.

Required

(a) Show the effect of this lease on the income statements and balance sheets of Shockers Ltd in each of the four years from 31 December 2010 to 31 December 2013 in accordance with the requirements of IAS 17.

(b) With reference to IA7 17 *Leases*, explain the difference between a finance lease and an operating lease, and discuss briefly the merits of capitalising a finance lease in the financial statements.

6. Level III

You have recently been appointed as finance director to a manufacturing company and are about to attend a board meeting to discuss the draft management accounts to 31 December 2009.

A change in company policy during the previous year saw a change from buying manufacturing equipment to leasing equipment. The book-keeper who prepares monthly management accounts for discussion at board meetings is unaware of the contents of IAS 17, and has treated all lease payments as expenses in the profit and loss account. A memorandum issued by the chairman to you and the other directors in response to the draft accounts detailed below advises of 'a substantial improvement in the company's performance. Our decision to lease rather than purchase outright our manufacturing equipment has had the desired effect on our financial statements. Our return on capital employed is now equal to the industry average and our gearing ratio is one of the lowest around. This is a clear indication of the success of our new strategy and our share price will no doubt reflect this once the statutory financial statements are made public.'

Draft income statement for year ended 31 December 2009	
	£
Turnover	3,500
Operating profit	1,500
Interest	25
Profit before tax	1,475
Tax	475
Profit after tax	1,000

Draft balance sheet at 31 December 2009	
	£
Fixed assets	500
Net current assets	1,500
	2,000
Bank loans due > 1 year	200
	1,800
Share capital	500
Reserves	1,300
	1,800

You are reviewing the draft financial statements with the senior book-keeper who provides the following information regarding two leases that were entered into on 1 January 2009.

Machine 1

Four annual instalments of £100,000 each, the first payment being made 1 January 2009. The cost of the machine were it to have been purchased was £348,680, and the finance cost implicit in the lease is 10% per year. The machine is expected to last five years.

Machine 2

A total of 24 monthly instalments of £1,000 per month payable in advance and terminable at any time by either party. The cash price of this machine would be £100,000 and its estimated useful life is ten years.

Company policy is to depreciate assets on the straight line basis. The effects on taxation can be ignored.

Required

(a) Explain, with reference to the two leases described above, the difference between a finance lease and an operating lease.
(b) Show the effect on the financial statements for the year ended 31 December 2009 of capitalising the company's finance lease in accordance with IAS 17. (Note: only leases that qualify as finance leases should be capitalised.)
(c) Calculate the following key ratios before and after capitalising the finance lease.

 (i) $\dfrac{\text{Operating profit}}{\text{Sales}}$

 (ii) Return on capital employed: $\dfrac{\text{earnings before interest and tax}}{\text{total assets less current libilities}}$

 (iii) Gearing: $\dfrac{\text{long-term debt}}{\text{shareholders' funds}}$

Draft a memorandum to the chairman explaining the impact of capitalising the finance lease on the ratios.

Further reading

G4+1 *Accounting for Leases – A New Approach.* July 1996

IAS 17 *Leases.* IASB, revised 2003

Allum *et al.* (1989) Fleet focus: to lease or not to lease. *Australian Accountant,* September.

Goodacre, A. (2003a) Assessing the potential impact of lease accounting reform: a review of the empirical evidence. *Journal of Property Research,* 20, 1, 49–66.

Goodacre, A. (2003b) Operating lease finance in the UK retail sector. *International Review of Retail, Distribution and Consumer Research*, 13, 1, 99–125.

McGregor, W. (1996) Lease accounting: righting the wrongs. *Accountancy*, September, 96.

Perera, R. (1986) To buy or not to buy – how to decide. *Certified Accountant*, December.

Appendix 1: Definitions of IAS 17

A lease is an agreement whereby the lessor conveys to the lessee, in return for a payment or series of payments, the right to use an asset for an agreed period of time.

A finance lease is a lease that transfers substantially all the risks and rewards incidental to ownership of an asset. Title may or may not eventually be transferred.

An operating lease is a lease other than a finance lease.

Economic life is either:

- the period over which an asset is expected to be economically usable by one or more users, or
- the number of production or similar units expected to be obtained from the asset by one or more users.

Useful life is the estimated remaining period, from the commencement of the lease term, without limitation by the lease term, over which the economic benefits embodied in the asset are expected to be consumed by the entity.

The lease term is the non-cancellable period for which the lessee has contracted to lease the asset, together with any further terms for which the lessee has the option to continue to lease the asset, with our without further payment, when, at the inception of the lease, it is reasonably certain that the lessee will exercise the option.

A non-cancellable lease is a lease that is cancellable in only one of the following four circumstances:

1. on the occurrence of some remote contingency
2. with the permission of the lessor
3. if the lessee enters into a new lease for the same or an equivalent asset with the same lessor
4. on payment by the lessee of an additional amount such that, at inception, continuation of the lease is reasonably certain.

The inception of the lease is the earlier of the date of the lease agreement and the date of commitment by the parties to the principal provisions of the lease. As at this date:

- a lease is classified as either an operating or a finance lease, and
- in the case of a finance lease, the amounts to be recognised at the commencement of the lease term are determined.

The commencement of the lease term is the date from which the lessee is entitled to exercise its right to use the leased asset. It is the date of initial recognition of the lease (i.e. the recognition of the assets, liabilities, income or expenses resulting from the lease, as appropriate).

Minimum lease payments are the payments over the lease term that the lessee is, or can be, required to make, excluding contingent rent, costs for services, and taxes to be paid by and reimbursed to the lessor, together with:

- in the case of the lessee, any amounts guaranteed by the lessee or by a party related to the lessee, or
- in the case of the lessor, any residual value guaranteed to the lessor by either:
  - (a) the lessee
  - (b) a party related to the lessee, or
  - (c) a third party unrelated to the lessor that is financially capable of discharging the obligations under the guarantee.

Fair value is the amount for which an asset could be exchanged or a liability settled, between knowledgeable, willing parties in an arm's length transaction.

From the viewpoint of the lessee, the guaranteed residual value that is part of the residual value that is guaranteed by the lessee or by a party related to the lessee (the amount of the guarantee) being the maximum amount that could, in any event, become payable.

From the viewpoint of the lessor, the guaranteed residual value is that part of the residual value that is guaranteed by the lessee or by a third party unrelated to the lessor who, is financially capable of discharging the obligations under the guarantee.

Unguaranteed residual value is that portion of the residual value of the leased asset, the realisation of which by the lessor is not assured or is guaranteed solely by a party related to the lessor.

The lessor's gross investment in the lease is the aggregate of the minimum lease payments receivable by the lessor under a finance lease and any unguaranteed residual value accruing to the lessor.

Net investment in the lease is the gross investment in the lease discounted at the interest rate implicit in the lease.

Unearned finance income is the difference between:

- the gross investment in the lease, and
- the net investment in the lease.

The interest rate implicit in the lease is the discount rate that, at the inception of the lease, causes the aggregate present value of (a) the minimum lease payments, and (b) the unguaranteed residual value to be equal to the sum of fair value of the leased asset and any initial direct cost of the lessor.

The lessee's incremental borrowing rate of interest is the rate of interest the lessee would have to pay on a similar lease or, if that is not determinable, the rate that, at the inception of the lease, the lessee would incur to borrow over a similar term, and with a similar security, the funds necessary to purchase the asset.

Contingent rent is that portion of the lease payments that is not fixed in amount but is based on the future amount of a factor that changes other than with the passage of time (e.g. percentage of sales, amount of usage, future price indices, future market rates of interest).

Inventories and Construction Contracts

Introduction

Inventories – also known as stocks – represent goods on hand at the year end that will be carried forward for sale in the next accounting period.

Section 1: Basic Principles

In the case of retail businesses, inventories are likely to consist of finished goods, while in the case of a manufacturing company these inventories may well comprise:

- raw materials (i.e. materials that will be subject to some manufacturing process prior to sale)
- work in progress (i.e. partially completed goods)
- finished goods (i.e. stocks that have been through the manufacturing process and are available for sale).

Some companies – particularly construction companies – have a further classification of year-end 'stock'. Such companies are often involved in projects that may last for more than one accounting period. Moreover, as these companies are normally hired to complete specific contracts (e.g. the construction of a bridge), they are unlikely ever to carry stocks of 'finished goods'. It is likely, however, that they will at the end of at least one accounting period, have a contract in progress and will, therefore, need to make appropriate accounting entries to reflect the work carried out to date. Furthermore, it may also be appropriate to recognise an element of the overall profit on the contract on an annual basis.

This chapter begins with an explanation of inventories, and in particular their accounting entries as far as double entry book-keeping is concerned, together with a review of stock valuation methods.

The detailed requirements of IAS 2 *Inventories* are then covered in the second section and, finally, the advanced section deals with the requirements of IAS 11 *Construction Contracts*.

5.1 Inventories

Depending on the type of organisation, there may be a perpetual record kept of inventory items – updated continually – or it may be that stocks are determined by means of a year-end stock take.

Whichever method is adopted, as far as financial reporting is concerned, a valuation will need to be made at each balance sheet date.

Progress Point 5.1

What main categories of stock are likely to be held by a manufacturing business?

Solution

A manufacturing business is likely to have the following categories of stock:

- raw materials (i.e. materials used in the manufacture of the particular product)
- work in progress (i.e. materials that have started but not completed the manufacturing process)
- finished goods (i.e. goods that are complete and available for sale).

5.2 The accounting issue involved

Inventories are a unique item within an organisation's financial statements as they appear in both the income statement, within cost of sales, and the balance sheet, within current assets. The profit for the year is calculated after charging appropriate costs against turnover. Any products that are unsold at the end of the year will be included within stock and carried forward to be charged against future years' turnover.

Example

Income statement extract		Balance sheet extract	
Costs of sales:		Current assets	
Opening stock	X	Stock	Y
Purchases	XX		
	XXX		
Less: closing stock	Y		
Cost of sales	XY		

Moreover, closing stock has a direct effect on profit and net assets as:

- an increase in closing stock will reduce cost of sales and increase profit, and result in an increase in net assets, and

■   a decrease in closing stock will increase cost of sales and reduce profit, and result in a decrease in net assets.

Consequently, inventory provides a rich area for the creative accountant. An increase in stock value will result in an increase in profit, and vice versa.

 Example

Dean commences in business selling fireplaces. In his first year of trading he buys 50 fireplaces costing £2,000 each (i.e. £100,000) and sells 45 of these for £3,000 each (i.e. £135,000). Five fireplaces remain in stock at the year end.

If the sales proceeds are simply compared with purchase costs (i.e. £135,000 − £100,000) it would appear that Dean has made a profit of £35,000. This is not the complete picture, however, as if the number of units bought is compared with number of units sold, it can be seen that Dean still has five fireplaces in stock at the year end, which he hopes to sell in the next accounting period.

If the matching concept is to be adhered to, then rather than comparing sales proceeds with absolute purchase costs, sales proceeds need to be compared with the comparative costs of the fireplaces that were sold (i.e. the cost of goods sold). This results in Dean's profit increasing to £45,000 (i.e. 45 × £3,000 − 45 × £2,000). The cost of goods sold is therefore the purchases made in the year – that is, 50 less the amount in stock at the year end (i.e. 5: (50 − 5 = 45)), giving a cost of goods sold of 45 × £2,000 = £90,000.

5.3 Accounting for stock

Double entry book-keeping

As noted above, many organisations determine year-end stocks by means of an annual stock take. This means that stocks will not automatically be included in the organisation's double entry system or, consequently, trial balance. To continue the example above, Dean will have stock on hand at year end with a cost of £10,000 (5 × £2,000). As far as Dean's trial balance is concerned it will simply show the sales value of the fireplaces sold and the purchase price of *all* fireplaces purchased, e.g. extract trial balance:

Extract trial balance	Dr	Cr
Sales		£135,000
Purchases	£100,000	

In order to account for the unsold items, a stock adjustment needs to be prepared to show the value of the stocks on hand at the year end – i.e. £10,000 (5 × £2,000). The journal entry to account for this is as follows:

Dr	Closing stock (balance sheet)	£10,000	
Cr	Closing stock (income statement)		£10,000
Being closing stock.			

and has the effect of crediting the income statement (and thus reducing costs) with the value of the unsold fireplaces. It also has the effect of deferring the expenditure on those fireplaces to the balance sheet, where it will be expensed in the next accounting period. Dean's income statement and balance sheet extracts will show the following:

Income statement (extract) For Year 1		
	£	£
Sales		135,000
Less: Cost of sales		
Purchases	100,000	
Less: closing stock	10,000	
		90,000
Gross profit		45,000

Balance sheet (extract) As At Year 1	
	£
Current assets	
Stock	10,000

Suppose that, in the next accounting period, Dean purchases a further 60 fireplaces but that the cost of these has now increased to £2,100 each (i.e. £126,000). He sells 53 fireplaces in the year for £3,200 each (i.e. £169,600), 12 fireplaces remain in stock at year end, all at a cost of £2,100 each (i.e. £25,200).

In order to calculate the profit made in the second accounting period, it is once more necessary to match the cost of the fireplaces sold with their purchase cost.

Dean has sold 53 fireplaces: five fireplaces from the purchases made in the first year and 48 from the purchases made in the second year. His profit is therefore:

	£	£
Sales 53 x £3,200		169,600
Less: costs		
5 x £2,000	10,000	
48 x £2,100	100,800	
		110,800
Profit		58,800

In this example, it has been possible to match sales exactly with the cost of the items sold. In practice, however, this may not be possible and, as noted above, stocks are often measured annually by means of a stock take. This brings in valuation issues and these will be covered in the next section. Continuing with this example, if the opening and closing stock figures are inserted within the cost of sales calculation, Dean's income statement and balance sheet extracts will show the following:

Income statement (extract) For Year 2		
	£	£
Sales		169,600
Less : Cost of sales		
Opening stock	10,000	
Add : purchases	126,000	
	136,000	
Less : closing stock	25,200	
		110,800
Gross profit		58,800

Balance Sheet (Extract) As at Year 2	
Current Assets	£
Stock	25,200

The journal entries required to account for the stock adjustments through cost of sales are as follows.

First, the closing stock at the end of Year 1 will require to be transferred to the income statement as an expense in Year 2 (i.e. these stocks have been sold in Year 2 and will therefore form part of the cost of sales calculation):

Dr	Opening stock (Income statement)	£10,000	
	Cr Stock (Balance sheet)		£10,000
Being transfer to cost of sales.			

Second, the stock on hand at the end of Year 2 needs to be accounted for as follows:

Dr	Closing stock (Balance sheet)	£25,200	
	Cr Closing stock (Income statement)		£25,200
Being closing stock.			

It can be seen that, because of the matching process, the cost of the unsold items at each year end is deferred to the next accounting period. Moreover, because of the cost of sales calculation, the higher the closing stock figure at the year end, the higher will be the reported gross profit, and vice versa.

Progress Point 5.2

What are the effects of omitting goods costing £1,000 from the year-end stock figure?

Solution

If stocks are omitted, this would increase cost of sales by £1,000 and consequently reduce profit by £1,000. Net assets would also be reduced by £1,000.

Valuation methods

The application of the matching principle requires the identification of the cost of goods sold to be charged against revenues received. The cost of goods sold calculation itself results in two complementary aspects of this problem: the first involves the identification of the cost of goods sold during each accounting period; the second involves the identification of the value (or cost) of goods unsold at the end of a period. The cost of goods unsold at the end of one period must be carried forward and allocated as expenses in the future periods in which revenues will be received from the ultimate sale of the goods.

It is worth noting at this stage that only those stocks that are expected to yield future economic benefits should be carried forward. Consequently, if any of the fireplaces in the previous example were, for instance, so badly damaged that a future sale would be impossible, then their cost would immediately be recognised in the income statement as an expense of that period. It should also be noted that increases in the value of closing stock are not recognised as it is not prudent to do so. This would be anticipating income in the hope of a future sale, which would conflict with the prudence concept.

Inventory cost recognition

In the earlier example, Dean was able to calculate the cost of sales by reference to the unit cost of the specific fireplaces sold. In many cases, however, stocks may be indistinguishable from one another and, if costs have altered over an accounting period, the accountant is faced with a problem of cost recognition. In such circumstances, where it is physically impossible to identify which units were purchased at which cost, it is necessary to introduce a systematic method of cost recognition that will identify the order in which costs are to be allocated or expensed. Without such a system, the accountant is faced with a bewildering array of potential cost of goods sold figures – and values for closing stock – as the following example shows.

 ## Example

Uno Retailing Ltd sells a single product line. Purchases and sales during the month of November 2009 were as follows:

Opening stock		Nil
Purchases	(i) 10 units @ £5 each	£50
	(ii) 25 units @ £6 each	£150
		£200
Sales: 25 units at a price of £10 each		£250

The retailer is therefore faced with two problems:

1. identifying which costs to set against revenues for the month of November, and
2. identifying which costs to assign to the closing stock of unsold goods.

First in first out (FIFO) method

The method that appeals intuitively is to recognise costs in the order in which they actually occur. That is, the costs of goods acquired first should be expensed first (i.e. first in first out); the units remaining will therefore be regarded as representing the latest units purchased. Calculation of gross profit for Uno Retailing Ltd using the FIFO basis of cost recognition is as follows:

	£
Sales revenue	250
Cost of goods sold:	
10 units @ £5	50
15 units @ £6	90
	140
Gross profit	110
Closing stock: 10 units @ £6	£60

Last in first out (LIFO) method

Here, the order of cost recognition is reversed so that the last costs incurred will be recognised first. It is argued that, in times of rising prices, this method produces a cost of goods sold figure that reflects a close approximation to replacement cost, while still retaining the historic cost system of valuation, and thus gives a more realistic profit figure. It should be noted, however, that this will produce a relatively

BASIC

INTERMEDIATE

ADVANCED

lower closing stock figure. Calculation of gross profit for Uno Retailing Ltd using the LIFO basis of cost recognition is as follows:

	£
Sales revenue	250
Cost of goods sold	
25 units @ £6	150
Gross profit	100
Closing stock: 10 units @ £5 each	50

Weighted average cost (AVCO) method

Using this method, the average cost is applied and weighted, according to the different proportions at the different cost levels, to the items in stock. Weighted average unit cost is calculated by dividing the total cost of units acquired during an accounting period by the number of units acquired.

The weighted average cost of goods purchased by Uno Retailing Ltd for the month of November 2009 is as follows:

$$\frac{(10 \times £5) + (£25 \times £6)}{35 \text{ units}}$$
$$= \frac{£200}{35 \text{ units}}$$
$$= £5.71$$

Calculation of gross profit for Uno Retailing Ltd using a weighted average system of cost recognition is as follows:

	£
Sales revenue	250.00
Cost of goods sold	
25 units @ £5.71	142.75
Gross profit	107.25
Closing stock: 10 units @ £5.71 each	57.10

Base inventory method

This final method is based on the argument that a certain minimum level of stocks is necessary in order to remain in business at all. It is argued therefore that some of the stocks viewed in the aggregate are not really available for sale and should instead be regarded as a fixed asset. This minimum level – defined by management – remains at its original cost and the remainder of the stock above this level is treated, as stock, by one of the other methods. Assume for Uno Retailing Ltd that the minimum level is five units. Calculation of gross profit for Uno Retailing Ltd based on a minimum stock level of five units and using FIFO is as follows:

	£
Sales revenue	250
Cost of goods sold	
5 units @ £5[1]	25
20 units @ £6	120
	145
Gross profit	105
Closing stock: base stock	
5 units @ £5 each	25
5 units @ £6 each	30
	55

[1] Of the original purchase of ten units, five are being treated as base stock.

Which method should be used?

The method chosen should provide the fairest practicable approximation to cost. In the UK, however, neither the use of LIFO nor base stock is permitted under SSAP 9 as these methods often result in stocks being stated in the balance sheet at amounts that bear little relationship to recent cost levels. When this happens, not only can the presentation of current assets be misleading, but subsequent periods' profits may also be distorted if stock levels reduce and out-of-date costs are transferred into cost of sales in the income statement.

FIFO and weighted average cost are both permitted methods under SSAP 9.

Progress Point 5.3

(a) Name three methods of stock valuation. Describe the differences between them, and the effects of those differences in terms of rising prices.

(b) Bedrock Supplies commenced trading on 1 April, supplying tarmac. During this month, the following transactions took place:

			Tonnes	Cost per ton
April	1	Purchased	10,000	£10
	9	Purchased	20,000	£13
	17	Sold	10,000	

Required

Calculate cost of sales and closing stocks for Bedrock Supplies using the FIFO, LIFO and AVCO methods of stock valuation.

Solution

(a) The three methods of stock valuation are as follows.

First in first out (FIFO)
Under this method, the costs of stocks that were acquired first are expensed first. In times of rising prices, this means that balance sheet stocks are carried at higher (up-to-date) values and this therefore gives a higher profit in the profit and loss account as cost of sales is based on lower (out-of-date) values.

Last in first out (LIFO)

Under this method, the costs of stock that are acquired last are expensed first. In times of rising prices this will give a lower profit figure as sales will be matched against up-to-date costs and the balance sheet will have a correspondingly lower stock figure as it will be valued at lower (out-of-date) values.

Average cost (AVCO)

Under this method, the cost of costs sold and closing stock figures are based upon a weighted average unit cost. In times of rising prices this would result in a profit and stock figure that is between the two identified under FIFO and LIFO. The balance sheet would therefore carry stocks at an understated value, and the correspondingly lower closing stock figure in the profit and loss account would result in an understated profit figure.

(b)   The cost of sales and closing stocks under the three methods would be as follows.

FIFO

Under the FIFO method, it is the first 10,000 tonnes that are assumed to be sold first. The remainder – which are the later purchases – will comprise the closing inventories.

Cost of sales	=	10,000 tonnes × £10	=	£100,000
Closing stock	=	20,000 tonnes × £13	=	£260,000

LIFO

Under the LIFO method, it is the later purchases that are assumed to be the first sold and so it will be the remainder of the later purchases plus the earlier purchases that will comprise the closing stocks.

Cost of sales	=	10,000 × £13	=	£130,000
Closing stock	=	(20,000 – 10,000) × £13 + 10,000 × £10	=	£230,000

AVCO

Under the AVCO method, the weighted average of the stocks purchased during the period will be used to determine a unit cost to be applied to the number of units sold in cost of sales and the number of units held in closing stock.

$$\text{Average cost per unit} = \frac{(10{,}000 \times £10) + (20{,}000 \times £13)}{(10{,}000 + 20{,}000)}$$

	=	£12 per tonne		
Cost of sales	=	10,000 x £12	=	£120,000
Closing stock	=	20,000 x £12	=	£240,000

Perpetual and periodic stock valuation

As was noted earlier, depending on the type of the organisation, there may be a perpetual record kept of stock items, maintained and updated continuously as items are purchased and sold. This has the advantage of providing stock information on a timely basis but requires the maintenance of a full set of stock records. In contrast, with a periodic system of stock valuation, stocks are determined by a physical count at a specific date. The stock shown in the balance sheet is determined by the physical count and is priced in accordance with the cost recognition method used. The net change between opening and closing stock enters in to the computation of cost of goods sold. The examples above all use periodic valuations. The journal entries required to record cost of purchases and goods sold are as shown within the Dean's Fireplaces example (page 258).

With the perpetual method of cost recognition and stock valuation, cost of goods sold will be identified immediately each sale has been made. Transfers from the stock account to cost of goods sold expense account will be made following a sale, with the result that the stock account will be continuously adjusted to the actual level of stocks held.

Example: periodic vs perpetual stock valuation

Purchases and sales made by Handy Stores for the first seven days of June 2009 are as follows:

Day			
	1	Purchases	20 units @ £5 each
	3	Sales	15 units
	5	Purchases	30 units @ £6 each
	7	Sales	10 units

The effect of the application of different approaches is illustrated below. FIFO, LIFO and weighted average are compared using a periodic basis and perpetual basis of cost recognition and stock valuation.

FIFO: periodic stock valuation

Cost of goods sold		Closing stock	
	£		£
20 units @ £5	100		
5 units @ £6	30	25 units @ £6	150
	130		150

FIFO: perpetual stock valuation

	Day	Units	Unit price	Stock balance	Cost of goods sold	
			£	£	£	
Goods in	1	20	5	100		
Goods out	3	(15)	5	75	75	(15 @ £5)
		5		25		
Goods in	5	30	6	180		
		35		205		
Goods out	7	(10)		(55)	25	(5 @ £5)
					30	(5 @ £6)
Balance		25	6	150	130	

LIFO: periodic stock valuation

Cost of goods sold		Closing stock	
			£
25 units @ £6	150	20 units @ £5	100
		5 units @ £6	30
			130

BASIC

INTERMEDIATE

ADVANCED

LIFO: perpetual stock valuation

	Day	Units	Unit price	Stock balance	Cost of goods sold
			£	£	£
Goods in	1	20	5	100	
Goods out	3	(15)	5	(75)	75 (15 @ £5)
		5		25	
Goods in	5	30	6	180	
		35		205	
Goods out	7	(10)	6	(60)	60 (10 x £6)
Balance		25		145	135
			Comprising 5 @ £5	25	
			20 @ £6	120	
				145	

Weighted average: periodic stock valuation

Cost of goods sold		Closing stock	
			£
25 units @ £5.60	£140	25 units @ £5.60	140

Weighted average cost $= \dfrac{(20 \times £5) + (30 \times £6)}{(20 + 50)}$

$= £5.60$ per unit

Weighted average: perpetual stock valuation

	Day	Units	Unit price	Stock balance	Cost of goods sold
			£	£	£
Goods in	1	20	5	100	
Goods out	3	(15)	5	(75)	75 (15 x £5)
		5		25	
Goods in	5	30	6	180	
Averaged to:		35	5.86	205	
Goods out	7	10	5.86	(58.60)	58.60 (10 x £5.86)
Balance		25		£146.40	£133.60

As the above comparisons show, under the FIFO method of cost recognition, the same figures for cost of goods sold and closing stock are produced whether calculated on a periodic or perpetual basis. The LIFO and weighted average (AVCO) methods, however, produce different results according to whether they are applied on a perpetual or periodic basis.

Progress Point 5.4

If a company maintains a perpetual inventory control system, is it necessary to have an annual stock take?

Solution

With an efficient and accurate perpetual inventory system, in theory, an annual stock take would not be necessary as closing stock figures at any date can be taken from the stock records. An annual stock take does provide, however – albeit at a cost – a useful independent check on the accuracy of the perpetual inventory system. This may highlight and bring to the attention of management irregularities, such as theft, that could otherwise go undetected.

The problems identified

As the above examples have illustrated, the calculation of cost of goods sold and closing stock is by no means clear cut. The use of different cost recognition methods results in different values and those differences are further compounded depending upon whether a periodic or perpetual stock system is maintained. The examples given above deal with finished goods. In reality, the problems will be much greater. It will not only be finished goods that will require valuation. In manufacturing businesses not only will the raw materials need to be valued but also the cost of converting raw materials into products and services for sale. This brings cost of purchase and cost of conversion into the valuation requirements. Cost of conversion brings the need to consider both direct and indirect overhead costs. Although direct costs ought to be easily identified, indirect overheads, by definition, will need to be assigned to particular units of product or service according to some reasonable allocation basis. This necessarily introduces assumptions and approximations to the equation – for example, the derivation of normal level of activity and the calculation of a reasonable overhead cost rate. As can be seen, therefore, the valuation of stocks is by no means straightforward, and it requires management to make several judgements.

Summary

It is a fundamental accounting principle that revenues earned are matched with the related costs incurred in earning them. In determining the profit or loss for a particular period, the costs of the goods sold need to be calculated; in determining the profit or loss for future periods the cost of unsold stocks at the end of one financial year needs to be carried forward to the next accounting period so that they can be matched with the revenue recognised on their future sale. The stock value is therefore a crucial element not only in the computation of profit, but also in the valuation of assets for balance sheet purposes. In the next section, the requirements of IAS 2 *Inventories* are reviewed in detail, together with how IAS 2 seeks to narrow the differences and variations that result from the array of valuation methods available.

Section 2: Intermediate Issues

5.4 IAS 2 *Inventories*

Objective

The objective of IAS 2 is to prescribe the accounting treatment for inventories. It provides guidance for determining the cost of inventories and for subsequently recognising an expense, including any write-down to net realisable value. It also provides guidance on the cost formulas that are used to assign costs to inventories.

Scope

IAS 2 defines (para. 6) inventories as assets that:

(a) are held for sale in the ordinary course of business (i.e. finished goods)
(b) are in the process of production for such sale (i.e. work in process), or
(c) are in the form of materials or supplies to be consumed in the production process or in the rendering of services.

However, IAS 2 excludes certain inventories from its scope (para. 2):

- work in progress arising under construction contracts (covered by IAS 11 *Construction Contracts*)
- financial instruments (covered by IAS 39 *Financial Instruments*)
- biological assets related to agricultural activity and agricultural produce at the point of harvest (covered by IAS 41 *Agriculture*).

In addition, while the following are within the scope of the standard, IAS 2 does not apply to the measurement of inventories held by:

- producers of agricultural and forest products, agricultural produce after harvest, and minerals and mineral products to the extent that they are measured at net realisable value (above or below cost) in accordance with well-established practices in those industries; when such inventories are measured at net realisable value, changes in that value are recognised in profit or loss in the period of the change
- commodity brokers and dealers who measure their inventories at fair value less costs to sell; when such inventories are measured at fair value less costs to sell, changes in fair value less costs to sell are recognised in profit or loss in the period of the change.

Fundamental principle of IAS 2

The standard accounting practice set out in paragraph 9 of IAS 2 is as follows:

Inventories shall be measured at the lower of cost and net realisable value.

This basic principle therefore requires that, in order to make such a comparison of cost and net realisable value, for each separate item of inventory the following needs to be determined:

- cost
- net realisable value (NRV).

The separate item point is significant, and para. 29 requires that inventories be written down to net realisible value on an item-by-item basis. It is allowable, however, for a group of similar items to be

accounted for together – for example, items coming from the same product line (e.g. 500 g and 1 kg bags of flour). Returning to the separate item point, if the total cost was compared to the total net realisable value – without regard to the individual items making up the total – there could be an imprudent set-off of losses against unrealised profits. The following example illustrates this point.

 ## Example

An enterprise has four products in its inventory with values as follows:

Product	Cost	NRV
	£	£
A	100	140
B	200	250
C	300	210
D	400	600
	£1,000	£1,200

At what value should the inventory be stated in the balance sheet in accordance with IAS 2?

Solution

The correct value is:

Product	Lower of cost and NRV	
	£	
A	100	(cost)
B	200	(cost)
C	210	(NRV)
D	400	(cost)
	£910	

If the inventory is not separated into each type it would be valued at the lower of cost of £1,000 and NRV £1,200 (i.e. £1,000). However, IAS 2 requires each type of inventory to be valued separately and therefore the correct value is £910.

Progress Point 5.5

IAS 2 requires that inventories should be measured at the lower of cost and net realisable value. Why is this necessary?

Solution

It is necessary to value stocks in this way to adhere to the prudence and realisation concepts. If net realisable value is less than cost, then to use cost would be to overstate the future benefits expected from the sale of the stock item. This will go against prudence. On the other hand, if net realisable value is higher than cost, to include the higher figure would mean that unrealised profits were being taken, would be contrary to the prudence concept.

In order to be able to correctly account for the value of stock, an understanding of the definitions of cost and net realisable value is necessary.

5.5 Cost

The cost of stock is defined in IAS 2 (para. 10) as comprising all costs of purchase, costs of conversion and other costs incurred in bringing the inventories to their present location and condition.

Costs of purchase

Paragraph 11 further extends the costs of purchase to include:

- the purchase price
- import duties and other taxes (other than those subsequently recoverable by the enterprise from the taxing authority)
- transport costs (to the current location)
- handling costs, and
- other costs directly attributable to the acquisition of finished goods, materials and services.

And to deduct:

- trade discounts (but not settlement discount for early payment, which should be taken directly to profit and loss)
- rebates, and
- other similar items (e.g. subsidies).

Costs of conversion (para. 12)

These include:

- direct costs (e.g. direct materials and direct labour found from manufacturing or costing records)
- the systematic allocation of fixed production overheads (e.g. depreciation, maintenance charges)
- the systematic allocation of variable production overheads (e.g. indirect materials and labour).

Production overheads can be based on a number of methods and can include a wide range of overheads. Fixed overheads are those indirect costs of production that remain relatively constant regardless of volume of production over a defined period of time, whereas variable overheads are those that vary directly with changes in volume over a defined period of time.

IAS 2, by stating that fixed costs should be included, therefore requires absorption costing for dealing with overheads. Absorption costing absorbs all production costs into products and the unsold inventory is valued at total cost of production. With marginal (or variable) costing, only variable costs of production are absorbed into products and the unsold inventory is valued at variable costs of production. With marginal costing, fixed costs of production are treated as a cost of the period in which they are incurred.

The allocation of fixed production overheads, however, must be based only on the normal capacity of the production facilities, taking into account the loss of capacity resulting from planned maintenance. Normal capacity is the production expected to be achieved on average over a number of periods. If production is below normal, fixed production overhead per unit should not be increased as a result of the low production or idle plant. The reason for this is straightforward. Stocks and cost of goods sold are being valued to adhere to the matching concept. If the increased cost per unit resulting from under-capacity or idle plant were to be absorbed into stock, the cost of such inefficiencies would be effectively masked and deferred to be recognised in some future accounting period.

The same principle does not, however, apply to abnormally high levels of production. Stock is never valued above the actual cost incurred.

The following examples illustrate these points.

Example: under recovery of overheads

A company has variable production costs of £200 per unit and total fixed production costs of £800,000. Normal capacity of production is 10,200 units but this is reduced by 200 units for planned maintenance.

During the year to 31 December 2009, actual production was 8,000 units, of which 550 were in closing stock. What is the cost of the closing stock?

Solution

	£
Variable cost per unit	200
Fixed cost per unit (£800,000/10,000)	80
Total cost per unit	280
Stock cost 550 units x £280	£154,000

Note that the fixed overheads have been allocated based on normal production levels after taking account of planned maintenance (i.e. 10,200 – 200 = 10,000 units). The under-recovered overheads are an expense of the period. That is, the overheads which would have been deferred had the fixed costs been allocated according to the *actual* level of production: £800,000/8000 = £100 × 550 = £55,000.

 ## Example: abnormally high production levels

Continuing with the above example, what would the cost of closing stock be if actual production was 11,200 units?

Solution

	£
Variable cost per unit	200
Fixed cost per unit (£800,000/11,200)	271
Total cost per unit	271
Stock cost 550 units x £271	£149,050

Note that when production is abnormally high, fixed costs per unit is based on actual production – resulting in a lower cost per unit figure. This ensures that the cost of closing stock is never higher than the actual cost incurred. Had a cost per unit based on normal production levels been used, this would, if all units remained in stock at the period end, result in the fixed costs being absorbed into the stock cost being higher than the actual fixed production costs incurred, i.e. (£800,000/10,000) × 11,200 = £896,000.

Other costs (para. 15)

Other costs should be included only if they are incurred in bringing the stock to its present location and condition. It may be appropriate to include certain non-production overheads.

BASIC

INTERMEDIATE

ADVANCED

Administration overheads

Administration overheads are in respect of the whole business so only that portion that is easily identifiable to production should form part of the valuation. For example, the costs of the personnel or payroll department could be apportioned to production on a head-count basis and that element would be included in the stock valuation. In addition, any production-specific administration costs (e.g. welfare costs, canteen costs) would also be included in the inventory valuation. Design costs related to a specific item of stock is another example. If the expense cannot be identified as forming part of the production process, it will not form part of the inventory valuation.

Selling and distribution overheads

These costs will not normally be included in the stock valuation as they are incurred after production has taken place. An exception to this rule exists, however, if the goods are on a 'sale or return' basis and are on the premises of the customer – but still belong to the supplier. In such circumstances the delivery and packing costs will be included in the stock value of goods held on a customer's premises.

Interest costs

It may be possible to include interest on borrowings under IAS 23, as interest may be capitalised on a qualifying asset.

A qualifying asset is an asset that necessarily takes a substantial period of time to get ready for its intended use or sale (IAS 23, para. 4). Most stocks do not take a substantial period. An exception is maturing whisky, which takes several years to get to a sellable condition.

Progress Point 5.6

The following cost, overhead and expenses data relate to Hogden Company for the year ended 31 December 2009.

	£
Direct material cost of trowel per unit	1
Direct labour cost of trowel per unit	1
Direct expenses cost of trowel per unit	1
Production overheads per year	600,000
Administration overheads per year	200,000
Selling overheads per year	300,000
Interest payments per year	100,000

At the year end there were 250,000 trowels in finished goods stock. You may assume that there were no finished goods at the start of the year and that there was no work in progress. The normal annual level of production is 750,000 trowels, but in the year ended 31 December 2009, only 450,000 were produced because of a labour dispute.

Calculate the cost of the stock of trowels at 31 December 2009.

Suggested solution

The direct costs of the stock are straightforward to identify and calculate:

	£
250,000 trowels at £1 direct material cost	250,000
250,000 trowels at £1 direct labour cost	250,000
250,000 trowels at £1 direct expenses cost	250,000
	750,000

The production overheads of £600,000 will be allocated according to normal levels of production (i.e. £600,000/750,000 = £0.80 per unit). No account will be taken of the selling overheads or the interest payments as these are not incurred in respect of a qualifying asset.

Closing stock will therefore be valued at:

	£
Direct costs	750,000
Production overheads 250,000 x £0.80	200,000
	£950,000

The abnormal costs associated with the labour dispute (i.e. £600,000 − (450,000 × £0.8) = £240,000) will be charged as an expense in the period they are incurred. Note that this is not an additional expense. The production overheads of £600,000 will remain. It is just that they will be allocated as follows:

	£
Cost of sales (200,000 units @ £0.80)	160,000
Closing stock (250,000 units @ £0.80)	200,000
Abnormal costs (300,000 units @ £0.80)	240,000
	£600,000

IAS 2 (para. 16) gives examples of items that should not be included in the cost of stock. These are:

- abnormal amounts of wasted materials, labour or other production costs
- storage costs (unless necessary in the production process prior to a further production stage, e.g. drying of wood before being made into furniture)
- administrative overheads that do not contribute to bringing stocks to their current location and condition
- selling costs (because the items are in stock and have not yet been sold unless, as noted earlier, these stocks are sale or return items held on a customer's premises), and
- interest cost when inventories are purchased with deferred settlement terms; when the transaction effectively contains a financing element, any difference between the purchase price on normal credit terms and the amount paid, is recognised as a finance cost over the period of the financing (para. 18).

BASIC

INTERMEDIATE

ADVANCED

Progress Point 5.7

Which of the following costs can be included in the cost of inventory under IAS 2?

- Discounts on purchase price
- Import duties
- Transport insurance
- Commission and brokerage costs
- Storage costs after receiving materials that are necessary in the production process
- Salaries of sales department
- Warranty cost
- Research for new products
- Audit fees

Suggested solution

Discounts on purchase price	Yes
Import duties	Yes
Transport insurance	Yes
Commission on brokerage costs	Yes
Storage costs after receiving materials that are necessary in the production process	Yes
Salaries of sales department	No
Warranty cost	No
Research for new products	No
Audit fees	No

It is worth pausing for a moment here to recap on the accounting issues at hand. In endeavouring to adhere to the matching concept, only those costs that are incurred in bringing the inventories to their present location and condition should be included. Abnormal amounts of wasted materials, labour or other production costs should not be included in the cost of stock. With this in mind, try working through Progress Point 5.8, which illustrates many of the issues covered so far in this chapter.

Progress Point 5.8

The following information relates to the actual production of vodka for the month of November.

	£
Cost of grain and other materials	30,000
Direct wages	4,000
Indirect production costs	6,000
Power	1,000
Administration – production	1,200
– general	1,350
Selling and marketing costs	3,400
Discount received for early payment	500
Depreciation	3,500

Notes

1. All administration costs and 40% of indirect production costs are fixed.
2. Included in depreciation is £1,850 relating to the distilling process. Depreciation is based on output.
3. 95% of the power relates to production.
4. Normal capacity is 300,000 litres per month.

Calculate the cost per litre of vodka in accordance with the requirements of IAS 2 assuming actual production in November was 240,000 litres.

Suggested solution

In tackling a problem such as this, a good approach is to 'simplify' the data by discounting any information that is not relevant. By following the requirements of IAS 2 (para. 16), the following details can immediately be erased:

	£
Administration – general	1,350
Selling and marketing costs	3,400
Discounts received for early payment	500

That is, general administration costs will not form part of the production process; selling and marketing costs will be incurred *after* production of the vodka has taken place; discounts received for early payment are treated as other income and do not affect the purchase price.

After taking account of the proportions of costs that are variable as given in the additional information notes, this leaves the following allowable costs that need to be allocated between fixed and variable costs:

	£
Costs of grain and other materials	30,000
Direct wages	4,000
Variable indirect production costs (60% x 6,000)	3,600
Power (95% x 1,000)	950
Depreciation	1,850
Total variable production costs	40,400
Fixed indirect production costs (40% x 6,000)	2,400
Fixed production administration	1,200
Total fixed production costs	3,600

The variable cost per litre can be calculated as follows:

Total variable costs/actual production
= 40,400 ÷ 240,000 = £0.1683 per litre

The allocation of fixed costs is more complex.

First, actual production needs to be compared with normal production, to determine whether or not there is an over- or under-recovery. In this instance, production is below normal and consequently the allocation of fixed overhead must be based on the level of normal capacity (i.e. 300,000 litres). (Remember that if actual production was greater than normal, we would have used the actual production volume.)

The fixed cost per litre can, therefore, be calculated as follows:

Total fixed production costs/normal production
= 3,600/300,000 = £0.012

The total cost per litre for November is as follows:

	£	
Variable cost	0.1683	
Fixed cost	0.012	
	£0.1803	i.e. 18.03 pence

Techniques for the measurement of cost

IAS 2 permits the use of the standard cost method, where normal levels of materials, supplies, labour, efficiency and capacity utilisation will be used to calculate a standard cost. A standard cost is a target cost that should be attained under specified operating conditions. In many cases this may be the only way to value manufactured goods in a high-volume/high-turnover environment. The standard also permits the use of the retail method. Under the retail method the cost of inventory is determined by reducing the sales value of the inventory by the appropriate gross profit margin. Problems can occur where a retailer deals in products of widely differing profit margins, or discounts slow-moving items.

Use of standard costs (para. 21)

The standard cost method may be used for the measurement of cost, provided that the results approximate to actual cost. Standard costs have to be reviewed regularly if this method is used. Adjustments will need to be made for significant variances. Variances that relate to abnormal events of the period should not be adjusted for as they relate to the period and should be written off in the period. They should not be carried forward in stock as this would simply defer the abnormality to a future accounting period and contravene the prudence principle.

 ### Example: standard cost method

Allandale Ltd estimated the following standard cost for product X at 1 January 2009, the beginning of its accounting year.

	£ per unit
Direct labour	50
Direct materials	200
Direct expenses	40
Production overheads	60
Selling and distribution	20
	370

The following variances (i.e. differences between the planned standard cost and actual cost), occurred during the year. (Note: an adverse variance arises when the actual cost is greater than the standard cost; a favourable variance arises when the actual cost is less than the standard cost.)

- Labour – £120,000 favourable: this resulted from a more efficient use of labour throughout the year.
- Material – £20,000 adverse: this was caused by an undetected machine fault leading to materials being damaged and scrapped.
- Direct expenses – £60,000 favourable: a new subcontractor was used from 1 September 2009 onwards; resulting in reduced subcontracting costs.

At 31 December 2009, 2,000 units of product X were in stock. Total production for the year was 12,000 units. Allandale uses the FIFO method for stock valuation purposes.

Required

Calculate the cost of the closing stock of product X.

Solution

As explained earlier, decide which of the information given is relevant. While selling and distribution costs may well be relevant to Allandale for internal control purposes, they are not permitted, under IAS 2, to be included in the stock valuation and so should be excluded from the calculation of closing stock.

Having decided which information is relevant, decide whether adjustments need to be made for the variances. If so, these will add to, or reduce, the standard cost.

	£
Cost of stock at standard cost	
2,000 units x (£370 – £20)	700,000
Labour variance (favourable)	
Adjustment should be made as standard was inaccurate	
Units in stock equal 1/6 of production (2,000/12,000)	
∴ 1/6 of variance = 1/6 x 120,000	(20,000)
Material variance (adverse)	
This was due to an abnormal event and no adjustment should be made.	
Expenses variance (favourable)	
This should be adjusted for as it is a normal event – it is just that it was not anticipated when the original standard was set.	
As the variance occurred over the last four months of the year and closing stock equals the last two months of production the adjustment is:	
(2,000/4,000) x £60,000	(30,000)
Closing stock of product X	£650,000

Consider in detail the adjustments made, as described below.

(i)   Selling and distribution costs, while no doubt invaluable information for internal control purposes, are not permitted to be included in closing stocks and so are removed from the initial unitary standard cost valuation (i.e. £370 – £20 = £350 per unit).

(ii) The favourable labour variance needs to be deducted from the standard cost as calculated. This is because the reduction in costs is due to greater efficiency. If no adjustment was made and the standard cost of £50 per unit was maintained there would be, by default, an element of inefficiency being included in the closing stock valuation.

(iii) The unfavourable material variance will not be adjusted for. It will already be included with the material purchased expense within cost of sales. It does not, therefore, require any further adjustment. The standard cost of £200 per unit for direct materials will continue to be used in the closing stock valuation.

(iv) Similar to the favourable labour variance, the use of the new subcontractor has resulted in a reduction in costs. This will result in a new standard cost being calculated for this particular element of production, which presumably will be incorporated in the next year's standard cost calculation. For the current year, this requires to be adjusted for as, otherwise, direct expenses would be being carried forward that are in excess of those that ought to be being accounted for in stock (i.e. subcontractor costs based on the standard would be in excess of the actual subcontractor costs incurred).

BASIC

INTERMEDIATE

ADVANCED

Progress Point 5.9

DRT Ltd manufactures a single product. It operates a standard costing system and updates these standards at the start of each financial year. At 1 January 2009, the following standard costs per unit were set:

	£ per unit
Direct materials	125
Direct labour	40
Direct expenses	30
Production overhead	35
Selling & distribution	10
	240

Information taken from the management accounts shows the following variances for the year to 31 December 2009.

	Price/cost increases		Usage		Efficiency		Total	
	£		£		£		£	
Direct materials	30,000	A	90,000	F			60,000	F
Direct labour	100,000	A			60,000	F	40,000	A
Production overhead					120,000	F	120,000	F
	130,000	A	90,000	F	180,000	F	140,000	F

A: adverse
F: favourable

Consultation with management has identified that the variances were caused by the following factors.

- Direct materials: a new production process was introduced from 1 September 2009. This required higher-quality and more expensive materials but led to reduced wastage.
- Direct labour: a higher than anticipated wage increase was made halfway through the year. This was partly offset by agreed new working practices, which led to efficiency savings.
- Production overhead: greater throughput in the year increased cost recovery.

At 31 December 2009, there were 2,000 units of finished goods in stock. The units in stock are equivalent to December production. Production arises evenly throughout the year. DRT Ltd uses the FIFO method in valuing stock.

Required

Calculate the closing stock value of DRT Ltd.

Solution

The use of standard costs is acceptable providing they reflect current conditions. As DRT Ltd sets its costs at the start of its accounting year, certain variances may require to be adjusted for in the stock valuation.

	£
Standard cost	240
Less: selling and distribution costs	10
	230
∴ stocks at standard cost = 2,000 x £230	460,000
Adjustments for variances:	
Direct material	(15,000)
Direct labour	6,667
Production overhead	(10,000)
Closing stock value	441,667

Workings

Selling and distribution

As these costs are not related to bringing the stock to its current location and condition they should be omitted from the stock valuation.

Direct materials

A net £60,000 favourable variance arose in the last four months following the introduction of a new production process. The existing standard would therefore overstate cost per unit. A reduction is therefore required of:

£60,000/4 mths = £15,000

That is, as production arises evenly throughout the year, the adjustment reflects one months production (i.e. 2,000 units).

Direct labour

A net £40,000 adverse variance arose over the last six months following a higher than expected wage increase. The existing standard would therefore understate cost per unit. An increase is therefore required of:

£40,000/6 mths = £6,667

Production overhead

The favourable increase of £120,000 arises from additional production and the existing standard would overstate stocks. A reduction is therefore required of:

£120,000/12 mths = £10,000

Retail price (para. 22)

As with the standard cost method, the retail method may be used provided that the results approximate to actual cost. The retail method, as its name would suggest, is used in the retail trade for dealing with stock valuations of businesses that have high volumes of various line items of stock, and where similar mark-ups are applied to all stock items or groups of items. Under the retail method a conventional stock count is carried out and the selling price is used to determine the cost of the inventory by reducing the sales value by the appropriate gross profit margin.

Example

Retco, a supermarket chain, achieves average mark-ups on goods sold of 50%.

At 31 December 2009, following its annual stock count, stocks with a retail price of £750,000 were identified.

Under the retail method, the cost of these stocks may be approximated by converting it to cost by removing the normal mark-up. That is:

$$\text{Cost} + (50\% \text{ cost}) = \text{retail price}$$
$$\text{Cost} = \frac{\text{retail price}}{1\frac{1}{2}}$$
$$= \frac{750{,}000}{1\frac{1}{2}}$$
$$= £500{,}000$$

Clearly, the problem in applying the retail method is in determining the margin to be applied to the stock at selling price to convert it back to cost. Because different lines and different departments may have widely different margins, it is normally necessary to subdivide stock and apply the appropriate margins to each subdivision. An additional problem can arise where stocks have been marked down to below original selling price. In such a situation, adjustments have to be made to eliminate the effect of these mark-downs so as to prevent any item of stock being valued at less than both its cost and its net realisable value.

 Example

Beachwear Plus uses the retail method for stock valuation. During December 2009, it marked down its swimwear lines to 75% of its normal selling price. At its year end of 31 December, it has stocks of swimwear amounting to a sale (after mark-down) price of £120,000. Beachwear Plus normally achieves a mark-up of 60% on cost. Assuming that all swimwear is expected to be sold following the winter mark-down, at what value should Beachwear Plus value the stock at 31 December 2009?

Solution

The mark-down adjusted selling price is £120,000. The sales price prior to the mark-down would therefore have been as follows:

$$\text{Full sales price} = \frac{120{,}000}{75\%} = \underline{\underline{£160{,}000}}$$

Assuming a normal mark-up of 60% on cost, this would equate to a cost of:

$$\frac{160{,}000}{160\%} = \underline{\underline{100{,}000}}$$

Beachwear Plus would therefore value its swimwear lines at £100,000.

The position in practice

In practice, companies that use the retail method tend to apply a gross profit margin computed on an average basis rather than apply specific mark-up percentages. This practice is acknowledged by IAS 2, which states that 'an average percentage for each retail department is often used'.

Cost formulas (paras 23 – 27)

The standard requires (para. 23) that for specific items that are not interchangeable, specific costs should be attributed to the specific items of inventory. In other words, costs should be identified for specific items of stock where each item can be separately identified and separately costed.

Where items are made to a particular specification, it is appropriate to cost each individually. In practice this method is rarely used due to the complexity of most manufacturing and retailing businesses and the interchangeability of many items. IAS 2 recognises this and allows the use of FIFO or weighted average cost formulas to value items that are interchangeable. The LIFO formula, which had been allowed prior to the 2003 version of IAS 2, is no longer permitted.

Para. 25 requires that the same cost formula should be used for all inventories having a similar nature or use to the enterprise. For other stock items with a different nature or use, an alternative cost formula may be justified.

Stock of a service provider

Thus far in this chapter, the analysis has concentrated on the valuations of physical items of stock (i.e. goods). IAS 2 defines inventories as including assets that are in the form of the rendering of services. The situation where an enterprise is involved not with the sale or manufacture of goods, but with the provision of services, needs to be considered.

Providers of professional services, such as accountants, solicitors and architects, may have commenced work for a client prior to the year end but may not be in a position at the year end to issue an invoice for the work carried out thus far and hence recognise the related revenue. This gives rise to service provider stock and the same matching principles require to be applied to it as for physical stock items.

The costs that will need to be identified and carried forward as stock to the next accounting period will be:

- labour costs of personnel directly engaged in providing the service
- other directly related costs (e.g. travelling costs)
- an appropriate allocation of supervisory costs and overheads, but not general administrative overheads.

As with items of physical stock, no profit element should be included in the valuation of service provider stock.

5.6 Net realisable value (NRV)

Net realisable value (NRV) is defined as the estimated selling price in the ordinary course of business less the:

- estimated costs of completion, and
- the estimated costs necessary to make the sale.

The prudence concept dictates that stock will be valued at NRV if it is lower than the cost. In general, cost will be lower than NRV, however there are a number of situations where NRV might be less than cost. These occasions will vary among organisations, but can be summarised as follows:

- there is a permanent fall in the selling price of the stock; short-term fluctuations should not cause net realisable value to be implemented
- there is an increase in the cost of the stock
- physical deterioration of stocks (e.g. in the food industry by reference to 'sell-by' dates)
- obsolescence of products as a result of technical advances, or due to the development of different marketing concepts within the organisation, or a change in market needs
- a decision by management to sell goods at below cost as part of a company's marketing strategy (e.g. the concept of a 'loss leader' is well known in supermarkets, but organisations may also sell below cost when trying to penetrate a new market)
- errors in production or purchasing.

BASIC

INTERMEDIATE

ADVANCED

When cost is higher than NRV, not all the cost incurred can be recovered and therefore stock should be valued at the lower amount. The effect of this is to recognise the write-down immediately, and the 'loss' is recognised as an expense in the period in which the write-down occurs. Any reversal should be recognised in the income statement in the period in which the reversal occurs.

The mechanics of a write-down of stock from cost to NRV are best illustrated with a numerical example.

Example: write-down of stocks from cost to NRV

Norbank carried out its annual stock count at 31 March 2009, which showed stocks at cost of £120,000. Included in that sum, however, were £40,000 of items that, because of technical advances, were effectively obsolete. These items would, however, be able to be sold as spare parts at an estimated net realisable value of £15,000.

Norbank will, therefore, need to value its stock at 31 March 2009 as follows:

	£
Stocks at cost as counted	120,000
Less: write-down to NRV of obsolete stocks	
(£40,000 – £15,000)	25,000
Revised stock value	£95,000

The cost of sales calculation (i.e. opening stock + purchases-closing stock) effectively ensures that the write-down is immediately recognised within cost of sales. In other words, cost of sales is reduced by the value of closing stock. In this instance, it is being reduced by a lesser amount (i.e. £95,000) than it would have been had the stock continued to be valued at cost (i.e. £120,000). Furthermore, the stock value being carried forward to the next accounting period will more accurately match the revenues generated from its sale as spare parts.

Estimates of NRV should be based on the most reliable evidence at the time the estimates are made as to the amounts the stocks are expected to realise.

The estimates are made at the year end but should take into account events after the balance sheet date if these confirm conditions existing at the balance sheet date (e.g. sales after the year end).

It must be remembered that net realisable value is the amount the business receives for its stock from the market. It may be the case that additional expenses are incurred in getting the stock to the market (e.g. packaging, advertising, delivery and even repair of damaged inventory). These additional costs must be deducted from the realisable value to arrive at the net realisable value.

Where stocks are held to service firm sales or service contracts, the NRV is based on the contract price. If additional stock is held over and above that required to service the agreed sales or contracts, this additional stock should be based on general selling prices.

Example: net realisable value

A company has the following items in stock at 31 December 2009:

Item	Units	Cost	Sales price
		£	£
No. 876	1,200	415	580
No. 997	610	148	150
No. 1822	200	720	810
No. 2076	416	510	430
No. 4732	508	930	1,400

All sales prices are stated before 6% commission paid to sales staff on the sale of an item.

The company has received and accepted an order for all 416 units of item no 2076. The goods would need to be reworked to the customer's specification, however, at a cost of £215 per unit. The sales price, before sales commission, would be £820 each for the completed units.

Required

Calculate the stock value at 31 December 2009.

Solution

Item	Units	Cost	NRV[1]	Lower of cost and NRV	Value
		£	£	£	£
No. 876	1,200	415	545	415	498,000
No. 997	610	148	141	141	86,010
No. 1822	200	720	761	720	144,000
No. 2076	416	500	556[2]	500	208,000
No. 4732	508	930	1,316	930	472,440
					1,408,450

1. Stock is valued on a line-by-line basis.
2. Costs to complete an item are deducted in arriving at NRV – they are not added to cost. Remember that these costs have not yet been incurred and so cannot be included in the cost at the balance sheet date. They are of relevance in determining the net realisable value so that this may be compared to cost at the balance sheet date. Only if there has been an error should the costs figures be changed.

Workings

(i) All sales prices have been reduced by the 6% sales commissions to arrive at net realisable value.
(ii) Item no. 2076: as the company has accepted the order for all the units, the NRV needs to be calculated on the revised selling price, taking account of the additional reworking costs:

	£
Selling price	820
Less: commission (6%)	49
Less: reworking costs	215
Net realisable value	556

Note that item no. 2076 is now profitable. Prior to the reworking, the NRV would have been as follows:

	£
Selling price	430
Less: commission (6%)	26
Net realisable value	404

Had the stock of item no. 2076 been sold at these amounts this would have resulted in a loss per unit of:

	£
Net realisable value	404
Cost	500
Loss per unit	96

The stock would have been valued at the lower of cost and NRV (i.e. £404).

Following the reworking, however, a profit will be made on the sale and it is therefore appropriate to value the stock of item no. 2076 at cost:

	£
Revised net realisable value (820 – 49 – 215) =	556
Less: cost	500
Profit per unit	56

Progress Point 5.10

The closing stock of Horne Products includes the following items:

Product A	£
5 units – costs incurred to date	140
Estimated sales revenue – 5 units	160
Selling and distribution expenses – 5 units	30
Product B	
10 units – costs incurred to date	230
Estimated sales revenue – 10 units	280
Selling and distribution expenses – units	20

Required

Calculate the stock value to be included in Horne Products' financial statements.

Solution

IAS 2 requires that individual types of stocks be valued separately. Therefore, for each product, the cost and net realisable value requires to be calculated and each product will be valued at the lower of the two amounts:

		£
Product A –	Sales revenue	160
	Less : selling and distribution expenses	30
	Net realisable value	130
	Costs incurred to date	140

∴ as NRV is lower than cost, Product A will be valued at £130.

Product B –	Sales revenue	280
	Less: selling and distribution expenses	20
	Net realisable value	260
	Costs incurred to date	230

∴ as cost is lower than NRV, Product B will be valued at £230.

5.7 Work in progress

Issues examined so far in this chapter have related to a single production process and stocks of finished goods. Also included within the IAS 2 definition of inventories are assets in the production process for sale in the ordinary course of business. Such inventories are classified as work in progress (W-I-P) and are mainly found in manufacturing organisations. Work in progress is simply the cost of partly completed goods or services at the end of the accounting period.

The valuation of W-I-P follows the rules laid out in IAS 2, and consequently must be valued at the lower of cost and net realisable value.

The accounting issue involved

The accounting issue with work in progress is, as with stock, deciding what to include in cost. Once more an allocation of total costs will need to be made to those goods and services that are at an intermediate stage of completion (i.e. direct materials, direct labour and appropriate overhead). Directly attributable costs can be assigned directly, after which indirect costs will be allocated by reference to one or more factors (e.g. direct labour cost, labour hours worked). Whichever method is chosen for the allocation procedure, it should attempt to relate the indirect costs as precisely as possible to the process that has given rise to them.

Direct materials

It is necessary to identify what proportion of direct materials has been used in work in progress.

The amount contained within work in progress will vary with different types of organisation, as the following examples illustrate.

- If the item is complex or materially significant (e.g. a custom-made car), the W-I-P calculation will be based on actual materials and components that have been booked to the job to date.
- If, however, there is a mass-production process, it may not be possible to identify each individual item within W-I-P. In such circumstances, the accountant will make a judgement and define the W-I-P as being a particular percentage complete in respect of raw materials and components. For example, a bolt manufacturer with 5 million bolts per week in W-I-P may decide that, in respect of raw materials, they are 100% complete. The W-I-P valuation would therefore proceed on that basis and include the full materials cost for the 5 million bolts.

However work in progress is valued, consistency is essential and the same method should therefore be applied consistently.

Direct labour

As with direct materials, it is necessary to identify how much direct labour has been consumed into W-I-P. Again, there are two broad approaches.

1. If the item of W-I-P is complex or materially significant, the actual time booked to the job will form part of the W-I-P valuation.

2.   In a mass production situation, it may not be possible to assign costs with such precision and an accounting judgement may have to be made as to the average percentage completion in respect of direct labour. In the example of the bolt manufacturer, it could be that, on average, W-I-P is 80% complete in respect of direct labour.

Appropriate overhead

The same two approaches as for direct labour can be adopted.

1.   With a complex or materially significant item, it should be possible to allocate the overhead actually incurred. This could be an actual charge – for example, subcontract work – or an application of the appropriate overhead recovery rate (ORR). The ORR is the overhead cost divided by a measure of activity, such as direct labour hours, to give a cost per unit of activity. For example, if a direct labour recovery rate is used and the ORR is £20 per direct labour hour, and the recorded labour time on the W-I-P is ten hours, then the overhead charge for W-I-P purposes is £200.

2.   With mass-production items, the accountant must either use an overhead recovery rate approach or, as with direct costs, adopt a percentage completion approach (e.g. in respect of overheads, W-I-P is 75% complete).

Whichever method is chosen, the company's auditors will check to ensure that application of the particular allocation process results in a true and fair view being achieved. In practice this can pose problems for the company accountant as well as the auditors. The responsibility for determining the percentage completion of W-I-P will often fall to a process engineer or a manager with technical knowledge of the product, rather than the accountant. The accountant may not have the technical expertise himself and so reliance on these other employees will be essential.

The following examples illustrate the allocation of total costs referred to above.

Example

Parkinson Products is a manufacturer of briefcases. The costs of a completed briefcase are:

	£	
Direct materials	12.00	
Direct labour	6.00	
Appropriate overhead	10.00	
Total cost	28.00	(for finished goods stock value purposes)

After consultation with the production manager, the company accountant takes the view that, for W-I-P, the following applies:

Direct materials	100% complete
Direct labour	80% complete
Appropriate overhead	60% complete

Therefore, for one briefcase in W-I-P, the following values will be assigned:

		£
Direct materials	£12.00 x 100%	12.00
Direct labour	£6.00 x 80%	4.80
Appropriate overhead	£10.00 x 60%	6.00
W-I-P value		22.80

If the company has 10,000 briefcases in work in progress, the value will be: $10,000 \times £22.80 = £228,000$.

This technique is particularly useful in processing industries such as petroleum, brewing, dairy products or paint manufacture, where it may be impossible to identify W-I-P items precisely. In such circumstances, the role of the auditor in verifying such practices is essential.

 ## Example

A custom chopper company making customised motorcycles has the following costs in respect of Project 907, an unfinished motorcycle, at the end of the month:

	£
Materials charged to Project 907	2,500
Labour: 100 hours at £25 per hour	2,500
Overheads: £22/DLH x 100 hours	2,200
W-I-P value of Project 907	7,200

This is an accurate work in progress value provided all the costs have been accurately recorded and an accurate overhead recovery rate established. The level of accounting work is not excessive as the information is required by a normal job costing system from stock records, timesheets, etc. An added advantage is that, for audit purposes, the work in progress figure can be verified and proven.

The net realisable value of work in progress

It is important not to forget the underlying principle of IAS 2 that inventories should be measured at the lower of cost and net realisable value. It follows therefore that, in order to make a comparison of cost and NRV, that NRV of work in progress needs to be considered.

This poses the accountant some additional problems. It is highly unlikely that there will be a market for partly completed goods, and consequently the NRV calculation will need to be made taking account of costs to completion and ultimate selling price. Given the assumptions made, however, in arriving at cost for W-I-P, such calculations would be at best cumbersome and in many instances, unnecessary. The enterprise will be producing the stock item with a view to making a profit and so the NRV is likely to be in excess of cost in any event. Consequently, in such circumstances, it is more appropriate to consider the NRV of the stock item in its finished state. Then, if any of the conditions apply to suggest that NRV might be less than cost – for example, an increase in costs or a fall in selling price, physical deterioration of stocks, obsolescence of products, a decision as part of a company's marketing strategy to manufacture and sell products at a loss – the carrying value of the related raw materials and work in progress must also be reviewed and a provision made if required.

5.8 Raw materials

The net realisable value of raw materials

Again, it would be easy to forget the underlying valuation principles of IAS 2 in respect of raw materials. Raw materials, by definition, are subjected to some form of process by an enterprise in becoming finished goods. Consequently, it is normally not possible to arrive at a particular NRV for each item of raw material based on selling price. In such circumstances, current replacement cost might be the best guide to NRV. If current replacement cost is less than historic cost, however, a provision is required to be made only if the finished goods into which they will be made are expected to be sold at a loss. No provision should be made just because the anticipated profit will be less than normal. Where

stocks of spares are held for resale, it may be possible to predict obsolescence – and identify the need for a provision – by reference to the number of units sold to which the spares are applicable. In forecasting net realisable value, events occurring between the balance sheet date and completion of the accounts need to be considered.

Progress Point 5.11

Oscar Industries manufactures one standard product. The following information is available in respect of stocks and work in progress at the year end.

1.   The inventory sheets at the year end show the following items:

> Raw materials:
> 100 tonnes of steel at cost £140 per ton
> Present price is £130 per tonne
>
> Finished goods:
> 100 finished units:
> Cost of materials   £50 per unit
> Labour cost   £150 per unit
> Selling price   £500 per unit
>
> Partly finished goods:
> 40 partly finished goods
>
> For work in progress, the company accountant has advised the following:
> Materials   100% complete
> Labour $66\frac{2}{3}$% complete
>
> Damaged finished units:
> 10 damaged finished units
> Costs to rectify the damage – £200 per unit
> Selling price when rectified   £500 per unit

2.   Manufacturing overheads are   100% of labour costs
3.   Selling and distribution costs are   £60 per unit

Required

From the information given, calculate the amounts to be included in the balance sheet of Oscar Industries Ltd in respect of stocks and work in progress. State also the principles applied in arriving at the valuations.

Solution

1.   Principles applied: stocks are valued at the lower of cost and net realisable value. Cost includes those overheads that have been incurred in bringing the stocks to their existing condition (i.e. manufacturing overheads).
2.   Valuation method:
      Raw materials
            Stock value = 100 tonnes @ £140 = £14,000

Note: as there is no indication that the finished goods will be sold at a loss it is appropriate to value the raw materials at £140 per tonne. Only if there had been such an indication would it have been appropriate to value the raw materials at the lower amount – that lower amount being the best guide to net realisable value.

BASIC

INTERMEDIATE

ADVANCED

Finished goods: 100 units		£
Cost	Direct materials: cost per unit	50
	Direct labour: cost per unit	150
	Manufacturing overheads: 100% of labour	150
	Cost per unit	350
NRV	Selling price per unit	500
	Less : selling and distribution costs	60
	Net realisable value per unit	440

The stocks of finished goods will, therefore, be valued at the lower of cost and net realisable value, i.e. £35,000 (100 units × £350).

Partly finished goods: 40 units	£
Cost (based on percentage complete)	
Direct materials 100% x £50	50
Direct labour 66⅔% x £150	100
Manufacturing overheads 100% of labour	100
Cost per unit	250
No. of units: 40 x £250	10,000

NRV (based on percentage method):

	£
Selling price	500
Less : selling and distribution costs	60
	440
Less: costs to complete:	
Direct labour 33⅓% x £150	50
Manufacturing overheads 100% of labour	50
	340
Less: costs incurred so far	250
Expected profit per unit	£90

As the partly finished goods are expected to be sold at a profit, they should be valued at cost (i.e. 40 units × £250 = £10,000).

Damaged finished goods: 10 units.

In order to value the damaged finished goods, we need to determine the net realisable value. The net realisable value is:

	£
Selling price	500
Less: selling and distribution costs	60
Less: costs to rectify	200
NRV per unit	240

BASIC

INTERMEDIATE

ADVANCED

The cost of these damaged units would have been the same as the finished units, i.e.:

	£
Direct materials	50
Direct labour	150
Manufacturing overhead	150
	£350

The damaged units should therefore be valued at the lower of cost and net realisable value, i.e.:

10 units × £240 = £2,400

Balance sheet extract:

	£	
Stocks: raw materials	14,000	
Work in progress	10,000	
finished goods	37,400	(35,000 + 2,400)
	£61,400	

5.9 Problems in practice

Establishing an accurate stock valuation can be extremely difficult. The calculation of unit cost is fraught with difficulties and is often an exercise in judgement, which, however expert, is essentially subjective in nature. For example, the separation of direct and indirect costs, the basis for allocation of indirect overheads, the level of activity for which standard costs are calculated, the measurement of the degree of completion of work in progress – all these decisions involve an element of judgement, and the resulting costs will only be as accurate as the judgements on which they are based.

Unfortunately, no area of accounting provides more opportunities for subjectivity and creative accounting than the valuation of inventory. Furthermore, because inventories feature on both the income statement and balance sheet – and because they can dramatically alter an enterprise's financial position, inventories are particularly susceptible to fraudulent manipulation. The practising accountant is faced with many problems relating to inventory valuation, and some of these are considered below.

While, in many instances, an auditor will attend a company's stock take, there will be far more instances when the accountant will not attend – and instead, be provided with stock valuations by the client companies themselves. This is particularly the case with sole traders and partnerships, as well as small to medium-sized limited companies. Such entities, if below a certain level of turnover limits, do not require an audit. It might well be the case that a stock valuation is simply provided to the reporting accountant for inclusion within the financial statements. The accountant is then faced with the dilemma of accepting a figure that he has little means of checking. Moreover, depending on the business's circumstances, this figure may well have been 'chosen' to fulfil that business's 'needs'. For example, a company which knows that it has had a successful trading year may deliberately value stock on the low side in order to reduce profits and consequently its income tax liability. On the other hand, a company having had a mediocre year may try to boost profits to keep its lenders happy or indeed, if there are external shareholders, to satisfy them that efficient returns are being made on their investment.

The question that naturally arises is, therefore, 'How can the accountant guard against such manipulations?'

First, the accountant should be aware of the pressures that are surrounding the particular business. If there has been a profitable year then it is likely that the company will wish to reduce the stock valuation; if the company has been under pressure from its lenders then the tendency will be for the company to value higher than normal.

Second, the accountant can calculate ratios such as gross profit percentage and rate of stock turnover, to help verify the cost of sales figures. Such ratios are considered in depth in Chapter 12 and will help to highlight any possible discrepancies by comparing the results against previous year's ratios or industry norms. Third, at a more detailed level, the accountant may look at the purchase and sales invoices in the last few months of the company's year to ascertain the level of stock purchases and sales, and confirm that the relationship between them is consistent with the closing stock level.

In larger organisations – particularly those where an audit opinion is required – there can be even more difficulties. A stock count may last many days and it is essential to determine the 'cut-off' date (i.e. the date when the trading year effectively ceases and the line is drawn after which any profits will be allocated to the next accounting year). In practice, the matching of sales with cost of sales can be problematic – particularly if the stock take does not happen on the year-end date and there continue to be physical flows of stock between the year-end date and the date of the actual stock take. This is particularly problematic for companies with year end dates of 31 December – not many auditors would wish to be attending stock takes on 1 January! The practical solution to this problem relies on having an accurate record of stock movements between the date of the stock count and the year-end date. An adjusted stock figure can then be calculated:

	£
Stocks at 7 January 2009	XXX
Less: purchases (1 January 2009 – 7 January 2009)	(XXX)
Add: sales (1 January 2009 – 7 January 2009)	XXX
Stocks at 31 December 2008	XXX

Continuing with the problems in determining the 'cut-off' date is linking physical stocks with the recorded flows of stocks in the company's financial records. The auditor must be aware that the recording of accounting transactions may not coincide with the physical flows of stock. Stocks may have been sold, a sale recorded in the financial records but the related items may be in the warehouse awaiting dispatch. It would be essential therefore to exclude any such stock from the closing stock valuation; similarly, a purchase of stock may have been recorded in the financial records but the related item may not have been delivered by the date of the stock count. It will be essential therefore to include the value of that as yet undelivered stock in the year-end valuation.

Further problems arise where goods are held on a sale or return basis – that is, goods may be on the company's premises but title still lies with the supplier – the purchase from the supplier not being required until the stocks have been sold. This happens frequently in the motor trade where a manufacturer will supply a dealership with several vehicles on a sale or return basis to assist the dealership by reducing stocking costs (i.e. the dealership would not have to fund the cost of stocking what might be hundreds of thousands of pounds, worth of vehicles). In such instances, this stock would require to be excluded from the dealer's year-end stock valuation.

The company itself may operate a sale or return system for its goods (i.e. the company may have stocks that it has supplied to its customers on a sale or return basis). Such stocks will not have been sold and consequently they require to be included in the year-end valuation at the lower of cost and net realisable value. This can pose significant problems for the auditor if these stocks are held at several different locations over a wide geographical area.

The auditor must be aware of all these possibilities and design appropriate procedures to test that controls are in place to ensure that stocks are dealt with correctly. In particular, the auditor will wish to be able to trace a sample of each stock entry through the accounting records so that:

- if a purchase is recorded, but no sale, then the item must be in stock
- if a sale is recorded, a purchase must also have been recorded, and the item should not be in stock.

Treatment of stock items		
Sales	*Stock*	*Warehouse*
If invoiced to customer	Remove from stock	Stock not counted
If returned from customer	Include in stock	Include
If not invoiced/returned	Include in stock	Include
Purchases		
If invoiced to company	Include in stock	Include
If returned by company	Remove from stock	Stock not counted
If invoiced/credited	Include	Include

Table 5.1 illustrates the various possibilities and required accounting treatment

Physical condition of stocks

The auditor will need to satisfy himself of the physical condition of the stocks. Damaged stocks will have a lower value than stocks in first-class condition. The auditor must ensure that the condition of the stock is recorded at the stock count so that the correct value is assigned to it. Damaged items and items that have been in stock for a long period will require to be written down to net realisable value.

Identification of high-value items

Clearly, stock items with a higher value will have a more significant effect on the valuation of stocks overall. It is important, therefore, that the auditor familiarises himself with the production process and has appreciation of the materials used, and their relative importance and their relative values. Distinguishing between two similar items can be crucial when there are large differences in value. For example, steel-coated brass rods look identical to steel rods but their relative values will be very different. It is important, therefore, that they are recorded correctly at the inventory count so that the correct values may be assigned to them.

Valuation of complex items

Some stock takes will consist of the measurement of large vats of chemicals. While the auditor may be able to calculate the volume of a cylinder, he may not have the expertise to confirm what stage in the production process the particular chemical is at. Again, knowledge of the industry is essential to ensure that an appropriate valuation is assigned.

Detailed audit trails

Tracing an item through an accounting system can often be time consuming and may require a great deal of effort (i.e. checking the order, the authority for the order, the purchase invoice, the pricing of the invoice, identifying the sale/identifying the item in stock). If the particular item is messy and indistinguishable, the auditor may not have the expertise – or indeed the will – to verify the measurements taken by the client's own employees. Frequently, the more tedious audit tests are given to audit juniors – it is not surprising how many positive audit conclusions are arrived at by such staff.

The problems noted above are all inherent problems (i.e. they are problems that exist simply as a result of the particular processes or nature of the companies concerned). What if, as may be the case, management sets out to deliberately manipulate the stock figures? The following sections give consideration to the types of manipulation management may try to implement.

Manipulating cut-off procedures

Determining the cut-off point is essential to ensure that purchases, sales and stocks are dealt with in the correct accounting period. One way of boosting closing stock, and hence profit and net assets, is to take goods into stock but not record the related purchase invoice.

Fictitious transfers

Again, relating to cut-off, year-end stocks may be inflated by recording fictitious transfers of non-existing inventory (i.e. by declaring that goods are 'in transit' between different depots of the same company, a physical count becomes very difficult). Moreover, if the transfer is between depots in different countries, then verification would be extremely costly.

Incorrect valuations

It may be the case that management attaches an unrealistic value to obsolete stock. Knowledge of the business on the part of the auditor should prevent such manipulations, but the auditor may lack sufficient expertise to challenge management's assertions.

Inaccurate inventory records

If inventory records are poorly maintained, this may mask theft from within the organisation. Such poor record-keeping may be deliberate and designed to 'hide' theft, or it may be that opportunistic employees have become aware of the shortcomings of the stock recording system and are using them to their advantage.

Downright dishonesty!

Within auditing literature is the example of the audit assistant who was sent to audit coal at a coal yard. The audit assistant was shown various stock piles of coal and, equipped with the formula for determining the volume of a cone, the audit assistant set about measuring the diameter and height of the various conical piles of coal. What the audit assistant had not appreciated was that 'hidden' underneath one of the piles was a concrete shed! The volume of coal had therefore been inflated by the volume of the concrete shed.

Creative accounting

As the above shows, where there is a will to manipulate, stocks are the ideal items with which to be creative. In fairness to the auditor, even the most diligent of individuals may fail to uncover such fraudulent activities if management is determined enough to mislead and misrepresent the reality of the situation.

5.10 Disclosure requirements

IAS 2 (para. 36) requires disclosure of:
(a)   the accounting policy adopted in measuring inventories
(b)   total stock, analysed into appropriate categories
(c)   the amount of stock carried at net realisable value
(d)   the amount of stock recognised as an expense in the period (this will normally be part or all of cost of sales)
(e)   the amount of any stock write-down
(f)   the carrying amount of stock held as security for liabilities
(g)   the amount of any reversal of write-down to NRV, and the circumstances that led to such reversal.

Disclosure in practice

In practice, the required disclosures of IAS 2 *Inventories* are dealt with in distinct sections. The accounting policies note is normally used to explain in narrative form the policies adopted by an

enterprise in measuring inventories, the types of inventories held, and the cost formula used, while the balance sheet discloses the total inventories, and the note to the balance sheet details the classification and numerical elements of the required disclosures.

Inventories

The following extract from the accounting policy note of Logica identifies the nature of its inventories held (computer equipment and materials), and states its compliance to IAS 2 in its declaration that inventories are stated at the lower of cost and net realisable value.

> Inventories represent computer equipment that, at the balance sheet date, had not yet been allocated to a specific customer contract and materials, including work-in-progress, used in document printing and finishing.
>
> Inventories are stated at the lower of cost and net realisable value. Cost comprises direct materials and, where applicable, direct labour costs and those overheads that have been incurred in bringing the inventories to their present location and condition. Cost is calculated using the first-in-first-out (FIFO) method. Net realisable value represents the estimated selling price less costs to be incurred in marketing, distribution and sale.
>
> Amounts recoverable on contracts represent revenue which has not yet been invoiced to customers on fixed price contracts. Such amounts are separately disclosed within trade and other receivables. The valuation of amounts recoverable on contracts is adjusted to take up profit to date or foreseeable losses in accordance with the Group's accounting policy for profit recognition.

The extract from the accounting policy of Logica identifies the nature of its inventories held (computer equipment and materials) and states its compliance to IAS 2 in its declaration that inventories are stated at the lower of cost and net realisable value. The note then defines both cost and net realisable value.

Current assets

Current assets			
Inventories	22	**1.4**	2.9
Trade and other receivables	23	**1,021.2**	1,070.2
Current tax assets		**40.5**	31.2
Cash and cash equivalents	34	**108.7**	177.3
		1,171.8	1,281.6

Figure 5.1 Current assets note of Logica plc

Inventories are included within the current assets section of Logica's balance sheet (see Figure 5.1) and have a total carrying amount of £1.4 million at 31 December 2007, with a comparative balance at 31 December 2006 of £2.9 million. Further information regarding inventories is given in note 22 to the financial statements.

Inventories

	2007 £'m	2006 £'m
Computer equipment not allocated to a customer contract	**1.2**	0.5
Materials used in document printing and finishing	**0.2**	2.4
	1.4	2.9
The Directors estimate that the carrying value of inventories approximated their fair value.		

Figure 5.2 Logica: detailed analysis of inventory items

The note to the financial statements provides further analysis of the total inventories figure in the balance sheet of £1.4 million. Here, the carrying amounts of the different types of inventories referred to in the accounting policy note are disclosed, together with a statement from the directors that the carrying values of inventories approximated their fair value.

Summary

The objective of IAS 2 is to prescribe the accounting treatment for inventories, and to provide guidance for determining their cost and for subsequently recognising an expense including any write-down to net realisable value.

The fundamental principle of IAS 2 is that inventories shall be measured at the lower of cost and net realisable value.

The calculation of unit cost is fraught with difficulties. IAS 2 allows expenses incidental to the acquisition or production cost of an asset to be included in its cost. This includes not only directly attributable production overheads but also those overheads that are indirectly attributable to production. Although IAS 2 provides guidelines on the classification of overheads to achieve an appropriate allocation, in practice it is difficult to make these distinctions, and the complexity of some manufacturing processes will result in auditors finding it difficult to challenge management on such matters. Moreover, if management is intent on fraud, then stocks are an ideal figure to manipulate.

Consequently, although the fundamental principle is straightforward, the valuation of inventories is by no means so. Furthermore, while the reporting requirements of IAS 2 no doubt go some way to defining practices, narrowing differences and variations in those practices, and ensuring adequate disclosure in the accounts, at the end of the day the valuation of inventory is still a subjective process relying heavily on the expertise and judgement of management. Unfortunately, this subjective judgement can have substantial effects on the reporting of financial information: financial information that may be manipulated to suit management's desired objectives.

Section 3: Advanced Aspects

5.11 Construction contracts

In the introduction to this chapter, a particular type of 'stock' was referred to that typically occurs within construction companies. Such companies are often involved in construction contracts that start in one accounting period and end in another. Consequently, at the end of an accounting period, a valuation must be made of the work carried out to date so that appropriate entries may be made in both the income statement and balance sheet in respect of this 'work in progress'. As was covered in the previous section, under IAS 2, stocks require to be valued at the lower of cost and net realisable value. This method concurs with both the prudence and realisation concepts in prohibiting income or profit to be recognised until it is realised. In the case of construction contracts, however, a strict adherence to this policy would mean that profit could not be recognised until the contract was completed and accepted by the customer. Moreover, since contracts could continue for several years, it is clear that companies would not show a true and fair view of their activities or performance during the period of the contract by adopting this principle.

BASIC

INTERMEDIATE

ADVANCED

5.12 The accounting issue involved

The accounting issue is the allocation of profit over the various accounting periods during which the construction contract is in progress. The realisation concept would argue against recognising profits before the contract was completed, as would prudence. However, this will not give a 'fair representation' of the results for each period. Moreover, it could be argued that, if it was 'reasonably certain' during the contract of at least some profit, then adherence to the matching principle would be of far more informational benefit than would a strict adherence to prudence. It follows, then, that an alternative method of accounting for such contracts must be considered. There is a trade-off between the accruals/matching principle and the prudence/realisation concepts, and this results in the need to exercise professional judgement and expertise in determining what amounts should be reported in the accounts. At its simplest level, it could be assumed that profits are accrued evenly as the contract progresses. While in practice this is unlikely to be the case, nevertheless it will enable a simple example to illustrate the accounting issues involved.

 ### *Example*

Shamac is contracted to build a motorway flyover for £15m. The following data are available in relation to the contract:

	2009	2010	2011
Percentage complete	45%	80%	100%
Contract costs £10m			
Estimated profits £5m (i.e. £15m – £10m)			

If profits are not recognised until the contract is completed, Shamac would not recognise the profit of £5m (£15m – £10m) until 2011. This is known as the completed contract method.

Assuming profits are accrued in direct proportion to the percentage completion, the income statements would show the following:

	2009 £000	2010 £000	2011 £000	Total £000
Turnover	6,750	5,250	3,000	15,000
Contract costs	4,500	3,500	2,000	10,000
Profit	2,250	1,750	1,000	5,000

Notes

1. Turnover, contract costs and profit in 2009 are calculated by multiplying the total figures by 45%.
2. In 2010, the totals are multiplied by the incremental level of completion (i.e. 80% – 45% = 35%).
3. In 2011, the totals are multiplied by the incremental level of completion (i.e. 100% – 80% = 20%).

As the above example illustrates, the amount of profit allocated to each accounting period is based on the percentage level of completeness of the overall contract. This is known as the 'percentage-of-completion' method, and requires allocation over accounting periods of the total profit on the contract. In this example, the turnover and contract costs are being recognised in proportion to the percentage completion. In practice, the actual invoices that are issued and expenses that are incurred as the contract progresses may not equate to the turnover and expenses being recognised. By their nature, contracts may take a considerable period to complete and will often be for considerable amounts. The contractor will not wish to bear the full cost of financing the contract, and the contract agreement will require that the customer will be invoiced for work done as the contract progresses. These amounts are referred to as 'progress billings'. These progress billings are normally ascertained by an external expert (e.g. engineer, architect or surveyor) who will confirm that the contract has reached a particular stage of completion.

These progress billings will normally be invoiced during the contract after work has been done, and may be after deduction of retentions. Retentions are usually held back by the customer as a safeguard to ensure that the work is completed and is up to standard. Retentions are usually a percentage of the amount billed (often 5%, but occasionally higher) that, under the terms of the contract, the customer does not pay until the contract is completed.

As these billings – also known as progress payments – are not for the completed project, they are not credited directly to sales or turnover, as would happen with a completed sale, but are recorded for each invoice raised as:

> Dr   Debtors
>   Cr   Contract account
> Being progress billings invoiced.

When cash is received from the customer it is recorded in the normal way:

> Dr   Bank
>   Cr   Debtors
> Being cash received from customer.

 ## Example: retention

Works carried out by a contractor give rise to progress billings of £100,000. It is accepted practice that the customer will hold back a 5% retention. The progress billing and related receipt will be dealt with as follows:

> Dr   Debtors   £100,000
>   Cr   Contract account   £100,000
> Being progress billing invoiced.

> Dr   Bank   £95,000
>   Cr   Debtors   £95,000
> Being cash received from debtor.

Note that the amount of the retention (i.e. 5% × £100,000) will remain as a debtor until it is ultimately received – usually on satisfactory completion of the contract.

5.13 Contract accounts

The contract account is a form of trading account for each contract. Each construction contract should have its own separate contract account. All expenditure traceable to the contract will be charged to the contract account. In practice this is far easier than ascertaining direct expenses in a factory, as any expenditure on the contract will be treated as direct. Typical costs include:

- wages and salaries
- materials
- hire of equipment
- depreciation charge
- subcontractor costs
- allocation of overheads.

BASIC

INTERMEDIATE

ADVANCED

At the year end, this will include accrual and prepayment adjustments.

The contract account is essentially a holding account in the balance sheet to which all invoices relating to the contract are posted during the year. At the year end, relevant amounts are transferred out to the profit and loss account.

Progress billings can be thought of as potential sales or turnover to be recognised. As we will see, however, progress billings invoiced are not necessarily the same as turnover, as the following example illustrates.

 ## Example

The following information relates to a contract in progress at the end of Year 1 by SBS Enterprises. An independent architect has been used to determine the level of completion of the contract, which has been agreed at 40%.

	£
Total contract revenue	1,300,000
Total contract expenses	1,125,000
Actual contract costs incurred (Year 1)	510,000
Progress billings (i.e. invoices issued)	400,000

Required

Calculate the turnover and cost of sales to be included in the profit and loss account, and show the relevant balance sheet extracts.

Solution

The amounts to be shown in the profit and loss account in respect of turnover and cost of sales will be determined by the level of completion, and will therefore be as follows:

	£
Turnover (1,300,000 x 40%)	520,000
Cost of sales (1,125,000 x 40%)	450,000
Gross profit	70,000

Note: the proportion of net income that is attributable to the work performed to date as ascertained by the architect has been credited to the profit and loss account. The actual costs so far incurred on this contract, however, amount to £510,000. There is therefore a difference between the actual costs and the costs recognised of £60,000 (i.e. £510,000 – £450,000). This is because the amount of costs recognised has been calculated as a percentage of the total contract costs to reflect the percentage level of completion, and not the actual costs incurred. An additional balance sheet entry requires to be made, therefore, to deal with this difference:

	£
Costs incurred to date	510,000
Contact expenses	450,000
Amounts due from customers	60,000

The difference is treated as a receivable – amounts due from customers – and will be shown in current assets.

A further difference exists between the value of contract revenue recognised as turnover and the amount of progress billings made (i.e. invoices issued):

	£
Contract revenue	520,000
Progress billings	400,000
Amounts due from customers	120,000

Again, this difference has arisen because the amount of revenue recognised has been calculated as a percentage of the total contract revenue and not the actual invoices issued. This difference is also treated as a receivable – amounts due from customers – and will be shown in current assets. The appropriate balance sheet extract will be:

	£
Current assets	
Amounts due from customers	180,000

Note that this figure can also be calculated as :

costs incurred £510,000 + recognised profits £70,000 less progress billings £400,000 = £180,000

To summarise the above example, the amounts to be included in the profit and loss account in respect of long-term contracts should reflect the proportion of the contract completed during the accounting period. The differences between the actual progress billings made and contract revenues recognised, and actual expenses incurred and contract expenses recognised are dealt with in the balance sheet, and shown as amounts due from (or to) customers.

This simple example assumes that, over the contract, the actual costs would be equal to the budgeted costs and that no unforeseen expenses are likely to arise in the future relating to work already completed or work not yet started. Neither assumption will necessarily be realised in practice.

Let us now consider what complications can arise in practice and look in detail at the requirements of IAS 11 *Construction Contracts*.

5.14 IAS 11 *Construction Contracts*

Objective

The objective of IAS 11 is to prescribe the accounting treatment of revenue and costs associated with construction contracts.

Definition

IAS 11 (para. 3) defines a construction contract as 'a contract specifically negotiated for the construction of an asset or a combination of assets that are closely interrelated or interdependent in terms of their design, technology and function or their ultimate purpose or use'.

Examples of a single asset would be a bridge, tunnel, building or ship.

Examples of closely interrelated combinations of assets would be oil refineries, power plants or chemical works.

A contract may extend to more than one year but this is not an essential feature. Some contracts with a shorter duration should be accounted for as long term if they are so material that exclusion of their turnover and results would result in the accounts not giving a fair representation of the results for that period. A contract to develop software would also be covered by the IAS, although contracts for services are covered by IAS 18 *Revenue*.

The standard identifies (para. 3) two types of contract.

1. A fixed price contract: a **fixed price contract** is a construction contract in which the contractor agrees to a fixed contract price or a fixed rate per unit of output, which may be subject to cost escalation claims (e.g. to allow for inflation).

2. A cost plus contract: a cost plus contract is a construction contract in which the contractor is reimbursed for allowable or otherwise defined costs, plus a percentage of these costs or a fixed fee.

Although the definitions would suggest that there are two types of contract, fixed price or cost plus, in practice the type of contract is not always so clear cut and many have characteristics of both types.

The standard also covers a separability issue. Under IAS 11, if a contract covers two or more assets, the construction of each asset should be accounted for separately if:

(a) separate proposals were submitted for each asset
(b) each asset has been subject to separate negotiations, and the contractor and customer have been able to accept or reject that part of the contract relating to each asset, and
(c) the costs and revenue of each asset can be measured.

However, in certain circumstances, a group of contracts may in substance be a single construction contract and required to be treated as such when:

(a) the group of contracts is negotiated as a single package
(b) the contracts are so clearly interrelated that they are in effect part of a single project with an overall profit margin
(c) the contracts are performed concurrently or in a continuous sequence.

If a contract gives the customer an option to order one or more additional assets, construction of each additional asset should be accounted for as a separate contract if either:

(a) the additional asset differs significantly from the original asset(s), or
(b) the price of the additional assets is separately negotiated.

Progress Point 5.12

Explain what is meant by the term construction contract.

Solution

A construction contract is defined in IAS 11 as a contract specifically negotiated for the construction of an asset or a combination of assets that are closely interrelated or interdependent in terms of their design, technology and function, or their ultimate purpose or use, where the time taken to complete the contract is such that the contract actively falls into different accounting periods. A construction contract may extend to more than one year but this is not an essential feature. Some contracts with a shorter duration should be accounted for as long term if they are so material that exclusion of their turnover and results would result in the accounts not giving a fair representation of the results for that period; such a policy must be applied consistently.

5.15 Accounting for construction contracts

Contract revenue and costs

Contract revenue (para. 11) should comprise:

(a) the initial amount of revenue agreed in the contract, and
(b) variations in contract work, claims and incentive payments
     (i) to the extent that it is probable that they will result in revenue, and
     (ii) they are capable of being reliably measured.

In other words, all the revenues that are expected to be received from the contract providing the basic criteria of probable receipt and measurability are satisfied.

A variation (para. 13) is an instruction from the customer for a change in the scope of work (e.g. change in design). This may result in an increase or decrease in revenue. Variations should be included as part of total revenue when it is probable that the customers will approve both the variation and the monetary value.

A claim (para. 14) occurs when the contractor seeks recompense from the customer for costs not included in the contract price arising from, for example, delays caused by the customer or errors in specification. Because of their contentious nature claims are included as part of revenue only when negotiations have reached an advanced stage, such that it is probable that the customer will accept the claim.

Incentive payments (para. 15) are additional amounts paid to the contractor if specified performance standards are met or exceeded (e.g. early completion). These should be included only when the contract is sufficiently advanced that it is probable that the specified standard will be met and the amount of the incentive payment can be measured reliably.

Possible penalties through failure to meet performance standards should also be considered and included if they can be measured reliably. Note that penalties are viewed as a reduction in turnover and not as additional costs. Penalties should be deducted from revenue when it is probable they will be incurred.

Contract costs (para. 16) include the following.

(a) Costs that relate directly to the specific contract (e.g. site labour costs, costs of materials, depreciation of assets used on construction, costs of moving assets and materials to and from the contract site, hire charges, costs of design and technical assistance that are directly related to the contract, the estimated costs of rectification and guarantee work, including warranty costs, claims from third parties).

(b) Costs that are attributable to contract activity and can be allocated to specific contracts, such as insurance, costs of design and technical assistance that are not directly related to a specific contract, construction overheads; costs of this nature need to be allocated on a systematic and rational basis, based on the normal level of construction activity.

(c) Such other costs as are specifically chargeable to the customer under the terms of the contract: examples of these would be general administration and development costs for which reimbursement is specified in the terms of the contract. Permissible costs follow the same rules as in IAS 2.

Specifically, however, IAS 11 excludes the following costs (para. 20):

(a) general administration costs not specified in the contract
(b) selling costs
(c) research and development costs not specified
(d) depreciation of idle assets not used on a specific contract.

Contract costs normally include relevant costs from the date the contract is secured to the date the contract is finally completed. Costs incurred in securing a contract are also included if they can be separately identified and measured reliably and it is probable that the contract will be obtained (para. 21). However, where such costs were previously written off as an expense in the period in which they were incurred, then they are not included in contract costs when the contract is obtained in a subsequent period (i.e. once these costs have been written off they stay written off).

Recognition of contract revenue and expenses

IAS 11 requires that, where the outcome of a construction contract can be estimated reliably, revenue and costs should be recognised in proportion to the stage of completion of contract activity. Under this process the proportion of net income that is attributable to the work performed to date will be credited in the income statement. This is known as the percentage of completion method of accounting.

To be able to estimate the outcome of a contract reliably, the enterprise must be able to make a:

- reliable estimate of total contract revenue, and assess that it is probable that the related economic benefits will flow to the enterprise
- reliable measurement of the total contract costs (both those incurred to date and those expected to be incurred in the future)
- reliable estimate of the stage of completion of the contract.

The stage of completion of a contract can be determined in a variety of ways. IAS 11 does not identify a single method that may be used to identify the stage of completion however, whichever method is chosen, it should measure reliably the work performed. For many contracts this may involve an external expert (e.g. architect, quantity surveyor) confirming that the contract has reached a particular stage of completion. However, alternative methods that might be appropriate include:

- the proportion that costs incurred for work performed to date bear to the total estimated costs
- completion of a physical proportion of the contract work.

If the outcome cannot be measured reliably, no profit should be recognised. This could be the case where, for example, the contract is at too early a stage for an accurate prediction of the overall result. In such circumstances, provided there is no reason to expect that the contract will make an overall loss, then the revenue that is recognised should be restricted to the costs incurred during the year that relate to the contract to the extent that they are expected to be recoverable. These contract costs should be expensed as incurred. In such circumstances, the net income recognised will be nil. Contract costs that are not likely to be recovered are recognised as an expense immediately. No revenue is recognised in respect of these items. Indications of doubt over recoverability include doubts over whether the customer will be able to pay, and costs on a contract that is subject to the outcome of pending litigation. IAS 11 (para. 34) gives further examples. An expected loss on a construction contract should be recognised as an expense immediately on the grounds of prudence. The expected loss should be provided for immediately, irrespective of:

- whether or not work has started on the contract
- the stage of completion of the contract, or
- the amount of profits expected to arise on other contracts.

Example

The following data are available in respect of a construction contract:

Costs to date	£3m
Total contract revenue expected	£3m
Further costs to completion	£0.7m

How should this contract be shown in the accounts?
From the information given, the contract is forecast to make a loss of £0.7m. This expected loss is required to be recognised immediately as a expense on the grounds of prudence.

Income statement entries

Having considered the recognition criteria for contract revenue and contract expenses, the following worked example will illustrate the accounting requirements of the standard and the related journal entry adjustments. It is perhaps worth pausing at this stage to remind ourselves of the overall objectives of the standard.

The standard prescribes the accounting treatment of revenue and costs associated with construction contracts.

It is necessary to first of all ascertain that a construction contract exists. Having confirmed that, it is then necessary to take a decision on the expected outcome based on available evidence at the time of estimated total revenue and estimated total costs. This will indicate whether the contract is estimated to make a profit or a loss. If that outcome is:

- profitable and the outcome can be estimated reliably, then revenue, costs and profit should be recognised in line with the stage of completion of the contract
- profitable but the outcome cannot be estimated reliably, then revenue and costs should be recognised but no profit
- loss making, then the full amount of the loss should be recognised immediately; an expected loss should be provided for immediately, irrespective of the stage of completion of the contract, whether or not work has started on the contract, or the amount of profits expected to arise on other contracts.

There are, therefore, three categories of contracts, and the accounting requirements will vary accordingly.

Example

Clarkstruction has three contracts in progress at 31 December 2009: Project A, Project B and Project C. All three contracts commenced during the year and the following information is currently available. Due to the nature of the contracts, Clarkstruction can usually determine the outcome of the contract reliably when the contract is 40% complete. All costs are considered recoverable.

Contract	Project A £000	Project B £000	Project C £000
Total contract value	800	400	700
Costs incurred to date	500	30	400
Estimated further costs to completion	70	300	390
%age completion	80%	10%	50%

What are the turnover and cost of sales figures to be included in the income statement of Clarkstruction for the year to 31 December 2009?

Step 1: calculate whether the contract will make an overall profit or loss

In order to determine the appropriate accounting treatment, the expected outcome of each contract needs to be determined. Using the available information, the expected profit or loss can be calculated as follows:

	Project A £000	Project B £000	Project C £000
Contract value	800	400	700
Less: costs incurred to date	(500)	(30)	400
costs to complete	(70)	(300)	390
Estimated profit/(loss)	230	70	(90)

Projects A and B are profit making and Project C is loss making.

When a project is 40% complete, Clarkstruction can reliably estimate the outcome. Consequently, while Project A is profitable and 80% complete, and therefore its outcome can be measured reliably; Project B, although profitable, is only 10% complete and therefore at such an early stage there is no certainty as to the project's overall outcome.

Step 2: calculate turnover

Having determined the expected outcomes of each of the projects, the appropriate accounting treatments can now be applied.

Project A

Project A is a profitable contract where the outcome can be estimated reliably.

$$\text{Turnover} = \text{estimated total revenue} \times \text{stage of completion}$$
$$= 800,000 \times 80\%$$
$$= £640,000$$

Project B

Project B is a profitable contract where the outcome cannot be estimated reliably.

As the outcome cannot be estimated reliably, no profit is recognised. Turnover is restricted to the extent of contract costs incurred that it is probable will be recoverable. Therefore:

$$\text{Turnover} = \text{costs incurred that are expected to be recovered}$$
$$= £30,000$$

Project C

Project C is a loss-making contract.

Turnover is calculated as a percentage of the stage of completion.

$$\text{Turnover} = \text{estimated total revenue} \times \text{stage of completion}$$
$$= 700,000 \times 50\%$$
$$= £350,000$$

The journal entry required to account for these contracts will be:

			£	£
Dr	Contract account – Project A		640,000	
Dr	Contract account – Project B		30,000	
Dr	Contract account – Project C		350,000	
	Cr	Turnover		1,020,000
Being turnover recognised on contracts.				

Step 3: calculate cost of sales

Project A

Project A is a profitable contract where the outcome can be estimated reliably.

$$\text{Cost of sales} = \text{total estimated costs} \times \text{stage of completion}$$
$$= 570,000 \times 80\%$$
$$= £456,000$$

Project B

Project B is a profitable contract where the outcome cannot be estimated reliably.

$$\text{Cost of sales} = \text{costs expensed as incurred}$$
$$= £30,000$$

Project C

Project C is loss-making.

Project C is expected to make an overall loss of £90,000. As turnover based on percentage of completion has been recognised of £350,000, the cost of sales figure requires to be set at a level that will give rise to a loss of £90,000, i.e:

$$\text{Cost of sales} = \text{turnover} + \text{expected loss}$$
$$= 350,000 + 90,000$$
$$= £440,000$$

The journal entry required to account for these contracts would be:

		£	£
Dr	Cost of sales	926,000	
	Cr Contract account – Project A		456,000
	Cr Contract account – Project B		30,000
	Cr Contract account – Project C		440,000
Being cost of sales recognised on contracts.			

Clarkstruction's income statement extract for the year ended 31 December 2009 will be as follows:

	£
Turnover	1,020,000
Cost of sales	926,000
Gross profit	94,000

Let us recap on the transactions thus far. The original expenses incurred on each contract were posted throughout the year to the individual contract accounts and then, at the year end, the appropriate revenues and expenses that were recognised were transferred to the income statement. Earlier in this section it was noted that a contract account was essentially a holding account in the balance sheet. With the information available to us thus far, the contract accounts for Projects A, B and C would be as follows:

Project A			
Costs incurred	£500,000	Cost of sales	£456,000
Contract revenue recognised	£640,000		

Project B			
Costs incurred	£30,000	Cost of sales	£30,000
Contract revenue recognised	£30,000		

Project C			
Costs incurred	£400,000	Cost of sales	£440,000
Contract revenue recognised	£350,000		

As has been noted, the invoices issued as the contract progresses may not equate to the turnover being recognised. In addition, if these 'progress billings' remain unpaid at the year end, this too will give rise to an outstanding amount. Let us now consider the balance sheet entries relating to construction contracts.

Balance sheet entries

At the year end, there may be two balances left relating to construction contracts:

1. trade debtors, i.e. progress billings invoiced – progress billings received
2. the balance on the 'contract account'.

If the balance on the 'contract account' is a debit, IAS 11 requires that this be shown as an asset and presented as:

Gross amount due from customers

If the balance is a credit, this would be shown as a liability and presented as:

Gross amount due to customers

The gross amount due from customers comprises:

costs incurred (i.e. the customer owes us for costs incurred on their behalf)	X
add recognised profits (i.e. we will be charging the customer a mark-up), or	X
less recognised losses (i.e. we cannot recoup all costs)	(X)
less progress billings invoiced (i.e. when we bill the customer it reduces what they owe us on the contract and becomes a debtor)	(X)
	X

This will be the case for all contracts in progress for which costs incurred plus recognised profits (less recognised losses) exceed progress billings. In other words, the customer still owes the company for costs incurred and/or work completed but not invoiced. It is, therefore, an asset.

The gross amount due to customers comprises:

Costs incurred	X
add recognised profits	X
less recognised losses	(X)
less progress billings invoiced	(X)
	(X)

This will be the case for all contracts in progress for which progress billings exceed costs incurred plus recognised profits (less recognised losses). In other words, the customer has been invoiced too much and is owed money back and/or the company is unable to recover all costs incurred. It is, therefore, a liability.

Continuing with the earlier example, Clarkstruction Ltd, suppose the following additional information is available regarding progress billings invoiced and received:

	Project A £000	Project B £000	Project C £000
Total contract value	800	400	700
Costs incurred to date	500	30	400
Estimated costs to complete	70	300	390
Progress billings invoiced	600	35	330
Progress billings received	510	–	270
%age completion	80%	10%	50%

What amounts should appear in the balance sheet of Clarkstruction at 31 December 2009?

Step 4: calculate the resultant balance sheet amounts

In journal entry form, progress billings invoiced will be entered as follows:

Dr   Trade debtors – progress billings
Cr   Contract account

The journal entry required to account for these contracts would be:

	£	£
Dr Trade debtors	965,000	
Cr Contract account – Project A		600,000
Cr Contract account – Project B		35,000
Cr Contract account – Project C		330,000
Being progress billing invoiced.		

BASIC

INTERMEDIATE

ADVANCED

Progress billings received will be accounted for like any other debtor, i.e.:

Dr   Bank
    Cr   Trade debtors
Being cash received from customer.

The journal entry required to account for these contract would be:

	£	£
Dr Bank	680,000	
Cr Trade debtors (510,000 + 270,000)		680,000
Being cash received from customers.		

The individual contract accounts for Projects A, B and C incorporating the progress billings invoiced will now be as follows:

Project A				
Costs incurred	£500,000	Cost of sales	£456,000
Contract revenue recognised	£640,000	Progress billings	£600,000
		Balance c/d	£84,000
	£1,140,000		£1,140,000
Balance b/d	£84,000		

This is a debit balance and will be presented as gross amount due from customers.

Project B				
Costs incurred	£30,000	Cost of sales	£30,000
Contract revenue recognised	£30,000	Progress billings	£35,000
Balance c/d	£5,000		
	£65,000		£65,000
		Balance b/d	£5,000

This is a credit balance and will be presented as gross amount due to customers.

Project C				
Costs incurred	£400,000	Cost of sales	£440,000
Contract revenue recognised	£350,000	Progress billings	£330,000
Balance c/d	£20,000		
	£770,000		£770,000
		Balance b/d	£20,000

This is a credit balance and will be presented as gross amount due to customers.
The summary debtor account will be as follows:

Trade debtors				
Project A – progress billings	£600,000	Bank (Project A)	£510,000
Project B – progress billings	£35,000	Bank (Project C)	£270,000
Project C – progress billings	£330,000		
		Balance c/d	£185,000
	£965,000		£965,000
Balance b/d	£185,000		

Alternatively, a columnar approach could have been adopted to determine the balance sheet position:

	Project A £000	Project B £000	Project C £000
Progress billings invoiced	600	35	330
Progress billings received	510	–	270
Trade debtors	90	35	60
Costs incurred	500	30	400
Profit/(loss) recognised	184	–	(90)
Progress billings invoiced	(600)	(35)	(330)
Amounts due from/(to) customers	84	(5)	(20)

Clarkstruction's extract balance sheet at 31 December 2009 would be as follows:

	£000
Current assets	
Trade debtors (receivables)	185
Gross amounts due from customers	84
Current liabilities	
Gross amounts due to customers	(25)

Notes

The gross amounts due to customers on Projects B and C have been added together. This is the correct presentation.

Amounts due to and from customers must be presented as current asset and liability, respectively. They must never be netted off to give a single amount.

The journals to account for construction contracts and the steps to follow in arriving at the appropriate profit and loss account and balance sheet entries are summarised in Appendices 1 and 2, at the end of this chapter. Check your understanding by working through the example in Progress Point 5.13.

Progress Point 5.13

DSM Ltd is a construction company. In the year to 31 December 2009, it started work on the following two contracts. Relevant details are:

		Contract 1 £000	Contract 2 £000
Contract value (total)		5,000	16,000
Costs incurred		3,050	7,300
Estimated costs to complete		1,150	9,100
Progress billings	– invoiced	3,600	5,200
	– received	3,100	4,800
%age completion		70%	40%

Relevant amounts are all regarded as recoverable and the outcomes of both contracts can be reliably estimated once they are 30% complete.

Required

(i) Prepare all necessary journal entries to record transactions relating to the contracts.

(ii) Prepare extracts of the profit and loss account of DSM Ltd for the year to 31 December 2009 and the balance sheet as at that date.

Suggested solution

(i)

Step 1: Calculate whether each contract will make an overall profit or loss.

	Contract 1 £000	Contract 2 £000
Contract value	5,000	16,000
Costs incurred	3,050	7,300
Estimated costs to complete	1,150	9,100
Estimated profit/(loss)	800	(400)

As both contracts are more than 30% complete the outcomes can be estimated reliably, i.e. Contract 1 is profitable while Contract 2 is loss-making.

Step 2: Calculate turnover.

Contract 1: Turnover = estimated total revenue × stage of completion

$$= 5,000,000 \times 70\%$$
$$= 3,500,000$$

Contract 2: Turnover

$$= 16,000,000 \times 40\%$$
$$= 6,400,000$$

Journal entry to record turnover:

Dr	Contract account – Contract 1	£3,500,000	
Dr	Contract account – Contract 2	£6,400,000	
	Cr Turnover		£9,900,000
Being turnover recognised on contracts			

Step 3: Calculate cost of sales.

Contract 1: Cost of sales = total estimated costs x stage of completion

$$= (3,050,000 + 1,150,000) \times 70\%$$
$$= 2,940,000$$

Contract 2: Contract 2 is expected to make an overall loss of £400,000. As turnover of £6,400,000 has been recognised, the cost of sales figure is calculated as:

$$= \text{turnover} + \text{expected loss}$$
$$= 6,400,000 + 400,000$$
$$= 6,800,000$$

Journal entry to record cost of sales:

Dr	Cost of sales	£9,740,000	
	Cr Contract account – Contract 1		£2,940,000
	Cr Contract account – Contract 2		£6,800,000
Being cost of sales recognised on contracts.			

Step 4: Calculate the resultant balance sheet amounts.

In respect of progress billings invoiced:

Dr	Trade debtors – progress billings	£8,800,000	
	Cr Contract account – Contract 1		£3,600,000
	Cr Contract account – Contract 2		£5,200,000
Being progress billings invoiced.			

In respect of progress billings received:

Dr	Bank (3,100,000 + 4,800,000)	£7,900,000	
	Cr Trade debtors		£7,900,000
Being cash received from customers.			

	Contract 1 £000	Contract 2 £000	Total £000
Costs incurred	3,050	7,300	
Profit/(loss) recognised	560	(400)	
Progress billings invoiced	(3,600)	(5,200)	
Gross amounts due from customers	10	1,700	1,710
Progress billings invoiced	3,600	5,200	
Progress billings received	3,100	4,800	
Trade debtors	500	400	900

(ii) DSM profit and loss account (extract)
For the year ended 31 December 2009

	£000
Turnover	9,900
Cost of sales	9,740
Gross profit	160

Balance sheet (extract)
At 31 December 2009

	£000
Current assets	
Trade debtors	1,710
Gross amounts due from customers	900

Reliable estimates

Contracts where the outcome can reliably be estimated have been dealt with. The question that does arise is how to decide whether an estimate is reliable or not. IAS 11 gives the following guidance.

The outcome can be estimated reliably (para. 23) when:

(a) total contract revenue can be assessed reliably
(b) it is probable that the economic benefits will flow to the company (i.e. the customer will pay)
(c) both contract costs to complete and stage of completion can be measured reliably, and
(d) contract costs can be clearly identified and measured reliably.

For a contract in its early stages or where there are significant risks remaining (e.g. on a contract using new technology or techniques) it will probably not be possible to meet criteria (c) above and the overall outcome cannot be estimated reliably. Such a contract will fall into the profitable not reliable category (i.e. the revenue that is recognised would be restricted to the costs incurred).

Contracts lasting several years

The examples thus far in this chapter have been concerned with contracts in their first year of construction. In practice, contracts may last for several years and the contract price and estimated total costs will undoubtedly be changing over the duration of the particular contract. In such circumstances it is important to keep track of the cumulative position.

 Example

Stadium Structures entered into a contract to build a sports stadium in 2008, which is due to be completed by 2010. Relevant information is:

	2008 £000	2009 £000	2010 £000
Contract price	15,000	15,000	15,000
Variations	–	200	400
Penalty	–	–	(100)
%age completion	35%	80%	100%

The variations and the penalty can be assumed to have been agreed, and have been measured reliably at each balance sheet date. Assume that the contract is profitable overall and the outcome can be estimated reliably at each balance sheet date.

What amounts should be recognised as turnover in 2008 to 2010?

	2008 £000	2009 £000	2010 £000	Total £000
Total contract revenue	15,000	15,200	15,300	
Percentage completion	35%	80%	100%	
Total revenue to be recognised	5,250	12,160	15,300	
Less: already recognised	–	5,250	12,160	
Turnover recognised	5,250	6,910	3,140	15,300

Notes

Variations should be included as part of total revenue only when it is probable that the customer will approve both the variation and the monetary value; penalties are viewed as a reduction in turnover and not as additional costs.

The approach adopted is therefore to: ascertain the total contract revenue at each balance sheet date; determine the percentage completion to ascertain the cumulative contract revenue recognisable at each balance sheet date; isolate the contract revenue to be recognised in each year by deducting the previously recognised cumulative turnover from the total revenue to be recognised at each balance sheet date. As far as the balance sheet is concerned, the figures presented will be based on the cumulative amounts.

Advances and retentions

Earlier in this section the accounting requirements in respect of retentions were explained and demonstrated. IAS 11 provides a formal definition of retentions as 'amounts of progress billings which are not paid until the satisfaction of conditions specified in the contract for the payment of such amounts or until defects have been rectified' (para. 41).

Advances received are amounts received by the contractor before the related work is performed. Advances are shown separately as payments on account. They are not offset against amounts due from customers until the relevant work is performed.

Progress Point 5.14

Show how the following information for construction contract Project 430 should be recorded in the financial statements.

	Project 430
	£
Contract revenue recognised	500
Contract expenses recognised	450
Progress billings	500
Progress billings received plus advance	525
Contract costs incurred	600

Project 430 is reliably estimated to be profitable.

Solution

Given the information provided, the income statement entries are straightforward (i.e. the contract revenue and contract expenses to be recognised have been given and so no further adjustments are required).

Therefore, the income statement entries will be:

	£
Contract revenue	500
Contract expenses	450
Gross profit	50

The balance sheet entries will have to be calculated to determine the position in respect to amounts due/from customers.

Using the steps detailed in Appendix 2 (at the end of this chapter) relating to the balance sheet gives:

	£
Costs incurred to date	600
Add: recognised profits	50
Less: progress billings invoiced	(500)
Gross amounts due from customers	150

This is a debit balance and will therefore be disclosed under current assets.

In respect of the advance received of £25, this will be disclosed under current liabilities.

The balance sheet extract entries will be:

Current assets	
Gross amounts due from customers	150
Current liabilities	
Advances received	25

BASIC

INTERMEDIATE

ADVANCED

5.16 Examination issues

As the examples in this section will have illustrated, there are a range of questions that may be asked in relation to construction contracts. Although there are two standard types of question, the situation and requirement in each can vary.

The two basic types of question are as follows.

1. One or more contracts started in the current year: here you will normally be tested to ensure you follow the correct steps to determine whether each contract is profitable, profitable but not reliable, or loss making, and apply the appropriate accounting treatment to each. Remember that in an exam it is likely that you would be given one of each. If, therefore, you are given three contracts and you think all are profitable, check again – this is an unlikely situation.
2. One contract that lasts for several years: here you will normally be asked to calculate the position for each year of the contract, or perhaps two or three years into the contract. Remember to keep track of the cumulative position, and remember also that the contract price and estimated contract cost is likely to alter over the duration of the contract.

Situation

The situation you are placed in, in the question, may also vary. You may have to do all the recording in some, but in many questions, the contract costs, payments on account invoiced and received will have been recorded but you will have to work out the amounts to be included in the profit and loss account and balance sheet. In a few the figures to be transferred to the profit and loss account will also be given and the emphasis will be on the balance sheet.

Requirement

The requirement may also vary. Some questions may require full journals for initial recording, year-end adjustments through to producing extracts from the balance sheet and profit and loss account. Others may ask only for figures for the profit and loss account and balance sheet.

5.17 Disclosure requirements

These are detailed at paras 39–45, and are as follows:

(a) amount of contract revenue recognised in the period (para. 39(a))
(b) method used to determine revenue (para. 39(b))
(c) method used to determine stage of completion (para. 39(c))
(d) for contracts in progress at the balance sheet date (para. 40)
   –   the aggregate amount of costs incurred and recognised profits (less recognised losses)
   –   the amount of advances received (if any)
   –   the amount of retentions (if any)
(e) the gross amount due from customers for contract work should be shown as an asset (para. 42)
(f) the gross amount due to customers for contract work should be shown as a liability (para. 42).

Disclosure in practice

In a similar manner to the disclosure of inventories, the disclosure requirements of IAS 11 *Construction Contracts* are satisfied in distinct sections.

Inventories

Incorporated along with the inventories notes, Logica includes its accounting policy on construction contracts. This extract from the policy note of Logica explains amounts recoverable on contracts and refers to the group's policy on revenue recognition:

> Inventories represent computer equipment that, at the balance sheet date, had not yet been allocated to a specific customer contract and materials, including work-in-progress, used in document printing and finishing.
>
> Inventories are stated at the lower of cost and net realisable value. Cost comprises direct materials and, where applicable, direct labour costs and those overheads that have been incurred in bringing the inventories to their present location and condition. Cost is calculated using the first-in-first-out (FIFO) method. Net realisable value represents the estimated selling price less costs to be incurred in marketing, distribution and sale.
>
> Amounts recoverable on contracts represent revenue which has not yet been invoiced to customers on fixed price contracts. Such amounts are separately disclosed within trade and other receivables. The valuation of amounts recoverable on contracts is adjusted to take up profit to date or foreseeable losses in accordance with the Group's accounting policy for profit recognition.

Revenue and profit recognition

The group's policy on revenue recognition is disclosed, together with the method used (percentage of completion) to determine the contract revenue recognised in the period. As the note states, Logica uses a level of completion of 50% to determine reliably the outcome of a contract:

> Revenue represents the fair value of consideration received or receivable from clients for goods and services provided by the Group, net of discounts, VAT and other sales-related taxes. Where the time value of money is material, revenue is recognised as the present value of the cash inflows expected to be received from the customer in settlement.
>
> Revenue from the sale of software products or hardware with no significant service obligation is recognised 100% on delivery. Revenue from the sale of software products or hardware requiring significant modification, integration or customisation is recognised using the percentage of completion method.
>
> The revenue and profit of contracts for the supply of professional services at predetermined rates is recognised as and when the work is performed, irrespective of the duration of the contract.
>
> The revenue and profit on fixed price contracts is recognised on a percentage of completion basis when the outcome of a contract can be estimated reliably. A contract's outcome is deemed to be capable of reliable estimation at the earlier of six months from contract commencement and the date at which the contract is 50% complete. If a contract outcome cannot be estimated reliably, revenues are recognised equal to costs incurred, to the extent that costs are expected to be recovered.
>
> The stage of contract completion is determined by reference to the costs of professional services incurred to date as a proportion of the total estimated costs of professional services, except in rare circumstances when measuring the stage of contract completion using total contract costs is more representative of the work performed, in which case total contract costs are used. Where a contract contains multiple elements, the individual elements are accounted for separately where appropriate.
>
> Provision is made for all foreseeable future losses in the period in which it is identified.

Trade and other receivables

	2007 £m	2006 £m
Trade receivables	619.4	626.2
Less: provision for impairment	(6.1)	(8.1)
Trade receivables – net	613.3	618.1
Amounts recoverable on contracts	219.9	297.7
Prepayments and accrued income	148.5	123.2
Derivative financial instruments	5.4	1.4
Other receivables	34.1	29.8
	1,021.2	1,070.2

Amounts recoverable on contracts included amounts due for settlement after more than one year of £42.4 million at 31 December 2007 (2006: £40.6 million).

Figure 5.3 Logica: amounts recoverable on contracts note

Contracts accounted for under the percentage-of-completion method

Contracts in progress at the balance sheet date:	2007 £m	2006 £m
Contract costs incurred plus recognised profits less recognised losses to date	4,349.7	3,823.8
Less: progress billings	(4,217.5)	(3,636.1)
	132.2	187.7
Recognised as:		
Amounts due from contract customers included in trade and other receivables	219.9	297.7
Amounts due from contract customers included in trade and other payables	(87.7)	(110.0)
	132.2	187.7

The Group's credit risk on trade and other receivables is primarily attributable to trade receivables and amounts recoverable on contracts. The Group has no significant concentrations of credit risk since the risk is spread over a large number of unrelated counterparties. The Directors estimate that the carrying value of financial assets within trade and other receivables approximated their fair value.

Figure 5.4 Logica: detailed contracts in progress disclosure note

The note to the balance sheet details the amounts recognised in the financial statements in respect of construction contracts. Note that the amounts due to and from customers is disclosed separately, the standard not allowing such balances to be netted off.

Progress Point 5.15

Morgan Henry Contracts Ltd has the following details in relation to a construction contract to build a motorway at the end of its financial year of 31 March 2009.

Contract M45	
	£000
Total contract price	26,000
Costs incurred to date	15,000
Costs to complete	4,000
Progress billings	12,000
Advance payments	3,000
%age complete 31 March 2009	60%
%age complete 31 March 2008	30%

The contract has been ongoing since June 2007 and Morgan Henry Contracts Ltd recognised revenue of £6.5 million and costs of £5 million in its financial statements to 31 March 2008. The company uses the stage of completion method to estimate revenues and expenses. Stage of completion is based on surveys of work performed.

Required

Prepare extracts of the Profit and Loss Account for Morgan Henry Contracts Ltd for the year to 31 March 2009 and the balance sheet as at that date. Show, as far as possible, the disclosure requirements in accordance with IAS 11.

Suggested solution

Step 1: Calculate whether the contract will make an overall profit or loss.

	Contract M45
	£000
Total contract price	26,000
Costs incurred to date	(15,000)
Costs to complete	(4,000)
Estimated profit	7,000

Step 2: Calculate turnover.

Turnover: estimated total revenue × stage of completion
= 26,000,000 × 60% = £15,600,000

∴ cumulative turnover to be recognised	£15,600,000
Less: recognised year to 31 March 2008	£6,500,000
Revenue recognised year to 31 March 2009	£9,100,000

Step 3: Calculate cost of sales.

Cost of sales = total estimated costs × stage of completion
= 19,000,000 × 60% = £11,400,000

∴ cumulative expenses recognised	£11,400,000
Less: recognised year to 31 March 2008	£5,000,000
Cost of sales recognised year to 31 March 2009	£6,400,000

Step 4 : Balance sheet entries:

	£000
Costs incurred	15,000
Profit recognised	4,200
Progress billings invoiced	(12,000)
Gross amounts due from customers	7,200

		31/3/08 £000	31/3/09 £000	Total £000
Profit recognised:	cumulative revenue	6,500	9,100	15,600
	cumulative expenses	5,000	6,400	11,400
	Profit	1,500	2,700	4,200

Morgan Henry Contracts Income statement (extract) Year to 31 March 2009	
	£000
Turnover	9,100
Cost of sales	6,400
Gross profit	2,700

Balance sheet (extract) As at 31 March 2009	
	£
Current assets	
Trade receivables	12,000
Gross amounts due from customers	7,200
Current liabilities	
Advance payments	3,000

Notes to the accounts

1. Turnover: turnover for the year on construction contracts amounted to £91,000,000. Turnover was calculated using the stage of completion and the total estimated revenue arising on contracts. Stage of completion was assessed based on surveys of work performed.

2. Costs:

	£000
Aggregate costs incurred	15,000
Aggregate profit less recognised losses	4,200

The effect of the disclosure requirements

The effect of the disclosure requirements in IAS 11 is to provide information both on the cumulative position of contracts – as in the aggregate costs incurred and aggregate profit recognised – but also on the turnover for the year under consideration.

It is worth pausing at this stage to consider what the balance sheet amounts in relation to construction contracts actually represent.

Gross amount due to/from customers – by its very calculation – involves the incorporation into the total of unrealised profits (i.e. the profit recognised to date). This means that in such a balance sheet figures will be incorporated that are not at lower of cost or net realisable value – but at some 'profit inclusive' value. In one sense, the accounting for construction contracts is akin to accounting for fixed assets, albeit in reverse. When accounting for fixed assets the net book value was found to be simply an accounting value representing the as yet unallocated cost of the fixed asset to the profit and loss account (i.e. the net book value is an intermediate stage in the allocation process).

Accounting for a long-term contract is very similar. Over the period of a contract, a given profit will be earned. By following the requirements of IAS 11, this profit can be allocated to accounting periods during which the contract is in process. Until the contract is completed, therefore, the recognised profits are simply an intermediate stage in the overall profit measurement.

5.18 Comparison between GAAPs

In the UK, both stocks and long-term contracts are dealt with in one standard: SSAP 9. The principles followed in SSAP 9 are similar to those in IAS 2 and IAS 11, except for some differences in relation to contracts. SSAP 9 has more detailed presentation in the balance sheet, although the net amounts in the profit and loss account and balance sheet are the same as IAS 11.

Under US GAAP, if an enterprise cannot determine contract revenue or costs, estimated costs to completion or the stage of completion, then the completed contract method is required. Under the completed contract method, net income is not recognised until the contract is complete. IAS 11 prohibits the use of the completed-contract method.

5.19 IAS 11: a critical appraisal

As was demonstrated in our study of stock valuations, the balance sheet figure for stock can be extremely subjective. The valuations carried as construction contracts are subject to all the problems associated with stock valuations – and more. It is easy to forget the principles that underpin accounting reporting – particularly when some of these principles conflict. A fundamental principle is that accounts are prepared following the historic cost convention; figures are recorded at their actual amounts and incorporated into the entity's financial reporting system at those historic amounts. In the case of construction contracts, this is what is being done in the recording of costs relating to specific contracts and recorded in the individual contract accounts. However, these contract accounts are not shown in the income statement but are instead held on the balance sheet pending adjustments made in relation to recognisable revenue, expenses and profits. This is because of the nature of long-term construction contracts and the reporting problems that would exist if firms engaged in such contracts were unable to recognise profits until after a contract was completed; they would be placed in a situation in which reported profits might be subject to wide fluctuations from year to year. Reported profits would depend on the volume of contracts actually completed during a particular time period, which may bear no relation to the level of activity of the organisation. Indeed, it is possible to envisage situations where a highly profitable firm is engaged in a small number of major contracts and yet appears to make heavy losses for a number of years followed by huge profits in the years in which the contracts terminate. In such circumstances the recognition of profit on construction contracts makes 'income smoothing' very desirable indeed. And therein lies the problem.

As has been demonstrated through our study of other areas in this book, as well as giving guidance to accountants in respect of the reporting of accounting transactions, standards also serve a regulatory function to try to prevent misleading users through the use of creative accounting. Unfortunately, income smoothing is just that – creative accounting. Moreover, if one considers just what is being recognised as revenue, it is clear that this in no way follows the historic cost recording principles. The amounts being recognised are an abstract based on the total contract revenue – revenue that no doubt has inflationary safeguards built in and that will be earned at some future date. Indeed, depending on the method chosen to determine the level of completion, the amount of contract costs recognised may bear very little resemblance to those costs actually incurred. Of course, it could be argued that all this information is available in the financial statements and the related notes, and that it is possible to extract from the accounts the detail required to make appropriate judgements on such activities. But

this is not an easy topic. The accounting for construction contracts is complicated enough before one considers the inherent difficulties in obtaining the information to be accounted for in the first place. IAS 11 does not specify a single method that may be used to identify the stage of completion. The stage of completion of a contract can be determined in a variety of ways – including the proportion that contract costs incurred for work performed to date bear to the estimated total contract costs, surveys of work performed or completion of a physical proportion of the contract work. In some circumstances, the use of each of these methods to determine a level of completion may give vastly different results – and each would be acceptable, the IAS proviso being that whichever method is chosen it should reliably measure the work performed.

It is clear therefore that the valuation of construction contracts is fraught with difficulty. From an auditor's perspective, it is unlikely that she or he will have the expertise to verify management's representations regarding stages of completion. The auditor's reliance on management will be great – and his auditor independence diminished. Fortunately, in many instances, the valuations will be made by independent, third-party valuers thus alleviating the auditor of this particular burden. From a user's perspective, however, an awareness of the principles underlying the reporting of construction contracts is essential to fully understand the figures within the financial statements. Moreover, since an element of subjectivity will once again be attached to the estimates made, however expertly calculated, the requirement to apply the chosen method of determining recognised profits in as consistent a manner as possible is essential if users of the financial statements are to place any credibility on them.

Summary

In the preceding section it was demonstrated how difficult it was to place an accurate valuation on inventories. The valuation of long-term contracts is even more difficult. The standard's emphasis is on what can be recognised as revenue rather than on the balance sheet figure, however the two are inextricably linked. The standard allows attributable profit to date on a long-term contract to be taken to the profit and loss account when the earnings process is sufficiently far advanced and there is reasonable certainty of making a profit. This permitted treatment forms one exception to the rule of not recognising profits until realised. This treatment also favours the accruals principle over prudence. Consequently, the analysis of a set of financial statements of a contracting business has to be approached in a very different way from a straight manufacturing business.

BASIC

INTERMEDIATE

ADVANCED

Chapter summary

IAS 2 *Inventories*

■ Inventories should be valued at the lower of cost and net realisable value.

■ Cost includes all costs to bring the inventories to their present condition and location.

■ Where specific cost is not appropriate, the benchmark treatment is to use FIFO or weighted average.

■ The standard cost and retail methods may be used for the measurement of cost, provided that the results approximate actual cost.

■ The same cost formula should be used for all inventories with similar characteristics as to their nature and use to the enterprise.

■ For inventories with a different nature or use, different cost formulas may be justified.

IAS 11 *Construction Contracts*

■ There is no reference to the length of a contract in its definition, but there is a requirement that the contract should be specifically negotiated.

■ Contract revenue should include the amount agreed in the initial contract, plus revenue from variations in the original contract work, plus claims and incentive payments that are expected to be received and that can be measured reliably.

■ Contract costs should comprise costs that relate directly to the specific contract, plus costs that are attributable to contract activity in general and can be allocated to the contract, and such other costs that can be specifically charged to the customer under the terms of the contract.

■ When the outcome of a construction contract can be estimated reliably, revenues and costs should be estimated by reference to the stage of completion of the contract.

■ To be able to make a reliable estimate, the enterprise must be able to make a reliable estimate of total contract revenue, the stage of completion and the costs to complete the contract.

■ If the outcome cannot be measured reliably, no profit should be recognised; instead costs should be expensed and revenues should be recognised in line with recoverable costs.

■ An expected loss on a construction contract should be recognised as an expense as soon as such a loss is probable.

■ The stage of completion of a contract may be determined in a variety of ways:
  – the proportion that contract costs incurred for work performed to date bear to the estimated total contract costs
  – surveys of work performed, or
  – completion of a physical proportion of the contract work.

 Key terms for review

Definitions can be found in the glossary at the end of the book.

Inventories

Net realisable value

Fair value

Construction contract

Fixed price contract

Cost plus contract

Review questions

1. Identify which costs should be included in the cost of inventories and which should be excluded from the cost of inventories.
2. Explain the effect an increase or decrease in the value of closing stock will have on the reported profit of a company.
3. Briefly outline each of the following methods of stock valuation:
    (a) first in, first out (FIFO)
    (b) last in, first out (LIFO)
    (c) weighted average cost (AVCO).
4. Explain the difference between *perpetual* and *periodic* bases of stock valuations.
5. What is the IAS 2 definition of *inventories*?
6. Explain how inventories should be measured to comply with IAS 2.
7. Explain how an under-recovery of overheads should be accounted for in arriving at a figure for closing stock.
8. Explain how an over-recovery of overheads should be accounted for in arriving at a figure for closing stock.
9. Identify the items that IAS 2 specifically excludes from the cost of stock.
10. How should the stock of a service provider be accounted for?
11. What is the IAS 11 definition of a *construction contract*?
12. Explain how revenue and costs should be recognised in accordance with IAS 11 where the outcome of a construction contract can be estimated reliably.

Exercises

1. Level I

BD Joiners stock transactions for the three months ended 31 March 2009 were as follows:

	Units	Unit cost £	Unit selling price £
Stock on hand: 1/1/09	60	30	
January purchases	90	34	
January sales	(40)		60
February purchases	55	60	
February sales	(45)		100
March purchases	60	75	
March sales	(75)		130
Stock on hand 31/3/09	105		

BD Joiners maintains its stock records on the perpetual system, and all purchases are made on the first day of the month.

Required

(i) Calculate cost of goods sold, gross profit and closing inventory for the three months ended 31 March 2009 under FIFO and LIFO cost flow assumptions.

(ii) With reference to your findings in (i) above, explain the effect each of the cost flow assumptions has on the income statement and balance sheet in times of rising prices.

2.   Level I

Purchases and sales of a certain product for the first seven days of June 2009 are as follows:

Day	1	Purchases	20 units @ £5 each
	3	Sales	15 units
	5	Purchases	30 units @ £6 each
	7	Sales	10 units

Required

 (i)   Determine the cost of goods sold for the week and closing stock at the end of the week under the FIFO, LIFO and weighted average methods of inventory valuation, assuming a periodic system of inventory control.
 (ii) Determine the cost of goods sold for the week and closing stock at the end of the week under the FIFO, LIFO and weighted average methods of inventory valuation, assuming a perpetual system of inventory control.
(iii) Discuss the advantages and/or disadvantages of FIFO, LIFO and the weighted average method.
(iv)   If a company maintains a perpetual inventory control system, is it necessary to have an annual stock take?

3.   Level II

Mod Transport Ltd manufacture four types of scooter: Models A, B, C and D. The following information relates to the value of finished goods and work in progress in inventories on 31 December 2009 (the company's financial year end):

Model	Number of items in stock	Production cost to date	Estimated further costs required to complete each item	Expected selling price per item
		£	£	£
A	10	150	–	140
B	15	70	–	110
C	23	65	20	100
D	7	110	30	150

It is estimated that further costs will necessarily be incurred in selling the scooters. These additional costs are estimated at 5% of each item's total cost (production and completion).

Required

Calculate the value at which inventories will be stated in the balance sheet at 31 December 2009.

4. Level III

Flofoam is a manufacturer of specialist lightweight padding for seating in passenger aircraft. As a result of the particular machinery required, Flofoam manufactures and sells only this one product. Raw materials are purchased in lots of 1,000 tonnes at the commencement of each week throughout the year ended 31 March 2009. The price per tonne was £100 for the first nine months and £130 thereafter. Transport costs to the factory amount to £20 per tonne and customs duty of £4 per tonne was paid throughout the year. Due to the volume of purchases, the supplier of raw materials gave a discount of £8 per tonne from 1 October 2008 onwards.

Direct costs of processing amount to £30 per tonne and fixed production overheads have been calculated at £27 per tonne on the basis of normal levels of activity.

Each tonne of raw material produces one tonne of finished goods.

Company general administration overheads amount to £5,000 per week and selling costs are estimated at £18 per tonne.

At the end of the year there were £4,000 tonnes of raw material and 1,500 tonnes of finished goods.

The selling price to customers per tonne was £300 throughout the year. Opening stock equalled £640,000 in total, made up of 3,000 tonnes of raw materials and 500 tonnes of finished goods.

Required

(i) Calculate the stock value of raw materials and finished goods as at 31 March 2009. Assume the FIFO method is used.

(ii) Calculate the gross profit for the year to 31 March 2009 assuming an operational year of 52 weeks.

5. Level III

Bennett Building Supplies Ltd ('BBS') is a building supply company. At 31 December 2009, a stock count was carried out of the eight main categories of stock held by the company. Relevant information is as follows:

Category	Units in stock	Cost per unit £	NRV per unit £
A	500	110	140
B	2,100	75	70
C	350	170	150
D	4,100	42	55
E	1,500	210	220

The calculation of NRV does not take into account a price cut equivalent to 5% of cost that will be applied from 1 January 2009 onwards.

All building supply materials are finished goods.

BBS has received a firm order for 100 of the category C items at a price of £220 per unit. Selling costs would be £8 per unit. The customer requires these to be modified to meet its specification. BBS estimates this will cost £32 per unit.

Required

Calculate the total value of the closing stock of BBS at 31 December 2009.

6. Level II

D & C Stores is a food retailer that values stock at a retail price less a margin. Stock at 30 November 2009 has been counted and categorised as follows:

Category	Units	Retail price per unit £	Average gross margin %
Perishable goods	800	1.20	40
Drinks	1,850	2.90	20
Household, cleaning	550	2.10	18
Tinned goods	6,300	0.65	15
Packaged dry goods	4,100	1.40	24

It is company policy to create a provision of 50% of the cost of perishable goods.

Required

Calculate the closing stock value to be included in the accounts of D & C stores at 30 November 2009.

7. Level III

MCL has manufactured summerhouses for a number of years and has a well-developed costing system. In anticipation of the forthcoming year's budgeted demand for its prestige model, the Postcode Penthouse, MCL has concentrated production on this one particular summerhouse. The standard costing information for the year ended 31 December 2009, which had been set on 1 January 2009, was as follows:

	Cost per summerhouse £
Raw materials	800
Direct labour	1,000
Production overheads	1,200
Distribution costs	100

The costing department has supplied the following information regarding variances.

1. A production fault occurred during August 2009, which resulted in a batch of doors being scrapped.
2. The price of raw materials increased on 1 November 2009.
3. A changed in working practices took effect from 1 October 2009, which increased direct labour pay rates.
4. The variances recorded for the Postcode Penthouse for the year ended 31 December 2009 are as follows:

	Production fault £	Price rise £	Change in working practices £	Total £
Raw materials	200,000 A	600,000 A	–	800,000 A
Direct labour	50,000 A	–	540,000 A	590,000 A
Production o/hds	50,000 A	–	480,000 F	430,000 F
	300,000 A	600,000 A	60,000 A	960,000 A

Note

A: adverse variance

F: favourable variance

Further information

1. Information regarding stocks of the Postcode Penthouse and work in progress at 31 December 2009 was as follows:

Finished goods	2,000 units
Work in progress	1,000 units

   Work in progress was 100% complete as to raw materials, and 50% complete as to direct labour and production overheads.

2. The normal monthly level of production of 4,000 units was achieved throughout the year ended 31 December 2009. Completed summerhouses were sold on the first in first out basis.
3. Since the year end, the finished goods have all been sold to retailers at £3,800 each, and the work in progress has all been completed and sold at a special price of £3,000 each.

Required

Prepare the stock valuations at 31 December 2009 for stocks and work in progress, in accordance with IAS 2 *Inventories*.

8. Level II

Stone By Stone Ltd ('SBS') is a construction company involved in several building contracts. Details of two of the contracts in progress at the company's year end of 31 December 2009 are as follows.

Patterson Palace

This contract was originally negotiated in March 2007 at a price of £10.5m. In a bid to ensure speedy completion, an additional 5% incentive payment was included in the contract for completion by 31 March 2009.

During 2008, Lady Patterson amended the specification and both parties agreed that an increase of £0.5m should be made to the contract price. The incentive payment was also to apply to this variation.

At 31 December 2009, the contract is 95% complete and the engineers are confident it will be completed by mid-March 2010.

McLeod Mansion

This contract to construct a futuristic building was secured in January 2008 after a long period of tender and negotiation. SBS has estimated the total costs of the contract to be:

	£000
Materials	9,650
Labour	4,200
Subcontracted work	1,560
Professional fees	710
Equipment hire	250
Depreciation of plant and equipment	410
General administration	520
Development costs	260
Costs of contract tender	620
Production overheads	3,100

The development costs of £260,000 relate to the estimated costs of finalising a new technique to be used to construct the building. As this technique is likely to be used on future contracts, SBS did not specify reimbursement of these in the terms of the contract.

It is company policy to provide 5% of total costs for rectification and guarantee work.

Of the £620,000 contract tender costs, £512,000 were incurred and written off to profit and loss in the year to 31 December 2008.

Required

Calculate the total revenue for the Patterson Palace contract and the estimated total costs of the McLeod Mansion contract.

9. Level III

The following data relate to a profitable contract – contract F360M:

Contract F360M	£000
Costs incurred on contract	1,000
Appropriate proportion of total contract value reported as turnover for year	1,500
Costs incurred in reaching stage of completion recognised in turnover	900
Progress payments invoiced to customers	1,200

Required

Prepare journal entries to record the relevant information for the profit and loss account and balance sheet in accordance with IAS 11 *Construction Contracts* requirements, and show the relevant profit and loss account and balance sheet extracts.

10. Level II

The following data relate to Contract RJC 19:

	£000
Total contract value	500
Value of work completed (certified)	400
Costs to date (all attributable to work completed)	500
Estimated costs to completion	80
Progress payments invoiced	540

Required

Prepare the relevant profit and loss account and balance sheet extracts in accordance with the requirements of IAS 11 *Construction Contracts*.

11. Level II

Metvon Ltd has a number of contracts in progress at its year end: 31 December 2009. Details of two of these are given below:

	Contract 1	Contract 2
	£000	£000
Contract price	16,000	36,000
Progress billings invoiced	6,300	21,400
Progress billings received	4,850	20,000
Costs incurred to date	4,300	25,000
Estimated costs to complete	10,100	13,000
% completion	30%	65%

Both contracts were started in the current year.

The company uses the stage of completion method, and all costs and outstanding billings invoiced are regarded as recoverable.

Metvon can estimate reliably the outcome of contracts once they are 40% complete.

Required

Calculate the amounts to appear in the profit and loss account of Metvon Ltd for the year to 31 December 2009, and the balance sheet as at that date (disclosure notes are not required).

12. Level II

On 1 February 2007, Arena Construction Ltd obtained a contract to build a sports complex. The complex was to be build at a total cost of £4,500,000 and was scheduled for completion by 1 September 2009. One clause of the contract stated that Arena Construction Ltd was to deduct £10,000 from the £6,000,000 total contract price for each week that completion was delayed. Completion was delayed five weeks, which resulted in a £50,000 penalty. Below are data pertaining to the construction period:

	2007	2008	2009
	£	£	£
Costs incurred to date (cumulative)	1,500,000	3,220,000	4,600,000
Estimated costs to complete	3,000,000	1,380,000	–
Progress billings invoiced (cumulative)	1,000,000	2,500,000	5,950,000
Progress billings received (cumulative)	800,000	2,300,000	5,950,000

Arena Construction determines the stage of completion of a contract by reference to the proportion that contract costs incurred for work performed to date bear to estimated total contract costs.

The outcome of contracts can be estimated reliably only when a contract is at least 40% complete.

Required

(i) Prepare extracts from the profit and loss account and balance sheet for each of the three years of the contract ending 31 December 2007, 31 December 2008 and 31 December 2009.

13. Level II

Buildwell Ltd commenced business on 1 April 2008 as building contractors. The following details relate to three contracts in progress at the company's year end of 31 March 2009:

Contract name	Station Road	Park Terrace	Castle Way
	£	£	£
Costs incurred to date	30,470	27,280	13,640
Value of work certified by			
Contractees' architects	38,250	22,015	14,300
Progress billings invoiced	33,000	17,600	11,000
Progress billings received	27,500	17,600	11,000
Estimate of:			
	£	£	£
Final cost including future costs of			
rectification and guarantee work	33,000	38,500	66,000
Final contract price	42,500	31,450	89,375

The company uses the stage of completion method to estimate revenues and expenses. Stage of completion is based upon surveys of works performed by the contractees' architects. Buildwell Ltd can estimate the outcome of a contract reliably only when it is at least 40% complete.

Required

Prepare extracts from the profit and loss account and balance sheet for the year ended 31 March 2009.

14. Level III

Alternative Power Solutions Ltd ('APS') is a firm of building contractors specialising in the construction of offshore wind farms. At 31 December 2009 the company had three contracts in progress: North Shores, Western Beaches and Philorth Flats. North Shores was started during the year ended 31 December 2008, and Western Beaches and Philorth Flats were started during the year ended 31 December 2009.

Details of the contracts are as follows:

	North Shores 31/12/08 £000	North Shores 31/12/09 £000	Western Beaches 31/12/09 £000	Philorth Flats 31/12/09 £000
Contract value	250	250	320	420
Agreed variation	–	30	–	–
Progress billings (cumulative)				
Progress billings invoiced	40	240	260	340
Progress billings received	40	200	210	340
Costs to date (cumulative)				
Materials	20	100	84	69
Labour	5	20	54	71
Production overhead	10	80	82	80
Estimated additional costs to complete:				
Materials	75	5	30	144
Labour	20	–	5	14
Production overhead	65	5	15	72
Percentage complete	20%	90%	80%	50%

Percentage complete is based upon surveyors' valuations. APS can estimate reliably the outcome of contracts once they are 30% complete.

Required

(i) Calculate, showing all workings, the amounts to be included in the financial statements for APS Ltd for the year ended 31 December 2009, in respect of each of the contracts for:
   (a) turnover
   (b) cost of sales
   (c) trade receivables, and
   (d) gross amount due from customers or due to customers for contract work.
(ii) Prepare the relevant profit and loss account and balance sheet extracts for the year ended 31 December 2009.

Further Reading
IAS 2 *Inventories*. IASB, 2003
IAS 11 *Construction Contracts*. IASB, 1993

Appendix 1: Journals for construction contracts

The following journal entries are used to record the accounting entries in respect of construction contracts.
   During the year:

(1)	Dr	Trade debtors (b/s)	X	
		Cr Contract account (b/s)		X
		Being progress billings invoiced.		

To record the progress billings invoiced to the customer.

(2)	Dr	Bank	X	
		Cr Trade debtors		X
		Being amounts received from customers.		

To record the amounts received from the customer.

(3)	Dr	Contract account (b/s)	X	
		Cr Bank/trade creditors		X
		Being contract costs incurred in year.		

To record the costs incurred in the year.
   At the year end, the relevant amounts are transferred from the contract account in the balance sheet to the profit and loss account on a work completed basis:

(4)	Dr	Contract account (b/s)	X	
		Cr Turnover (p&l)		X
		Being turnover recognised on contracts.		

To record recognised turnover.

(5)	Dr	Cost of sales (p&l)	X	
	Cr	Contract account (b/s)		X
		Being cost of sales recognised on contracts.		

To record recognised cost of sales.

Depending on the information provided, you may have to calculate some of the relevant amounts.

Appendix 2: Steps for construction contracts

Appendix 2 summarises the steps to be followed in respect of construction contracts to ascertain the recognised turnover and cost of sales amounts, and to determine the balance sheet entries.

Profit and loss account

Step 1: calculate overall profit/loss on the contract.

Step 2: calculate turnover for each year of contract.

For profitable/reliable or loss-making contracts:

turnover = contract price × stage of completion (less previous recognised turnover)

For profitable/not reliable:

turnover = costs incurred (less previously recognised turnover)

Step 3: calculate cost of sales for each year of contract.

For profitable/reliable:

cost of sales = total estimated costs × stage of completion (less previously recognised cost of sales)

For profitable/not reliable:

cost of sales = costs incurred which are recoverable (less previously recognised cost of sales)

For loss making:

cost of sales = recognised turnover + full loss

That is, the full loss must be recognised immediately and the cost of sales is the balancing figure.

Stage of completion if not specified can be calculated as follows:

$$\text{Cost basis} = \frac{\text{costs to date}}{\text{total costs}}$$

$$\text{Survey of work to date} = \frac{\text{work certified to date}}{\text{contract value}}$$

Balance sheet

Step 4: calculate the resultant balance sheet amount.

Current assets	
Trade debtors	
Progress billings invoiced to date	X
Less: progress billings received to date	(X)
	X
Gross amounts due from customers*	
Costs incurred to date	X
Profit/(loss) recognised to date	X/(X)
Less: progress billings invoiced to date	(X)
	X
Creditors: amounts falling due within one year	
Gross amounts due to customers*	
Costs incurred to date	X
Profits/(loss) recognised to date	X/(X)
Loss: progress billings invoiced to date	(X)
	(X)
Advance payments received	X

*   Note that these are calculated the same way. If the resultant amount is a positive figure, it should be disclosed as gross amounts due from customers within current assets. If it comes out as a negative, it should be disclosed as gross amounts due to customers within current liabilities.

6

Share Capital and Reserves

LEARNING OUTCOMES

After studying this chapter you should be able to:

☑ define share capital and reserves

☑ compare different classes of shares and explain key terms relating to share capital

☑ explain the concept of limited liability

☑ describe what is meant by capital maintenance, and how this is achieved in practice

☑ distinguish between distributable and non-distributable reserves

☑ describe and apply the rules in relation to the reduction of share capital for public and for private companies

☑ explain the uses to which non-distributable reserves may be put

☑ identify specific situations where a reduction in capital may be desirable

☑ prepare the appropriate entries to account for a reduction in capital

☑ gain an understanding of the complexities of the existing legislation in relation to limited companies, and the proposals for its simplification.

Introduction

Having looked in detail at the assets and other resources held by a business, it is perhaps now appropriate to consider what a business owes and what claims exist again those assets.

Section 1: Basic Principles

Share capital, reserves and liabilities all represent claims against the assets of a business. Liabilities – for example, trade payables or accruals – represent claims from those who trade or transact with the entity, whereas share capital and reserves represent the claims on the assets by the owners.

This chapter begins by defining share capital and explaining the accounting entries in respect of the issue of shares. There is then a brief explanation of limited liability in relation to companies limited by shares and an introduction to the doctrine of capital maintenance. Reserves are then defined and illustrated, and the accounting issues introduced. Liabilities are dealt with in the following chapter.

BASIC

INTERMEDIATE

ADVANCED

6.1   Share capital

In accounting, the term capital is used frequently, and consequently it is difficult to define it generally. However, it may mean the original fund with which a business was started and over time represents the claim by the business owner on the net assets of the business. This claim – also known as the ownership interest – will increase if the net assets increase and decrease if the net assets decrease. The ownership interest applies to the entire net assets (i.e. the total assets less the total liabilities).

In the case of a sole trader, this ownership interest would be represented by the capital account. In the case of a limited company, although the same broad principles apply, the situation is usually a little more complicated.

With a limited company, the ownership interest is split between the original investment and the subsequent changes in net assets made through profits and gains. The original investment is usually made in return for shares in the company, and the subsequent profits and gains are known as reserves. The ownership interest in a limited company will therefore consist of shares and reserves. These ownership or equity shares are known as ordinary shares. When a company is first formed, those who take steps to form it will decide how much needs to be raised by the potential shareholders in order to set up the company with the necessary assets to operate. Shares represent the basic units of ownership of a business and each share has a named value, which is called its nominal or par value.

This par value is at the discretion of the people who start up the company. In practice, £1 tends to be the maximum nominal value for shares, and 25 pence and 50 pence are common nominal values. Whatever amount is chosen, it will be written on the share certificate, which is the document given to each investor as evidence of being a shareholder.

It is important to note that the par value has little significance as it does not necessarily relate to the price that the share could be bought or sold for. It is simply the value that is attached to the divided units of total share capital. Indeed, for an existing company, any new shares issued after the company has started trading are likely to be issued at a price in excess of the nominal value.

 ### *Example*

Suppose a company has share capital of £100,000. This could comprise:

- 100,000 shares of £1
- 200,000 shares of £0.50
- 400,000 shares of £0.25.

Authorised share capital

For a company formed under the Companies Act 1985, at the date of incorporation, it would have been set up with a specified authorised share capital. This is the maximum amount of shares that may be issued by the company. The members of the company can, at a later date, increase the authorised share capital should the need arise. There is no upper limit on what a company may choose to set as its authorised share capital. The Companies Act 2006 has abolished the concept of authorised share capital for new companies but it continues to operate as a restriction for existing companies.

Issue of shares at the date of incorporation

When a company is first formed, shares will be issued to raise the appropriate funds required by the company to operate. It is likely that, at commencement, these shares will be issued at their par value. For example, 50,000 shares of £1 par value will raise £50,000. The accounting entry to record such an issue is:

Dr	Bank	£50,000	
	Cr Share capital		£50,000
Being issue of ordinary shares at par.			

This would give rise to a balance sheet on incorporation as follows:

	£
Cash at bank	50,000
Net assets	50,000
Capital	
Share capital	
50,000 shares of £1 each	50,000

Note that the share capital represents the owners' interest in the net assets. That is, the claim that the owners – the shareholders – have, is the amount of the net assets.

Let us assume that the company buys the necessary fixed assets and stocks and begins to trade. During the first year, the company makes a profit of £10,000. This, by definition, increases net assets by £10,000. At the end of this first year the balance sheet would appear as follows:

	£
Net assets (assets less liabilities)	60,000
Capital and reserves	
Share capital	
50,000 shares of £1 each	50,000
Revenue reserve	10,000
	60,000

The profit made by the company is shown as a revenue reserve – it has arisen from generating revenues. Note, however, that the ownership interest is now £60,000 and that this is made up of:

- share capital, and
- revenue reserve.

The ownership interest in this company is called the shareholders' equity. That is, the residual interests in the assets of the company after deducting all its liabilities.

It is worth pausing here to consider the position regarding the shares. One year on, the net assets have a value of £60,000. Given that there are 50,000 shares in issue, this would suggest that each share would have a value of £1.20 (60,000/50,000 = £1.20). Note that the par value is not affected by this – it will remain at £1 per share. This difference between the par value and the net asset value gives rise to a specific accounting adjustment where shares are issued at a higher price than their par value and is most likely to happen after incorporation.

Issue of further shares after incorporation

As time goes by, a company will, it hopes, generate profits and increase net assets. This will have the effect of increasing the value of each share in issue. Indeed, the value of each share will, in an efficient market, be influenced not only by the underlying net assets in the company, but also the future expectations of the earnings of the company. This may mean that the market value attached to each share will be substantially higher than its par value.

If the company wishes to expand further, say by buying new non-current (fixed) assets, it may wish to raise finance by issuing new shares. Providing the company has sufficient authorised share capital, it can issue further shares to raise the required funds. Note, however, that while the par value remains the same, the market value may be somewhat different.

BASIC

INTERMEDIATE

ADVANCED

⚙ *Example*

A company has shares with a nominal value of £1 but finds that its shares are selling in the stock market for £5. The company decides to issue 20,000 new shares. These shares will be issued for their market value of £5 per share, thus raising £100,000.

Nominal value and premium

Company law requires that the company shows separately the nominal value of the shares and any amount extra over the nominal value. The nominal value is £1 and as the total amount collected is £5; this means that the extra amount is £4 per share. This extra amount is known as a premium. The increase of £100,000 in ownership interest will be recorded therefore as two separate items, namely the nominal value of £20,000 and the share premium of £80,000.

The accounting entry is:

Dr	Bank	£100,000	
	Cr	Share capital – ordinary	£20,000
	Cr	Share premium	£80,000
Being issue of ordinary shares.			

Subsequent share transfers: buying and selling

The issue of shares, whether it be at incorporation or some later date, will result in a cash inflow to the company. The shareholders', or members', details will be recorded in the Register of Members, which is maintained in public companies by the Company Secretary.

Subsequent share dealings between existing and new shareholders will not result in cash inflows to the company. Once the shares have been issued, and the funds received by the company in respect of the issue, there will be no further cash inflows to the company, irrespective of the price attached to the shares in the trading share market. The only involvement by the company will be to ensure that the details of the shareholders are correctly recorded in the Register of Members.

The role of shares

Shares are a form of company funding; a shareholder invests in a company and gets shares in return. A person who holds shares in a company does not own a share of the assets of that company. Instead, the shares carry certain rights from which the shareholder can benefit. The exact nature of those rights will depend upon the type, or 'class', of share.

Types of shares

The rights attached to shares depend upon the type of share held. Broadly speaking there are two types of shares: ordinary shares and preference share. Those shareholders holding ordinary shares will be entitled to a share of any dividend declared by the company and a share in the net assets of the company when it closes down or is wound up. In addition, ordinary shareholders will be able to vote on issues that affect the company (e.g. who should be the directors).

Preference shares, unlike ordinary shares, usually have a fixed dividend that is paid before dividends are paid to ordinary shareholders. Preference shares guarantee that, if a dividend is paid, the preference shareholders will be entitled to the first part of it up to a maximum value. The maximum is usually defined as a fixed percentage of the nominal value of the shares issued. For example, if a company has 100,000 preference shares of £1 each with a dividend rate of 9%, this means that the preference shareholders are entitled to receive the first £9,000 (i.e. 9% × £100,000) of any dividend that is paid by the company for a year. Any excess over £9,000 will be available to the ordinary shareholders.

In addition, preference shares normally carry a right to a preference in the order of payment in the event of the company going into liquidation. The rights of preference shareholders will be set out in the Articles of Association of the company. Some preference shareholders may have the right to share in a surplus of net assets on a winding up, but others may only be entitled to the amount of capital originally invested. Preference shares do not normally carry the rights to vote.

The accounting issue involved

From an accounting perspective, the rights attached to preference shares give rise to a particular accounting issue, that issue being whether they should be classified as equity or debt. Preference shares may be redeemable (i.e. into cash) or non-redeemable; they may carry a right to dividends on a cumulative basis (i.e. if the directors do not pay dividends in a year, the preference shareholders will have a right to receive that year's dividend and any others that have not been paid before the ordinary shareholders can be paid any dividend). Some preference shares – known as participating preference shares – get a share of profits if the profit is over a certain figure. The fixed-return nature of preference shares tends to suggest they should be treated as a form of debt, however, from a legal viewpoint, preference shares are seen as more akin to equity.

Progress Point 6.1

Explain the following terms:

(a)   nominal or par value
(b)   share premium
(c)   preference shares.

Solution

(a)   The nominal or par value is the value put on a share when the company is initially formed.
(b)   Share premium is the difference between the price at which a share is issued and the par value.
(c)   Preference shares are a type of share that normally carry a right to preference over the ordinary shares in the payment of dividends, and to priority in terms of repayment in the event of liquidation. They may have cumulative rights with respect to dividends, be redeemable, or have rights to participate in profits under certain conditions.

6.2   Doctrine of capital maintenance

The doctrine of capital maintenance is a judge-made doctrine that concerns protecting the level of capital investment in a company by its shareholders.

A limited liability company is recognised as a separate legal entity that is distinct from its owners. The identifying feature of a company limited by shares is that the liability of the shareholders for the debts of the company is limited to the amount unpaid on the shares held by them. Because shareholders normally pay fully for their shares when they are issued, shareholders are rarely held liable for the company's debts.

The privilege of limited liability status requires some counter-measures to protect creditors' interests.

Limited liability

A limited company is, for legal purposes, treated as being a separate legal entity: it can sue and be sued; it can own property and can enter into contracts in its own name. This contrasts greatly with other

BASIC

INTERMEDIATE

ADVANCED

types of business (e.g. sole traders or partnerships), where it is the owner or owners rather than the business that must sue, enter into contracts and so on, because these types of business have no separate legal identity.

In the event that a sole-trader business finds itself in a position where it is insolvent (i.e. where the liabilities exceed the business assets), the law gives creditors the right to demand payment from whatever other assets the sole trader may have, whether it be his personal bank accounts, investments or indeed his house. The sole trader could, in theory, lose everything and this is because the law makes no distinction between the sole trader as a business and the sole trader as a private individual.

With a limited company, because it is treated as being a separate legal entity, it is the company itself that has responsibility for its debts – not the owners of the company. It is this important distinction that distinguishes limited liability companies from other types of businesses. Moreover, once a shareholder has paid to the company that amount which has been agreed for the shares, that shareholder's obligation to the company – and indeed to the company's creditors – is satisfied. Consequently, shareholders' liabilities are limited to that amount which they have paid, or have agreed to pay, for their shares.

While this is clearly advantageous to shareholders and potential shareholders in that they know exactly what they may lose, it is not necessarily advantageous to the other possible stakeholders of the business. Limited liability is attractive to shareholders because they can, in effect, walk away from the company's debts. In practice, as well as equity finance, a company may also have loan finance and is likely to have other stakeholders, such as trade creditors. While it is probable that banks advancing loan funds to a company will have the debt secured on a specific asset – or group of assets, held by the company, it is unlikely that a supplier of goods will be able to obtain such a security. It is because of this inability to secure debts and the added limitation on the rights of creditors to claim against the private assets of the shareholders that there is a statutory requirement for a company to retain within the company specific amounts of net assets. This requirement is known as capital maintenance and involves placing restrictions on the amount of shareholders' equity that can be distributed to shareholders. As a general rule, a company's issued **share capital** is not repayable to shareholders and neither are any capital, non-distributable reserves. The doctrine of capital maintenance is considered in more detail later in this chapter.

Share capital and company accounts

The balance sheet of a company shows, on the one hand, the resources held by a company, i.e. the current and non-current assets, and on the other the sources from which they were derived or who has a claim on them. The resources (i.e. the assets), will have debit balances, and the sources or claims on those assets will have credit balances. Liabilities, share capital and **reserves** are all credit balance items. Liabilities represent claims from those who trade and transact with the business on the resources the business holds; share capital and reserves represent claims by the owners on the net resources that the business holds.

✸ *Example*

(i)   Total sources/claims:

Total assets	500	Shareholders' equity	300
		Long-term debts	105
		Current liabilities	95
	500		500

(ii)   Long-term sources/claims

Total assets less Current liabilities	405	Shareholders' equity	300
		Long-term debts	105
	405		405

(iii) Shareholders' sources/claims:

Net assets	300	Shareholders equity	300

As the above example shows, the accounting equation is satisfied in each of the three cases, depending on the presentation adopted.

Example (i) shows the total assets and the total claims against those total assets.

Example (ii) shows the total assets less current liabilities and the long-term claims (including shareholders') against those total assets less current liabilities.

Example (iii) shows the net assets, i.e. the total assets less current and long-term liabilities and the shareholders' claims against those net assets. Note that the shareholders' claim is a residual one (i.e. it is the amount remaining after all liabilities have been deducted from total assets). In order to be able to correctly quantify shareholders' funds, it is necessary to correctly classify and quantify a company's liabilities. Moreover, a correct quantification and classification is essential if capital maintenance rules are to be adhered to.

Progress Point 6.2

Why is it important to distinguish between liabilities, share capital and reserves?

Solution

Liabilities are amounts owed by the business to third parties, whereas share capital and reserves are amounts owed by the business to the owners. The distinction is important as when such items are included within the accounting equation, they have a direct effect on the net assets, and worth, of a business.

6.3   Reserves

With a limited company, the ownership interest (i.e. shareholders' equity) is split between the original investment, the share capital, and the subsequent changes in net assets made through profits and gains, the reserves.

Reserves created from trading profits are known as revenue reserves or retained earnings. Revenue reserves represent the retained trading profits of a business at the end of the financial year. It is important to understand what this balance represents. The profits earned by the company will have resulted in a corresponding increase in net assets. The amount retained is therefore being employed by the company among the various net assets. In this respect the term 'reserve' is perhaps misleading. It does not mean that a corresponding amount of money is being kept available to meet contingencies or future requirements. Retained profits form part of the equity of the owners, and therefore represent a claim on the assets of the business, and these assets are likely to include various items apart from cash.

Reserves are classified as either revenue reserves or capital reserves. Revenue reserves arise from trading profits. They also arise from gains made on the disposal of fixed assets.

Capital reserves are quite different from revenue reserves. A company may issue shares at a premium (i.e. where shares are issued at a price greater than their par value). The par value of the new shares is credited to the share capital account and the premium to a share premium account. The share premium account represents a part of the proceeds of the share issue. The only reason it is not included in the share capital account is that UK law requires that the excess of the issue price over the nominal value be shown separately. The premiums can be regarded as capital profits and, like retained profits, the amount adds to the total claims of the ordinary shareholders. The share premium account is an example of a capital reserve, and the main difference between a capital reserve and a revenue reserve is that a capital reserve cannot be used for a dividend distribution. Money is raised by a share issue specifically to provide additional resources and it would be inappropriate to pay back part of the proceeds to the same or other shareholders.

A revaluation reserve is another example of a capital reserve. A revaluation reserve is created when a non-current (fixed) asset is revalued upwards in the financial statements. When a revaluation takes place, the financial statements recognise the increase in value of the asset, and the uplift in value within the asset schedule is matched with a corresponding increase in the revaluation reserve. Such a recognition of increase in value is an unrealised gain. As the gain has not been realised it cannot be shown as revenue. It has not been represented by any cash receipt and depends upon the subjective view of the valuer. Moreover, although the recognition of the increase in value does increase shareholders' equity, the increase is not one that has been created through trading operations and cannot therefore be distributed. Again, it would be inappropriate to try to distribute some or all of such a reserve as this could mean that the asset giving rise to the revaluation itself would require to be sold in order to fund the distribution.

The accounting issue involved

Limited companies are required by law to distinguish between that part of their capital that may be distributed to the shareholders and that part that may not. The distributable part is that which has arisen from trading profits and from realised gains on the disposal of fixed assets less any taxes and previously distributed profits (i.e. revenue reserves).

The non-distributable part normally consists of that which has arisen from funds injected by shareholders in respect of share issues and that which has arisen from upward revaluations in company assets that remain in the company (i.e. share capital and capital reserves).

The reason for this distinction is the limited liability status that company shareholders enjoy. With a limited company, the business and the owners are legally separate and, in order to protect the company's creditors, the law insists that the shareholders cannot legally withdraw a specific part of the capital of the company. In other words, that part of the capital must be maintained. Section 2 of this chapter looks in detail at the concept of capital maintenance.

Progress Point 6.3

Why is it important to distinguish between capital and revenue reserves?

Solution

The concept of capital maintenance involves placing restrictions on the amount of shareholders' equity that can be distributed to shareholders. It is important to make the distinction because revenue reserves can be distributed to shareholders, whereas capital reserves can not.

Summary

Share capital, reserves and liabilities represent claims on the assets of a business.

The separate legal status of a limited liability company means that it is important to distinguish between those claims that arise from the owners (i.e. ownership interest), and those that arise from those who trade and transact with the business.

Share capital represents part of the original funding of a limited liability company. Each share that has been issued will have a par (or nominal) value, although this may be very different from the value at which the share could be traded in a stock market. Shares traded independently of a company do not result in any cash flows to the company.

Reserves are classified as revenue reserves or capital reserves. Revenue reserves may be distributed to shareholders, whereas capital reserves are non-distributable.

The concept of capital maintenance and creditor protection means that the distinction between liabilities, share capital and distributable and non-distributable reserves is essential.

Section 2: Intermediate Issues

In the introductory section to this chapter share capital was explained and defined, the issue of shares at incorporation and subsequent to incorporation was dealt with, and the two broad categories of shares – equity or preference – were introduced.

In addition, both revenue reserves and capital reserves were defined, and it was explained that only revenue reserves could be distributed to shareholders. Finally, creditor protection in relation to transacting with limited companies was introduced, along with the concept of capital maintenance.

This section now looks in more detail at share capital, capital maintenance and distributable profits.

6.4   Reduction of share capital

Once shares have been issued by a company, the share capital account is credited with the par (or nominal) value of the shares. This value forms part of the permanent capital of the company – capital that requires to be maintained in the interests of creditor protection.

There may, however, be genuine reasons why a company would wish to reduce its capital. In the UK, the Companies Act has provision for share capital to be reduced, however as the intention is that this amount should not be reduced, for public companies such a reduction can only take place subject to the consent of the court. On 1 October 2008 the Companies Act 2006 introduced a new procedure for private companies to make share capital reductions. As an alternative to obtaining court approval, private companies have the option of reducing the amount of their share capital by a special resolution supported by a solvency statement made by the directors.

A reduction of capital is most commonly undertaken where:

- the company's share capital exceeds the fair value of its underlying assets
- the company has liquid assets surplus to its needs, or
- the company redeems its shares.

The principle of capital maintenance requires that if any part of the permanent capital base is repaid to members, it must be:

- replenished by a transfer out of profits, or
- replaced by new capital.

However, subject to this rule, limited companies may reduce their share capital if:

- there is authority for the reduction in the Articles or, if not authorised, there is no restriction of prohibition of a reduction in the articles
- a special resolution is passed by the shareholders
- in respect of public companies, the court confirms the transaction.

In arriving at its decision, the court will consider whether the reduction of capital would prejudice the rights of creditors, and will usually require an undertaking from the company that it will not make any distributions until all creditors outstanding at the time of the transaction have been settled.

A typical capital reduction involves the transfer of an amount from share capital, share premium or capital redemption reserve either to a special reserve or to make good past losses. Capital reduction means that the share capital is subjected to a lessening of its nominal value, i.e. reducing a share nominal value from £1.00 to, say, £0.50.

The first two situations noted above will be considered in detail. The redemption of shares is covered later in this chapter.

Share capital exceeds fair value of underlying assets

This situation normally occurs when a company has accumulated trading losses that prevent it from making dividend payments under the distributable profits rules.

A typical balance sheet might show the following:

Share capital 200,000 ordinary shares of £1	£200,000
Profit and loss account	(180,000)
	£20,000

The accounting issue involved is that a company that was loss making may well return to profitability but that, in the absence of any correction to the balance sheet, the company would not be able to make future distributions based on the future profits until the accumulated losses had been eliminated. The Companies Act 2006 allows a company to reduce its capital where it has incurred losses and the share capital is no longer represented by available assets (i.e. the capital is reduced to reflect the actual level of asset backing).

The following example illustrates the mechanics of such a reduction.

 *Example*

Assume that the capital and reserves of Fairfield plc were as follows at 31 December 2008:

Share capital 200,000 ordinary shares of £1	£200,000
Profit and loss account	(180,000)
	£20,000

The directors are confident that the company can return to profitability, and estimate that it will make profits in the year to 31 December 2009 of £4,000 and subsequent annual profits of £5,000.

The directors have presented their case for a reduction in share capital to the shareholders, and have obtained a special resolution and court approval to reduce the £1 ordinary shares to ordinary shares of 10p each. The reduction is dealt with through a 'capital reduction' account, which is debited with accumulated losses and credited with the amount written off the share capital. The accounting entries will be:

Dr Capital reduction account	£180,000	
Cr Profit and loss account		£180,000
Being transfer of accumulated losses.		

Dr Share capital	£180,000	
Cr Capital reduction account		£180,000
Being reduction of share capital.		

The balance sheet of Fairfield plc immediately after the reduction will be:

Share capital 200,000 ordinary shares of 10p	£20,000
Profit and loss account	0
	£20,000

The advantages of this to the shareholders of Fairfield are immediately apparent. If the reduction of share capital had not taken place then the profits earned in 2009 and subsequent years would have to have been used to reduce the accumulated losses. This would mean that the company would be unable to pay a dividend for approximately 36 years if it continued at that level of profitability (i.e. until the accumulated profits had been eliminated and distributable reserves became available).

The advantages of this to the company are also immediately apparent – it would be extremely difficult to attract equity investment in the company if shareholders could not expect a dividend for over 30 years!

As for the creditors, then, as can be seen from the balance sheets before and after the reduction, the net asset position remains the same (i.e. £20,000). The assurances given by the company to the courts so that existing creditors will be paid before any distributions are made should ensure that they are left no worse off.

Company has liquid assets surplus to its needs

In contrast to a company that has accumulated losses, it may be the case that a company has excess cash or other liquid reserves (i.e. it has assets that are no longer needed). This can happen following a contraction in the company's activities. It may be appropriate, therefore, for the company to reduce its capital by returning these excess funds to shareholders.

A typical balance sheet might show the following:

	£
Excess cash	1,000,000
Other net assets	2,000,000
	3,000,000
Share capital 2,000,000 ordinary shares of £1	2,000,000
Profit and loss account	1,000,000
	3,000,000

The accounting entries for the repayment are to credit cash and debit share capital. The directors have presented their case for a reduction to the shareholders to reduce the £1 ordinary shares to ordinary shares of £0.50 each. The accounting entries will be:

Dr	Share capital (2,000,000 x 50p)	£1,000,000	
	Cr Cash		£1,000,000
Being repayment of excess funds to shareholders.			

The balance sheet immediately after the reduction will be:

Other net assets	£2,000,000
Share capital 2,000,000 ordinary shares of £0.50	£1,000,000
Profit and loss account	£1,000,000
	£2,000,000

The benefits to the shareholders are again immediately apparent. They have been refunded one half of the par value of their shares – £1,000,000 in total.

From the company perspective, it has been able to effectively reduce its unwanted liquid resources.

The creditors, on the other hand, have been left exposed to a greater risk. The net assets prior to the reduction were £3,000,000 but reduced to £2,000,000 after the payment to the shareholders. This illustrates the need for creditor approval to be sought and obtained prior to such actions.

6.5   Capital maintenance and creditor protection

The concept of capital maintenance in relation to limited liability companies was explained in the introductory section to this chapter. The limitation of shareholders' liabilities to the amounts invested in their shares requires that additional protection is needed for creditors dealing with limited companies as opposed to dealing with unincorporated businesses. Such unincorporated businesses do not require specific capital maintenance rules as the business owners can themselves be held to account for their business's debts, with the only limits being the value of their personal assets.

The examples shown above are a good illustration of the two extremes faced by companies, their shareholders and their creditors. At the one extreme there was a loss-making company with accumulated losses and little in the way of net assets. At the other extreme there was a company with surplus liquid funds. In both instances, however, creditor protection rules required the permission of the courts before any capital reductions could be made which could potentially affect the claims on the net assets by the creditors. Note that the illustrations assumed that the companies were public companies. Private companies no longer need court approval.

The creditor perspective is now considered and we look in detail at the risks the creditor groups are exposed to, and the measures put in place to minimise those risks.

Risks faced by creditors

Broadly speaking, creditors are faced with two types of risk. First, there is the risk that a company will operate unsuccessfully and will not be in a position to settle its obligations; second, there is the risk that a company will be profitable and in a position to settle its obligations but will instead pay its shareholders rather than its creditors.

Creditor protection rules are not designed to protect against ordinary business risks (e.g. a company incurring trading losses that render it unable to meet its debts). The rules do, however, aim to protect the latter type of risk, and the Companies Act 2006 requires the amount available to meet creditors' claims to be calculated by reference to the company's annual financial statements. The question is how should the amounts available to meet creditors' claims be quantified?

There are two possible approaches to ensuring creditor protection by reference to a company's balance sheet.

1. The assets could be considered in relation to the liabilities and limits set, to ensure that there are always assets with a realisable value sufficient to cover all outstanding liabilities. This is known as the direct approach.

2. The liability side of the balance sheet could be considered in relation to reserves and these could be classified into distributable and **non-distributable reserves**, i.e. reserves that are and are not available to shareholders by way of dividend distributions. This is known as the indirect approach.

At first glance, the direct method would appear to have greater merit – it attempts to ensure that there are sufficient assets to cover the liabilities. On further consideration, however, the problems of asset valuation become very apparent. As was illustrated in Chapter 2, the book values of assets often bear little or no resemblance to their realisable values. Consequently, if the direct method were to be adopted, there could potentially be several different results as to the level of creditor cover, depending on whether historic cost, replacement cost or realisable values were adopted for asset valuation. As a result, the Companies Act opts for the indirect approach by specifying capital maintenance in terms of the shareholders' funds.

It is worth noting, however, that certain creditors effectively minimise their risk by adopting a direct approach and securing their debts on specific assets of the company. For example, it is common

practice for a mortgage to be secured on the asset for which the loan was granted; indeed, banks often take out what is known as a 'floating charge' over all the assets in a company. This effectively secures one or more mortgages or loans over all the company's assets. Unfortunately, while this minimises the risk to the banks, it nevertheless disadvantages the trade creditors, whose claims would be considered only once these priority rights have been settled.

We continue with our study of capital maintenance and creditor protection, and once more consider the importance of share capital. We have already seen that reduction of capital is an important issue – so too are a company's minimum capital requirements.

Minimum share capital

The minimum share capital requirement for a limited company depends on whether it is a public company or a private company. The main difference between these is that a public company can offer its shares for sale to the general public, whereas a private company is prohibited from doing so.

A public limited company – identified as such by having the words 'public limited company' or the abbreviation 'plc' after its name – requires to have a minimum share capital of £50,000. Indeed, a 'plc' is not permitted to commence trading unless it has issued this amount.

The minimum share capital requirement refers to the nominal (par) value of the share capital and not the market value of the shares in issue. The nominal value is used for identification but also, more importantly, for capital maintenance. It is questionable, however, whether this figure of £50,000 is adequate. Most 'plcs' tend to be very large indeed and, in relative terms, £50,000 is a small figure to be maintained.

There is effectively no minimum capital requirement for private companies. These can be set up with a very limited number of shares – a single £1 share is not uncommon and this clearly affords very little in the way of creditor protection. Furthermore, private companies form about 99% of the total of 1.5 million UK limited companies. Most private companies tend to be smaller businesses where the ownership is divided among relatively few shareholders, often family members. Given the number of such private companies, and the particularly low minimum capital requirement, it is questionable whether any creditor protection exists at all.

Creditor protection: distributable profits

A company can make distributions only out of revenue (distributable) reserves. A distribution is every transfer of a company's assets to its members, in cash or otherwise, except:

(a) bonus issue of shares
(b) redemption or purchase of own shares out of capital
(c) reduction in share capital through eliminating unpaid share capital, and
(d) a distribution of assets on a winding up.

By far the most common form of distribution is the payment of a dividend.

Profits available for distribution

These are distinguished between private and public companies, as follows.

Private companies

The definition of distributable profits under the Companies Act 2006 is:

> Accumulated, realised profits, so far as not previously utilised by distribution or capitalisation, less its accumulated, realised losses, as far as not previously written off in a reduction or re-organisation of capital.

This means that:

- unrealised profits cannot be distributed (i.e. on, say, a revaluation)
- there is no difference between realised revenue and realised capital profits (i.e. if a company sells a fixed asset at a profit then because the gain is realised it can still be distributed even though it is a capital gain)
- all accumulated net realised profits (i.e. realised profits less realised losses) on the balance sheet must be considered (i.e. it is the balance sheet reserve figure that is important and not the fact that a profit was made in a particular year); consequently, a company need not make a profit in the year that it pays a dividend as it can use reserves brought forward; on the other hand, a company may make a profit one year but not be able to pay a dividend as it has accumulated losses brought forward.

Public companies

The Companies Act specifies the reserves of a company which are undistributable.

The undistributable reserves of a public company are:

- its share capital
- its share premium
- its capital redemption reserve (covered in detail later in this chapter)
- the excess of accumulated unrealised profits over accumulated unrealised losses at the time of the intended distribution, and
- any reserves not allowed to be distributed under the Act or by the company's own Memorandum or Articles of Association.

This means that, when dealing with a public company, the distributable profits have to be reduced by any net unrealised loss. The following example illustrates the difference between a private and public company's distributable reserves.

 ## Example

Shareholders' funds		
	£000	£000
Share capital		3,000
Share premium		700
Capital redemption reserve		200
		———
Permanent capital at beginning of year		3,900
Unrealised gain	200	
Unrealised losses	(300)	
	———	
		(100)
		———
Permanent capital at end of year		3,800
Realised: current years profits	600	
current years losses	(100)	
	———	
	500	
Retained profits b/f	1,100	
	———	
		1,600
Net assets		5,400

BASIC

INTERMEDIATE

ADVANCED

Private company

The profits available for distribution were the above details to apply to a private company would be £1,600,000 (i.e. its accumulated net realised profit). No account need be taken of the accumulated net unrealised gain or losses.

Public company

The undistributable reserves of a public company are:

	£000
Share capital	3,000
Share premium	700
Capital redemption reserve	200
Excess of unrealised profits over unrealised losses	–
	3,900

The amount of distributable reserves were the above details to apply to a public company will be £5,400,000 – £3,900,000 (i.e. £1,500,000). That is, the distributable profits have to be reduced by any net unrealised loss, i.e. £1,600,000 – £100,000 = £1,500,000.

Progress Point 6.4

Greval Ltd had a profit and loss reserve credit of £100,000 at 31 December 2006. Its results for the next three years were as follows:

2007	£50,000	Loss
2008	£60,000	Loss
2009	£35,000	Profit

Assuming all amounts are distributable, what is the maximum dividend the company could pay in respect of each year?

Solution

The accumulated reserves require to be calculated.

	2007	2008	2009
	£	£	£
Balance b/f	100,000	50,000	(10,000)
Profit/(loss) for year	(50,000)	(60,000)	35,000
Balance c/f	50,000	(10,000)	25,000

The balance carried forward at each year-end date represents the maximum that can be paid out in each period. If, however, £50,000 is paid out in 2007, the cumulative losses at the start of 2009 would be £60,000 and no dividend would be payable in 2009. The balance carried forward on accumulated reserves at the end of 2009 if a £50,000 dividend had been paid in 2007 would be £25,000 loss.

A company cannot lawfully make a distribution out of capital. Consequently, the directors, when proposing and making a dividend, must ensure that losses made since the last balance sheet was drawn up do not make the distribution illegal.

In addition, directors have a fiduciary duty to protect the assets of the company and to ensure that the company can pay its debts when they fall due. Directors must therefore specifically consider whether the company will remain solvent following a proposed dividend.

Realised profits and losses

The Companies Act states that references to realised profit and realised loss are to such profits or losses as fall to be treated as realised in accordance with principles generally accepted, at the time the accounts are prepared.

A profit is realised when it arises from a transaction where the consideration received by a company is 'qualifying consideration'.

Qualifying consideration includes cash, an asset for which a liquid market exists (e.g. gilts), and amounts due to be settled in either of these where the debtor is capable of settling within a reasonable period of time, it is reasonably certain that the debtor will be capable of settling when called upon and there is an expectation the receivable will be settled.

Therefore, a profit arising on a normal cash or credit sale will be a realised profit. Other realised profits arise from:

- a foreign currency gain on a monetary asset or liability
- a reversal of a loss previously regarded as realised (e.g. reversal of an impairment loss).
- a profit previously regarded as unrealised becoming realised due to sale for qualifying consideration (e.g. sale of a previously revalued asset)
- if a revalued asset is depreciated, an amount equal to the excess depreciation over the historical cost equivalent is treated as a realised profit.

Almost all losses are realised losses although a revaluation loss that cancels out a previous unrealised revaluation gain is not realised.

 ## Example

Salton Ltd had the following balances at 31 December 2008.

	£000
Share capital	5,000
Share premium	4,000
Revaluation reserve	1,000
Profit and loss reserve	7,000
	17,000

At 31 December 2008 there were no distributable profits other than the £7 million balance on the profit and loss reserve. During the year to 31 December 2009 the following occurred.

1. Salton Ltd made an after tax profit of £900,000.
2. Dividends on ordinary shares of £200,000 and £80,000 were paid in July and October 2009 respectively.
3. The asset to which the £1 million revaluation reserve balance related was sold for a gain of £120,000. The gain is included in the profit after tax for the year.
4. Salton acquired a new business, Creatart Ltd, which was valued at £2 million. The consideration given was an investment that Salton had acquired for £1.4 million several years ago. The gain of £600,000 has been included in the profit after tax for the year.

Required

(a) Calculate the distributable profits of Salton Ltd at 31 December 2009.
(b) Prepare an extract of the capital and reserves section of the balance sheet of Salton Ltd at 31 December 2009.

BASIC

INTERMEDIATE

ADVANCED

Solution

(a) Distributable profits:

	£000
At 31 December 2008	7,000
Add: profit for the year	900
Less: dividends	(280)
Add: realised revaluation gain	1,000
Less: unrealised gain	(600)
	£8,020

Notes

1. The revaluation gain was unrealised until the asset was sold.
2. The gain on the investment is unrealised as it was not sold for qualifying consideration.

(b) Balance sheet:

Workings:	Profit and loss reserve	Revaluation reserve
	£000	£000
At 31 December 2008	7,000	1,000
Add: profit for year	900	–
Less: dividends	(280)	
Sale of revalued asset	1,000	(1,000)
	8,620	–

Balance sheet extract 31 December 2009	
	£000
Share capital	5,000
Share premium	4,000
Revaluation reserve	–
Profit and loss reserve	8,620
	17,620

This example illustrates a very important point. The realised profits of a company may be a different figure from the balance on its profit and loss reserve.

In this instance the difference is £600,000, that difference being the unrealised gain on the disposal of the investment that was sold for a non-qualifying consideration.

Non-distributable reserves: capital redemption reserve

In the introductory section to this chapter, two examples of non-distributable reserves were given, namely share premium and revaluation reserve. Both these are capital reserves and as they are not created by trading operations, are not available for distribution to shareholders.

The capital redemption reserve is a further capital reserve. Before looking in detail at the capital redemption reserve, it will be beneficial to once more consider the reasoning behind the Companies Act capital maintenance requirements.

The general idea is that capital should not be returned to the shareholders except under certain circumstances. However, where a company has surplus assets and receives creditors and court approval, capital can be reduced and a return of capital made to shareholders. In addition, where a company has accumulated trading losses and its share capital exceeds the underlying net assets then again, subject to creditors and court approval, share capital can be reduced.

The Companies Act restrictions are designed to prevent shareholders withdrawing their capital from the business, thus prejudicing the claims of creditors. There are, however, two further instances whereby a company can reduce its share capital and this is when it purchases or redeems its own shares.

6.6   Purchase and redemption of own shares

As far as the accounting entries are concerned, these are the same for both redemption and purchase of own shares. It will be helpful, however, to look at the distinction between the two.

'Redeeming' means the buying back of shares that were originally issued as being redeemable in that the company stated when they were issued that they would be, or could be, redeemed (i.e. bought back by the company). The terms of the redemption (the buying back) would be stated at the time the shares were issued.

In contrast, when shares are issued that are not stated to be 'redeemable' then, when they are bought back by the company, it is said to be the 'purchase' of its shares by the company.

The Companies Act permits a company, if it is authorised to do so by its Articles of Association, to:

(i)   issue redeemable shares of any class (i.e. preference, ordinary), but subject to the proviso that the company can issue redeemable shares only if it also has in issue shares that are not redeemable; the reason for the restriction is that if a company issued only redeemable shares it could, in theory, if all the shares were redeemed, end up with no shareholders

(ii) purchase its own shares (i.e. shares that were not issued as being redeemable shares); again, there is a proviso that the company must, after the purchase, have other shares in issue at least some of which are not redeemable; this is to prevent the company redeeming its whole share capital and therefore ceasing to have members.

Advantages of purchase and redemption of shares

The advantages of a company being able to buy back its own shares rest primarily with private companies. For public companies, the main advantage is that those with surplus cash resources are able to return some of this surplus cash back to their shareholders by buying back some of their own shares.

For private companies the main advantage is that this facility helps to overcome the disadvantages of not having a ready market on which to trade the companies' shares, i.e. a stock exchange.

(i) It will help shareholders who have difficulty in selling their shares to another individual to be able to realise the value of their shareholding on, say, retirement or leaving the company.

(ii) It helps private companies raise finance as there is an exit route for those investors who previously purchased shares in the company. The fear of not being able to dispose of shares previously led to finance being relatively difficult for private companies to obtain from people other than the original main shareholders of the company.

(iii) Should a shareholder in a smaller family company die, the shares can be purchased and the proceeds used to assist with the settlement of any taxes on the shareholder's death.

(iv) Shareholders with grievances against the company can be bought out, thus eliminating future problems and contributing to the smooth running of the company.

(v) Should a family shareholder with a large number of shares die or retire, the facility to buy back some or all of the shares by the company may help the remaining shareholders keep control of the company (i.e. they will feel less pressured to sell the shares in the company to outsiders if they know that the company itself can be a source of funds to pay the exiting shareholder's estate).

(vi) Similar to public companies, the company could return surplus cash back to its shareholders.

(vii) Should a company, either private or public, whose shares are not listed on the stock exchange introduce a share scheme for employees, the employees would know that they could easily dispose of the shares instead of being stuck with them.

Companies act requirements

The safeguards for the protection of 'capital' contained in the Companies Act are as follows:

- no redemption can take place unless the shares are fully paid up; this is to protect those creditors who regard any uncalled capital as part of the capital base of the company
- no redemption can take place that would result in there being no shareholders; this would in effect be a winding up or liquidation of the company and other rules would then apply.

Different rules apply to the redemption of shares by public companies and by private companies. Each will be considered in turn.

6.7   Redemption of shares by a public company

Although a public company is permitted to redeem or buy back shares, there is the overriding requirement that it maintain the same overall level of permanent capital for the protection of creditors. There are two ways in which this can be achieved, and these are illustrated below. Remember that the accounting entries will be same for redemption and buy back of shares – the only difference will be in the titles of the accounts used (i.e. in practice the accounts would state which shares were redeemable).

General rules and procedures

There is no restriction on the price that a company may pay on purchasing its shares (except for the following rules). If the shares are being purchased for more than nominal value the total payment is split into:

- the nominal value of shares purchased
- the premium on purchase (note that this is different to any share premium on issue).

The general rules applying to all companies are in Part 17, Chapter 10, of the Companies Act 2006. The main provisions for protecting the permanent capital are as follows.

(i) The nominal value of the shares purchased must be replaced by either:
   (a) the proceeds of a fresh (new) issue of shares for the purpose (this includes the nominal value and any share premium raised in the new issue), or
   (b) a transfer from distributable profits to the capital redemption reserve (CRR); the CRR, like share capital and share premium, becomes part of 'permanent' capital; it can only be used to pay up a bonus issue, or
   (c) a combination of (a) and (b) if the proceeds in (a) are insufficient to replace the nominal value redeemed.

(ii) The premium (if any) paid on the purchase of shares must be charged wholly to distributable profits, unless the shares being purchased were originally issued at a premium *and* the purchase is being financed wholly or partly out of the proceeds of a new issue.

   In this case, some or all of the premium on purchase can be charged to the share premium account. The maximum that can be charged is the smaller of:
   (a) the premium on the issue of the original shares, and
   (b) the balance on the share premium account (after crediting any premium on the new issue).

   Any amount of the premium on purchase that cannot be charged (debited) to share premium should be debited to distributable profits.

If the company has an insufficient amount of distributable profits to write off any premium and transfer to the capital redemption reserve the scheme is illegal and should not be carried out. This may limit either the number of shares that can be purchased or the price that can be paid.

The following examples all assume that distributable profits equals the balance on the profit and loss reserve.

Shares purchased or redeemed must be cancelled and removed from issued share capital unless they are to be held as treasury shares. (Treasury shares are covered later in this chapter.) This does not alter the authorised share capital.

The following steps should be followed in any share purchase/redemptions.

Step 1: check legality

Check whether there are sufficient distributable profits to fund the purchase. If not, the proposal will be illegal.

Step 2: record the purchase/redemption

Split the purchase price being paid for the shares into nominal value of the shares being purchased and any premium element, and record:

```
Dr      Share capital (nominal value)
Dr      Premium on purchase (if any)
        Cr      Bank
Being purchase of shares.
```

Step 3: record any new issue

This is recorded as a normal new issue.

```
Dr      Bank
        Cr      Share capital
        Cr      Share premium (if any)
Being issue of shares.
```

Step 4: eliminate the premium on purchase

Calculate if any of the premium on purchase can be charged to the share premium account, and record. Any amount that cannot be debited to share premium must be debited to distributable reserves.

```
Dr      Share premium (if permissible)
Dr      Profit and loss reserve (balance)
        Cr      Premium on purchase
Being elimination of premium on purchase.
```

Step 5: replace the nominal value of the shares purchased (*if not met fully by the proceeds of a new issue*)

```
Dr      Profit and loss reserve
        Cr      Capital redemption reserve
Being transfer to CRR.
```

Step 6: Prepare balance sheet after purchase

That is, simply process the above transactions.

Redemption out of distributable profits

Where shares are redeemed (or, remember, bought back) by a company out of distributable profits, the Companies Act requires that an amount equal to the nominal value of the shares redeemed be transferred to a capital redemption reserve. Such a transfer is described as a capitalisation, which means that profits have been capitalised and the permanent capital has been maintained. The following examples show the accounting adjustments required depending on whether the shares are redeemed at par or at a premium, and whether the shares being redeemed were originally issued at par or at a premium.

 ## Example: redemption of shares at par out of distributable profits

The balance sheet of the company prior to capitalisation is as follows:

	£
Other net assets	7,500
Bank	2,500
	10,000
Ordinary share capital (£1 shares)	7,000
Profit and loss account	3,000
	10,000

A total of 2,000 ordinary shares of £1 each are to be redeemed at par out of distributable profits. The journal entries to effect the transaction are as follows:

Dr Ordinary share capital	£2,000	
Cr Bank		£2,000
Being ordinary shares purchased.		

Dr Profit & loss a/c – reserve	£2,000	
Cr Capital redemption reserve		£2,000
Being transfer as required by Companies Act.		

The balance sheets before and after redemption are as follows:

	Balances before £	Purchases £	Transfer to CRR £	Balance after redemption £
Other net assets	7,500			7,500
Bank	2,500	(2,000)		500
	10,000			8,000
Ordinary share of £1	7,000	(2,000)		5,000
Capital redemption reserve	–		2,000	2,000
Profit & loss account	3,000		(2,000)	1,000
	10,000			8,000

Note that the permanent capital (i.e. share capital) and (non-distributable) capital redemption reserve remain the same at £7,000.

Example: redemption of shares at a premium out of distributable profits

The balance sheet of the company prior to capitalisation is as follows:

	£
Other net assets	7,500
Bank	2,500
	10,000
Ordinary share capital (£1 shares)	7,000
Profit & loss account	3,000
	10,000

A total of 1,500 ordinary shares of £1 are to be redeemed at a premium of £0.50 each (i.e. £1.50 per share) out of distributable profits, making a capital repayment of £2,250. The Companies Act requires that if shares are to be redeemed at a premium (and they had not originally been issued at a premium) then an amount equal to the premium must be transferred from distributable profits to the credit of the ordinary share redemption account. Again, this is to divert profits away from being distributable to part of the company's permanent capital.

The journal entries to effect the transaction are as follows:

Dr	Share capital	£1,500	
	Premium on purchase	£750	
	Cr Bank		£2,250
Being purchase of shares.			

Dr	Profit and loss reserves	£750	
	Cr Premium on purchase		£750
Being elimination of premium on purchase.			

Dr	Profit & loss reserves	£1,500	
	Cr Capital redemption reserve		£1,500
Being transfer as required by the Companies Act.			

BASIC

INTERMEDIATE

ADVANCED

The balance sheets before and after redemption are as follows:

	Balance before redemption £	Purchase £	Write-off premium £	Transfer to CRR £	Balance after redemption £
Other net assets	7,500				7,500
Bank	2,500	(2,250)			250
	10,000				7,750
Ordinary share capital (£1 shares)	7,000	(1,500)			5,500
Capital redemption reserve				1,500	1,500
Profit and loss account	3,000		(750)	(1,500)	750
Premium on redemption		(750)	750		–
	10,000				7,750

Note once again that the permanent capital, i.e. share capital, and capital redemption reserve remain the same before and after the capitalisation at £7,000. The premium on redemption has been written off distributable profits.

Example: shares previously issued at a premium being redeemed at a premium out of distributable profits

This final example is used to illustrate a very important point. The Companies Act allows the write off to the share premium account of any premiums payable on the redemption or purchase of own shares provided the shares being redeemed were themselves issued at a premium but with an additional proviso that a new issue of shares is being made for the purpose. In this example the shares are being redeemed out of distributable profits and consequently the share premium account cannot be used.

The balance sheet of the company prior to capitalisation is as follows:

	£	
Other net assets	7,500	
Bank	4,500	
	12,000	
Ordinary shares of £1	7,000	
Share premium	1,750	(shares originally issued for £1.25)
Profit & loss account	3,250	
	12,000	

A total of 1,500 ordinary shares of £1 are to be redeemed at a premium of £0.50 each (i.e. £1.50 per share) out of distributable profits, making a capital payment of £2,250.

The journal entries to effect the transaction are as follows:

Dr	Share capital	£1,500	
	Premium on purchase	£750	
	Cr Bank		£2,250
Being purchase of shares.			

Dr	Profit & loss reserve	£750	
	Cr Premium on purchase		£750
Being elimination of premium on purchase.			

Dr	Profit & loss reserve	£1,500	
	Cr Capital redemption reserve		£1,500
Being transfer as required by the Companies Act.			

The balance sheet before and after redemption is as follows:

	Balance before redemption £	Purchase £	Write-off £	Transfer to CRR £	Balances after redemption £
Premium on redemption	–	750	(750)		–
Other net assets	7,500				7,500
Bank	4,500	(2,250)			2,250
	12,000				9,750
Ordinary share capital (£1 shares)	7,000	(1,500)			5,500
Share premium	1,750				1,750
Capital redemption reserve	–			1,500	1,500
Profit & loss account	3,250		(750)	(1,500)	1,000
	12,000				9,750

Again, the permanent capital, i.e. share capital, and share premium and capital redemption reserve remains the same before and after capitalisation at £8,750. Note, however, that the share premium account remains unaltered. Because the redemption was funded out of distributable profits and not a new issue of shares, the Companies Act prevented the share premium account being used to provide for the premium payable of £750 on the redemption of the shares – instead, this was written off the distributable reserves (i.e. profit and loss account).

Progress Point 6.5

Rollrock plc is a successful manufacturer of decorative stones. The company is owned by the Johnston family, one of whose members wants to sell his 100,000 shares and retire. The other shareholders are keen to keep all the company's shares in the family, but none can afford to buy the retiring shareholder's shares. It has been decided, therefore, that the company will purchase the 100,000 £1 ordinary shares for £180,000.

Rollrock plc has the following balance sheet at 30 September 2009.

	£000
Net assets	4,000
Capital and reserves	
Share capital – £1 shares fully paid	2,000
Share premium	500
Permanent capital	2,500
Profit and loss reserve	1,500
	4,000

Required

(a) Prepare journal entries to record the purchase of shares.
(b) Prepare the balance sheet of Rollrock plc after the share purchase.

Solution

(a) Journal entries:

Step 1: check legality

The purchase will cost £180,000; the company has distributable profits of £1,500,000. It is, therefore, a legal proposal.

Step 2: record the purchase

Dr	Share capital	£100,000	
Dr	Premium on purchase	£80,000	
	Cr Bank		£180,000
Being purchase of shares at a premium.			

Step 3: record any new issue

There is no new issue – the entire purchase is being funded out of distributable profits.

Step 4: eliminate the premium on purchase

Dr	Profit & loss reserve	£80,000	
	Cr Premium on purchase		£80,000
Being charge of premium to distributable profits.			

Step 5: replace the nominal value of shares purchased

Dr	Profit & loss reserve	£100,000	
	Cr Capital redemption reserve		£100,000
Being transfer to CRR in respect of nominal value of shares purchased.			

The first journal reduces both bank and share capital by the appropriate amounts. The premium on purchase account is used to maintain the double entry. The balance on this account is cancelled with the next step.

The second journal is required by the Companies Act. As no new shares are being issued the premium on purchase has to be written off against distributable profits.

The third journal replaces the nominal value of the shares purchased with a transfer to the capital redemption reserve. None of this is funded by a new issue and the transfer is required by the Companies Act.

(b)   Rollrock plc:

Balance sheet at 30 September 2009	
	£000
Net assets	3,820
Capital and reserves	
Share capital – £1 shares fully paid	1,900
Share premium	500
Capital redemption reserve	100
Permanent capital	2,500
Profit and loss reserve	1,320
	3,820

Both the company's total net assets and capital and reserves have been reduced by £180,000. The transfer to the CRR has, however, used part of the company's distributable profits to replace the permanent (share) capital reduced by the purchase.

Although the creditors' security has been affected by the outflow of cash and reduction in total equity, the important point is that the permanent capital has been maintained at £2,500,000. Note that the company could have paid a dividend of £180,000 and would have been in the same net asset position.

From a creditor perspective, it is never in their interests for the company to return equity to the shareholders, whether this is accomplished either by dividend or the repurchase of shares. There is, however, some protection in that distributable profits place an upper limit on such payments.

Redemption out of the proceeds of a new share issue

Instead of shares being redeemed out of distributable profits, in practice, shares are often redeemed out of the proceeds of a new issue – or indeed partly out of profits and partly out of the proceeds of a new issue.

Again, the following examples show the accounting adjustments required depending on whether the shares are redeemed at par or at a premium and whether those shares being redeemed were originally issued at par or at a premium.

Example: redemption of shares at par funded by new issue of shares at par

The balance sheet of the company prior to the capitalisation is as follows:

	£
Net assets	7,500
Bank	2,500
	10,000
Ordinary share capital (£1 shares)	7,000
Profit & loss account	3,000
	10,000

A total of 2,000 ordinary shares of £1 are to be redeemed at par – a new issue of 2,000 ordinary £1 shares at par being made for the purpose.

The journal entries to effect the transaction are as follows:

Dr Share capital	£2,000	
Cr Bank		£2,000
Being purchase of own shares.		

Dr Bank	£2,000	
Cr Share capital		£2,000
Being proceeds of new issue of shares.		

The balance sheets before and after redemption are as follows:

	Balances before redemption £	New issue £	Purchase £	Balances after redemption £
Net assets	7,500			7,500
Bank	2,500	2,000	(2,000)	2,500
	10,000			10,000
Ordinary share capital	7,000	2,000	(2,000)	7,000
Profit & loss account	3,000			3,000
	10,000			10,000

As can be seen, the permanent capital remains the same at £7,000.

✸ Example: redemption of shares at par funded by new issue of shares at a premium

The balance sheet of the company prior to the capitalisation is as follows:

	£
Net assets	1,250
Bank	250
	1,500
Ordinary share capital (£1 shares)	1,200
Profit & loss account	300
	1,500

A total of 100 ordinary shares of £1 are to be redeemed at par – a new issue of 80 ordinary £1 shares at a premium of £0.25 (i.e. £1.25) being made for the purpose.

The summarised journal entries to effect the transaction are as follows:

Dr Share capital	£100	
Cr Bank		£100
Being payment on redemption.		

Dr Bank	£100	
Cr Share capital		£80
Share premium		£20
Being issue of shares at a premium.		

The balance sheets before and after redemption are as follows:

	Balances before redemption £	Dr £	Cr £	Balances after redemption £
Net assets	1,250			1,250
Bank	250	100	100	250
	1,500			1,500
Ordinary share capital	1,200	100	80	1,180
Share premium	–		20	20
Profit & loss account	300			300
	1,500			1,500

Once again, the permanent capital, i.e. share capital, and share premium remains the same before and after redemption at £1,200.

 ## Example: shares previously issued at a premium being redeemed at a premium and funded by new issue of shares at a premium

As was noted above, where shares are redeemed at a premium, such a premium must be paid out of distributable profits except that where the shares being redeemed were themselves issued at a premium and a new issue of shares is being made for the purpose. In such instances, all or part of the premium now payable may be charged against the share premium account. The amount that may be charged against the share premium account is the lower of:

- the amount of the premium which the company received on the shares now being purchased, and
- the current balance on the share premium account, including any premium on the new issue of shares.

The balance sheet of the company prior to the capitalisation is as follows:

	£	
Net assets	1,250	
Bank	250	
	1,500	
Share capital (£1 shares)	1,000	
Share premium	200	(Shares originally issued at premium of £0.20 per share)
Profit & loss account	300	
	1,500	

A total of 100 ordinary shares of £1 are to be redeemed at a premium of £0.80 (i.e. £180). The redemption price of £180 is to be funded by the issue of 90 ordinary shares of £1 at a premium of £1 per share.

Because the redemption is funded by a new issue, part of the premium payable on the redemption may be charged against the share premium account, i.e. the lower of:

■ the original premium on the shares being purchased, i.e. 100 × £0.20 = £20, and
■ the balance on the share premium account, including the premium on the new share issue, i.e. £290 (£200 + £90).

Therefore, £20 can be charged against the share premium account. The balance (£80 – £20) £60 must come from distributable profits.

The summarised journal entries to effect the transaction are as follows:

Dr	Share capital	£100	
Dr	Premium on purchase	£80	
	Cr Bank		£180
Being payment on redemption.			

Dr	Bank	£180	
	Cr Share capital		£90
	Share premium		£90
Being issue of shares at a premium.			

Dr	Share premium	£20	
Dr	Profit & loss reserve	£60	
	Cr Premium on purchase		£80
Being share premium account used for redemption and write-off of remaining premium.			

The balance sheets before and after the redemption are as follows:

	Balances before redemption £	Dr £	Cr £	Balances after redemption £
Premium on purchase	–	80	80	–
Net assets	1,250			1,250
Bank	250	180	180	250
	1,500			1,500
Share capital (£1 shares)	1,000	100	90	990
Share premium	200	20	90	270
Profit & loss account	300	60		340
	1,500			1,600

Note that the permanent capital, i.e. share capital, and share premium has in fact increased (i.e. £1,200 to £1,260). This is because of the Companies Act restriction on the amount of share premium payable which may be charged against the share premium account. Although capital maintenance is the main aim of the legislation, as this example shows, circumstances can arise that result in an increase in permanent capital. Circumstances may also arise that result in a decrease.

Progress Point 6.6

Using the balance sheet information from Progress Point 6.5, suppose that the 100,000 £1 shares that Rollrock plc is buying back had originally been issued at a premium of £0.25 each and are being redeemed at £1.80 (i.e. at a premium of £0.80 each). The new issue is of 120,000 shares, issued at a premium of £0.50 per share.

Required

(a) Prepare journal entries to record the purchase of shares.
(b) Prepare the balance sheet of Rollrock plc after the share purchase.

Solution

(a)   Journal entries:

Step 1: check legality
There are sufficient distributable profits. The scheme is legal.

Step 2: record purchase
The premium on purchase is £80,000 (100,000 × 80p). The nominal value is £100,000.

Dr	Share capital	£100,000	
Dr	Premium on purchase	£80,000	
	Cr Bank		£180,000
Being purchase of own shares.			

Step 3: record new issue

Dr	Bank	£180,000	
	Cr Share capital		£120,000
	Cr Share premium		£60,000
Being recording of new issue of shares.			

Step 4: eliminate premium

Dr	Share premium	£25,000	
Dr	Profit & loss reserve	£55,000	
	Cr Premium on purchase		£80,000
Being write-off of premium on purchase.			

The original share premium on the issue of the shares being bought back was £25,000 (100,000 × £0.25). The balance on the share premium account after the issue will be £500,000 + £60,000 = £560,000. Thus, the maximum premium that can be offset against the new issue will be £25,000 (i.e. the lower of the premium on the original issue of shares £25,000 and the balance on the share premium account £560,000).

Step 5: replace nominal value

The nominal value is fully replaced by the new issue. There is no need to transfer anything to the CRR.

(b)   Balance sheet:

> Rollrock plc
> Balance sheet at 30 September 2009
>
> | | £000 |
> |---|---|
> | Net assets | 4,000 |
> | | |
> | Share capital – £1 shares fully paid | 2,020 |
> | Share premium | 535 |
> | | |
> | Permanent capital | 2,555 |
> | Profit and loss reserve | 1,445 |
> | | |
> | | 4,000 |

Note that, in this case, the permanent capital has increased as a result of the new issue.

At the beginning of this section it was noted that there were two ways in which a public company could redeem shares: out of distributable profits or out of the proceeds of a new issue. In practice, a redemption is likely to be made out of both (i.e. partly out of profits and partly out of the proceeds of a new issue). The final two examples in this section illustrate the accounting entries required when redemption is made partly out of profits and partly out of the proceeds of a new issue.

Example: redemption of shares at par – partly out of distributable profits, partly from issue of shares

The balance sheet of a company prior to capitalisation is as follows:

	£
Other net assets	7,500
Bank	2,500
	10,000
Ordinary share capital (£1 shares)	7,000
Profit & loss account	3,000
	10,000

A total of 2,000 ordinary shares of £1 are to be redeemed at par – a new issue of 1,200 ordinary shares of £1 being made at par to raise £1,200 and the balance to be funded out of distributable profits. The summarised journal entries to effect the transaction are as follows:

Dr Ordinary share capital	£2,000	
Cr Bank		£2,000
Being payment on redemption.		

Dr Bank	£1,200	
Cr Ordinary share capital		£1,200
Being issue of ordinary shares at par.		

Dr Profit & loss reserve	£800	
Cr Capital redemption reserve		£800
Being element of redemption not covered by new issue being transferred as per the Companies Act.		

The balance sheets before and after the redemption are as follows:

	Balances before redemption £	Dr £	Cr £	Balances after redemption £
Net assets	7,500			7,500
Bank	2,500	1,200	2,000	1,700
	10,000			9,200
Share capital (£1 shares)	7,000	2,000	1,200	6,200
Capital redemption reserve	–		800	800
Profit & loss account	3,000	800		2,200
	10,000			9,200

Note that the permanent capital, i.e. share capital, and capital redemption reserve remains the same before and after redemption at £7,000. The other accounting entries are what we would expect (i.e. the amount of the redemption not being funded by the new issue (£2,000 – £1,200 = £800) requires the transfer of an amount equal to the nominal value of the redeemed shares from distributable profits to the capital redemption reserve).

 ### Example: shares previously issued at a premium being redeemed at a premium and being funded partly out of distributable profits and partly from a new issue of shares.

The balance sheet of a company prior to capitalisation is as follows:

	£	
Net assets	1,250	
Bank	250	
	1,500	
Share capital (£1 shares)	1,000	
Share premium	200	(shares originally issued at a premium of £0.20 per share)
Profit & loss account	300	
	1,500	

A total of 100 ordinary shares, which had originally been issued at a premium of £0.20 per share, are to be redeemed for £180. The redemption price of £180 is to be funded from the issue of 40 ordinary shares at a premium of £1 per share (i.e. £2 × 40 = £80) with the balance coming from distributable profits.

The premium payable on the purchase of the shares is £80 (£180 – £100) and because a new issue of shares is being made for the purpose, then part of the premium can be charged to the share premium account. The amount that may be charged is the lower of:

■   the original premium on the shares being purchased (i.e. 100 × £0.20 = £20), and

■ the balance on the share premium account, including the premium on the new share issue (i.e. £240 (£200 + £40)); therefore £20 can be charged against the share premium account and the balance (£80 − £20), £60, must be charged to distributable profits.

As part of the purchase price is being met from distributable profits, it is necessary to make a transfer between distributable profits and the capital redemption reserve. The Companies Act requires the amount to be transferred to be calculated by deducting the aggregate amount of the proceeds of the new issue from the nominal value of the shares purchased.

In this example the amount of the transfer is therefore:

	£
Nominal value of shares purchased (100 x £1)	100
Less: proceeds of new issue	80
Required transfer	20

The summarised journal entries required to effect the transaction are as follows:

Dr	Share capital	£100	
	Premium on purchase	£80	
Cr	Bank		£180
Being payment on redemption.			

Dr	Bank	£80	
Cr	Share capital		£40
	Share premium		£40
Being issue of new shares at a premium.			

Dr	Share premium	£20	
	Distributable profits	£60	
Cr	Premium on purchase		£80
Being share premium account used for redemption and write-off of remaining premium.			

Dr	Distributable profits	£20	
Cr	Capital redemption reserve		£20
Being transfer required by the Companies Act.			

The balance sheets before and after the redemption are as follows:

	Balances before redemption £	Dr £	Cr £	Balances after redemption £
Premium on purchase		80	80	–
Net assets	1,250			1,250
Bank	250	80	180	150
	1,500			1,400
Share capital (£1 shares)	1,000	100	40	940
Capital redemption reserve	–		20	20
Share premium	200	20	40	220
Profit & loss account	300	60		220
		20		
	1,500			1,400

Note that the permanent capital, i.e. share capital and share premium and capital redemption reserve, has reduced from £1,200 to £1,180. The reason for this is that the proceeds of the new issue are treated as financing part of both the nominal value and the premium payable, but this is not recognised by the legislation in specifying the computation of the transfer to the capital redemption reserve. Let us reconsider the above workings. The proceeds of the new issue are £80, of which £20 is used to fund the premium on purchase. This therefore leaves £60 to replace the nominal value of the shares purchased. In order to maintain the permanent capital at £1,200, the transfer to capital redemption reserve would need to be £40. This would be calculated as follows:

		£
Nominal value of shares purchased		100
Less: net proceeds of new issue:		
total proceeds	80	
less: utilised to finance part of premium	20	
		60
Necessary transfer to capital redemption reserve		40

Why, then, has this reduction in permanent capital arisen? It is as a result of the wording of the Companies Act in relation to the transfer to the capital redemption reserve. As noted above, the Companies Act 2006 requires the amount to be calculated by deducting the aggregate amount of the proceeds of the new issue from the nominal value of the shares purchased (Section 733). Unfortunately, the Act does not take account of the amount of the proceeds used to finance the premium payable (in this case £20). Had the legislation referred to 'net' proceeds of the new issue then it would have had the desired effect in maintaining permanent capital by diverting sufficient reserves from distributable profits to the capital redemption reserve. That is:

	£
Nominal value of shares purchased	100
Less: net proceeds of new issue (80 – 20)	60
Required transfer	40

As it stands, therefore, the law seems to permit such a reduction in capital for both public and private companies. The law, it appears, has been poorly drafted.

Progress Point 6.7

Again, using the balance sheet information from Progress Point 6.5, suppose that Rollrock plc purchased the 100,000 shares that had originally been issued at a premium of £0.25 each, for £1.80 per share. This time, however, Rollrock plc issues only 60,000 shares at a premium of £0.50, raising £90,000. The remainder of the purchase is funded out of profits.

Required

(a) Prepare journal entries to record the purchase of shares.
(b) Prepare the balance sheet of Rollrock plc after the share purchase.

Solution

(a) Journal entries:

Step 1: check legality
Scheme is legal.

Step 2: record purchase

Dr	Share capital	£100,000	
Dr	Premium on purchase	£80,000	
	Cr Bank		£180,000
Being purchase of own shares.			

Step 3: record new issue

Dr	Bank	£90,000	
	Cr Share capital		£60,000
	Cr Share premium		£30,000
Being recording of nerw issue of shares.			

Step 4: eliminate premium

Dr	Share premium	£25,000	
Dr	Profit & loss reserve	£55,000	
	Cr Premium on purchase		£80,000
Being write-off of premium on purchase of shares.			

That is, the lower of the premium on the original share issue and the balance on the share premium account is written off the share premium account.

Step 5: replace nominal value

Dr	Profit & loss reserve	£10,000	
	Cr Capital redemption reserve		£10,000
Being transfer of distributable profits to the CRR.			

This transfer is required as the new issued raised only £90,000 of the £100,000 nominal value of shares purchased (i.e. there is a shortfall of £10,000).

(b)   Balance sheet:

Rollrock plc	
Balance sheet at 30 September 2009	£
	000
Net assets	3,910
Capital and reserves	
Share capital – £1 shares fully paid	1,960
Share premium	505
Capital redemption reserve	10
Permanent capital	2,475
Profit & loss reserve	1,435
	3,910

Note that there has been a reduction in the permanent share capital of £25,000 (2,500,000 − £2,475,000). This is because there is a certain amount of double counting in the application of the proceeds of the new issue to offset both the nominal value and the premium on the shares being repurchased. As noted earlier, this is probably an error in the way in which the rules have been drafted rather than an exception to the general principle that permanent capital should not be reduced.

In order to have maintained the permanent capital, the transfer to the CRR should have been calculated as follows:

	£	£
Nominal value of shares purchased		100,000
Less: net proceeds of new issue:		
total proceeds	90,000	
less: utilised to finance part		
of premium (100,000 × 25p)	25,000	
		65,000
Necessary transfer to CRR		35,000

6.8 Redemption of shares by a private company

Although the overriding aim of company law in relation to the redemption or buying back of shares is to maintain permanent capital, an unintended effect of the legislation is that there may be an increase or decrease in that permanent capital figure.

Private companies are, however, specifically permitted by the Companies Act to purchase their shares out of capital. This facility enables a private company to reduce its permanent capital without the formality and expense of undertaking a capital reduction scheme. This ability to purchase shares is of considerable benefit to, for example, a family-owned company where one shareholder wishes to realise his or her investment but the other shareholders are unwilling, or indeed unable, to purchase it.

Because a purchase of shares out of capital results in a fall in the resources potentially available to creditors, the legislation in the Companies Act 2006 provides a number of safeguards to protect their interests, as described below.

First of all, the payment out of capital must be permitted by the company's Articles of Association and authorised by a special resolution of the company. The directors also require to make a declaration of solvency to the effect that the company will still be able to pay its creditors after the redemption and during the year following redemption. As the protection of creditors rests on the validity of this declaration (i.e. the continuing solvency of the business), the law requires that the declaration be agreed and reported upon by the company's auditors. The auditors' report is to be addressed to the directors (not to the company or shareholders), which states that the auditor has enquired into the affairs of the company, the amount stated in the declaration as the permissible capital payment is in his view properly determined, and that he is not aware of anything to indicate that the opinion expressed by the directors is unreasonable in all the circumstances. Furthermore, once the payment out of capital has been authorised, the company must publicise it in an official gazette or by individual notice to each creditor who may object to such a redemption through the courts. Finally, in the event that the declaration of solvency proves not to have been well founded and the company commences to wind up within a year of the payment out of capital and is unable to pay all its liabilities and the costs of winding up, then directors and past shareholders may be liable to contribute. The directors who have signed the declaration of solvency and/or the past shareholders whose shares were purchased, may have to pay an amount not exceeding in total the permitted capital payment.

Note that a payment out of capital will arise only if the company cannot fund the purchase out of distributable profits and the proceeds of any fresh value.

The mechanics of the share purchase itself also provide protection of creditors' interests. The first condition is that the company must use all its distributable profits before it may reduce its capital. Similarly, if a company issues shares to finance the purchase, either wholly or in part, then these proceeds must be used before any capital reduction may occur. In other words, the permanent capital will be the last element of the funding of the purchase. This is known as the 'permissible capital payment' and is the maximum amount by which the permanent capital may be reduced. The permissible capital payment is the amount by which the total amount paid on redemption of shares exceeds the aggregate of the distributable profits of a company and the proceeds of any new share issue specifically made for the purposes of redemption.

	£	£
Amount payable to purchase shares		X
Less: distributable profits	X	
proceeds of new share issue	X	
	—	
		X
		—
Permissible capital payment		X
		=

The accounting entries required to limit the reduction in permanent capital to the permissible capital payment are as follows:

- if the nominal value of shares redeemed exceeds the permissible capital payment, an amount equal to the excess must be transferred from distributable profits to the capital redemption reserve account.
- if the nominal value of shares redeemed is less than the permissible capital payment, an amount equal to this plus the proceeds of any new share issue may be used to reduce any undistributable reserves, e.g. revaluation reserve, capital redemption reserve, share premium account, or fully paid share capital; these should be used in order of least 'restriction' (e.g. revaluation reserve before share premium, share premium before share capital); as profit will have been eliminated by this there will be nothing to transfer to CRR.

As noted above, the general effect is that, in limiting the reduction in permanent capital to the permissible amount, a private company first utilises its distributable profit before reducing any undistributable reserves. As before, this is best illustrated by examples.

Example: nominal value of shares redeemed exceeds the permissible capital payment

The balance sheet of a private company prior to redemption is as follows:

	£
Other net assets	240
Cash	260
	500
Share capital (£1 shares)	100
Share premium	240
Profit & loss account	160
	500

The company agrees to buy 50 of its shares of £1 each from a retiring director and shareholder at a premium of £3 per share, i.e. 50 × (£1 + £3) = £200. No new shares are to be issued for the purpose.

Step 1
The first step is to calculate the permissible capital payment:

	£
Amount payable to redeem shares	200
Less: distributable profits	160
Permissible capital payment	40

Step 2

The next step is to determine how much of the distributable profits require to be diverted from the profit and loss account to the capital redemption reserve:

	£
Nominal value of shares redeemed	50
Less: permissible capital payment	40
Capital redemption reserve	10

The journal entries required to effect the transaction are as follows:

Dr	Ordinary share capital	£50	
	Premium on redemption	£150	
	Cr Cash		£200
Being cash paid at redemption.			

Dr	Profit and loss reserve	£150	
	Cr Premium on redemption		£150
Being premium funded from distributable reserves.			

Dr	Profit & loss reserve	£10	
	Cr Capital redemption reserve		£10
Being transfer to capital redemption reserve.			

The balance sheets before and after redemption are as follows:

	Balances before redemption £	Dr £	Cr £	Balances after redemption £
Other net assets	240			240
Cash	260		200	60
Premium on redemption		150	150	
	500			300
Share capital (£1 shares)	100	50		50
Capital redemption reserve	–		10	10
Share premium	240			240
Profit & loss account	160	150		–
		10		
	500			300

Note that the permanent capital has reduced from £340 to £300 (i.e. by the amount of the permissible capital payment).

Looked at another way, the company paid £200 to redeem the shares. It had to use all of its distributable profits before it could reduce its capital. The company had distributable profits of £160 and therefore the difference (£200 – £160) had to come from permanent capital.

Example: nominal value of shares redeemed is less than the permissible capital payment

The balance sheet of a private company prior to redemption is as follows:

	£
Other net assets	240
Cash	260
	500
Share capital (£1 shares)	100
Share premium	240
Profit & loss account	160
	500

The company agrees to buy 50 of its shares of £1 each from a retiring director/shareholder at a premium of £5 per share (i.e. 50 × (£1 + £5) = £300). A total of 20 ordinary shares of £1 each are to be issued at a premium of £2 per share to help finance the redemption (i.e. 20 × (£1 + £2) = £60).

Step 1
The first step is to calculate the permissible capital payment:

	£	£
Amount payable to redeem shares		300
Less: distributable profits	160	
proceeds of new issue	60	
		220
Permissible capital payment		80

Step 2
The next step is to determine how much of the distributable profits requires to be diverted from the profit and loss account to the capital redemption reserve:

	£
Nominal value of shares redeemed	50
Less: permissible capital payment	80
Allowed reduction in permanent capital	(30)
Proceeds of new issue	(60)
Total allowed reduction in permanent capital	(90)

Remember that this example is illustrating the accounting procedures to be adopted where the nominal value of shares redeemed is less than the permissible capital payment. The permanent capital can therefore be reduced by the difference. However, the issue of the new shares has itself increased the permanent capital, and consequently the total reduction in undistributable reserves includes this new issue also.

The journal entries required to effect the transaction are as follows:

Dr	Share capital	£50	
	Premium on redemption	£250	
	Cr Cash		£300
Being cash paid at redemption.			

Dr	Cash	£60	
	Cr Share capital		£20
	Share premium		£40
Being cash received from new issue.			

Dr	Profit & loss account	£160	
	Cr Premium on redemption		£160
Being part of premium funded from distributable profits.			

Dr	Share premium	£90	
	Cr Premium on redemption		£90
Being part of premium funded from permanent capital.			

The balance sheets before and after the redemption are as follows:

	Balances before redemption £	Journals Dr £	Cr £	Balances after redemption £
Other net assets	240			240
Cash	260	60	300	20
Premium on redemption		250	160	–
			90	
	500			260
Share capital (£1 shares)	100	50	20	70
Share premium	240	90	40	190
Profit & loss account	160	160		–
	500			260

Note that the permanent capital has reduced from £340 to £260, which in this case is the permissible capital payment. Consider what has happened. The company has bought back shares costing £300 and has partly financed this by issuing new shares for £60. There is therefore a shortfall to be funded of (£300 − £60) = £240. The company has distributable profits of £160 and these must be used first to finance the purchase. There is therefore a shortfall of £240 − £160 (i.e. £80), which requires to come from permanent capital. As can be seen from the movements on the accounts above, share capital has been reduced by £30 and share premium by £50.

Progress Point 6.8

Ferbrew Ltd has decided to buy 10,000 of its £1 ordinary shares from a retiring director at a price of £1.25 each (i.e. £12,500). The shares were originally issued at par. The purchase is to be partly financed by the issue of 2,000 new ordinary £1 shares at £1.30 each.

The balance sheet of Ferbrew Ltd prior to the purchase is:

	£
Net assets	33,000
Capital and reserves	
Share capital	25,000
Share premium	–
Permanent capital	25,000
Profit & loss reserve	8,000
	33,000

Required

(a) Prepare journal entries to record the purchase of shares.
(b) Prepare the balance sheet of Ferbrew Ltd after the share purchase.

Solution

(a) Journal entries:

Step 1: calculate permissible capital payment (PCP)

			£
	Amount payable to purchase shares		12,500
Less:	distributable profits	8,000	
	proceeds of new issue	2,600	
			10,600
	Permissible capital payment		1,900

Step 2: record purchase

Dr Share capital	£10,000	
Premium on purchase	£2,500	
Cr Bank		£12,500
Being purchase of shares.		

Being purchase of shares.

Step 3: record new issue

Dr Bank	£2,600	
Cr Share capital		£2,000
Cr Share premium		£600
Being issue of new shares.		

▶

Step 4: eliminate premium

Dr Profit & loss reserve	£2,500	
Cr Premium on purchase		£2,500
Being elimination of premium on purchase.		

Step 5: transfer to CRR

The nominal value of shares redeemed (£10,000) exceeds the PCP (£1,900) and therefore a transfer must be made from distributable profits to the capital redemption reserve.

The remaining balance on the profit and loss reserve is:

	£
Profit & loss reserve	8,000
Less: premium on shares purchased	2,500
Remaining balance	5,500

Because the premium on purchase is debited to profit and loss reserve, only the remaining balance can be transferred to CRR.

Alternatively, the required transfer could have been calculated as follows:

	£	
Nominal value of shares redeemed	10,000	
Less: permissible capital payment	1,900	
	8,100	
Less: proceeds of new issue	2,600	
Required transfer to CRR	5,500	
Dr Profit and loss reserve	£5,500	
Cr CRR		£5,500
Being transfer to CRR.		

(b)   Balance sheet:

Step 6

This gives a balance sheet of:

	£
Net assets	23,100
Capital and reserves	
Share capital	17,000
Share premium	600
CRR	5,500
Permanent capital	23,100

The reduction in permanent capital is £1,900 (£25,000 – £23,100), which is the amount of the PCP.

Progress Point 6.9

Using the same balance sheet and funding information from Progress Point 6.8, suppose the shares are purchased for £2.00 each (i.e. for £20,000).

Required

(a) Prepare journal entries to record the purchase of shares.
(b) Prepare the balance sheet of Ferbrew Ltd after the share purchase.

Solution

(a) Journal entries:

Step 1: – Calculate permissible capital payment (PCP)

	£	£
Amount payable to purchase shares		20,000
Less: distributable profits	8,000	
Proceeds of new issue	2,600	
		10,600
Permissible capital payment		9,400

Step 2: Record purchase

Dr	Share capital	£10,000	
	Premium on purchase	£10,000	
	Cr Bank		£20,000
Being purchase of shares.			

Step 3: record new issue

Dr	Bank	£2,600	
	Cr Share capital		£2,000
	Cr Share premium		£600
Being issue of shares.			

Step 4: eliminate premium

The premium to be eliminated is £10,000. The balance on profit and loss reserve is only £8,000. There is therefore, insufficient in the profit and loss reserve to write off the premium. Other accounts must be used. These should be used in order of least restriction (e.g. revaluation reserve before share premium, share premium before share capital) – that is:

Dr	Profit and loss reserve	£8,000	
Dr	Share premium	£600	
Dr	Share capital	£1,400	
	Cr Premium on purchase		£10,000
Being elimination of premium on purchase.			

Step 5: transfer to CRR

As the profit and loss reserve has been fully eliminated in writing off the premium there is nothing to transfer to CRR.

BASIC

INTERMEDIATE

ADVANCED

▶

(b)   Balance sheet:

Step 6
This gives a balance sheet of:

	£
Net assets	15,600
Share capital	15,600
Share premium	–
CRR	–
Profit & loss reserve	–
Permanent capital	15,600

The reduction in permanent capital is £9,400 (£25,000 – £15,600), which is the amount of the PCP. Note, however, how this has been achieved. The balance on the share capital account is only £15,600 despite there being 17,000 £1 shares in issue.

6.9   Treasury shares

Earlier in this section it was stated that shares redeemed or purchased must be cancelled.

In Europe and the USA, companies have been able to buy back shares and hold them for reissue. In the UK, regulations introduced in 2003 (now S724 of the Companies Act 2006) allow listed (full listing or AIM) companies to purchase their own shares and to hold them as **treasury shares** for sale at some future date. Under these regulations, purchased or redeemed shares do not need to be cancelled and they are not removed from issued share capital. Instead, these treasury shares are shown as a deduction from the existing shareholders' funds. To qualify, the company must have sufficient distributable profits to cover the purchase.

A maximum of 10% of any class of shares can be held as treasury shares at any one time. Treasury shares carry no rights to dividends or to vote. The company is recorded as holder of these shares in the register of members.

IAS 32 *Financial Instruments: Presentation*, paras 33 and 34, deals with this topic (see Chapter 7).

The amount of any treasury shares should be deducted from shareholders' funds. No gain or loss should be recognised in the income statement on the purchase, sale, issue or cancellation of treasury shares. If treasury shares are cancelled, the usual rules for purchase of shares apply.

Accounting requirements

There are two common methods for accounting for treasury shares: the cost method and the par value method.

The most common method is the cost method, which provides that:

(i) **On purchase**
The treasury shares are debited at gross cost (i.e. purchase price not par value) to a treasury shares account, which is to be deducted from equity.

Journal:

Dr   Treasury shares
    Cr   Bank
Being purchase of treasury shares.

The treasury shares account records the consideration paid. Note that as the shares are not cancelled there is no debit to share capital.

(ii) **On resale**

The position on resale depends on whether the sales proceeds are greater than the purchase price.

(a) If the sales proceeds are higher than the purchase price, the treasury shares account is credited at cost and the excess is credited to share premium.

```
Dr    Bank
        Cr      Treasury shares
        Cr      Share premium
Being sale of treasury shares.
```

(b) If the sales proceeds are lower than the purchase price, the treasury shares account is credited with the original purchase price, and the deficit is debited to the profit and loss reserve.

```
Dr    Bank
Dr    Profit & loss reserve
        Cr      Treasury shares
Being sale of treasury shares.
```

Note that, in both instances, no gain or loss is recognised in profit and loss – any gains or losses are recognised directly in equity.

Example

Exbere plc has 10 million 50p ordinary shares in issue. These were originally issued at a price of £1.50 each. On 1 January 2009, it purchased 1 million of these shares for £2.00 each. The shares are to be held as treasury shares.

The company resold the shares as follows:

■   15 April 2009 – 400,000 shares at £2.20 per share
■   25 October 2009 – 250,000 shares at £2.50 per share.

The company has a 31 December year end.
The journals to record the purchase and resale of the treasury shares during the year would be:

Purchase of treasury shares:

```
January 2009
Dr    Treasury shares                           £2,000,000
        Cr    Bank                                              £2,000000
Being purchase of treasury shares.
```

```
April 2009
Dr    Bank                                         £880,000
        Cr      Treasury shares                            £800,000
        Cr      Share premium                              £80,000
Being sale of treasury shares.
```

That is, the treasury shares account is credited with the original purchase price of the shares subsequently sold (i.e. 400,000 × £2.00), with the excess being credited to share premium.

October 2009		
Dr Bank	£625,000	
Cr Treasury shares		£500,000
Cr Share premium		£125,000
Being sale of treasury shares.		

That is, again, the treasury shares account is credited with the original purchase price of the shares sold (250,000 × £2.00) with the excess being credited to share premium.

If a company holds shares as treasury shares and reissues some of these at below the initial purchase price it is prudent to write off the difference to profit and loss reserve (not profit and loss account). Not to do so would be to anticipate the remaining shares being issued at an amount to cover the shortfall.

Example

A company purchases 2 million 50p ordinary shares for £2.50 each on 1 March 2009 and holds these as treasury shares. The shares are subsequently sold as follows:

- 1 August 2009 – 500,000 shares at £2.30
- 1 November 2009 – 1,500,000 shares at £2.80.

The company has a 31 December year end.

The journals to record the purchase and resale of the treasure shares during the year would be:

Purchase of treasury shares

March 2009		
Dr Treasury shares	£5,000,000	
Cr Bank		£5,000,000
Being purchase of treasury shares.		

Sale of treasury shares

August 2009		
Dr Bank	£1,150,000	
Profit and loss reserve	£100,000	
Cr Treasury shares		£1,250,000
Being sale of treasury shares.		

Note that the treasury shares account is credited with the original purchase price of the shares sold, i.e. (500,000 × £2.50), the deficit is charged to profit and loss reserve.

November 2009		
Dr Bank	£4,200,000	
Cr Treasury shares		£3,750,000
Share premium		£450,000
Being sale of treasury shares.		

Again, the treasury shares account is credited with the original purchase price of the shares sold (1,500,000 × £2.50), with the excess being credited to share premium.

Note that the £100,000 remains debited to profit and loss reserve. It is not cancelled by part of the premium raised on the November sale.

The effect of the accounting treatment of treasury shares is as follows.

- If the disposal proceeds are equal to or less than the purchase price, the proceeds are treated as realised profit. This requires further explanation. Because the shares were originally purchased out of distributable profits, any proceeds received for their ultimate disposal – up to their purchase price – are credited back to realised profit. Note that this is not recognising that a profit has been made when it clearly has not – it is just that it is returning to distributable profits some of the original purchase price that had been charged to distributable profits.
- If the disposal proceeds exceed the purchase price, an amount equal to the purchase price is treated as a realised profit and the excess is transferred to a share premium account. Again, there is a reversal of the amount that had originally been charged to distributable profits with the excess – the 'gain' – being credited to share premium.

Reasons for holding treasury shares

By holding treasury shares a company has greater flexibility to respond to investors' attitudes to gearing. Gearing is the measure of interest-bearing liabilities in relation to shareholders' equity. Consequently if a company holds treasury shares and investors perceive the level of gearing to be too high, the company can reissue the shares, thus increasing shareholders' equity and reducing the level of gearing.

In addition, by holding treasury shares a company has the capacity to satisfy loan conversions and employee share options without the need to issue new shares that would dilute the existing shareholdings.

Disclosure

The amount of treasury shares held should be disclosed as a deduction from shareholders' funds either on the face of the balance sheet or in a note.

 ## Example

Continuing with the information in the Exbere plc example, of the 1 million shares originally held as treasury shares, by the year end of 31 December 2009, 650,000 shares had been sold and £1.3 million (£800,000 + £500,000) credited to treasury shares. This left 350,000 shares at purchase price of £2.00 per share (i.e. £700,000 sitting as a debit in the treasury shares account).

Assume that at 31 December 2008 the company had the following balances:

	£
Ordinary share capital	5,000,000
Share premium	1,000,000
Profit & loss reserve	3,500,000
	9,500,000

The retained profit for the year to 31 December 2009 was £400,000.

Assuming that the company discloses treasury shares on the face of the balance sheet, the shareholders' funds section of the balance sheet at 31 December 2009 would be as follows:

Shareholders' funds
At 31 December 2009

	£
Ordinary share capital	5,000,000
Share premium	1,205,000
Profit & loss reserve	3,900,000
	10,105,000
Treasury shares	(700,000)
	9,405,000

Notes

Note that the share capital remains the same as the purchased shares have not been cancelled; the treasury shares held at the year end are shown as a deduction from shareholders' funds.

Share premium = balance b/f + premiums on reissue.

$$= £1,000,000 + £80,000 + £125,000$$

$$= £1,205,000$$

Profit & loss reserve = balance b/f + retained profit.

$$= £3,500,000 + £400,000$$

$$= £3,900,000$$

6.10   Capital reserves put to use

The preceding examples have illustrated that capital reserves, once created, can be utilised. This is an important point to note. Our review of reserves thus far has effectively distinguished between distributable and non-distributable reserves, with capital reserves falling within the category of non-distributable. This does not mean that these reserves are not usable – it is just that they cannot be used from which to make distributions. The Companies Act specifies how capital reserves can be used and, in addition, a company's Articles of Association must also allow their use.

This is perhaps an appropriate point to look once more at capital reserves and how they may be used. As is often the case in accountancy, a full understanding of a particular topic often necessitates the introduction of a concept, and reference made to other concepts which, although essential to the understanding of the initial concept, have themselves not been explained. This has been the case with reserves, and in particular the capital redemption reserve, where the creation and subsequent use of the reserve have already been illustrated. Various capital reserves are now summarised, how they may be used is explained, and, as can be seen, this in itself leads to new issues requiring further illustration.

Capital redemption reserve

(a)   As previously illustrated, the capital redemption reserve can be reduced in the case of a private company where the permissible capital payment is greater than the nominal value of shares purchased/redeemed.

(b)   It can be applied in paying up un-issued shares of a company as fully paid shares. These are known as bonus issues, capitalisation issues or scrip issues. These are looked at in detail following this section.

Share premium account

(a)   As with the capital redemption reserve, the share premium account can be used to issue bonus shares.

(b)   Where an issue of shares resulted in a transfer to the share premium account, to write off expenses incurred on that issue.

(c)   Where an issue of shares resulted in a transfer to the share premium account, to write off any commission paid on that issue.

BASIC

INTERMEDIATE

ADVANCED

Revaluation reserve

(a) The revaluation reserve can be reduced if, at any time, the asset whose increase in value gave rise to the revaluation falls in value.

(b) The revaluation reserve, as illustrated above, may also be reduced where the permissible capital payment exceeds the nominal value of the shares redeemed/purchased by a private company.

6.11   Bonus issues

Bonus issues – also referred to as capitalisation issues or scrip issues – involve a transfer from one of the reserve accounts, distributable or non-distributable, to the share capital account to convert these reserves into shares. These shares can then be given to the existing shareholders in proportion to their holdings at the time of the issue. The shares will be treated as fully paid and usually do not include a premium element.

A bonus issue is often made when the market value of a share has grown to such an extent that it becomes difficult to trade on the stock market. It has the effect of lowering the value of each share without reducing the shareholders' collective or individual wealth. No new resources enter the company as a result of a bonus issue (i.e. there is no consideration received).

 **Example**

The balance sheet of a company is as follows:

	£
Net assets	128,000
Share capital (£1 shares)	50,000
Profit and loss account	78,000
	128,000

The company decides to make a bonus issue of one new share to existing shareholders for every share owned by each shareholder. The journal entries required to effect the transaction are as follows:

Dr Profit & loss reserve	£50,000	
Cr Share capital		£50,000
Being bonus issue – 50,000 shares.		

The balance sheet of the company immediately after this will be as follows:

	£
Net assets	128,000
Share capital (£1 shares) (50,000 + 50,000)	100,000
Profit and loss account (78,000 – 50,000)	28,000
	128,000

As can be seen, the reserves have reduced by £50,000 and the share capital increased by £50,000. In other words, the reserves have been capitalised. Note that, in real terms, the shareholders are not any better off. Although they may own twice as many shares as they did previously, the total value of the company has remained the same at £128,000. The shares themselves will each be worth one half of the market price of an old share at the time of the issue.

If a company's articles of association give the power, a company can use any of its reserves to make a bonus issue (i.e. revaluation reserves, share premium account and capital redemption reserve).

Progress Point 6.10

The directors of Rosellie plc have decided to make a bonus issue from profit and loss reserve of one new share for every three previously held. The company's balance sheet at 31 December 2009, just before the issue, was as follows:

	£m
Fixed assets	14
Net current assets	4
Non-current liabilities	(5)
	13
Share capital (£1 ordinary)	9
Profit & loss reserve	4
	13

Required

Prepare the journal entry required to record the bonus issue, and redraft the balance sheet of Rosellie plc taking account of the bonus issue.

Solution

The bonus issue will be £9m/3 = £3m giving the following journal:

Dr	Profit and loss reserve	£3m	
	Cr Share capital		£3m
Being the nominal value of shares created on bonus issue.			

The balance sheet would become:

Rosellie plc
Balance sheet at 31 December 2009

	£m
Fixed assets	14
Net current assets	4
Non-current liabilities	(5)
	13
Share capital (£1 ordinary)	12
Profit & loss reserve	1
	13

Note that net assets are unchanged as no new resources are raised in a bonus issue.

6.12   Share splits

There is another mechanism to reduce the market value per share, and that does not involve the use of any reserve accounts. A company can split its shares into shares with a smaller par value. As with bonus issues, the effect is to reduce the market price per share but for each shareholder to hold the same total value.

⚙ *Example*

100,000 ordinary shares of £1 each could be subdivided into:

■   200,000 ordinary shares of £0.50, or
■   400,000 ordinary shares of £0.25 each.

6.13   Disclosure

The following disclosure is required by IAS 1.
    For each class of share capital:

■   the number of shares authorised
■   the number of shares issued and fully paid, and issued but not fully paid
■   par value per share
■   reconciliation of number of shares outstanding at the beginning and end of the period
■   rights, preferences and restrictions attaching to each class of share
■   shares of the entity held by the entity or by its subsidiaries and associates, and
■   shares reserved for issue under options and contracts for the sale of shares, including the terms and amounts.

    In addition, para. 97 of IAS 1 requires the amounts of transactions with shareholders and a reconciliation of the carrying amount for each class of share at the beginning and end of the period, separately disclosing each change.

Disclosure in practice

The reporting requirements in relation to share capital are dealt with in IAS 1. The relevant disclosures can be found within the accounting policies note and the notes to the balance sheet.

Share capital

    Ordinary shares are classified as equity. Incremental costs directly attributable to the issue of new shares or options are shown in equity as a deduction from the proceeds.

Logica discloses in its policy note on share capital, the company's treatment of costs attributable to the issue of shares and that ordinary shares are classified as equity (see figure 6.1).

BASIC

INTERMEDIATE

ADVANCED

		2007	2006
	Authorised	£m	£m
2,250,000,000 (2006: 2,250,000,000) ordinary shares of 10 pence each		225.0	225.0

		2007		2006
Allotted, called-up and fully paid	Number	£m	Number	£m
At 1 January	1,535,698,482	153.6	1,146,238,652	114.6
Allotted under share plans	5,538,792	0.6	2,595,389	0.3
Shares purchased and cancelled	(83,591,195)	(8.4)	–	–
Allotted to acquire WM – data shares	–	–	377,848,632	37.8
Allotted to acquire WM – data convertible debentures	–	–	9,015,809	0.9
At 31 December	1,457,646,079	145.8	1,535,698,482	153.6

Figure 6.1 Logica: share capital note

The Company has one class of authorised and issued share capital, comprising ordinary shares of 10 pence each. Subject to the Company's Articles of Association and applicable law, the Company's ordinary shares confer on the holder: the right to receive notice of and vote at general meetings of the Company; the right to receive any surplus assets on a winding-up of the Company; and an entitlement to receive any dividend declared on ordinary shares.

During the period 25 June 2007 to 2 November 2007, the Company purchased and subsequently cancelled 83.6 million ordinary shares at an average price of £1.55, with a nominal value of £8.4 million, for consideration of £130.8 million. Consideration included stamp duty and commission of £0.8 million.

The share capital note from the Logica financial statements illustrates the disclosure requirements of IAS 1 in relation to share capital. A reconciliation of the number of shares at the beginning and end of the period is given, and the narrative element of the note gives details of the class of share in issue, the par value of those shares, the rights attaching to the shares and also that the company bought back and cancelled 83.6 million ordinary shares.

Other reserves

	Retained earnings £m	Treasury shares £m	Translation reserve £m	Capital redemption reserve £m	Merger reserve £m	Other £m	Total £m
At 1 January 2006	(344.0)	(35.9)	0.6	–	–	(0.8)	(380.1)
Net profit for the year	82.0	–	–	–	–	–	82.0
Dividends paid	(61.1)	–	–	–	–	–	(61.1)
Share-based payment, net of tax	9.1	–	–	–	–	–	9.1
Actuarial gains	17.5	–	–	–	–	–	17.5
Acquisition of WM-data	–	–	–	–	617.1	–	617.1
Cash flow hedges - transferred to income statement	(2.0)	–	–	–	–	–	(2.0)
Tax on items taken to equity	(3.9)	–	–	–	–	–	(3.9)
Other	(0.1)	–	–	–	–	–	(0.1)
Exchange differences	–	–	(6.8)	–	–	2.7	(4.1)
At 1 January 2007	(302.5)	(35.9)	(6.2)	–	617.1	1.9	274.4
Net profit for the year	169.9	–	–	–	–	–	169.9
Dividends paid	(85.9)	–	–	–	–	–	(85.9)
Share-based payment, net of tax	9.5	–	–	–	–	–	9.5
Shares purchased and cancelled	(130.8)	–	–	8.4	–	–	(122.4)
Actuarial gains	3.6	–	–	–	–	–	3.6
Recycled on disposal of foreign operations	–	–	5.1	–	–	–	5.1
Other	–	0.8	–	–	1.9	–	2.7
Exchange differences	–	–	95.0	–	–	0.4	95.4
At 31 December 2007	(336.2)	(35.1)	93.9	8.4	619.0	2.3	352.3

Figure 6.2 Logica other reserves note

Treasury shares

The Group holds shares in LogicaCMG plc in three discretionary trusts which were set up for the benefit of Logica employees. The trusts purchase the Company's shares in the market for use in connection with the Group's employee share plans. The amount shown in the treasury shares reserve at 31 December 2007, which related solely to shares purchased and disposed of by the trusts, would be deducted in determining the amount the Company had available for distribution at that date.

At 31 December 2007, the employee trusts owned 14,575,290 ordinary shares (2006: 15,588,650) with a nominal value of £1.5 million (2006: £1.6 million). The trustees of the CMG ESOP Trust and the Logica ESOP Trust have agreed to waive the right to future dividends on ordinary shares held by the trusts except for a nominal amount. At 31 December 2007 and 2006, the nominal amount payable to both trusts was 0.001 pence per share.

Translation reserve

The translation reserve represented the accumulated exchange differences arising from the following sources:

- the impact of the translation of the income statement and net assets of subsidiaries with a functional currency other than pounds sterling
- exchange differences recycled on disposal of foreign operations
- exchange differences arising on the translation of net investments in a foreign operation where any subsidiary of the Group may have a receivable from or a payable to a foreign operation and settlement is neither planned nor likely, and
- exchange differences arising on hedging instruments that are designated hedges of a net investment in foreign operations, net of tax where applicable.

Capital redemption reserve

The capital redemption reserve was a non-distributable reserve and contained the nominal value of the shares repurchased and cancelled.

Merger reserve

The merger reserve represented the excess of the fair value over the nominal value of shares issued by the Company to acquire at least 90% equity interest in an acquiree company. A purchaser company acquiring at least 90% equity interest in an acquiree company under an arrangement, which provides for the allotment of equity shares by the purchaser in return for the equity interest in the acquiree must apply Section 131 of the Act. When applicable, the section required that the premium on the issue of equity shares by the purchaser company be disregarded. Accordingly, the Company did not record a premium on the share it issued but recognised a merger reserve in the consolidated balance sheet.

The capital redemption reserve note explains that the reserve comprises the nominal value of the repurchased shares. In addition to buying back and cancelling shares, Logica also holds treasury shares as the extract above from the other reserves note discloses. As the note explains, these treasury shares are held for use in connection with employee share plans.

6.14   The position in practice

It is useful at this point to consider the position with share capital and reserves in practice.

The legislation governing share capital and reserves will be unique to the countries in which the accountant is based. The alteration of share capital as covered in this section has shown the importance of following the legislation prevalent in the reporting jurisdiction.

While an in-depth knowledge of the rules is not the aim of this book, an awareness of the possibilities to alter share capital very much is – particularly in relation to private companies. As noted earlier in this chapter, private companies form about 99% of the total of 1.5 million UK limited companies and it is therefore highly probably that, at some time, an issue in relation to the alteration of share capital will be encountered by the reader. Consequently, an awareness of the possible alterations that can be made to share capital is essential. Also essential is to be aware that before advising on any course of action in relation to such alterations, the Articles of Association must permit it, and the law prevailing in the reporting jurisdiction must be read in detail to establish exactly the correct procedures to be adopted.

Summary

Share capital has been covered in detail, and in particular the rather complex topics of capital reduction, redemption and reconstruction.

The reasons why a company might wish to reduce its share capital and the legal process that must be undergone before such action can be taken was considered; after which we looked at the concept of

capital maintenance and creditor protection, and how this affects companies' abilities to alter share capital and make distributions. Distributable profits were then defined, and non-distributable reserves introduced and explained in detail.

The purchase and redemption of shares by both public and private companies was illustrated, and it was explained that only private companies were permitted to purchase their shares out of capital. Finally, the chapter looked at how capital reserves could be put to use, and other forms of alteration of share capital, such as bonus issues and share splits.

The advanced section of this chapter now goes on to consider proposals for changes to company law, and how these changes could impact on alterations to share capital.

Section 3: Advanced Aspects

The topics covered in the previous section have been rather complex, and the mechanics themselves of effecting such actions as reducing share capital are themselves both cumbersome and complex, involving application to the court and the associated costs.

In 1999, the Company Law Review Steering Group (the Group) was appointed by the government to look into the possibilities of making changes to company law required for a competitive economy. A number of consultation documents were issued, one of which is on the formation of companies and the maintenance of their capital.

The Group made some important proposals for changes regarding the documents that companies should produce on their formation, and also regarding the question of their capital maintenance for the protection of their creditors.

The Companies Act 2006 incorporated many of the proposals.

6.15   Company formation

Prior to the Companies Act 2006 changes, when a company was formed there was a written document, the Memorandum and Articles of Association, which set out the powers of the company and was filed with the Registrar of Companies.

The Memorandum of Association describes and governs the relationship between the company and the outside world. The memorandum states the name of the company, the country in which the registered office is situated, the objectives of the company (i.e. activities the company may pursue), the authorised share capital, the nominal (par) value of the shares, a list of initial subscribers, and whether the liability of the members (i.e. shareholders) is limited.

The Articles of Association lay down the internal rules within which the directors run the company. The main items covered are:

(i)   the issue of shares, the rights attaching to each class of share, the consent required for the alteration of the rights of any class of shareholders, and any restrictions on the transfer of shares
(ii)   the procedure for board and general meetings, and for altering the authorised share capital
(iii)   the election and retirement of directors, their duties and their powers, including borrowing powers
(iv)   the declaration of dividends
(v)   the procedure for winding up the company.

The Companies Act 2006 has now replaced the Memorandum and Articles of Association with two different documents and made it easier for companies to alter some of the contents of these. The

Memorandum has been replaced with the 'Registration Form', which has broadly the same information but it is easier to change the contents; and the Articles with the 'Company Constitution', which again broadly resembles the previous document.

6.16   Capital maintenance

At present, any kind of shares issued by UK companies are required to have a nominal value. The Group proposed to allow companies to issue shares of no par value (NPV shares), i.e. shares without nominal values. This would affect the way a share is recorded and the way the permanent capital of a company is maintained. This proposal has not, however, been adopted by the Companies Act 2006.

6.17   Shares of no par value

It can be seen that the idea of a fixed par value for a share can be very misleading, particularly to non-accountants. The value for which a share may be traded on the open market may vary considerably from the par value and this can be very confusing.

The requirement to have a nominal value is a legal requirement and is contained within the Companies Act. Similarly, it is the Companies Act that requires that, where shares are issued at a premium (i.e. at an amount higher than their par value), the share premium is kept separate.

The main argument for retaining nominal values of shares is that the share capital can be determined and therefore can be maintained. The nominal value is, however, an arbitrary value that was attached to each share when the company was first formed. The issue of shares at a premium on a later date will increase the permanent capital at that date. It is only by looking at the two together (i.e. share capital and share premium), that the permanent capital can be determined. The argument put forward, therefore, that by having a nominal value the capital can be determined and maintained, is flawed; it can only be determined by looking at both the share capital *and* the share premium. Moreover, the only reason that the issue of shares at a premium is split between share capital and share premium is because of a legal requirement. The permanent capital could be determined and maintained, therefore, if there were only one entry for the entire receipt.

A second argument put forward for having a nominal value attached to shares is that dividends paid by a company can be based on the nominal value of its shares. This argument, too, has flaws. If a par value is kept to and the dividend based on this, then, over time, the dividend can look excessive, particularly in times of inflation.

BASIC

INTERMEDIATE

ADVANCED

✦ *Example*

Lido bought 100 ordinary shares 40 years ago for £100. The dividend paid on the shares was 5% and this was sufficient, 40 years ago, to purchase a certain amount of goods. Forty years later, let us assume that the goods that are to be purchased now cost 20 times as much as they did (i.e. 40 years ago they cost £5 and now they cost £100). In order to keep Lido's dividends at the same rate of purchasing power, he would need a dividend of 100%. That is:

$$\frac{£100}{100 \text{ shares}} \times 100 = 100\%$$

Note that if the dividend was based on the current value it would probably be at a more realistic level – indeed, probably very close to the average return for the particular industry. It is just that the very misleading convention in accounting in the UK of calculating dividends in relation to the nominal amount of share capital gives this dramatic result.

The current report by the Group backs up study findings in 1952, which recommended the introduction of shares of no par value. Unfortunately, the then government failed to legislate for it. It is still not possible for the UK government to allow companies to issue NPV shares as the Directive requires public companies to have nominal values for their shares. The Group has expressed its wish for the Directive to be changed so that all companies are allowed to issue NPV shares. Until then, it is proposed that the new Statute should retain the requirements for shares to have a nominal or par value.

6.18   Share capital: authorised, minimum and share issue

Previously, companies had to have an authorised share capital, which limited the maximum number of shares they could issue. In practice, this limit was set much higher than was ever required and, because it could be raised with shareholders' agreement, it served no useful purpose. The Act abolished the concept of authorised share capital, for both public and private companies for new companies from October 2008. Existing companies will, however, continue to be constrained by their authorised share capital, and will need to amend their Articles to abolish reference to authorised share capital if they want to allow the company to allot beyond that ceiling. The new rules instead require companies to deposit an initial statement of capital when incorporating, which will need to be updated when appropriate, such as when new shares are issued.

Currently, there is no requirement for private companies to have a minimum amount of share capital and no changes are proposed to this. There are no changes either to the minimum share capital of £50,000 required for public companies, although the Group does seek further consultation on this given that it is questionable whether this amount is adequate for creditor protection.

Shares will still be required to have a nominal value and, consequently, accounting for share issues will not change. Nominal values will continue to be credited to share capital account, and any excess of net receipt over this value to share premium account.

Simpler procedure for reducing share capital

The second section of this chapter explained that a company could reduce its share capital to:

- eliminate or reduce the part that has not been called up
- pay back that part which is in excess of its needs
- write off accumulated losses.

In all the above cases, prior to the passing of the Companies Act 2006, the court's consent was required to protect the interests of creditors.

Following implementation of the Companies Act 2006, private companies are now permitted to reduce their share capital by passing a special resolution but without the need for court approval.

Directors of all companies have to issue a formal solvency statement confirming that the company is solvent and will be able to pay its debts at all times within a year of the capital reduction. A director who makes a solvency statement without having reasonable grounds for the opinion expressed in it will be guilty of a criminal offence.

6.19   Repeal of restriction on assistance for acquisition of shares in private companies

The Companies Act 1985 prohibited private companies from giving financial assistance for the acquisition of their own shares unless certain conditions were satisfied. Under the Companies Act 2006 the prohibition has been wholly lifted for private companies but remains in place for public companies.

Implementation

The Companies Act 2006 was, after much publicity, passed by Parliament on 8 November 2006. It is a lengthy document, running to 1,300 sections. The aim of the Act is to consolidate most of the existing companies legislation and provide a focus on small businesses, using simplified language.

BASIC

INTERMEDIATE

ADVANCED

All parts of the Companies Act will be enforced by October 2009, however some aspects were implemented earlier. Provisions relating to electronic communication were, for instance, introduced in January 2007.

The government introduced these changes in an effort to make Britain an attractive place to set up and run a business, and to promote long-term investment. Time will tell whether the changes will have the desired effect.

Summary

Much of the legislation relating to share capital has been cumbersome and complex.

The Companies Act 2006 has been implemented to simplify many of the procedures that companies require to undertake in relation to company formations and subsequent alterations to share capital. The recognition by government that easing administrative burdens and providing flexibility to companies will help to promote long-term investment is welcomed, however the protection of creditors' rights must also be maintained. Nevertheless, many of the issues covered in this chapter have illustrated the complexities caused by the historic legislation and also, in relation to minimum share capital, where the requirements are decidedly inadequate and out of date. The next few years offer a true indication of the success or otherwise of the changes.

Chapter summary

Companies Act: share capital and reserves

- Share capital is recorded at nominal value with any excess being recorded as share premium.
- A distribution can only be made from distributable reserves.
- The permanent capital of a company is made up of its share capital plus non-distributable reserves.
- In order to protect creditors, the permanent capital of a company must be maintained.
- If a company reduces its share capital by purchasing or redeeming its shares, the redemption must be from distributable profits or the proceeds of a new issue.
- The nominal value of the shares purchased must be replaced by either:
    - the proceeds of a new issue, or
    - a transfer from distributable profits to capital redemption reserve.
- Where shares are purchased at a premium the normal rule is that the premium is debited to distributable profits.
    - An exception is available where there is:
        - a new issue, and
        - the shares being redeemed were originally issued at a premium.
    - In such cases the premium on the repurchase can be debited to the share premium account up to the lower of:
        - the premium on the original issue, and
        - the balance on the share premium account (including the premium on the new issue).
- Private companies are allowed to reduce permanent capital by the amount of the permissible capital payment (PCP).
- The permissible capital payment is calculated as follows:

Amount payable to repurchase shares	X
Less: distributable profits	(X)
Less: proceeds of new issue	(X)
PCP	X

- The amount of any treasury shares should be deducted from shareholders' funds.
- No gain or loss should be recognised in the profit and loss account on the purchase, sale, issue or cancellation of treasury shares.

Key terms for review

Definitions can be found in the glossary at the end of the book.

Preference shares	*Ordinary shares*
Limited liability company	*Distributable reserves*
Share capital	*Non-distributable reserves*
Reserves	*Permanent capital*
Nominal value	*Treasury shares*
Share premium	

Review questions

1. What are the advantages and disadvantages to a potential investor of investing in the following types of security:
   (a) ordinary shares
   (b) preference shares.
2. Explain the doctrine of capital maintenance.
3. Under what circumstances is a company permitted to reduce its capital?
4. Distinguish between profits available for distribution in private companies from those in public companies.
5. Outline the steps that should be followed in the event of a share purchase or share redemption by a public company.
6. What are the advantages to a private company of being permitted to buy back its own shares?
7. To what uses can a share premium account be put?
8. Explain what is meant by *share splits* and explain how they affect a company's share price.

 # Exercises

1. Level II

Rollside plc was incorporated on 15 March 2009 and issued 5,000,000 ordinary shares of 50p at par to raise capital to commence trading on 1 April 2009.

Authorised		£
5,000,000	ordinary shares at 50p each	2,500,000
Issued and fully paid		
4,100,000	ordinary shares of 50p each	2,050,000

During the year to 31 March 2010 the following occurred:

(i) in order to fund the construction of a new factory, in August 2009, 600,000 ordinary shares of 50p were each issued for £3.20 cash.

(ii) at a special general meeting the authorised share capital was increased by 800,000 shares

Required

(a) Prepare journal entries to record the initial issue of shares and the subsequent issue in August 2009.
(b) Prepare the disclosure note for share capital for inclusion in the 31 March 2010 financial statements, including comparatives.

2. Level II

Denside Ltd has the following summarised balance sheet:

	£000
Cash	20
Other net assets	320
	340
Share capital (400,000 ordinary shares of 25p)	100
Share premium	40
Profit & loss reserve	200
	340

The company is considering three possible changes to its capital structure:

(i)   issue for cash 50,000 additional ordinary shares at £1 per share, fully paid, or
(ii) make a bonus issue from profit and loss reserve of one ordinary share for every four previously held, or
(iii) make a 1-for-5 rights issue at £3 per share.

Required

(a)   Prepare journal entries to record each of the above transactions.
(b)   Show separately the impact of each change on the balance sheet of the company.

3.   Level II

Kenmac Ltd has decided to purchase shares with a nominal value of £110,000 (originally issued for £120,000) for £140,000. The purchase is to be funded out of distributable profits.

The balance sheet of Kenmac Ltd immediately prior to the purchase of the shares is as follows:

	£
Net assets	950,000
Share capital (£1 shares)	500,000
Share premium	250,000
Profit & loss reserve	200,000
	950,000

Required

(a)   Prepare journal entries to give effect to the above transaction.
(b)   Prepare the balance sheet of Kenmac Ltd immediately after the purchase.

4.   Level II

Timor Ltd makes a fresh issue of ordinary shares to finance the purchase of its £1 ordinary shares, as follows:

Shares issued (£1 shares)	
Nominal value	£75,000
Issue price	£150,000
Shares purchased	
Nominal value of shares	£150,000
Originally issued at a premium of	£7,000
Premium on redemption	£30,000

The balance sheet of Timor Ltd immediately before these transactions took place was as follows:

	£
Net assets	665,000
Share capital	450,000
Share premium (including the original	
premium on the shares to be redeemed)	35,000
Distributable profits	180,000
	£665,000

Required

(a)   Prepare journal entries to record the above transactions.

(b)   Prepare the balance sheet of Timor Ltd after the repurchase of its shares.

(c)   Comment on the permanent capital position of Timor Ltd after the repurchase of its shares.

5.   Level III

The shareholders of Ustraco Ltd, a private company, wish to buy back 250,000 shares with a nominal value of £250,000 from a retiring director at a premium of £100,000. The company makes a fresh issue of 50,000 ordinary shares of £1 for £125,000.

Before the transactions, the company's balance sheet was as follows:

	£
Net assets	1,150,000
Share capital (£1 shares)	500,000
Share premium (note 1)*	500,000
Profit and loss reserve	150,000
	£1,150,000

*Note 1: None of the share premium is attributable to the shares being redeemed.

Required

Calculate the permissible capital payment (PCP), the transfer to CRR (if any) and draft journal entries, and a balance sheet that incorporates the above transactions.

6.   Level III

Novaton plc purchased 5 million of its £1 ordinary shares for £6.40 each on 29 March 2009. The shares were held as treasury shares.

On 10 September 2009, Novaton sold 1.4 million of these shares at a price of £6.60 each.

The remaining treasury shares were sold at £6.33 on 13 October 2009.

Required

Prepare journal entries to record the above transactions.

7.   Level III

The abbreviated balance sheet of Netherfin plc, a listed company, at 31 March 2008, was as follows:

	£000
Net assets	25,000
Capital and reserves	
Share capital (25p ordinary)	2,000
Share premium	4,000
Revaluation reserve	2,500
Profit and loss reserve	16,500
	25,000

The retained profit for the year to 31 March 2009 was £240,000. During the year to 31 March 2009 the following transactions took place:

22 June 2008	Netherfin plc purchased 4 million of its ordinary shares at £3.20 each to be held as treasury shares
17 September 2008	Sold 1 million of the treasury shares for £3.10 each
1 March 2009	Sold 1.5 million of the treasury shares for £3.40 each

Required

(a) Prepare journal entries to record the above transactions.

(b) Prepare the capital and reserves section of the balance sheet as at 31 March 2009.

8. Level III

Cairnhall Ltd had the following balances at 31 March 2008.

	£000
Share capital (£1 shares)	10,000
Share premium	4,000
Capital redemption reserve	2,500
Revaluation reserve	1,500
Profit and loss reserve	6,000
	24,000

The following information is available.

1. The profit after tax of Cairnhall Ltd for the year to 31 March 2009 was £1,100,000.
2. Dividends of £400,000 and £300,000 were paid on 1 October 2008 and 18 March 2009, respectively.
3. Cairnhall Ltd revalues fixed assets but does not make transfer from revaluation reserve to profit and loss reserve in respect of excess depreciation. At 31 March 2008, depreciation on revalued assets was £120,000 higher than the depreciation on the historical cost amount. In the year to 31 March 2009, depreciation on the revalued amount was £50,000, and depreciation would have been £30,000 based on historic cost.
4. A revaluation at 31 March 2009 gave rise to a revaluation loss of £350,000. This was debited to the revaluation reserve as it related to assets that had previously been revalued upwards.
5. In March 2009, Cairnhall sold engineering equipment to a customer in China. In return, Cairnhall received electrical goods that it would use in its east European factories. As the value of the electrical goods exceeded the cost of the engineering equipment, £50,000 profit was included in Cairnhall's profits for the year.
6. On 30 June 2008, Cairnhall made a 1-for-10 bonus issue out of the profit and loss reserve.
7. At 31 March 2008 all the profits in the profit and loss reserve were distributable.

Required

(a) Calculate the distributable profits of Cairnhall Ltd as at 31 March 2009.

(b) Prepare an extract of the capital and reserves section of the balance sheet of Cairnhall Ltd as at 31 March 2009.

Further reading

Companies Act 2005

Companies Act 2006

IAS 1 *Presentation of Financial Statements*. IASB, revised 2004

IAS 1 *Presentation of Financial Statements*. IASB, revised 2007

Liabilities

Introduction

Liabilities represent claims against the assets of a business. This chapter considers the definition of liabilities and the importance of the correct classification of the various types of liabilities that may exist.

Section 1: Basic Principles

A liability is an amount owing at the balance sheet date which a business is under an obligation to pay. There will usually be an invoice or other contractual document stating the liability. Monies owing for stock, goods or other assets that have been received by the business at the balance sheet date are liabilities. A bank overdraft (i.e. money owing to the bank because the account has usually, by prior arrangement, been overdrawn), is a liability; the outstanding amount of a loan to the business is a liability. These liabilities all arise because some benefit, whether in the form of goods, services or indeed money, has been received by the business, but has not yet been fully paid for. Furthermore, whoever supplied the benefit in the first instance has a claim on the assets of the business equal to the amount outstanding. A key characteristic of a liability is that it is an amount owing that can be determined with substantial accuracy.

Liabilities can be classified according to the period for which they are likely to be outstanding; current liabilities are those payable within a short period – usually within the next accounting period – likely to be one year; long-term liabilities are those payable in the future but not within the next accounting period (i.e. after one year).

7.1 The accounting issue involved

The prudence (conservatism) principle refers to the accounting practice of recognising all possible losses but not anticipating possible gains. Adoption of this principle will tend to lead to an understatement of profits, with an understatement of asset values and with no corresponding understatement of liabilities.

Sometimes, however, the amount of an obligation may not be certain. When a known liability exists but cannot be determined with substantial accuracy, a provision may be made to account for the best estimate of the amount in order to adhere to the prudence principle. A provision is an amount recognised in a set of financial statements for future expenditure that is certain or likely to be incurred but for which there is uncertainty about the amount that will be paid and/or when it will be paid. A provision is an amount written off by way of providing for depreciation, renewals or diminution in value of assets; or retained by way of providing for any known liability of which the amount cannot be determined with substantial accuracy (e.g. doubtful debts).

The difference between a provision and a liability often depends upon what is meant by substantial accuracy. The amount owing for electricity at the balance sheet date would normally be known with precision – this would clearly be a liability; legal charges for a court case that has been heard but for which the lawyers have not yet submitted their bill, would be a provision.

Occasionally, it may be the case that an obligation may exist only if some future event happens, i.e. neither the existence nor the amount of the obligation is known with certainty at the balance sheet date. Such obligations are known as contingent liabilities. The accounting treatment of such contingent liabilities will be covered in Section 2 of this chapter.

Progress Point 7.1

Explain the difference between a liability and a provision.

Solution

A liability is an amount owing, the timing and amount of which can be determined with substantial accuracy. A provision is a liability of uncertain timing or amount.

Summary

Liabilities represent claims on the assets of a business. Liabilities may be exact amounts in the case of trade payables as there is likely to be a legal document such as an invoice that will detail the amount outstanding. In the case of contingent liabilities they may also be extremely difficult to determine and to quantify.

Section 2: Intermediate Issues

In the introductory section to this chapter a liability was defined as being 'an amount owing at the balance sheet date which a business is under an obligation to pay'.

In this section the IAS Framework definition of liabilities is considered, together with the detailed reporting requirements of the IASs in relation to liabilities.

7.2 Definition: liabilities

A liability is defined as: (Framework, para. 49b):

> a *present obligation* of the entity arising from *past events*, the settlement of which is expected to result in an *outflow* from the entity of resources embodying *economic benefits*.

This definition is deliberately wide so that it can encompass all possible liabilities. As with the Framework definition of an asset, however, in order to understand this definition fully, each phrase must be considered separately.

(i) **Present obligation**

A necessary condition for a liability is that the entity should have a present obligation. An obligation is a duty or responsibility to act or perform in a certain way. A legal obligation is evidence that a liability exists (e.g. under the law of contract there will be a binding obligation to make payment for goods and services).

The duty or responsibility may arise, however, from expectation of normal business practice (i.e. a constructive obligation). An example of a constructive obligation is to extend the benefits of a warranty for some period beyond the contractual warranty period, because this is an established practice (para. 60).

Note, however, that a present obligation is not the same as a future commitment. An entity may have a commitment to purchase an asset in the future at an agreed price. This does not, however, involve a net outflow of resources. The commitment itself does not give rise to a liability; it is only when the purchase has actually taken place and title has passed to the entity that the obligation to pay for it arises.

(ii) **Past events**

A liability does not arise from a decision to buy goods and services. While it could be argued that the decision is an event creating an obligation, the verification of such an event is extremely difficult, and likely to be subjective.

Accounting relies on objective measurement and, because most liabilities are related to a transaction, there tends to be documentary evidence that a transaction has taken place, e.g. taking delivery of a non-current asset, borrowing funds from a lender.

It may be the case that the existence of a liability is in doubt at the balance sheet date. In such cases, subsequent events may help to confirm the position.

For example, when a company offers to repair goods under a warranty agreement, the liability exists from the time that the warranty is offered. Once a pattern of warranty repairs and costs is established, a company will be able to make an allowance for such warranty repairs. Until that pattern is established, however, the company will have to make an estimate of the liability – perhaps based on experience from other product lines. Where such an estimate is made, this is known as a provision. The Framework requires that, where a provision involves a present obligation and satisfies the rest of the definition of a liability, it is a liability even if the amount has to be estimated.

BASIC

INTERMEDIATE

ADVANCED

(iii) Outflow of economic benefits

Cash is the usual economic benefit that is used in the settlement of obligations. There are other ways, however, in which a liability may be settled or discharged. For example, instead of a transfer of cash, there may be the transfer of a non-current asset or even the 'transfer' of a resource such as labour to settle an obligation. It is also possible to have a liability settled by replacement with another obligation – for example, a bank overdraft that is replaced by a bank term loan.

As was noted earlier, the definition of a liability has been made deliberately wide. By being so, it goes a long way to preventing liabilities from being 'hidden', perhaps by way of carefully worded agreements.

Table 7.1 gives examples of liabilities commonly found in company balance sheets, and illustrates the test aspects of the definition being satisfied.

Liability	Obligation	Transfer of economic benefits	Past events
1. Bank overdraft	To repay the overdraft on demand	Cash	Overdrawing the bank account
2. Trade payables	To pay the suppliers for the goods or services received	Cash	Taking delivery of the goods or services and receiving the supplier's invoice
3. Taxation payable	To pay the cash to the tax authorities	Cash	The making of the profits giving rise to the tax payable
4. Bank loan (term loan)	To repay the loan by a due date – usually after one year	Cash	Receiving the borrowed funds
5. Debenture loan (long-term loans)	To repay the loan by a due date – usually after one year	Cash	Receiving the borrowed funds

Table 7.1 Liabilities commonly found on balance sheets

It is conventional to classify liabilities into current liabilities and non-current (or long-term) liabilities.

A **current liability** is a liability that satisfies any of the following criteria:

■   it is expected to be settled in the entity's normal operating cycle
■   it is held primarily for the purpose of being traded
■   it is due to be settled within one year of the balance sheet date.

A **non-current (or long-term) liability** is any liability that does not meet the definition of a current liability. In Table 7.1, items 1 to 3 would be classified as current liabilities, and items 4 and 5 would be classified as non-current liabilities because they will remain due by the business for longer than one year.

Recognition of liabilities

Although an item may have passed the definition tests of a liability, this in itself does not qualify the item as a liability for inclusion in the balance sheet. The item still requires to pass **recognition** tests, however, the prudence concept requiring **provision** for anticipated future losses in full usually means that it is more difficult for a liability not to be disclosed on the balance sheet.

A liability is recognised in the balance sheet when:

- it is probable that an outflow of resources embodying economic benefits will result from the settlement of a present obligation, and
- the amount at which the settlement will take place can be measured reliably.

In order to satisfy the first criterion for recognition, an entity is likely to have strong evidence to prove the existence of a liability. For current liabilities, such as trade payables, there will be a payment made soon after the balance sheet date and a past record of making such payments on time (e.g. within 30 days). In the case of non-current (long-term) liabilities such as a bank loan, there will be an agreement confirming the terms and dates of repayment.

The second criterion is usually satisfied by the existence of the document giving rise to the obligation in the first instance. For example, if goods or services have been supplied there will be an invoice from the supplier showing the amount due; in the case of a bank loan, there will be a bank statement showing the amount outstanding.

Non-recognition

It is worth pausing at this point to consider the types of item that pass the definition tests of liabilities but fail the recognition tests. In the main, these items fail because there is insufficient documentary evidence to allow confirmation of their existence or to quantify the measurable amount.

Examples of liabilities that pass the definition test but fail the recognition tests are:

- a commitment to purchase non-current assets next year (but not a legally binding contract)
- a remote, but potential, liability for a defective product, where no court action has yet commenced
- a guarantee given to support the bank overdraft of another company, where there is very little likelihood of being called upon to meet the guarantee.

The prudence concept requiring the provision for all anticipated future losses means that although an item may not be recognised as a liability, it may well be disclosed in a note to the accounts. Recognition means reporting an item by means of words and amounts within the main financial statements in such a way that the item is included in the arithmetic totals. In the case of non-recognised liabilities, these are normally disclosed in a note to the accounts under the heading of contingent liabilities.

The above list of non-recognised liabilities all have some degree of uncertainty attached to them and, as a result, fail one or both of the recognition tests.

A commitment to purchase is not legally binding and there may not be an outflow of resources; the claim based on a product defect may go no further (i.e. there may not be court action and the amounts involved are uncertain); in the case of the guarantee, the facts as given would suggest that an outflow of resources is unlikely. These examples are designed to illustrate the accounting issue involved (i.e. recognition or disclosure – or indeed non-recognition and non-disclosure). In practice, the classification of items may not always be as clear cut and a great deal of subjectivity may be required.

7.3 IAS 37 *Provisions, Contingent Liabilities and Contingent Assets*

Objective

The objective of IAS 37 is to ensure that appropriate recognition criteria and measurement bases are applied to provisions, contingent liabilities and contingent assets, and that sufficient information is disclosed in the notes to the financial statements to enable users to understand their nature, timing and amount.

Traditional book-keeping methods tend to follow an objective, transaction-based system for recording financial data. Once accumulated, this data is then classified between revenue and capital following rules laid down within the accounting conventions, and then reported to users via the income statement and balance sheet.

Unfortunately, even the most sophisticated accounting systems are transaction based and this means that judgements still have to be made – not only in the classification of items whose existence at the balance sheet date is certain – but, in addition, of items whose existence at the balance sheet date is uncertain. Furthermore, the outcomes of those uncertain events themselves often require to be considered.

Company balance sheets are being used more and more by investors and lenders to determine the riskiness of their investments and, consequently, a greater level of information is being demanded than simply a summary of balances, many of them residual, at the balance sheet date.

Given the importance of the balance sheet in the decision-making process, it is essential that safeguards are in place to prevent presenting information in such a way as might mislead or misrepresent.

The key principle established by IAS 37 is that a provision should be recognised only when there is a liability (i.e. a present obligation arising from past events). Furthermore, the standard aims to ensure that only genuine obligations are dealt with in the financial statements, recognising that the accounting or not for such conditions can have a marked effect on both the balance sheet and income statement of an enterprise. In particular it targets 'big bath' provisions, which companies had creatively used in the past to influence future profits. 'Big bath' accounting is covered in more detail later in this chapter (Section 7.9).

Scope

IAS 37 is to be applied to all enterprises when accounting for provisions, contingent liabilities and contingent assets, except those arising from:

- non-onerous executory contracts (see below)
- items covered by another IAS (e.g. IAS 11 *Construction Contracts*, IAS 12 *Income Taxes*, IAS 17 *Leases* and IAS 19 *Employee Benefits*).

Non-onerous executory contracts

A non-onerous executory contract is a contract where neither party has performed any of its obligations or both parties have performed obligations to an equal amount. Such contracts generally cover delivery of future services. For example:

- electricity, gas, rates
- purchase orders.

Key definitions

IAS 37 defines a provision as: 'a liability of uncertain timing or amount'.

Provisions are a sub-class of liabilities. The Framework defines liabilities as: 'obligations of an entity arising from past events, the settlement of which is expected to result in an outflow of resources embodying economic benefits'.

It is clear, therefore, that intention without an obligation is insufficient to justify the creation of a provision.

Provisions could be made for a variety of items, including:

- reorganisation costs
- warranties
- environmental costs
- major refits/refurbishments

- decommissioning costs
- legal cases against the company
- deferred tax
- losses on contracts.

It should be noted that certain 'provisions' are not covered by IAS 37. It is common practice for the word 'provision' to be applied to:

- provision for depreciation
- provision for bad debt
- provision for impairment.

In these cases, the word provision does not mean 'a liability of uncertain timing or amount'; instead it refers to adjusting the carrying amount of the asset.

Uncertainty is a key feature of a provision. IAS 37 identifies four types of liabilities, as described below.

1   *Trade creditors*: liabilities to pay for goods or services that have been received or supplied, and have been invoiced or formally agreed with the supplier (i.e. there is very little uncertainty).
2   *Accruals*: liabilities to pay for goods or services that have been received or supplied but have not been paid, invoiced or formally agreed with the supplier. Although it may be necessary to estimate the amount or timing of an accrual (e.g. telephone bill), the uncertainty is generally much less than for provisions. Accruals are often reported as part of trade and other creditors, while provisions are reported separately.
3   *Provisions*: liabilities because they are present obligations and it is probable that an outflow of resources embodying economic benefits will be required to settle the obligation.
4   *Contingent liabilities*: These are not recognised as liabilities because they are either:
    (a)   possible obligations, as it is yet to be confirmed whether the entity has an obligation that could lead to the transfer of economic benefits, or
    (b)   present obligations that do not meet the recognition criteria of IAS 37 because, either it is not probable that a transfer of economic resources will be required, or a sufficiently reliable estimate of the amount of the obligation cannot be made.

It is worth pausing at this stage to consider the differences between a provision and a contingent liability.

A *provision* requires:

- a present obligation from past events
- a probable outflow of economic benefits
- an evaluation of timing and amount.

A *contingent liability* occurs when one or more of the requirements for a provision are not met. That is:

- a possible obligation exists, and/or
- an outflow of economic benefits is not probable, and/or
- a reliable estimate of outflow cannot be made.

IAS 37 provides in an appendix a useful decision tree to determine whether a provision or contingent liability exists in a given set of circumstances.

BASIC

INTERMEDIATE

ADVANCED

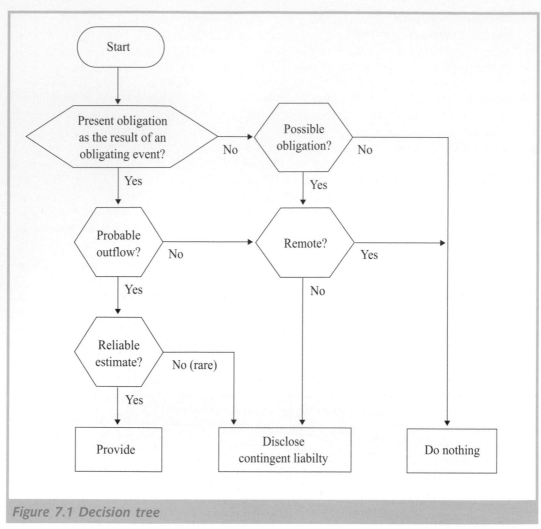

Figure 7.1 Decision tree

Contingent asset

A contingent asset is:

- a possible asset that arises from past events, and
- whose existence will be confirmed only by the occurrence or non-occurrence of one or more uncertain future events not wholly within the control of the enterprise.

Recognition of a provision

As with assets and liabilities, a provision will require to pass recognition tests before it can be accrued in the financial statements.

An enterprise must recognise a provision if, and only if:

- a present obligation (legal or constructive) has arisen as a result of a past event (the obligating event)
- payment is probable (more likely than not), and
- the amount can be estimated reliably.

An obligating event is an event that creates a legal or *constructive obligation* and, therefore, results in an enterprise having no realistic alternative but to settle the obligation. A *constructive obligation* arises if past practice creates valid expectation on the part of a third party – for example, a retail store that has a long-standing policy of allowing customers to return merchandise within, say, a 30-day period.

A possible obligation (i.e. a contingent liability), is disclosed but not accrued. However, disclosure is not required if payment is remote.

In rare cases, for example in a lawsuit, it may not be clear whether an enterprise has a present obligation. In such cases, a past event is deemed to give rise to a present obligation if, taking account of all available evidence, it is more likely than not that a present obligation exists at the balance sheet date. A provision should be recognised for that present obligation if the other recognition criteria described above are met. If it is more likely than not that no present obligation exists, the enterprise should disclose a contingent liability, unless the possibility of an outflow of resources is remote.

A contingent asset is not recognised in the accounts but it is disclosed if the inflow of economic benefits is probable.

A contingent liability is not recognised in the financial statements but is disclosed as follows:

- a brief description of the nature
- an estimate of its financial effect
- an indication of the uncertainties relating to the amount or timing of outflow
- the possibility of any reimbursement.

Progress Point 7.2

Valentino Ltd has a number of retail clothes outlets. Explain how the following situations will be viewed under IAS 37 in the preparation of the accounts to 31 December 2009.

(a) Goods were delivered to the Knightsbridge branch in December 2009. No invoice has been received as yet, but there are no disputes surrounding the delivery.

(b) A competitor is claiming that Valentino Ltd infringed its copyright on a garment design, and has raised a court action. Valentino's lawyers believe it is probable that the competitor will not be successful in its court action.

(c) Although under no statutory obligation to do so, Valentino Ltd has a long-established policy of refunding customers for goods they return within one month of purchase, irrespective of whether they are faulty or not.

(d) The directors decided in October 2009 to close a branch of the company in Luton. The decision was minuted with closure due to take place following the summer season sales in August 2010. No official announcement has been made. Redundancy costs are estimated to be £750,000.

Solution

(a) Uninvoiced goods: there is no dispute with the delivery of the goods or the amount. It is simply that the invoice has yet to be received by Valentino Ltd. This should be treated as an accrual as there is little uncertainty as to the event.

(b) Competitor court action: Valentino's lawyers believe that it is probable that the competitor's court action will fail. There is therefore no present obligation and consequently no creditor, accrual or provision. However, Valentino's lawyers cannot be certain that the court action will fail and therefore there is a possible obligation that should be disclosed as a contingent liability.

(c) Refund policy: Valentino's established pattern of past practice gives rise to a constructive obligation. Although not a legal obligation, shoppers will have a valid expectation that Valentino will accept responsibility for refunding returned goods. Because of the uncertainty surrounding the amount and timing of refunds for the return of goods bought prior to 31 December 2009, a provision is required rather than an accrual or trade creditor.

(d) Closure of Luton branch: although the branch is scheduled for closure and the directors' intentions have been minuted prior to the year end, there is no liability as the company has neither a legal nor constructive obligation. No announcement has been made to affected parties and therefore no valid expectation has been created in those parties (e.g. employees, suppliers). Furthermore, the directors could, if they wished, reverse their decision. There has been no obligating event and therefore no provision, or any other form of liability, should be created.

Probable transfer of economic benefits

The accounting treatment of events depends upon their probability. IAS 37 defines *probable* as meaning that the event is more likely than not to occur. When it is not probable, the company discloses a contingent liability unless the possibility is remote.

The accounting treatment is, therefore, dependent on how the preparer of the accounts defines the words probable, possible and remote – ultimately, a matter of personal degree.

The following examples will help to further illustrate the above. All information is at the enterprise's year end of 31 December 2009 unless otherwise stated.

 ### *Example 1*

An airline enterprise is required by law to overhaul its aircraft every three years. The aircraft was purchased a year ago. At the balance sheet date there is no obligation to overhaul the aircraft – indeed the enterprise could sell the aircraft to avoid the overhaul cost. This is neither a provision nor a contingent liability.

 ### *Example 2*

An enterprise has guaranteed a loan taken out by one of its subsidiaries. The subsidiary has placed itself in liquidation and it appears that it has insufficient funds to repay the loan. The enterprise has an obligation to fulfil the guarantee and therefore it is probable that there will be an outflow of funds. A provision should be recognised in the accounts.

 ### *Example 3*

The enterprise catered for a wedding reception in September 2009. Following the wedding, several people have died of food poisoning. The enterprise is disputing liability and its lawyers have advised that it is probable that it will not be found liable. There is no obligation and therefore no provision should be made. It is a contingent liability, which should be disclosed in the accounts unless the probability of any transfer of funds is remote.

Example 4

The enterprise has not received its electricity bill for the power supplied in the last quarter of the year. This is an accrual as there is very little uncertainty in respect of the timing on the amount due.

Progress Point 7.3

Andox Ltd, a supplier of medical equipment, is preparing its accounts for the year to 31 December 2009. The following information is available.

(a) Andox gives a one-year warranty on one of its products. Experience shows that these products are extremely reliable and none has ever been returned within the warranty period.

(b) Andox is defending a court case brought against it by a government department, claiming inadequate labelling on one of its products. The court upheld the department's complaint and, although not fining the company, instructed Andox Ltd to amend the labelling on all products produced from 1 December 2009. This led to the scrapping of stocks of labels, which cost £150,000.

Required

Explain whether a provision should be created for the above events.

Solution

(a) Warranty: although there is a present obligation arising from the issue of the warranty, it is not probable that an outflow of resources will take place. No provision should be recognised.

(b) Court ruling: there is a present obligation to comply with the court ruling. As there is no fine there is no outflow of resources. The loss of £150,000, although arising from the court case, is not an outflow of resources – it is a stock write-off. No provision should be created.

Measurement of Provisions

So far the recognition of a provision or contingent liability has been considered. In order for a provision to be recognised in the financial statements, there must also be a reliable estimate made of the amount.

The amount recognised as a provision should be the best estimate of the expenditure required to settle the present obligation at the balance sheet date (i.e. the amount that an enterprise would rationally pay to settle the obligation at the balance sheet or to transfer it to a third party). This means that:

■ provisions for one-off events (restructuring, environmental clean-up, settlement of a lawsuit) are measured at the most likely amount

■ provisions for large populations of events (warranties, customer refunds) are measured at a probability-weighted expected value

■ both measurements are at discounted present value using a pre-tax discount rate that reflects the current market assessments of the time value of money and the risks specific to the liability.

In reaching its best estimate, the enterprise should take into account the risks and uncertainties that surround the underlying events. Expected cash outflows should be discounted to their present values, where the effect of the time value of money is material.

If some or all the expenditure required to settle a provision is expected to be reimbursed by another party, the reimbursement should be recognised as a reduction of the required provision when, and only when, it is virtually certain that reimbursement will be received if the enterprise settles the obligation. The amount recognised should not exceed the amount of the provision. The reimbursement should be treated as a separate asset. An example of this would be where a company has insurance cover relating to an obligation (e.g. to cover legal costs). In the income statement the expense relating to a provision may be presented net of the amount recognised for a reimbursement.

Some obligations will not involve an outflow of resources – for example, a warranty may be given on a company's products but if no products develop any defects then no outflow of resources will occur; a court case may result in a company having to issue an apology but not to make any payments to the wronged party.

Other measurement issues

- Future events that may affect the amount required to settle an obligation should be reflected in the amount of a provision where there is sufficient objective evidence that they will occur. For example, new technology may reduce the costs of decommissioning major assets. The standard permits reasonable expectations of technically qualified observers as to the impact of new or better-used technology, but not the assumption that a completely new technology will be developed in the future that will reduce costs. Similarly, changes in legislation should not be anticipated unless there is sufficient objective evidence that the legislation is virtually certain to be enacted.
- Gains from the expected disposal of assets should not be taken into account when measuring a provision as this would be anticipating a gain.
- Provisions should be reviewed at each balance sheet date and eliminated if no longer required.

The following examples will help to illustrate the above.

 ## *Example 1*

A company has an obligation to pay £4m due to a past event to clean up a waste site. It is possible that technological developments could decrease this cost. These developments are nearing completion and should decrease the cost to £3m. There is also the possibility to reduce this cost further due to new research findings, however these research findings are not at a sufficiently advanced stage to reliably measure their effects.

At what amount should the provision for clean-up costs be shown in the accounts?

Given that the technological developments are near completion, the provision should be shown at £3m. The other research is too uncertain at this stage to estimate any further reductions in costs.

 ## *Example 2*

Goods are sold by a company under warranty. Previous claims experience shows that 75% of goods sold will have no defects, 20% will have minor defects and 5% major defects. The cost of rectifying the defects in all goods sold are as follows:

- £8m for minor defects
- £12m for major defects.

The probability-weighted expected value of the provision to be recorded in the financial statements of the company at the balance sheet date is:

$$75\% \times £0 + 20\% \times £8m + 5\% \times £12m = £2.2m$$

 ## *Example 3*

A company is facing a legal claim for £8m. The lawyers estimate that there is a 40% chance of successfully defending the claim. At what value should this provision be shown in the accounts?

It is tempting to apply the probability percentage against the claim and accrue 40% × £8m. Note, however, that if the claim against the company is successful it will have to pay £8m. The provision, therefore, requires to be based upon the most likely outcome. As the most likely outcome (i.e. 60%) is for the claim to be paid then the best estimate of the provision required is £8m.

✺ *Example 4*

A company has undertaken to replace under warranty a generator on an oil rig. The generator costs £1.0m to replace and six of these generators are used on the oil rig. Experience shows that there is a 45% chance of one generator failing, a 30% chance of two failing and a 25% chance of three failures. It has never been known for more than three to fail. What is the value of the provision that should be shown in the accounts of the company?

Again, it is tempting to base the provision on the most likely outcome (i.e. the costs of one failure), as this is the most likely outcome at 45% occurrence. The probability that more than one failure would occur is 55% (30% + 25%). Based on this, then, the best estimate is £2m (i.e. two failures). Note that if the probabilities had been 25% one failure, 35% two and 40% three, then the best estimate would still be £2m, two failures. This is because there is only a 40% chance of three failures and a 60% chance of fewer than three. Where a single obligation is being considered, the individual most likely outcome may be the best estimate of the liability (para. 40). Where, however, there are significant chances that the outcome will be lower or higher than the most likely outcome, these should be taken into account in making the best estimate.

✺ *Example 5*

Prohair Suppliers Ltd is being sued over the supply of a faulty hairdryer that injured a customer. The company's solicitors believe that the company will lose the case and have to meet the claimant's legal costs. There is uncertainty, however, as to the damages that will be awarded against the company. The company's solicitors estimate that there is a 60% chance that the damages will be at most £100,000, but a 30% chance they will be £150,000 and a 10% chance they will be £175,000. The legal costs of the claimant are estimated at £50,000.

Although the most likely payment is £100,000, there are significant (40%) chances that it will be more.

The provision in this instance should be calculated as follows:

Damages	£
60% x £100,000	60,000
30% x £150,000	45,000
10% x £175,000	17,500
	122,500
Legal costs	50,000
Total provision required	£172,500

Note that the full amount of the legal costs should be provided as the solicitors believe the company will lose the case and thus will have to meet the claimant's legal costs.

The risks and uncertainties surrounding the event in question should be taken into account in reaching the best estimate of a provision. This does not mean that an overly prudent view should be taken, but care should be exercised to ensure that liabilities are not understated.

Provisions are measured before the effect of any tax consequences. The tax effect will be shown in accordance with IAS 12 *Income Taxes* (see Chapter 8).

BASIC

INTERMEDIATE

ADVANCED

Progress Point 7.4

Fraselectric sells 10,000 washing machines each year, offering a one-year warranty. Past experience shows that 500 machines will require repair.

In addition, it sells two models of television: Standard and Deluxe. Sales for the year to 31 December 2009 were as follows:

	Sets	Sales price per set
		£
Standard	18,000	180
Deluxe	9,000	210

Engineers estimate that 5% of the Standard and 4% of the Deluxe sets sold will require repair within one year of sale. An additional 5% of the Deluxe sets will require to be repaired in the second year after sale. The Standard sets come with a one-year warranty, whereas the Deluxe sets have a two-year warranty. The average cost of repair is 20% of sales price. During 2009 the company spent £30,000 on warranty repairs of sets sold in the year.

Required

(i) Explain whether a provision should be recognised for washing machine repairs.
(ii) Calculate the provision for television warranties required at 31 December 2009 for sales made in that year.

Solution

(i) In the case of the washing machines, the chance of an individual machine requiring repair is 5% (i.e. 500/10,000). Nevertheless it is reasonable to expect that around 500 of the machines sold will require repair. This should be used as the basis for the provision.
(ii) The provision is calculated as follows:

Standard	18,000 x 5% x £180 x 20%	=	32,400
Deluxe	9,000 x (4% + 5%) x £210 x 20%	=	34,020
			66,420
Less: paid in year			30,000
Provision required at year end			£36,420

Accounting for provisions

While the recognition and measurement of provisions can be complex, fortunately the actual accounting entries to create and utilise a provision are straightforward. A reorganisation provision of £250,000 created in the 2009 accounts of a company is used to illustrate the entries.

Creation of a provision

Dr	Income statement	£250,000	
	Cr Provision for reorganisation		£250,000
Being provision for reorganisation.			

Most provisions are created by charging the income statement with the expense while in the balance sheet the item will appear under either non-current or current liabilities depending on when the provision is payable.

Note that it will not always be the case that the debit entry will be an expense. Sometimes a provision may form part of the cost of an asset. IAS 37 cites the example of the obligation for environmental clean-up when a new mine is opened or an offshore oil rig is installed (IAS 37, Example 3).

Utilisation of a provision

As the expenditure in relation to a provision is incurred, it is debited directly to the provision that has been set up.

Continuing with the above example, assume that £120,000 was spent on reorganisation in 2009.

The £120,000 should be charged to the provision as follows:

Dr Provision for reorganisation	£120,000	
Cr Bank		£120,000
Being utilisation of provision.		

If the cost of the reorganisation has been charged to the income statement, £120,000 should be released from the provision and credited to the income statement as follows:

Dr Provision for reorganisation	£120,000	
Cr Income statement		£120,000
Being release from provision.		

The effect being to cancel out the original charge to the income statement.

Review of a provision

The provision should be reviewed at the end of each year to see whether it should be reduced or increased by crediting or debiting the income statement.

Continuing with the above example, assume that the reorganisation was complete and that the remaining £130,000 was no longer required. The balance on the provision account should be transferred back to the income statement as follows:

Dr Provision for reorganisation	£130,000	
Cr Income statement		£130,000
Being writing back of provision.		

Discounting

IAS 37 (para. 45) requires that where the effect of the time value of money is material, the provision should be discounted to its present value. This is consistent with the balance sheet approach in that it recognises what it would cost to settle the provision now. Provisions of equal monetary amount are more onerous the nearer they are to settlement.

Note that discounting is not optional. IAS 37 requires discounting if the effect is material.

The discount rate used should be a pre-tax rate that reflects current market assessments of the time value of money and the risks specific to the liability.

The unwinding of the discount is normally treated as an interest cost in the income statement.

⚙ *Example*

At 31 December 2007 a company involved in the manufacture of concrete products, estimates that the cost of cleaning up a production site will be £10m in ten years' time. The risk adjusted discount rate is 5%.

Required

Calculate the provision in the balance sheets at 31 December 2007, 2008 and 2009 and the entries in the income statement for 2008 and 2009.

Solution

	£
31 December 2007	
Balance sheet (£10,000,000/(1.05)10)	6,139,133
31 December 2008	
Balance sheet (£10,000,000/(1.05)9)	6,446,089
Income statement (6,446,089 – 6,139,133)	306,956
31 December 2009	
Balance sheet (£10,000,000/(1.05)8)	6,768,394
Income statement (6,768,394 – 6,446,089)	322,305

The income statement charge is a finance charge and represents the cost of not settling the obligation at the outset. A larger provision is required as the discount unwinds due to the cash outflow getting closer. The journal for 2008 would be:

Dr Income statement (finance costs)	£306,956	
Cr Provision		£306,956
Being increase in provision.		

Care should be taken where the estimate of the final obligation is changed for a provision that is discounted.

Where this happens:

(i)   calculate the unwinding of the discount up to the year end and add to the opening provision; this is an interest expense

(ii) calculate the present value of the provision based on the new estimate

(iii) the difference between (i) and (ii) is a movement in the provision and is not a finance item. Normally it would be charged to the income statement as an increase in provision.

Specific examples in IAS 37

Although a general standard, IAS 37 identifies three specific applications of recognition and measurement of provisions within the standard itself, as discussed below.

Future operating losses

Future operating losses do not meet the definition of a liability as there is no present obligation and therefore no liability. The loss will be recognised as it occurs. An expectation of future losses is an indication, however, of impairment and an entity should therefore test for this under IAS 36 *Impairment of Assets*.

Onerous contracts

An onerous contract is one in which the unavoidable costs of meeting the obligations under the contract exceed the economic benefits expected to be received under it. Onerous contracts will normally be for the long-term supply of goods of services. For example, an enterprise leases a factory under an operating lease. During the year it moves production to a new factory but the old factory lease cannot be cancelled and it cannot be relet. There is, therefore, a present obligation and a provision is required of the unavoidable lease payments in total.

If the contract can be cancelled without having to pay compensation, it is not onerous. IAS 37 requires that the present obligation under the onerous contract should be recognised and measured as a provision. The unavoidable costs reflect the net cost of exiting from the contract, i.e. the lower (i) of the cost of fulfilling the terms of the contract and (ii) any compensation or penalties arising from failure to fulfil it.

Note that the contract has to be loss making. A contract that is merely uneconomic in terms of earning a below-average expected rate of return is not classified as onerous.

 ## Example

Esdaile Engineering Ltd, a manufacturer of specialist metal castings, prepares accounts annually to 31 December. At 31 December 2009, it had four contracts, W, X, Y and Z, which it believes to be onerous.

Contract W is for the future purchase of 1,000 tons of zinc, which were to be used in bronze manufacture. Esdaile Engineering Ltd sold off its bronze manufacturing business but was unable to assign this future contract. The contract price is £350 per tonne and at the year end the spot price is £280 per tonne. The terms of the contract specify that a cancellation fee of £100,000 is payable.

Contract X is for the purchase of 200 tonnes of titanium at a price of £1,500 per tonne. A change in processing technology means that Esdaile Engineering Ltd requires only 50 tonnes. The supplier is prepared to accept cancellation of the remainder of the contracted amount for a payment of £25,000. The year-end spot price is £1,300 per tonne.

Contract Y is for the purchase of 2,000 tonnes of special steel ingots at a cost of £600 per tonne. The company intends to use the ingots in manufacture where the processing costs will be £200 per tonne and the final product will be sold for £720 per tonne. Due to the high quality of these ingots there is minimal wastage in the manufacturing process. The spot price on 31 December 2009 is £500 per tonne.

Contract Z is for the purchase of aluminium at a price of £25 per kg. The spot price of aluminium at 31 December 2009 is £21 per kg. The metal is to be used in the manufacture of blades for wind turbines. As a result of the fall in the price of aluminium, the selling price of these blades has fallen to £400. Costs of manufacture amount to £240 per blade. Each blade uses 5 kg of aluminium.

Required
How should the contracts be dealt with in the accounts of Esdaile Engineering Ltd for the year to 31 December 2009?

Solution

Contract W

Esdaile is unable to assign this contract to purchase zinc. Esdaile should, however, be able to sell zinc at the spot rate ruling on the date it requires to purchase it. As the spot rate is lower, the contract will be loss making and classified as onerous. The provision should be set at the lower of:

(i) the cost of fulfilling the terms of the contract:
$$1,000 \times (£350 - £280) = £70,000$$
and

(ii) the compensation payable arising from failure to fulfil it:
cancellation fee = £100,000

A provision for Contract W of £70,000 should be provided.

Contract X

The surplus quantity is 150 tonnes. Again, the contract is loss making and will be classified as onerous. The provision should be set at the lower of:

(i) the cost of fulfilling the terms of the contract and selling on the spot market:
$$150 \times (£1,500 - £1,300) = £30,000$$
and

(ii) the compensation payable arising from failure to fulfil the contract:
Cancellation fee £25,000

Esdaile should opt to cancel the contract and provide the lower figure of £25,000.

Contract Y

A comparison requires to be made of the outcome were Esdaile Engineering Ltd to manufacture and sell the final product and the costs of selling the steel ingots on the spot market.

	£	£
Sales price		720
Production cost:		
Materials	600	
Processing	200	
		800
Loss per tonne		(80)

The costs of selling on the spot market would be:

	£
Contract price	600
Spot price	500
Loss per tonne	(100)

Esdaile Engineering Ltd should use the steel ingots rather than sell them as this results in a lower loss.

A provision should be made of 2,000 tonnes × £80 = £160,000.

Contract Z

Again, a comparison requires to be made of the outcome were Esdaile Engineering Ltd to manufacture and sell the blades and the costs of selling the aluminium on the spot market.

	£	£
Sales price		400
Production cost:		
Materials (5kg x £25)	125	
Manufacture	240	365
Profit		35

As a profit can be made on the use of the aluminium, the contract cannot be classified as onerous. No provision should be made.

Restructurings

IAS 37 (para. 10) defines restructurings as:

a programme that is planned and controlled by management and materially changes either:

(a)   the scope of a business undertaken by an enterprise; or

(b)   the manner in which that business is conducted.

Examples given in paragraph 70 are:

- sale or termination of a line of business
- closure of business locations in a country or region, or the relocation of business activities from one country or region to another
- changes in management structure
- fundamental reorganisation of a company that has a material effect on the nature and focus of the entity's operations.

The kind of expenditure covered by such restructuring programmes includes redundancy costs, lease termination payments, the costs of breaking contracts and other direct costs of carrying out the reorganisation. Such costs may not be capitalised as an asset.

The accounting issue involved

The accounting issue involved with restructurings concerns the point at which a present obligation arises as a result of a past event. IAS 37 (para. 72) gives guidance on restructuring provisions as follows.

A constructive obligation to restructure arises only when an entity

(a)   has a detailed formal plan for the restructuring identifying at least
   (i)   the business or part of a business concerned
   (ii)   the principal locations affected
   (iii)   the location, function and approximate numbers of employees who will be compensated for terminating their services
   (iv)   the expenditures that will be undertaken, and

(b)   has raised a valid expectation in those affected that it will carry out the restructuring by starting to implement that plan or announcing its main features to those affected by it.

Those affected by a constructive obligation are likely to be customers, employees and suppliers. Note that both (a) and (b) are necessary to create a constructive obligation.

Use of provisions

Provisions should be used only for the purpose for which they were originally recognised. They should be reviewed at each balance sheet date and adjusted to reflect the current best estimate. If it is no longer probable that an outflow of resources will be required to settle the obligation, the provision should be reversed. Note the effect of this requirement: it prevents the set-off of expenditures against a provision that was originally required for another purpose, which would conceal the impact of two different events.

7.4 Contingent liabilities

IAS 37 defines a contingent liability (para. 10) as:

(a)   a possible obligation that arises from past events and whose existence will be confirmed only by the occurrence of one or more uncertain future events not wholly within the control of the entity, or

(b)   a present obligation that arises from past events but is not recognised because
    (i)   it is not probable that an outflow of resources embodying economic benefits will be required to settle the obligation, or
    (ii)   the amount of the obligation cannot be measured with sufficient reliability.

Points (b)(i) and (ii) were covered earlier in the chapter and relate to actual obligations. Point (a) refers not to a present or actual obligation but to a possible obligation. This arises where it is more likely that no present obligation exists at the balance sheet date but, because there is a possibility that a liability exists, it is described as a contingent liability and disclosed, with explanation, in the notes to the accounts. If the possibility of an outflow of resources is remote, no liability note is required.

For example, a competitor has raised a claim against the company for unauthorised use of a design. The company's solicitors advise that the claim is frivolous and the possibility of the claim being successful is remote. In this case, no disclosure is required.

Contingent liabilities are disclosed in the accounts (i.e. they are reported in the notes to the accounts). No amount is recognised (included in the arithmetic totals) for a contingent liability.

Given the uncertainty surrounding contingent liabilities, it may not be clear whether a present obligation arises from a past event. Changes in circumstances may make past events that were not obligations at the time they occurred, obligations now (e.g. changes to legislation with a retrospective effect create a legal obligation). Furthermore, contingent liabilities may develop in a way not initially expected. IAS 37 requires that contingent liabilities be assessed continually to determine whether an outflow of resources embodying economic benefits has become probable. If it becomes probable that an outflow of future economic benefits will be required for an item previously dealt with as a contingent liability, a provision should be recognised in the financial statements of the period in which the change in probability occurs.

Unless the possibility of any transfer in settlement is remote, an entity should disclose (para. 86) for each class of contingent liability:

(a)   an estimate of its financial effect
(b)   an indication of the uncertainties relating to the amount or timing of any outflow, and
(c)   the possibility of any reimbursement.

7.5 Contingent assets

A contingent asset is defined (para. 10) as:

> a possible asset that arises from past events and whose existence will be confirmed only by the occurrence or non-occurrence of one or more uncertain future events not wholly within the control of the enterprise.

Contingent assets usually arise from unplanned or other unexpected events that give rise to the possibility of an inflow of economic benefits to the entity. IAS 37 (para. 32) gives the example of a claim that an entity is pursuing through legal processes, where the outcome is uncertain.

A contingent asset should not be recognised because it could result in the recognition of profit that may never be realised. When the realisation of profit is virtually certain then the related asset is not a contingent asset and its recognition is appropriate. In other words, a contingent asset can never be recognised; an asset can only be recognised when it is no longer contingent and the future economic benefits are certain.

Where an inflow of economic benefits is probable, an entity should disclose a brief description of the nature of the contingent assets at the balance sheet date and, where practicable, an estimate of their financial effect. The disclosure should not give a misleading indication of the likelihood of a profit arising.

Contingent assets should be assessed continually to ensure that developments are appropriately reflected in the financial statements. If it has become virtually certain that an inflow of economic benefits will arise, the asset and the related income are recognised in the financial statements of the period in which the change occurs.

7.6 IAS 37: disclosure requirements

The disclosure requirements of IAS 37 are, as would be expected, designed to provide relevant information to users:

For each class of provision, an entity shall disclose:

- the carrying amount at the beginning and the end of the period
- additional provisions made in the period, including increases to existing provisions
- amounts used (amounts charged against the provision)
- unused amounts reversed during the period.

For each class of provision, a brief description of:

- the nature of the obligation
- the uncertainties about the amount or timing of the outflows
- the amount of any expected reimbursement.

Disclosure in practice

IAS 37 requires both narrative and numerical disclosures.

Provisions

Logica outlines its policy on provisions in the accounting policies note where it identifies two specific items, namely restructurings and future committed property lease payments. In keeping with the requirements of the standard (para. 45), Logica measures provisions at their present value where the time value of money is material.

Provisions are recognised for restructuring costs when the Group has a detailed formal plan for the restructuring that has been communicated to affected employees. Provisions are recognised for future committed property lease payments when the Group receives no benefit from the property through continuing usage and future receipts from any sub-letting arrangements are not in excess of the Group's future committed payments.

Where the time value of money is material, provisions are measured at the present value of expenditures expected to be paid in settlement.

	Vacant properties £m	Restructuring £m	Other £m	Total £m
At 1 January 2007	15.7	13.5	4.8	34.0
Charged in the year	11.5	2.6	6.7	20.8
Utilised in the year	(5.6)	(12.4)	(5.7)	(23.7)
Unused amounts reversed	(2.5)	(0.8)	(0.2)	(3.5)
Unwinding of discount	0.4	–	–	0.4
Disposal of subsidiaries/businesses	(1.4)	–	–	(1.4)
Exchange differences	0.5	0.3	0.6	1.4
At 31 December 2007	**18.6**	**3.2**	**6.2**	**28.0**
ANALYSED AS:				
Current liabilities				**9.1**
Non-current liabilities				**18.9**
				28.0

Figure 7.2 Logica: provisions note

Vacant properties

At 31 December 2007, provisions for vacant properties represented residual lease commitments, together with associated outgoings, for the remaining period on certain property leases, after taking into account sub-tenant arrangements. The property costs provided for are mainly on properties located in the United Kingdom and Sweden. At 31 December 2007, non-current vacant property provisions amounted to £14.0 million of which £10.9 million was payable within five years and the balance thereafter.

Restructuring

At 31 December 2007, the restructuring provision mainly related to the restructuring of the businesses in France and Germany following the acquisition of Unilog and the restructuring in the Nordics following the acquisition of WM-data. The restructuring programme comprised a reduction in headcount and other measures to reduce the cost base. At 31 December 2007, £2.5 million of the restructuring provision was payable within one year with the remaining balance payable between one and two years.

Other

At 31 December 2007, the other provision mainly related to the value of legal claims brought by ex-employees. At 31 December 2007, £2.0 million of the other provision was payable within one year with the remaining balance payable between one and two years. The timing of the outflows could differ from management's estimates depending on the actual timing of the settlements of the legal claims.

The provisions note from the Logica financial statements highlights the importance of both narrative and numerical disclosure. As required by IAS 37, for each class of provision, Logica has prepared a movements table showing the charges and credits being made during the year to 31 December 2007.

Note the references to the unwinding of discounts, which indicate clearly that Logica does discount its provisions to present value. The narrative element of the disclosure note gives a brief description of each provision and includes, as IAS 37 requires, details of the timing, amount and uncertainties surrounding these provisions. Only by including both the narrative and numerical disclosures is the user in a position to determine the future cash flow effects of the various provisions.

Contingent liabilities

The Group's subsidiaries and the Company are currently, and may be from time to time, involved in a number of legal proceedings including inquiries from or discussions with governmental and taxation authorities. Whilst the outcome of current outstanding actions and claims remains uncertain, it is expected that they will be resolved without a material impact on the Group's financial position.

Logica's disclosure of contingent liabilities is short. It is difficult to determine much from such a note other than perhaps to conclude that none of the legal proceedings currently ongoing has any likelihood of any significant outflows of economic resources.

7.7 International comparison

The equivalent UK standard is FRS 12 *Provisions, Contingent Liabilities and Contingent Assets*. It was developed jointly with the international standard and there are no substantial differences between the two. Indeed, the examples and decision trees used in both standards are identical.

US GAAP is similar again, but with the following minor differences.

- Measurement:
    - discount rate is pre-tax, reflecting current market assessment of time value of money (i.e. no account of risk is taken).
    - where a range of estimates of the outflow are available and all are equally likely, then the lowest is taken (not the midpoint as per IAS).
- Restructuring:
    - management approval and commitment is sufficient to recognise the restructuring; accordingly, under US GAAP, restructuring provisions are likely to occur at an earlier point than under IAS.
- Contingent asset:
    - under US GAAP insurance recoveries will be recognised when probable – IAS requires virtual certainty; accordingly, US GAAP will recognise the contingent asset at an earlier stage than IAS.

7.8 Problems in practice

As has been illustrated, the topic of provisions, contingent liabilities and contingent assets is controversial and involves a great deal of subjective judgement. The professional accountant, in attempting to adhere to the standard, may require to effectively interrogate management in an attempt to uncover any such potential items. It is worth bearing in mind that management may have strong reasons for including particular items (or not) as liabilities, as such liabilities can dramatically alter a set of financial statements. In practice, therefore, the most important quality that the reporting accountant must have is to be free from bias when evaluating such issues. The accountant's decision will necessarily be subjective. However, if that decision has been based on an objective application of the definition and recognition rules (without being overly pessimistic) then this should ensure that only useful information is reported or disclosed. If not the alternative would be to take prudence to the extreme and use the words of the standard to report every possible eventuality whether probable, possible or remote.

7.9 'Big bath' accounting

Earlier in this chapter, reference was made to 'big bath' accounting, and in particular that IAS 37 was primarily designed to target big bath provisions. Having now covered in detail the nature of provisions and contingent liabilities, it will be easier to explain and illustrate the term 'big bath' accounting.

Big bath accounting involves making provisions in order to smooth profits without any reasonable certainty that the provision will actually be required in subsequent periods.

 Example

An enterprise with expected future profits of £25 million decides to recognise a provision (on the grounds of prudence) for reorganisation of future costs for future years of £2.0 million in the current year when its expected profits are £4.5 million.

The actual reorganisation costs incurred are £0.5 million in the next year and £0.5 million in the year following. Thereafter, no further costs arise.

The effect of the proposed accounting treatment for the reorganisation costs on the profits for the company for the current and future years is as follows:

	Year 1	Year 2	Year 3	Year 4
Profits	£4.5	£2.5	£2.5	£2.5
Provision (charged)/credited to income statement	(2.0)	0	1.0	0
Profits after provision	£2.5	£2.5	£3.5	£2.5
Provision b/f	0	2.0	1.5	0
Expense	0	(0.5)	(0.5)	0
Income statement charge/(credit)	2.0	0	(1.0)	0
Provision c/f	£2.0	£1.5	£0	£0

As can be seen, the enterprise has charged the full amount of the provision in Year 1, when it has expected profits of £4.5 million. In Years 2 and 3, instead of charging the reorganisation costs to the income statement, the enterprise is able to charge these costs against the provision and so the profits in Years 2 and 3 are not reduced. Moreover, in Year 3, as the whole provision of £2.0 million was not required, the excess (£2.0 million provided – £1.0 million incurred) has been released back to the income statement, increasing profits to £3.5 million. The enterprise has effectively taken a 'big bath' in Year 1, when the profits were substantial, and has protected future profits.

This potential for creative accounting highlights the need for a standard in this area. Indeed, without regulation, if the recognition of a provision were allowed to proceed on the intention to incur expenditure rather than an obligation to do so, then, this could result in even more creativity in accounting.

Sir David Tweedie, the chairman of the IASB has said:

A main focus of [IAS 37] is 'big bath' provisions. Those who use them sometimes pray in aid of the concept of prudence. All too often however the provision is wildly excessive and conveniently finds its way back to the [income statement] in a later period. The misleading practice needs to be stopped and [IAS 37] proposes that, in future, provisions should only be allowed when the company has an unavoidable obligation – an *intention* which may or may not be fulfilled *will not be enough*. Users of accounts can't expect to be mind readers.

Summary

The Appendix to IAS 37 summarises the main requirements of the standard (see Tables 7.2 and 7.3).

Summary of provisions and contingent liabilities

Obligation	Accounting effect	Disclosure
Present obligation that probably requires an outflow of resources	A provision is recognised	Amounts, nature, uncertainties, assumptions, reimbursements
Possible obligation or present obligation that may, but probably will not, require an outflow of resources	No provision recognised; contingent liability disclosed	Nature, estimate of financial effect, uncertainties, reimbursement
Possible obligation or present obligation where the outflow of resources is remote	No provision recognised; no contingent liability disclosed	No disclosure is required

Table 7.2 Summary of IAS 37 (1)

Summary of contingent assets

Economic benefits	Accounting effect	Disclosure
Inflow virtually certain	Asset rules apply, i.e. the asset is not contingent	N/A
Inflow probable but not virtually certain	No asset recognised; contingent asset disclosed	Nature, financial effect
Inflow not probable	No asset recognised; no contingent asset disclosed	Nil

Table 7.3 Summary of IAS 37 (2)

The underlying requirements can be summarised more simply as follows:
IAS 37 effectively bans:

- big bath accounting
- creation of provisions where no obligation to a liability exists
- use of provisions to smooth profits

and requires greater disclosure in relation to provisions to aid the user's understanding and present a true and fair view.

7.10 IAS 10 *Events After the Balance Sheet Date*

It is the uncertainty surrounding certain liabilities existing at the balance sheet date that gives rise to the accounting issues covered above. As time passes beyond the balance sheet date, however, the certainty of some obligations may become clearer and, indeed, may even become confirmed. The process of preparing financial statements for publication, can often take weeks – or even months – and the information that is available to the reporting accountant after the balance sheet date can be very useful in determining the appropriate accounting treatment for certain items.

BASIC

INTERMEDIATE

ADVANCED

Moreover, for the financial statements to be true and fair, any events occurring after the balance sheet date and before the signing of the annual accounts must be considered if these events give significant and further information relevant to those financial statements. These events are described as events after the balance sheet date. The decision as to whether information is significant or not will be made in the first instance by the directors. If this information is not provided then the accounts will potentially be misleading.

IAS 10 *Events After the Balance Sheet Date* gives guidance on such matters. IAS 10 defines an event after the balance sheet date as an event that could be favourable or unfavourable, which occurs between the balance sheet date and the date that the financial statements are authorised for issue.

An *adjusting event* is an event after the balance sheet date that provides further evidence of conditions that existed at the balance sheet date, including an event that indicates that the going concern assumption in relation to the whole or part of the enterprise is not appropriate.

A *non-adjusting event* is an event after the balance sheet date that is indicative of a condition that arose after the balance sheet date.

The key distinction, therefore, is whether the event in the post-balance sheet period (from the balance sheet to the date the accounts are authorised for issue) relates to a condition existing at the balance sheet date.

Accounting for adjusting events

If information becomes available that gives further evidence of the conditions that existed at the balance sheet date, the financial statements should be adjusted to include that information. There is no additional disclosure required. Examples are the subsequent determination of the purchase price or proceeds of sale of fixed assets sold before the year end, and a valuation of property that provides evidence of impairment in value.

Non-adjusting events

The financial statements should not be adjusted for non-adjusting events (i.e. those events or conditions that arose after the balance sheet date). Non-adjusting events should, however, be disclosed if they are of such importance that non-disclosure would affect the ability of users to make proper evaluations and decisions. The required disclosure is:

- the nature of the event, and
- an estimate of its financial effect or a statement that a reasonable estimate of the effect cannot be made.

 ## *Example*

Consider the following list of events after the balance sheet date and decide which should be classified as adjusting events and which are non-adjusting events in light of the above definitions:

(a)   the receipt of a copy of the financial statements of an unlisted company, which provides evidence of an impairment in the value of a long-term investment at the balance sheet date

(b)   the receipt of proceeds of sales after the balance sheet date concerning the net realisable value of stocks held at the balance sheet date

(c)   issues of shares and debentures

(d)   purchases and sales of fixed assets and investments

(e)   the renegotiation of amounts owing by debtors, or the insolvency of a debtor

(f)   losses of fixed assets or stocks as a result of a catastrophe such as fire or flood

(g)   changes in rates of foreign exchange

(h)   announcement of a major restructuring

(i)   a valuation that provides evidence of an impairment in the value of a property

(j)   the announcement of changes in the rates of tax

(k)   the discovery of errors or frauds, which show that the financial statements to be issued were incorrect

(l)   mergers and acquisitions.

Solution

Items (a), (b), (e), (i) and (k) would normally be adjusting events. The remainder are normally non-adjusting.

In deciding whether to disclose a non-adjusting event, a subjective decision will ultimately require to be made by the directors as to whether the information is significant or not. IAS 10 (para. 9) gives examples of adjusting events, while paragraph 22 gives examples of non-adjusting events that are of such importance that non-disclosure would influence the economic decisions of users of the financial statements.

Dividends

Paragraph 12 states, 'if an entity declares dividends to holders of equity instruments after the balance sheet date, the entity shall not recognise these dividends as a liability at the balance sheet date'.

Consequently, if dividends are declared after the balance sheet date but before the financial statements are authorised for issue, they are treated as a non-adjusting event whose disclosure is required under the provisions of IAS 1 *Presentation of Financial Statements*. Under IAS 1 they will be disclosed in the notes to the accounts. Such dividends are not recognised as a liability at the balance sheet date because they do not meet the criteria of a present obligation in IAS 37. Only dividends declared before the year end are accrued as a liability, as only then do they meet the criteria of a present obligation.

Going concern

Paragraph 14 states, 'an entity shall not prepare its financial statements on a going concern basis if management determines after the balance sheet date either that it intends to liquidate the entity or to cease trading, or that it has no realistic alternative but to do so'.

If the going concern basis is no longer appropriate, the effect is so pervasive that the IASB sees this as a fundamental change in the basis of accounting rather than an adjustment to the financial statements in the manner of adjusting events.

The preparation of accounts when the company is not a going concern is beyond the scope of this textbook.

7.11 Disclosure in practice

Events after the balance sheet date

The following disclosure by Logica is a non-adjusting event after the balance sheet date. The fact that it has been disclosed indicates that it is a material event and that non-disclosure could influence the economic decisions of users.

On 15 February 2008, Energias de Portugal S.A. (EDP) notified the Group of its exercise of the EDP Put Option, under the terms of the shareholders agreement entered into between EDP and Logica on 20 April 2005. Accordingly, EDP gave notice that it will sell to Logica the remaining 40% interest in the equity shares of Edinfor – Sistemas Informáticos S.A. and the outstanding shareholder loans for the fixed price of €55.0 million. On 7 March 2008, the transaction completed resulting in Logica owning a 100% equity interest in Edinfor.

7.12 The position in practice

It is useful at this point to consider the position with liabilities and contingent liabilities in practice.

Liabilities ought to be relatively simple to determine. The Framework definition, by including reference to a 'past event', goes a long way to guiding the accountant in determining both the existence and quantification of a liability (e.g. the purchase of goods giving rise to the existence of a liability and the invoice giving the amount). Contingent liabilities are more difficult both to ascertain and to determine. Business today has moved on greatly from the times when accounting standards were first being developed to give guidance on how to account for certain situations. An unavoidable consequence of this is that accountants have been expected to develop also, with the result that it is no longer sufficient to simply report on the obvious. In practice, accountants are expected to consider not only the figures that are included within the reporting system but also to consider those figures which have not been included in that system. Moreover, the accountant needs to consider situations with a broadened commercial awareness; in reviewing and discussing financial statements with management, the accountant needs to look beyond the figures and to the environment – social, economic and legal – in which the particular company operates in order to fully provide for any items whether requiring to be recognised, disclosed or not reported at all. Companies do not operate in a vacuum – and neither can the accountant.

Summary

In this long intermediate section, liabilities have been looked at in detail and the Framework definition used to help identify items that may require to be recognised, disclosed or simply ignored. IAS 37 has been covered in detail, and its objectives identified and appraised. IAS 10 identifies how to deal with events after the balance sheet date.

Section 3: Advanced Aspects

7.13 Financial Instruments

Introduction

In the preface to this text, it was noted that business is becoming increasingly complex and that the accounting for business transactions has also become increasingly complex. This is particularly apparent when dealing with financial instruments. Broadly speaking, a financial instrument is a means of raising finance; in practice, the term covers a wide range of complex financial arrangements, but common examples include loans of various types and share issues.

The market for financial instruments has expanded tremendously over the past 20 years. Many companies have moved from using only straightforward financial instruments (such as cash, trade debtors and creditors, long-term debt and investments in bonds and shares) to the adoption of sophisticated risk management strategies using derivatives and complex combinations of financial instruments. It is now possible to manage virtually any financial risk or speculate on key rates and prices in the increasingly global economy. However, while the types and availability of financial instruments have advanced considerably, traditional accounting recognition, measurement and disclosure principles have struggled to keep pace. Three standards have been issued by the IASB in response, to deal with these issues:

1.　IAS 32 *Financial Instruments: Presentation*
2.　IAS 39 *Financial Instruments: Recognition and Measurement*
3.　IFRS 7 *Financial Instruments: Disclosures.*

These standards define the term financial instrument, identify several types of financial instrument and prescribe the accounting treatment of each type.

This area of accounting can be extremely complex and a detailed coverage of financial instruments is beyond the scope of this book. The aim of this section therefore is simply to provide a basic introduction to the accounting issues involved. It is important to bear in mind, however, that while these standards are detailed they become complex only when dealing with more complex situations. They make no significant difference to accounting for more basic items such as cash, trade debtors, trade creditors and straightforward borrowings.

Definitions

The three standards use the same definition for a financial instrument. For a detailed definition, refer to IAS 32 paragraph 11.

■   A financial instrument is any contract that gives rise to a financial asset of one entity and a financial liability or equity instrument of another entity.

■   A financial asset is any asset that is:
(a) cash
(b) an equity instrument of another entity (e.g. an investment in the shares of another company)
(c) a contractual right
(i)   to receive cash or another financial asset from another entity (e.g. a debtor, loan made to a supplier), or
(ii) to exchange financial instruments with another entity under conditions that are potentially favourable to the entity (e.g. in the money option).

Physical assets such as property, plant and equipment or stock are not financial assets as they do not give a right to receive cash or another financial asset. It is important to note, however, that it would be expected that they would ultimately generate cash. Similarly, intangible assets such as brands and patents are not financial assets. Finally, prepayments are not financial assets as they will not be settled for cash or another financial instrument. Their settlement is by the delivery of goods and services.

■   A financial liability is any liability that is:
(a) a contractual obligation to deliver cash or another financial asset to another entity
(b) a contractual obligation to exchange financial instruments with another entity under conditions that are potentially unfavourable.

Examples include:
■   trade creditors and accruals – settlement will normally involve a transfer of cash
■   forward contract to acquire $1m dollars at £1 = $1.50 when current exchange rate is £1 = $1.60; that is, there is an unfavourable exchange resulting in a contract to pay $1m/1.50 = £666,667 when it could be acquired for $1m/1.60 = £625,000
■   bank loan.

Tax liabilities and deferred income are not financial liabilities as they do not derive from contractual obligations. Tax is a statutory obligation, not a contractual obligation. Deferred income is not a financial liability as there is no obligation relating to deferred income. It exists because of the revenue recognition policy of the company.

■   An equity instrument is any contract that evidences a residual interest in the assets of an entity after deducting all of its liabilities. This definition includes shares (ordinary and some preference), and warrants and options to acquire shares.

BASIC

INTERMEDIATE

ADVANCED

■   A derivative is a financial instrument that changes in value with an underlying economic item (e.g. interest rate, exchange rate or share price), requires no or relatively little investment, and is settled at a future date. Common types of derivatives include forward exchange contracts, interest rate swaps and options.

Example

On 31 December 2009 a company acquires an option to purchase 20,000 shares in ABC plc at 50p per share. The option is exercisable on 31 March 2010. The cost of the option is £750. The share price of ABC plc on 31 December 2009 is 48p.

Required

Explain whether the option meets the definition of a derivative.

Solution

The tests to see whether the option meets the definition of a derivative are as follows.

(a)   *Change in value*: the value of the option will change in response to changes in the share price of ABC plc. If the share price increases between 31 December and 31 March the value of the option will increase, and vice versa.

(b)   *Initial investment:* the cost of the option (£750) is relatively little compared to what would have to be paid for the shares themselves (£9,600, i.e. 20,000 × 48p).

(c)   *Settled at a future date:* if the option is exercised it will be in March 2010 (i.e. in the future).

All the above tests are satisfied and the option therefore meets the definition of a derivative.

Progress Point 7.5

Explain whether the following transactions give rise to a financial instrument as defined by IAS 32:

(a)   a company sells goods to a customer on credit
(b)   a company has a corporation tax bill outstanding of £250,000
(c)   a company makes an issue of ordinary shares
(d)   a company prepays rates of £50,000
(e)   a company buys goods from a supplier on credit.

Solution

(a)   The sale of goods on credit results in a contractual obligation on the part of the customer to pay for the goods. The contract is a financial instrument because:
    (i)   the company now has a trade receivable (a financial asset)
    (ii) the customer now has a trade payable (a financial liability).

(b)   The payment of taxation is a statutory obligation, not a contractual one. Because the payment of taxation does not derive from a contractual obligation it is not a financial liability.

(c)   The issue of ordinary shares creates a contract between the company and its shareholders, which entitles them to a residual interest in the assets of the company after deducting all of its liabilities. The contract is a financial instrument because:
    (i)   the shareholders now own the shares (a financial asset)
    (ii) the company has additional share capital (an equity instrument).

BASIC

INTERMEDIATE

ADVANCED

(d)   The prepayment is not a financial asset as it will not be settled for cash or another financial instrument. The prepayment will be settled by the delivery of services. This contract is not a financial instrument.

(e)   The purchase of goods on credit creates a contractual obligation on the part of the company to pay for the goods. This contract is a financial instrument because:
 (i)   the supplier now has a trade receivable (a financial asset)
 (ii) the company now has a trade payable (a financial liability).

The accounting issue involved

The accounting issue involved is that an industry evolved in the development of 'new financial instruments' that were designed to exploit loopholes in tax regulations and/or the Companies Act definitions, so that companies could pay less tax or have stronger-looking balance sheets. Some of these instruments have features of capital and liabilities. The intention behind IAS 32 and IAS 39 is to clarify the accounting treatment of these items. If the requirements of IAS 32 did not exist, an entity, might be able to incur a financial liability but then present this liability as equity, and consequently improve the gearing ratio but at the same time reduce the reliability of the reported information.

7.14 IAS 32 *Financial Instruments: Presentation*

Classification of financial instruments

The fundamental principle of IAS 32 is that a financial instrument should be classified as either a financial liability or an equity instrument according to the substance of the contract, not its legal form. Consequently, even though the legal form of a financial instrument might be a share issue, the instrument could still be regarded as giving rise to a financial liability if the underlying substance of the transaction indicates that this is the case.

A key distinction between a financial liability and an equity instrument is whether a contractual obligation exists. A financial instrument should be classified as an equity instrument if, and only if, the instrument includes no contractual obligation to deliver cash or another financial asset to another entity.

Example

A company has the following items in issue at 31 December 2009

- 5 million £1 4.5% bonds 2012
- 12 million ordinary shares of 25p.

Required
Explain how these should be classified in the balance sheet of the company at 31 December 2009.

Solution
Bonds
The bonds represent a financial liability as they contain contractual obligations. The first is in respect of the annual interest payable on them of £225,000 (£5,000,000 × 4.5%) and the second is the obligation to repay the bonds in 2012. Either obligation is sufficient to identify the bonds as debt.

Ordinary shares

The ordinary shares are an equity instrument. Although the ordinary shareholders will expect to receive dividends, and indeed, once any dividends have been properly declared the company has a legal obligation to pay these to the shareholders, the key point is that the company is under no obligation to declare a dividend in the first place. No obligation means no liability. Similarly, the shareholders do not have a right to receive back the money they paid for the shares.

Redeemable preference shares

In judging whether an obligation exists, IAS 32 requires a substance over form approach to distinguish between liabilities and equity. This leads to most preference shares and some ordinary shares being classified as liabilities.

Preference shares or ordinary shares that either the company is obliged to redeem at a certain date or redeem at the option of the holders are liabilities because there is an obligation to transfer financial assets to the holder.

In the event that preference shares are not redeemable, an assessment of the substance of the contractual arrangements needs to be made. Where distributions are at the discretion of the issuer, the shares are equity. Most preference shares, however, carry an obligation to pay a stated dividend (e.g. 5%). This obligation is contingent only on the company having sufficient reserves legally to pay the dividend. The standard clarifies this point by stating that the decision to classify as a liability or equity item is not affected by the amount of the company's reserves or its history of making distributions. Such preference shares will, therefore, be classified as liabilities.

It is worth covering at this stage how the dividends from such preference shares should be dealt with. IAS 32 adopts a consistent approach and requires that interest and dividends relating to financial liabilities should be recognised as an expense in the income statement. Consequently, any dividends paid to the holders of redeemable preference shares must be treated as an expense. Furthermore, any accrued dividends unpaid at the end of an accounting period should be treated in the same way as accrued interest. This should be compared with dividends on equity instruments, which are required to be dealt with through equity. Dividends proposed at the year end will not be recognised.

Compound financial instruments

Some financial instruments, known as compound financial instruments, have both a liability component and an equity component from the issuer's perspective. Where an instrument has both an equity and liability element, IAS 32 requires that the two should be accounted for and presented separately.

The most common is convertible debt (i.e. loan stock), which is convertible to ordinary shares at the option of the lender. Legally this is one instrument but in substance combines a financial liability (the contractual obligation to transfer cash on repayment and normally to pay interest up until that point) and an equity instrument (a call option granting the holder the right, for a specified period, to convert to ordinary shares). The two elements should be classified separately – one within liabilities and the other as part of reserves in equity (a separate reserve should be used to record this part). The option to convert is termed an 'embedded derivative' in IAS 39.

IAS 32 does not address measurement issues but suggests (para. 31) a method for separating the total amount of a convertible instrument into the liability and equity elements.

(a) The carrying amount of the liability element should first be calculated by measuring the fair value of a similar liability that does not have conversion rights.

(b) The fair value of the equity element is then determined by deducting the fair value of the liability element from the fair value of the whole instrument. IAS 39 states that the fair value of the whole instrument is normally equal to the amount of the consideration that was received when the instrument was issued.

IAS 32 defines fair value as 'the amount for which an asset could be exchanged, or a liability settled, between knowledgeable willing parties in an arm's length transaction'.

Example

A company issued the following instrument at par on 31 March 2009:

> 2 million 50p 3% convertible bonds 2015

The value of 2 million 50p 3% bonds 2015 without the conversion rights is estimated to be £960,000.

Required

State the amounts that should appear for the above items in the accounts of the company as at 31 March 2009.

Solution

Bonds	£
Total amount raised (2 million x 50p)	1,000,000
Allocated to liability (fair value of bond w/o rights)	960,000
Allocated to equity (difference)	40,000

Note that the classification of the liability component is made at issuance and is not revised for subsequent changes in market interest rates, share prices or other event that changes the likelihood that the conversion option will be exercised (para. 28).

7.15 IAS 39 *Financial Instruments: Recognition and Measurement*

The objective of IAS 39 is to establish principles for recognising and measuring financial assets, financial liabilities and some contracts to buy or sell non-financial items. The recognition principles determine when a financial asset or liability should be shown on an entity's balance sheet while the measurement principles determine the amount at which a financial asset or liability should be shown.

Recognition and derecognition

IAS 39 states that an entity should recognise a financial asset or a financial liability on its balance sheet when, and only when, it becomes a party to the contractual provisions of the instrument.

This means that derivatives (e.g. forward contracts) will be included on the balance sheet from the date of the commitment, rather than on the date on which settlement takes place. In many cases, however, these will have no initial monetary value as there is no cost attached to them at the outset. They may have a value in the future as the underlying variable changes or due to the time value of money.

The rules within IAS 39 in relation to derecognition are very detailed (paras 15–42).

The main requirements are as follows:

(a) a financial asset is derecognised when the entity's contractual rights to receive cash flows from the asset expire

(b) a financial liability is derecognised when the entity's contractual obligations expire, are discharged or cancelled

Initial measurement of financial assets and liabilities

IAS 39 requires that all financial assets and liabilities are initially measured at fair value (with the exception of financial assets at fair value through the profit and loss account) plus transaction costs directly attributable to the acquisition or issue of the financial asset or financial liability. Fair value is the amount paid for the asset or received for the liability.

Transaction costs include fees and commissions paid to advisers, agents, brokers, and so on, as well as transfer taxes (e.g. stamp duty). They do not include internal administrative or holding costs.

Transaction costs are an addition to the cost of a financial asset and a reduction in a net liability.

Example

A company had the following transactions in the year to 31 March 2009:

(i)   entered into a forward contract to acquire $20m in 3 months' time at £1: $1.65; there were no costs or fees arising

(ii) acquired 300,000 shares in Ulpas plc for £5 per share; commission and stamp duty totalled £15,000

(iii) issued 5 million £1 3.5% bonds 2017 at a discount of 25%; the bonds will be redeemed at 110p in 2017; arrangement fees of £45,000 were paid.

Required

Prepare journal entries to record the initial measurement of the above items.

Solution

(i)   Forward contract: although the company is party to a contract there is no cost to record on initial measurement. No journal entry is required.

(ii) Acquisition of shares: the cost of the shares (300,000 × £5 = 1,500,000), together with the commission and stamp duty (£15,000), would be recorded.

Dr	Investment	£1,515,000	
	Cr Bank		£1,515,000
Being cost of acquisition of shares.			

(iii) Issue of bonds: the issue of bonds is at a discount and raises 5 million × £1 × 75% = £3,750,000. The costs of the issue are £45,000.

Dr	Bank	£3,750,000	
	Cr Non-current liability bonds		£3,750,000
Being issue of bonds at discount.			

Dr	Non-current liabilities – bonds	£45,000	
	Cr Bank		£45,000
Being cost of issuing bonds.			

The bonds would be initially recorded at £3,705,000 (£3,750,000 less £45,000).

Subsequent measurement of financial assets

Many financial instruments will change in value after initial recognition. IAS 39 identifies and defines four categories of financial instrument and prescribes how each category should be measured after its initial recognition.

Financial assets at fair value through profit or loss

These are usually financial assets that have been acquired for the purpose of generating a profit from short-term fluctuations. However, on initial recognition, an entity may designate any financial asset as being 'at fair value through profit or loss' if this would result in more relevant information.

After initial recognition, financial assets that fall into this category should be measured at their fair value, with any gains or losses arising from fluctuations in fair value being recognised in the income statement.

Fair value should not include any deduction for transaction costs that might arise on the disposal of the asset. Market value is the best indicator of fair value but, in the absence of a reliable market value, a valuation technique (e.g. dividend valuation model) should give a reliable figure. Where available, bid prices should be used.

Held-to-maturity investments

These are financial assets with fixed or determinable payments and fixed maturity that the entity has the positive intent and ability to hold to maturity. After initial recognition, held-to-maturity investments should be measured at their amortised cost using the effective interest method (see below).

Loans and receivables

These are financial assets with fixed or determinable payments that are not quoted in an active market. This category will mainly comprise trade receivables and other debtors and loans made by a company.

After initial recognition, loans and receivables should be measured at their amortised cost using the effective interest method. This method involves discounting the amounts expected to be received when the loan or receivables is settled. The standard does not required amortised cost to be applied to short-term receivables unless the effect of discounting would be material. In respect of short-term receivables, usually it would not be.

Available-for-sale financial assets

These are any other financial assets that do not fall into the above categories. Common examples are investments in shares and debt of other companies. Shares in private companies, whose fair value cannot be measured reliably, are included in this category.

After initial recognition, available-for-sale financial assets should generally be valued at their fair value with gains or losses arising from fluctuations in fair value being recognised in other comprehensive income (reserves). In cases where it is impossible to measure the fair value of unquoted shares reliably (e.g. private companies), these should be valued at cost.

 ## *Example*

A company purchased 100,000 ordinary shares of 25p in A plc, a listing company, for £3.60 per share on 24 February 2009. Broker's commission on the purchase was £3,000.

At 31 December 2009, the year end of the company, the shares of A plc were quoted at a bid/offer price of £3.95 – £3.98. Selling costs are estimated at 0.5% of the sales proceeds.

The shares are in the available-for-sale category.

Required

State the amounts at which the shares would be recorded on 24 February and 31 December 2009.

Solution

The shares would initially be recorded at their purchase price and acquisition costs. That is:

100,000 × £3.60 + 3,000 = £363,000

As the investment is in the available-for-sale category it should be included at fair value at the balance sheet date. At 31 December, the investment in A plc would be included at £395,000 (100,000 × £3.95, i.e. the bid price). No deduction would be made for selling costs.

Subsequent measurement: financial assets at amortised cost

As noted above, financial assets that are categorised as held-to-maturity investments or loans and receivables should be measured subsequent to initial recognition at their amortised cost using the effective interest method.

The amount under amortised cost is as follows:

	The amount on initial recognition (or balance b/f from a previous period)
plus	Amortisation (i.e. the finance income for the period)
minus	Repayments
minus	Any reduction for impairment or uncollectibility (e.g. bad debt provision)
=	Balance carried forward at end of period

The effective interest method uses the internal rate of return to calculate the amortisation each year. The effective interest rate is the rate that exactly discounts estimated future cash receipts through the expected life of the financial asset to the net carrying amount of the financial asset.

 ## Example

AB plc makes a loan of £600,000 to YZ plc on 1 February 2009. Interest of 3% per annum is due annually in arrears. YZ plc must repay £738,000 on 31 January 2014. This gives an effective interest rate of approximately 7% per annum. The loan is classified as loans and receivables.

Required

State the amounts at which the loan to YZ plc would be disclosed in AB plc's accounts for the years ended 31 January 2010, 2011, 2012, 2013 and 2014.

Solution

The amortised cost of the loan at the end of each year is calculated as follows:

Year to 31 Jan	Opening carrying value	Finance income (7%)	Received in year (3%)	Closing carrying value
	£	£	£	£
2010	600,000	42,000	(18,000)	624,000
2011	624,000	43,680	(18,000)	649,680
2012	649,680	45,478	(18,000)	677,158
2013	677,158	47,401	(18,000)	706,559
2014	706,559	49,459	(18,000)	738,018
Rounding		(18)		(18)
				738,000

Notes

(i) The loan carries 3% interest but yields a higher return as an additional £138,000 will be received in 2013. The effective interest method spreads this premium over the life of the loan.

(ii) The finance income would be recorded in the income statement each year.

(iii) The annual repayments made by XY plc are £18,000 (£600,000 × 3%).

Impairment and uncollectibility of financial assets

Although IAS 36 (covered in Chapter 3) deals with impairment of assets, it excludes financial assets from its scope. IAS 39 has its own rules for impairment, covered in paragraphs 58–70.

IAS 39 requires an entity to assess at each balance sheet date whether there is any objective evidence of impairment. If any such evidence exists (e.g. borrower enters liquidation), the entity is required to do a detailed impairment calculation to determine whether an impairment loss should be recognised. The amount of this loss should be measured as the difference between:

- the carrying amount of the asset, and
- the present value of the estimated cash flows discounted at the financial asset's original effective interest rate.

The carrying amount of the asset should be reduced by the amount of the impairment loss with the loss, itself being written off in the income statement.

If, in a subsequent period, the amount of the impairment loss relating to a financial asset carried at amortised cost or a debt instrument carried as available-for-sale decreases due to an event occurring after the impairment was originally recognised, the previously recognised impairment loss is reversed through the income statement. Impairments relating to investments in available-for-sale equity instruments are not reversed.

Progress Point 7.6

Castle Contracts plc has the following financial assets at 31 December 2009.

> Trade debtors of £2,257,000
> 250,000 ordinary shares of 25p in Airthfield Ltd

Additional information

(i) Credit sales are due for settlement within 30 days of the invoice date. At 31 December 2009 a bad debt provision of 1.5% of debtors was required.

(ii) The shares in Airthfield Ltd cost £140,000. Airthfield is unlisted and the directors of Castle Contracts plc are unable to determine a reliable fair value at 31 December 2009.

> The shares are designated as available for sale.

Required

State the amounts at which the above financial assets should be included in the financial statements of Castle Contracts plc at 31 December 2009.

Solution

(i) Trade debtors: there is an obvious indicator of impairment (i.e. the bad debt provision). There is no need to discount the balance as this would not be material given the credit terms.

BASIC

INTERMEDIATE

ADVANCED

> Carrying value = 2,257,000 – (2,257,000 x 1.5 = 33,855) =   £ 2,223,145

(ii)   Investment in Airthfield Ltd: this should be valued at cost as there   £
is no reliable fair value, i.e.   140,000

Subsequent measurement of financial liabilities

After initial recognition, all liabilities should be measured at amortised cost using the effective interest method. There are exceptions to this rule, two of which are considered below.

Financial liabilities at fair value through profit and loss

These consist mainly of financial liabilities that are held for trading. In a similar manner to financial assets, however, an entity may designate any financial liability as being 'at fair value through profit and loss' if doing so would result in more relevant information.

After initial recognition, these should be measured at fair value, with gains or losses arising from fluctuations in fair value being recognised in the income statement.

Trade payables

Short-term payables (e.g. trade payables), may be measured at the original invoice amount if the effect of discounting is not material.

 ## Example

Metston plc issued 5 million 50p 7% bonds on 1 January 2009. The bonds are issued at a 10% discount (so only £2,250,000 is received) from the lenders, and costs of issue amount to £120,000. Interest is to be paid annually at the end of each year and the bonds are to be repaid at a premium of 20% on 31 December 2013. The effective rate of interest has been calculated at approximately 14.3%.

Required

(i)   State the amount at which the bonds should be measured on 1 January 2009.
(ii) Calculate the amortisation of the cost of the bond over the five years to 31 December 2013.

Solution

(i)   The bonds should initially be measured at £2,130,000. This is calculated as follows:

	£
Face value of bonds 5,000,000 x 50p	2,500,000
Less: 10% discount	(250,000)
Less: costs of issue	(120,000)
	£2,130,000

That is, the consideration received less costs directly attributable to the issue

(ii)   The bonds should be measured at cost using the effective interest method. The cost can be calculated by multiplying the amount outstanding for the period by the effective interest rate. Any payments of principal or interest should be deducted in calculating the carrying value. Workings are as follows:

Year to 31 Dec	Opening carrying value £	Finance cost (14.3%) £	Payments in year £	Closing carrying value £
2009	2,130,000	304,590	(175,000)	2,259,590
2010	2,259,590	323,121	(175,000)	2,407,711
2011	2,407,711	344,303	(175,000)	2,577,014
2012	2,577,014	368,513	(175,000)	2,770,527
2013	2,770,527	404,473*	(3,175,000)	–
		£1,745,000		

* Balancing amount

Notes

1.   The finance cost is a constant percentage of the carrying value (14.3%).
2.   The annual payments are those determined by the bond rate (i.e. 7% × 5m × 50p = £175,000).
3.   The liability progressively increases to the amount that will be repaid at the end of 2013 (i.e. the interest charge for the year of £175,000, the face value of the bonds, £2,500,000, and the premium of £500,000 (£2,500,000 × 20%)).
4.   The total finance costs amounted to:

	£
Issue costs	120,000
Discount	250,000
Interest (5 yrs x £175,000)	875,000
Premium	500,000
	£1,745,000

Note how these have been spread over the life of the bond by the use of the effective interest rate. This rate takes account of all the costs to the company and is therefore higher than the rate at which the annual interest rate payments are calculated (7%).

7.16 IFRS 7 *Financial Instruments: Disclosures*

Disclosure requirements

There are extensive disclosure requirements in IFRS 7 *Financial Instruments: Disclosures*. The two main categories of disclosures required by IFRS 7 are:

1.   information about the significance of financial instruments
2.   information about the nature and extent of risks arising from financial instruments.

   The purpose of these disclosures is to enhance a user's understanding of the entity's exposures to financial risks and how the entity manages those risks.

Significance of financial instruments

The main disclosures to evaluate the significance of financial instruments for an entity's financial position and performance are as follows.

BASIC
INTERMEDIATE
ADVANCED

Balance sheet (paras 8 – 19)

The carrying amount of each of the following categories of financial assets and liabilities should be shown either on the face of the balance sheet or in a note:

- financial assets at fair value through profit and loss
- loans and receivables
- available-for-sale financial assets
- financial liabilities at fair value through profit and loss
- financial liabilities measured at amortised cost.

Income statement and equity

The following should be disclosed on the face of the financial statements or in the notes:

- net gains and losses on
    - financial assets or liabilities at fair value through profit and loss
    - available-for-sale assets showing the amount recognised in equity and the amount removed from equity (on disposal)
    - loans and receivables, and
    - financial liabilities measured at amortised cost
- total interest income and total interest expense for financial assets and liabilities
- the amount of any impairment loss for each class of financial asset.

Other disclosures

These might include:

- accounting policies (i.e. the measurement bases and other accounting policies used in relation to financial statements)
- fair value of each class of financial assets and liabilities should be disclosed in a way that facilitates comparison with carrying amounts.

Nature and extent of risks

IFRS 7 requires entities to disclose information that enables the users of the financial statements to evaluate the nature and extent of the risks arising from financial instruments. Qualitative and quantitative disclosures of exposures to the following risks are required.

- **Credit risk**, including an analysis of the age of assets past their due date but not impaired, and an analysis of individual assets that are not impaired. Credit risk is the risk that one party to a financial instrument will cause a financial loss for the other party by failing to discharge an obligation.
- **Liquidity risk**, including a maturity analysis for financial liabilities that shows the remaining contractual maturities. Liquidity risk is the risk that an entity will encounter difficulty in meeting obligations associated with financial liabilities.
- **Market risk**, including a sensitivity analysis. Market risk is the risk that the fair value or future cash flows of a financial instrument will fluctuate due to changes in market prices.

Summary

Accounting standards are generally about measurement, presentation and disclosure. All three issues are usually covered within a single standard.

   The fact that there is a separate accounting standard for each issue is a measure of the complexity of accounting for financial instruments. As business transactions have become increasingly complex, the need for standards regulating such transactions is paramount if financial statements are to be relied upon.

Chapter summary

IAS 37 *Provisions, Contingent Liabilities and Contingent Assets*

- A provision is defined as a liability of uncertain timing or amount.
- A liability requires there to be an obligation at the balance sheet date.
- A provision should be recognised if:
  - a present obligation has arisen as a result of a past event
  - a payment is probable (i.e. more likely than not)
  - the amount can be estimated reliably.
- A contingent liability is a possible obligation that arises from past events and whose existence will be confirmed only by the occurrence or non-occurrence of one or more uncertain future events not wholly within the control of the entity.
- Contingent liabilities should not be recognised as liabilities but disclosed, unless the possibility of an outflow of resources is remote.
- A contingent asset is a possible asset that arises from past events, and whose existence will be confirmed only by the occurrence or non-occurrence of one or more uncertain future events not wholly within the control of the enterprise.
- Contingent assets should not be recognised but should be disclosed where an inflow of benefits is probable:
  - when the realisation of income is virtually certain, then the related asset is not a contingent asset and its recognition (as an asset) is appropriate.
- A provision should be recognised at the best estimate of the expenditure required to settle the present obligation at the balance sheet date.
- The risks and uncertainties that surround many events and circumstances should be taken into account in reaching the best estimate of a provision.
- Where the effect of the time value of money is material, the amount of a provision should be the present value of the expenditures expected to be required to settle the obligation.
- Provisions should be reviewed at each balance sheet date and adjusted to reflect the current best estimate. If it is no longer probable that an outflow of resources will be required to settle the obligation, the provision shall be reversed.
- Provisions should be used only for the purpose for which they were originally recognised.
- Provisions should not be recognised for future operating losses.
- If an entity has a contract that is onerous, the present obligation under the contract should be recognised and measured as a provision.
- A constructive obligation to restructure arises only when an entity has a detailed formal plan for the restructuring and has raised a valid expectation in those affected that it will carry out the restructuring.

IAS 10 *Events After the Balance Sheet Date*

- Events after the balance sheet date are those events that occur between the balance sheet date and the date when the financial statements are authorised for issue.
- Adjusting events after the balance sheet date provide additional evidence of conditions that existed at the balance sheet date and require figures to be adjusted accordingly.
- Non-adjusting events after the balance sheet date are material events that occur in the period between the balance sheet date and the date when the financial statements are authorised for issue, and are sufficiently important to be brought to the attention of users by way of a note.
- Proposed dividends should not be recognised as a liability at the balance sheet date.

IAS 32 *Financial Instruments: Presentation*

- A financial instrument is a contract that gives rise to a financial asset for one entity and a financial liability (or equity instrument) for another.
- Financial instruments should be classified as either a financial liability or an equity instrument according to the substance of the contract, not its legal form.

- An equity instrument is a financial instrument that includes no contractual obligation to deliver cash (or any other financial asset) to another entity.
- Redeemable preference shares are generally classed as financial liabilities. Dividends from preference shares classified as financial liabilities should be treated as an expense.
- A compound financial instrument should be separated into its two components by evaluating the liability component first and then deducting this from the fair value of the whole instrument to give the equity component.
- The entity must make the decision as to classification at the time the instrument is initially recognised.
- The classification is not subsequently changed based on changed circumstances.

IAS 39 *Financial Instruments: Recognition and Measurement*

- A financial asset or a financial liability should be recognised when (and only when) the entity becomes a party to the contractual provisions of the instrument.
- Financial assets and financial liabilities should be measured initially at their fair value plus transaction costs.
- Financial assets should be held at fair value except that the following should be held at amortised cost using the effective interest method:
  - (a) loans and receivables
  - (b) held-to-maturity investments.
- Financial assets whose fair value cannot be measured reliably should be held at cost.
- Gains and losses should be recognised in the income statement except those arising from available-for-sale financial assets, which should be recognised in the statement of changes in equity (statement of other comprehensive income, as per IAS 1 revised).
- Financial liabilities should be measured at amortised cost using the effective interest method, except that fair value should be used for those held for trading.
- Gains and losses should be recognised in the income statement.
- A financial asset is derecognised when the entity's contractual rights to receive cash flows from the asset expire.
- A financial liability is derecognised when the entity's contractual obligations expire, are discharged or cancelled.

IFRS 7 *Financial Instruments: Disclosures*

- An entity must group its financial instruments into classes of similar instruments.
- The two main categories of disclosures required are:
  1. information about the significance of financial instruments
  2. information about the nature and extent of risks arising from financial instruments.

 Key terms for review

Definitions can be found in the glossary at the end of the book.

Liability	*Financial liability*
Current liability	*Equity instrument*
Non-current (*long-term*) *liability*	*Derivative*
Recognition	*Compound financial instruments*
Provision	*Fair value*
Contingent liability	*Credit risk*
Restructurings	*Liquidity risk*
Financial instrument	*Market risk*
Financial asset	

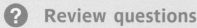

Review questions

1.   What is the definition of a liability according to the IASB Framework?
2.   When should a liability be recognised in a balance sheet?
3.   According to IAS 37, what is the definition of a *contingent asset*?
4.   Explain how the amount of a provision should be measured.
5.   What are the accounting entries required to:
      (a)   create a provision?
      (b)   utilise a provision?
6.   Explain the term '*big bath*' accounting.
7.   Explain, according to IAS 10, what is meant by an *event after the balance sheet date*.
8.   Define the term *financial instrument*.
9.   At what point should a company recognise a financial asset or liability on its balance sheet?
10.   What is meant by the term *amortised cost*?
11.   Explain what is meant by the terms:
      (a)   credit risk
      (b)   liquidity risk
      (c)   market risk.

Exercises

1.   Level I

Briefly explain the differences between creditors, accruals, provisions and contingent liabilities.

2.   Level II

Cragg Cycles Ltd is an outdoor pursuits company operating a number of retail outlets. The finance director is unsure how the following should be dealt with under IAS 37 in the preparation of the financial statements for the year to 31 December 2009.

(a)   At a board of directors meeting on 30 November 2009, it was decided to close one of the company's three outlets in Inverness. Redundancies and other costs will arise. The staff and customers have been advised of the closure by 31 December 2009 and the company has informed the landlord that the lease of the property will not be renewed at the end of its current term (March 2010).

(b)   Cragg Cycles Ltd has a subsidiary company, Hangliders 4 U Ltd. Cragg Cycles Ltd has guaranteed the borrowings of its subsidiary, which is currently very profitable and in a sound financial state.

(c)   In October 2009, a member of staff was injured while demonstrating a mountain bicycle. The Health & Safety Executive has alleged that the company was at fault. Cragg Cycles Ltd's solicitors believe the company will lose any case brought against it.

Required

Advise the finance director on the status of the above situations in relation to the accounts of Cragg Cycles Ltd for the year to 31 December 2009.

3.   Level II

Andlaw Ltd has produced the following figures at its year end of 31 December:

	2007 £	2008 £	2009 £
Operating profit after charging	200,000	180,000	170,000
Reorganisation costs paid	–	20,000	30,000

The reorganisation was approved by the directors in 2006.

Required

(a) Assuming a provision for reorganisation costs of £50,000 was created in the year to 31 December 2007, show the effect on the profits of the three years and compare this with the situation where no provision is created.

(b) Comment on your findings.

4. Level II

As the financial director of Bellrock plc, you have the following to consider in the accounts for the year to 31 December 2009.

 (i) A customer has made a claim against Bellrock for defective goods. The claim is nearing settlement and Bellrock's legal advisers think it is probable that a sum of £300,000 will be paid by Bellrock in settlement, in addition to all legal costs.

 (ii) Bellrock sells goods with a warranty. If minor defects arose in all products sold, repair costs of £2 million would arise. If major defects arose in all products sold, repair costs of £8 million would arise. Bellrock's experience is that 20% of sales lead to claims for minor defects and 5% lead to claims for major defects.

(iii) In September 2009 Bellrock relocated to new office premises. The lease on the old premises runs to 31 December 2011 at a rent of £180,000 per year. Bellrock has been unable to find a tenant to sub-let the old office premises.

(iv) A law passed in October 2009 requires the fitting of new smoke filters at a cost of £150,000 by March 2010. This work has not yet been carried out.

 (v) Bellrock has a provision of £200,000 brought forward at 1 January 2009 against a legal claim. During the year to 31 December 2009, Bellrock won this court action and therefore the provision is no longer needed. However, environmental penalties of some £200,000 have been threatened by the Health & Safety Executive and it is probable that this cost will have to be paid. The directors have therefore proposed that the provision be carried forward.

Required

Explain, quantifying your answer where possible, how the above should be accounted for in accordance with IAS 37.

5. Level II

Watfield Engineering Ltd sells and services forestry equipment. Provisions, have to made in the accounts of Watfield Engineering Ltd for the year to 30 September 2009.

(a) As part of the servicing schedule of forestry vehicles, Watfield is required to replace the engine oil. A special tank is used to collect the old oil, which is emptied on a regular basis and recycled. A leak developed in the tank, causing environmental damage to a nearby river. The company has spent £50,000 on clear-up costs at the year end but further work requires to be done. Advisers estimate that there is a 50% likelihood that the additional work will cost £75,000, a 30% chance it will cost £90,000 and a 20% chance it will cost £110,000.

(b) Watfield Engineering Ltd sells log splitters. The following details are available:

Model	Warranty period	Number of units sold in year
Basic	1 year	400
Standard	1 year	310
Super	2 years	250

The company estimates that 15%, 12% and 20% of Basic, Standard and Super, respectively, will require repair within the warranty period. Estimated repair costs are £150, £200 and £220 for Basic, Standard and Super, respectively. During the year the company spent £15,500 on repairing log splitters sold in the year.

(c)   At 30 September 2008, the accounts contained a provision of £195,000 relating to potential damages arising from a court case being brought against the company. The company reached an out-of-court settlement in December 2008, with Watfield making a full and final payment of £148,000.

Required

 (i)   Explain, using appropriate figures, the effect of the above on the financial statements of Watfield Engineering Ltd for the year to 30 September 2009.
(ii)   Prepare the provisions disclosure note for inclusion in the 30 September 2009 accounts.

6.   Level II

Davpet Ltd built an oil rig in 2007. A decommissioning provision was created at 30 June 2007 based on:

Estimated decommissioning costs	£5.5 m
Discount rate	6%
Estimated decommissioning date	30 June 2019

Due to changes in legislation in June 2009, it is now estimated that decommissioning costs will be £7.0m in 2019. It is company policy to capitalise the decommissioning costs.

Required

(a)   Calculate the provision required in the accounts of Davpet Ltd at 30 June 2009 and prepare journal entries to show all movements on the provision for the year to 30 June 2009.
(b)   Prepare the provisions disclosure note for inclusion in the 30 June 2009 accounts.

7.   Level III

Brownbev Ltd is a brewer of specialist beers. During the audit of the accounts to 31 March 2009 the following items have been brought to your attention as audit manager. The financial accountant has asked you to provide him with some notes so that he can discuss them with the finance director. The company's annual general meeting is held in July each year and the accounts are normally approved in June.

 (i)   At 31 March 2009 a provision of £100,000 was made for the cost of a court case against the company. During April 2009 an out-of-court settlement of £125,000 was agreed. Legal fees, which had not been provided for, of £10,000 were also incurred.
(ii)   On 15 March 2009 a contract was signed for the purchase of new brewing equipment costing £750,000 to be delivered and paid for on 30 June 2009. The equipment will be brought into use immediately on delivery.
(iii) During March 2009 Brownbev Ltd began legal proceedings against a competitor company whose website was using a domain name registered by Brownbev. On 28 March 2009, Brownbev's solicitors filed a claim for £100,000 in damages. The solicitors have advised that the case is likely to take several months to settle and the outcome is uncertain at this stage. Legal fees, for which no provision has as yet been made, are expected to be £20,000.
(iv)   On 25 April 2009, the board of directors proposed a final dividend of £1 per ordinary share be paid for the year ended 31 March 2009, subject to approval at the shareholders' AGM.
 (v)   At the AGM, the board of directors will announce the amalgamation of two of its microbreweries in Scotland on 30 September 2009. This will result in initial redundancy costs of £200,000, but annual savings of £450,000.

Required

Prepare notes for the financial accountant, setting out and explaining how the above matters should be accounted for and disclosed in the financial statements of Brownbev Ltd for the year ended 31 March 2009.

8.   Level II

Brax plc has the following transactions in the year to 31 December 2009.

 (i) Purchased plant and machinery for £75,000 in October 2009. The estimated useful life of the plant and machinery is five years. The invoice from the supplier was still outstanding at 31 December 2009.

 (ii) Issued 2 million ordinary shares of £0.50 at £3.20 each in May 2009.

 (iii) Accrued £15,000 of electricity costs as at 31 December 2009.

 (iv) Borrowed £300,000 from a bank as a five-year term loan.

 (v) Received a government grant of £20,000 in relation to the plant and machinery mentioned in (i) above.

Required

Identify any financial assets, financial liabilities and equity instruments arising from each of the above transactions.

9.   Level II

Emack plc acquired 570,000 ordinary shares of £1 each in Amber Ltd in January 2007 for £1,700,000. Broker's commission and stamp duty amounted to £33,000. Emack holds the shares as an available for sale asset.

 The fair value of the shares was as follows:

■   31 December 2007 – £3.10 per share

■   31 December 2008 – £3.23 per share.

The shares were sold in March 2009 for £3.15 per share.

Required

State how the above would be dealt with in the accounts of Emack plc for the years to 31 December 2007, 2008 and 2009.

10.   Level II

Edsant plc has the following financial instruments at 1 January 2008.

■   Financial asset interest-free loan to a supplier of £450,000. The loan was originally made on 1 January 2006 and is due to be repaid in 2010 with an internal rate of return of 2.5%. The loan is included under loans and receivables.

■   Financial liability 5,000,000 £1 4% bonds 2016 were issued on 1 January 2005. These bonds were issued at par with issue costs of £100,000. The effective interest rate is 4.5% per annum. Interest on the bonds is payable annually in arrears. The bonds were not designated as financial liabilities at fair value through profit or loss.

Required

Calculate the amounts to appear in the income statement of Edsant plc for the year to 31 December 2008 in relation to the above items.

Further reading

IAS 10 *Events after the Balance Sheet Date.* IASB, 2003

IAS 32 *Financial Instruments: Presentation.* IASB, revised 2003

IAS 38 *Provisions, Contingent Liabilities and Contingent Assets.* IASB, 1998

IAS 39 *Financial Instruments: Recognition and Measurement.* IASB, revised 2003

Chapter 8

Taxation

LEARNING OUTCOMES

After studying this chapter you should be able to:

- ☑ prepare the accounting entries required to account for corporate income taxes
- ☑ explain why differences arise between accounting profits and taxable profits
- ☑ explain deferred tax
- ☑ explain and appraise the arguments for and against providing for deferred tax
- ☑ identify several methods of accounting for deferred tax
- ☑ apply the requirements of IAS 12 *Income Taxes*
- ☑ critically appraise whether IAS 12 is effective in providing useful information to user groups.

Introduction

Taxation and the payment of tax is probably the one business issue that evokes a great deal of interest and emotion. Taxation, unlike other expenses that are incurred *in earning* profits, and indeed are matched with the revenues they generate, is charged *as a result of* earning profits. In practice, paying taxation is seldom welcomed and more often resented by all concerned.

This chapter deals with accounting for taxation, together with the reporting of the tax liability for a business. The chapter will not deal directly with the calculation of the tax liability itself, however some knowledge and understanding about taxation is inevitably required.

In practice, depending on the size of the particular organisation, a company may have its own tax department responsible for the calculation of the annual tax charge. Alternatively, the company may employ a firm of taxation specialists to calculate its annual liability for taxation.

Once the tax charge has been established, the details will be passed over to the reporting accountant for inclusion within the financial statements. Consequently, although taxation rates and rules may change, and so affect the calculation of the tax liability, the accounting treatment of the calculated liability will remain broadly the same.

Section 1: Basic Principles

8.1 Corporate income taxes

The tax charged on a company's profits – corporate income tax – is governed by the law prevailing in any given country. In the United Kingdom, this is known as corporation tax and is calculated under rules and rates set by the UK Parliament each year in the Finance Act. The date of payment of the corporation tax is dependent upon whether a company is classified as small or large. A company is large for tax purposes when its taxable profits exceed £1.5m.

The corporation tax of small companies is due in one payment and is to be paid nine months and one day after the end of its accounting period. For example, a small company with a year ending on 31 March 2009 will be required to pay its corporation tax on 1 January 2010. In this instance, corporation tax payable would be classified as a current liability.

A large company must pay corporation tax in instalments. These instalments are based on the company's own estimates of its corporation tax liability for the accounting year. Payments are made in four equal instalments due on the fourteenth day of the seventh, tenth, thirteenth and sixteenth month after the *start* of the accounting year.

For example, a large company with an accounting year *ended* on 31 December 2008 would require to pay its corporation tax in four equal instalments based on the *start* of the accounting year. In this case the start of the accounting year is 1 January 2008, and so corporation tax would be payable as follows:

- Instalment 1 – 14 July 2008
- Instalment 2 – 14 October 2008
- Instalment 3 – 14 January 2009
- Instalment 4 – 14 April 2009

At 31 December 2008, the company would disclose the 14 January and 14 April 2009 amounts as current liabilities. It is important to note that this system imposes upon companies the problem of estimating taxable profits as the year proceeds, in order to calculate the instalments payable.

 Example

A small company for tax purposes has a corporation tax liability of £19,000 in respect of its profits for the year of £100,000. The corporation tax rate is 19%.

Income statement extract	
	£
Profit on ordinary activities before tax	100,000
Tax on profit on ordinary activities (Note 1)	19,000
Profit on ordinary activities after tax	81,000

Notes to the accounts extract	
	£
Note 1: Taxation	
UK corporation tax on the profits for the year at 19%	19,000

Balance sheet extract	
	£
Current liabilities	
Other creditors including taxation and Social Security	19,000

The journal entry required to record a company's corporate income tax liability is as follows:

Dr	Corporation tax charge (income statement)	£19,000	
	Cr Corporation tax payable (balance sheet)		£19,000
Being corporation tax charge.			

Progress Point 8.1

Castle Coaches Ltd has an estimated corporation tax charge of £3.2 million for the year to 31 December 2008. It paid £800,000 (the instalments being calculated based on the estimated profits, i.e. £3.2 million/4 = £800,000) of the tax on 14 July and 14 October 2008. The profit before tax was £9,400,000.

Required

(a)   Prepare journal entries to record the corporation tax transactions arising in the year to 31 December 2008.
(b)   Prepare extracts from the income statement of Castle Coaches Ltd for the year to 31 December 2008 and the balance sheet at that date.

Solution

(a)   Journal entries
       The transactions in 2008 would be recorded as:

Dr	Tax expense (I.S.)	£1,600,000	
	Cr Bank		£1,600,000
Being first and second instalments paid.			

Dr	Tax expense (I.S.)	£1,600,000	
	Cr Corporation tax payable		£1,600,000
Being corporation tax outstanding at year end (i.e. third and fourth instalments).			

Income statement extract:

	£
Profit on ordinary activities before tax	9,400,000
Tax on profit on ordinary activities	3,200,000
Profit on ordinary activities after tax	6,200,000

Balance sheet extract:

Creditors: amounts falling due within one year	
Corporation tax	1,600,000

NB: The third and fourth instalments would be paid on 14 January 2009 and 14 April 2009. These will be recorded as:

Dr	Corporation tax creditor	
	Cr Bank	
Being cr position tax paid.		

8.2 The accounting issue involved

The complicating factor when accounting for taxation is that while accounting profits form the starting point for the computation of taxable profits and the resulting taxation charge, accounting profits and taxable profits are seldom the same. Consequently, the actual taxation paid by a company can often bear no resemblance to the expected payment based upon a user's knowledge of the prevailing tax rate and the accounting profits earned by a company.

For example, a company reporting accounting profits of £1,000,000, when the prevailing tax rate is 30%, might be expected to show a corporation tax charge of £300,000 (i.e. £1,000,000 × 30%), but may actually show a quite different tax figure.

This is because the tax rules for allowing expenses to be charged against profit differ from the accounting rules. This means that, from an accounting point of view, all expenses, including provisions and adjustments for accruals and prepayments, will be included in the calculation of the accounting profit. However, this profit as stated in the income statement may not be acceptable to the authorities as the basis for the taxation charge.

8.3 Differences between accounting profits and taxable profits

In arriving at accounting profits, accountants will deduct those expenses that have been incurred in earning those profits. Unfortunately, the tax authorities specifically disallow certain items of expenditure and allow others, which accounting profits do not. This gives rise to two types of differences.

1. Permanent differences: these are items that, while allowable deductions in arriving at accounting profits, will *never* be allowed as a deduction for tax purposes.
2. Timing differences: these are items that are legitimate deductions in arriving at both accounting and taxable profits, but in different time periods.

Permanent differences

Permanent differences arise in respect of expenditure that is deductible in arriving at accounting profits but is specifically prohibited from being a deduction in arriving at taxable profits.

Examples of such expenses are:

- entertaining, and
- company formation fees.

In the case of entertaining expenses, the tax authorities do not allow this as a taxable deduction because it is open to abuse. For example, suppose Businessman A took out B for lunch and claimed the cost of the meal as a business expense for tax purposes. This is effectively giving A tax relief on normal living expenditure, the rationale being that everyone has to eat! Company formation fees are deemed to be of a capital nature and are therefore not deductible against revenues.

⚙ *Example*

	£	£
Gross profit		100,000
Expenses		
Rent	10,000	
Rates	8,000	
Entertainment	2,000	
		20,000
Net accounting profit		80,000
Taxation (see note)		24,600
Profit after tax		55,400

Note: The taxation charge is calculated as follows, assuming a corporation tax rate of 30%:

	£
Net accounting profit as reported	80,000
Add disallowable expenditure:	
Entertainment	2,000
Taxable profit	82,000
Corporation tax at 30%	24,600
Profit after tax	55,400

In this instance, with the knowledge that entertainment is not permitted as a deduction in arriving at taxable profits, a user would be able to reconcile the tax charge to the accounting profits.

Timing differences

Timing differences arise in respect of items that are legitimate credits or deductions in arriving at both accounting and taxable profits, but in different time periods.

The most common example of a timing difference is the difference between the accounting reliefs given in respect of the depreciation charges of a fixed asset and the statutory tax reliefs granted in respect of the purchases of such assets.

Depreciation can be a very subjective calculation since it depends upon several factors, such as the life of the asset and residual value. A different depreciation charge may be calculated in respect of the same asset. It is for this reason, and indeed to avoid manipulating taxable profits, that depreciation is not an allowable expense for tax purposes. Instead, tax allowances, known as capital allowances, are given as deductions in arriving at taxable profits.

Capital allowances are in effect 'statutory depreciation charges', which are given at predetermined rates set by governments. Such rates do not take account of factors, such as useful economic life, pattern of benefit or expected residual value. Moreover, capital allowances are often given at enhanced rates to encourage investment in plant and equipment, which often means that the timing of the accounting and taxation reliefs may differ.

Over the lifetime of any particular asset, a company will receive the same amount of reliefs for accounting purposes (through the income statement in a combination of depreciation and profit or loss on disposal) as it will for tax purposes (in a combination of capital allowances and balancing adjustments on disposal). It is because of the way the capital allowances are given that the timing of the

BASIC

INTERMEDIATE

ADVANCED

reliefs may differ. Indeed, if the differences in any particular year are significant, this can have a considerable bearing on the tax payable by a company, and on the relationship between the accounting profit and the tax payable.

Progress Point 8.2

Explain what is meant by timing differences.

Solution

Timing differences are differences between an entity's taxable profits and its results as stated in the financial statements that arise from the inclusion of gains and losses in tax assessments in periods different from those in which they are recognised in financial statements. Timing differences originate in one period and are capable of reversal in one or more periods.

 Example

A company buys a van for £3,000, which is to be depreciated over four years at £750 per annum. At the end of Year 4, the company disposes of the van for £200.

The statutory tax reliefs given on the van are as follows:

Year 1:	40% first year allowance (FYA)
Year 2 onwards:	25% writing down allowance (WDA) on written-down value (WDV)

The accounting deductions given will be as follows:

	Year 1 £	Year 2 £	Year 3 £	Year 4 £	Relief £
Depreciation	750	750	750	750	3,000
Gain on disposal	–	–	–	(200)	(200)
	750	750	750	550	2,800

Note that the accounting deductions over the four years equal the net cost of the van to the company, i.e. cost less residual proceeds received (3,000 − 200 = £2,800).

The taxation reliefs given will be as follows:

		Year 1	Year 2	Year 3	Year 4	Total
Cost	3,000					
FYA (40%)		1,200				1,200
WDV		1,800				
WDA (25%)			450			450
WDV			1,350			
WDA (25%)				338		338
WDV				1,012		
Sales proceeds					200	
Balancing allowance*					812	812
		1200	450	338	812	2,800

*In the year of disposal there is no writing-down allowance; instead, the sales proceeds are set against the written-down value at the beginning of that year (i.e. £1,012 − 200 = £812).

Note again that the taxation reliefs granted equal the net cost of the van to the company.

Comparison of reliefs:

	Year 1	Year 2	Year 3	Year 4	Total
Accounting reliefs	750	750	750	550	2,800
Taxation reliefs	1,200	450	338	812	2,800

Assume that, in Year 1, the company has accounting profits (after charging depreciation) of £9,250. If the rate of corporation tax ruling is 30% then the company will pay corporation tax as follows:

	£	
Accounting profits	9,250	
Add: depreciation	750	(disallowable accounting relief)
Profit before depreciation	10,000	
Less: capital allowances	1,200	(allowable taxation relief)
Taxable profits	8,800	
Corporation tax (30%)	2,640	

The company accounts will show the following:

	£
Accounting profits	9,250
Taxation	2,640
Profit after tax	6,610

However, the expected tax charged based on the accounting profit is £2,775 (i.e. £9,250 × 30% = £2,775). The difference between the actual tax charge of £2,640 and the expected tax charge of £2,775 (i.e. £135) is the timing difference. This timing difference arises as a result of the taxation reliefs in Year 1 being greater than the accounting reliefs (i.e. (1,200 − 750) × 30% = £135).

Assume that the company, over the four years of owning the asset, has the following results.

If the taxation charge was based on the accounting profits then the expected tax charges would be as follows:

	Year 1	Year 2	Year 3	Year 4	Total
Profit before depreciation	10,000	11,000	9,500	12,000	
Depreciation (as calculated)	750	750	750	550	
Accounting profits	9,250	10,250	8,750	11,450	
Expected tax charge (30%)	2,775	3,075	2,625	3,435	11,910

The taxable profits, however, would be calculated as follows:

	Year 1	Year 2	Year 3	Year 4	Total
Profit before depreciation	10,000	11,000	9,500	12,000	
Capital allowances	1,200	£450	£338	£812	
Taxable profits	2,775	10,550	9,162	11,188	
Actual tax charge (30%)	2,640	3,165	2,749	3,356	11,910

Comparison	Year 1	Year 2	Year 3	Year 4	Total
Expected tax charge	2,775	3,075	2,625	3,435	11,910
Actual tax charge	2,640	3,165	2,749	3,356	11,910
Difference	135	(90)	(124)	79	–

As can be seen, in each of the years, there is a difference between the expected tax charge found by multiplying the accounting profit by the appropriate corporation tax rate, and the actual tax charge. The difference is a result of the timing of the capital allowances (reliefs available as deductions against taxable profits) being different from the depreciation (deductions against accounting profits). However, as the example illustrates, the total tax charge for the period as a whole remains the same at £11,190. It is simply that the timing of the tax payments differs.

The difference between the depreciation charge in any year and the tax allowance for that year is referred to as the 'timing difference'. In the above example, the tax allowances have the effect of reducing the actual tax charge to below the expected tax charge in Years 1 and 4, and increasing the actual tax charge above the expected tax charge in Years 2 and 3. The difference in Year 1 is known as the 'originating difference', caused by the capital allowances given being *higher* than the depreciation disallowed (i.e. accelerated capital allowances). The differences in Years 2 to 4 are known as 'reversing differences', caused by the capital allowances given being *lower* than the depreciation disallowed.

8.4 Deferred tax account

It is possible to account for this distortion in the tax charge by creating a special account called a deferred tax account. A deferred tax account recognises the tax effects of timing differences in the current period and is used to make appropriate adjustments to the tax charge in future periods.

Continuing with our earlier illustration, the additional tax charge required in Year 1 to equalise the expected tax charge with the actual tax charge would be £135 (i.e. £2,775 – £2,640). This is the amount that requires to be transferred *into* the deferred tax account and is calculated as follows:

Tax rate × (tax allowances given – deprecation disallowed)
i.e. 30% × (1,200 – 750) = £135.

In Year 1, the effect of this adjustment on the tax charge in the income statement would be as follows:

Income statement (Year 1)	£	£
Profits		9,250
Taxation: actual	2,640	
deferred	135	
Total tax charge		2,775
Profit after tax		6,475

By making the deferred tax adjustment, the taxation charge and after-tax profit figure becomes the same as if the accounting profit had been multiplied by the tax rate and had itself been used in the tax calculation.

Note, however, that the deferred tax adjustment does not affect the tax payable to the tax authorities – it is merely an accounting adjustment that effectively equalises the tax charge to the expected tax charge that would have resulted had there been no timing differences.

The journal entry required to record this transfer is as follows:

	£	£
Tax expense (profit and loss) Dr	135	
To provision for deferred tax		135
Being originating differences.		

The provision for deferred tax would be shown separately in the balance sheet under the heading 'Provision for liabilities and charges'.

Balance sheet extract	£
Current liabilities	
Corporation tax payable	2,640
Provision for liabilities and charges	
Deferred tax	135

What does the provision for deferred tax represent?

The provision for deferred tax represents the additional tax that would have become due had the timing differences not arisen. The taxable profits are lower than the accounting profits because the capital allowances are higher that the depreciation charge. The provision for deferred tax equalises the total tax charge with the expected tax charge. Given that, over the lifetime of the asset, these timing differences will reverse, the amount in the provision for deferred tax account will be used to make the total tax charge equal to the expected tax charge in subsequent accounting periods. This procedure follows the accruals principle and matches the tax charge with the accounting profits earned in a particular accounting period.

Year 2

Carrying on with the example, the position in Year 2 is as follows:

Transfer to/(from) deferred tax
= tax rate × (tax allowances given – depreciation disallowed)
= 30% × (450 – 750)
= (90)

In Year 2, the timing difference is the opposite from that in Year 1. Rather than a transfer into the provision for deferred tax account being required, a transfer out of the provision account is required. This is because, in Year 2, the capital allowances given are *less* than the depreciation charge disallowed, which means the actual tax charge is *higher* than the expected tax charge. This transfer is made into the profit and loss account. Such a transfer is known as a 'reversal'.

The journal adjustment required to record this transfer is as follows:

	£	£
Dr Provision for deferred tax	90	
Cr Taxation expense (profit & loss account)		90
Being transfer from deferred taxation.		

The income statement and balance sheet extracts would be as follows:

Income statement: Year 2	£	£
Profits		10,250
Taxation: actual	3,165	
deferred	(90)	
Total tax charge		3,075
Profit after tax		7,175

Again, the transfer from deferred tax results in the tax charge shown in the income statement as being the same as that which would have occurred had depreciation been allowed as a deduction for tax purposes and no timing differences had therefore arisen.

Balance sheet: Year 2	£
Current liabilities	
Corporation tax payable	3,165
Provision for liabilities and charges	
Deferred tax (135 − 90)	45

Year 3

Adopting the same procedure for Year 3 gives the following:

$$\text{Transfer to/(from) deferred tax}$$
$$= \text{tax rate} \times (\text{tax allowances given depreciation disallowed})$$
$$= 30\% \times (338 - 750)$$
$$\text{Transfer (from) deferred tax} = \underline{\underline{(124)}}$$

The journal entry required to record this transfer is as follows:

	£	£
Dr Provision for deferred tax	124	
Cr Taxation expense (profit and loss account)		124
Being transfer from deferred taxation.		

The income statement extract will be as follows:

Income statement: Year 3	£	£
Profits		8,750
Taxation: actual	2,749	
deferred	(124)	
Total tax charge		2,625
Profit after tax		6,125

The balance sheet for Year 3 is slightly more complex. At the end of Year 2 the balance on the deferred tax provision was £45. As a result of the transfer made to the income statement of £124, this means that a deferred tax asset of £79 (£124 – £45) needs to be created.

Balance sheet extract: Year 3	
Deferred tax asset	79
Current liabilities	£
Corporation tax payable	2,749
Provision for liabilities and charges	
Deferred tax	–

Year 4

Finally, in Year 4, the van that was originally purchased, and that has given rise to the timing differences, is sold. The deferred tax adjustment is as follows:

Transfer to/(from) deferred tax
= tax rate × (tax allowances given depreciation disallowed)
= 30% × (812 – 550)
Transfer (from) deferred tax = (79)

In Year 4, the tax allowance is greater than the depreciation charge and consequently a transfer to deferred tax is required. The actual tax charge is lower than expected as a result of the tax allowances being greater than the depreciation deduction.

The journal entry required is as follows:

	£	£
Dr Taxation expense (profit & loss account)	79	
Cr Provision for deferred tax		79
Being transfer to deferred taxation.		

The income statement extract will be as follows:

Income statement: Year 4		
	£	£
Profits		11,450
Taxation: actual	3,356	
deferred	79	
Total tax charge		3,435
Profit after tax		8,015

The balance sheet extracts will be as follows:

	£
Balance sheet: Year 4	
Deferred tax asset (79 – 79)	–
Current liabilities	
Corporation tax payable	3,356
Provision for liabilities and charges	
Deferred tax	–

By the end of Year 4, the timing differences have equalised and no further deferred tax adjustments are required.

Overview

As a result of the timing differences between the tax allowances given and the depreciation charged on the van, the actual tax charge for each of the years did not bear any relationship to the accounting profits earned. By utilising the deferred tax account, and making appropriate transfers to and from that account, the total tax charge and after-tax profit figures became the same as if the accounting profits had themselves been used in the tax calculations (i.e. and no timing differences had therefore arisen).

The accounting issue involved

The earlier example has demonstrated the effects of timing differences. As a consequence of taxation reliefs being granted in different time periods from depreciation being claimed, and the resulting difference between taxable profits and accounting profits, the actual tax paid by a company often bears no relationship to the accounting profit earned.

Why it matters

The example was based on the assumption that first year allowances of 40% were granted. In practice, initial allowances can be as much as 100%. In such cases, all the tax relief in respect of an asset purchase is claimed in Year 1, while the depreciation charges may be allocated over two, three or more years. The deferred tax adjustment effectively allocates the tax relief over the lifetime of the asset and in a manner reflecting the consumption of that asset.

This can result in the tax charge in the year of purchase being unexpectedly low and the subsequent years' tax charges being higher than expected.

Advantages of providing for deferred tax

A key accounting indicator used by investors is that of earnings per share (EPS); this is calculated using after-tax profits.

Taxation is a function of the profit for the period together with the company's tax circumstances. These circumstances may result in higher or lower taxable profits. As a result, the total tax charge will, if comparison between other companies/years is to be possible, require to be adjusted to remove the distortions caused by timing differences.

Consequently, unless an adjustment is made within the total tax charge, the actual tax charge will not accurately reflect the total tax cost of a company's current profits. In the year in which an asset is purchased, and where significant initial allowances have been granted, a low tax rate will be recorded. This low rate will not be sustainable, however, as the tax charge in future years increases. Therefore, without making an adjustment to account for the timing differences, the future tax cost of the accelerated capital allowances claim is ignored, and the profit after tax figure will not reflect the true performance of the company.

A further benefit of providing for deferred tax is that it reduces shareholder pressure for dividends. By smoothing after-tax reported profits, less pressure will be put on directors to pay dividends than would be the case were a company to show a low tax charge and hence higher after-tax profits. Moreover, the paradox of such a situation is that in arriving at the capital allowances claim, the company may well have invested heavily in capital expenditure and would not have cash resources left. In other words, it is as a result of spending its cash resources that the company has managed to reduce its tax liability.

It would also appear to be desirable to show the true liability for tax based on accounting profits as opposed to taxable profits, by showing a combination of actual tax charge and the deferred tax element that remains as a provision.

To provide for deferred tax in full would therefore appear to adhere to both the prudence and accruals concepts. This is known as full provisioning for deferred tax.

Disadvantages of providing for deferred tax

There is no requirement for a company's tax charge to bear a relationship to its reported income. As was noted in the Introduction to this chapter, taxation is an expense that is unique. It is not incurred in earning profits, but rather is incurred as a result of earning profits and consequently the accruals concept would appear not to be applicable to such a rogue expense.

Moreover, the tax payable by a company is that tax which has been calculated in respect of its taxable profits. The deferred tax adjustment does not affect the tax payable and, consequently, providing the actual tax liability is disclosed then the prudence concept is effectively satisfied.

Providing for deferred tax may also mask any perceived tax benefits given by the government. The government may try to encourage investment in capital equipment by offering incentives such as initial allowances, but if the reduced actual tax charge is effectively masked by the overall tax charge (i.e. current tax and deferred tax), then any perceived tax benefits will not be readily evident from the financial statements.

At the individual company level, the benefits of good tax planning (i.e. investment strategies) are not reflected in the financial statements.

A real-life example will illustrate the problem.

 ## *Example*

A few years ago, I met with a client just before the company's year end. The company had traded very successfully during the year and was to invest heavily in new equipment in order to take advantage of the initial allowances available at that time and which would substantially reduce the company's tax liability. The company duly invested in the equipment and the financial statements were compiled shortly after the year end. The company's actual tax charge had been significantly reduced, however the provision for deferred tax returned the total tax charge back to the expected tax charge based on the accounting profit. At a meeting held to discuss the draft accounts, the CEO was extremely unhappy. He questioned the advice that had been given to him in respect of the investment in the equipment since the tax charge did not appear to reflect the tax savings that had been discussed at the time.

It took a great deal of time and effort to convince the CEO that the investment strategy had worked and the company's tax liability had been reduced. The provision for deferred tax had most certainly been unhelpful in this instance.

As an alternative, the 'flow through' approach ignores the effects of timing differences and accounts only for that tax payable in respect of the period in question.

Summary

Although accounting profits form the basis for the computation of taxable profits, **accounting profits and taxable profits** are seldom the same. This is because the tax rules for deductibility of expenses differ from accounting rules, and means that the profit or loss as stated in the income statement may not be that which the tax authorities will accept as the basis for the taxation charge.

It is possible to account for the distortions caused by the differences by creating a deferred tax account and providing in full for the future tax consequence of **current tax** savings. This approach is known as full deferred tax accounting. The flow through approach, on the other hand, ignores the effects of timing differences and accounts only for that tax payable in respect of the period in question.

Section 2: Intermediate Issues

8.5 Deferred tax

Section 1 explained how the deferred tax adjustment could be used to remove distortions in calculated tax figures caused by accelerated capital allowances. Some of the advantages of providing for deferred tax were outlined, however, there were also advantages in adopting the 'flow through' approach, which ignores the effects of timing differences and instead accounts only for the tax payable in respect of the period in question.

The examples presented were concerned with the deferred tax position in relation to individual assets only. This section now considers the position in relation to a collection of assets held by a company, and looks at the deferred tax implications.

The accounting issue involved

At the individual asset level, it is possible to estimate, over the lifetime of the asset, the originating and reversing differences, and account for the deferred tax adjustments accordingly. The position with regard to all the assets that a company may acquire is somewhat more complex. Most businesses will tend to replace assets regularly and, over time, inflationary pressures will tend to push up the prices of the replacement assets. In addition, companies are not static and will tend to grow over time.

If the taxation rules in place are such that initial allowances in the year of acquisition are greater than the depreciation being charged then there is the possibility that each year there will be an originating difference and therefore no reversing differences. Moreover, where such circumstances prevail, providing in full for deferred tax will result in the balance on the deferred tax account becoming larger and larger each year with no net reversing differences to reduce that balance.

Following a full provision approach may well cause difficulties when interpreting financial statements. As was noted in Section 1, deferred tax is disclosed separately on the balance sheet under the heading 'Provision for liabilities and charges'. Consequently, such a classification results in the net assets figure in the balance sheet being reduced by a 'liability' that will never crystallise. Moreover, by its inclusion in the balance sheet, an item that will not be payable in the foreseeable future, would appear to be inconsistent with the going concern concept – that is, if the going concern concept applies then investment will continue and therefore originating differences will continue to be created. Only cessation of the company or contraction of its business and reduced investment would result in there being reversals to the provision.

Partial provision: a partial solution

In order to avoid the problems caused by providing in full for deferred tax, and the disadvantages caused by following the 'flow through' approach, a partial provision approach could be adopted. As its name suggests, a partial provision provides only for that part of the deferred tax liability that is likely to become payable in the future, or to 'crystallise in the foreseeable future'.

This partial provision approach estimates how much of the provision is likely to crystallise into a liability. This crystallisation is assumed to happen when the depreciation charge in succeeding years exceeds the capital allowances (i.e. when there are reversing as opposed to originating differences).

 **Example**

Neat plc is calculating the necessary provision for deferred tax using partial provision of the end of Year 5. It has forecast the following information, taking account of expected expenditure, capital allowances and depreciation for the next four years. Corporation tax is expected to remain at 30% throughout the period.

	Year 6 £000	Year 7 £000	Year 8 £000	Year 9 £000
Capital allowances	1,600	1,750	1,100	2,400
Depreciation	1,400	1,600	1,670	1,000
Net originating differences	(200)	(150)	–	(1,400)
Net reversing differences	–	–	570	–

In this illustration, the depreciation charge exceeds the capital allowances claim in Year 8. It will be in this year, therefore, that the taxable profits will exceed the accounting profits by £570,000. Given that the tax rate in Year 8 is expected to be 30%, the amount of tax involved is 30% of £570,000, which is £171,000.

Consequently the provision required for deferred tax at the end of Year 8 needs to be £171,000.

The income statement charges and balance sheet extracts would be as follows:

Income statement extract				
	Year 5 £	Year 6 £	Year 7 £	Year 8 £
Deferred tax	171,000	–	–	(171,000)

Balance sheet extract				
	Year 5 £	Year 6 £	Year 7 £	Year 8 £
Provision for liabilities and charges				
Deferred tax	171,000	171,000	171,000	0

However, it could be argued that to make all the required provision in Year 5 is being excessively prudent. Indeed, this approach is known as the 'most prudent partial provision'.

Based on Neat plc's forecasts, the provision could be built up as follows, taking a cumulative view of the position in future years. Instead of providing for all of the deferred tax balance in Year 5, only an amount that results in the required provision being accumulated by the beginning of Year 8 need be provided for. Given this approach, the net reversing difference in Year 8 is preceded by net originating differences in Year 7 and Year 6. Therefore, it will be possible to make additional provisions in those two years in order to determine the amount of the provision required in Year 5:

			£000
i.e.	Net reversing differences in Year 8		570
	Less: future net originating differences		
	Year 6	200	
	Year 7	150	
		350	
			220

	£
Minimum provision necessary at Year 5	
£220,000 x 30% =	66,000

Using this minimum partial provision approach results in the following income statement and balance entries being reported.

BASIC
INTERMEDIATE
ADVANCED

Income statement extract	Year 5	Year 6	Year 7	Year 8
Deferred tax	66,000	60,000	45,000	(171,000)

Balance sheet extract	Year 5	Year 6	Year 7	Year 8
Provision for liabilities and charges	£	£	£	£
Deferred tax	66,000	126,000	171,000	–

In Year 5, the provision is set to £66,000 and if the forecasts on expenditure, tax and depreciation are met, net originating differences in Year 6 of £60,000 (£200,000 × 30%) and Year 7 of £45,000 (£150,000 × 30%) will result in there being an accumulated provision of £171,000 by the beginning of the year in which the reversal takes place.

In Year 8 there is a net originating difference and no further details available, therefore no further calculations using partial provisioning can be made.

Comparison of methods

Income statement extracts	Year 5	Year 6	Year 7	Year 8
	£	£	£	£
Most prudent provision				
Deferred tax	171,000	–	–	(171,000)
Minimum partial provision				
Deferred tax	66,000	60,000	45,000	(171,000)

Balance sheet extracts	Year 5	Year 6	Year 7	Year 8
	£	£	£	£
Most prudent partial provision				
Provision for deferred tax	171,000	171,000	171,000	–
Minimum partial provision				
Provision for deferred tax	66,000	60,000	45,000	(171,000)

As can be seen from the comparison, there are marked variations between the two.

Partial arts

So which one is correct?

Both are!

Unfortunately, both methods are perfectly acceptable. Adopting a partial provision approach to providing for deferred tax necessarily involves making estimates, taking judgements and making assumptions about future investment plans, future tax rates as well as the inherent subjectivity in determining depreciation charges and estimating useful lives, patterns of benefit and residual values. Full provisioning, on the other hand, is made on the basis of the knowledge of what has happened in the past. Regrettably, given the level of potential variation, partial provisioning could also allow for manipulation of deferred tax and, consequently, reported after-tax profits.

Changes in tax rates

The analysis thus far has assumed that tax rates over time have remained the same. Further complications, and choices, arise when the rate of tax changes. There are effectively two rates that could be adopted:

1. the rate ruling at the time the original timing difference occurred; this approach is known as the deferral method
2. the current rate of tax ruling at the date the balance sheet is prepared; this is known as the liability method.

Deferral method

Under the deferral method, the tax effects of the timing differences that have arisen in each year are calculated. The tax effect is then debited or credited to the income statement as part of the annual tax charge and the corresponding adjustment made to the deferred tax provision in the balance sheet. The balances on the deferred tax account are regarded as deferred credits or deferred charges rather than as amounts payable or recoverable, and are not revised on changes in the rate of tax. The deferral method places an emphasis on the income statement charge. In principle, all reversing timing differences in respect of an asset are reversed at the same rate of tax that applied to the originating timing difference on that asset. This approach, known as the 'strict deferral method', inevitably involves extensive recording of dates and rates – particularly when more than one asset is concerned. In practice, as a consequence of the extremely onerous record-keeping requirements, a 'net change method' is used instead, whereby the net amount of all originating and reversing timing differences is calculated. If this produces a net originating difference then the current tax rate will be applied. If, however, there is a net reversing difference then either:

■ a first in, first out (FIFO) basis is used, whereby the rate applying to the earlier timing differences making up the deferred tax account is used, or
■ an average basis is applied, the rate being arrived at by comparing the balance on the deferred tax account at the beginning of the period with the total of related timing differences.

Liability method

Under the liability method, the tax effects of timing differences are regarded as liabilities for taxes payable in the future. Whenever there is a change in the rate of tax, the balance on the deferred tax account is adjusted to that current rate of tax on accumulated timing differences. The corresponding income statement charge will normally be shown as part of the taxation charge. The liability method places an emphasis on the balance sheet liability on the basis that the most recent rate of tax is the best available estimate of the tax payable if timing differences reverse. This approach allows calculations to be made in total and therefore it is not necessary to keep such detailed records as would be required for the deferral method.

 *Example*

An asset attracts capital allowances as follows: £200,000 in 2008 and £150,000 in 2009. Depreciation on the asset, calculated using the straightline method is £100,000 per annum. The tax rate is 30% in 2008 and 25% in 2009.

	2008	2009
	£	£
Depreciation charge	100,000	100,000
Tax allowance	200,000	150,000
Timing difference	100,000	50,000

Deferral method

	2008	2009
	£	£
Deferred tax charge	30,000	12,500
Deferred tax balance	30,000	42,500 (100,000 x 30% + 50,000 x 25%)

Liability method

	2008	2009
	£	£
Deferred tax charge	30,000	7,500 (25% x 50,000) + (100,000 x (25% – 30%))
Deferred tax balance	30,000	37,500 (25% x 150,000)

Summary

Three approaches to accounting for the tax effects of timing differences arising from accelerated capital allowances have been put forward:

1.   the flow through approach
2.   the full deferral approach
3.   the partial deferral approach.

Two further methods have been put forward to calculate a deferred tax balance:

1.   the liability method
2.   the deferral method.

The remainder of this section considers what other variations between accounting practice and taxation law give rise to timing differences and how these should be accounted for under IAS 12 *Income Taxes*.

8.6 IAS 12 *Income Taxes*

IAS 12 and current tax

IAS 12 applies to current tax as well as deferred tax.

Definition (*para. 5*)

Current tax is the amount of income taxes payable (recoverable) in respect of the taxable profit (tax loss) for a period.

Recognition and measurement

Current tax for the current and prior periods should be recognised as a liability to the extent that it has not been settled, and as an asset to the extent that the amounts already paid exceed the amount due.

The benefit of a tax loss that can be carried back to recover current tax of a prior period should be recognised as an asset.

Current tax assets and liabilities should be measured at the amount expected to be paid to (recovered from) taxation authorities, using the rates that have been enacted or substantially enacted at the balance sheet date.

Current tax should be recognised as income or expense in the income statement except if it arises from a transaction that is or has been taken directly to reserves, when it should be taken to reserves and reported through the statement of recognised income and expenses.

IAS 12 and deferred tax

IAS 12 is based on a balance sheet approach and requires a liability measurement of deferred tax together with the full provision method for all temporary differences.

IAS 12 extends the principles outlined earlier in relation to timing differences, which were illustrated using depreciation and tax allowances, and requires that deferred tax be accounted for on the future tax consequences of all items that are included within the financial statements and are dealt with for accounting purposes differently than for tax purposes. In other words, the matching principle is being extended further to include taxation adjustments that are implied by the valuations of the assets and liabilities included within the financial statements. Items whose accounting treatments and taxation treatments differ – income or expenses – by their very nature must be unsettled at the balance sheet date (otherwise they would be permanent differences), and will therefore appear as assets or liabilities in the balance sheet. IAS 12 requires that where those assets and liabilities are recognised, then the taxation effects of their inclusion as assets and liabilities must also be recognised.

Consequently, where a company recognises, for example, a debtor in respect of an overseas dividend receivable, which will be taxed on receipt, it should also recognise the corresponding tax that will fall due once the dividend has been received. This would give rise to a deferred tax liability.

Temporary differences

The overseas dividend situation illustrated above is an example of a temporary difference.

A temporary difference is the difference between the **tax base** of an asset or liability and its carrying amount in the balance sheet.

The tax base of an asset or liability is the amount attributed to that asset or liability for tax purposes.

One way of understanding this concept is to consider what amount would appear in the balance sheet if it was drawn up based on tax rules as opposed to accounting principles.

It follows that, in order to calculate the deferred tax expense (or benefit) and the related deferred tax liability (asset), a company will require to determine the tax values of its assets and liabilities and then compare them with their carrying amounts in the published accounts.

Assets

It is assumed that assets in a balance sheet will generate future income or benefits at least equal to their carrying amounts – otherwise the assets will be overstated.

If it is probable that the recovery of the asset will make future tax payments larger (smaller) in the future, a deferred tax liability (deferred tax asset) should be recognised.

⊛ Example

Tartan plc accrued dividend income from Sodik Inc (a foreign company) of £150,000 as at 31 December 2008. The amount was received during 2009. Under UK tax law, overseas dividend income is taxed on a receipts basis and, consequently, Tartan plc is not subject to corporation tax until the dividend is received in 2009.

However, the company has a potential tax liability at 2008 in respect of the accrued income. Indeed, by accruing the income as receivable, Tartan plc is confident of its ultimate receipt. Tartan plc therefore has a liability for the related tax, which will fall due on receipt. This tax is accounted for not as current tax, but as deferred tax.

The journal entry to record this will be:

		£	£
Dr	Taxation expense (income statement)	45,000	
	Cr Deferred tax liability (balance sheet)		45,000
Being deferred tax on dividend receivable.			

Liabilities

It is assumed that liabilities will be settled (benefits transferred) at least equal to their carrying amounts. If it is probable that the settlement of a liability will make future tax payments smaller (larger) a deferred tax asset (liability) should be recognised.

 ## Example

A company has a pension liability of £100,000 recognised in its balance sheet at the year end. Under UK tax rules, pension contributions are deducted for tax purposes when they are paid.

This company will require to make the appropriate pension contributions to clear the liability in future years by increasing its contributions. This will result in future years' tax liabilities being reduced as the contributions are paid and the taxable profits reduced. This future tax relief will be shown in the accounts now as a deferred tax asset (i.e. £100,000 × 30% = £30,000).

The journal entry to record this will be:

		£	£
Dr	Deferred tax asset (balance sheet)	30,000	
Cr	Deferred tax expense (income statement)		30,000
Being deferred tax asset on pension liability.			

Note, however, that there are only a few assets and liabilities that may give rise to temporary differences. Where the economic benefits (income) are not taxable then the tax base of the asset is equal to its carrying amount.

 ## Example

A company has dividends receivable of £1,000 in its balance sheet. The tax legislation to which the company is subject does not tax dividends.

Because the dividend is not taxable then its tax base is £1,000, and therefore no temporary differences arise.

	Tax base	Carrying amount	Temporary difference
Dividends receivable	1,000	1,000	–

Temporary differences may be either one of the following:

- Taxable temporary differences: these will result in taxable amounts in future periods when the carrying amount of the asset or liability is recovered or settled. These will give rise to deferred tax liabilities. Overseas dividend is an example of a taxable temporary difference.
- Deductible temporary differences: these will result in amounts that are deductible in arriving at taxable profits in future periods when the carrying amount of the asset or liability is recovered or settled. These will give rise to deferred tax assets. The pension liability is an example of a deductible temporary difference.

Progress Point 8.3

Norwood plc accrued dividend income from a foreign company of £100,000 at 31 December 2008 – the dividend being received in February 2009. This dividend is taxable on receipt in the UK. Given a corporation tax rate of 30%, calculate and record any deferred tax asset or liability arising.

Solution

Under the tax legislation the dividend would not be subject to corporation tax until the year to 31 December 2009 (i.e. the year of receipt). Its tax effect would not therefore be recognised in the corporation tax charge for the year to 31 December 2008 in the profit and loss account. However, assuming that the asset (i.e. the accrued income), will generate income at least equal to its carrying amount, the asset will make future tax payments higher (i.e. in the year to 31 December 2009). A deferred tax liability at 31 December 2008 should therefore be created of £100,000 x 30%, as follows:

Dr	Deferred tax (income statement)	£30,000	
	Cr Deferred tax liability (balance sheet)		£30,000
Being deferred tax on dividend receivable.			

This liability will be reversed in the year to 31 December 2009, when the foreign dividend is received and subject to corporation tax.

The UK position

The following are examples of temporary differences under UK tax legislation.

Tangible fixed assets held at cost and on which capital allowances are available

The temporary difference equals:

		£
Carrying amount	NBV (net book value)	X
Tax base	Tax WDV (written down value)	X
Temporary difference		X

If NBV > Tax WDV = deferred tax liability.
If NBV < Tax WDV = deferred tax asset.

Tangible fixed assets held at value

The same principles apply as those for assets held at cost, except net book value is based on revalued figures.

Note that where there is a revaluation, deferred tax is provided even if there is no intention to sell the asset. If such assets were sold at the revalued amount then a profit would arise that could be subject to tax. Although no actual tax is payable in respect of the upward revaluation, IAS 12 requires that the implicitly deferred tax be accounted for. The deferred tax on the revaluation gain is recognised in the statement of recognised income and expense (SORIE) rather than the income statement – the reason being that as the revaluation itself is not realised, it will be recognised in the SORIE and not the income statement.

The journal entry to record this will be:

```
Dr    Revaluation reserve
    Cr      Deferred tax liability
Being deferred tax on revalued assets.
```

Accrued income

There are no deferred tax consequences unless the income is taxed when received (i.e. on a cash basis). If income is taxed on a cash basis, the temporary difference equals:

Carrying amount (accrued income)	X
Tax base	0
Taxable temporary difference	X

Note that while, for accounting purposes, the accrued income has been included at the balance sheet date, for tax purposes, the income will be taxed when received; in other words, in the financial statements for the following year. As far as the tax authorities are concerned, the tax base will be nil. In the following year, the position will be reversed and the tax base will take on the value of the amount received while the carrying value in the balance sheet will be nil (i.e. it has now been received).

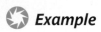 ## Example

Ferdz provided for deferred tax of £60,000 in respect of accrued income receivable of £200,000 in the year to 31 December 2008. This income was received in February 2009 and is subject to tax on receipt. In the financial statements to 31 December 2009, the credit would be released to the tax expense in the income statement.

i.e.	Carrying value (2009)	0
	Tax base	200,000
	Temporary difference	(200,000)
	Deferred tax @ 30%	£60,000 Dr

The journal entry will be:

	£	£
Dr Deferred tax liability (balance sheet)	60,000	
Cr deferred tax income (income statement)		60,000
Being reversal of deferred tax liability.		

The effect of this is that the tax expense in 2008 is set to that level that is implied by including the accrued income within those financial statements. And in 2009, when the actual tax is paid on the amounts received, the tax expense is reduced by the deferred tax previously accounted for. The distorting effects of the temporary differences are therefore removed and the tax expense reflects that level of charge which is implied by the level of profit.

Pension asset

In respect of defined benefit plans (i.e. plans that specify the amounts payable to pensioners on retirement), a pension asset may be recognised in the balance sheet. A pension asset represents a recognised surplus of invested funds, which means that the company may pay reduced contributions in the future or may even receive a refund of contributions paid. Consequently, by recognising the pension asset now, the future tax consequences of this recognition, i.e. lower future pension payments and therefore higher taxable profits and higher tax, also have to be recognised. This will result in a deferred tax liability calculated as follows:

BASIC

INTERMEDIATE

ADVANCED

Carrying amount: pension asset	X
Less: tax base	0
Taxable temporary difference	X

In this instance the tax base is nil as the tax authorities will not recognise the surplus until the refund or reduced contribution takes place. (Remember that tax relief for pension premiums is granted when the premium is paid).

Provisions

Certain provisions are not allowable deductions for tax purposes. While specific bad debt provisions are acceptable deductions, general bad debt provisions are not allowable until the debt is specifically provided for or written off. General bad debt provisions can therefore give rise to temporary differences.

The deductible temporary difference is calculated as follows:

	£
Carrying amount: general bad debt provision	X
Tax base	0
Deductible temporary difference	X

This gives rise to a deferred tax asset as the tax relief in respect of the provision will be receivable in the future when the bad debts are either specifically provide for or written off. The journal entry will be:

Dr	Deferred tax asset	
	Cr	Deferred tax income
Being deferred tax asset on provisions.		

Example

Included in arriving at the accounting profit of £900,000 of Emerson for the year to 31 December 2008, is a general bad debt provision of £50,000. The extract tax expense entries are as follows:

	£	£
Profit before tax		900,000
Current tax	285,000	
Deferred tax	(15,000)	
Total tax expense		270,000
Profit after tax		630,000

Note that the general bad debt provision is not deductible for tax purposes and the current tax charge is calculated as follows (£900,000 + £50,000 = £950,000 × 30% = £285,000). The deferred tax credit is calculated as follows (£50,000 × 30% = £15,000), with the corresponding debit being shown as a deferred tax asset.

Suppose that in the year to 31 December 2009, the customer's debts, which gave rise to the general provision of £50,000, are now written off. Assuming Emerson had accounting profits of £800,000, the extract tax expense entries would be as follows:

	£	£
Profit before tax		800,000
Current tax	225,000	
Deferred tax	15,000	
Total tax expense		240,000
Profit after tax		560,000

Note that the bad debts written off would now be deductible for tax purposes and the current tax charge would be calculated as follows (£800,000 – £50,000 = £750,000 × 30% = £225,000). The deferred tax asset created at 31 December 2008 would now be reversed in the year to 31 December 2009.

As can be seen, for each of the years concerned, the total tax expense becomes that charge which is expected or implied by the level of profits and the prevailing tax rate. In the year to 2008, the tax expense is reduced – a lower tax charge is expected given the level of profits but the non-deductibility of the general bad debt provision results in a higher current tax charge. In the year to 2009, the tax expense is increased – a higher tax charge is expected given the level of profits, however the actual bad debts written off now become tax deductible expenses and result in there being a lower current tax charge than the profits would imply.

Pension liability

A pension liability for a defined benefit plan relates to a recognised deficit. This means that the fund has insufficient investments to meet its future pension obligations and will require additional contributions in the future in order to rectify the situation. As pension contributions are deductible when they are paid, the recognition of the pension deficit now gives corresponding rise to a deferred tax asset (i.e. the future tax relief that will result from the future contributions paid).

The deductible temporary difference is calculated as follows:

Carrying amount: pension liability	X
Tax base: nil	0
Deductible temporary difference	X

Progress Point 8.4

Majestic plc has the following items in its balance sheet at 31 March 2009:

	£
Tangible fixed assets	
Buildings	2,200,000
Plant and machinery	1,300,000
Current assets	
Stock	280,000
Debtors	505,000
Prepayments and accrued income	85,000
Bank	110,000
Pension asset	200,000

Additional information:

1. The buildings have a tax written-down value of £1,590,000. They were revalued from their net book value of £1,800,000 to £2,200,000 on 31 March 2009.
2. Plant and machinery has a tax written-down value of £410,000.

3. Debtors are stated net of bad debts of £8,000, a specific provision of £5,000 and a general provision of £4,500.
4. Prepayments and accrued income include accrued foreign dividends of £40,000. The dividends will be taxed on receipt.
5. At 31 March 2008, Majestic plc had a deferred tax liability of £95,000, which related solely to accelerated capital allowances.

Required

Calculate, assuming a corporation tax rate of 30%, the required deferred tax balance at 31 March 2009. Prepare the appropriate journal entry at 31 March 2009 to record deferred tax for the year and the relevant disclosure note.

Solution

Step 1
The first stage in the calculation is to determine the temporary differences:

	Carrying amount £	Tax base £	Taxable/(deductible) temporary differences £
Fixed assets			
Buildings	2,200,000	1,590,000	610,000
Plant and machinery	1,300,000	410,000	890,000
Current assets			
Stock	280,000	280,000	–
Debtors	505,000	509,500	(4,500)
Prepayments	45,000	45,000	–
Accrued income	40,000	–	40,000
Bank	110,000	110,000	–
Pension asset	200,000	–	200,000
			1,735,500

Note that stocks, prepayments and bank have a tax base equal to the carrying amount. Debtors have been adjusted for the non-deductible general provision; accrued income has a tax base of nil as it will not be taxed until received; the pension asset represents a surplus of funds, indicating that future pension contributions will be lower – its tax base is therefore nil.

Step 2
Calculate the deferred tax liability at 31 March 2009 as follows:

Temporary differences x tax rate	
1,735,500 x 30% =	£520,650
Deferred tax liability at 31 March 2008	£95,000
∴ Increase required	425,650

Step 3
Prepare journal.
NB: the amount of tax relating to the revaluation should be charged to the revaluation reserve. That is:
(2,200,000 – 1,800,00) x 30% = £120,000

Journal:

		£	£
Dr	Revaluation reserve	120,000	
Dr	Deferred tax expense (income statement)	305,650	
	Cr Deferred tax liability (balance sheet)		425,650
Being increase in deferred tax liability for the year.			

Step 4

Disclosure note: the detail of temporary differences of deferred tax requires to be disclosed.

	Accelerated capital allowances	Revaluation	Overseas dividends	Pension asset	Total liabilities	Assets: bad debt provn
	£	£	£	£	£	£
At 31/3/08	(95,000)				(95,000)	
(Charged) to p&l a/c	(235,000)[1]		(12,000)[2]	(60,000)[3]	(307,000)	
Credited to p&l a/c						1,350[4]
Charged to equity		(120,000)			(120,000)	
	(330,000)	(120,000)	(12,000)	(60,000)	(522,000)	1,350
					Net £520,650	

Notes

[1] Buildings: (1,800,000 − 1,590,000)   = 210,000
   Plant and machinery (1,300,000 − 410,000)   = 890,000
                                                                                          1,100,000 × 30% = 330,000

   Balance at 31 March 2008   95,000

   Increase in deferred tax   235,000

[2] Overseas dividend:
   40,000 × 30% = £12,000

[3] Pension asset:
   £200,000 × 30% £60,000

[4] Bad debt provision:
   £4,500 × 30% = £1,350

Deferred tax assets: tax losses

So far in this chapter, our discussion of deferred tax assets has centred on when, as a result of temporary differences, the tax benefits of a transaction are deferred to a future period rather than being recognised in the current period.

There are, however, specific business situations that may also give rise to the creation of deferred tax assets. Such situations arise when the company in question has made a tax loss.

Tax losses may be used to offset against future taxable profits and therefore reduce future tax payable.

IAS 12 requires that a deferred tax asset in respect of the carry forward of unused tax losses should only be to the extent that it is possible that future taxable profits will be available against which the unused tax losses can be used. This means that deferred tax assets may be recognised on a partial basis.

Example

A company has calculated deferred tax assets of £1,000,000 at 31 March 2008, resulting from trading losses incurred in the year. Taxable profits for the next year are estimated at £200,000, however due to market uncertainties, no profits can be anticipated in the following year to 31 March 2010.

Given a tax rate of 30%, the amount of deferred tax asset that should be recognised is £60,000 (i.e. 30% × £200,000). The deferred tax asset would be set to the level of the future tax liability, which would be implied from the next year's profit of £200,000.

Suppose, however, that in the year to 2010, and for the foreseeable future, the company is expected to make significant profits. In this event, the restriction on the amount of deferred tax asset to be created would be lifted and the company would account for the tax effects of the full deferred tax assets of £1,000,000.

As the above example illustrates, the calculation may be very subjective and can only ever be an estimate – an estimate based on a forecast of future profitability. IAS 12 requires an enterprise to assess, at each balance sheet date, unrecognised deferred tax assets. Consequently, where tax losses exist that previously were unrecognised as deferred tax assets, they may subsequently be recognised to the extent that it has become probable that future taxable profit will allow the deferred tax asset to be recovered.

For example, an improvement in trading conditions may make it more probable that the enterprise will make sufficient taxable profit in the future for the deferred tax asset.

Other factors to consider include:

- whether the enterprise has sufficient taxable temporary differences that will result in taxable amounts against which the losses/credits can be used
- whether it is probable that the enterprise will have taxable profits before the losses/credits expire
- whether the unused tax losses result from identifiable causes that are unlikely to recur
- whether tax planning opportunities are available that will create taxable profits against which the losses/credits can be used.

Progress Point 8.5

At 31 March 2009, Obsidian plc had calculated the following amounts in respect of deferred tax:

	2009 £000	2008 £000
Accelerated capital allowances	(964)	(993)
Revaluations	(430)	(360)
	(1,394)	(1,353)

In addition, following an unexpected change in the market in the year to 31 March 2008, Obsidian had recognised unrelieved trading losses of £1,500,000, which were expected to be able to be used against future taxable profits and temporary difference reversals. During the year to 31 March 2009, Obsidian made a trading profit (before loss relief) of £600,000, and £600,000 of the available trading losses will be utilised to eliminate the taxable profits.

At 31 March 2009, it is estimated that only £700,000 of the remaining trading losses are useable in the foreseeable future as part of the trade has been discontinued. Deferred tax has been calculated at 30%.

Required

Prepare the balance sheet note for deferred tax for the year to 31 March 2009.

Solution

The first step in preparing the balance sheet note is to ascertain the balances at 31 March 2008 (i.e. the opening balance for the year to 31 March 2009). In terms of the deferred tax liability balances, these are as outlined in the example (i.e. £993,000 in respect of accelerated capital allowances and £360,000 in respect of revaluations).

The deferred tax asset at 31 March 2008 is calculated as follows: Obsidian has unrelieved trading losses of £1,500,000 and *at that time* it believed that these would be able to be used against future profits. The deferred tax asset recognised is therefore £1,500,000 x 30% (i.e. £450,000).

At 31 March 2009, the closing deferred tax liability balances have been given in the example and consequently the differences need only be accounted for in the disclosure note.

The deferred tax asset to be recognised *at 31 March 2009* is calculated as follows: Obsidian has estimated that only £700,000 of the unrelieved losses will be able to be used against future profits. The deferred tax asset recognised at this time will be £700,000 × 30% = £210,000. Again, the change will be disclosed in the note.

Deferred tax liability and asset:

	Liability Accelerated capital allowances £000	Revaluations £000	Total £000	Asset Unrelieved trading losses £000
At 31 March 2008	(993)	(360)	(1,353)	450
(Charged)/credited to Income statement	29		29	(240)
Charged to equity		(70)	(70)	
At 31 March 2009	(964)	(430)	(1,394)	210

Note that the charge to the income statement in respect of unrelieved trading losses of £240,000 is made up of:

(a)   the charge resulting from the use of the trading losses in the year of £600,000

	£
i.e. £600,000 × 30%	= 180,000

(b)   the charge resulting from the write-off of the losses, which are now deemed to be unrelievable of £200,000

i.e. (£1,500,000 – 600,000 – 700,000) × 30%	= 60,000
	240,000

8.7 Disclosure

The disclosure requirements in IAS 12 are extensive and the standard must be read in detail. The main disclosure requirements are:

■   tax assets and liabilities must be shown separately from other assets and liabilities in the balance sheet
■   deferred tax should be distinguished from current tax
■   deferred tax should always be classified as non-current

- current tax assets and current tax liabilities should be offset on the balance sheet only if the enterprise has the legal right and the intention to settle on a net basis
- deferred tax assets and deferred tax liabilities should be offset on the balance sheet only if the enterprise has the legal right to settle on a net basis and they are levied by the same taxing authority
- separate major components of the tax expense (tax income) in the income statement (e.g. current tax, deferred tax, changes in either due to tax rates)
- charges in respect of tax charged to equity
- tax relating to extraordinary items
- reconciliation between tax charge and that calculated by applying the tax rate to accounting profit
- detail of temporary differences of deferred tax.

Disclosure in practice

As noted above, the disclosure requirements in respect of IAS 12 *Income Taxes* are extensive, and disclosures can be found within the accounting policies, income statement and balance sheet, and notes to the accounts.

Taxation

Logica's policy note on taxation details the rates at which tax is recognised, and its policies on providing for deferred tax assets and liabilities. Note that Logica does not discount deferred tax liabilities.

Current tax is recognised based on the amounts expected to be paid or recovered under the tax rates and laws that have been enacted or substantively enacted at the balance sheet date.

Deferred tax is provided in full on temporary differences that arise between the carrying amounts of assets and liabilities for financial reporting purposes and their corresponding tax bases. Liabilities are recorded on all temporary differences except in respect of investments in subsidiaries and joint ventures where the timing of the reversal of the temporary difference is controlled by the Group and it is probable that it will not reverse in the foreseeable future.

Deferred tax assets are recognised to the extent that it is probable that future taxable profits will be available against which the asset can be offset.

Deferred tax is measured on an undiscounted basis using the tax rates and laws that have been enacted or substantively enacted at the balance sheet date.

Current and deferred tax are recognised in the income statement, except when the tax relates to items charged or credited directly to equity, in which case the tax is also dealt with directly in equity.

Profit before tax	12	**84.1**	116.6
Taxation	13	**(5.4)**	(31.2)
Profit for the year from continuing operations		**78.7**	85.4
DISCONTINUED OPERATION:			
Profit from discontinued operation	14	**89.4**	3.7
Net profit for the year		**168.1**	89.1

Figure 8.1 Logica: income statement extract

	2007 £m	Restated 2006 £m
CURRENT TAX:		
UK corporation tax	(3.8)	17.2
Overseas tax	50.5	28.4
	46.7	45.6
DEFERRED TAX:		
UK corporation tax	1.8	2.4
Overseas tax	(43.1)	(16.8)
	(41.3)	(14.4)
Continuing operations	5.4	31.2
Discontinued operation	7.5	9.1
	12.9	40.3

Figure 8.2 Logica: taxation note

The effective tax rate on continuing operations for the year, before the share of post-tax profits from associates, exceptional items and amortisation of intangible assets initially recognised on acquisition, was 17.6% (2006: 25.4%), of which a credit of £0.4 million (2006: charge of £19.6 million) related to the United Kingdom. The effective tax rate for 2007 was lower than 2006 due to the use of unrecognised losses brought forward.

The effective tax rate on exceptional items was 9.5% (2006: 7.1%) and the effective tax rate on amortisation of intangible assets initially recognised on acquisition was 32.4% (2006: 32.7%).

The tax charge from continuing operations is lower than the standard rate of corporation tax in the UK applied to profit before tax.

The differences are explained below.

	2007 £m	Restated 2006 £m
Profit before tax	84.1	116.6
Less: share of post-tax profits from associates	(1.2)	(0.3)
Profit before tax excluding share of post-tax profits from associates	82.9	116.3
Tax at the UK corporation tax rate of 30% (2006: 30%)	24.9	34.9
Adjustments in respect of previous years	(7.7)	(7.0)
Adjustment for foreign tax rates	2.9	2.0
Tax loss utilisation	(9.9)	(5.5)
Income not taxable	(7.6)	(3.2)
Deferred tax assets not recognised	2.8	10.0
Tax charge from continuing operations	**5.4**	**31.2**

Figure 8.3 Logica: analysis of taxation charge

In addition to the amounts charged to the income statement, a deferred tax charge of £nil (2006: £4.5 million) relating to retirement benefit schemes, a deferred tax credit relating to items transferred to the income statement on settlement of £0.6 million in 2006 and a deferred tax charge of £0.1 million (2006: £0.4 million) relating to share-based payment arrangements were recognised directly in equity. In the prior year a deferred tax credit of £0.6 million relating to items transferred to the income statement was also recognised in equity.

The current tax related to exceptional items for the year ended 31 December 2007 was a tax credit of £2.2 million (2006: £1.7 million).

The reduction in the statutory corporation tax rate in the UK from 30% to 28% from 1 April 2008 was reflected in calculating the UK deferred tax assets and liabilities. The effect on the results for the year ended 31 December 2007 was an additional tax charge of £0.7 million.

The tax charge for the year to 31 December 2007 as recognised in Logica's income statement is £5.4 million. The accompanying note to the income statement charge shows how this tax charge is made up and there is also a reconciliation of the tax charge to the accounting profit.

	Property, plant and equipment £m	Intangible assets £m	Retirement benefits £m	Tax losses £m	Goodwill £m	Other £m	Total £m
At 1 January 2006	3.6	(0.4)	13.4	6.1	(35.5)	(7.5)	(20.3)
Credit/(charge) to profit or loss for the year	(3.0)	12.3	(4.0)	5.0	9.9	(7.7)	12.5
(Charge)/credit to equity	–	–	(4.5)	–	–	0.2	(4.3)
Reclassification from current tax	–	–	–	–	–	(0.7)	(0.7)
Acquisition of subsidiary	3.0	(103.6)	1.2	1.3	–	(2.4)	(100.5)
Exchange differences	–	(0.6)	–	(0.2)	–	0.3	(0.5)
At 1 January 2007	3.6	(92.3)	6.1	12.2	(25.6)	(17.8)	(113.8)
(Charge)/credit to profit or loss for the year	(1.1)	24.2	(1.4)	9.3	15.6	(4.0)	42.6
Charge to equity	–	–	(0.1)	–	–	–	(0.1)
Reclassification from current tax	–	–	–	–	–	0.6	0.6
Acquisition of subsidiaries	–	–	–	–	–	(0.6)	(0.6)
Disposal of subsidiaries/ businesses	0.5	–	–	–	–	5.5	6.0
Exchange differences	0.2	(9.3)	0.2	0.5	(1.1)	4.3	(5.2)
At 31 December 2007	3.2	(77.4)	4.8	22.0	(11.1)	(12.0)	(70.5)

Figure 8.4 Logica: deferred tax disclosure note

The credit to profit or loss for the year includes a £1.3 million credit (2006: charge of £1.9 million) which is included in the profit from discontinued operation.

The deferred tax liability for goodwill arises as deductions are allowed for tax purposes in certain territories.

Deferred tax assets and liabilities are offset where there is a legally enforceable right of offset and the Group intends to settle the balances on a net basis. An analysis of the deferred tax balances for financial reporting purposes is shown in the table below:

	2007 £m	2006 £m
Deferred tax assets	54.5	50.6
Deferred tax liabilities	(125.0)	(164.4)
	(70.5)	(113.8)

Figure 8.5 Logica: analysis of deferred tax balances

The reduction in the statutory corporation tax rate in the UK from 30% to 28% from 1 April 2008 was reflected in calculating the UK deferred tax assets and liabilities. The effect on the results for the year ended 31 December 2007 is an additional tax charge of £0.7 million.

At 31 December 2007, the Group had unused tax losses of £245.6 million (2006: £298.4 million) available for offset against future taxable profits for which no deferred tax asset had been recognised. At 31 December 2007, £82.6 million (2006: £88.3 million) of the unused losses are subject to time expiry rules and will expire in full on or before 31 December 2022.

No deferred tax liability was recognised in respect of the unremitted earnings of overseas subsidiaries, joint ventures and associates as the Group is in a position to control the timing of the reversal of the temporary differences and it is probable that such differences will not reverse in the foreseeable future. The Group estimated that tax of £62.7 million (2006: £14.6 million) would arise in respect of remitting all earnings of overseas subsidiaries to the United Kingdom to the extent legally possible.

The deferred tax provisions note discloses the amount of deferred tax assets and liabilities recognised in the balance sheet for each type of temporary difference and in respect of unused tax losses. Note that Logica has netted off its deferred tax assets and liabilities. This is because it intends to settle the balances on a net basis.

8.8 Discounting

In some countries (e.g. the Netherlands, the UK) companies are allowed under national accounting rules to discount their deferred tax balances.

A major conceptual issue is whether the objective of discounting deferred tax is to reflect the fair value of deferred tax (for which discounting can be seen as a surrogate) or to reflect the time value of money. If the objective is to reflect the time value of money then problems can arise in determining the future cash flows to be discounted, and the discount rate to be used.

With regard to future cash flows, some argue that it is unrealistic to discount the deferred tax inherent in timing differences at the balance sheet date since it may well be that these timing differences have no effect on tax cash flows in the year that they reverse. For example, future investment and the related capital allowances may postpone the deferred tax liability.

Another view is that discounting may give rise to double counting since the purchase price of an asset already reflects the net present value of future income earned from the asset. If depreciation is already discounted, then it is not appropriate to discount further the deferred tax arising from it.

IAS 12 does not permit the discounting of deferred tax balances, with one exception. It allows discounting of deferred tax where it relates to a pre-tax amount that is itself discounted – that is, the application of a tax rate to an already discounted item will automatically result in a deferred tax charge that is discounted.

Section 3: Advanced Aspects

8.9 Deferred tax: a critical appraisal

Many of the ideas introduced so far in this chapter have, by the very complexity of their nature, been relatively advanced. This section, and the remainder of the chapter, take an overview of the concepts and arguments put forward earlier and make a critical appraisal of the deferred tax issue.

Deferred tax is not a liability. It is not, as is stated in the Framework, a 'present obligation' of an enterprise, and consequently it could be argued that deferred tax should not appear in the financial statements. Moreover, it could be argued that only the actual amount of tax payable by an enterprise should be incorporated within the financial statements. This would avoid any confusion over what the taxation charge represents and the potential to mislead users with tax charges that bear little resemblance to actual tax payable, i.e. the tax disclosed would be that tax that was actually payable – not the tax that would have been payable had the adjustments required by taxation law not occurred. Furthermore, taxation rules are quite separate and distinct from accounting standards requirements. Tax is calculated on taxable income, not accounting income, and it could be argued that there is no requirement for the tax charge to bear any relationship to reported income.

Additional information could be made available in the notes to the accounts, which would explain the difference between the actual tax payable and the expected tax charge based on the operating results.

We have seen, however, the distorting effects that timing differences can have on an enterprise's taxation charges. In times of enhanced taxation allowances, which may be to encourage investment in fixed assets, an actual tax charge can be significantly lower than an implied tax charge based on the level of profit. This in turn, if no deferred tax adjustments are made, will give rise to an increased after-tax profit, which in turn may result in pressure from shareholders for the enterprise to pay dividends. Paradoxically, given that the investment in the assets giving rise to the tax allowances may have used up the enterprise's cash reserves, such shareholder pressure comes at a time when the enterprise may have little or no cash reserves left. The ability, therefore, to smooth out the distortions can be seen as desirable.

But is income smoothing desirable?

Is this ability by preparers of financial statements to dramatically alter an overall taxation charge by the use of a deferred tax charge desirable? Financial statements should be free from bias and objective – however, as we have seen, the very nature of the deferred tax calculation and the inherent subjectivity within opens to question the effectiveness of the deferred tax charge in meeting this reporting requirement.

However, one of the most fundamental of accounting concepts is that financial statements are prepared on the accruals basis of accounting. The use of deferred tax adjustments effectively takes accrual accounting to the maximum possible degree by accounting for the taxation implications of all temporary differences. For example, if a balance sheet includes an asset at a revalued amount then it seems perfectly plausible to argue that the implicit taxation arising on this future economic benefit should be provided for at the same time.

Should deferred tax be provided for?

There are strong arguments for and against this question, but perhaps the question can best be answered by once more taking a critical look at the user of the financial statements.

The business owner, the supplier, the creditor, the unsophisticated investor – for these groups deferred tax is likely to cause as much confusion and mislead as much as its intention is to remove confusion and provide more useful information. We are not, therefore, any further forward in obtaining an answer to our question.

Consider, however, the board of directors of a capital-intensive listed company who will be judged by shareholders on their efforts in increasing stock prices and profits. Full provisioning for deferred tax may, as we have illustrated, result in the creation of ever increasing liability balances that reduce reserves and, consequently, stock prices. Moreover, their investment strategies – and related successes – may be masked by the deferred tax charges when they may well have planned for investment at tax-opportune moments. In such circumstances, we may conclude that management may well be opposed to deferred tax accounting.

BASIC

INTERMEDIATE

ADVANCED

Consider, however, the sophisticated investor who bases investment decisions on the basis of future cash flows. The inclusion of the deferred tax adjustments allowing the timing of tax payments to be incorporated within the investors' analysis is doubtless invaluable. We have, therefore, a strong argument for deferred tax accounting.

Arguments for and against deferred tax accounting can be found when considering any user group. Is it possible, therefore, to rely on the Framework to provide an answer?

The answer is probably yes – but perhaps not in the obvious definitions of assets and liabilities, future economic benefits or present obligations. One of the other most fundamental of accounting concepts is that of consistency of accounting treatment: consistency between similar transactions between one year and the next, and between one company and another. It seems reasonable to suggest therefore that, regardless of the arguments for and against deferred tax accounting, provided that companies treat similar transactions in a similar manner – which adherence to the IASs should ensure – and adequate disclosure of the nature of the taxation balances is made, then all users of the financial statements will be able to extract the information they require and discard that which they do not.

BASIC

INTERMEDIATE

ADVANCED

Chapter summary

IAS 12 *Income Taxes*

- Current tax for the current and prior periods should be recognised as a liability to the extent that it has not been settled, and as an asset to the extent that the amounts already paid exceed the amount due.
- The benefit of a tax loss that can be carried back to recover current tax of a prior period should be recognised as an asset.
- Current tax assets and liabilities should be measured at the amount expected to be paid to (recovered from) taxation authorities, using the rates/laws that have been enacted by the balance sheet date.
- Deferred tax liabilities should be recognised for all taxable temporary differences and measured at the tax rates that are expected to apply to the period when the liability is settled (liability method).
- Deferred tax assets should be recognised for deductible temporary differences, unused tax losses and unused tax credits to the extent that it is probable that taxable profit will be available against which the deductible temporary differences can be utilised, and measured at the tax rates that are expected to apply to the period when the asset is realised.
- Current and deferred tax should be recognised as income or expense, and included in net profit or loss for the period.

 Key terms for review

Definitions can be found in the glossary at the end of the book.

Accounting profit	*Tax base*
Taxable profit	*Temporary differences*
Accounting profits and taxable profits	*Taxable temporary differences*
Current tax	*Deductible temporary differences*

 Review questions

1. Why does the charge to taxation in a company's accounts not equal the profit multiplied by the current rate of corporation tax?
2. Explain and distinguish between the *flow through*, *full deferral* and *partial deferral* approaches to providing for deferred tax.
3. Explain and distinguish between the *liability method* and *deferral method* of providing for deferred tax.
4. Define the term *current tax*, and explain how it should be accounted for under IAS 12.
5. Define the term *temporary differences*, and explain the difference between taxable temporary differences and deductible temporary differences.
6. What is the tax base of an asset or a liability?
7. Is *income smoothing* a sufficient reason to provide for deferred tax?

Exercises

1. Level II

Company A has a piece of machinery bought for £100,000 on 1 January 2009. It adopts the straight line method of providing for depreciation and estimates that the asset has a useful life of 10 years with no residual value.

Company B also bought an asset for £100,000 on 1 January 2009. It also adopts the straight line method of providing for depreciation, and estimates that the asset it purchased has a useful life of three years and no residual value.

Tax allowances of 25% are available on both assets and the rate of corporation tax is 30%. Neither company has deferred tax balances at 31 December 2008.

Required

(a) For each company:
   (i) calculate the deferred tax asset/liability at 31 December 2009 and prepare the necessary journal entry, and
   (ii) repeat (i) at 31 December 2010 and 2011. Assume that Company B does not sell the asset until 2012.
(b) For Company A, calculate the year in which the temporary difference reverses (i.e. begins to decline).

2. Level II

Dambysil plc is a profitable company that manufactures greenhouse accessories. On 31 December 2008, the net book value of fixed assets in the published accounts was £5,000,000. The tax written-down value of these assets was £4,250,000. Previously no deferred taxation has been provided.

Dambysil plc has produced a budget indicating the likely expenditure over the next few years and, from this, the following information regarding depreciation and tax allowances (capital allowances) has been derived.

Year ended 31 December	WDA £000	Depreciation £000
2009	125	25
2010	25	50
2011	25	75
2012	175	50

From 2012 onwards, it is expected that tax allowances will be well in excess of depreciation.

Required

(a) Assuming that the corporation tax rate is 30%, calculate the deferred tax charge (or credit) for each of the four years to 31 December 2012, and the deferred tax asset or liability for inclusion in the balance sheet at each year end, and show the relevant income statement and balance sheet extracts, under each of the following:
   (i) on a full provision basis
   (ii) on a partial provision basis.
(b) IAS 12 *Income Taxes* recommends full deferral when providing for deferred tax. Critically appraise this approach and explain what other methods could be used.

3. Level III

Herbox plc prepares accounts to 31 December each year. The following information has been provided by the directors of Herbox as at 31 December 2008.

(i) At 31 December 2008, the net book value of plant and machinery was £50m. The tax written-down value at that date was £38m.

(ii) The directors revalued land from £25m to £35m on 31 December 2008.

(iii) The figure of debtors in Herbox plc's balance sheet at that date consisted of:

	£
Gross debtors	18
Less: bad debts	(2)
Less: specific provision	(1)
Less: general provision	(3)
Net debtors	12

(iv) Herbox had £1m accrued overseas dividend income at 31 December 2008. This dividend is taxable on receipt.

(v) Herbox had no deferred tax asset or liability at 31 December 2007.

(vi) Assume a corporation tax rate of 30%.

Required

Calculate the required deferred tax balance at 31 December 2008.

4. Level III

Rivendell plc is a manufacturer of loft ladders. At 31 March 2008 Rivendell had a deferred tax provision of £2.25m, made up as follows:

	£
Accelerated capital allowances	1.95m
Accrued interest receivable	0.30m
	2.25m

At 31 March 2009, the balance sheet showed plant and machinery costing £120m with a net book value of £70m. Capital (tax) allowances so far given on these assets amount to £58m.

In 1999 Rivendell had purchased some land costing £6m, with a view to building a new display showroom. Planning permission had been difficult to obtain – however, following a change in local authority policy, this has now been granted. At 31 March 2009 the land was valued at £7.8m and as the directors intend to use this land as security for loan purposes, they have decided to incorporate the revalued amount in the financial statements.

Rivendell received £1,000,000 in interest during the year to 31 March 2009 from funds held in a foreign bank account. This interest had been accrued in the financial statements to 31 March 2008. Corporation tax is payable on receipt of this interest.

The company incurred taxable losses in the year to 31 March 2009 of £4.8m. Rivendell has been consistently profitable for the last ten years and the loss arose from the closure of an old product range. The new range was introduced late in the year and the company is now trading profitably. Indeed, budgets indicate that the company will be profitable for the foreseeable future.

Assume a tax rate of 30%.

Required

(a) Calculate the required deferred tax provision as at 31 March 2009.

(b) Prepare the relevant income statement and balance sheet extracts for deferred tax as required by IAS 12 for the year ended 31 March 2009.

(c) Prepare the deferred tax disclosure note.

5. Level III

Arkling plc had recognised the following deferred tax balances at 31 March 2008.

Type of temporary difference	Temporary difference £m	Deferred tax asset/(liability) £m
Accelerated capital allowances	(10)	(3)
Revaluations	(10)	(3)
Tax losses	35	10.5
Other	(15)	(4.5)

At 31 March 2008, Arkling had additional tax losses of £8,500,000, which had not been recognised. At that time, it was not certain that there would be future taxable profits against which these losses could be utilised. Consequently, Arkling recognised only the amount of losses sufficient to cover the deferred tax liabilities in respect of the taxable temporary difference relating to accelerated capital allowances, revaluations and the other taxable temporary differences existing at that date.

Additional information

1.   At 31 March 2008, the net book value of assets qualifying for capital allowances was £90m and the tax written-down value was £80m. During the year to 31 March 2009, Arkling acquired new assets qualifying for capital allowances, costing £15m. The depreciation charge for the year to 31 March 2009 was £20m and the capital allowances claimed amounted to £24m. All the assets qualifying for capital allowances are plant and equipment.

2.   The company acquired a new office block in June 2008 costing £9.5m. There were no capital allowances available on this building.

3.   Following a general downturn in the property market, properties that had previously been revalued upwards in the year to 31 March 2008 were revalued downwards as at 31 March 2009. A downward revaluation of £5m occurred.

4.   The other temporary differences existing at 31 March 2008 reversed during the current year.

5.   During the year to 31 March 2009, Arkling had accounting profits before tax of £29m. The taxable profits came to £41.5m, arrived at after adjusting for depreciation, capital allowances, other temporary difference and disallowable expenditure. The tax losses brought forward have been set off against the taxable profits to fully eliminate the tax payable. Disallowable expenditure in the tax computation amounted to £1.5m.

Required

(a)   Calculate the required deferred tax balance as at 31 March 2009, and the amounts to be taken to the income statement and to equity.

(b)   Prepare an extract of the income statement of Arkling for the year to 31 March 2009.

(c)   Prepare the deferred tax liability disclosure note as at 31 March 2009.

(d)   Prepare a tax reconciliation for the year to 31 March 2009.

Further reading

IAS 12 *Income Taxes*. IASB, 2000

FRS 19 *Deferred Tax*. ASB, 2002

FRS 16 *Current Tax*. ASB, 1999

Stylianou, J. (1997) Deferred tax – partial arts. *Accountancy Age*, April.

Chapter 9

Cash Flow Statements

LEARNING OUTCOMES

After studying this chapter you should be able to:

- ☑ explain the difference between cash and profit
- ☑ identify cash flow from operating activities
- ☑ explain the additional information a cash flow statement can give
- ☑ explain the difference between the direct method and indirect method of determining cash flow
- ☑ distinguish between cash and cash equivalents
- ☑ identify non-cash transactions
- ☑ outline and explain the requirements of IAS 7 *Statement of Cash Flows*
- ☑ prepare a cash flow statement in accordance with IAS 7 *Statement of Cash Flows*.

Introduction

It is widely recognised that the ability to generate cash is essential for a company's survival. Indeed, it is often said that cash is the 'lifeblood' of a business. A business that cannot pay its suppliers or employees will not survive. The ability to earn profits, however, does not necessarily result in a healthy cash balance.

This chapter first of all considers the differences between cash and profit (profit vs cash flow) and explores the reasons why these differences arise. A simple example is used to illustrate these differences. The next section shows how a cash flow statement is constructed, providing step-by-step guidance on how to prepare a cash flow statement from a profit and loss account and balance sheet. The final section outlines the requirements of IAS 7 *Statement of Cash Flows*, and discusses in detail the specific requirements of this standard.

Section 1: Basic Principles

Accountants frequently meet with clients to review their financial statements. When the level of profit made is being considered, the discussion almost always results in the comment from the clients to the effect that it is a pity that the bank balance does not appear to reflect the level of the profit achieved. It can be quite puzzling for clients to understand why, after a year of good profits, their bank overdraft is bigger at the end of the year than it was at the start. Or indeed why the bank balance has increased more than profit.

9.1 Cash vs profit

The ability to generate cash is crucial to the survival of a business. Indeed, many profitable businesses fail because they cannot generate enough cash to meet short-term commitments. Other things being equal, in the longer term profits do have the effect of increasing the bank balance. However, in the short term, the making of a profit will not necessarily result in an increased cash balance.

Consider the following scenario.

A fruit seller has a market stall and £100 cash. He buys some apples for £100 and during the day sells them all for £130.

His profit and loss account for the day would be as follows:

Sales	£130
Purchases	£100
Profit	£30

Suppose all the transactions were for cash. How much *cash* is left at the end of the day?

Sales (all for cash)	£130
Purchases (all for cash)	£100
Profit	£30

Because all the transactions were for cash, the profit earned will be reflected in the cash position at the end of the day.

Cash at start of day	£100
Less cash purchases	£100
	0
Add cash from sales	£130
Cash at end of day	£130
Cash at start of day	£100
Cash at end of day	£130
Increase in cash	£30

So in this instance profit and increase in cash are equal.

Consider the situation where all purchases are for cash, and some of the sales are for cash and some on credit. Suppose cash sales are £100 and credit sales are £30. As before, profit will still be £30.

Sales (cash)	£100
Sales (credit)	£30
	£130
Purchases (all for cash)	£100
Profit	£30

However, this time, cash at the end of the day will be £100.

Cash at start of day	£100
Less cash used for purchases	£100
	0
Add cash from sales	£100
Cash at end	£100
Cash at start	£100
Cash at end	£100
Increase in cash	£0

Profit and increase in cash are not equal.

It can be seen that the reason for this is that some sales were made on credit during the day. These credit sales had no effect on cash but were included in arriving at the profit figure. It is possible to reconcile the profit figure with the change in cash as follows:

Profit per accounts	£30
Less: credit sales	(30)
Change in cash	0

In other words, the sales that are on credit do not increase cash, instead they increase debtors. Therefore, the following reconciliation can also be made:

Profit per accounts	£30
Less: increase in debtors	(30)
Change in cash	0

Consider the situation where the purchases are for cash, but all the sales are on credit. Again, as before, profit is still £30.

Sales (all on credit)	£130
Purchases (all for cash)	£100
Profit	£30

However, this time, cash at the end of the day will be zero since no cash will have been received from sales.

Cash at start of day	£100	
Less cash purchases	£100	
	0	
Add cash from sales	0	(all sales are on credit)
Cash at end of day	£0	
Cash at start	£100	
Cash at end	£0	
Decrease in cash	£100	

BASIC

INTERMEDIATE

ADVANCED

Given that all the cash was spent on apples and no cash was collected from selling them, cash at the end of the day will be zero. However, a profit of £30 has been made. Again, in this instance, profit and increase in cash are not equal.

Once more, reconciliation can be made of the profit with the change in cash. In this scenario, all the sales were on credit, therefore cash is not affected. Instead there is an increase in debtors of the full amount of the credit sales. Therefore:

Profit per accounts	£30
Less: increase in debtors	(130)
Change in cash (decrease)	(100)

The market trader would be in difficulty if he is not able to buy more apples on credit to sell the next day because he has no cash left.

This simple example leads to two important issues:

1. the important distinction between cash and profit
2. the usefulness of the information provided by the profit and loss account and the balance sheet in helping the business identify whether or not it will be able to generate sufficient cash to finance its operations.

Balance sheet

The balance sheet discloses the cash/bank balances, the near cash assets, such as debtors, and the short-term liabilities, such as creditors. However, the balance sheet provides an overview at a specific point in time so it is a static picture. The balance sheet does not show how the business has financed its activities during the period under review.

Profit and loss account

The profit and loss account shows revenues and expenses rather than cash receipts and payments. The profit shown in the profit and loss account is the difference between the revenues and expenses for the period. This may have little or no relationship to the cash generated for the period.

Progress Point 9.1

Why does the making of a profit not necessarily result in an increase in cash?

Solution

The reason a profit does not necessarily result in an increase in cash is due to the fact that profit is determined by comparing income with expenditure and not receipts with payments. Where a business has sold goods on credit this will be recorded as income, however it will not result in an inflow of cash until that cash is received from the debtor.

This anomaly identified above can be illustrated as follows.

Current assets and current liabilities of a business at the start of a period are as follows:

Stock	£200
Debtors	£30
Cash	£50
Creditors	£20

During the year the following transactions took place.

1. 100 items bought on credit costing £2 each
2. 180 items sold on credit for £4 each
3. Cash paid to creditors £180
4. Cash received from debtors £700

The information given above can be put together in the following summary statement

Summary statement:				
	Opening position			**Closing position**
Stock	£200	+ £200 (1)	- £360 (2)	£40
Debtors	£30	+ £720 (2)	- £700 (4)	£50
Cash	£50	- £180 (3)	+ £700 (4)	£570
Creditors	£20	+ £200 (1)	- £180 (3)	£40
Net current assets	£260			£620

Net current assets is the total of current assets (stock, debtors and cash) less the current liabilities (creditors). Net current assets are more commonly referred to as working capital. In this case net current assets have increased by £360 (£620 – £260) over the period.

The transactions may be explained as follows.

1. Items bought on credit for £200 (100 × £2). This will have the effect of increasing stock and increasing creditors by £200.
2. Items sold on credit for £720 (180 × £4). This will have the effect of increasing debtors by £720 and decreasing stock by £360, that is at cost (180 × £2).
3. Cash paid to creditors. This will decrease creditors and decrease cash by £180.
4. Cash received from debtors. This will increase cash by £700 and decrease debtors by £700.

Profit versus cash

Using the above summary statement, a profit and loss account can now be prepared:

Profit and loss account For the period ended ...		
Sales		£720
Less cost of sales		
Stock at start	£200	
Add purchases	200	
	400	
Less stock at end	40	£360
Profit		£360

This is the same as the increase in net current assets (working capital) over the same period.

What has happened to cash? Cash at the start is £50 and cash at the end is £570, so cash has gone up by £520 but profit has gone up by only £360. What is the explanation for the difference?

In general terms the reason for the difference is one of timing. For example, some of the cash has still to be received from debtors. However, credit sales will already have been taken account of as part of total sales and so will already have been taken into account in the calculation of profit.

The specific reasons for the difference between cash and profit can be identified and measured separately. The cash flow statement combines these individual changes and measures the overall change.

Consider each possible change in isolation.

Stock

If stock increases over the period, the implication is that the business is buying more stock, so the likely impact of this would be to decrease cash. If stock decreases over the period, the opposite would be true. It could be implied that the company is selling stock and so cash would increase. In this instance, stock has decreased, implying that it has been sold, so increasing cash.

Debtors

If debtors increase over the period it is as though the debtors are not paying. Cash is not coming in as quickly. This situation will have a negative impact on cash and so will notionally decrease cash. However, if debtors are falling over the period it is as though debtors are paying more quickly. This will have a positive impact on cash and so will notionally increase cash. In the illustration given, debtors have increased. This suggests that while sales have been made, the amount of cash generated from these sales has been less than the sales. In the example, debtors have increased, so notionally decreasing cash.

Creditors

If creditors are increasing over the period it is as though the business is not paying its creditors and so is retaining cash in the business. This will have a positive impact on cash and will increase cash. Conversely, if creditors are decreasing over the period, it is as though the company is paying the creditors more quickly. This will have a negative impact on cash and will lead to a cash decrease. In the example, creditors have increased. Purchases have been recognised in the profit and loss account as an expense, thus reducing profit. However, since these purchases were on credit the impact of this is to increase creditors and so notionally increase cash.

Then changes can now be combined as follows:

Cash flow statement	
Profit for the period	£360
Changes having positive impact on cash	
Decrease in stock	£160
Increase in creditors	£20
	£540
Changes having a negative impact on cash	
Increase in debtors	£20
Increase in cash	£520
Opening cash	£50
Closing cash	£570
Increase in cash	£520

This example also shows how valuable information about the profit of a business can be extracted. From the computation above, the cash generated from the trading activities of the business can be seen. The business has made a profit, which will increase working capital (net current assets). The composition of the current assets and current liabilities will determine whether sufficient cash has been generated to allow a business to survive. The cash flow statement allows the *quality* of the profit to be tested.

Progress Point 9.2

Explain whether each of the following statements is true or false.

(a)   Accounting profit is the difference between cash received and cash paid.
(b)   A decrease in debtors increases the cash position.
(c)   An increase in creditors decreases the cash position.
(d)   An increase in stocks increases the cash position.

Suggested solution

(a)   False: accounting profit is the difference between revenues earned and expenses incurred whether or not they have been received or paid.
(b)   True: if debtors have decreased, this means that money has been received from debtors.
(c)   False: if creditors have increased, this means that creditors are not being paid, so cash is being retained in the business.
(d)   False: if stocks are increasing this means that the business is buying more stock and so this is likely to decrease the cash position.

   The cash flow statement now combines these individual changes and shows the overall impact of them on the cash position. While profit and cash rarely equal each other, the fact that a company makes a profit will tend to have a positive impact on net assets and therefore on cash. Profit will contribute to the change in cash over the period.

   Continuing with the example, suppose the company has depreciating assets and the depreciation charge for the period is £100.
   The profit will be reduced by £100, from £360 to £260. What is the impact on cash?
   There is no impact on cash. This is because depreciation represents a charge for using fixed assets and is matched against the revenues generated from using such assets. However, the business does not actually pay depreciation in cash, so there is no effect on cash.
   Depreciation reduces the profit but has no effect on cash. In order to reconcile profit with the change in cash, any factors that distort one, but not the other must be eliminated. Given that depreciation reduces profit and not cash then depreciation must be added back on to profit.
   Building on the earlier example:

Cash flow statement	
Profit for the period (after depreciation)	£260
Add back depreciation	£100
	£360
Changes having positive impact on cash	
Decrease in stock	£160
Increase in creditors	£20
	£540
Changes having a negative impact on cash	
Increase in debtors	£20
Increase in cash	£520
Opening cash	£50
Closing cash	£570
Increase in cash	£520

Other items that have an impact on profit but not on cash

Loss on sale of fixed asset

This arises when cash received from the sale of an asset is less than the net book value of the asset. This loss on sale will be deducted from the profit figure in the profit and loss account and so has the effect of decreasing profit. However, it has no impact on cash. As with depreciation, this loss on sale will have to be added back on to profit.

Gain on sale of fixed asset

This arises when cash received from the sale of an asset is greater than the net book value of the asset. This gain on sale is added to the profit in the profit and loss account, and so has the effect of increasing profit. However, it has no impact on cash. This time, it will have to be deducted from profit.

In both the above cases, it is the actual cash received from disposing of the assets that will have an impact on cash.

Progress Point 9.3

(a) Explain the effect of each of the following on the balance sheet, profit and loss account, and cash flow statement.
   (i) Depreciation of £10,000 is charged
   (ii) Credit sales of £8,000 are made
   (iii) Stocks costing £13,000 are purchased on credit
   (iv) A fixed asset with a net book value of £5,000 is sold for £3,000
   (v) Land is revalued from its original cost of £130,000 to £200,000
(b) The information relating to current assets and current liabilities of a business is as follows.
   At start of year.

Stocks (100 items at £3 each)	£300
Debtors	£50
Cash	£75
Creditors	£35

During the year, the following transactions took place:
1. 80 items bought on credit, each costing £3
2. 150 items sold on credit for £5 each
3. Cash paid to creditors £175
4. Cash received from debtors £600

Calculate the change in the cash balance and net current assets, and reconcile these using a cash flow statement.

Solution

(a) (i) Balance sheet: the depreciation charge will reduce the net book value of fixed assets by £10,000.
   Profit and loss account: profit is reduced by £10,000 depreciation.
   Cash flow statement: no effect as no cash flow has occurred.
   (ii) Balance sheet: there will be an increase in debtors of £8,000.
   Profit and loss account: there will be an increase in sales revenue of £8,000.
   Cash flow statement: no effect as no cash flow has occurred.

(iii) Balance sheet: there will be an increase in creditors of £13,000.

Profit and loss account: there will be an increase in purchases of £13,000.

Cash flow statement: no effect as no cash flow has occurred.

(iv) Balance sheet: the fixed assets are reduced by £5,000 and the cash is increased by £3,000.

Profit and loss account: profit is reduced by the £2,000 loss on the sale of fixed asset.

Cash flow statement: there will be a cash inflow of £3,000 from the sale of the fixed asset.

(v) Balance sheet: the carrying value of the land is increased by £70,000 and the same amount is credited to a revaluation reserve.

Profit and loss account: no effect as the gain is not realised.

Cash flow statement: no effect as no cash flow has occurred.

(b)

Net current assets	At start		At end
Stocks	£300	+ 240 – 450	£90
Debtors	£50	+ 750 – 600	£200
Cash	£75	+ 600 – 175	£500
Creditors	(£35)	+ 240 – 175	(£100)
	£35		£690

∴   Change in cash balance = £75 – £500: increase £425

Change in net assets = £390 – £690: increase £300

Cash flow statement	
	£
Profit for the period (increase in net assets)	300
Add: decrease in stocks	210
increase in creditors	65
	575
Less: increase in debtors	150
increase in cash	£425

Section 2: Intermediate Issues

This section extends and expands some of the basic principles introduced in the previous section. In particular it will demonstrate how to prepare and present a cash flow statement in accordance with international accounting standards. It will compare and contrast two methods of identifying cash flows: the direct method and the indirect method.

BASIC

INTERMEDIATE

ADVANCED

9.2 Balance sheet changes

The balance sheet enables the change in working capital between one accounting period and the next to be calculated. It also helps to identify the change in the cash position. The profit and loss account, on the other hand, shows whether or not a profit has been made.

It has already been explained that making a profit does not necessarily lead to an equivalent increase in cash. The profit and loss account measures the profit or loss for an accounting period by matching the revenues with the expenses for that period, using the realisation principle and the accruals basis.

Sales are therefore recognised in the profit and loss account even though some or all of the sales is on a credit basis (i.e. debtors may not have paid in full by the year end). Purchases on credit are recorded in the profit and loss account even though the business may owe money to its suppliers (creditors) at the year end.

The profit and loss account does not record the cost of purchasing fixed assets. Instead the costs of these fixed assets are allocated to the profit and loss account over their estimated useful economic lives in the form of the annual depreciation expense.

The profit and loss account does not detail other items affecting cash, such as:

- cash coming into the business through the introduction of capital (e.g. additional shares issued)
- the business obtaining a loan or repaying a loan
- the purchase and sale of fixed assets.

All these different receipts and payments can be brought together in the form of a statement that summarises the sources of the cash and the uses of cash. Such a summary statement is known as a cash flow statement.

Cash flows within a business can be categorised as arising from three main activities.

1. Operating activities: these are ongoing trading activities of a business, which include sales, purchases, and the payment of taxation.
2. Investing activities: these include payments made to acquire fixed assets and also receipts from the sale of fixed assets.
3. Financing activities: these include cash received from the issue of shares and payments of dividends.

A definitive list, as given by IAS 7, is shown in the final section of this chapter (see page 502).

Progress Point 9.4

Explain the effect of each of the items below on the balance sheet, profit and loss account, and cash flow statement.

(a) During the year the company purchased a new piece of machinery costing £15,000
(b) A loan of £12,000 was taken out to help finance the purchase of the machine
(c) The company paid back a long-term loan to the bank of £80,000
(d) The company made an issue of 100,000 8% £1 preference shares at a price of £1.20 per share
(e) The company received bank interest of £1,000

Solution

(a)   Balance sheet: the fixed assets are increased by £15,000 and the cash is reduced by £15,000.

Profit and loss account: no effect.

Cash flow statement: the cash flow statement will show cash outflows from investing activities of £15,000.

(b)   Balance sheet: cash is increased by £12,000 and liabilities (loans) will increase by £12,000.

Profit and loss account: no effect.

Cash flow statement: the cash flow statement will show cash inflows from financing activities of £12,000.

(c)   Balance sheet: long-term liabilities are reduced by £80,000 and the bank balance is reduced by a similar amount.

Profit and loss account: no effect as we are merely using an asset to discharge a liability.

Cash flow statement: the financing section of the cash flow statement will show a cash outflow of £80,000.

(d)   Balance sheet: increase issued preference share capital by £100,000 and increase the share premium account by £20,000.

Profit and loss account: no effect.

Cash flow statement: cash flows from financing activities will show an inflow of £120,000 (i.e. 100,000 shares at £1.20 each).

(e)   Balance sheet: cash will increase by £1,000.

Profit and loss account: included in arriving at profit from operating activities.

Cash flow statement: included in arriving at net cash inflow from operating activities.

Comprehensive example

The following information comprises the profit and loss account of XYZ for the year ended 31 March Year 4, together with balance sheets of the business as at 31 March Year 4 and Year 3

Profit and loss account		
Year ended 31 March Year 4	£	£
Sales		100
Cost of sales		30
Gross profit		70
Expenses		
Depreciation	5	
Loss on disposal	2	
Wages and salaries	13	20
Operating profit		50
Taxation		10
		40
Dividends proposed		5
Retained profit		35
Profit & loss account balance b/f		20
Profit & loss account balance c/f		55

Balance sheets					
As at 31 March		Year 4		Year 3	
	£	£	£	£	£
Fixed assets (cost)		98		80	
Less depreciation		33		30	
		65		50	
Current assets					
Stock	10		15		
Debtors	34		21		
Cash	12		3		
	56		39		
Current liabilities					
Creditors	6		9		
Taxation	10		8		
Dividends	5		7		
	21		24		
Total net current assets		35		15	
Net assets		100		65	
Share capital		45		45	
Profit & loss account		55		20	
		100		65	

The following additional information is also given.

Assets, which originally cost £12 and had a net book value at time of sale of £10, were sold for £8.

9.3 Preparation of a cash flow statement

From the information given above, a cash flow statement will now be prepared.

The cash flows will be calculated for each of the headings of *Operating activities, Investing activities* and *Financing activities.*

Working notes

In order to prepare the cash flow statement it is necessary to group the items into the above headings. To do this, some additional information needs to be extracted from the information given.

Step 1: analyse the changes in fixed assets

In order to find out the how much depreciation has been charged and how much has been spent on fixed assets, it helps to construct a schedule of fixed assets, a little 'magic square', as follows:

	Cost	Depreciation	Net book value
	£	£	£
Position at start (Year 3)	80	30	50
Assets sold	12	2	10
	68	28	40
Position at end	98	33	65
Increase in assets	30	5	25

Explanation of the statement

The increase in assets of £30 represents the amount of fixed assets bought during the year.

An increase in deprecation of £5 represents the depreciation for the year.

Assets that cost £12 with a net book value of £10 at the time of sale were sold for £8. This means that there was a loss on the sale of these assets of £2 (£10 – £8). There was also a cash inflow of £8 associated with the sale of these assets.

Step 2: find out how much tax has been paid.

From the balance sheets and profit and loss accounts the following information can be determined:

Tax owing in Year 3	8	(from balance sheet)
Amount of tax for end year 4	10	(from profit and loss account)
	18	
Tax owing in Year 4	10	(from balance sheet)
Therefore tax paid during the year	8	

Step 3: identify the changes in current assets and current liabilities other than cash

Decrease in stock of	£5 (£15 – £10)
Increase in debtors	£13 (£21 – £34)
Decrease in creditors	£3 (£9 – £6)

Step 4: combine the information to determine the cash flow from operating activities

Cash flow from operating activities	
	£
Operating profit before tax and dividends	50
Add: depreciation	5
loss on disposal	2
	57
Add: decrease in stock	5
Less: increase in debtors	(13)
decrease in creditors	(3)
	46
Less: taxation paid	8
Net cash flows from operating activities	38

Step 5: identify the cash flows from investing activities

	£
Purchase of fixed assets	(30)
Proceeds from sale of fixed assets	8
Net cash used in investing activities	(22)

BASIC

INTERMEDIATE

ADVANCED

Step 6: identify the cash flow from financing activities

In this example, the company had declared dividends for the year of £5. We need to calculate what amount of dividends the company actually paid in cash.

Dividend owing at the start	£7	(balance sheet Year 3)
Dividend proposed	£5	(profit and loss account)
	£12	
Dividend owing at the end	£5	(balance sheet Year 4)
Therefore dividend paid	£7	

Step 7: combine all the above information to produce the complete cash flow statement

Cash flow statement	
Cash flow from operating activities (step 4)	£38
Cash flow from investing activities (step 5)	(£22)
Cash flow from financing activities (step 6)	(£7)
Net cash inflow	£9

This net cash inflow can be verified by comparing the change in the cash over the period:

Cash at start	£3	(balance sheet Year 3)
Cash at end	£12	(balance sheet Year 4)
Increase in cash	£9	

9.4 Operating cash flows: direct or indirect

The method shown above of calculating cash flows from operating activities is known as the indirect, or net, method. It involves starting with the operating profit and adjusting it for non-cash charges and credits so that one figure of operating cash flow is shown.

Another method exists, however, known as the direct or gross method, which involves showing the individual operating cash receipts from customers, and cash payments to suppliers and employees.

In order to use the direct method of calculating operating cash flows using our earlier example, cash receipts from customers and cash payments made to suppliers and other cash payments made will have to be calculated.

Calculation of direct cash flows

Cash receipts from customers		
Debtors at start of period	£21	(balance sheet Year 3)
Sales for period	£100	(profit and loss account)
	£121	
Debtors at end of period	£34	(balance sheet Year 4)
Therefore cash received	£87	

Cash paid to suppliers

This needs to be done in two stages. First of all the purchases for the year need to be calculated. From the profit and loss account the cost of sales figure of £30 is given. From the balance sheet the opening and closing stocks can be identified. This information can be used to calculate the purchases:

Opening stock	£15	(balance sheet Year 3)
Add purchases	£x	(missing number)
Less closing stock	£10	(balance sheet Year 4)
Cost of sales	£30	(profit & loss account)

The missing number, purchases, is deduced to be £25.
$(£15 + £x - £10) = £30 \therefore = £25$.

Stage 2:

Creditors at start of period	£9	(balance sheet Year 3)
Purchases	£25	(stage 1)
	£34	
Creditors at end of period	£6	
Therefore cash paid	£28	

Other cash paid

This will be the amount shown in the profit and loss account for wages and salaries of £13.

Cash flow from operating activities (direct method)	
Cash receipts from customers	£87
Cash paid to suppliers	(£28)
Cash paid to employees	(£13)
Cash generated from operations	£46
Taxation paid	£8
	£38

The operating cash flow figure is the same regardless of the method used. This example allowed the calculation to be made using either method. In practice, companies operate accounting systems that are geared towards accrual accounting and, consequently, the detailed information required to enable the calculation to be made using the direct method may not always be available.

Progress Point 9.5

(a) The direct method of preparing the cash flow statement is the easiest to understand but most companies use the indirect method. Why do you think this might be so?
(b) The cash flows below were extracted from the accounts of Gemmill Ltd, a landscaping business.

	£
Loan repaid	25,000
Purchase of office equipment	15,000
Sale of property	25,000
Interest paid	350
Dividend received	1,150
Payments to suppliers	175,000
Payments to employees	55,000
Expenses paid	10,000
Receipts from customers	250,000

Prepare a cash flow statement using the direct method for the year ended 31 December 2009.

Solution

(a)   The main difference between the direct and indirect methods of preparing the cash flow statement is in the calculation of operating cash flow. Under the direct method, cash inflows and outflows are directly reported, starting with the major categories of gross receipts and payments. This means that cash flows such as receipts from customers and payments tosuppliers are stated separately within the operating activities. By contrast, the indirect method starts from operating profit, and adjusts for movements in working capital and for non-cash items such as depreciation. Because the direct method deals with the natural cycle of cash flows (i.e. receipts and payments), it is easier to understand. Again, by contrast, it is less easy to grasp the adjustments to operating profit required by the indirect method.

The reason most companies use the indirect method is primarily because the cash flow statement is prepared from the existing profit and loss account and balance sheet.

It is therefore a matter of putting through a set of overall adjustments. In addition, the direct method potentially requires a lot of work to analyse the constituent cash flows from the cash book. This will involve additional expense, which companies may not wish to incur. Finally, for reasons of confidentiality, companies may not wish to reveal comprehensive details of their cash flows from customers or to suppliers.

(b)   Gemmill Ltd

Cash flow statement (direct method) Year ended 31 December 2009		
Cash flow from operating activities	£	£
Receipts from customers	250,000	
Payments to suppliers	(175,000)	
Payment to employees	(55,000)	
Expenses paid	(10,000)	
Net cash inflow from operating activities		10,000
Cash flow from financing activities		
Loan repaid	(25,000)	
Interest paid (i)	(350)	
Net cash flow from financing activities		(25,350)
Cash flow from investing activities		
Dividend received (ii)	1,150	
Purchase of office equipment	(15,000)	
Sale of property	25,000	
		11,150
Decrease in cash		(£4,200)

Notes:
    (i)   interest paid may be classified as either an operating or financing activity
    (ii) dividends received may be classified as either operating or investing activities.

This is explained more fully in the following section.

Progress Point 9.6

The following information relates to Runstone Ltd.
  Profit and loss account for year ended 31 December Year 4

	£ 000s	£ 000s
Sales		500
Cost of sales		350
Gross profit		150
Expenses	121	
Depreciation	10	
		131
Net profit		19

Balance sheet as at 31 December		
	Year 4 £000	Year 3 £000
Fixed assets	130	130
Less depreciation to date	20	10
	110	120
Stock	32	25
Trade debtors	60	40
Bank	–	5
	92	70
Trade creditors	36	48
Bank overdraft	5	–
	41	48
	161	142
Issued share capital	100	100
Retained profit	61	42
	161	142

Prepare a cash flow statement showing the cash receipts and payments that explain the changes in the bank account of Runstone Ltd between Year 3 and Year 4.

Solution

	(£000)
Profit from profit & loss account	19
Add: depreciation	10
	29
Changes having a positive impact on cash		
Changes having a negative impact on cash		
Increase in stock	7	
Increase in debtors	20	
Decrease in creditors	12	39
Decrease in cash		10
Cash in Year 3		£5
Bank overdraft in Year 4		£5

Cash has moved from £5 in Year 3 to an overdraft in Year 4, a decrease of £10 over the period. Although Runstone made a profit of £19,000, a £10,000 depreciation charge had been deducted in arriving at that profit figure. The depreciation charge does not involve a flow of cash and must be added back to the profit figure in order to compensate for the fact that there is no cash impact. Stock increased by £7 over the period, implying that some cash was used to buy this stock. Trade debtors increased by £20,000, which meant that although sales had been made, no cash was generated from £20,000 of these sales In other words, no cash income. Creditors decreased over the period, implying that some of the cash has been used to pay them and so depleting the cash balance further. The net effect of all of the above has been to turn a positive bank figure of £5 – into an overdraft of £5 – a reduction of £10.

9.5 Disclosure in practice

The disclosure requirements of IAS 7 *Statement of Cash Flows* are contained with the statement itself together with notes to the financial statements.

Logica's cash flow statement (Figure 9.1) reports, as required by IAS 7, cash flows for the year ended 31 December 2007, classified by operating, investing and financing activities.

	Note	2007 £m	Restated* 2006 £m
Consolidated cash flow statement			
For the year ended 31 December 2007			
Cash flows from continuing operating activities			
Net cash inflow from trading operations		**261.0**	242.5
Cash outflow related to restructuring and integration activities		**(28.6)**	(33.0)
Cash generated from continuing operations	33	**232.4**	209.5
Finance costs paid		**(40.2)**	(26.3)
Income tax paid		**(45.8)**	(31.5)
Net cash inflow from continuing operating activities		**146.4**	151.7
Net cash inflow/(outflow) from discontinued operating activities		**7.0**	(1.3)
Cash flows from continuing investing activities			
Finance income received		**7.0**	5.1
Dividends received from associates		**1.0**	–
Proceeds on disposal of property, plant and equipment		**2.2**	2.2
Purchases of property, plant and equipment		**(35.3)**	(28.2)
Expenditure on intangible assets		**(13.0)**	(17.1)
Purchase of minority interests		**2.2**	–
Deferred consideration and acquisition of subsidiaries, net of cash acquired		**(34.2)**	(398.3)
Disposal of subsidiaries and other businesses, net of cash disposed		**42.0**	1.9
Disposal of discontinued operation, net of cash disposed		**213.2**	–
Net cash inflow/(outflow) from continuing investing activities		**180.7**	(434.4)
Net cash outflow from discontinued investing activities		**–**	(5.5)
Cash flows from continuing financing activities			
Proceeds from issue of new shares		**2.5**	3.4
Payment for share issue costs		**–**	(5.4)
Purchase of own shares		**(130.8)**	–
Proceeds from transfer of shares by ESOP trust		**0.8**	–
Proceeds from bank borrowings		**34.5**	480.6
Repayments of bank borrowings		**(204.2)**	(208.0)
Repayments of finance lease principal		**(4.7)**	(2.1)
Repayments of borrowings assumed in acquisitions		**–**	(3.8)
Proceeds from other borrowings		**–**	0.4
Repayments of other borrowings		**–**	(0.4)
Payments on forward contracts designated as a net investment hedge		**(6.3)**	–
Dividends paid to the Company's shareholders		**(85.9)**	(61.1)
Dividends paid to minority interests		**(0.4)**	(1.8)
Net cash (outflow)/inflow from continuing financing activities		**(394.5)**	201.8
Net decrease in cash, cash equivalents and bank overdrafts		**(60.4)**	(87.7)
Cash, cash equivalents and bank overdrafts at the beginning of the year	34	**150.9**	245.3
Net decrease in cash, cash equivalents and bank overdrafts	34	**(60.4)**	(87.7)
Effect of foreign exchange rates	34	**9.1**	(6.7)
Cash, cash equivalents and bank overdrafts at the end of the year		**99.6**	150.9

* Restated as described further in Note 33.

Figure 9.1 Logica: consolidated cash flow statement

	2007 £m	Restated 2006 £m
Operating profit from continuing operations	109.7	141.9
ADJUSTMENTS FOR:		
Share-based payment expense	8.5	9.3
Depreciation of property, plant and equipment	38.7	29.2
Loss on disposal of non-current assets and subsidiaries	2.1	1.0
Loss on disposal of businesses	9.7	–
Amortisation of intangible assets	84.0	44.1
Impairment of financial assets	1.8	–
Derivative financial instruments	(1.0)	0.6
Defined benefit plans	(4.2)	(13.4)
	139.6	70.8
Net movements in provisions	(18.1)	3.6
MOVEMENTS IN WORKING CAPITAL:		
Inventories	0.6	(0.2)
Trade and other receivables	33.3	(51.3)
Trade and other payables	(32.7)	44.7
	1.2	(6.8)
Cash generated from continuing operations	232.4	209.5
Add back: Cash outflow related to restructuring and integration activities	28.6	33.0
Net cash inflow from trading operations	261.0	242.5

Figure 9.2 Logica: reconciliation of operating profit to cash generated from continuing operations

The consolidated cash flow statement for the year ended 31 December 2006 was restated to show the Telecoms Products business as a discontinued operation to allow a more meaningful comparison with the current period.

Cash generated from continuing operations is detailed further in this note to the statement. The adjustments made include many of those that have been dealt with in this chapter. The complexities of Logica's operating activities mean that additional adjustments are required in respect of defined benefit plans, share-based payments and defined benefit plans.

	At 1 January 2007 £m	Cash flows £m	Acquisitions and disposals* £m	Other non-cash movements £m	Exchange differences £m	At 31 December 2007 £m
Cash and cash equivalents	177.3	(78.2)	–	–	9.6	**108.7**
Bank overdrafts	(26.4)	17.8	–	–	(0.5)	**(9.1)**
	150.9	(60.4)	–	–	9.1	**99.6**
Finance leases	(6.5)	4.7	0.1	(4.7)	(0.8)	**(7.2)**
Bank loans	(498.0)	169.5	–	(1.9)	(24.3)	**(354.7)**
Other loans	(1.1)	0.2	–	–	–	**(0.9)**
Convertible bonds	(202.4)	–	–	0.2	(17.8)	**(220.0)**
Net debt	(557.1)	114.0	0.1	(6.4)	(33.8)	**(483.2)**

* Excludes cash and cash equivalents assumed on acquisition of businesses, amounting to £5.6 million and cash and cash equivalents disposed of £41.4 million and bank overdrafts disposed of £1.3 million.

Figure 9.3 Logica: reconciliation of movements in net debt

	2007	2006
	£m	£m
Cash at bank and in hand	**100.9**	141.2
Short-term deposits	**7.8**	36.1
Bank overdrafts	**(9.1)**	(26.4)
Cash, cash equivalents and bank overdrafts	**99.6**	150.9

Figure 9.4 Logica: cash and cash equivalents

> The Group's credit risk on cash, cash equivalents and bank overdrafts is limited because the counterparties are well-established banks with high credit ratings. Included in cash at bank and in hand were overdrafts that were part of cash pooling arrangements for which a legal right of off-set existed against positive cash balances that were of an equal or greater amount at the balance sheet date.
>
> The Directors estimate that the carrying value of cash and cash equivalents approximated their fair value.
>
> The Group's policy for cash investments requires that cash and deposits only be placed with counterparties that have a minimum A1/P1 short-term rating and AA-equivalent long-term credit rating. The reference to ratings must include at least one from either Standard & Poor's or Moody's. Cash and deposits are limited to £25 million per bank. No credit limits were exceeded during the reporting period and management does not expect any losses from non-performance by any of these counterparties.

The reconciliation of movements in net debt discloses the classifications of finances and borrowings adopted by Logica. Note that Logica takes a prudent view with its cash investments; no more than £25 million is deposited with any one bank.

Section 3: Advanced Aspects

This section extends and expands the previous two sections. It explains the development of the cash flow statement in terms of the publication of SFAC No. 1 *Objectives of Financial Statements*. The section goes on to identify and explain the requirements of the international accounting standard (IAS 7).

9.6 Development of cash flow statements

In November 1987 the requirement to produce a statement of cash flow was required in the USA when SFAS 95 was issued by the FASB. This requirement by the USA started a trend in financial reporting that extended worldwide. It had been long recognised by the FASB, since the publication of SFAC No. 1 *Objectives of Financial Reporting by Business Enterprises* in 1978, that investors, potential investors, creditors and other users of financial information needed information to assess the amounts, timing and uncertainty of prospective net inflows to the related enterprise.

SFAC No. 5 *Recognition and Measurement in Financial Statements of Business Enterprises*, published in December 1984, stated that a 'full set of financial statements for a period should show: ... cash flows during the period.

In July 1977 the IASC originally approved IAS 7 *Statement of Changes in Financial Position*, which required the presentation of a statement of sources and use of funds. IAS 7 was revised in 1992 and renamed *Cash Flow Statements*; it required businesses to prepare a cash flow statement. An amended version of IAS 7 is now mandatory for financial periods beginning on or after 1 January 2005. In September 2007, IAS 7 was retitled *Statement of Cash Flows* as a consequential amendment resulting from revisions to IAS 1.

9.7 IAS 7 *Statement of Cash Flows*

Objective

The objective as stated by IAS 7 is 'to require the provision of information about the historical changes in cash and cash equivalents of an entity by means of a cash flow statement which classified cash flows during the period from operating, investing and financing activities' (IAS 7). The aim of the standard is to give users of financial statements a basis on which to evaluate the ability of a business to generate cash and cash equivalents.

A number of benefits of a cash flow statement are outlined in the standard, as follows.

- It gives the business the ability to influence cash flows in light of changing circumstances.
- It enables the operating performance of different businesses to be compared.
- Historical cash flow information is often used as an indicator of the amount, timing and uncertainty of future cash flows.
- It is useful for checking the accuracy of past assessments of future cash flows.
- It is useful for examining the relationship between profitability and net cash flow, and the impact of changing prices.

However, although these benefits are outlined in the standard it is questionable if all those benefits referred to can really be derived from the cash flow statement. After all, a cash flow statement shows only the changes in the cash of a business on a historic basis.

The cash flow statement is useful in that it highlights the differences and the similarities between the various elements of profitability and net cash flow. Also, cash flow information is less easily manipulated or influenced by the effect of different accounting treatments. It has to be said that, even in conjunction with the other information obtainable for the financial statements, it would be difficult for a user of accounting information to assess the extent to which an organisation could adapt to changing financial circumstances, the timing and certainty of future cash flows and indeed the impact of changing prices.

What is needed in addition is some additional management commentary to accompany the financial statements. In the future, this may be provided by the operating and financial review (OFR).

Scope of IAS 7

IAS 7 applies to all businesses regardless of size, ownership structure or industry. This includes wholly owned subsidiaries, banks, insurance companies and other financial institutions.

Cash and cash equivalents

The examples used thus far in this chapter have been worked on the basis of cash flows being actual flows of cash. A wider definition of cash flows is required, however, to include cash and cash equivalents. Cash is defined by IAS 7 as 'cash on hand and demand deposits'. Cash equivalents are defined as 'short-term highly liquid investments that are readily convertible to known amounts of cash and which are subject to an insignificant risk of changes in value'.

The decision on how to classify such items can be difficult and involves a degree of subjectivity. For example, many businesses put surplus funds on deposit, perhaps for a number of months, and the decision as to how to classify such items can be difficult. Cash equivalents are held for the purpose of

meeting short-term cash commitments rather than for investment or other purposes. For an investment to qualify as a cash equivalent it must be readily convertible to a known amount of cash and be subject to an insignificant risk of changes in value.

Normally, only an investment with a short maturity of, say, three months or less would qualify under the definition. Equity investments are excluded unless they are cash equivalents in substance – for example, redeemable preference shares acquired within a short period of their maturity and with a specified redemption date.

Bank borrowings can be equally problematic. A bank overdraft, repayable on demand, could be viewed as part of cash and cash equivalents where it forms an integral part of a business's cash management policy. A mortgage over ten years, say, would almost certainly be a financing activity.

The decision of how to classify such items can be subjective: one business may classify an investment as a cash equivalent, while another may treat the same investment as an investing item. In general terms, however, an investment normally qualifies as a cash equivalent only where it is readily convertible to a known amount of cash, is not subject to a significant risk of changes in value, and where it has a short maturity (three months or less) from date of acquisition.

Note that cash flows under IAS 7 exclude movements between cash in hand and highly liquid investments because these are components of a business's cash management rather than part of the operating, investing and financing activities.

Non-cash transactions

In the examples so far, the only illustrations of non-cash transactions have been depreciation, losses on disposal or gains on disposal of assets. Consider now how some assets used in a business are obtained. This will show that there are other possibilities of non-cash transactions.

An example of non-cash transactions

The notes to the accounts of Roughwall show the following fixed asset note:

	Freehold property £	Plant and machinery £	Total £
Cost at 1 January 2009	750,000	200,000	950,000
Additions	–	150,000	150,000
Disposals	–	–	–
Cost at 31 Dec. 2009	750,000	350,000	1,110,000

Assume that included in the additions to fixed assets figure of £150,000 is an amount of £100,000 in respect of assets held under finance leases.

These assets held under finance leases will not involve a flow of cash and will not therefore show in the investing section of the cash flow statement. The £50,000 asset additions will, however, show as part of the investing activities of the business. The payments required under the finance lease will be shown in the financing section of the cash flow statement.

Example: non-cash transaction where debt is converted to equity

Balance sheet extract		
	Year 4 £000s	Year 3 £000s
Debentures	100	200
Share capital	200	100

Notes to the accounts

During the year £100,000 10% debentures were converted to £100,000 ordinary shares.

In this example, from an initial examination of the movement in the share capital in the balance sheet it would appear that there has been a share issue. The notes to the accounts, however, will explain the reason for the change in share capital. The conversion from debentures into share capital has been made in this example, so no flows of cash have taken place.

9.8 Formal presentation of the cash flow statement

The cash flow statement reports inflows and outflows of cash and cash equivalents during the period. Such inflows and outflows are classified under the following headings:

- Operating activities
- Investing activities
- Financing activities.

This classification is to allow users to assess how these types of activity impact on the financial position of the business. The various components of the classifications will be those most appropriate to the business. The standard notes that a single transaction may fall into different classifications. For example, where the repayment of a loan includes both interest and capital, the interest payment may be included in operating activities, whereas the capital repayment is a financing cash flow.

Individual components of cash flow statements

Cash flow from operating activities

Operating activities are defined as the 'principal revenue-producing activities of the business and other activities that are not investing or financing activities'. So, by definition, all cash flows that are neither investing nor financing will be deemed to be part of operating activities. The standard states that operating cash flow information is valuable since:

- it provides an important indication of the extent to which a business has generated enough cash flows from its operating activities to pay dividends, to make investments, to repay debts and to increase its scale of operating activity without borrowing
- it may assist in forecasting future cash flows.

Examples of cash flows from operating activities given in the standard include:

- cash receipts from sale of goods or performing a service
- cash receipts from fees, royalties, commissions and other revenue
- cash payments to suppliers for goods and services
- cash payment to employees
- cash payments or refunds of taxes (unless they can be specifically identified with financing and investing activities).

Cash flows from operating activities may be reported on a gross basis (direct method) or net basis (indirect method). At the present time the IASB is considering whether or not to make reporting cash flow using the direct method mandatory. Most businesses, particularly those preparing consolidated financial statements, choose to use the indirect method since this avoids the additional administrative cost arising from the need to collect and analyse cash transactions across the whole group.

To obtain cash flow information for the indirect method, the balance sheet figures have to be analysed according to the three standard headings in the cash flow statement. The reconciliation of profit or loss resulting from operating activities will include only those elements of changes in debtors and creditors that relate to operating activities. For example, if there are any amounts payable in respect of the acquisition of property, plant and equipment, or any accrued interest, this will be excluded from the movement in creditors to be included in the reconciliation. Where a group of companies has made an acquisition of a subsidiary during the year, the change in the working capital items will have to be allocated between the increase due to the acquisition and that due to operating activities, which will be shown in the reconciliation.

Cash flow from investing activities

IAS 7 defines investing activities as 'the acquisition and disposal of long-term assets and other investments not included in cash equivalents'. According to the standard, this classification allows users of the financial statements to understand the extent to which expenditures have been made for resources intended to provide future income and cash flows. Cash flows from investing activities include:

■   payments made to acquire, and receipts from the sale of long-term assets, including those payments and receipts relating to capitalised development costs and self-constructed assets
■   payments made to acquire and receipts from the sale of equity or debt instruments of other businesses and interests in jointly controlled entities
■   advances and loans made to and repaid by other parties
■   cash payments for and receipts from futures, forward, option and swap contracts (except when these contracts are held for trading purposes).

Cash flow from financing activities

IAS 7 defines financing activities as 'those activities that result in changes in the size and composition of the contributed equity and borrowings of the entity'. Examples of cash flows arising from financing activities include:

■   share issues
■   redemption of shares
■   issue and repayment of debentures and other long-term borrowing
■   payments made under a lease.

Allocation of items to operating, investing and financing activities

There may be situations where it is not clear how cash flows should be classified. IAS 7 provides additional guidance on the classification of interest, dividends and taxation.

Interest and dividends

IAS 7 notes that there is no consensus on the classification of these cash flows, and suggests that interest paid can be classified either as operating or financing activities. Interest and dividends received can be included in either operating or investing cash flows. The standard allows dividends paid to be classified as a financing cash flow, since such dividends are a cost of obtaining financial resources, or as an operating cash flow.

BASIC

INTERMEDIATE

ADVANCED

The standard requires the total amount of interest paid to be disclosed whether it has been recognised as an expense or has been capitalised as part of the cost of an asset (as allowed under IAS 23).

Taxation

Cash flows arising from taxes on income should be disclosed separately within operating cash flows unless they can be specifically identified with investing or financing activities. In general terms, tax paid is usually classified as an operating cash flow since it is often impractical to match such cash flows with specific investing and financing activities.

Conclusion

Both preparers and users of financial statements can generally understand IAS 7. The objective of the standard is to require information about the changes in cash and cash equivalents to be disclosed. The application is relatively straightforward in that it requires cash flows to be classified under one of three headings. Businesses have some discretion over the treatment of interest and dividend cash flows provided these are separately disclosed and are treated consistently from period to period.

Chapter summary

IAS 7 *Statement of Cash Flows*

- Requires the presentation of information about the changes in cash and cash equivalents by means of a statement of cash flows.
- Statement classifies cash flows according to operating, investing and financing activities.
- Operating activities are the principal revenue-producing activities of the entity.
- Investing activities are the acquisition and disposal of long-term assets and other investments not included in cash equivalents.
- Financing activities are activities that alter the equity capital and borrowing structure of the enterprise.
- Cash flows from operating activities may be reported using either:
  - (a) the direct method, whereby major classes of gross cash receipts and gross cash payments are disclosed, or
  - (b) the indirect method, whereby profit or loss is adjusted for non-cash charges and credits, changes in working capital and items of income or expense associated with investing or financing cash flows.
- Cash and cash equivalents are disclosed and reconciled with the amounts in the cash flow statement.

 Key terms for review

Definitions can be found in the glossary at the end of the book.

Profit vs cash flow   **Operating activities**
Cash   **Investing activities**
Cash flows   **Financing activities**
Cash equivalents

Review questions

1. Why is it that a profitable business can find itself short of cash?
2. Is it possible for a business to make losses year after year but still increase its bank balance?
3. What is the main aim of a cash flow statement?
4. How does an increase in the depreciation charge affect the operating profit and the net cash flow from operating activities?
5. Distinguish between the *direct method* and *indirect method* of calculating the net cash flow from operating activities.
6. Explain what is meant by *cash and cash equivalents*.
7. Explain each of the following terms, which are defined in IAS 7:
   - (a) operating activities
   - (b) investing activities
   - (c) financing activities.

Exercises

1. Level I

(a) A company has the following income statement for the year ended 31 December 2009 and balance sheet extracts at that date.

Income statement Year to 31 December 2009	
	£
Turnover	1,200,000
Cost of sales	(840,000)
Gross profit	360,000
Distribution and administration expenses	(120,000)
Profit before tax	240,000

Balance sheet extracts at 31 December 2009		
	2009	2008
	£	£
Current assets		
Stocks	160,000	140,000
Debtors	288,000	235,000
Current liabilities		
Trade creditors	168,000	138,000

You are given the following information.
1. Expenses includes depreciation of £36,000.
2. During the year the company disposed of an item of plant for £24,000, which had a net book value of £18,000. The profit had been netted off expenses.

Required

Show how the net cash flow from operating activities would be presented on the cash flow statement under the direct method.

(b) Using the same information, show the net cash flow from operating activities using the indirect method.

2. Level II

The following are extracts from the income statement and the balance sheets of Croft Ltd ('Croft').

Income statement Year to 30 April 2009	
	£
Turnover	4,200,000
Cost of sales	(2,870,000)
Gross profit	1,330,000
Distribution costs	(280,000)
Administrative expenses	(473,000)
Operating profit	577,000
Interest	(23,000)
Profit before tax	554,000

Balance sheet As at 30 April		
	2009	2008
	£	£
Current assets		
Inventory	318,000	292,000
Trade receivables	416,000	389,000
Cash and cash equivalents	71,000	25,000
Current liabilities		
Trade payables	373,000	320,000
Accruals	61,000	85,000

Notes

1. Operating profit includes a gain of £5,000 on the disposal of a fixed asset and £12,000 amortisation of a government grant. These were deducted in arriving at net administrative expenses.
2. Accruals at 30 April 2009 includes £16,000 accrued interest (for 2008 the amount was £14,000).
3. Cost of sales includes depreciation of £215,000.

Required

(a) Prepare the cash generated from operating activities under the indirect method.
(b) Using the following additional information, produce the cash generated from operating activities under the direct method.
    1. Cost of sales, distribution costs and administrative expenses include wage and salary costs, all of which were paid by the year end
    2. Administrative expenses includes £17,000 bad debt written off in the year.

3. Level II

Margot Ltd had the following fixed asset balances at 1 January 2009:

	Land	Machinery
	£	£
NBV	1,000,000	2,800,000

During the year to 31 December 2009 the following occurred:
  (i) land was revalued upwards by £600,000
 (ii) depreciation of £1,016,000 at 20% straight line was charged on machinery
(iii) a piece of machinery, bought in 2006 for £410,000 was sold for £120,000
(iv) machinery with a fair value of £70,000 was obtained under a new finance lease during the year.

At 31 December 2009 the company had the following fixed asset balances:

	Land	Machinery
	£	£
NBV	1,850,000	3,110,000

It is the policy of the company to charge a full year's depreciation in the year of purchase and none in the year of disposal.

Required

Calculate purchases of fixed assets for the year to 31 December 2009.

4. Level II

Sharma plc's draft income statement for the year ended 31 December 2009 and balance sheets at 31 December 2009 and 31 December 2008 were as follows:

Sharma plc
Income Statement for the year ended 31 December 2009

	£000s
Sales	360
Distribution and administrative expenses	186
Operating profit	174
Interest payable	14
Profit before tax	160
Taxation	62
Profit for year	98

Balance sheet as at 31 December 2009

	2009 £000	2009 £000	2008 £000	2008 £000
Fixed assets:				
Property, plant and equipment at cost		798		780
Depreciation		159		112
		639		668
Current assets:				
Stock	12		10	
Trade debtors	33		25	
Bank deposit account	24		28	
	69		63	
Current liabilities:				
Bank overdraft	10		8	
Trade creditors	6		3	
Taxation	51		43	
	67		54	
Net current assets		2		9
		641		677
Long-term loans		100		250
		541		427
Share capital (£1 shares)		180		170
Share premium		18		12
Profit and loss		343		245
		541		427

In addition, the following information is available.
1. Included within distribution and administration expenses were:
   - Depreciation   £59,000
   - Loss on disposal   £9,000
2. During the year, the company paid £45,000 for a new piece of machinery.

Required

Prepare a cash flow statement for Sharma plc for the year ended 31 December 2009 as required by IAS 7, using the indirect method to calculate cash flows from operating activities.

5. Level II
The following information has been extracted from the draft financial statements of T plc:

T plc Profit and loss account for the year ended 30 September 2009	
	£000
Sales	15,000
Cost of sales	(9,000)
	6,000
Other operating expenses	(2,400)
	3,600
Interest	(24)
Profit before taxation	3,576
Taxation	(1,040)
Dividends	(1,100)
	1,436
Balance brought forward	4,400
	5,836

T plc
Balance sheet at 30 September

		2007		2006
	£000	£000	£000	£000
Fixed assets:	18,160		14,500	
Current assets:				
Stock	1,600		1,100	
Debtors	1,500		800	
Bank	150		1,200	
	3,250		3,100	
Current liabilities:				
Creditors	(700)		(800)	
Proposed dividend	(700)		(600)	
Taxation	(1,040)		(685)	
	(2,440)		(2,085)	
Net current assets		810		1,015
		18,970		15,515
Long-term loans		(1,700)		(2,900)
		17,270		12,615
Deferred tax		(600)		(400)
		16,670		12,215
Ordinary share capital		2,500		2,000
Share premium		8,334		5,815
Profit and loss		5,836		4,400
		16,670		12,215

Fixed assets schedule	Land and buildings £000	Plant and machinery £000	Total £000
Cost			
30 September 2008	8,400	10,800	19,200
Additions	2,800	5,200	8,000
Disposals	–	(2,600)	(2,600)
30 September 2009	11,200	13,400	24,600
Depreciation			
30 September 2008	1,300	3,400	4,700
Disposals	–	(900)	(900)
Charge for year	240	2,400	2,640
30 September 2009	1,540	4,900	6,440
Net book value			
30 September 2009	9,660	8,500	18,160
30 September 2008	7,100	7,400	14,500

The plant and machinery that was disposed of during the year was sold for £730,000.

Required

Prepare T plc's cash flow statement using the indirect method to arrive at cash flows from operating activities for the year ended 30 September 2009.

6. Level III

You have been provided with the following information relating to Belgar plc for the year to 31 March 2009.

Income statement for the year to 31 March 2009	
	£000s
Turnover	4,850
Cost of sales	600
Gross profit	4,250
Distribution and administration expenses	2,875
Operating profit	1,375
Interest	300
Profit before tax	1,075
Taxation	670
Profit for the period	405

Balance sheets at 31 March 2009				
	2009 £000s	£000s	2008 £000s	£000s
Fixed assets:				
Land and buildings at cost		3,500		1,800
Plant and machinery at cost	6,100		5,800	
Less: depreciation	3,900		3,850	
		2,200		1,950
		5,700		3,750
Current assets				
Stock and work in progress	3,435		3,150	
Debtors	2,200		1,900	
Bank	160		500	
	5,795		5,550	
Current liabilities				
Bank overdraft	(1,750)		(1,500)	
Trade creditors	(1,450)		(1,550)	
Taxation	(820)		(1,150)	
	(4,020)		(4,200)	
Net current assets		1,775		1,350
		7,475		5,100
Debentures – 8% £1		2,000		–
		5,475		5,100
Share capital – fully paid ordinary £1 shares	1,200		1,000	
Share premium	550		600	
Retained profits	3,725		3,500	
	5,475		5,100	

Additional information

1. The ordinary dividend paid during the year and charged against the profit after tax was £180,000.

2.   Interest of £300,000 was made up of:

- Debenture interest   £160,000 (£80,000 accrual included in creditors)
- Overdraft interest   £140,000 (all paid in year)

3.   During the year, plant and equipment that had cost £1,200,000, and on which depreciation of £590,000 had been provided, was sold for £565,000.

4.   There had been a rights issue of ordinary shares at the rate of 1 for 10 at a price of £1.50 per share payable in full on 1 April 2008.

5.   Subsequently, a bonus issue of 1 for 11 shares had been made utilising the share premium account.

6.   The 8% debentures had been issued at par on 1 April 2008, payable in full.

Required

Prepare the cash flow statement for the year to 31 March 2009 for Belgar plc in accordance with IAS 7, using the indirect method to calculate the cash flows from operating activities.

Further reading

IAS 7 *Statement of Cash Flows*. IASB, amended 2009

Business Combinations

Introduction

Companies, as well as individuals, can be investors. Such companies may buy and sell shares issued by other companies. The way a company accounts for such investments depends, in part, on why an investment was acquired and the power an investment gives to the investor company. Investments in other companies need to be accounted for. This chapter will introduce the different methods of investing in other companies, and illustrate the methods of accounting for such investments. It will then go on to deal with basic group structures and discuss the accounting regulations governing the preparation of group accounts. The final section will examine the theoretical rationale underlying the alternative methods of preparing group accounts.

There are different ways in which one company can combine with another company. For example, the various assets and liabilities of two or more businesses may be acquired by a newly formed business and the original business cease to exist. This is called an *amalgamation*. An alternative way of combining is by *absorption*. This is where various assets (and sometimes liabilities) of a business are acquired by another business and are part of the acquiring company's own assets (and liabilities). A third way is where one company acquires shares in another company, with each continuing to exist independently. It is this third method that will be the subject of this chapter.

Section 1: Basic Principles

A company can make an investment by acquiring shares in another company. These investments can be at different levels – for example, 1%, 10%, 100%. The level of investment gives different degrees of 'power' to the acquiring company.

10.1 Initial recording of an investment

An investment arises when one company, the investor, buys shares in another company or undertaking, the investee. The investor is acquiring a new asset and will have to pay for this 'asset'. The payment is often referred to as the *consideration*.

 Example 1

Alpha Ltd buys 25,000 £1 ordinary shares of Beta Ltd at £4 each. Alpha pays cash. In the accounts of Alpha there will be a 'new' asset, the investment in Beta, and, in order to acquire this asset, Alpha will have used up cash. So, this transaction will be recorded as follows:

Dr	Investment in Beta	£100,000	
	Cr Bank		£100,000
Being investment in Beta.			

Note that although the par value of the shares is £1, the price paid for each share is £4.

It would also be possible for one company to pay for the shares in another company by issuing new ordinary shares of its own.

 Example 2:

Alpha buys 25,000 £1 ordinary shares of Beta at £4. To finance the purchase, Alpha issues 20,000 of its 25p ordinary shares. The market value of each Alpha share is £5.

The 'cost' of the investment in Beta is what Alpha had to give up to acquire the shares. Alpha has to give up shares worth £100,000 (25,000 × £4) to acquire its shares in Beta. These shares are worth £5 each – that is, £100,000 (20,000 × £5) in total. To record this transaction, Alpha will have a 'new' asset, the investment in Beta, but this time will have issued shares to pay for it. The issue of shares will result in the share capital being increased. The share capital account can only be increased by the par value of the shares. The difference between the market value of the shares, £5.00, and the par value, 25p, is classed as a share premium (£5.00 − £0.25) of £4.75.

So, the transaction will be recorded as follows:

Dr	Investment in Beta	£100,000	
	Cr Share capital (20,000 x £0.25)		£5,000
	Share premium (20,000 x £4.75)		£95,000
Being investment in Beta.			

The shares in Beta will be bought from existing shareholders, perhaps through the stock exchange. It is important to realise that the balance sheet of Beta (the investee company) will not be affected. This is because the transaction is between the investor company (Alpha) and the shareholders of Beta. All Beta has to do is to record the change in its register of members.

10.2 The investors' accounts

Once an investment has been made, the investor must decide how to classify this in its balance sheet. If the investment is to be held for a short period of time it should be classified as a current asset investment. If, on the other hand, it is to be held for a long period of time, it will be classified as a non-current asset.

In the balance sheet, the investment will be initially recorded at cost. The investment can remain at this amount or can be revalued to fair value every year (see Chapter 2).

The investor company (Alpha in the example above) will be entitled to received a dividend from Beta. This will constitute investment income in the income statement of the investor company (Alpha). Only dividends that are realised from the investor's point of view should be included. While it is prudent to include only those dividends actually received, any dividend that has been declared by the investee company, but has not actually been received, will normally be shown as a dividend receivable.

✴ *Example*

Alpha Ltd owns 100% of the ordinary shares of Beta Ltd. On 15 October Year 8, Beta pays a dividend of £60,000. On 31 December Year 8, Beta declares a dividend of £100,000. Assuming that the dividend declared on 31 December will be paid, and that there is no intention on the part of Alpha to sell the shares in Beta, the accounting entries will be as follows:

Dr	Bank	£60,000	
	Cr Investment income (profit and loss)		£60,000
Being dividend received.			

Dr	Debtors (dividend receivable)	£100,000	
	Cr Investment income (profit and loss)		£100,000
Being dividend received accrued.			

10.3 Investments that give control or influence

It may be that the purchase of shares in one company by another gives the investing company some degree of control or influence over the other company. The relationship between the two companies will depend on this degree of control. The degree of control may be linked to the percentage shareholding. There are four categories of investment that can be determined. These can be identified as follows.

1. Where Company A acquires a small stake in Company B – for example, 0.1%: this will constitute a simple investment and will be recorded on the balance sheet of Company A as an asset. Examples 1 and 2 (page 516) relate to this situation.
2. Where Company A has a substantial stake in Company B such that it is able to exercise total control over the operating and financial policies of Company B in other words, where Company A can exert a 'dominant influence' over Company B. Such control normally exists when Company A has more than 50% of Company B. If 'dominant influence' exists, then Company B is by definition a subsidiary company.
3. Where Company A has a stake in Company B, but this stake is not large enough to give Company A total control, but does allow Company A to participate in the operating and financial policy decisions, but not to control these: this gives Company A a 'significant influence' and usually arises from a holding of between 20% and 50% of the shares. If such a degree of influence was held by Company A, then Company B would be by definition an associate company.
4. Where Company A has a stake in Company B and shares control jointly with others (venturers), through some contractual arrangement. All the venturers will have to agree on key operating and financial policies with no single venturer in a position to exercise total control. In this case a joint venture would exist.

BASIC

INTERMEDIATE

ADVANCED

Progress Point 10.1

X Ltd buys a stake in Y Ltd, comprising 100,000 ordinary shares of £1. In order to finance this purchase, X Ltd issues 40,000 ordinary shares of £1. The current market price of the shares in X Ltd is £5 and in Y Ltd is £2.

(a)   How would X Ltd record its investment in Y Ltd?

(b)   If Y Ltd paid an interim dividend of £10,000 and declared a final dividend of £50,000, show how this would be recorded in the accounts of X Ltd.

(c)   Under what circumstances would Y Ltd be:
- (i) an associate
- (ii) a subsidiary
- (iii) a joint venture?

Solution

(a) Cost of investment in Y Ltd = (100,000 × £2) = £200,000.

Shares issued by X Ltd = 40,000.

Value of the 'consideration' = 40,000 × £5 = £200,000.

To record this share issue, share capital would be increased at par (40,000 × £1) and the excess (£5 – £1) would be put into the share premium (40,000 × £4).

So the transaction would be recorded in the books of X Ltd as follows:

Dr	Investment in Y Ltd	£200,000	
	Cr Share capital		£40,000
	Share premium		£160,000
Being cost of investment in X Ltd.			

(b)

Dr	Bank account (dividend received)	£10,000	
	Cr Investment income (profit & loss)		£10,000
Being dividend received.			

Dr	Debtors (dividend receivable)	£60,000	
	Cr Investment income (profit & loss)		£60,000
Being dividends receivable accrued.			

(c)

(i)   Y Ltd would be an associate if X Ltd had a participating interest, and was able to exert a significant influence over its operating and financial policies. Such an influence would be deemed to exist if X Ltd held a stake of between 20% and 50%.

(ii)   Y Ltd would be a subsidiary if X Ltd was able to exert a dominant influence and so have total control over its operating and financial policies. Total control would tend to exist if X Ltd had a stake of more than 50%.

(iii)   Y Ltd would constitute a joint venture if it was jointly controlled by X Ltd and other venturers, such that no one venturer was in a position to control Y Ltd unilaterally.

10.4 Subsidiary companies

As was noted above, a subsidiary company is one in which another company (called the parent or holding company) has total control over the operating and financial policies. When one company acquires a substantial stake in another company then this has to be accounted for. If the relationship that exists between those companies is that of parent and subsidiary, then a special technique of accounting is used. This accounting technique is called acquisition accounting, sometimes called the purchase method.

Acquisition of a subsidiary

Company H plc is interested in acquiring Company S plc. The balance sheet of S plc is as follows:

Balance sheet of S plc As at 31 December Year 1	
	£m
Fixed assets	150
Current assets:	
Cash	100
Creditors due within one year	
Trade creditors	(50)
	200
Capital and reserves	
Ordinary shares of £1	150
Retained earnings	50
	150

From this balance sheet it can be seen that the net assets of S plc are worth £200.

The balance sheet of H plc is as follows:

Balance sheet of S plc As at 31 December Year 1	
	£m
Fixed assets	600
Current assets:	
Cash	440
Creditors: due within one year	
Trade creditors	(40)
	1,000
Capital and reserves	
Ordinary shares of £1	£800
Retained earnings	200
	1,000

On the 31 December Year 1, H plc decides to buy all of S plc and is prepared to pay £300m. Assuming that the purchase was for cash, how would the balance sheet of H plc change? H plc will now have a new asset, Company S, and will have used up cash in acquiring this 'asset'. The balance sheet of H plc after the acquisition of S plc will now be as follows:

Balance sheet of H plc (after acquisition of S plc) As at 31 December Year 1	
	£m
Fixed assets	600
Investment in S	300
Current assets:	
Cash	140
Creditors: due within one year	
Trade creditors	(40)
	1,000
Capital and reserves	
Ordinary shares of £1	800
Retained earnings	200
	1,000

After the acquisition by H plc, the balance sheet of S plc won't change. All that has happened is that the ownership of the shares has passed to H plc. At this stage it is important to appreciate that H plc and S plc are still separate companies, and will continue trading as such. They will maintain their own accounting records. However, H plc will have to account for its interest in S plc by preparing group financial statements.

Using the balance sheets of H plc and S plc, the group balance sheet can now be prepared.

 ## Example

Summary balance sheets As at 31 December year 1		
	H plc	S plc
Fixed assets	£600	£150
Investment in S	300	
Current assets: cash	140	100
Trade creditors	(40)	(50)
	£1,000	£200
Share capital	£800	£150
Retained earnings	200	50
	£1,000	£200

Some initial points to note:

1. the group is a single entity and a single entity cannot have an investment in itself, nor can it issue share to itself
2. the assets *controlled* by H plc should be reflected in the group accounts.
3. any profits earned as a result of H plc's control should be shown in the group accounts. These are the profits earned after acquisition – that is, *post-acquisition*.

Some preliminary points

Showing an *Investment in S* in the group balance sheet does not make sense, since this would imply the group has an investment in itself. This cannot be, since the group is a single entity. This Investment in S must be eliminated from the group balance sheet.

The Investment in S, represents the price paid by H plc to acquire the net assets of S plc.

Since H plc controls all the fixed assets of S plc in order to give a true and fair view, the total assets of both companies will be shown in the group balance sheet.

Stage 1

Compare the price paid to acquire S plc (i.e. the Investment in S), with the 'value' of S plc at the date it was acquired (i.e. the **date of acquisition**).

H plc paid £300 for S plc. At the time of the purchase the 'value' of S plc was £200. So H plc was prepared to pay an additional £100 for something that is not shown in the balance sheet. This 'something' could be the reputation of S plc, its experienced staff, its market position, established customers, and so on. This additional amount paid to acquire control of S plc is called **goodwill**.

Goodwill is measured as the excess of the cost of the investment over the 'value' of the proportion of net assets acquired. The net assets acquired can be measured either as fixed assets plus net current assets, or as share capital and reserves. Usually in the preparation of group accounts it is easier to use the share capital and reserves measure, so this measure will be used in the examples that follow.

The calculation of goodwill will be:

'Value' of S plc at the date of acquisition	
Share capital	£150
Retained earnings	50
	200
Proportion acquired (100%)	£200
Price paid	£300
Therefore goodwill	£100

Stage 2

Calculate the total retained earnings of the group. The retained earnings of the group will comprise the profits of H plc plus H's share of the profit of S plc which have been earned since acquisition. This is because at the date of acquisition, H plc acquired the net assets of S plc, which are represented by the share capital and reserves. So the goodwill figure of £100 has already taken account of any profits which existed at the date of acquisition. Such profits are referred to as pre-acquisition profits.

The calculation of the profits of the group will be:

Profit of H plc	£200
H's share of the profit of S earned since date of acquisition	0 (all the profit of S is pre-acquisition)
	£200

The group balance sheet can now be prepared.

BASIC

INTERMEDIATE

ADVANCED

Balance sheet of H group As at 3 December Year 1		
Fixed assets	£750	(total of H and S, since H controls these)
Goodwill	100	
Current assets: cash	240	(total of H and S)
Trade creditors	(90)	(total of H and S)
	£1,000	
Share capital	£800	(only share capital of H)
Retained earnings	200	(profit of H and any pre-acquisition profit of S)
	1,000	

Goodwill is dealt with in full in Chapter 3. However, it is useful to note as a reminder that goodwill can be either positive, as in this example, or negative. Positive goodwill arises when the price paid is greater than the value of the net assets acquired. In other words, the acquiring company pays a premium.

When the price paid is less than the value of the net assets acquired, then negative goodwill arises. This is not very common.

Note that positive goodwill should remain in the balance sheet at cost but should be tested annually for impairment, while negative goodwill is taken to the income statement (see Chapter 3).

When the holding is less than 100%

Up to now the assumption made is that H plc owns 100% of S plc. Suppose that H plc had acquired only 75% of S plc. Who owns the other 25%? This other 25% may be held by many different shareholders. Collectively, this other ownership is called the non-controlling interest (NCI) (**minority interest**). If there is a non-controlling interest of 25% this has to be accounted for. The fact that H plc owns 75% of S plc means that H plc still has control over S plc.

Applying the same principles as indicated above, the group balance sheet can now be prepared.

Stage 1: goodwill calculation

Goodwill is calculated in the same way as before. However, this time the proportion of the assets acquired is less than 100% . The calculation is as follows:

'Value of S at date of acquisition		
Share capital	£150	
Retained earnings	50	
	£200	
Proportion acquired	150	(75% of £200)
Price paid	300	
Goodwill	150	

Stage 2: calculate the total retained profit of the group

This is done as follows:

Profit of H plc	£200
H's share of the profit of S earned since date of acquisition (75% x £0)	0 (all the profit of S is pre-acquisition)
	£200

Given that H plc has less than 100% of S plc, the minority interest must be accounted for.

Stage 3: calculate the non-controlling (minority interest)

As indicated above, the non-controlling interest is 25%. If the net assets of S plc are 'valued' at £200, then the non-controlling interest in these will be £50 (25% of £200).

The balance sheet of the H group can now be prepared.

Balance sheet of H group As at 31 December Year 1		
Fixed assets	£750	(total of H and S, since H controls these)
Goodwill	150	
Current assets: cash	240	(total of H and S)
Trade creditors	(90)	(total of H and S)
	£1,050	
Share capital	£800	(only share capital of H)
Retained earnings	200	(profit of H and any pre-acquisition profit of S)
Non-controlling interest	50	(the part on net assets not controlled by H)
	1,050	

BASIC

INTERMEDIATE

ADVANCED

Progress Point 10.2

The balance sheets of A plc and S plc are given as follows:

Balance sheets as at 30 June, Year 2				
		A plc		S plc
Tangible fixed assets		£200		£140
Investment in S		175		–
		375		140
Current assets:				
Stock	60		40	
Debtors	30		15	
	90		56	
Creditors due within 1 year				
Trade creditors	(70)	20	(35)	20
		395		161
Capital and reserves				
Ordinary share capital of £1	150		100	
Retained profit	245		60	
	395		160	

(a) Prepare the consolidated balance sheet of the A group, assuming A plc has acquired 100% of S plc.

(b) Prepare the consolidated balance sheet of the A group, assuming A plc has acquired 80% of S plc.

Solution

(a) Calculation of goodwill

'Value' of S at date of acquisition	
Share capital	100
Retained profit	60
	160
Proportion acquired (100%)	160
Price paid	175
Goodwill	15

Retained profit of group
    Profit of A   £245
Add A's share of post-acquisition profit of S   £0 (all profit is pre-acquisition)
                                     £245

Consolidated balance sheet of A group as at 30 June Year 2		
Tangible fixed assets (£200 + £140)		£340
Goodwill		15
Current assets		
Stock (£60 + £40)	100	
Debtors (£30 + £15)	45	
	145	
Creditors (£70 + £35)	(105)	40
		£395
Capital and reserves		
Ordinary share capital		£150
Retained profit		245
		£395

(b)   Where control is 80%, calculation of goodwill is as follows.

'Value' of S at date of acquisition		
Share capital	£100	
Retained profit	60	
	160	
Proportion acquired (80%)	128	
Price paid	175	
Goodwill	47	

Non-controlling interest

If the majority acquire 80% then the minority proportion is 20%. So non-controlling interest is 20% of £160 = £32.

Group retained earnings will be the same as in (a).

Consolidated balance sheet of A group as at 30 June Year 2		
Tangible fixed assets (£200 + £140)		£340
Goodwill		47
Current assets		
Stock (£60 + £40)	100	
Debtors (£30 + £15)	45	
	145	
Creditors (£70 + £35)	(105)	40
		£427
Capital and reserves		
Ordinary share capital		£150
Retained profit		245
Non-controlling interest		32
		£427

BASIC

INTERMEDIATE

ADVANCED

Consolidation in period after acquisition

So far consolidation at the date of acquisition has been considered. This section will consider the preparation of consolidated balance sheets when the subsidiary was acquired some time ago. An important date in the preparation of the group financial statements is the date at which acquisition takes place.

To illustrate this point, assume that company S was formed in Year 0. In Year 3 it was acquired by Company H. Profits reported by Company S are as follows:

- Year 3: £10,000 (date of acquisition)
- Year 5: £25,000

The total accumulated profit in Year 5 can be allocated as shown in Figure 10.1.

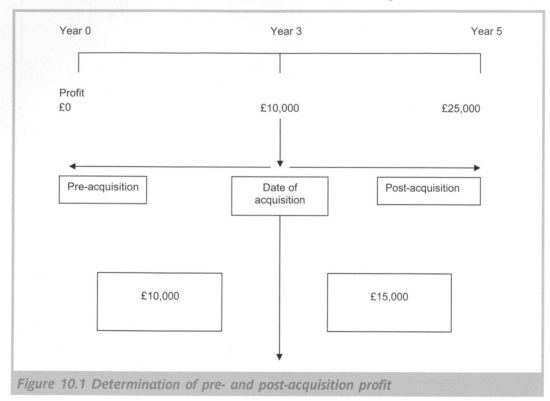

Figure 10.1 Determination of pre- and post-acquisition profit

From Figure 10.1, it can be seen that the total profit of Company S at Year 5 (i.e. at the **date of consolidation**) is £25,000. However, at the date Company S was acquired (i.e. date of acquisition) the accumulated profit was £10,000. This means that, since acquisition, profits have increased from £10,000 to £25,000, an increase of £15,000. The date of acquisition divides the life of the company into two: the period before acquisition, or *pre-acquisition*, and the period after acquisition, or *post-acquisition*. This means that any profits earned since the date of acquisition (i.e. the post-acquisition profit) will amount to £15,000 (£25,000 − £10,000).

Why is the distinction important?

The distinction is important because profits earned before the date of acquisition are accounted for differently to those earned after the date of acquisition. Pre-acquisition profits are used in the calculation of the goodwill figure – in other words, capitalised – while post-acquisition profits become part of the group profit.

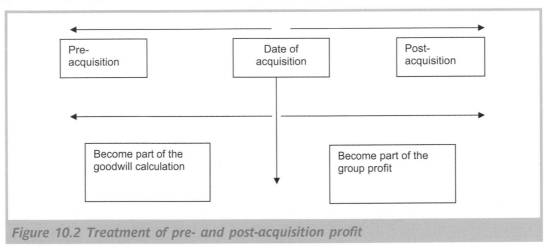

Figure 10.2 Treatment of pre- and post-acquisition profit

Note that non-controlling interest will not be affected. Minority is entitled to a share in both pre- and post-acquisition profits.

 ## Example

Matthew Ltd and Mark Ltd

On 31 March Year 3 Matthew Ltd acquired 40,000 of the £1 ordinary shares in Mark Ltd. On this date, the retained profit of Mark Ltd was £27,000. The balance sheets of the two companies a year later are as follows:

	Matthew Ltd £000	Mark Ltd £000
Investment in Mark Ltd	83	
Net assets	659	153
	586	153
Share capital £1 ordinary shares	150	50
Retained profit	592	103
	742	103

Prepare the consolidated balance sheet at 31 March Year 4.
This can be done through the stages indicated above.

Stage 1: calculate and record the goodwill

Matthew has acquired 40,000 shares out of the 50,000 shares of Mark. This is 80%. This implies that the non-controlling interest is 20%.

'Value' of Mark at date of acquisition		
Share capital	£50	
Retained profit	27	(this is the pre-acquisition profit)
	77	
Acquired 80%	61.6	(non-controlling interest = 20% = £15.4)
Price paid	83.0	
Goodwill	21.4	

Stage 2: calculate the group retained profit

This is the retained profit of Matthew plc plus Matthew's share of the post-acquisition retained profit of Mark plc. It can be calculated as follows:

Retained profit of Matthew		£592.0	
Total retained profit of Mark	£103.0		
Less pre-acquisition	£27.0		
Post-acquisition portion	£76.0		
Portion due to Matthew =	80% =	£60.8	(non-controlling interest = £15.2)
		£652.8	

Stage 3: calculate and record the non-controlling interest

The minority are entitled to a share in both the pre- and post-acquisition profits.

'Value' of Mark at date of consolidation		
Share capital	£50	
Retained profit	103	(this is, both pre- and post-acquisition)
	153	
Minority = 20% =	30.6	(£15.4 + £15.2)

The group balance sheet can now be prepared:

Matthew Group Balance sheet as at 31 March, Year 4.	
Net assets (£659 + £153)	£812.0
Goodwill (Stage 1)	21.4
	£833.4
Capital and reserves	
Share capital	£150.0
Retained profit (Stage 2)	652.8
Minority (Stage 3)	30.6
	£833.4

Consolidated income statement

The consolidated income statement shows the profit generated by all the resources disclosed in the consolidated balance sheet. In other words, the resources of the net assets of the parent company and its subsidiaries.

The consolidated income statement follows two basic principles.

1.   All the items shown in the income statement, down to profit after tax, will add together the income and expenses of both the parent and the subsidiary.
2.   If the subsidiary is only partly owned, there will be a non-controlling interest in the profit for the year of the subsidiary (after taxation). The profit attributable to the non-controlling interest will be deducted from the group profit.

 Example

P acquired 80% of the ordinary share capital of S. The income statements for the year ended 30 November 2009 were as follows:

	P	S
Sales revenue	£8,500	£2,200
Cost of sales and expenses	7,650	£1,980
Profit before tax	850	220
Taxation	400	100
Profit after tax	450	120

The subsidiary is partly owned (80%) so there will be a non-controlling interest in the profit for the year (after tax) of the subsidiary. This is calculated as follows:

20% of £120,000 = £24,000

As indicated above, all the items in the income statement of both the parent and subsidiary are added together, down to the profit after tax. In this example, the consolidated income statement would be as follows:

Consolidated income statement	
Sales revenue (£8,500 + £2,200)	£10,700
Cost of sales and expenses (£7,650 + £1,980)	9,630
Group profit before tax	1,070
Taxation (£400 + £100)	500
Net profit for the period	£570
Amount attributable to:	
Equity holder of the parent (£570 – £120 minority)	£546
Minority interest (20% of £120)	24
	£570

Section 2: Intermediate Issues

This section will develop the basic principles identified in Section 1. It will consider additional adjustments necessary to calculate the goodwill figure. In addition, it will consider the treatment of inter-company transactions and how these impact on the group financial statements.

10.5 Fair value adjustments

When one company is acquired by another company, any price paid will reflect the underlying values of the net assets of the company being acquired. It is likely therefore that, at the date of acquisition, the assets of the company being acquired will be revalued. This will mean adjusting the values of each individual asset and liability on the balance sheet and bringing them up to date. In other words, the net assets of the company being acquired will be restated to current values at the date of acquisition. Although there is no specific requirement to do so, it is likely that the acquiring company will also take the opportunity to bring its balance sheet up to date too. The following example continues the one on page 520.

 Example

P plc bought 3,200 ordinary shares in S plc several years ago. At the time P plc bought the holding in S plc, the balance in retained profits of S plc was £1,200. The balance sheets of P plc and S plc at 31 December Year 6 (i.e. now) are as follows:

Balance sheets As at 31 December Year 6		
	P plc	S plc
Fixed assets	£1,900	£4,000
Investment in S plc	8,500	
Current assets	800	2,500
Current liabilities	(700)	(500)
	£10,500	£6,000
Share capital (£1 shares)	£9,000	£4,000
Retained profits	£1,500	£2,000
	£10,500	£6,000

At the date of acquisition the fixed assets of S plc were revalued to £6,000. All the other net assets did not require any adjustment.

The balance sheet of S plc does not reflect this adjustment. In order to take account of the revaluation, the fixed assets of S plc will need to be increased to £6,000 and a revaluation reserve of £2,000 will need to be created.

BASIC

INTERMEDIATE

ADVANCED

Balance sheet of S plc after the fair value adjustment:

	S plc
Fixed assets	£6,000
Current assets	2,500
Current liabilities	(500)
	£8,000
Share capital (£1 shares)	£4,000
Retained profits	£2,000
Revaluation reserve	£2,000
	£8,000

Note that, since the adjustment to fair value occurred at the date of acquisition, it will be treated as pre-acquisition and so will become part of the goodwill figure.

The group balance sheet can now be prepared using the stages discussed above.

Stage 1: goodwill calculation

This time the fair value of the assets is taken and compared with the cost of the investment, as follows:

Fair value of S at date of acquisition		
Share capital	£4,000	
Retained profits	1,200	
Revaluation reserve	2,000	
	£7,200	
80% acquired	£5,760	(3,200 shares out of 4,000)
Price paid	8,500	
Goodwill	£2,740	

Stage 2: calculate the total retained profit of the group

This is done as follows:

Profit of P plc		£1,500
P's share of the profit of S earned since date of acquisition:		
Total profit of S plc	£2,000	
Less pre-acquisition	1,200	
Post-acquisition	800	
Whereof	80%	£640
		£2,140

Stage 3: calculate the non-controlling interest

Minority will be entitled to 20% of the 'fair value' of the company at date of consolidation = 20% of £8,000 = £1,600.

The balance sheet of the P group can now be prepared:

```
Balance sheet of P group
As at 31 December Year 1
Fixed assets              £7,900    (£1,900 + £4,000 + £2,000)
Goodwill                  £2,740
Current assets            £3,300
Trade creditors          (£1,200)
                         ─────────
                         £12,740
                         ═════════

Share capital             £9,000
Retained earnings         £2,140
Minority interest         £1,600
                         ─────────
                         £12,740
                         ═════════
```

10.6 Acquisition for consideration other than cash

Often when a company acquires another company, instead of paying cash, the acquiring company will issue shares to substitute for the shares it acquires. When there is a non-cash acquisition the investment in the subsidiary will be recorded at fair value. In this case the fair value of the investment in a subsidiary will be based on the number of shares issued and the current market price of each share.

 Example

Balance sheets of:	H plc	S plc
Net assets	£1,600	£1,200
Share capital (£1 shares)	£1,000	£800
Retained profit	600	400
	£1,600	£1,200

H plc is to acquire 100% of S plc. The terms of the acquisition are that H plc will issue shares on a 1 for 2 basis to acquire S plc. The fair value of the net assets of S plc at date of acquisition is £1,500. The market value of each share in H plc at date of acquisition is £5.

The figures for the group financial statements can be determined as before.

Stage 1: calculate the goodwill

In this case the fair value of the net assets of S plc will be measured and compared with the fair value of the shares given by H plc – that is, the 'consideration'. In order to acquire its stake in S plc, H plc gives up shares currently worth £5 each. In other words:

Number of shares in S plc = 800 (par value £1)

H plc gives 1 of its shares for every 2 in S plc, so H plc will issue 400 shares.

Fair value of those shares = £5 × 400 = £2,000

This is called the 'fair value of the consideration'

In order to calculate goodwill, the fair value of the consideration needs to be measured against the fair value of the net assets.

Fair value of net assets:		
Share capital	£800	
Retained profit	£400	
Revaluation reserve	£300	
	£1,500	
Fair value of consideration	£2,000	
Therefore: goodwill =	£500	

The issue of shares by H plc will be recorded in the accounts of H plc as normal. The share capital will be increased by the amount of shares issues, as par. Any excess will be transferred to the share premium. In this case the issue of 400 at a market price of £5 per share will be recorded as follows:

Dr	Investment in S plc	£2,000	
	Cr Share capital		£400
	Cr Share premium		£1,600
Being investment in S.			

Stage 2: calculate the group profit

In this example the group profit will only be the profit of H plc since all of the profit of S plc is pre-acquisition.

Stage 3: calculate the non-controlling interest

In this case there is no non-controlling interest since it was a 100% acquisition.

So the group balance sheet is as follows:

Balance sheet of H Group		
Net assets	£3,100	(£1,600 + £1,200 + £300)
Goodwill	500	
	£3,600	
Share capital	£1,400	(£1,000 + £400)
Share premium	£1,600	
Retained profit	£600	
	£3,600	

10.7 Dividend paid by subsidiary after acquisition

Care has to be taken when a subsidiary pays a dividend around the time of acquisition. After a subsidiary has been acquired the payment of a dividend by the subsidiary usually has no impact on the price paid or the goodwill element of the purchase.

The parent company is acquiring the assets that existed at the date of acquisition, which will equal the share capital and reserves at that date. Any dividends paid after the date of acquisition should have no impact on the reserves acquired at this date. However, any dividend paid before the date of acquisition will not be reflected in the 'value' of the company acquired.

In other words, the parent company will be paying for assets that in essence, don't really exist. In order to rectify this situation, any dividend from profits that existed at the date of acquisition should be deducted from the profit reserve and from the payment made to acquire the subsidiary.

✦ Example

Company H acquires Company S on 31 December Year 0. At this date the retained profit of S was £40. For the year ending 31 December Year 1 the income statement of Company S is as follows:

Profit for the year	£10
Retained profit at 31 December Year 0	£40
	£50
Dividend paid	£20
Retained profit at 31 December Year 1	£30

At the date S was acquired, the cost of control (i.e. goodwill) calculation would be based on the profit of £40, which is the profit at 31 December Year 0, the date of acquisition.

However, further analysis of the profit of S would reveal:

	Total	Pre	Post
Profit for year ending 31 December Year 1	£10		£10
Balance at 31 December Year 0	£40	£40	
	£50	£40	£10

So the total retained profit of £50 at 31 December is made up of pre-acquisition profit of £40 and post-acquisition profit of £10. Company S pays a dividend of £20. Where does this dividend come from? There are not enough post-acquisition profits available to pay the dividend. Some or this entire dividend has to come from **pre-acquisition profits**. It would be usual to use up the post-acquisition profits first, then the pre-acquisition profits. So in this example the dividend of £20 would be offset against the post-acquisition profits first, then the pre-acquisition profits, as follows:

	Total	Pre	Post
Profit for year ending 31 December Year 1	£10		£10
Balance at 31 December Year 0	£40	£40	
	£50	£40	£10
Dividend paid	£20	£10	£10
Retained profit at 31 December Year 1	£30	£30	£0

At the date of acquisition H acquired reserves (net assets) of £40, which would reflect the price H would pay for these assets. Would H have paid the same price if the reserves (i.e. asset values) of S were less than £40? Probably not.

Treatment of this dividend

Since this dividend has already been received by H it will be credited in the income statement of H. Unless an adjustment is made, the group income statement will contain some pre-acquisition profits in the form of dividend received by H. In order to rectify this situation, it is necessary to remove this pre-acquisition profit element by reducing the profit reserve and by reducing the amount paid by H to acquire company S, the Investment in S.

Adjustment required:

- Reduce the profit reserve
- Reduce the Investment in S.

With the amount of dividend from pre-acquisition profit.

This has the effect of reducing profit and reducing the purchase price by the amount of dividend from pre-acquisition profits.

10.8 Inter-company trading

Where there is a transfer of goods from one company to another at *cost*

 Example

P has a subsidiary: S. P transfers (sells) goods to S at cost: £10,000. Normally, each company will keep a record of its transactions with the other company using current accounts. So P will keep a record of its transaction with S in 'Current Account S' and S will keep a record of its transactions with P in 'Current Account P'. Because they are inter-company, these accounts will represent the amounts owing to, and from, each of the companies. The balances in them should be equal and opposite, and will be eliminated on consolidation.

Where there is a transfer of goods from one company to another at profit

In this situation one company will sell goods to the other company at selling price.

 Example holding company sells to subsidiary

H has a 60% interest in S. H buys an item of stock for £100 and sells it to S for £125. S subsequently sells this item for £140.

As far as the individual companies are concerned, each will make a profit. H's profit is calculated as follows:

Cost of item of stock	£100
Sold to S for	£125
Profit made by H	£25

S's profit will be calculated as follows:

Cost of item of stock from H	£125
Sold for	£140
Profit	£15

As far as the group is concerned, the profit will be:

Profit of H	£25
Profit of S	£15
Group profit	£40

This is the profit that would be expected since the cost of the item is £100 and was ultimately sold for £140, giving a profit of £40.

Since this item is subsequently sold, all of the group profit would be realised. However, what happens if, at the end of the year, the item is not sold by S but remains in the inventory of S? As far as the *group* is concerned, the profit made by H has not been realised, since it is still in the stock of S. Both the group profit and group stock figures will be overstated and will require to be adjusted as follows:

- reduce the group profit by the amount of the unrealised profit
- reduced the group inventory by the amount of the unrealised profit.

If instead of the sale being from H to S, it was the other way round – from S to H – how would the situation change?

The principle is exactly the same. The amount of unrealised profit must be eliminated, but this time there will be a non-controlling interest to be accounted for. The unrealised profit element, using the above example, is £40. The non-controlling interest in this is 40%, which is £16. The adjustment required is as follows:

- reduce group profit by majority share (60%) – £24
- reduce non-controlling interest – £16
- reduce group inventory – £40.

Progress Point 10.3

H acquired 90% of S on 1 January 2008. S sold some goods to H at a selling price of £18,000, and a mark-up of 25% on cost. Two-thirds of these goods remained in stock at the year end. How would this be accounted for in the group financial statements?

Solution

The first thing to notice is that the sale is from subsidiary to holding (i.e. from S to H), so there will be a non-controlling interest to account for. S sells to H at a mark-up of 25% on cost, so cost plus 25% of cost equals selling price. Therefore:

```
Let cost = C
      C + 25% of C  = £18,000
      C + 0.25C     = £18,000
      1.25C         = £18,000
      C             = £14,400 (£18,000 / 1.25)
      Profit = £18,000 – £14,400 = £3,600
```

Given that two-thirds of the stock remains unsold implies that two-thirds of the profit will be unrealised.

Amount of unrealised profit = two-thirds of £3,600 = £2,400

So, in the group financial statements:

- reduce group profit by majority share (90%)   £2,160
- reduce minority interest (10%)   £240
- reduce inventory   £2,400.

10.9 Transfer of non-current assets

Transfer of fixed assets between group companies causes similar problems to those concerned with internal stock transfers. The objective is to make adjustments on consolidation, which will show the assets at cost to the group – in other words, as if the transfer had not taken place.

Where a non-current asset transfer occurs within a group at an amount greater than the net book value of the asset in the books of the transferor, any profit made on the transfer must be eliminated since this profit is unrealised.

However, the transaction has an additional effect as far as the group is concerned since the asset will have been subject to depreciation in the books of both companies. The depreciation charged by each company may be different, which means that the same asset will be subject to both a different amount and different pattern on depreciation as a result of the transfer.

✦ Example

T Ltd owns 75% of the ordinary shares of H Ltd. In April 2009, H Ltd sold a piece of machinery to T Ltd for £450,000. H Ltd had bought this machinery in 2005 for £700,000. The policy of both companies is to depreciate machinery over a total useful life of ten years using the straight line method. When assets are transferred it is group policy to depreciate over the remaining useful life of the assets. A full year's depreciation is charged in the year of acquisition, and none in the year of disposal.

When the asset was owned by H Ltd the pattern of depreciation would have been as follows:

1/1/05	Cost of asset		£700,000
31/12/05	Depreciation	£70,000	
31/12/06	Depreciation	£70,000	
31/12/07	Depreciation	£70,000	
31/12/08	Depreciation	£70,000	£280,000
	Net book value		£420,000
	Sold for		£450,000
	Profit on sale		£30,000

When the asset is transferred to T Ltd, the cost is £450,000 and the asset will be depreciated over the remaining six years at a depreciation charge of £75,000 p.a. So, at 31 December 2009, the asset will be shown in the books of T Ltd as follows:

Cost of asset	£450,000
Depreciation	75,000
Net book value at 31 December 2009	£375,000

As far as the *group* is concerned, the profit of £30,000 is unrealised and must be eliminated. Also, the depreciation by T is based on the transfer price, and not on the cost to the group. In order to restore the carrying amount of fixed assets to that which would have existed had the inter-company transfer not taken place, four adjustments may have to be made.

1. The asset must be adjusted back to the original cost to the group.
2. The profit on sale must be removed since, from a group point of view, it is unrealised.
3. The depreciation charge for the year must be adjusted to what it would have been, based on the cost to the group.
4. Aggregate depreciation needs to reflect the amount it would be had all the depreciation calculations been based on the original cost of the asset.

The profit made by H Ltd is unrealised and must be eliminated from the group accounts. This is done as follows:

■ Reduce the group profit by (75% of £30,000)   £22,500 Dr
■ Reduce non-controlling interest by (25% of £30,000)   £7,500 Dr
■ Reduce the fixed assets by   £30,000 Cr.

The depreciation charged by T Ltd will be higher than it ought to be since it will be based on the 'new' cost of the asset to T Ltd. Had the asset not been transferred it would have been depreciated by £70,000. When it was transferred the depreciation increased to £75,000. Therefore there is an excess depreciation of £5,000 that must be adjusted.

The adjustment is made to both the income statement (profit will be understated), and to the provision for depreciation (which will be overstated). So:

- reduce the provision for depreciation   £5,000 Dr
- increase group profit (75% of £5,000)   £3,750 Cr
- increase non-controlling interest (25% of £5,000)   £1,250 Cr.

These adjustments will have the effect of restoring the asset to the position it would have been in had the transfer not taken place.

Progress Point 10.4

Alpha Ltd owns 80% of the ordinary shares of Beta Ltd. On 1 January Year 3 Beta sold a machine to Alpha for £7,000. Its original cost in Year 0 was £8,000 and it was depreciated by Beta at 10% straight line. The policy of both companies is to depreciate machinery over a total useful life of ten years using the straight line method. When assets are transferred it is group policy to depreciate over the remaining useful life of the assets. A full year's depreciation is charged in the year of acquisition, and none in the year of disposal.

The fixed assets schedules of Alpha and Beta at 31 December Year 6 show the following:

	Alpha	Beta
Non-current assets at cost	£38,000	£27,000
Depreciation	£14,000	£10,000
Net book value	£24,000	£17,000

Show how this asset transfer would be shown in the group accounts at 31 December Year 6.

Solution

In this example the transfer is from Beta (subsidiary) to Alpha (parent). As far as the asset is concerned, the pattern of depreciation will be as follows:

In the books of Beta			
Year 0	Cost of asset		£8,000
31/12 Year 0	Depreciation	£800	
31/12 Year 1	Depreciation	£800	
31/12 Year 2	Depreciation	£800	£2,400
Net book value when sold			£5,600
Sold to Alpha for			£7,000
Profit on sale			£1,400

When the asset is sold to Alpha the cost to Alpha will be £7,000. The asset has a life of ten years, and has already been depreciated for three years, so there are seven years left of the asset's life. The depreciation in the books of Alpha will be spread over the remaining life of seven years, and will be charged at the rate of 1/7 (i.e. £1,000 p.a.).

In the books of Alpha		
Cost of asset from Beta		£7,000
31/12 Year 3 Depreciation	£1,000	
31/12 Year 4 Depreciation	£1,000	
31/12 Year 5 Depreciation	£1,000	
31/12 Year 6 Depreciation	£1,000	£4,000
Net book value at 31 December Year 6		£3,000

1. Unrealised profit of £1,400 needs to be eliminated

Reduce the profit by (80% of £1,400)	£1,120 Dr		
Reduce non-controlling interest (20% of £1,400)	£280 Dr		
Reduce fixed assets		£1,400	Cr

2. Adjust for excess depreciation

If the asset had not been transferred to Alpha, then Beta would have continued to charge depreciation at £800 p.m. However, Alpha charged depreciation at £1,000 p.m. So:

Depreciation that ought to be charged (£800 x 4)	£3,200
Depreciation actually charged (£1,000 x 4)	£4,000
Excess depreciation charges	£800

The adjustment will be made as follows:

Reduce provision for depreciation	£800 Dr		
Increase group profit (80% of £800)		£640	Cr
Increase non-controlling interest (20% of £800)		£160	Cr

Cost of assets to the group

As far as the group is concerned, it is as though the transfer had not taken place.

Beta	Cost	Depreciation	Net book value
Balance at start	£27,000	£10,000	£17,000
Add back asset	£8,000	£5,600	£2,400
	£35,000	£15,600	£19,400

Alpha			
Balance at start	£38,000	£14,000	£24,000
Remove asset	£7,000	£4,000	£3,000
	£31,000	£10,000	£21,000

Group			
Alpha	£31,000	£10,000	£21,000
Beta	£35,000	£15,600	£19,400
	£66,000	£25,600	£40,400

10.10 Transfer at a loss

Where the asset is transferred at a loss, the same principles apply, except that transfer below net book value may imply impairment, in which case the asset should be carried at the reduced amount and the loss retained. This would be a 'realised' loss and so no consolidated adjustment would be required.

10.11 Debentures

Holding bonds, debentures, loan stock in a subsidiary does not give ownership rights and normally does not give any control, as such items are liabilities and not capital. Therefore the parent does not require to hold any of the subsidiary's debt. However, the parent may hold some or all of the subsidiay's debt, as there is nothing to stop this happening.

Where debt of a group company is held by another member of the group, then such a holding is deemed to be inter-company and must be eliminated on consolidation.

Any balance outstanding after elimination will represent the holding outside the group and must be shown in the consolidated balance sheet. Remember that external debt holders are long-term creditors and not shareholders. In the consolidated balance sheet they should be shown as long-term creditors and not included in the minority interest.

10.12 Preference shares

It may be that the parent company acquires some preference shares in a subsidiary. Normally, preference shares are not required for control since they do not carry any voting rights. However, the purchase of preference shares in an existing subsidiary requires that the goodwill on acquisition be calculated. This calculation is the same as that required for the acquisition of ordinary shares. The net assets acquired are equivalent only to the nominal value of the shares acquired because preference shareholders do not have ownership rights over the reserves of a company.

 Example

XY Ltd is a subsidiary of AB Ltd. AB Ltd purchased 75% of the preference share capital of XY Ltd for £375,000. The preference share capital of XY Ltd comprises 400,000 shares of £1 each.

Goodwill is calculated as before:

Nominal value of preference shares	£400,000
Proportion acquired = 75% =	£300,000
Price paid	£375,000
Goodwill	£75,000

This goodwill on acquisition of preference shares is not separately identified in the balance sheet. It is combined with goodwill arising on acquisition of ordinary shares. Any balance of preference shares not held by the group is included in the consolidated balance sheet as part of minority interest. In this case the minority interest element would be £100,000 (25% of £400,000).

10.13 Consolidated income statement: development of issues

Impairment of goodwill

Once any impairment has been identified during the year, the charge for the year will be shown in the consolidated income statement. This will usually be done through the operating expenses.

Dividends

A payment of a dividend from a subsidiary to a parent company will need to be eliminated. This is in essence an intra-group transaction. Only dividends paid by the parent company to its own shareholders will appear in the consolidated financial statements. Any dividend income shown in the consolidated income statement must only be investments other than in a subsidiary.

The principles outlined relating to the cancellation of internal dividends on ordinary shares also apply to preference dividends on consolidation. However, since preference shareholders are entitled to their dividends before ordinary shareholders, preference dividends must be deducted before calculating the minority interest in profits available to ordinary shareholders.

✸ *Example*

H plc holds 60% of the ordinary shares of S plc and 80% of the preference shares. The following information relates to the year ending 31 December Year 1.

Profit after taxation of S plc is £15,000.

Dividends:		
	£	£
Ordinary	5,000	2,000
Preference	2,000	4,000

In order to calculate the non-controlling interest in the profit for the year of S plc, the preference dividend must be taken into account. The non-controlling interest would be calculated as follows:

Profit for the year of S plc after tax	£15,000	
Less preference dividend	4,000	minority = 20%
Available for ordinary shareholders	£11,000	minority = 40%
Total minority interest:		
20% of £4000	£800	
40% of £11,000	£4,400	
	£5,200	

Progress point 10.5

The income statements of P Ltd and S Ltd for the year ended 31 August 20 Year 4 are shown below. P acquired 75% of the ordinary shares capital of S several years ago.

Income statements	P Ltd	S Ltd
	£	£
Sales revenue	2,400	800
Cost of sales and expenses	(2,160)	(720)
Trading profit	240	80
Dividend from S	2	–
Profit before tax	242	80
Taxation	(115)	(40)
	127	40

Prepare the consolidated income statement for the year ended 31 August Year 4.

Solution

Working 1: non-controlling interest

Non-controlling interest will be 25% of profit of S for the year, after tax:

= 25% of £40 = £10

P consolidated income statement for year ended 31 August Year 4	
Sales revenue (£2,400 + £800)	£3,200
Cost of sales and expenses (£2,160 + £720)	£2,880
Group profit before tax	£320
Taxation (£115 + £38)	£155
Profit for the year	£165
Attributable to:	
Group	£155
Minority interest	£10

Sales, purchases and inventories

The general principle that applies to the above items is that any intra-group trading must be eliminated from the consolidated income statement. In the case of sales and purchases, the sales from one company in the group will be the purchases of another company within the group. So for the consolidated income statement:

> *Consolidated sales revenue*
> Revenue of the parent company
> Add revenue of the subsidiary company
> Less any intra-group sales
>
> *Consolidated cost of sales*
> Cost of sales of the parent company
> Add cost of sales of the subsidiary
> Less intra-group sales

If there are any intra-group goods sold that are still in the closing inventory, their value must be adjusted to the lower of cost and net realisable value to the group, as is the case with the consolidated balance sheet. In other words, any unrealised profit must be removed. This is usually done in practice by increasing the cost of sales figure.

Example

The income statements of P Ltd and its subsidiary L Ltd for the year ended 31 December Year 5 are given as follows:

	P Ltd	L Ltd
	£000	£000
Sales revenue	3,200	2,560
Cost of sales	2,200	1,480
Gross profit	1,000	1,080
Distribution costs	160	120
Admin costs	400	80
	440	880
Dividend income	160	0
	600	880
Taxation	400	480
Net profit for the year after tax	200	400

BASIC

INTERMEDIATE

ADVANCED

Additional information

1. P Ltd acquired 80% of the ordinary shares of L Ltd on 31 December Year 1, when the share capital was £800,000 and the balance on L's retained earnings was £600,000.
2. A goodwill impairment of £38,000 was necessary. Impairments are to be included within administrative expenses.
3. P Ltd sold goods to L Ltd, at a selling price of £600,000. Not all of these goods had been sold externally by the year end. The profit element included in the closing inventory of L was £30,000.

In order to prepare the consolidated income statement the sales revenue and cost of sales need to be adjusted to take account of intra-company trading. The unrealised profit will also have to be eliminated from the closing stock. As was stated above, this is usually achieved by increasing the cost of sales. The goodwill impaired will be accounted for by increasing the administration expenses by the amount impaired. Finally, the non-controlling interest in the profit for the year of L will be disclosed.

The consolidated income statement would be as follows:

Sales revenue (£3,200 + £2560 − £600)	£5,160
Cost of sales (£2,200 + £1,480 − £600 + £30)	3,110
Gross profit	2,050
Distribution costs	280
Admin costs (£400 + £80 + £38 (goodwill))	518
Profit before taxation	1,252
Taxation (£400 + £480)	880
Profit after tax	372
Amount attributable to:	
Equity shareholders of P	£290
Minority interest	80

Note: the minority interest is calculated as 20% of the profit for the year after tax of L. This equals: 20% of £400 = £80.

10.14 Interest

If loans are outstanding between group companies, intra-group loan interest will be paid and received. Both the loan and the loan interest must be excluded from the consolidated financial statements.

10.15 Acquisition of a subsidiary during its accounting period

Up to now the acquisition of a subsidiary happened at the end of the accounting period. In practice it is unlikely that the date of acquisition will coincide precisely with the end of the accounting period. It is more likely that the date of acquisition will occur during the accounting period.

When a parent company acquires ordinary shares in a subsidiary during the accounting period it will not be necessary to prepare consolidated financial statements immediately. These statements will be prepared at the normal year end of the company. However, the principles of consolidation are unchanged in that it is necessary to calculate goodwill based on conditions existing at the date of acquisition. Where the subsidiary has been acquired during the accounting period, some of the reserves at the balance sheet date will be attributable to post-acquisition, and some to pre-acquisition.

BASIC

INTERMEDIATE

ADVANCED

The objectives of the adjustments in this situation are:

- to ensure that all reserves at the date of acquisition are capitalised as part of the calculation of goodwill so that the purchase price is compared with the net assets at the date of acquisition
- to ensure that the consolidated income statement includes the results of the new subsidiary only from the date of acquisition

If a separate set of accounts is not prepared for the subsidiary at the date of acquisition, the balance on reserves at that date will have to be estimated. Time apportionment of the profit of the subsidiary for the relevant accounting period is acceptable.

In addition, it should be noted that to ensure that the consolidated income statement only includes the results of the new subsidiary, it will be necessary to apportion the items in the income statement on a time basis also.

However, if the circumstances suggest that apportionment on a time basis would be unacceptable, then a basis that reflects the circumstances should be used – for example, if there is some kind of seasonality in the business cycle of the company. The objective is to calculate as accurately as possible the net assets of the company at the date of acquisition.

 ## Example

Bright Ltd purchased 80% of Spark Ltd on 30 June 2009 for £600,000. The accounts for Spark Ltd for the year ended 31 December 2009 were as follows:

Income statement for period ended 30 December 2009	
Sales revenue	£400,000
Cost of sales and expenses	235,000
Profit before taxation	£165,000
Taxation	60,000
Profit after tax	£105,000

Balance sheet as at 30 December 2009	
Net assets	£790,000
Share capital	£50,000
Retained earnings	£740,000
	£790,000

The following information is available.

1. The trade of Spark Ltd is seasonal, and the timing of the profit is such that 75% of the profit arises in the last six months of the year.
2. Goodwill is not impaired.

The goodwill on acquisition will be calculated as follows.

Fair value of net assets acquired at date of acquisition:

Share capital	£50,000
Retained earnings at 31 December 2008	
= £740,000 – £105,000	£635,000
Retained earnings from 1 Jan 2009 to	
30 June 2009 are split 25%/75%. So	
pre-acquisition part = 25% of £105,000	£26,250
	£711,250
Whereof 80%	£569,000
Price paid	£600,000
Goodwill	£31,000

As far as non-controlling interest is concerned, this would normally be calculated at the last balance sheet date. However, if the subsidiary is acquired during the year, there would not be minority at the start of the year because there would be no subsidiary. In this situation, the non-controlling interest is calculated at the date of acquisition.

In the example given, the non-controlling interest at date of acquisition is 20% of £711,250 = £142,250. However, minority will also be entitled to a share in the profits earned since acquisition. These are the profits earned from 1 July 2009 to 31 December 2009 = 75% of £105,000 = £78,750. Non-controlling interest will be 20% of this, which is £15,750 (20% of £78,750). Total non-controlling interest shown in the group balance sheet would be £158,000 (£142,250 + £15,750).

In the group income statement, 75% of the sales revenue and costs of the subsidiary will be added to those of the parent, so that only the results of the new subsidiary from date of acquisition will be included. So, using the figures from the above example, the amounts to be included in the consolidated income statement from Spark Ltd will be as follows:

Sales revenue (75% of £400,000)	£300,000
Cost of sales and expenses	(176,000)
Profit before taxation	123,750
Taxation	(45,000)
Profit after tax	78,750

Progress Point 10.6

Kay Ltd acquired 60% of Gregor Ltd on 30 June 2009.

The financial statements of the two companies for the year ended 30 September 2009 are as follows:

	Kay Ltd £	Gregor Ltd £
Income statement		
Sales revenue	900,000	750,000
Cost of sales	(650,000)	(450,000)
Gross profit	250,000	300,000
Operating expenses	(100,000)	(80,000)
Interest expense	(60,000)	(20,000)
Profit before tax	90,000	200,000
Taxation	(30,000)	(65,000)
Profit after tax	60,000	135,000

Balance sheet:	£	£
Tangible fixed assets	784,000	485,000
Investment in Gregor	460,750	
Current assets	215,250	210,000
Creditors: amounts owing for less than one year	(100,000)	(25,000)
	1,360,000	670,000
Share capital £1 ordinary shares	400,000	150,000
Share premium	350,000	50,000
Retained profit	610,000	470,000
	1,360,000	670,000

Additional information

1. There has been no impairment of goodwill.
2. Kay paid a dividend in the year of £20,000.
3. Profits of Gregor accrue evenly throughout the year.

Required

Prepare the consolidated income statement for the year ended 30 September 2009 together with a consolidated balance sheet as at that date.

Solution

Kay acquired Gregor on 30 June. Group financial statements have to be prepared on 30 September, so the revenues and costs will have to be apportioned 9/12 (pre-acquisition) and 3/12 (post-acquisition). In addition, the revenues and costs of Gregor shown in the income statement will have to be apportioned from date of acquisition to date of consolidation. The adjusted income statement of Gregor will therefore be as follows:

Adjusted income statement of Gregor	
Sales (3/12th of £750,000)	£187,500
Cost of sales (3/12th of £450,000)	(£112,500)
Gross profit	£75,000
Operating expenses (3/12th of £80,000)	(£20,000)
Interest (3/12th of £20,000)	(£5,000)
Profit before tax	£50,000
Taxation (3/12th of £65,000)	(£16,250)
Profit after tax	£33,750

The information required for the consolidated balance sheet can be prepared in accordance with the stages outlined previously.

Stage 1: calculate and record goodwill

Fair value of Gregor at date of *acquisition*		
Share capital		£150,000
Share premium		£50,000
Profit and loss account		
This can be split into two time periods:		
(i) at 1/10/08 (£470,000 – £135,000)	£335,000	
(ii) from 1/10/08 to 30/09 (£135,000 x 9/12)	101,250	436,250
		£636,250
Portion acquired = 60%		£381,750
Price paid		460,750
Goodwill		£79,000

Stage 2: calculate total retained profit of the group

Retained profit of Kay		£610,000
Add Kay's share of the post-acquisition profit of Gregor		
In this example only 3/12th of £135,000 is post-acquisition.		
So post-acquisition profit	£33,750	
Share of this attributable to Kay = 60%		20,250
Total group retained profit		£630,250

▶

Stage 3: calculate total non-controlling interest

Remember there is no need to divide reserves into pre- and post-acquisition as far as the minority are concerned. Minority are entitled to a share in both pre- and post-acquisition profits.

Fair value of Gregor at date of *consolidation*	
Share capital	£150,000
Share premium	50,000
Retained profit	470,000
	£670,000
Minority share = 40%	£268,000

The non-controlling interest can be shown to comprise two components, as follows.

1. Minority at date of acquisition: .
    Share capital   £150,000
    Share premium   £50,000
    Profit   £436,250   (from Stage 1 above)
                                                  £636,250
    Minority share = 40%   £254,500
2. Non-controlling interest in the profit for
    the year of Gregor.
    = 9/12th of £135,000 × 40%   £13,500

Total minority   £268,000

The group financial statements can now be prepared.

Group income statement	
Sales revenue (£900,000 + £187,500)	£1,087,500
Cost of sales (£650,000 + £112,500)	(762,500)
Gross profit	325,000
Operating expenses (£100,000 + £20,000)	(120,000)
Interest (£60,000 + £5,000)	(65,000)
Profit before tax	£140,000
Taxation (£30,000 + £16,250)	£46,250
Profit after taxation	£93,750
Attributable to:	
Group shareholders	£80,250
Non-controlling interest	£13,500

Group balance sheet	
Tangible fixed assets (£784,000 + £485,000)	£1,269,000
Goodwill	79,000
Current assets (£215,250 + £210,000)	425,250
Current liabilities (£100,000 + £25,000)	(125,000)
	£1,648,250
Share capital	£400,000
Share premium	350,000
Retained profit	630,250
Minority interest	268,000
	£1,648,250

10.16 Accounting for associates and joint ventures

The definitions of associates and joint ventures have already been given in the first section. This part will now deal with the accounting issues relating to associates and joint ventures.

Associates

As an investor has significant influence over an associate it has a measure of responsibility for the performance of the associate, and for the return on its investment. Significant influence is the power to participate in the financial and operating policy decisions of the investee company by the investor, but does not give the investor control over those policies.

Significant influence would not be evidenced merely by retaining the investment at cost and recording the dividends received. Neither is consolidation, either full or partial, appropriate, since the investor company does not control the net assets of an associate.

In terms of accounting for an associate an investor accounts for its stewardship by including its share of the profits and net assets of an associate in its consolidated financial statements using a method of accounting called equity accounting.

Equity accounting is a method of accounting that brings an associate investment into the parent company's financial statements initially at cost. The carrying amount of the investment is then adjusted in each period for the group share of the profit of the associate less any impairment losses. The investment in the associate is calculated at:

- cost of investment
- add group share of post-acquisition retained profit
- less any impairment losses

or

- share of the net assets of the associate
- add premium on acquisition (goodwill)
- less any impairment losses.

The equity method of accounting requires that the consolidated income statement does not include any dividend income from the associate, but instead includes the group's share of the associate company's profit for the year.

The following example illustrates these two basic points.

🔅 *Example*

H plc acquired 25% of A plc when the share capital of A was £40 and its profits were £12.

Balance sheets as at 31 December 2009		
	H plc	A plc
	£	£
Assets	105	72
Investment in A	20	0
	125	72
Share capital	60	40
Retained profits	40	20
	100	60
Current liabilities	25	12
	125	72

Income statement for the year ending 31 December 2009		
	H plc	A plc
	£	£
Trading profit	20	8
Dividend received	1	0
Profit for the year	21	8

Under the equity method of accounting the investment in the associate will be calculated as follows:

Cost of investment	£20	
Add share of post-acquisition profit	2	(25% of £20 – £12)
	£22	

Alternatively, the investment in the associate can be calculated by adding the goodwill figure to the share of net assets acquired.

Calculation of goodwill:

Fair value of A at date of acquisition	
Share capital	£40
Retained profit	£12
	£52
Share acquired = 25%	£13
Cost	£20
Goodwill	£7

So, investment in associate:

Share of net assets (25% of £72 – £12)	£15
Add goodwill	£7
	£22

Income statement	
Profit (H only)	£20
Share of profit of A (25% of £8)	£2
	£22

Balance sheet	
Assets (only assets of H)	£105
Investment in associate	£22
	£127
Share capital	£60
Retained profit (£40 + 25% of £8)	£42
	£102
Current liabilities	£25
	£127

Progress Point 10.7

The following question brings together some aspects of accounting for subsidiary companies and incorporating the results of an associate.

The following are the balance sheets of D, L and P as at 31 December 2009.

	D £000	L £000	P £000
Tangible assets	1,120	980	840
Investments:			
672,000 shares in L	744		
168,000 shares in P	224		
	2,088		
Current assets:			
Inventory	280	640	190
Receivables	190	310	100
Cash	35	58	46
	505	1,008	336
	2,593	1,988	1,176
Equity and liabilities			
Capital and reserves			
Ordinary shares	1,120	840	560
Retained profits	1,232	602	448
	2,532	1,442	1,008
Current liabilities			
Payables	150	480	136
Taxation	91	66	32
	241	546	168
	2,593	1,988	1,176

The following information is also relevant.

1.   D acquired its shares in L on 1 January, 2009 when the retained profit of L was £56,000.
2.   D acquired its shares in P on 1 January, 2009 when the retained profit of P was £140,000.
3.   An impairment test at the year end shows that goodwill for L has been impaired by £3,360 and the investment in P by £2,800.

Required

Prepare the consolidated balance sheet at 31 December 2009.

Solution

The solution to this question can be prepared using the stages as already outlined in previous examples.

D in L

D holds 672,000 shares out of 840,000 shares in L. This is a holding of 80%, therefore L would be a subsidiary of D.

Stage 1: calculate the goodwill

Fair value of L at date of acquisition:	
Share capital	£840,000
Retained profit	56,000
	896,000
Whereof 80%	£716,800
Price paid	£744,000
Goodwill	£27,200

Stage 2: calculate the group retained profit

This will comprise the profit of D, plus D's share of the post-acquisition profits of both L and P.

Profit of D		£1,232,000
Profit of L	£602,000	
Less pre-acquisition	56,000	
Post-acquisition	546,000	
80%		436,800
Profit of P	£448,000	
Less pre-acquisition	140,000	
Post-acquisition	308,000	
30%		92,400
		£1,761,200

Stage 3: non-controlling interest

Fair value of D at date of consolidation:

Share capital	£840,000
Retained profit	602,000
	£1,440,000
Whereof 20%	£288,400

There is no non-controlling interest in an associate.

Associate company (D in L)

D owns 168,000 shares out of 560,000 shares in P, this is 30%. P; is deemed to be an associate. The value of the investment in the associate needs to be calculated as was explained above.

It can be calculated in one of two ways:

Share of net assets of P (30% of £1,008,000)	£302,400
Add goodwill	14,000
	£316,400

Value of P at date of acquisition	
Share capital	£560,000
Retained profit	140,000
	£700,000
Whereof 30%	£210,000
Price paid	£224,000
Goodwill	£14,000

or

At cost	£224,000
Add share of post-acquisition profit	£92,400
	£316,400

Group balance sheet		
Tangible assets (£1,120,000 + £980,000)		£2,100,000
Investment in associate		316,400
Goodwill		27,200
Current assets:		
Inventory (280,000 + £640,000)	£920,000	
Receivables (£190,000 + £310,000)	£500,000	
Cash (£35,000 + £58,000)	93,000	1,513,000
		£3,956,600
Capital and reserves		
Ordinary shares		£1,120,000
Retained profits		£1,761,200
Minority interest		288,400
Current liabilities:		
Payables	£630,000	
Taxation	£157,000	£787,000
		£3,956,600

10.17 Associate companies: development of issues

Fair values and the associate

If the fair value of the net assets of the associate at date of acquisition is materially different from their book values, then the net assets of the associate should be adjusted in the same way as for a subsidiary.

Balances with the associate

The associate company is considered to be outside the group, so any balances between group companies and the associate will remain in the consolidated balance sheet.

Unrealised profit in inventory

This is treated in the same way as was illustrated for subsidiaries in that it has to be eliminated, as follows.

(i) If parent company sells to associate:
   in this case the profit element is included in the accounts of the parent company, so
   remove from group retained earnings (Dr)
   remove from investment in associate (Cr)

(ii) If associate sells to parent:
   in this case the profit element is included in the accounts of the associate, so
   remove from group retained earnings (Dr)
   remove from group inventory (Cr).

In addition, since the associate is considered to be outside the group any sales or purchases between group companies and the associate are not normally eliminated. These will remain part of the consolidated figures in the income statement.

Progress Point 10.8

The income statements of the B group for the period ending 31 December 2009 are given below.

	B £000	K £000	S £000
Sales revenue	385	100	60
Cost of sales	(185)	(60)	(20)
Gross profit	200	40	40
Operating expenses	(50)	(15)	(10)
Profit before tax	150	25	30
Taxation	(50)	(12)	(10)
Profit after tax	100	13	20

The following information is also given.

1. B acquired a 30% stake in S a number of years ago.
2. B acquired a 90% stake in K a number of years ago.
3. During the year, S sold goods to B for £28,000. None of these goods was in the inventory at the end of the year.
4. Goodwill and the investment in the associate were impaired for the first time during the year as follows:
   - S £2,000
   - K £3,000.

   Impairment of the goodwill of the subsidiary should be charged to operating expenses.

Required

Prepare the consolidated income statement for B group incorporating the results of the associated company.

Solution

Consolidated income statement (incorporating the results of the associate)	
Sales revenue (£385 + £100)	£485
Cost of sales (£185 + £60)	(245)
Gross profit	240
Operating expenses (£50 + £15 + £3 impairment)	68
Profit before tax	172
Share of profit of associate (30% of £20 – impairment £2)	4
	176
Less taxation	£62
	£114
Attributable to	
Equity holders of the parent	£112.7
Non-controlling interests (10% of £13,000)	£1.3

BASIC

INTERMEDIATE

ADVANCED

10.18 Joint ventures that are jointly controlled entities

The recommended treatment for jointly controlled entities is by an accounting technique called *proportionate consolidation* (although equity accounting is permitted).

 Example

H acquired 50% of S plc on 31 December 2008. The balance sheets of the two companies are as follows:

	H plc	S plc
Fixed assets	600	150
Investment in S	300	
Current assets	140	100
Current liabilities	(40)	(50)
	£1,000	£200
Share capital	800	150
Retained profit	200	50
	£1,000	£200

As the name suggests, this does not involve consolidating all the assets, liabilities and income of the joint venture. Only the proportion that belongs to the group is consolidated. The consolidated balance sheet would be as follows:

Consolidated balance sheet	
Fixed assets (£600 + 50% of £150)	£675
Goodwill (see calculation below)	200
Current assets (£140 + 50% of £100)	190
Current liabilities (£40 + 50% of £50)	(65)
	£1,000
Share capital	£800
Retained profit	£200
	£1,000

Note: The retained profit is only that of H plc because the profit of S plc is all pre-acquisition. There are no post-acquisition retained profits of S.

The goodwill figure will be calculated as follows:

Fair value of S at date of acquisition:	
Share capital	£150
Retained profit	£50
	£200
Acquired 50%	£100
Price paid	£300
Goodwill	£200

As far as the profit and loss account is concerned, the same broad principles apply. The figures in the profit and loss account for revenues and costs will be the revenues and costs of the parent company plus the proportion of revenue and costs attributable to the parent company.

Progress Point 10.9

Ron plc has a number of subsidiaries. Group accounts for the year to 31 December 2009 have been prepared and are given below. R is one of four venturers who each have an equal share in Riv Ltd, a joint venture. The financial statements of Riv Ltd are also given below:

	Ron plc £000	Riv Ltd £000
Balance sheet		
Tangible fixed assets	9,200	2,200
Investment in Riv	450	–
	9,650	2,200
Current assets		
Stock	900	400
Receivables	1,300	450
Cash	240	100
	2,440	950
Creditors: due with one year		
Trade creditors	2,500	460
Taxation	850	100
	3,350	560
Creditors: due more than one year	3,100	600
	£5,640	£1,990
Share capital	1,200	600
Share premium	2,650	800
Profit and loss reserve	1,790	590
	5,640	1,990

Income statements		
Income statements	£000	£000
Sales revenue	7,700	2,000
Cost of sales	(5,000)	(1,580)
Gross profit	2,700	420
Operating expenses	(500)	(60)
Operating profit	2,200	360
Interest	(200)	(40)
Profit before tax	2,000	320
Taxation	(850)	(100)
	1,150	220

Notes
1. All the subsidiaries of Ron are wholly owned.
2. Ron acquired its interest in Riv in 2002 for £450,000, when the reserves of Riv were £200,000 and share premium was £800,000.
3. Goodwill has not been impaired since Riv was acquired
4. Riv pays a dividend of £100,000 in October 2009.

Required

Prepare the consolidated profit and loss account of the Ron group for the year ended 31 December 2009 together with a consolidated balance sheet as at that date.

Solution

Stage 1: calculate goodwill

Fair value of net assets acquired at date if acquisition:

Share capital	£600,000
Share premium	800,000
Profit and loss	200,000
	£1,600,000
Whereof 25%	£400,000
Price paid	£450,000
Goodwill	£50,000

Stage 2: group profit

Profit of Ron	£1,790
Add Ron's share of post-acquisition	
Profit fof Riv (25% of £590 – £200)	97
	£1,887

Stage 3: non-controlling interest

There is no need to adjust for minority interest, since in this method, the group share only is included in the statements. So, in effect, minority interest is being accounted for on an item-by-item basis.

Ron plc
Consolidated balance sheet as at 31 December 2009

	£000	£000
Fixed assets (£9,200 + 25% of £2,200)		9,750
Goodwill		50
		9,800
Current assets		
Stock (£900 + 25% of £400)	1,000	
Debtors	1,412	
Cash	265	
	2,677	
Creditors: amounts due within one year		
Trade creditors	(2,615)	
Taxation	(875)	
	(3,490)	(813)
Net current liabilities		8,987
Creditors: amounts due in more than one year		(3,250)
		5,737
Share capital		1,200
Share premium		2,650
Profit and loss reserve		1,887
		5,737

Income statement	
	£000
Sales	8,200
Cost of sales	(5,395)
Gross profit	2,805
Operating expenses	(515)
Operating profit	2,290
Interest	(210)
Profit before tax	2,080
Taxation	(875)
Profit after tax	1,180

10.19 Disclosure in practice

In terms of the information given in the financial statements, if the company has subsidiaries, then group accounts will be prepared. These group accounts will include a consolidated income statement, balance sheet and cash flow statement for the group. Each of these statements will be prepared in accordance with the principles outlined in this chapter.

An example of the consolidated income and balance sheet can be seen in the financial report of Logica (see Figure 10.3).

Consolidated income statement For the year ended 31 December 2007			
	Note	2007 £m	Restated* 2006 £m
Continuing operations:			
Revenue	5	3,073.2	2,420.7
Net operating costs	6	(2,963.5)	(2,278.8)
Operating profit		109.7	141.9
ANALYSED AS:			
Operating profit before exceptional items		132.9	165.8
Exceptional items	7	(23.2)	(23.9)
Operating profit	5	109.7	141.9
Finance costs	10	(37.8)	(34.3)
Finance income	11	11.0	8.7
Share of post-tax profits from associates		1.2	0.3
Profit before tax	12	84.1	116.6
Taxation	13	(5.4)	(31.2)
Profit for the year from continuing operations		78.7	85.4
DISCONTINUED OPERATION:			
Profit from discontinued operation	14	89.4	3.7
Net profit for the year		168.1	89.1
ATTRIBUTABLE TO:			
Equity holders of the parent		169.9	82.0
Minority interests		(1.8)	7.1

Figure 10.3 Logica: example of consolidated income statement

Note that the profit for the year is allocated to the equity holder of the parent and to the minority interests.

Consolidated balance sheet 31 December 2007	Note	2007 £m	2006 £m
Non-current assets			
Goodwill	17	1,604.0	1,552.1
Other intangible assets	18	358.0	415.1
Property, plant and equipment	19	132.1	136.6
Investments in associates	20	2.4	6.0
Financial assets	21	11.0	10.1
Retirement benefit assets	38	12.0	18.7
Deferred tax assets	28	54.5	50.6
		2,174.0	2,189.2
Current assets			
Inventories	22	1.4	2.9
Trade and other receivables	23	1,021.2	1,070.2
Current tax assets		40.5	31.2
Cash and cash equivalents	34	108.7	177.3
		1,171.8	1,281.6
Current liabilities			
Convertible debt	25	(220.0)	(202.4)
Other borrowings	25	(97.2)	(33.1)
Trade and other payables	24	(868.2)	(886.4)
Current tax liabilities		(56.1)	(32.3)
Provisions	27	(9.1)	(20.8)
		(1,250.6)	(1,175.0)
Net current (liabilities)/assets		(78.8)	106.6
Total assets less current liabilities		2,095.2	2,295.8
Non-current liabilities			
Borrowings	25	(274.7)	(498.9)
Retirement benefit obligations	38	(50.6)	(64.1)
Deferred tax liabilities	28	(125.0)	(164.4)
Provisions	27	(18.9)	(13.2)
Other non-current liabilities		(0.7)	(0.8)
		(469.9)	(741.4)
Net assets		1,625.3	1,554.4
Equity			
Share capital	29	145.8	153.6
Share premium account	30	1,098.9	1,097.0
Other reserves	31	352.3	274.4
Total shareholders' equity		1,597.0	1,525.0
Minority interests	32	28.3	29.4
Total equity		1,625.3	1,554.4
Effect of foreign exchange rates	34	9.1	(6.7)
Cash, cash equivalents and bank overdrafts at the end of the year		99.6	150.9

Figure 10.4 Logica: example of consolidated balance sheet

Additional information on the basis of consolidation is given in the accounting policy section of Logica. Note that this gives information on how Logica accounted for its interest in its associates and joint ventures, using the equity method as described in this chapter. The business combinations are accounted for using the 'purchase method', that is acquisition accounting. Notice too that inter-company transactions are eliminated on consolidation.

Basis of consolidation

The consolidated Financial statements include those of the Company and all of its subsidiary undertakings (together, the Group), and the Group's share of the results of associates and joint ventures. Investments in associates and joint ventures are accounted for using the equity method.

Subsidiary undertakings are those entities controlled directly or indirectly by the Company. Control arises when the Company has the ability to direct the financial and operating policies of an entity so as to obtain benefits from its activities.

All business combinations are accounted for using the purchase method.

On acquisition, the interest of any minority shareholders is stated at the minority's proportion of the fair value of the assets and liabilities recognised. Subsequently, the minority interest in the consolidated balance sheet reflects the minority's proportion of changes in the net assets of the subsidiary.

Information specific to any investment in associate companies is disclosed separately. The information given by Logica in Figure 10.5 is fairly detailed. It is likely that this is an overseas associate since there is an exchange difference shown. Note that the share of the post-tax profit of the associate is given.

Investments in associates		
The carrying value of the Group's investments in associates at 31 December is shown below:		
	2007	2006
	£m	£m
Associates	2.4	6.0
Investments in associates		£m
At 1 January 2007		6.0
Increase in stake to subsidiary		(2.0)
Disposals		(2.3)
Share of post-tax profits of associates		1.2
Dividends received		(0.7)
Exchange differences		0.2
At 31 December 2007		2.4
Summarised information in respect of associates at 31 December is provided below on a 100% interest basis and, where relevant, after provisional fair value adjustments.		
	2007	2006
	£m	£m
Assets	11.0	27.8
Liabilities	(4.7)	(15.7)
Revenue	32.2	13.1
Net profit	2.3	0.5

Figure 10.5 Logica: investment in associates

In the notes to the accounts of Logica, full details are given of the non-controlling interests (see Figure 10.6).

Minority interests		
	2007	2006
	£m	£m
At 1 January	29.4	17.2
Share of net profit for the year	(1.8)	7.1
Share of actuarial gains on defined benefit schemes, net of tax	–	0.1
Acquisitions and buy out of minority interests	(0.9)	7.5
Dividends paid to minority interests	(0.4)	(1.8)
Disposals of subsidiaries	–	(0.7)
Exchange differences	2.0	–
At 31 December		

Figure 10.6 Logica: minority interests

Overview

Subsidiary

This is defined in IAS 27. The method of accounting used is acquisition accounting. The accounts of the subsidiary are combined with those of the parent to produce the consolidated financial statements. Any goodwill arising is shown in the balance sheet and is tested for impairment. All aspects of intra-company trading are eliminated so that the figures remaining are at 'cost to the group'.

Associate

Defined in IAS 38 and accounted for using the equity method. This method estimates the value of the investment in the associate and is calculated by adding cost of the investment to the parent company's share of any post-acquisition profit.

Joint venture

This is defined in IAS 31. At the moment the required treatment of a joint venture is by using proportionate consolidation. However, according to ED 9, the use of proportionate consolidation is likely to be eliminated.

All these techniques of accounting for business acquisitions have been dealt with elsewhere in this chapter.

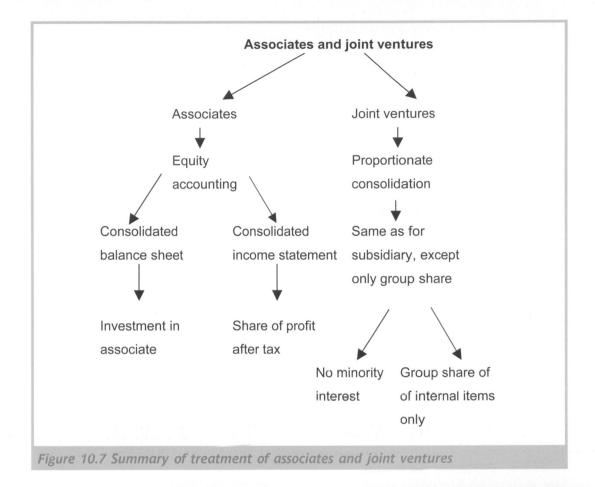

Figure 10.7 Summary of treatment of associates and joint ventures

Section 3: Advanced Aspects

The previous two sections have concentrated heavily on the preparation of consolidated financial statements. Various technical aspects were explored in greater detail, and the examples and progress points given have focused mainly on the construction of consolidated financial statements incorporating these adjustments. This section now goes on to examine the rationale for group accounts, and explores the underlying conceptual thinking behind group accounts. It also identifies aspects of the regulatory framework, in particular international accounting standards, as they apply to the preparation of group accounts.

10.20 Background to the preparation of consolidated accounts

In 1983 the Seventh Council Directive of the European Communities was issued. This directive specifies that a member state should require any parent undertaking that is subject to its national laws to prepare consolidated accounts. Furthermore a consolidated annual report needs to be prepared if such an undertaking has control of another undertaking, either by ownership of shares, voting rights or through a dominant influence.

BASIC

INTERMEDIATE

ADVANCED

Concepts underlying group accounts

A parent company is a company that has one or more subsidiary companies. The shareholders of a parent company are not entitled to receive any information from the subsidiary companies because they are not shareholders of these companies. However, in order to give the holding company shareholders information on the financial position of a group of companies, consolidated financial statements are prepared.

Consolidated financial statements are designed to give effect to the economic substance of intra-group relationships rather than the strict legal form of such relationships. The traditional approach to preparing group accounts focuses on providing information for the equity investors for the parent company. Any interests that the minority shareholder has is seen as of secondary importance. This approach is sometimes referred to as the parent company concept. Under this concept there is an assumption that the parent company has the power to exercise control over the subsidiary company.

Consolidation is the process whereby the individual accounts of the parent company and each of the subsidiaries are combined as though it were a single company. This combination requires that each item in the individual company accounts is aggregated on a line-by-line basis, eliminating in the process any double counting.

Control

Control is important in determining how a particular investment is to be classified. Under the Seventh Directive, two concepts of control are identified: legal concept and entity (economic) concept.

Legal concept

Formerly, legal definitions of control were based on an ownership holding of more than 50% of equity (rather than voting) shares. In addition to this, control of the composition of the board of directors would have given a parent–subsidiary relationship. This legal concept of control is evident in the Seventh Directive's definition of subsidiary undertaking. However, the Seventh Directive's definition of control is much broader and takes into account the economic concept of control.

Entity (economic) concept

This concept focuses on the existence of the group as an economic unit, rather than looking at it only through the eyes of the dominant shareholder group. The main focus of this concept is on the resources controlled by the company, and it views the identity of owners with claims on such resources as being less important. No distinction is made between the treatment given to different classes of shareholders, whether majority or minority, and all transactions between the shareholders are regarded as internal to the group.

Proprietary (parent entity) concept

This concept emphasises ownership through a controlling shareholding interest. Consolidated financial statements are therefore prepared for the shareholders of the holding company. This means that the minority shareholders are treated as 'outsiders' and the interests of this group of shareholders are reflected in the consolidated financial statements as a kind of liability. An alternative is to omit the minority altogether and consolidate the parent company's proportion of the assets and liabilities of the subsidiary. This approach is the proportionate consolidation method, as described in previous section. The propriety concept is sometimes known as the 'parent entity' concept and there is a variant of it known as the 'parent entity extension' concept.

The parent company approach to consolidation was used extensively in the UK, where it was known as acquisition accounting. This is the method of accounting that has been demonstrated in the earlier sections of this chapter.

Recent changes to international accounting standards seem to be moving the accounting for groups away from the parent company approach and towards the entity approach. In terms of the accounting regulation, which will be discussed in more detail later, it is the parent company concept that is required by international accounting standards (IFRS 3). However, some changes to the new international standard on *Presentation of Financial Statements* (IAS 1), as illustrated in Chapter 2, have introduced a slight movement towards the entity concept. This is because IAS 1 now requires that the consolidated profit and loss account be analysed to show only the parent share of the profit for the year, and the minority interest in that profit. Previously, the non-controlling interest was deducted on the face of the profit and loss account.

IAS 1 also requires that non-controlling interest also be shown on the consolidated balance sheet as part of equity. Before, the parent company approach showed this minority outside of equity.

Regulatory framework

The content of consolidated financial statements is dealt with in IAS 27 (revised in 2008). The methods of accounting for business combinations and how to deal with goodwill arising on consolidation are deal with by IFRS 3 (Revised), which we will look at now.

10.21 IFRS 3 (revised) *Business Combinations*

IFRS 3 (Revised) *Business Combinations* was published in January 2008 and has created significant changes in accounting for business combinations. Some of the more significant changes are in relation to the purchase consideration, which now includes the fair value of all the interests that the acquirer may have held previously in the acquired business. This includes any interest in an associate or joint venture, or any other equity interest.

If an acquiree has held a previous stake in a business, this is seen as being 'given up' to acquire the entity, and a gain or loss is recorded on its disposal. If the acquirer already held an interest in the acquired entity before acquisition, the standard requires that this existing stake is re-measured to fair value at the date of acquisition. If the value of the stake has increased, there will be a gain recognised in the statement of comprehensive income of the acquirer at the date of the business combination. (Note that it is possible for a loss to occur if the existing interest has a book value in excess of the proportion of fair value obtained and no impairment had previously been recorded. This loss situation is not expected to occur very often).

Goodwill and non-controlling interests

The revised standard given entities the option, on an individual transaction basis, to measure non-controlling (minority) interest at either:

(a)   the fair value of their proportion of identifiable assets, or
(b)   full fair value.

If option (a) is chosen, then this will result in a goodwill calculation that is basically the same as the original IFRS. If option (b) is chosen, the goodwill will be recorded on the non-controlling interest as well as on the acquired controlling interest. Goodwill continues to be a residual, but it will be a different residual under IFRS 3 (Revised) if the full fair value method is used. This is partly because all of the consideration (including any previously held interest in the acquired business) is measured at fair value, but also because goodwill can be measured in two different ways, as described below.

Partial goodwill method

This is the difference between the consideration paid and the purchaser's share of the identifiable net assets acquired. This is classed as a partial goodwill method because the non-controlling interest (minority) is recognised at its share of identifiable net assets and does not include any goodwill.

Full goodwill method

This approach results in the recognition of the whole goodwill of the acquired business and not just the acquirer's share of goodwill. Under this method goodwill is measured as the difference between the aggregate of:

- the consideration transferred (generally measured at fair value at the date of acquisition)
- the amount of any non-controlling (minority) interest
- the fair value at date of acquisition of any previously held equity interest in the acquiree (if any)
- the identifiable net assets at date of acquisition.

Non-controlling interests can be measured in one of two ways:

1. at fair value (this results in the full goodwill approach)
2. at the non-controlling interest's proportionate share of the acquiree's net assets (this is the same as the purchased goodwill approach as per the previous IFRS 3 method).

The following examples will illustrate the point.

Example 1

On 1 September Year 10, A plc acquires 60% of B plc for £10,000. Prior to the acquisition it has been determined that:

- the fair value of the non-controlling interest in B plc is £6,000
- the fair value of the identifiable net assets of B plc is £9,000.

Show the calculation of goodwill under previous IFRS 3 and IFRS 3 (Revised).

IFRS 3 (previous)	
Fair value of identifiable net assets	£9,000
Non-controlling interest (40%)	3,600
	5,400
Fair value of consideration	£10,000
Goodwill	£4,600

IFRS (Revised)

Under this method, non-controlling interest can be measured either:

(a) at fair value, or
(b) at proportionate share (as before).

	Fair value	Proportionate share	
Fair value of identifiable net assets	£9,000	£9,000	
Non-controlling interest	6,000	3,600	(40% of £9,000)
	3,000	5,400	
Fair value of consideration	£10,000	£10,000	
Goodwill	£7,000	£4,600	

✦ Example 2

On 1 September Year 10, A plc acquires 50% of B plc for £10,000 Prior to this, A plc held 10% of the equity of B plc, which had a fair value of £1,000 immediately prior to the acquisition of the additional 50% of B plc. A plc has determined the following:

■ the fair value of the non-controlling interest in B plc is £6,000
■ the fair value of the identifiable net assets of B plc is £9,000.

Show the calculation of goodwill under previous IFRS 3 and IFRS 3 (Revised).

IFRS 3 (previous)	
Fair value of identifiable net assets	£9,000
Non-controlling interest (50%)	4,500
	4,500
Fair value of consideration	£10,000
Goodwill	£5,500

IFRS (Revised)

Under this method, non-controlling interest can be measured either:

(a) at fair value, or
(b) at proportionate share (as before).

	Fair value	Proportionate share	
Fair value of identifiable net assets	£9,000	£9,000	
Non-controlling interest	6,000	3,600	(40% of £9,000)
	3,000	5,400	
Previously held equity at fair value*	1,500	1,500	
	1,500	3,900	
Fair value of consideration for 50%	£10,000	£10,000	
Goodwill	£8,500	£6,100	

* Previously held equity at fair value.

The fair value of the 40% non-controlling interest is now £6,000. So a holding of 10% would have a fair value now of £1,500. This is an increase of £500 (£1,500 – £1,000) over the previous fair value and will be recorded as a profit.

Fair value aspects

The revised IFRS 3 has introduced some changes to both assets and liabilities recognised in the acquisition balance sheet. The existing requirement to recognise all the identifiable assets and liabilities is retained. With the exception of certain items, such as pension obligations and deferred taxation, most assets are recognised at fair value. Additional clarification has been given by the IASB, which might result in more intangible assets being recognised. Acquirers are required to recognise brands, licences and customer relationships, and other intangible assets. Other ongoing projects on standards linked to business combinations may affect their recognition or measurement. Such projects are on provisions (IAS 37) and on deferred tax (IAS 12).

Summary of the main changes to IFRS 3

These are presented in Table 10.1.

Previous IFRS	'New' IFRS
Used the term 'minority interest'	Uses the term 'non-controlling interest'
Negative goodwill is described as 'excess of net assets over the cost of the business acquisition'	Negative goodwill is referred to as 'gain from a bargain purchase' (but still take to profit or loss)
At date of acquisition the minority in the acquiree is stated at the minority's proportionate share of the identifiable net assets of the acquiree	At acquisition, the non-controlling interest in the acquiree is measured at fair value (of the NCI) or at the NCI's proportionate share of the acquiree's identifiable net assets (i.e. same as the previous IFRS); the choice is applicable on a transaction-by-transaction basis.
Used the term 'cost of business combination', which = the fair values (at date of acquisition) of assets given, liabilities assumed and equity issued + any directly related costs	Uses the term 'consideration transferred', which = sum of the fair values of assets transferred, liabilities incurred and equity interest issued (including contingent consideration) at date of acquisition; note that directly attributable costs are not included
Goodwill is initially measured as the excess of the cost of the business combination over the acquirer's interest in the net fair value of the identifiable net assets (i.e. only the acquirer's attributable share of goodwill is recognised)	Recognise goodwill at date of acquisition, measured as the excess of (a) over (b), where (a) is the total of ■ consideration transferred ■ amount of any NCI ■ in a business combination achieved in stages, the fair value of the acquirer's previously held equity interest in the acquiree at date of acquisition and (b) is the ■ total fair value of identifiable net assets acquired
Business combinations achieved in stages (piecemeal acquisition); acquirer treated each acquisition separately, using the cost of the transaction and fair value information at the date of each exchange transaction to determine goodwill	Business combinations achieved in stages (piecemeal acquisition); an acquirer must re-measure its previously held equity interest at fair value at date of acquisition; any resulting gain (or loss) should be recognised in the profit or loss

Table 10.1 Summary of the main changes to IFRS 3

Disclosure requirements of IFRS 3

IFRS requires disclosures such that users of financial statements can evaluate the nature and financial effect of business combinations. Disclosure is required as follows:

- names of combining entities
- date of acquisition
- proportion of company acquired
- cost of the combination, together with components of the cost
- any operations disposed of due to the combination
- details of fair values and carrying values of assets, liabilities and contingent liabilities acquired
- any negative goodwill
- amount of post-acquisition profit included in the profit and loss account of the acquirer.

As a result of IFRS 3 (Revised), financial statements will require some new disclosures. Examples of such disclosures include:

- where non-controlling interest is measured at fair value, the valuation methods used will need to be disclosed
- in a step acquisition, the fair value of any previously held equity interest will require to be disclosed, and any gain or loss resulting from re-measurement will need to be recognised in the income statement.

10.22 IAS 27 (Revised) *Consolidated and Separate Financial Statements*

This standard requires a parent company to prepare consolidated financial statements except when:

- the parent is a wholly owned or partly owned subsidiary of another company
- the company's shares are not publicly traded
- the ultimate or any intermediate parent produces consolidated financial statements available for public use that comply with IFRS.

The definition of what constitutes a subsidiary is given in IAS 27. A subsidiary is defined as an entity that is controlled. Control is defined under IAS 27 and is presumed to exist if a parent holds more than half the voting power of a company. Subsequent revisions have been made to IAS 27 in light of changes to IFRS 3.

Summary of main changes to IAS 27

These are presented in Table 10.2.

Previous IAS 27	IAS 27 (Revised)
No guidance on accounting given in situations where there are changes in the parent's ownership interest that do not result in loss of control	Specifies that changes in the ownership interest of the parent that do not result in the loss of control must be accounted for as equity transactions; this means that any profit or loss attributable to the parent resulting from the sale of shares where control is retained goes to the statement of changes in equity and not to the statement of comprehensive income
The carrying amount of an investment retained in a former subsidiary must be shown at its cost on initial measurement of financial assets (in terms of IAS 39)	There are now specific requirements on how an entity measures any gain or loss arising on the loss of control of a subsidiary; any such gain or loss is recognised in the income statement; any gain or loss on the re-measurement of the retained non-controlling equity investment to fair value (at the date control is lost); any investment retained in the former subsidiary at the date control is lost is measured at its fair value
Excess losses in a subsidiary were not allocated to minorities but to the owners of the parent (except where minorities had a binding obligation and were able to make additional investment to cover such losses)	Requires that total comprehensive income be attributed to the owners of the parent, and to the non-controlling interests, even if this results in the non-controlling interests having a deficit balance

Table 10.2 Summary of main changes to IAS 27

New disclosure requirements include:

- any gain or loss arising from the loss of control of a subsidiary
- movements between controlling and non-controlling interest.

10.23 IAS 28 *Investments in Associates*

An associate is defined in IAS 28 as an entity over which the investor has significant influence. Significant influence is deemed to apply where the investor holds, directly or indirectly, 20% or more of the voting power of the investee unless it be can clearly demonstrated that this is not the case. Significant influence is usually in evidence where there is:

- some representation on the board of directors
- some participation in the policy-making process
- interchange of managerial personnel.

The major disclosure requirements under IAS 28 are as follows:

- fair value of investments in associates
- aggregate amounts of assets, liabilities, revenues and profit (or loss)
- reasons why the investor has significant influence despite holding less than 20% (if applicable).

Where an associate has not been accounted for using the equity method, this fact should be disclosed.

If there is any goodwill arising on consolidation this is included in the carrying amount of the investment, according to IAS 28. In this case goodwill is not separately identified, nor is it subject to a separate impairment test.

BASIC

INTERMEDIATE

ADVANCED

10.24 IAS 31 *Interests in Joint Ventures*

IAS 31 categorises joint ventures (JV) into three areas:

1   jointly controlled operations
2   jointly controlled assets
3   jointly controlled entities.

Jointly controlled operations

This involves the use of the assets and other resources of the venturers rather than the establishment of a corporation, partnership or other entity. Each venturer uses its own property, plant and equipment and inventories. It also incurs its own expenses and liabilities, and raises its own finance. The JV agreement usually provides a means by which the revenue from the sale of the joint product and any expenses incurrent in common are shared among the venturers.

An example of this is where venturers combine their operations, resources and expertise to manufacture jointly a particular product (e.g. a ship). Jointly controlled operations are accounted for by recognising in the financial statements of the venturer:

■   the assets that it controls and the liabilities that it incurs
■   the expenses it incurs and its share of the income earned from sale of goods or services.

This treatment is appropriate since the jointly controlled operation is not purchasing assets or raising finance in its own right.

Jointly controlled assets

This is where venturers jointly own and control specific assets for the purpose of a joint venture. As with jointly controlled operations there is no separate JV entity or financial structure separate from the venturers themselves. Each venturer has control over its share of future economic benefits through its share in the jointly controlled asset. Many examples of this type of joint venture occur in the oil and gas industries.

Jointly controlled entities

This is where a distinct entity is formed in which each venturer has an interest. The JV has a financial structure separate from the venturers. The JV enterprise controls the assets of the JV, incurs liabilities and expenses, and earns income. It may enter into contracts and raise finance in its own right. The JV will keep its own financial records and produce financial statements, which will be included in the group financial statements. IAS 31 recommends accounts for jointly controlled entities by proportionate consolidation in group accounts.

Accounting for jointly controlled entities is a bit different to the other two forms of joint venture. Legally the entity must maintain its own accounting records and prepare financial statements. At the moment IAS 31 requires either proportionate consolidation, the benchmark treatment or the equity method, the allowed alternative treatment. The IASB published ED 9 *Joint Arrangements* in September 2007. This exposure draft proposed that proportionate consolidation be eliminated.

Chapter summary

IFRS 3 (Revised) *Business Combinations*

- Uses the term 'non-controlling interest'.
- Negative goodwill is referred to as 'gain from a bargain purchase' (but still take to profit or loss).
- At acquisition, the non-controlling interest in the acquiree is measured at fair value (of the NCI) *or* at the NCI's proportionate share of the acquiree's identifiable net assets (i.e. same as the previous IFRS). The choice is applicable on a transaction-by-transaction basis.
- Uses the term 'consideration transferred', which = sum of the fair values of assets transferred, liabilities incurred and equity interest issued (including contingent consideration) at date of acquisition. Note: directly attributable costs are not included.
- Recognises goodwill at date of acquisition, measured as the excess of (a) over (b), where (a) is the total of consideration transferred plus amount of any NCI plus the fair value of the acquirer's previously held equity interest in the acquiree at date of acquisition (where the business combination is achieved in stages), and (b) is the total fair value of identifiable net assets acquired.
- Where business combinations are achieved in stages (piecemeal acquisition) an acquirer must re-measure its previously held equity interest at fair value at date of acquisition. Any resulting gain (or loss) should be recognised in the profit or loss.

IAS 27 (Revised) *Consolidated and Separate Financial Statements*

- Specifies that changes in the ownership interest of the parent that do not result in the loss of control must be accounted for as equity transactions. This means that any profit or loss attributable to the parent resulting from the sale of shares where control is retained goes to the statement of changes in equity and not to the statement of comprehensive income.
- There are now specific requirements on how an entity measures any gain or loss arising on the loss of control of a subsidiary. Any such gain or loss is recognised in the income statement. Any gain or loss on the re-measurement of the retained non-controlling equity investment to fair value (at the date control is lost).
- Any investment retained in the former subsidiary at the date control is lost is measured at its fair value.
- Requires that total comprehensive income be attributed to the owners of the parent, and to the non-controlling interests, even if this results in the non-controlling interests having a deficit balance.

IAS 31 *Interests in Joint Ventures*

- Jointly controlled operations involve the use of assets and other resources of the venturers rather than the establishment of a separate entity.
- Requires that the venturer should recognise in its financial statements the assets it controls and the liabilities it incurs; also the expenses it incurs and the share of the income from the sale of goods or services by the joint venture.
- Jointly controlled assets involve the joint control of assets dedicated to the joint venture.
- Requires that the venturer should recognise in its financial statements its share of the joint assets, any liabilities, income from sale of use of its share of the output of the joint venture, and share of expenses incurred in respect of interest in the joint venture.
- Two treatments are permitted for the accounting for an investment:
  - proportionate consolidation
  - equity method of accounting.

Key terms for review

Definitions can be found in the glossary at the end of the book.

Subsidiary company	*Goodwill*
Associate company	*Minority interest*
Joint venture	*Date of consolidation*
Acquisition accounting	*Pre-acquisition profits and reserves*
Date of acquisition	*Equity accounting*

Review questions

1. What is the philosophy underlying the *proprietary* approach?
2. What is the philosophy underlying the *entity* approach?
3. Explain how negative goodwill may arise and how it should be accounted for.
4. Explain why it is only the net assets of the subsidiary that are adjusted to fair value at the date of acquisition for the purpose of consolidated accounts, and not those of the parent.
5. Explain why the minority interest is calculated at the year end, while goodwill is calculated at the date of acquisition.
6. Explain why pre-acquisition profits of a subsidiary are treated differently from post-acquisition profits.
7. Why is it important to remove unrealised profits arising from transactions between companies in a group?
8. Explain the treatment of dividends paid by a subsidiary to a parent company on consolidation.
9. Explain how dividends paid out of pre-acquisition profits of a subsidiary are treated on consolidation.
10. Explain how associated companies are accounted for in a consolidation, and how this differs from the treatment of a subsidiary.

Exercises

1. Level II

The balance sheets of Parent plc and Daughter plc as at 31 December 2008 were as follows:

	Parent £	Daughter £
Net assets	45,000	10,800
Share capital (£1 shares)	40,500	9,000
Retained profit	4,500	1,800
	45,000	10,800

On 31 December 2008, Parent plc acquired all the ordinary shares in Daughter plc. The purchase consideration was satisfied by the issue of one new ordinary share in Parent plc for every three held in Daughter plc. The fair value of a £1 ordinary share in Parent plc was £2. The fair value of the net assets in Daughter plc was £15,000.

Required

Prepare the consolidated balance sheet at 31 December 2008.

2. Level II

Red plc acquired 80,000 shares in Blue plc on 31 December 2005. At that date, the retained profit of Blue plc was £200,000 and the revaluation reserve was £50,000. The summarised balance sheets of the two companies at 31 December 2008 are as follows:

	Red plc £	Blue plc £
Investment in Blue	315,000	
Fixed assets	400,000	250,000
Net current assets	135,000	200,000
	850,000	450,000
Share capital (£1 shares)	250,000	100,000
Revaluation reserve	100,000	50,000
Retained profit	500,000	300,000
	850,000	450,000

Required

(a)   Prepare the consolidated balance sheet for the Red Group as at 31 December 2008.
(b)   If Red plc has acquired 20,000 shares in Blue plc, instead of 80,000, and had appointed a member to the board of directors of Blue plc, how would this affect the consolidated balance sheet under (a) above. Show the new balance sheet.

3. Level II

On 31 March 2009 Jardine plc declared unconditional its offer for the entire share capital of Walker plc. The agreed consideration was in the form of five new ordinary shares of 50p each issued by Jardine plc for every four held in Walker plc. The fair value of the shares issued by Jardine plc was £1.30 per share.

The balance sheets of the two companies at 31 March 2009, prior to the implementation of the business combination, were as follows:

	Jardine £000	Walker £000
Tangible fixed assets	4,500	1,200
Net current assets	1,700	1,300
	6,200	2,500
Creditors	2,000	900
	4,200	1,600
Share capital (par value 50p each)	2,000	800
Share premium	400	–
Profit and loss account	1,800	800
	4,200	1,600

In the course of negotiations it was established that the fair value of the tangible fixed assets of Walker plc was £700,000 greater than the existing book value.

Required

Show the balance sheet after the business combination.

4. Level II

T plc acquired 75% of the ordinary share capital of S plc when shareholders' funds of S plc were:

	£000
Ordinary share capital £1 shares	400
Reserves	800
	1,200

T plc acquired 25% of the ordinary share capital of a plc when shareholders' funds of a plc were:

	£000
Ordinary share capital £1 shares	200
Reserves	360
	560

The balance sheets of the three companies at 31 December 2008 were:

	T plc £000	S plc £000	A plc £000
Fixed assets	2,200	1,400	700
Investment in S	1,600		
Investment in A	168		
Net current assets	1,200	1,000	500
	5,168	2,400	1,200
Share capital	1,000	400	200
Reserves	2,168	1,200	600
14% debentures	2,000	800	400
	5,168	2,400	1,200

Required

Prepare the consolidated balance sheet for the T group as at 31 December 2008, assuming T plc appoints a member to the board of A plc.

5. Level II

The following information concerns Landlord Ltd and its subsidiary undertaking Tennant.

Trial balance as at 31 December 2008

	Landlord £	Tennant £
Land and buildings at cost	35,000	
Machinery at cost	80,000	30,000
Accumulated depreciation on machinery	(35,000)	(17,000)
Investment in Tennant (9,000 shares) at cost	16,000	
Amount due by Tennant	8,000	
Inventories	27,000	9,000
Accounts receivable	20,000	6,000
	£151,000	£28,000
Ordinary shares of £1 each	120,000	12,000
General reserve		4,000
Retained profits	21,000	8,000
Accounts payable	10,000	4,000
	£151,000	£28,000

Additional notes

1. Landlord bought 9,000 shares in Tennant at a time when the general reserve of Tennant was £2,000 and retained profits were £4,000.
2. Six years earlier, Tennant bought a machine for £20,000 and immediately transferred it to Landlord for £40,000. This machine had an estimated life of ten years and has been depreciated at 10% per annum in the books of Landlord.
3. The amount due by Tennant at 31 December 2008 represents goods in transit that were received and recorded by Tennant in January 2009. These goods were priced so as to give Landlord a gross profit of 25%.

Required

Prepare the consolidated balance sheet as at 31 December 2008 for Landlord and it subsidiary, Tennant.

6. Level II

The following are the summarised accounts of A, D and G for the year ended 31 December 2009.

Income statements	A	D	G
Sales revenue	£573,600	£314,000	£150,000
Operating costs	(300,000)	(200,000)	(90,000)
Operating profit	273,600	114,000	60,000
Interest payable	(20,000)	(14,000)	(8,000)
Dividend income from D	14,400		
Dividend income from G	4,000		
Other dividend income	10,000	–	–
Profit before tax	282,000	100,000	52,000
Tax	(72,000)	(30,000)	(16,000)
Profit for the year	£210,000	£70,000	£36,000
Balance sheets	A	D	G
Investment in D (60%)	60,000		
Investment in G (25%)	50,000		
Other assets	300,000	120,000	100,000
	410,000	120,000	100,000
Ordinary shares	20,000	30,000	10,000
Retained earnings	330,000	66,000	70,000
Current liabilities	60,000	24,000	20,000
	410,000	120,000	100,000

Additional information

1. The shares in D and G were acquired on 1 January 2009.
2. Goodwill in the subsidiary has suffered an impairment of 20% of its value, and the associate has suffered an impairment of £7,000.
3. A has accounted for the dividends from both the subsidiary and associate.

Required

Prepare the consolidated income statement for the year ended 31 December 2009, together with a balance sheet as at that date.

7. Level II

Hook plc is a well-established firm in the fishing industry. The summary balance sheet of Hook plc on 1 January 2009 is as follows:

Summary balance sheet	£000
Assets:	
Cash	40
Other assets	180
	220
Share capital	100
Reserves	60
Liabilities	60
	220

On 1 January 2009, Hook plc enters into a joint venture with Line plc. They establish a new firm, Sinker, and each invests cash of £10,000 in it. Sinker raises a long-term loan to finance the purchase of fixed assets. When the investment is made in Sinker the summary balance sheet is as follows:

Summary balance sheet of Sinker		£000
Assets:		
Cash		10
Other assets		90
		100
Share capital:		
Hook	10	
Line	10	20
Long-term debt		80
		100

For the period ended 31 December 2009, Sinker reports revenues of £70,000 and a profit of £10,000. It pays a dividend of £8,000. In the same period Hook plc reports revenues of £150,000 and a profit from its own activities of £20,000. It pays a dividend of £12,000. Year end liabilities are still £60,000. There are no inter-company transactions between Hook plc and Sinker, except for the dividend.

Required

(a) Explain the circumstances under which Hook plc would account for its investment in Sinker, under:
  (i) the equity method of consolidation
  (ii) proportional consolidation
  (iii) acquisition accounting.
(b) For each of the methods listed in (a) above, prepare income statements for the year ended 31 December 2009, together with balance sheets as at that date.

Further reading

Deloitte: Business Combinations and Changes in Ownership Interests. Deloitte, 2008
IAS 27 *Consolidated and Separate Financial Statements*. IASB, revised 2008
IAS 31 *Interests in Joint Ventures*. IASB, revised 2003
IFRS 3 *Business Combinations*. IASB, revised 2008
KPMG: Business Combinations. IFRS 3, revised January 2008
RSM International: The New Approach to Business Combination Introduced by the Revised IFRS 3 and the Revised IAS 27

Foreign Currency Translation

After studying this chapter you should be able to:

☑ record transactions denominated in a foreign currency

☑ calculate any exchange gain or loss arising in the accounts of the individual company

☑ describe the regulations governing foreign currency transactions for individual companies

☑ translate the accounts of overseas subsidiaries

☑ describe the disclosure requirements of IAS 21 in terms of foreign currency translation.

Introduction

This chapter will look at the issues that arise when one company has dealings with another company located overseas. This other company could simply be a customer or supplier of goods or services, or it could be an overseas subsidiary. There will be an impact on the accounts given that the rate of exchange between domestic and foreign currencies is not stable. The reporting requirements of IAS 21, which looks at the accounting aspects of overseas dealings, will be examined. In the first instance, this chapter will deal with situations where companies have individual dealings with another company in terms of individual transactions. The intermediate section will consider the situation when a company located in one country has a subsidiary company located in another country. In order to prepare the group financial statements, the accounts of the overseas company must be converted, or translated, into the holding company's currency. Finally, the advanced section looks in detail at the reporting requirements of IAS 21 *The Effects of Changes in Foreign Exchange Rates*.

Section 1: Basic Principles

Businesses are becoming increasingly international. It is not unusual for firms to import or export goods and services to firms in other countries. These transactions may involve the purchase of, for example, raw materials from a foreign supplier. In order to pay for such materials, the purchaser will have to acquire some foreign currency. A similar situation would arise if a company sold to an overseas buyer and received payment in a foreign currency.

Most exchange rates are not fixed but vary from day to day. This fluctuation can pose problems for a company dealing with overseas suppliers or customers. When a foreign currency transaction is completed within an accounting period then currency conversion will be required. This currency conversion can be regarded as comprising two separate aspects: the purchase or sale of an asset, and the receipt or payment of cash for these assets.

11.1 Conversion and translation of currency

Conversion is the exchange of one currency for another, while translation is the expression of another currency in terms of the currency of the reporting entity.

Functional currency

In terms of foreign currency translation requirements, the functional currency concept is central. IAS 21 defines the functional currency as 'the currency of the primary economic environment in which the entity operates'. In general terms, the primary economic environment in which an entity operates is normally the one in which it mainly generates and spends cash. Although the functional currency is not necessarily the 'local' currency of the country in which the entity operates, in most cases it will be. The currency in which the financial statements are presented is called the presentation currency.

Foreign currency transactions

In order to record foreign currency transactions in its own accounts, a company has to convert (i.e. translate) these transactions into the currency in which the financial statements are presented.

Monetary and non-monetary items

The distinction between monetary items and non-monetary items is important, since the rate used in the translation of these items differs.

The general approach taken is as follows.

1. When a company enters into a transaction with an overseas company, the exchange rate to be used is the one in operation at the date the transaction took place. This rate is referred to as the '*spot*' rate.
2. Items in the balance sheet that can be classified as monetary assets, or monetary liabilities – for example, cash, accounts payable, accounts receivable, loans – should be translated at the rate ruling at the balance sheet date. This rate is referred to as the '*closing*' rate.
3. Items that are classified as non-monetary items – for example, property, plant and equipment, inventory – are generally measured in terms of historic cost and will be translated at the rate ruling at the date these items were acquired. This rate is referred to as the '*historic*' rate. However, it should be noted that, if the carrying amount of an asset is determined by comparing two or more amounts – for example, lower of cost or net realisable value in the case of inventory, then:
   (i) cost (or carrying amount) will be translated at the spot rate
   (ii) net realisable value will be translated at the closing rate.
   Sales and purchases of goods will be translated at the rate ruling when the sale or purchase was made.
4. If any non-monetary item is carried at fair value, then the exchange rate used should be that at the date the fair value was determined.

Gain and losses arising on exchange rate movements

Gains and losses will arise when there is a movement in the exchange rate between the date of transaction, the date of preparation of the financial statements and the date of settlement.

For example, a UK company buys an item of stock from an overseas company in the USA. The item costs $100 and at the date of purchase the exchange rate is £1 = $1.5. If payment is made immediately, then no problem arises. The amount to be paid will be $100/1.5 = £66.67. However, if payment is not made until one month later and the exchange rate at this time was £1 = $1.6, then the amount owing to the US company would be £62.50 ($100/1.6). This means that a payment of £62.50 is required to be made, instead of £66.67. The difference of £4.17 is the 'gain' the company has made because of the exchange rate movement. This exchange difference needs to be accounted for, and the regulations governing the treatment of exchange gains and losses are contained in IAS 21.

11.2 Accounting treatment of exchange gains and losses

As indicated above, exchange gains and losses arise when there is a delay between entering into a transaction and receiving payment, and during this period of 'delay' the exchange rate moves.

These problems are illustrated further in the following examples.

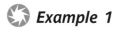 *Example 1*

A UK company buys goods for resale from a US company at a cost of $450,000. When the transaction was entered into, the exchange rate ruling was £1 = $1.5. This initial purchase will be recorded at £300,000 ($450,000/1.5) and the amount to be paid to the US company will be the same.

Dr	Purchases	£300,000	
	Cr Accounts payable (US company)		£300,000
Being goods purchased.			

When the accounts payable are settled, then the rate at date of settlement will be used. So, using the above example, if the US supplier was paid when the rate was £1 = $1.2, then the amount paid would be £375,000 ($450,000/1.2).

Dr	Accounts payable	£375,000	
	Cr Bank		£375,000
Being payment made to settle debt.			

This is more than the initial liability of £300,000. The fact that the payment was made when the rate moved from 1.5 to 1.2 meant that the company had to pay more to settle the account. This difference of £75,000 (£375,000 – £300,000) is a loss on exchange as more was paid to the US supplier than originally recorded. In accordance with IAS 21, this loss on exchange should be taken to the income statement for the year:

Dr	Income statement (loss on exchange)	£75,000	
	Cr Accounts payable		£75,000
Being loss on exchange.			

The above entries can be combined as follows:

Dr	Income statement (loss on exchange)	£75,000	
Dr	Accounts payable	£300,000	
	Cr Bank		£375,000

The purchases remain at the historic amount.

If the supplier is paid when the rate is £1 = $1.8 then a different situation emerges. The amount to be paid this time would be £250,000 ($450,000/1.8). This is less than the initial payment recorded, so in this situation a gain on exchange arises. The gain amounts to £50,000 (£300,000 – £250,000) and arises because less was paid to the US supplier than originally recorded. In accordance with IAS 21, this gain is also taken to the income statement for the year. The accounting entries for this would be:

Dr	Accounts payable		£300,000	
	Cr	Bank		£250,000
	Cr	Income statement (gain on exchange)		£50,000
Being gain in exchange				

As indicated above in the general approach to foreign currency translation, any non-monetary items, such as fixed assets, inventory and equity investments, should be recorded at the rate ruling at the date of the transaction. These items are not re-translated at any time in the future unless there is a fair value adjustment. However, if there are monetary assets and liabilities in existence at the year end, then these should be re-translated at the rate of exchange ruling at the balance sheet date. This is referred to as the 'closing rate'. By using the closing rate, this means that those monetary items are shown in the balance sheet at an up-to-date rate. In other words, as though they were payable (or recoverable) at the balance sheet date.

If there are any exchange gains or losses arising on transactions and outstanding monetary items, then these gains or losses should be reported in the income statement for the year.

 ## Example 2

A UK company buys a fixed asset on credit from a US company on 1 November 2008. The asset cost $3 million and the rate of exchange at the date of purchase was £1 = $1.5. Assume the company's financial year is from 1 January to 31 December.

This transaction will be recorded at the rate ruling when the transaction was undertaken. The fixed asset will be recorded at £2 million ($3 million/1.5) and the corresponding account payable will be recorded at the same amount.

Dr	Fixed asset		£2,000,000	
	Cr	Accounts payable		£2,000,000
Being purchase of fixed asset				

At the year end, when the balance sheet is to be prepared, the accounts payable, a monetary item, will be shown at the rate ruling at the balance sheet date – that is, the closing rate. The fixed asset, on the other hand, will not be re-translated. It is a non-monetary item and so will remain recorded at the rate of the original transaction – in other words, the historic rate.

If the rate of exchange at the balance sheet date was £1 = £1.6, then at the balance sheet date, the accounts payable would be £1.875 million (£3 million/1.6). The difference between the original accounts payable of £2 million and the £1.875 million represents an exchange gain of £125,000. At the date of purchase the amount owed was £2 million and at the balance sheet date the amount owed is £1.875 million – a 'saving' of £125,000. This would be recorded in the accounts as follows:

Dr	Accounts payable		£125,000	
	Cr	Income statement (exchange gain)		£125,000
Being exchange gain				

Note that the gain is taken to the income statement, in accordance with IAS 21.

To take this scenario to its logical conclusion. If the account payable was paid on 15 January 2009, when the exchange rate was £1 = $1.55, then at 15 January, the account payable would now be £1.935m ($3 million/1.55) and it is this amount that will require to be paid. The account payable at the year end was shown as £1.875 million and at the date of payment is £1.935 million, resulting in an exchange loss of £60,000 (£1.935 – £1.875). The transaction will be recorded as follows:

Dr	Accounts payable	£1,875,000	
Dr	Income statement (exchange loss)	60,000	
	Cr Bank		£1,935,000

As before, the loss will be included in the income statement for the year ended 2009 since it arises from exchange movements from 1 to 15 January 2009.

Progress Point 11.1

ABC is a UK company that sells goods in the USA. An invoice is raised on 15 December 2008 for $100,000 in respect of the goods sold. On 10 January 2009, the invoice was paid. The financial year of ABC runs from 1 January to 31 December. The relevant exchange rates are as follows:

15 December 2008	£1 = $1.75
31 December 2008	£1 = $1.80
10 January 2009	£1 = $1.78

Required

Show how any exchange movements will be recorded in the financial statement of ABC.

Solution

(a)   to record the initial transaction:
    at date of transaction the amount owing from the US company will be £57,143 ($100,000/1.75),

| Dr | Accounts receivable | £57,143 | |
| | Cr   Sales | | £57,143 |

(b)   When the accounts are prepared at 31 December, the accounts receivable, a monetary item, will be re-translated at the rate ruling at that date. The amount will be £55,556 ($100,000/1.80). This will mean that there is a loss on exchange of £1,587 (£57,143 – £55,556). It is a loss because less will be received from the debtor than was originally anticipated.

| Dr | Income statement (loss on exchange) | £1,587 | |
| | Cr   Accounts receivable | | £1,587 |

(c)   At the date of settlement the actual amount received will be £56,179 ($100,000/1.78). There will now be a gain on exchange of £623 (£56,179 – £55,556). It is a gain this time because more will be received (£56,179) than was anticipated (£55,556).

Debit	Bank	£56,179	
	Cr Income statement (gain on exchange)		£623
	Cr Accounts receivable		£55,556

Hedging

One of the ways in which companies minimise the risk of exchange rate movements is to take out hedges against individual transactions. For example, a UK company wants to buy a piece of machinery from a US company for $10,000. If the exchange rate at the date the transaction was undertaken was £1 = $2 then the UK company would be required to pay £5,000 ($10,000/2).

BASIC

INTERMEDIATE

ADVANCED

However, if the machine was not to be delivered for six months, then by the time the payment is required to be made the exchange rate may have moved to, say, £1 = $1.8. This would mean that the UK company would be liable now to pay £5,556 (rounded) [$10,000/1.8], which is more than would have been paid initially (had the exchange rate remained fixed).

In order to avoid this risk, the company can enter into a deal to buy dollars in advance, and so fix the rate. This is known as buying forward. In other words, if the UK company bought dollars forward at the time it entered into the transaction with the US company, then the exchange rate would have been fixed at the outset at £1 = $2. This technique is known as hedging. When such a transaction takes place, the asset would be recorded in the UK company's books at the exchange rate built in to the forward contract, not at the rate in existence when the asset is delivered.

If there is no hedge, then the individual transactions are translated at the rate ruling when the transaction took place.

Section 2: Intermediate Issues

A company may conduct foreign operations through an overseas subsidiary company. This overseas subsidiary will maintain its own accounting records in the currency of the foreign country; this will be in the local currency. In order for the results of the foreign operation to be included in the overall results of the parent company, the financial statements of the foreign operation need to be translated into the currency used by the parent company. How this translation process is done depends on the nature of the relationship between the subsidiary company and the parent company.

This section outlines the different relationships between the subsidiary and the parent company, and illustrates the different methods used for translating and presenting the results of overseas operations.

11.3 Monetary and non-monetary items

In the introductory section there was a brief explanation of how exchange gains or losses arise. This now needs to be formalised and related to what will be described later as monetary items. Monetary items refer to monetary assets and liabilities such as cash, accounts receivable and payable, loans and overdrafts. These items are important since if a company holds them over a period during which the rate of exchange changes, then a gain or loss will arise.

To illustrate this, consider the following example. A company has overseas accounts receivable in the USA of $100,000 at a time when the exchange rate is £1 = $2. The company could reasonably expect to receive £50,000. However, if by the time the monies are to be received, the exchange rate becomes £1 = $1.8 then the amount receivable will now be £55,555. The company will receive £5,555 more than expected. This represents a gain from holding accounts receivable. Of course the situation would be reversed if the rate became £1 = $2.2. This time the amount to be received would be £45,454, which is lower by £4,545, resulting in a loss.

The same general principle can be applied to all monetary assets.

In terms of monetary liabilities the situation would be similar. If the same company had outstanding accounts payable of $80,000 at a time when the exchange rate is £1 = $2 then the company would reasonably expect to pay £40,000. If, however, by the time payment was made the rate had become £1 = $1.8 then the amount to be paid would become £44,444. This is not good news since the company will have to pay £4,444 more than expected and so will result in a loss from holding a monetary liability. If, however, the rate became £1 = $2.2 then the amount required to settle the liability would become £36,363. This is less than was originally owed and so results in a gain to the company from holding a monetary liability.

The same general principle can be applied to all monetary liabilities.

The distinction between monetary and non-monetary assets and liabilities becomes important later when dealing with what is known as the temporal method of translation. In this method it is necessary to identify the gain or loss from holding net monetary items. This is described in more detail later in this section.

Functional and presentation currencies

At this stage it is necessary to further develop an understanding of functional and presentation currencies. There are two areas in which these currencies are applied:

1. in translating the results of foreign operations to be included in the consolidated financial statements of the entity, and
2. in translating the financial statements of foreign operations into a presentation currency.

In essence there are two different types of translation process. To help understand this it is necessary to distinguish between three different 'types' of currency.

1. Local currency: this is the currency in which the foreign operation measures and records its transactions.
2. Functional currency: this has already been defined above, as the currency of the primary economic environment in which the entity operates. It is the currency that affects the economic wealth of the entity.
3. Presentation currency: this is the currency in which the financial statements are presented.

 ## *Example*

Home Ltd is a UK company that has an overseas subsidiary, Overseas Ltd, which operates in France. The operations in France are to sell goods manufactured in Singapore. In this scenario, Overseas Ltd would probably maintain its accounts in euros (the local currency) while the functional currency could be the Singaporean $ (reflecting the major economic operations in Singapore). However, for presentation of the financial statements of Home Ltd, the presentation currency could be the £ sterling.

As the accounts are maintained in euros, they may have first of all to be translated into the functional currency, the Singaporean $, and then translated into £ sterling for presentation purposes.

It is these two translation processes that are referred to in IAS 21.

Choice of functional currency

As the foreign subsidiary operates in another country, it is important that any financial effects on the parent entity of a change in the exchange rate are apparent from the process of translation. Given that the parent entity has an investment in a foreign operation, it is exposed to a change in the exchange rate since it has assets in that other country. Any choice of translation method must deal with the extent to which the parent company is exposed to exchange rate movements. The impact of any exchange rate movements will have an effect depending on the economic relationship between the parent and the subsidiary.

Consider the following examples, which illustrate the case of a UK company that wishes to sell its product in the USA.

 ## *Example 1*

On 1 January 2009 the UK company acquires premises in the USA to be used as a distribution depot. The building cost $1.2 million. The UK company also put £60,000 into a business bank account in the USA. This £60,000 is equivalent to $90,000 (£60,000 × 1.5). At the end of January 2009 total sales on credit in the USA amounted to $450,000 and these good had cost £275,000 to manufacture. The rate of exchange during January was £1 = $1.5. The accounts receivable were collected in February 2009 when the rate of exchange was £1 = £1.6.

The UK company has no subsidiary but has acquired an overseas asset, put money into an overseas bank and has sold goods. These can be looked at as a series of transactions (as was shown in the introductory section) and would be recorded by the UK company in £ sterling as follows.

(a)   Acquiring the building:

Dr	Building ($1,200,000/1.5)	£800,000	
	Cr Cash		£800,000
Being purchase of buildings.			

(b)   Paying cash into the bank account:

Dr	Bank (US bank)	£60,000	
	Cr Cash		£60,000
Being cash paid into bank account.			

(c)   Selling goods on credit:

Dr	Accounts receivable ($450,000/1.5)	£300,000	
	Cr Sales		£300,000
Being goods sold on credit.			

(d)   Cost of goods sold:

Dr	Cost of sales	£275,000	
	Cr Inventory		£275,000
Being cost of sales.			

Assume that the cash is received from the customers in February 2009 and that the exchange rate has moved to £1 = $1.6. The amount received would be $450,000/1.6 = £281,250. The amount originally receivable was £300,000 so there is a loss on exchange of £18,750 (£300,000 − £281,250). It is a loss on exchange because less was actually received than was expected (see introductory section).

This loss on exchange would be taken to the profit and loss account. The transactions would be recorded as follows:

(e)	Dr	Loss on exchange	£18,750	
	Dr	Cash	£281,250	
		Cr Accounts receivable		£300,000
Being exchange loss taken to income statement.				

In addition to this there would be an exchange difference arising from the fact that the US company has $90,000 in the bank account. The bank account is a monetary asset and, as such, any movement in the exchange rate will affect the 'value' of such an asset.

The $90,000 in the bank account was put in when the rate was £1 = £1.5, so this was equivalent to £60,000. However, when the rate moved to £1 = $1.6, the equivalent amount was now £56,250 ($90,000/1.6). The monetary asset has therefore lost 'value' to the extent of £4,850 (£60,000 − £56,250). This loss in 'value' has arisen because of an exchange rate movement and will be recorded as a loss on exchange. The bank account will have to be reduced and a loss on exchange recorded.

(f)	Dr	Loss on exchange	£4,750	
		Cr Bank		£4,750
Being loss from holding monetary asset.				

Example 2

Instead of dealing with customers in the USA, the UK company formed an overseas subsidiary company, Overseas Ltd, to deal with the US operations. This situation is similar to the one above in that all the goods are transferred from the UK parent company to the US subsidiary at cost. The goods are sold in the USA by the subsidiary and the profits are sent back to the UK parent.

The underlying transactions are the same as for Example 1. The fact that a subsidiary has been formed does not change the underlying economic effects of the transactions. The translation of the US subsidiary must show the position as if the parent had undertaken the transactions itself. This is the purpose behind the choice of the functional currency approach.

The basic underlying transactions would be as follows.

(a) On receipt of inventory at cost:

Dr	Inventory	$412,500	
	Cr Accounts payable		$412,500

(b) On sale of inventory on credit:

Dr	Accounts receivable	$450,000	
	Cr Sales		$450,000

(c) Cost of goods sold:

D	Cost of sales	$412,500	
	Cr Inventory		$412,500

The opening balance sheet of the US subsidiary would be as follows:

Building	$1,200,000
Inventory (transferred at cost) (£275,000 x 1.5)	412,500
Accounts payable (amount owing for inventory)	(412,500)
Bank account	90,000
	$1,290,000
Capital	$1,290,000

Assume:

(i)   all the inventory is sold on credit at the end of January 2009
(ii) the financial statements of the subsidiary have to be prepared at the end of February 2009 when the exchange rate is £1 = $1.6.

At the end of February the financial statements of the US company would be as follows:

Income statement (local currency)	
Sales	$450,000
Cost of sales	412,500
Profit	37,500

Balance sheet (local currency)	
Building	$1,200,000
Accounts receivable	450,000
Bank	90,000
Accounts payable	(412,500)
Net assets	$1,327,500
Capital	$1,290,000
Profit for period	37,500
	$1,327,000

Although the financial statements are shown in the *local currency*, the *functional currency* is the £ sterling since this is the currency of the primary economic environment affecting the overseas subsidiary. The inventories are manufactured in the UK, the parent is financing the subsidiary and the cash flows that influence the parent to continue to trade in the US come from the UK.

In this scenario, the subsidiary is simply an extension of the parent company and is used for transforming foreign currency transactions into cash flows. In this situation, the financial statements of the subsidiary must now be translated into the functional currency, the £ sterling, and must show:

- the assets of the subsidiary at cost to the parent – in other words, what the parent would have paid in its own currency to acquire the asset
- the revenues and expenses of the subsidiary at what it would have cost the parent at the date the transactions occurred
- any gain or loss from holding monetary items (monetary assets and monetary liabilities); any gains or losses on holding monetary items should be shown in the income statement since they affect the parent directly.

The financial statements of the subsidiary would be translated into the functional currency as follows:

Income statement			
		Rate	
Sales	$450,000	1.5	£300,000
Cost of sales	412,500	1.5	275,000
Profit	37,500		25,000
Loss on holding net monetary assets (see Note 1)			5,312
			£19,688

Balance sheet			
Building	$1,200,000	1.5	£800,000
Accounts receivable	450,000	1.6	281,250
Bank	90,000	1.6	56,250
Accounts payable	(412,500)	1.6	(257,812)
	$1,327,500		£879,688
Capital	$1,290,000	1.5	860,000
Profit for period	37,500		19,688
	$1,327,500		£879,688

Notes 1: net monetary items

As explained above, monetary items comprise items such as cash, accounts payable and, accounts receivable. In the above scenario the monetary items are as follows:

Cash	$90,000	monetary asset
Accounts receivable	$450,000	monetary asset
Accounts payable	$412,500	monetary liability

So overall the company has net monetary assets of $127,500 ($90,000 + $450,000 – $412,000). These net monetary assets are in existence at the end of January when the exchange rate is £1 = $1.5. When the financial statements are prepared at the end of February, the exchange rate is now £1 = $1.6.

So, net monetary assets:

- At end of January   £85,000 ($127,500/1.5)
- At balance sheet date   £79,688 ($127,500/1.6)

The 'value' of these assets has fallen by £5,312, which represents the loss from holding net monetary items and is shown in the income statement.

 ## Example 3

Assume in this scenario that the UK company sets up a subsidiary company in the USA with $1,290,000 as in Example 2, the money being used to buy a building and set up a bank account. However, this time, the US subsidiary is established to manufacture products in the USA for sale in the USA. Also, US workers are used in the manufacturing process and any profits made by the company are used to expand the business in the USA. The parent company receives remittances from the subsidiary in the form of dividends.

This is a completely different scenario from that presented in Example 2. The subsidiary is not just an extension of the parent. The cash flows for the subsidiary are dependent this time on the economic environment of the USA not the UK. If there is a change in exchange rate between the £ and the $, then there will not be an immediate effect on the operations of the US subsidiary. In this case the functional currency will be the US$ not the UK£. However, given that the US company is a subsidiary of the UK company, the accounts of the US subsidiary will have to be translated into the *presentation* currency.

In analysing the success or otherwise of the overseas subsidiary, the interrelationships between sales, profits, assets and equity should be the same whether expressed in $s or £s. The translation process should adjust all such items by the same exchange rate to retain these interrelationships. In this case the closing rate would be used.

Where the functional currency of a subsidiary is different to the presentation currency of the group, then the financial statements should be translated into the presentation currency as follows:

- balance sheet – items should be translated at the rate of exchange at the balance sheet date, the closing rate
- income statement – items should ideally be translated at the rate of exchange ruling at the date of each transaction, but for practical purposes is usually an average rate is usually used
- any exchange differences arising are taken directly to a translation reserve (not to the income statement).

Since translation differences do not have much effect on the present and future cash flows from foreign operations, they are not recognised in the income statement.

Using the information from Example 2:

Income statement		Rate	
Sales	$450,000	1.5	£300,000
Cost of sales	412,500	1.5	275,000
Profit	37,500		25,000

Balance sheet		Rate	
Building	$1,200,000	1.6	£750,000
Accounts receivable	450,000	1.6	281,250
Bank	90,000	1.6	56,250
Accounts payable	(412,500)	1.6	(257,812)
	$1,327,500		£829,688
Capital	$1,290,000	1.5	860,000
Profit for period	37,500		25,000
Translation reserve (exchange loss)			(55,312)
	$1,327,500		£829,688

How can the exchange difference (the amount in the translation reserve) be explained? It can be verified as follows.

The balance sheet of both years can be linked as follows;

Opening net assets	+	Profit	=	Closing net assets
$1,290,000	+	$37,500	=	$1,327,500

The opening net assets 'come in' when the rate is £1 = £1.5, and 'go out' as part of closing net assets when the rate is £1 = £1.6. The same is true of the profit. Profit is calculated when the transactions take place. At this time the rate is £1 = $1.5. However, the profit of $37,500 is part of the closing net asset figure of $1,327,500 and the closing net assets have been translated at the rate of £1 = $1.6. So the exchange difference may be explained as follows.

Explanation of exchange difference

Opening net assets

At opening rate	$1,290,000/1.5	=	£860,000
At closing rate	$1,290,000/1.6	=	£806,250
Exchange loss (assets have decreased)			£53,750

Profit for the year

At rate	£37,500/1.5	=	£25,000
At closing rate	£37,500/1.6	=	£23,437
Exchange loss (profit has gone down)			£1,562
Total loss to translation reserve		=	£55,312

Examples 2 and 3 give rise to two different methods of translation. In Example 2 the overseas subsidiary was seen as an extension of the parent company and as such the functional currency was that of the parent company. In this scenario the accounts of the subsidiary were translated into that currency. If an overseas subsidiary is an 'extension' of the parent company then the currency of the parent company is the functional currency. The method illustrated in Example 2 is referred to as the temporal method of foreign exchange translation.

In Example 3 the overseas subsidiary is independent of the parent. The functional currency will most likely be the 'local' currency: the US$. Once in the functional currency, the accounts of the subsidiary have to then be translated from functional currency to presentation currency. The method illustrated in Example 3 is referred to as the closing rate method, or the net investment method of foreign exchange translation.

The methods of foreign currency translation illustrated above are dealt with formally in IAS 21 *The Effects of Changes in Foreign Exchange Rates*.

11.4 IAS 21 *The Effects of Changes in Foreign Exchange Rates*

Translation into the functional currency: the temporal method

The process of translating one currency into another is detailed in paragraphs 21 and 23 of IAS 21. Paragraph 21 deals with items reflected in the income statement that concern transactions occurring in the current period. IAS 21 does not use the term 'temporal method' to describe these translation procedures. According to the standard, accounting for non-autonomous foreign operations is considered to be equivalent to the accounting for foreign currency transactions. According to the standard, a foreign currency transaction shall be recorded on initial recognition in the functional currency. This is done by applying the spot rate of exchange between the functional currency and the foreign currency at the date of the transaction.

Strictly speaking, then, in translating revenues and expenses in the income statement each item of revenue and expense should be translated at the spot rate of exchange between the functional currency and the foreign currency on the date that the transaction occurred. In the real world, given the very large number of transactions that a company would have, IAS 21 provides for an averaging system to be used. A rate that approximates the actual rate at the date of the transaction can be used. An average rate for the month might be used for all transactions occurring within this period.

Basic principles of translation

Balance sheet items

- Assets and liabilities: assets and liabilities need to be first of all classified as either monetary or non-monetary. Monetary assets and monetary liabilities are translated at the rate existing at the balance sheet date, the closing rate. Non-monetary assets are recorded at the rate ruling when the asset was acquired, the historic rate. If a non-monetary asset has been revalued then the rate ruling at the date of revaluation would be used. Non-monetary liabilities are translated at the date of valuation.
- Share capital: if this is capital created by an investment or that exists at the date of acquisition then this is translated at the rate ruling when the investment was made (or at date of acquisition).
- Retained earnings and other reserves: if these reserves are on hand at the date of acquisition, then they are translated at the rate existing at acquisition. If the reserves result from internal transfers then the rate to be used is the one that existed at the date the amounts transferred were originally recognised in equity.

Income statement items

- Income and expenses: in general these are translated at the rates in existence when the transactions were entered into. For items that relate to non-monetary items, such as depreciation, the rates to be used are those used to translate the related non-monetary item.
- Dividends paid: translated at the rate ruling at the date of payment.
- Dividends declared: translated at the rate ruling at the date the dividend was declared.
- Transfers to and from reserves: if internal transfers are made, then the rates applicable are those existing when the amounts transferred were originally recognised in equity.

Given that non-monetary items are translated at the historic rate then no exchange difference will arise on these items. Any exchange difference that does arise will be from holding monetary items. In addition, items such as sales, purchases and expenses give rise to monetary items such as cash, and accounts receivable and payable. Exchange differences can be explained therefore by looking at movements in the monetary items over the period.

In accordance with IAS 21, any exchange differences arising are to be recognised in profit or loss in the period in which they arise.

⊛ *Example*

H plc has a wholly owned overseas subsidiary S Ltd, which it acquired on 1 January 2009. The summary financial statements of S as at 1 January 2009 and at 31 December 2009 are as follows:

Balance sheets as at				
As at	1 Jan 2009		31 Dec 2009	
	AUS$	AUS$	AUS$	AUS$
Tangible fixed assets		450		330
Current assets:				
Inventory	240		360	
Accounts receivable	120		240	
	360		600	
Accounts payable	210		240	
		150		360
		600		690
Share capital		600		600
Retained profit		0		90
		600		690

Income statement For the year ending 31 December 2009		
	AUS$	AUS$
Sales revenue		1,500
Cost of sales		
Opening inventory	240	
Purchases	1,200	
	1,440	
Closing inventory	360	1,080
Gross profit		420
Depreciation	120	
Taxation	150	
Dividend	60	330
		90

Assuming that the functional currency of S Ltd is that of the UK, translate the financial statement of S Ltd into the functional currency using the temporal method. Identify and explain any exchange difference arising.

The movements in the exchange rate are as follows:

1 January 2009	£1 = AUS$3
Average rate for opening inventory	£1 = AUS$3
Average for the year	£1 = AUS$2.5
Average rate for closing inventory	£1 = AUS$2
31 December 2009	£1 = AUS$2

Explanation

The temporal method described above uses a mixture of rates:

- non-monetary items are translated at historic rate
- monetary items are translated at closing rate
- profit and loss account items are translated at the date the transaction occurred.

Depreciation will be translated at the rate that applied when the asset to which the depreciation related was acquired. In this case it is the opening rate.

	AUS$	AUS$	Rate	£	£
Income statement					
For the year ending 31 December 2009					
Sales revenue		1,500	2.5		600
Cost of sales					
Opening inventory	240		3	80	
Purchases	1,200		2.5	480	
	1,440			560	
Closing inventory	360	1,080	2	180	380
Gross profit		420			220
Depreciation	120		3	40	
Taxation	150		2	75	
Dividend	60	330	2	30	145
		90			75*

At this stage the income statement is incomplete. The exchange difference is missing. The exchange difference can be identified from the translated balance sheet.

	AUS$	AUS$	Rate		£
Balance sheets					
Tangible fixed assets		330	3		110
Current assets:					
Inventory	360		2	180	
Accounts receivable	240		2	120	
	600			300	
Accounts payable	(240)		2	(120)	
		360			180
		690			290
Share capital		600	3		200
Retained profit		90			90*
		690			290

* At this stage, in order to make the balance sheet balance, the retained profit needs to be £90. However, the profit shown in the income statement is £75. The profit from the profit statement is lower than it ought to be. The difference, £15, is the amount that needs to be added to the profit of £75 to bring it up to £90. The £15 is the gain on exchange that needs to be shown in the income statement.

The complete income statement can now be shown as follows:

Income statement For the year ending 31 December 2009					
	AUS$	AUS$	Rate	£	£
Sales revenue		1,500	2.5		600
Cost of sales					
Opening inventory	240		3	80	
Purchases	1,200		2.5	480	
	1,440			560	
Closing inventory	360	1,080	2	180	380
Gross profit		420			220
Depreciation	120		3	40	
Taxation	150		2	75	
Dividend	60	330	2	30	145
		90			75
Gain on exchange					15
					90

This is one way of determining the exchange difference. However, the exchange difference can also be calculated separately. As was described above, any exchange difference can arise only from the monetary items, since the non-monetary items are translated at the historic rate (i.e. the rate in existence when these items were acquired), so no exchange difference arises. Monetary items, on the other hand, are translated at the closing rate.

Calculation of the exchange difference

From the opening balance sheet the opening net monetary position can be established:

Accounts receivable	120
Accounts payable	210
Net monetary liabilities	(90)

During the year sales were made and inventory was purchased. This would have an impact on the opening monetary position. Sales would have a positive impact (increase accounts receivable) and purchases would have a negative impact (increase accounts payable) on the monetary position.

Also, when payments are made for tax and dividends, this too would have a negative impact since it would reduce cash (a monetary asset). A statement can be prepared as follows:

Statement of net monetary position:	AUS$	AUS$
Opening net monetary liabilities		(90)
Sales during year	1,500	
Purchases during year	(1200)	300
		210
Payments at year end		
Tax	150	
Dividends	60	210
		0
Closing monetary position		
Accounts receivable		240
Accounts payable		240
		0

Keep in mind that the assumption made for sales and purchases is that since they occurred during the year, an *average* rate has been used in this example to translate these items. This impact can be seen in Figure 11.1.

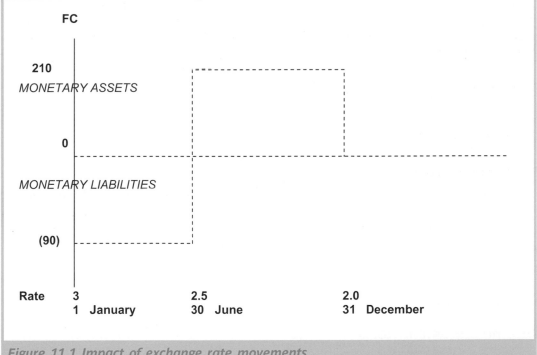

Figure 11.1 Impact of exchange rate movements

From Figure 11.1, it can be seen that the company holds net monetary liabilities until transactions are undertaken. Remember it is assumed that these transactions are averaged over the year, so the mid-year point is taken.

Once sales and purchases have been made, the net monetary position changes from (90) to 210 and remains at that point until the final payments are made for tax and dividends. Using this figure, the exchange difference can be calculated as follows:

Opening net monetary liabilities	
(90/3)	£30
(90/2.5)	£36
Exchange loss	(£6)

This is a loss on exchange since when the rate moves from 3 to 2.5, liabilities increase from £30 to £36, so the company has to pay more than anticipated.

When the sales and purchases are made, the net monetary liabilities changes to net monetary assets.

Net monetary assets	
(210/2.5)	£84
(210/2.0)	£105
Exchange gain	£21

This is an exchange gain since more will be received than was expected.

Overall there is an exchange gain of £15 (£21 − £6) from holding net monetary items. It is this gain of £15 that appears in the income statement.

Translation into the presentation currency: the net investment (closing rate) method

Once the financial statements of a subsidiary are prepared in the relevant functional currency these statements have now to be translated into the presentation currency. The principles of translation are given in IAS 21, paragraph 39.

Basic principles of translation

Balance sheet items

- Assets and liabilities: all assets and liabilities (whether monetary or non-monetary) are translated at the exchange rate ruling at the reporting date; this is the closing rate.
- Share capital: if this capital is created by an investment, or exists at the date of acquisition this is translated at the rate that existed at the date of acquisition; this is the historic rate.
- Retained earnings and other reserves: if these reserves are on hand at acquisition date then they are translated at the rate current at this acquisition date. If reserves are post-acquisition and created by an internal transfer within equity, they are then translated at the rate existing at the date the reserve from which the transfer was made was originally recognised in the accounts. If the reserves are post-acquisition, and not created as a result of an internal transfer – for example, an asset revaluation surplus – then the rate to be used is that which is in existence when the reserve is created.

Income statement items

- Income and expenses: these should be translated at the rates current at the date at which the transactions took place. For such items as sales and purchases of inventory, which will occur on a regular basis throughout the period, average rates may be used. In relation to items such as depreciation, which are in essence allocations for a period, an average exchange rate may be used.
- Dividends paid: these are translated at the rates current when the dividends are paid.
- Dividends declared: these are translated at the rate ruling when the dividend is declared.
- Transfers to and from reserves: if these transfers are internal then the rate used is the one ruling when the amounts transferred were originally recognised in equity.

Using the previous example, the financial statements can now be translated into the presentation currency. The example is repeated here for convenience.

Example

H plc has a wholly owned overseas subsidiary S Ltd, which it acquired on 1 January 2009. The summary financial statements of S as at 1 January 2009 and at 31 December 2009 are as follows. These statements are presented in the functional currency.

Balance sheets as at				
	1 Jan 2009		31 Dec 2009	
	AUS$	AUS$	AUS$	AUS$
Tangible fixed assets		450		330
Current assets:				
Inventory	240		360	
Accounts receivable	120		240	
	360		600	
Accounts payable	210		240	
		150		360
		600		690
Share capital		600		600
Retained profit		0		90
		600		690

Income statement For the year ending 31 December 2009		
	AUS$	AUS$
Sales revenue		1,500
Cost of sales		
Opening inventory	240	
Purchases	1,200	
	1,440	
Closing inventory	360	1,080
Gross profit		420
Depreciation	120	
Taxation	150	
Dividend	60	330
		90

Assuming that the *presentation* currency of S Ltd is that of the UK, translate the financial statement of S Ltd into the *presentation* currency using the *closing rate method*. Identify and explain any exchange difference arising.

The movements in the exchange rate are as follows:

1 January 2009	£1 = AUS$3
Average rate for opening inventory	£1 = AUS$3
Average for the year	£1 = AUS$2.5
Average rate for closing inventory	£1 = AUS$2
31 December 2009	£1 = AUS$2

This time the income statement will be translated using rates in existence when the transactions were undertaken. In general this is usually the average rate for the period. In this example the average rate is used except for opening and closing inventory, and taxation and dividends, since it is known when those items were paid/acquired.

Income statement For the year ending 31 December 2009				
	AUS$	AUS$	Rate	£	£
Sales revenue		1,500	2.5		600
Cost of sales					
Opening inventory	240		3.0	80	
Purchases	1,200		2.5	480	
	1,440			560	
Closing inventory	360	1,080	2.0	180	380
Gross profit		420			220
Depreciation	120		2.5	48	
Taxation	150		2.0	75	
Dividend	60	330	2.0	30	153
		90			67

The balance sheet will be translated using the closing rate, except for the share capital. Retained profit is the profit for the year, so in this the profit shown in the income statement will be carried forward into the balance sheet.

Balance sheets				
	AUS$	AUS$	Rate	£
Tangible fixed assets		330	2	165
Current assets:				
Inventory	360		2	180
Accounts receivable	240		2	120
	600			300
Accounts payable	(240)		2	(120)
		360		180
		690		345
Share capital		600	3	200
Retained profit		90		67
		690		267
Difference (translation reserve)				78
				345

The translated balance sheet does not balance; the difference of £78 (£345 − £276) is the amount of the exchange difference. In this case it is an exchange gain of £78 and would be put into a translation reserve.

This is one way of determining the exchange difference, by simply using the balancing figure in the balance sheet. However, the exchange difference can also be calculated separately. This example is slightly more complicated than that shown in the example on page 592, but the basic principle explained there still applies. Remember, the opening balance sheet and the closing balance sheet are linked by the profit for the year.

Opening net assets	+	Profit	=	Closing net assets
AUS$600	+	AUS$90	=	AUS$690

Note that the figure for closing net assets contains both the opening net assets plus the profit. Under the closing rate method, the opening net assets would 'come in' at a rate of 3 and 'go out' at a rate of 2.

An exchange difference will arise as follows:

Opening net assets

$600/3 (opening rate)	£200
$600/2 (closing rate)	£300
Gain on exchange	£100

This is an exchange gain because assets have increased in 'value', i.e. are shown at a higher amount.

The profit for the year is slightly more complicated this time, because of the different rates used to translate the opening and closing inventory, and also the payment of the dividend and taxation at the year end. All other items of revenue and expenditure are taken at the average rate for the year. In general terms an increase in revenue will result in an exchange gain, while an increase in a cost will result in an exchange loss.

The exchange difference relating to the profit for the year can be deconstructed as follows.

Sales revenue

£1,500/2.5	£600
£1,500/2	£750
Exchange gain	£150

Opening inventory

$240/3	£80
$240/2	£120
Exchange loss	£40

Purchases

$1,200/2.5	£480
$1,200/2	£600
Exchange loss	£120

Closing inventory

No exchange difference arises since it is translated at the closing rate in the income statement and in the closing balance sheet.

Depreciation

$120/2.5	£48
$120/2	£60
Exchange loss	£12

Taxation and dividends

Again no exchange difference since they are translated at the closing rate both in the income statement and in the closing balance sheet.

Overall exchange difference in the profit	
Exchange gain on sales	£150
Exchange loss on opening inventory	(£40)
Exchange loss on purchases	(£120)
Exchange loss on depreciation	(£12)
Net exchange loss in profit	(£22)

Total exchange gain	
Opening net assets	£100
Profit	(£22)
Translation reserve	£78

Progress Point 11.2

Alba plc has a subsidiary, NS Ltd, a company incorporated in the USA. The following information relates to the subsidiary for 2009.

Balance sheet as at 31 December 2008 and 2009		
	2008	2009
	$000	$000
Tangible fixed assets	32,200	32,000
Monetary assets	5,300	7,600
Monetary liabilities	(6,500)	(5,000)
	31,000	34,600
Share capital	28,000	28,000
Retained profit	3,000	6,600
	31,000	34,600

Income statement for period ended 31 December 2009	
	$000
Sales revenue	10,080
Cost of sales	(3,960)
Gross profit	6,120
Depreciation	(200)
Other operating expenses	(240)
Operating profit	5,680
Taxation	(2,080)
Profit for the year	3,600

Sterling exchange rates were:

31 December 2008	£1 = $2.00
Average rate for 2009	£1 = $1.8
31 December 2009	£1 = $1.6

Required

(a) Translate the balance sheet and income statement into:
    (i) the functional currency of Alba plc using the temporal method
    (ii) the presentation currency of Alba plc using the net investment method.
(b) For each of (i) and (ii) above, calculate the exchange difference, and explain how the exchange difference is to be treated in the financial statements.
(c) Prepare a statement showing how the exchange difference is calculated.

Solution

(i) Translation into functional currency (temporal method)

(a)

Balance sheet	$000	Rate	£000
Tangible fixed assets	32,000	2.0	16,000
Monetary assets	7,600	1.6	4,750
Monetary liabilities	(5,000)	1.6	(3,125)
	34,600		17,625
Share capital	28,000	2.0	14,000
Retained profit			
2008	3,000	2.0	1,500
2009	3,600	Balancing figure	2,125
	34,600		17,625

Income statement			
	$000		£000
Sales revenue	10,080	1.8	5,600
Cost of sales	(3,960)	1.8	2,200
Gross profit	6,120		3,400
Depreciation	(200)	2.0	(100)
Other operating expenses	(240)	1.8	(133)
Operating profit	5,680		3,167
Taxation	(2,080)	1.6	1,300
Profit for the year	3,600	1.8	1,867
		Exchange gain	258
			2,125

(b) The exchange gain is £258 and can be determined from the balance sheet figure for retained profit for the year. The figure required to 'balance' the balance sheet is £2,125, while the translated figure in the income statement is £1,867. This results in a difference of £258, which is the amount of the exchange gain. In the temporal method this exchange gain is shown as part of the profit for the year.

(c) As has been seen before, any exchange difference under this method results in an exchange difference from holding monetary items. Since other assets and liabilities are translated at the historic rate, then there is no exchange difference arising from these items.

Statement of net monetary position

Opening monetary position:	
Monetary assets	$5,300
Monetary liabilities	$6,500
Net monetary liabilities	($1,200)
Sales	$10,080
Cost of sales	($3,960)
Expenses	($240)
	$5,880
Net monetary assets	$4,680
Taxation	(2,080)
Closing net monetary assets	$2,600

This can be verified from the closing balance sheet:

Net monetary assets	$7,600
Net monetary liabilities	$5,000
	$2,600

Determination of gain or loss from holding net monetary items.

The gain from holding net monetary assets can be shown diagrammatically, as in Figure 11.2

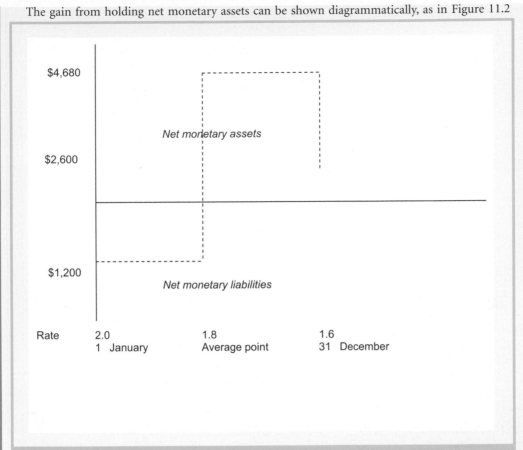

Figure 11.2 Gain from holding net monetary assets

Opening net monetary liabilities	
$1,200/2	£600
$1,200/1.8	£667
Loss from holding NML	(£67)
Monetary assets	
$4,680/1.8	£2,600
$4,680/1.6	£2,925
Gain from holding NMA	£325
Total gain (£325 – £67)	£258

This gain is shown in the income statement as part of profit for the year.

(ii) Translation into presentation currency (net investment method)

(a)

Balance sheet	$000	Rate	£000
Tangible fixed assets	32,000	1.6	20,000
Current assets	7,600	1.6	4,750
Current liabilities	(5,000)	1.6	(3,125)
	34,600		21,625
Share capital	28,000	2.0	14,000
Retained profit			
2008	3,000	2.0	1,500
2009	3,600	1.8	2,000
	34,600		17,500
Translation reserve (balancing figure)			4,125
			21,625

Income statement			
Sales revenue	10,080	1.8	5,600
Cost of sales	(3,960)	1.8	2,200
Gross profit	6,120		3,400
Depreciation	(200)	1.8	(111)
Other operating expenses	(240)	1.8	(133)
Operating profit	5,680		3,156
Taxation	(2,080)	1.8	(1,156)
Profit for the year	3,600	1.8	2,000

(b)

Opening net assets	+	Profit	=	Closing net assets
$31,000	+	$3,600	=	$34,600

This would be translated

$31,000/2.0	+	$3,600/1.8	=	$34,600/1.6
£15,500	+	£2,000		£21,625

The closing net assets should be £17,500 and not £21,625. Over the period the net assets have increased in 'value' by £4,125 (£21,625 − £17,500). The difference represents a gain on exchange, and will go to the translation reserve.

(c)
Explanation of exchange difference
Opening net assets

At opening rate	$31,000/2	=	£15,500
At closing rate	$31,000/1.6	=	£19,375
Exchange gain			£3,875

Profit for year			
At average rate	$3,600/1.8	=	2,000
At closing rate	$3,600/1.6	=	2,250
Exchange gain			250
Total gain to translation reserve			£4,125 (£3,875 + 250)

11.5 Disclosure in practice

The main source of information concerning the disclosure of information regarding foreign currency is contained, mainly, in the policy notes and in the notes to the group financial statements. As far as Logica is concerned, information is given on both the choice of functional currency and of the presentation currency. The functional currency is the pound sterling, presumably reflecting the primary economic environment in which the company operates.

The note concerning the functional currency is given in the accounting policy section, as follows:

Foreign currencies

The functional currency of the Company is pounds sterling. Transactions denominated in foreign currencies are translated into the functional currency of the Company at the rates prevailing at the dates of the individual transactions. Foreign currency monetary assets and liabilities are translated at the rates prevailing at the balance sheet date. Exchange gains and losses arising are charged or credited to the profit and loss account within the net operating costs.

This clearly follows the requirement of IAS 21, translating the monetary items at the closing rate and putting any exchange gains or losses into the profit and loss account (income statement).

In terms of the presentation currency, again the pound sterling, the notes to the group financial statements, accounting policy section, show the following:

Foreign currencies

The presentation currency of the Group is pounds sterling. The Group also presents primary statements in euros.

Items included in the separate Financial statements of Group entities are measured in the functional currency of each entity. Transactions denominated in foreign currencies are translated into the functional currency of the entity at the rates prevailing at the dates of the individual transactions. Foreign currency monetary assets and liabilities are translated at the rates prevailing at the balance sheet date. Exchange gains and losses arising are charged or credited to net operating costs or finance costs/income in the income statement, as appropriate, except when deferred in equity as qualifying cash flow hedges and qualifying net investment hedges.

The income statement and balance sheet of foreign entities are translated into pounds sterling on consolidation at the average rates for the period and the rates prevailing at the balance sheet date respectively. Exchange gains and losses arising on the translation of the Group's net investment in foreign entities, and of financial instruments designated as hedges of such investments, are recognised as a separate component of shareholders' equity.

In this section reference is further made to the policy regarding functional currency. Note this time that, in terms of translation into the presentation currency, the net investment method is followed, in that the income statement is translated using average rates for the period, while the rate ruling at the balance sheet date is used for balance sheet items. The exchange difference this time is shown as a separate component of equity.

Some additional information on the exchange differences is given in the statement of recognised income and expense, as shown in Figure 11.3.

Exchange differences on translation of foreign operations	**97.4**	(4.1)
Exchange differences recycled on disposal of foreign operations	**5.1**	–
Cash flow hedges transferred to income statement on settlement	–	(2.0)
Actuarial gains on defined benefit plans	**3.6**	17.5
Tax on items taken directly to equity	–	(3.9)
Net income recognised directly in equity	**106.1**	7.5
Profit for the year	**168.1**	89.1
Total recognised income and expense for the year	**274.2**	96.6
ATTRIBUTABLE TO:		
Equity holders of the parent	**274.0**	89.4
Minority interests	**0.2**	7.2
	274.2	96.6

Figure 11.3 Logica: exchange differences

The company also gives an indication of the most important currencies for the group: the euro and the Swedish krona. This is given as part of the accounting policy section, as shown in Figure 11.4.

The most important foreign currencies for the Group are the euro and the Swedish krona. The relevant exchange rates to pounds sterling were.

	2007		2006	
	Average	Closing	Average	Closing
£1 = €	1.46	1.36	1.47	1.48
£1 = SEK	13.51	12.87	13.57	13.39

Figure 11.4 Logica: foreign currencies used

Section 3: Advanced Aspects

This section will outline in a little more detail some of the issues raised in the previous sections. In particular it will look at the specific requirements of IAS 21 *The Effects of Changes in Foreign Exchange Rates*. It will outline the specific requirement for the identification of the functional currency, and the rationale for the differences in treatment of some items under the temporal and closing rate methods of translation. Some of these requirements have already been illustrated in Section 2 of this chapter. Hedging transactions will be examined further.

11.6 Functional currency: further aspects

In the intermediate section of this chapter, the functional currency was defined as that currency of the primary economic environment in which the entity operates. This tends to oversimplify the issue. In reality it might not be so simple to determine the functional currency of an entity. Some criteria need to be identified and this has been done in terms of IAS 21.

For example, in general terms the functional currency is normally the one in which the entity generates and spends cash (para. 9). So it is important to consider:

- the currency in which the sales prices are denominated or the currency that influences sales prices
- the currency of the country that influences the sales prices through specific regulations or through various competitive forces

■ the currency in which manufacturing costs are determined, either in terms of how such costs are settled or in terms of how such costs are influenced.

According to paragraph 10, there are two factors to consider:

1. the currency in which funds from financing activities are generated
2. the currency in which receipts from operating activities are retained.

It is also important to consider the following questions (under para. 11).

■ Are the activities of the foreign operation carried out as an extension of the reporting entity?
■ Are the number of transactions with the reporting entity a high or low proportion of the activities of the foreign operation?
■ Do the cash flows of the foreign operation directly affect the cash flows of the reporting entity?
■ Are the cash flows from the foreign operation readily available for remittance to it?
■ Are the cash flows from the foreign operation sufficient to service existing or expected debt obligations (without funds being made available from the reporting entity)?

Finally, paragraph 12 indicates that management should use judgement to determine which currency most faithfully reflects the economic effects of the underlying transactions and events.

Translation methods: further discussion

Temporal method (*translation into the functional currency*)

As described above, the temporal method views the subsidiary as an extension of the parent and treats the transactions as though they were carried out by the parent. This method requires translation into the functional currency by applying the spot rate of exchange at the date of the transactions. This has been illustrated in the intermediate section of this chapter. However, what is the situation at the next and subsequent balance sheet dates?

This is particularly important in the case of borrowings in foreign currencies. These loans may be over a number of years and will by necessity have to appear in several balance sheets before final repayment. The accounting question that arises is at what amount should the loan liability be stated in each of the balance sheets between the receipt of the loan and the final repayment? Depending on how the exchange rate moves, it may be that a company has to repay more than it borrowed. If this is the case, then the difference will need to be recognised as a loss at some point. The question is how, and when should the loss be recognised?

From a shareholder's perspective, the most useful information would be how much has to finally be paid to settle the loan and what is the amount of the total loss over the period. The question is, therefore, should the exchange loss be recognised only at this time? Suppose it was an exchange gain, what then? IAS 21 takes the view that such items should be translated at the rate existing at the balance sheet date. This is the closing rate. Any difference arising because of a movement in the exchange rate is to be taken to the income statement. What is the rationale for this treatment? The view is that the closing rate gives the best approximation of the future repayment and is the best information available.

According to IAS 21 the treatment of items depends on the nature of the item (i.e. whether monetary or non-monetary). This means that all exchange differences arising on such items, whether gains or losses, are to be recognised in the income statement. Of course, any such gains will be unrealised until the monetary item is settled (e.g. when a loan is repaid). This is one of the few cases when an unrealised gain is taken to the income statement. That said, it is open to question whether or not a difference on translation is truly a gain or a loss. Given that exchange rates may fluctuate both up and down, is there any reason to suppose that any translation difference is purely temporary? For example, the rate of exchange may be, for example, £1 = $2 at the date of the balance sheet, but the very next week may have changed to £1 = $1.8. How valid is it to recognise a gain or loss at the balance sheet date if the position has already changed when the statements are in the process of being prepared? Again, if the gain or loss is temporary, should it be recognised in the income statement at all?

Closing rate method: translation into the presentation currency

This method of translation recognises the subsidiary as an independent entity. The method of translation used the closing rates to translate the items in the balance sheet. As regards the mechanics of translation, if the subsidiary is 'independent' then the assets and liabilities of such an entity will interact with each other rather than with those of the parent. Assume the assets of the subsidiary were acquired by means of a long-term loan. If these assets were translated at the rate ruling when they were acquired, and long-term loans at the rate ruling at the balance sheet date, then different rates would be being used to translate items that are interdependent. In this case the rationale for the closing rate method seems to make sense, in that it preserves this interrelationship.

However, there is one major conceptual flaw in this approach. By consolidating the subsidiary using the current (closing) exchange rate the assets of the subsidiary will be 'imported' into the group accounts at current values. This represents some form of hidden revaluation. According to the purchasing power parity theory, exchange rates move in response to inflation and the use of current rates for fixed assets means that an inflation adjustment is being automatically built in to the group accounts. In terms of pure historical cost accounting, it is not acceptable to revalue some assets and not others. Revaluation should be applied systematically and not on the haphazard basis of currency inflation. Surely in this instance the correct rate ought to be the historic rate!

Comparison of temporal method and closing rate method

Temporal method

The following example will be used to illustrate the main differences.

 ### Example

A UK company invests $6m in a US subsidiary on 1 January 2009. The subsidiary borrows $4 from a local bank and buys assets for $10m. At 31 December 2009 the US subsidiary made a profit of $1m.

During the year to 31 December 2009, the exchange rates moved as follows:

At 1 January 2009	£1 = £1.8
Average for the year	£1 = £1.5
At 31 December 2009	£1 = £1.4

The balance sheet of the subsidiary in 'local' currency at the start and end of the period will be as follows:

	At start		At end
	$000		$000
Assets	10,000		10,000
		Monetary assets	2,500
		Monetary liabilities	(1,500)
			11,000
Long-term loan	(4,000)		(4,000)
	6,000		7,000
Share capital	6,000		6,000
Retained profit	0		1,000
	6,000		7,000

As far as the subsidiary is concerned, this is quite a good set of results. Net assets have increased by 17% from $6,000 to $7,000. Now consider the situation when the results of the subsidiary are translated using the temporal method:

	At start		At end	Rate
	£000		£000	
Assets	5,555		5,555	1.8
		Monetary assets	1,786	1.4
		Monetary liabilities	(1,071)	1.4
			6,270	
Long-term loan	(2,222)		(2,857)	1.4
	3,333		3,413	
Share capital	3,333		3,333	
Retained profit	0		667	1.5
	3,333	Exchange loss	(587)	
			3,413	

When translated, the results do not look nearly so good. Net assets have only grown by a modest 2.4% in comparison with the 17% shown in the local currency accounts. Why has this situation arisen? The reason is that the long-term loan has been translated at the current (closing) rate of 1.4 while the assets to which the loan relates have been translated at the historic rate of 1.8. This is because the assets and liabilities are viewed from the parent company viewpoint. Prudence requires that the growth in the liability be shown at current value if the liability is recognised, whereas the assets should be shown at historic cost. Should the liability also be shown on the same basis as the asset to which it relates, thus ignoring prudence, or should the asset be revalued?

This example of a local loan to finance the purchase of a local asset is common practice in international business. If the parent company had not borrowed but had invested $10m directly, then it would have experienced greater exposure to exchange rate movements. What has happened in this situation is that the company has acquired assets of $10m with a currency risk of $6m. The loan is balanced by the asset, since any rate change will affect the loan (liability) and the asset in opposite ways, so cancelling each other out. This has been referred to in the previous section as a currency hedge. The problem with the temporal method in this regard is that it fails to recognise the economic existence of the hedge in so much as the rate change is reflected in the accounts only in so far as it affects the liability and not where it affects the asset.

Closing rate (net investment) method

 Example

	At start £000		At end £000	Rate
Assets	5,555		7,142	1.4
		Monetary assets	1,786	1.4
		Monetary liabilities	(1,071)	1.4
			7,857	
Long-term loan	(2,222)		(2,857)	1.4
	3,333		5,000	
Share capital	3,333		3,333	
Retained profit	0		667	1.5
	3,333	Exchange gain	1,000	
			5,000	

The use of the closing rate method ties the rate change to both assets and liabilities, and so reflects the current exchange value for both.

Comparison of translated balance sheets at the end of the period:

	Temporal £000		Closing rate £000
Assets	5,555		7,142
Monetary assets	1,786		1,786
Monetary liabilities	(1,071)		(1,071)
	6,270		7,857
Long-term loan	(2,857)		(2,857)
	3,413		5,000
Share capital	3,333		3,333
Retained profit	667		667
Exchange loss	(587)	Exchange gain	1,000
	3,413		5,000

The numbers chosen in the example showed a picture of a situation in which sterling was weakening against the dollar. Under the temporal method, the impact was to show an increased liability.

Note that if the exchange rate had moved in the other direction, then the impact would have been the complete opposite. The asset would have remained at its 'old' sterling value, while the liability would have decreased. The exchange difference would have been positive. Under the net investment method, if this had been the case, both the asset and liability would have declined and so would have given a negative exchange difference.

Impact of exchange differences on performance

Using the example above to measure return on equity gives the following measures:

	Return on equity (%)
In local currency ($)	16.67
Temporal method	2.4
Closing rate method	50.0

Three different measures of performance are shown, depending on the method of translation chosen. From an interpretation point of view this can present problems for the analyst. The effect of translation differences can be highlighted in two ways.

1. The differences will be reflected in the analysis of fixed assets. When the closing rate method is used it will change the value of the assets. This change ought to be disclosed in the note to the fixed assets.

2. It is also important to look at the translation difference taken to reserves. Is it material?

In the accounting policy notes companies need to disclose the method used to translate foreign subsidiaries. The amounts written off must also be disclosed, showing details of what has been taken directly to equity. This will appear in the statement of changes in equity.

Hedging a net investment

A description of the mechanics of hedging was given in the introductory section. There is, however, a major loophole in IAS 21, concerned with currency hedges. It is likely that a multinational company will have investments in many countries. These investments will be denominated in many different currencies and will potentially be exposed to exchange rate movements. Multinational companies will try to minimise this exposure by borrowing in foreign currencies. If, for example, a UK company wants to invest in a subsidiary in the USA, it will try to borrow the money in the USA to finance the deal. The cash flow from the investment in the overseas subsidiary may be used to pay interest on the borrowing, and may ultimately be used to repay the debt. Any movement in the exchange rate will have no impact since both the loan and the investment will 'cancel' each other out.

Companies will hedge their investments and will borrow in those currencies that will reflect their future expected cash flows. As was indicated above, such borrowings will have to be translated into the functional currency using the closing rate, while the underlying investment will be translated at the historic rate. If this were the case, then the borrowing and the investment would not 'balance' out.

However, IAS 39 *Financial Instruments: Recognition and measurement*, allows any translation gains and losses on loans that are hedges to be taken directly to equity, without going through the income statement. Multinational companies, however, tend not to hedge individual investments, but rather take out a 'basket' of currency loans to hedge a 'basket' of investments. It is not possible therefore to link individual assets to individual loans. At the year end it is up to the company to disclose which items are trading debts and so will be taken to the income statement, and which are hedges. This system is clearly open to abuse.

Foreign operations in a high inflationary economy

This is a special situation and is subject to special rules under IAS 21. If the foreign operation is an autonomous unit and is based in an economy experiencing a very high rate of inflation, the closing rate method may distort the financial results of the foreign company. In particular, the tangible fixed assets may be severely understated. There are two ways of dealing with this problem:

1. adjust the financial statements in the local currency to take account of the impact of inflation before they are translated;

2.   assume that the overseas operation is an integral part of the parent company, and use the temporal method to translate the accounts.

While both approaches are in use, the first must be used where a company has an autonomous subsidiary in a country experiencing hyperinflation.

Overview

Group financial statements of multinational companies may contain information that is aggregated and contain a combination of financial statements denominated in many difference currencies. Where there are fluctuating exchange rates this gives rise to accounting problems in terms of the exchange rate to be used, and in the treatment of any gain or loss that arises on translation.

In terms of the accounting regulation, IAS 21 sets the functional currency of a foreign subsidiary, which is integrated with the operations of the parent, and for which the temporal method is more appropriate, to that of the parent. IAS 21 refers only to the closing rate method as the method to be used when translating financial statements of overseas subsidiaries into the presentation currency of the parent. Any difference on exchange arising is then treated as an adjustment to shareholders' equity.

Chapter summary

IAS 21 *The Effects of Changes in Foreign Exchange Rates*

- Where there are transactions denominated in foreign currencies, such transactions denominated in the 'local' currency need to be translated into the functional currency.
    - Business transactions are translated at the rate ruling at the date of the transaction.
    - Monetary items are translated at the rate ruling on the balance sheet date.
    - Any exchange differences, whether a gain or a loss, are taken to the income statement.
- For consolidation purposes there are two methods that have been put forward for translation purposes depending on the relationship between the parent and the subsidiary.
- If the subsidiary is seen to be an extension of the parent then the translation of the subsidiary is done as though the transactions were those of the parent itself. The method applied in this case has been referred to as the temporal method. Under this method a mixture of different rates will be applied.
    - Non-current assets are translated at the rate ruling when the asset was acquired.
    - Monetary items are translated at the rate ruling at the balance sheet date.
    - Revenues and expenses are translated at the average rate for the period.
    - Any exchange differences are taken to the consolidated income statement.
- If the subsidiary is seen to be an independent entity, then the method of translation applied is referred to as the closing rate (net investment) method. Under this method:
    - assets and liabilities are translated at the rate ruling at the balance sheet date, the closing rate
    - revenues and expenses are translated (usually) at the average rate for the period
    - any exchange differences arising are shown as a separate component of equity.
- While the closing rate method preserves the relationship between assets and liabilities within the balance sheet of the company, there may be a problem with assets that have been 'revalued' in terms of the foreign currency exchange rate movement. Such 'revalued' assets will then be incorporated into a historical cost balance sheet, so the information given may be misleading.

Key terms for review

Definitions can be found in the glossary at the end of the book.

Translation	*Exchange difference*
Functional currency	*Hedge*
Presentation currency	*Local currency*
Transaction	*Temporal method*
Monetary items	*Closing rate method*
Non-monetary items	*Translation reserve*

Review questions

1. Distinguish between a company's *functional* currency and its *presentational* currency.
2. What factors should a company take into account when determining which is its functional currency?
3. Identify the circumstances under which IAS 21 permits the use of the closing rate method and the temporal method for translation of financial statements.

4.   Explain the differences in treatment and the effect of translating financial statements using the temporal and closing rate method.

5.   Explain what is meant by 'hedge accounting', and give an example of when a company may use a hedge transaction.

6.   Explain the difference between foreign currency translation and foreign currency conversion.

 # Exercises

1. Level 1

X Inc is a wholly owned US subsidiary of A plc and was acquired on 31 December 2007. The balance sheets of X are as follows:

	Dec 07	Dec 08
	$	$
Net assets	10,000	14,000
Share capital	4,000	4,000
Retained profit	6,000	10,000
	10,000	14,000
Income statement		
Revenues		10,000
Net revenues		6,000
Profit for the year		4,000

Exchange rates were as follows:

At 31 December 2007	£1 = $2.00
Average for year	£1 = $1.94
At 31 December 2008	£1 = $1.90

Required

(a)   Translate the balance sheet of X at 31 December 2008 into the presentation currency of the pound, for inclusion in the group accounts of A plc.

2. Level II

This extends the previous example. The balance sheet of X Inc one year on is added so that the statements for three years are as follows:

Balance sheet			
	Dec 07	Dec 08	Dec 09
	$	$	$
Net assets	10,000	14,000	19,000
Share capital	4,000	4,000	4,000
Retained profit	6,000	10,000	15,000
	10,000	14,000	19,000

Income statement	
Net revenues for the year	$5,000
Exchange rates were as follows:	
At 31 December 2007	£1 = $2.00
Average for 2008	£1 = $1.94
At 31 December 2008	£1 = $1.90
Average for 2009	£1 = $1.80
At 31 December 2009	£1 = $1.75

Required

Translate the balance sheet of X at 31 December 2009 into the presentation currency of the pound, for inclusion in the group accounts of A plc.

3. Level II

ABC plc is a trading company that has its head office in London and operates in the UK, Japan and eastern Europe. One of its investments is a wholly owned subsidiary company, XYZ Ltd, which is registered and operates in the Czech Republic. This subsidiary was acquired on the 1 April 2008 at which time the share capital and reserves amounted to 2.4 Czech crowns. During the year to 31 March 2009, XYZ Ltd made a profit of 600,000 crowns.

Exchange rate movements during the year to March 2009 were as follows:

- 1 April 2008   £1 = 41.8 crowns
- Average for year   £1 = 48.0 crowns
- 31 March 2009   £1 = 48.5 crowns.

Required

(a) Prepare a summary balance sheet of XYZ Ltd translated into the presentation currency (sterling) for inclusion in the group financial statements.
(b) Calculate the difference arising on exchange and explain how this difference has arisen.
(c) Explain how the accounting treatment of XYZ Ltd would have differed if its operations were a direct extension of the parent company rather than a separate independent operation.

4. Level II

Sterling Engineering acquired Pathfoot Products Ltd, a Latvian-based manufacturing company, on 31 March 2008. The balance sheets of the new company are given below. No new assets have been acquired by Pathfoot products since the date of acquisition.

	31 March 2008		31 March 2009	
	Lats (m)	Lats (m)	Lats (m)	Lats (m)
Fixed assets		24.5		20.3
Current assets				
Inventory	34.5		39.5	
Accounts receivable	24.2		15.8	
Cash	3.5	62.2	16.5	71.8
		86.7		92.1
Account payable		45.2		22.6
		41.5		69.5
Long-term loan		16.5		51.5
		25.0		18.0
Share capital		15.6		15.6
Reserves		7.0		7.0
Retained profit (loss)		2.4		(4.6)
		25.0		18.0

Income statement for the year ended 31 March 2009		
		Lats (m)
Sales		8.0
Cost of sales		
Opening inventory	34.5	
Purchases	10.0	
	44.5	
Closing inventory	39.5	5.0
		3.0
Other costs (including depreciation)		(10.0)
Loss for the year		(7.0)

Exchange rate movements

31 March 2008   £1 = 6.5 lats

Average for year   £1 = 7.8 lats

31 March 2009   £1 = 10.4 lats

Required

Translate the balance sheet of Pathfoot Products at 31 March 2009, together with the income statement, into:

(i) functional currency

(ii) presentation currency

in accordance with IAS 21.

5. Level II

The following are the summary accounts of Overseas Ltd, in foreign currency (limas).

Balance sheet as at 31 December 2009	
	Limas
Ordinary share capital	630,000
Retained profits	80,000
	710,000
Plant and machinery at cost	700,000
Less depreciation	70,000
	630,000
Stocks at cost	210,000
Net monetary current assets	40,000
	880,000
Less long-term loan	170,000
	710,000

Profit and loss account for year ended 31 December 2009		
		Limas
Cash sales		900,000
Less: cost of sales:		
Purchases	960,000	
Closing inventory	(210,000)	
	750,000	
Depreciation	70,000	
		820,000
Operating profit before tax		80,000

During the year the relevant exchange rates were:

	Limas to the £1
1 January 2009	14
Average for the year	12
Average at the acquisition of closing stock	11
31 December 2009	10

Your UK company, Sterling Ltd, had acquired Overseas Ltd on 1 January 2009 by subscribing £45,000 of share capital when the exchange rate was 14 limas to the £1. The long-term loan had been raised on the same date. On that day, Overseas Ltd had purchased the plant and equipment for 700,000 limas. It is being depreciated by the straight line method over ten years.

Required

(a) Translate the balance sheet and profit and loss account of Overseas Ltd into the functional currency.
(b) Translate the balance sheet and profit and loss account of Overseas Ltd into the presentation currency.
(c) For each of the requirements (a) and (b) above, provide a detailed explanation of any exchange difference that arises.

Further reading

IAS 21 *The Effects of Changes in Foreign Exchange Rates*. IASB, revised 1993.

Nobes, C. (1980) A review of the translation debate. *Accounting and Business Research*, 40, Autumn. London: ICAEW.

Revsine, L. (1987) The rationale underlying the functional currency choice. In R. Bloom and P.Y. Elgers (eds) *Accounting Theory and Policy*. Orlando: Harcourt Brace Jovanovich.

12

Interpretation of Financial Statements

Introduction

Interpretation of financial statements is probably one of the most interesting aspects of financial reporting, but will present many challenges. In order to judge the extent to which a company has performed over a number of years requires a good understanding of how the accounting numbers have been compiled and also what can cause an accounting number to change.

Having gained an understanding of the individual figures making up a set of financial statements, it is now appropriate to consider these individual figures in the overall context of a set of financial statements. A constant theme throughout this text is that decision making is the main use to which financial statements are put. In order to make decisions based on financial statement information there must be standards, budgets, expectations or benchmarks against which the reported financial information is compared and assessed. The study of such relationships, interpretation of financial statements, is the subject of this chapter.

In particular this chapter describes the techniques of analysis available, including horizontal, vertical and ratio analysis, to evaluate a company's performance. It will evaluate these techniques and develop an understanding of how the accounting numbers interact with each other to give an indication of the financial health of a company.

Section 1: Basic Principles

Interpretation of financial statements is useful in providing information for decision making. For example:

- How much would a bank be prepared to lend to the company?
- Would an investor be prepared to buy shares in the company?
- Should a supplier be willing to supply goods to the company?

These kinds of questions can be answered, to an extent, by using accounting information. However, it is important to realise at the outset that the technique of interpretation can be used in conjunction with any additional information available that is not necessarily disclosed in the financial statements – for example, general economic conditions, inflation, state of the industry.

The application of financial statement analysis provides only part of the information used by decision makers. In order to produce a good analysis, what is needed is an enquiring frame of mind. What exactly do the accounting numbers tell? In order to build up a methodology for analysis, it is useful to start with a general overview of the company.

12.1 The interpretation process

There are various 'tools' available to the user in the interpretation process. Techniques such as horizontal analysis, vertical analysis and ratio analysis can all be used to extract data from a set of financial statements. The best 'tool' is, however, to have an inquisitive and enquiring frame of mind.

In practice, before applying any specialist techniques the interpretation process should begin with a general overview of the financial statements to be analysed. This will allow the figures to be put into context – for example, have sales increased/decreased? Has the overdraft gone up/reduced? What is particularly important at this stage is to remember that a company does not operate in a vacuum; the reported figures must be put in context of the wider economy and, in particular, the economic conditions that persist in the industry of which the company is a part.

General overview

Information disclosed in financial reports may relate to an individual company or to a group of companies. This information will show, for example:

- different kinds of assets and how they are financed
- relationship between items (e.g. debt/shareholders' funds, current assets/current liabilities)
- level of sales and profits
- earnings per share, dividends.

From the information given in the financial statements of a company it is possible to get an overview of how successful the company has been over the period under review. The main financial statements need to be examined but it is important to note that any analysis must be set in context. It is important to:

- compare like with like in terms of companies in the same industry – it is not much use comparing a company in the retail sector with one in the manufacturing sector; any analysis would be flawed
- it is also a good idea to compare with industry norms, to ensure that the comparison is like with like.

In terms of the information provided, two broad techniques of analysis are available: horizontal analysis and vertical analysis.

Horizontal analysis

The is where trends can be examined over a number of accounting periods. Horizontal analysis is useful where comparisons are for periods greater than two years. Companies do publish historical summaries covering five years, and in some cases, ten years.

Consider the following example.

 ## *Example*

	Year 1	Year 2	Year 3	Year 4	Year 5
Sales (£m)	630	819	1,046	1,298	1,562
Profit	45	48	56	73	94
Net assets	500	600	700	850	900
Dividends	2	4	5	6	8

These figures do not give an immediate indication of how well, for example, the company's sales performance is. In order to get a better picture of movements in numbers, indexing may be used.

The way indexing works is that a base year is chosen, and this is set at 100. All the other figures are then adjusted to correspond with this figure. So if Year 1 is chosen as the base year, the £630 sales figure is set equal to 100. The corresponding numbers are adjusted as follows.

If £630 = 100, then the Year 2 sales of £819 will be equal to:
£819 × 100 / £630 = 130

Each sales figure is then related to the base year of Year 1.
Year 3 sales will be equal to:

£1046 × 100 / 630 = 166

So a table can be compiled as follows:
Year 1 = 100

	Year 1	Year 2	Year 3	Year 4	Year 5
Sales	100	130	166	206	248

In terms of how the information is presented it is much easier to see the growth in sales. However, care should be taken when looking at growth rates. In the above example, although sales are growing, the rate of growth year on year may not be growing. Continuing with the above example:

Example	Year 1	Year 2	Year 3	Year 4	Year 5
Sales	100	130	166	206	248
Increase over previous year		30	36	40	42
% increase over previous year		30%	28%	24%	20%

This shows that, although there is a growth in sales over the five-year period, the rate of growth is slowing down, from 30% in Year 1 to only 20% in the final period.

In addition to this, there are some problems with historical summaries.

- There is nothing to compare them with, so they suffer from a lack of comparability
- The information given is not audited so there is no independent verification of the numbers contained in the historical summary.
- If the company changes an accounting policy – for example, on revaluation – there is no indication as to how this accounting policy change affects the accounting numbers.

- If the company acquires a new subsidiary during the year, it may be difficult to detect this since acquisitions are not always reported.
- The figures give will not be adjusted to take account of inflation, although this can be done as a separate exercise using some inflation index, such as the Retail Price Index.
- The information contained in a historical summary is not mandatory, so directors can choose its contents. Information given in historical summaries is not standard across companies.

Vertical analysis

While year-on-year analysis tends to work year on year, comparing each item with the previous year to get the percentage change, or as was indicated above to see the trend in a particular item, it is also possible to work vertically: vertical analysis. This is done by equating the total to 100 and then producing what are known as 'common size' statements. This can be done for both balance sheets and income statements. The following example illustrates a common size statement for a balance sheet. The individual balance sheet figures are shown as a percentage of the total net assets of the company.

 Example

Balance sheet as at . . .		
	£000	% of total net assets
Fixed assets		
Land	32,300	127
Machinery	3,100	12
Vehicles	9,500	38
	44,900	177
Current assets		
Stock	8,600	34
Debtors	2,600	10
Cash	600	2
	11,800	46
Current liabilities		
Creditors	17,700	70
Net current liabilities	(5,900)	(24)
Total assets less current liabilities	39,000	153
Long-term loan	(13,700)	(53)
Net assets	25,300	100
Share capital	20,000	79
Reserves	5,300	21
	25,300	100

This method has some advantages in that inter-company comparison is made easier since the items in the financial statements are reduced to a common scale. This shows more clearly any changes in the financial structure of the company. Vertical analysis can be used over several years to show how the sales and profitability pattern, or the financial structure of a company, is changing.

Section 2: Intermediate Issues

Once a general overview of the company is undertaken using trend analysis, it is possible to do a more detailed analysis using accounting ratios. These ratios will direct the focus of the user to highlight areas of good and bad performance, and identify any significant change. Once change has been identified this is only the first step: it is very important to know the reason why the change has taken place.

12.2 Ratio analysis

Ratios describe the relationship between different accounting numbers in the financial statements. At the outset it is important to note that some ratios are more useful than others, so care must be taken in interpreting these, otherwise the results may be misleading. It is also important to set the ratios in context. A ratio by itself will be meaningless. Ratios need to be compared with:

■   the same ratios in the preceding period
■   budgeted ratios for the same period
■   ratios for other companies in the same sector.

In order that comparison is possible it is important to compare 'like with like'. The precise implications of a given ratio are only possible if it is accompanied by a clear definition of its constituent parts. Before the reliability of a ratio can be assessed, the reliability of the underlying business operations must be ascertained.

The definitions of ratios themselves may vary. There is no universal definition of an accounting ratio. No accounting standards have ever been published on the subject of ratios. Other textbooks may give different definitions of the same ratios. What is important is to ensure that when calculating ratios a consistent approach is used.

Purpose of ratio analysis

The annual financial statements of an organisation can provide a lot of financial information that is difficult to interpret. Looking at the income statement, this may show an increase in profit before tax. However, this does not mean that the company is making efficient use of all its resources. In general ratio analysis has the following uses:

■   it helps to review the performance of an organisation over time
■   it makes it possible to compare the performance of an organisation with that of its competitors
■   it makes it possible to compare the performance of an organisation with the industry average
■   it enables any problems within a company to be highlighted and corrective action can then be taken.

Ratio analysis is a useful tool for any of the stakeholders in an organisation. For example, a supplier may want to ensure that any new customer will be able to pay for goods and services. The liquidity of the business will be important in this context. The efficiency of an organisation in generating profits will be of interest to potential shareholders. Lenders will be interested in the risk of the organisation, to ensure that the business is not overexposed to long-term debt and can afford to meet any interest payments when they become due. Management of the business will be interested in those ratios that highlight the efficiency of the business.

BASIC

INTERMEDIATE

ADVANCED

Limitations of accounting data

Before looking in detail at the various ratios commonly used to analyse financial statements, it is perhaps appropriate to look at their limitations, which arise mainly from the limitations that are inherent in the accounting data being used.

Our studies thus far in the course have shown that there is scope for differences in accounting treatment for the same transaction, which can lead to tremendous variation in reported figures. For example, the use of the straight line method of providing for depreciation can give a significantly different charge from that obtained by using the reducing balance method. In addition, account must be taken of the distortions that may arise when comparing accounts based on historic cost principles and where one company has chosen to revalue its assets. The figures contained in financial statements themselves can contain assumptions and estimates that can be very subjective.

In practice it is not always possible to obtain all the required accounting information in order to calculate a desired ratio. As has been seen, the content and presentation of limited company financial statements are summarised and prescribed, and it may not be possible to extract the required information to prepare the ratio.

Moreover, the use of year-end figures extracted from financial statements may not be representative of the year as a whole; many companies choose a quiet time of year for their year end, and consequently stock, debtor and creditor levels may be uncharacteristically low. Any seasonal factors may be missed entirely.

Problems can also arise due to the time lag in preparation and publication of the accounts following a company's year end. Unless information is available in a timely fashion it may be too late to take corrective or preventative actions.

Finally, traditional accounting statements deal only with those items that are measurable in money terms and therefore cannot disclose important facts that are not monetary (e.g. a loyal workforce).

Limitations of ratio analysis

It is important to note that the ratios in themselves are of little informational benefit; it is only when they are compared against other years or other firms, or perhaps against budgeted figures or other profit centres within a firm, that they provide the information necessary to interpret what has happened and to predict what will happen. Problems often arise with inter-temporal analysis in establishing a normal base year with which to compare other years, or in selecting an industry norm if inter-firm comparisons are being attempted.

It is important that like-for-like comparisons are made. In the case of inter-temporal analysis this should be readily achievable but care will still need to be taken to ensure that no changes in accounting policy have taken place that could distort the results. In addition, changes in technology make time comparisons difficult where prices and asset efficiency have changed – what was once an acceptable ratio may not be now.

International comparisons can be even more problematic as there is the added problem of the different accounting policies that may exist in different countries.

In the case of inter-firm comparisons within the same industry, provided that each company uses exactly the same basis in calculating ratios, this provides a controlled and objective means of evaluation. This is because every company is subject to identical economic and market conditions in the review period and this therefore allows a much truer comparison than a single company's fluctuating results over several years.

The precise implication of a given ratio is possible only if it is accompanied by a clear definition of its constituent parts. Unfortunately, the use of accounting information in published accounts is generally summarised and there may not be sufficiently detailed information available to calculate the ratios required. In addition, the definitions of ratios themselves may vary from source to source as they are not universally defined.

Finally, it must be remembered that ratios only identify symptoms and not causes of problems and, as such, must be used in conjunction with other available information.

12.3 The use of ratios in practice

Having collected the data, the information provided by the ratios can be used to interpret what has happened and to predict what will happen.

As noted earlier, ratios in themselves provide little informational benefit. They need to be compared against other years' ratios, other companies' ratios, budgeted ratios or against other profit centres within the same firm.

This comparison of ratios will direct attention to key areas requiring analysis, and identify areas of good and bad performance. The ratios may highlight areas of significant change, and provide an indication of the profitability and cash position of a company.

By highlighting areas of good and bad performance, ratios can assist management in identifying where their strengths and weaknesses are and where further effort should be directed. Ratios help in identifying the success or otherwise of particular choices of action as comparison can be made of the pre- and post-action results. Although there can be differences in accounting treatment of particular items between different companies, such variations should not exist when making inter-temporal comparison and therefore a comparison of like for like can be made. The use of historic costs can also be overcome in certain circumstances and current values used to replace outdated asset values.

While ratios in themselves are of little benefit, ratio analysis as a technique should not be used in isolation either. It is essential that the findings are incorporated into an overall analysis. It is necessary to establish *why* there has been a change and not simply identify that there *has* been a change. Any interpretation or analysis must be taken in context with all the other available information about the company and its environment. Companies do not operate in a vacuum and are instead part of the industries in which they operate, the economy and, indeed, the world economy. As such, the sources of information available with which to assist in any analysis are numerous.

Accounting ratios

The accounting ratios most often used can be grouped as follows:

- profitability
- liquidity
- management (or activity)
- risk.

In order to illustrate the calculation and interpretation of the ratios, the following example will be used.

Example

Choclatier Ltd is a company that makes luxury confectionery. The following is a summarised extract from the financial statements of the company.

Income statements for the year ended 30 June			
	Notes	2009 £000	2008 £000
Turnover		6,200	5,800
Cost of sales		(4,800)	(4,600)
Gross profit		1,400	1,200
Operating expenses		(668)	(650)
Operating profit		732	550
Net interest payable	1	(45)	(30)
Profit before tax		687	520
Tax		(180)	(91)
Profit after tax		507	429
Dividend		(40)	(20)
Retained profit for the year		467	409

Balance sheets as at 30 June			
		2009 £000	2008 £000
Fixed assets			
Intangible fixed assets		200	200
Tangible fixed assets		1,400	1,100
		1,600	1,300
Current assets			
Inventory		400	350
Accounts receivable	2	1,825	1,721
Cash		3	120
Creditors: amounts falling due within one year	3	(1640)	(1,790)
Net current assets		588	401
Total assets less current liabilities		2,188	1,701
Creditors: amounts falling due after one year			
12% debentures		(250)	(250)
Provision for liabilities and charges	4	(40)	(20)
Total net assets		1,898	1,431
Capital and reserves			
Share capital		450	450
Share premium		120	120
Retained profit		1,328	861
		1,898	1,431

Notes to the accounts

Note 1: interest

Payable on overdrafts and other loans	17	10
Payable on debentures	30	30
Receivable on short-term deposits	(2)	(10)
	45	30

Note 2: accounts receivable

Amounts falling due within one year		
Trade receivables	1,590	1,537
Prepayments	190	90
	1,780	1,627
Amounts falling due after one year		
Trade receivables	25	80
Prepayments	20	14
	45	94
Total receivables	1,825	1,721

Note 3: payables

Trade payables	1,200	1,090
Accruals	141	560
Taxation	210	75
Other taxes	89	65
	1,640	1,790

Note 4: provisions for liabilities and charges

Deferred tax	40	20

When analysing the financial performance of an organisation it is rarely possible to produce a good analysis without making use of the notes to the accounts in addition to the income statement and the balance sheet. Ratios will give a better analysis if the numbers used in them are meaningful.

Profitability ratios

The most commonly calculated ratios that consider the profitability and trading activities of an organisation are:

- return on capital employed (ROCE)
- return on shareholders' capital
- net profit margin
- asset turnover
- gross margin.

Return on capital employed (*ROCE*)

Return on capital employed (ROCE) measures the return made by the organisation from using its capital resources. This is sometimes referred to as the primary ratio and gives an indication of how efficient the organisation is at generating profits from its capital. It is calculated by:

$$\frac{\text{Profit before interest and taxation (PBIT)}}{\text{Capital employed}} \times 100\ \%$$

Capital employed refers to the funds provided by shareholders and long-term lenders. It will include provision for liabilities and charges as these are essentially long-term debt, and also minority interest. It can be measured from both sides of the balance sheet, viz:

Total assets less current liabilities

or

Share capital + reserves + creditors (due more than 1 year) + minority interests + provisions for liabilities and charges.

For Choclatier Ltd, in the above example, the ROCE will be calculated as follows:

2009	2008
$\frac{£732}{£2,188} \times 100$	$\frac{£550}{£1,701} \times 100$
33%	32%

These figures indicate that an investment in this organisation gives a higher return than that available from, say, a deposit account. So from that point of view these ratios are good. However, one major problem with ROCE is that it is particularly sensitive to the valuation of the fixed assets of the organisation. A company that does not revalue assets on a regular basis will show a high ROCE. If the assets were to be shown at market value (assuming it is higher than original cost) then the ROCE will fall. It is important when making comparisons therefore to adjust for any differences in valuation policies.

The question is whether the bank overdraft of a company is being used to partly finance its long-term activities. If so, then it ought to be included as part of capital employed.

As well as looking at the movement from previous years and comparing it with other organisations, the analyst may compare the calculated ROCE with commercial bank deposit rates. If the ROCE is higher than these rates, then the company is making a better return from trading than it would have had it (theoretically) invested its capital in deposit accounts.

Overall, ROCE will be improved by reducing costs and increasing sales, which will improve the PBIT part of the ratio.

In terms of how useful the measure is, it should be noted that:

- if the return is low, then it may be wiped out if there is a downturn in the fortunes of the company or in the economy
- in terms of the cost of borrowing, if ROCE is lower then any increase in borrowing will reduce earnings per share (EPS)
- it can be a useful guide in assessing possible acquisitions; if potential ROCE is not good, then it would not be a good idea to go ahead with the acquisition
- any persistent low ROCE for any part of a business may suggest it should be disposed of (provided it is not an integral part of the business).

It is useful to note the effect on the ratio of acquiring a new subsidiary. In accordance with acquisition accounting, the total assets of subsidiary will be included but only profits since date of acquisition (post-acquisition) will be included. In a year in which an acquisition is made, ROCE may fall.

Return on shareholders' capital (ROSC)

Return on shareholders capital (ROSC) is similar to ROCE but considers the profit made by the company in relation to the capital contributed by shareholders. Note that the long-term debt and the costs associated with this are excluded. The ratio is calculated as follows:

$$\frac{\text{Profit after interest but before tax}}{\text{Shareholders' funds}} \times 100$$

For Choclatier, the ratio is as follows:

2009	2008
$\frac{£687}{£1,898} \times 100$	$\frac{£520}{£1,431} \times 100$
36%	36%

Shareholders in this instance should be satisfied with what appears to be a healthy return on their invested capital. However, it would be necessary to compare with similar ratios from competitors and the industry average to determine whether or not this ROCE is as healthy as it appears.

Net profit margin

Net profit margin simply considers PBIT as a percentage of sales and is calculated as follows:

$$\frac{\text{PBIT (profit before interest and tax)}}{\text{Sales}} \times 100$$

Generally, low margins show poor performance, but care needs to be taken in interpreting this, since low margins:

■ may be set by management to increase market share
■ may be caused by expansion costs (new product launching).

On the other hand, high margins show good performance, but may mean that the company will attract competition.

Note that the trading profit margins are important since both management and investment analysts tend to base their forecasts of future profitability on projected turnover multiplied by estimated future margins.

For Choclatier, net profit margin is as follows:

2009	2008
$\frac{£732}{£6,200} \times 100$	$\frac{£550}{£5,800} \times 100$
= 11.8%	10%

Asset turnover

Before interpreting the net profit margin ratio is it important also to calculate the asset turnover ratio. Asset turnover is calculated as:

$$\frac{\text{Turnover}}{\text{Capital employed}}$$

The answer this time is not a percentage, but the number of times turnover exceeds capital employed. This ratio provides useful information about the efficiency of the company at generating sales from its capital. However, it is important to examine the underlying causes of any change in this ratio. For example, any increase in asset turnover may be due to various factors, such as:

■ *An increase in sales*: if so, then this is acceptable since the company will be generating a higher turnover so using the asset base efficiently.

- *A reduction in capital employed* will increase asset turnover, but this would not be acceptable since this would imply a failure by the company to maintain its asset base, so there may be problems arising in the future.
- *A drop in stock level*: again this would not be a good indicator of financial health.

In addition to this it is important to watch out for signs of overtrading. Overtrading occurs when a business expands too rapidly on an insufficient capital base. More on this later.

For Choclatier, asset turnover is as follows:

	2009	2008
	$\dfrac{£6.200}{£2,188}$	$\dfrac{£5,800}{£1,701}$
=	2.83 times	3.41 times

Profit margin and asset turnover ratios are, in essence, subdivisions of the ROCE:

ROCE	=	Net profit margin	×	Asset turnover
$\dfrac{\text{PBIT}}{\text{Capital employed}} \times 100$	=	$\dfrac{\text{PBIT}}{\text{Turnover}} \times 100$	×	$\dfrac{\text{Turnover}}{\text{Capital employed}}$
For 2009				
33%	=	11.8%	×	2.83

This indicates that there is a trade-off between net profit margin and asset turnover. Consequently some companies can afford to squeeze profit margins if they are certain that they can achieve consistent and high levels of sales. Two separate companies could have the same ROCE but quite different profit margins and asset turnovers. The following example will illustrate this.

Example

	Company A	Company B
Capital employed	£100	£100
Turnover	£500	£200
Profit before interest and tax	£50	£50
ROCE	50%	50%
Net profit margin	10%	25%
Asset turnover	5 times	2 times

Although company A has a lower profit margin that company B, A uses its assets more efficiently. A has a higher asset turnover. B will make a great profit per item sold but will sell fewer goods during the year. This example is typical of food retailers: A could be an example of a supermarket, whereas B could be an example of a more specialised food shop with few outlets.

For Choclatier, net profit margin has increased from 10% to 11.8% but this has been offset by a decline in asset turnover, which has declined from 3.41 times to 2.83 times: a fall of 17%. The increase in the available capital has not been matched by an equivalent increase in sales. This implies that the efficiency of the management at generating sales from available resources has fallen over the last year. On the basis of sales made, Choclatier has improved its profit per item sold.

Gross margin

Gross margin measures the ability of the business to sell goods for more than they cost to make. However, it is not always possible to calculate this ratio given the information published in the statutory financial statements. It is calculated as follows:

$$\frac{\text{Gross profit}}{\text{Turnover}} \times 100$$

It is to be expected that this ratio will remain fairly stable over time. Competitors are likely to show similar gross margins. If this ratio is declining, then it may mean that the company is unable to control its production costs or achieve an optimum sales price or sales quantity.

For Choclatier the gross margin is as follows:

	2009	2008
	$\frac{£1,400}{£6,200} \times 100$	$\frac{£1,200}{£5,800} \times 100$
=	23%	21%

The figures show that the gross margin has increased from 21% to 23%, an improvement of nearly 10% over the period. This increase may have arisen from the rationalisation of production costs or perhaps from a sales contract with a good sales value.

Liquidity ratios

The ratios most often calculated when assessing the liquidity of a company are:

- current ratio
- liquidity ratio.

These ratios are designed to provide information regarding the ability of the company to meet its short-term commitments when they fall due. Liquidity is crucial for the survival of an organisation. Organisations can survive even if they make losses (at least in the short to medium term), but an organisation cannot survive without cash.

Current ratio

Current ratio looks at the working capital of the business. It asseses the ability of the company to meet its short-term debts. The thinking behind this is that the company could in theory sell its current assets to pay its current liabilities.

The ratio is calculated as follows: current assets : current liabilities.

This ratio is a broad indicator of a company's short-term financial position. A prudent ratio is usually given as 2 : 1, but this should be treated with caution since the ideal level will depend on the type of business.

Rather than focusing on the actual number, it is more important to consider the trend in this ratio over time. What should the ratio be? There is no simple rule to apply. It is important to consider the nature of the business in which the company is engaged, the quality of the current assets, and how volatile working capital requirements are. Some businesses may survive on a lower current ratio. Supermarkets can operate and survive comfortably with a current ratio of less that 0.5 : 1. This is because supermarkets have a regular cash inflow. Companies in heavy engineering, on the other hand, may operate with a level greater than this because of high levels of work in progress.

The most informative feature is the trend from year to year. An increasing ratio may not necessarily be a good sign: it may show excessive stocks or a very large amount of cash that could be put to better use. A continuing decline in the ratio is a warning signal that should not be ignored.

The current ratio of Choclatier is calculated as follows:

	2009	2008
CA : CL	£2,183 : £1,640	£2,097 : £1,790
=	1.33 : 1	1.17 : 1

Receivables due after one year have been excluded.

The figures show that the current ratio of Choclatier appears to be reasonable. The ratio has increased from 1.17 to 1.33, but this hides the fact that the company has considerably less cash in 2009 than in 2008, as is apparent from the balance sheet.

Liquidity ratio

Not all current assets are readily converted into cash to meet debts (e.g. stock and work in progress may take time to convert into cash). The liquidity ratio sometimes called the 'acid test' or 'quick ratio', recognises this, eliminates stock and applies the 'acid test' to see what would happen if the company had to settle all its creditors straight away. If the current ratio is less than 1: 1 it would not be able to do so.

The liquid ratio is calculated as follows:

current assets less stock : current liabilities

Some companies which normally sell for cash (e.g. supermarkets), may operate with a quick ratio of less than 1: 1. In fact some supermarket chains have a liquidity ratio of around 0.15 : 1. It is also worth noting that neither the current ratio nor the liquidity ratio take into account any overdraft limit the company may have. The fact that the organisation can have access to liquid funds (not apparent from the balance sheet) can significantly change the overall view of the liquidity of the organisation.

However, there are problems indicated if the ratio is poorer when compared to other companies or if there is a declining trend in the ratio. A low and declining ratio often indicates a rising overdraft, so it is important to consider the bank's position.

As far as Choclatier is concerned, the liquid ratio is:

	2009	2008
CA – Stock : CL	£1,783 : £1,640	£1,747 : £1,790
=	1.09 : 1	1 0.98 : 1

As with the current ratio, there is nothing to suggest that there are any problems with liquidity.

If there are liquidity problems it would be important for the analyst to examine the cash flow statement. This statement would let the analyst see if there are any potential problems with the movement of cash.

While the cash flow statement might highlight a deteriorating cash situation it still does not tell the analyst how near the company is to its overdraft limit. Nor does it give any indication of whether any of the borrowing agreements have been broken or whether the bank is happy with the situation. There is some further discussion of the cash flow statement in the advanced section of this chapter.

Activity ratios

Activity ratios are designed to provide some information about the efficiency with which management controls the business. The ratios that are considered most helpful are:

- stock (or inventory) turnover
- collection period for receivables
- payment period for payables.

Stock turnover

Also known as inventory turnover, this ratio calculates how quickly the company is turning over its stock during the year. This can give an indication of slow-moving stocks, or how efficient the stock control policy of the company is. The ratio is calculated as follows:

$$\frac{\text{Cost of sales}}{\text{Stock}}$$

It is better to use the average stock figure for this ratio, but the year-end figure would be acceptable. Again different industries will show different numbers for stock turnover. For example, a company in heavy engineering may have a stock turnover of 1, whereas a company in the retail industry may have a stock turnover of 10.

Again it is the trend in the number that is important. A decrease in the ratio may highlight a slowdown in trading or a build-up in the levels of stock, which would indicate that too much money may be tied up in stock.

As an alternative to the rate of stock turnover, it is possible to calculate the number of days stock is held for. This is done as follows:

$$\text{Stock days} = \frac{\text{Stock}}{\text{Cost of sales}} \times 365$$

Adding together the number of debtor days and stock days gives an indication of how long it takes the company to convert stock into cash. A continual increase in this number could indicate liquidity problems.

Stock turnover of Choclatier:

	2009	2008
	£4,800	£4,600
	£400	£350
=	12 times	13 times

Stock turnover has fallen from 13 to 12, which may be as a result of a slowdown in demand for the product. It is important to monitor the trend in this since, if the ratio continues to fall, this would be an indication of serious problems for the company.

Collection period for receivables

The collection period of receivables ratio measures how effective the business is in collecting its debts. The ratio is a measure of how many days' credit customers are taking to pay. It is calculated as follows:

$$\frac{\text{Accounts receivable}}{\text{Credit sales}} \times 365$$

In calculating this ratio, problems can arise in what should be included – for example:

- should the average or year-end receivables be used?
- should credit sales or total sales be used?
- should total receivables be used, or only those due within one year?

As before, it is the trend that is important here. If the ratio is seen to be continually increasing over time, this could be an indication of a problem with credit control and with bad debts. On the other hand, a falling collection period is generally a good sign, but could reflect a shortage of cash and may be as a result of debtors being pressured to pay or extra discounts being given for prompt payment.

Other factors to consider when interpreting this ratio are as follows:

- What is the composition of debtors? Is there an undue proportion of debt due from one major customer? If so, what would happen if this customer had problems paying?
- What would be the impact on debtors if one or two of the debtors failed to pay?
- What is the age pattern of debtors? How long have some of the debts been outstanding?
- Is there adequate provision for bad and doubtful debts?

Collection period for Choclatier:

	2009	2008
	$\frac{£1,615}{£6,200} \times 365$	$\frac{£1,617}{£5,800} \times 365$
=	95 days	102 days

This ratio includes long-term debtors.

If the long-term debtors were excluded, the collection period still appears to be rather high (although this needs to be compared to the industry as a whole). The 2009 figure is better than the previous year's, but there is still an indication of poor credit control. It may also mean that there are significant bad debts, but this is not apparent from the financial information.

It is sometimes helpful to see how much cash could be released if the collection period was reduced. So if the company reduced the collection period from 95 days to, say, 70 days how much cash would be released? The debtor days figure is reduced by 25 days. The value of one day's sales is calculated by dividing the year-end debtor of £1,615 by 95. So the value of 25 days' sales is:

$$\frac{£1,615}{95} \times 25 = £425$$

So Choclatier could release approximately £425,000 if it reduced the collection period from 95 days to 70 days.

Payment period for payables

The **payment period for payables** (or payment period taken) ratio calculates how many days credit the business is taking from suppliers. This ratio is calculated as follows:

$$\frac{\text{Trade payables}}{\text{Credit purchases}} \times 365$$

The figure for credit purchases is often difficult to obtain and the cost of sales figure is often used as a substitute.

As has been stated before, it is the trend in the ratio that is important. A steady increase in the ratio may highlight the fact that the company is making better use of interest-free credit, or it could be that the business has no cash to pay its suppliers. It just might mean that the business is taking longer to pay its suppliers, which may damage its credit standing.

Payment period of Choclatier:

	2009	2008
=	$\frac{£1,200}{£4,800} \times 365$	$\frac{£1,090}{£4,600} \times 365$
	91 days	86 days

Given that the cost of sales has been used for this calculation the ratio is only approximate. Note that the company is taking longer to collect debts than it is to pay debts. This means the company is a net provider of funds: not good working capital management. It would also help to quantify any changes in cash terms (as was the case with the receivables).

Risk ratios

In general shareholders and lenders will be interested in those ratios that provide a measure of risk. If a company if financed partly by borrowing, it will be exposed to a degree of risk. The higher the borrowing the higher will be the exposure to risk. This is because interest must be paid whether or not a company has made profits. The ratios considered most useful in this connection are:

- gearing ratio, and
- interest cover.

Gearing ratio

Gearing is concerned with the capital structure of the company and has been defined in a number of ways. The intention of gearing is to show what proportion of the assets of the company has been financed by lenders rather than shareholders.

There are different ways of calculating the gearing ratio, but they all measure the proportion of capital employed that is borrowed. The problem is in defining what is meant by 'capital employed' and what is meant by 'borrowing'. There are two generally accepted ways of measuring gearing:

1. Debt/equity
   Debt   Interest-bearing loans + preference share capital (include short-term borrowing
              where interest is payable, e.g. bank overdraft)
   Equity   Ordinary shareholders' funds (i.e. share capital + reserves + minorities)

2. Debt/capital employed
   Debt is same as in (1) above
   Capital employed   Shareholders' funds + minority interest + provisions + all long-
                        and short-term borrowing + preference shares (if redeemable)

In both of the above definitions, preference shareholders have essentially been classified as debt rather than equity. Strictly speaking, preference shareholders are not really debt. However, the holders of preference shares do have a prior claim on the profits and net assets of the company over the ordinary shareholder. Preference shares are therefore included in order to show the risks the ordinary shareholders are exposed to.

Which is the better measure? 'It depends' would be the obvious answer. The debt/equity ratio is a more sensitive measure of gearing. That said, high gearing is risky, while low gearing may provide scope to increase borrowing. The higher the level of gearing, the greater the risk that there will not be enough profits available for dividend payments to shareholders. In addition, the more highly geared a company is, the more sensitive it is to changes in interest rates. If interest rates increase, then highly geared companies will have a higher interest charge to pay, and so profits may suffer. However, the converse is also true. If interest rates fall, then profits of a highly geared company will improve and so shareholders will gain.

Also, in periods of profit fluctuation, a highly geared company will experience a much greater impact with regard to this. Consider the following example.

Example: gearing effect

The capital structure of two companies, A and B, is given as:

	Company A	Company B
Share capital	600	200
Reserves	300	300
	900	500
Long-term borrowing (10%)	100	500
	1,000	1,000

Gearing ratios:

(a) Debt/equity

$$\frac{£100}{£900} \times 100 \qquad \frac{£500}{£500} \times 100$$

$$11\% \qquad\qquad 100\%$$

(b) Debt/capital employed

$$\frac{£100}{£1,000} \times \qquad \frac{£500}{£1,000} \times 100$$

$$10\% \qquad\qquad 50\%$$

Company A would be a low-geared company, while company B is a high-geared company. A further analysis of Company A shows the following income statements for two years:

	Year 1	Year 2
Profit (before interest)	£100	£80
Interest	£10	£10
	£90	£70
Less taxation (assume 30%)	£27	£21
	£63	£49

This shows that, when profits fall from £100 to £80 (20%), the profit after taxation is only marginally affected: falls from £63 to £49 (22%). However, the situation as far as company B is concerned is more dramatic.

Company B:

	Year 1	Year 2
Profit (before interest)	£100	£80
Interest	£50	£50
	£50	30
Less taxation (assume 30%)	£15	9
	£35	£21

This time, when profit drops by 20%, profit after taxation falls by 40% (£35 to £21).

The converse of this is also true. If profits increase from £80 to £100 a similar effect is seen. For company A, the increase in profit is 25% (£80 to £100), while the increase in profit after taxation is 28%. For company B, the effect is more dramatic. Profits go up to 25% as before, but profit after taxation rises by 66% (£21 to £35).

There is no one particular level of gearing that is deemed to be 'risky', and high gearing is not necessarily bad. As long as the company is generating sufficient and increasing profits, and will be able to meet interest costs, then a highly geared company will survive. The danger for highly geared companies arises when profits start to decline, as is seen in the example above.

For Choclatier:

	2009	2008
Debt/equity	$\frac{£250}{£1,898} \times 100$	$\frac{£250}{£1,431} \times 100$
	13.1%	17.5%
Debt/capital employed	$\frac{£250}{£2,188} \times 100$	$\frac{£250}{£1,707} \times 100$
	11.4%	14.6%

These figures show a relatively low level of borrowing, so clearly Choclatier is not exposed to a high level of risk. If the company wished to borrow more for expansion, then it looks as though this would be easy to do.

Interest cover

This ratio shows how many times the company can pay its interest charges. In other words, how much the profits of the company can fall before the interest payments are threatened. Interest cover is calculated as follows:

$$\frac{\text{Profit before interest and tax}}{\text{Interest}} = \text{number of times}$$

The ideal level of cover depends on the current economic climate of a country. If economic conditions are tight, then interest cover should be higher than when the economy is stable or in a state of growth.

For Choclatier:

		2009	2008
Interest cover		$\frac{£732}{£47}$	$\frac{£550}{£40}$
	=	15.6 times	13.8 times

These figures show that Choclatier is exposed to very little risk. The interest cover is good, showing that it can easily afford the interest charges.

Complete analysis of Choclatier

The ratios calculated above for Choclatier can now be summarised:

Ratio	2009	2008
ROCE	33%	32%
ROSC	36%	36%
Net profit margin	12%	10%
Asset turnover	2.83 times	3.41 times
Gross margin	23%	21%
Current ratio	1.33 : 1	1.17 : 1
Liquid ratio	1.09 : 1	0.98 : 1
Receivable days	95 days	102 days
Payable days	91 days	86 days
Inventory turnover	12 times	13 times
Debt/equity	13%	17%
Debt/capital employed	11%	15%
Interest cover	15.6 times	13.8 times

When the above ratios are reviewed together it allows the analyst to build up a picture of the main strengths and weaknesses of a company. It is important to realise that the ratios interlink and any conclusion reached should take all the relevant ratios into account.

BASIC

INTERMEDIATE

ADVANCED

However, before reaching any conclusions it is import to remember that these ratios have been calculated for only two years, therefore it is not possible to determine whether the movement indicated is part of an overall trend or whether it is a one-off movement. Further details to support the conclusions may be available from other sources of information. There are no industry averages given.

Overall summary of Choclatier

The company appears to be in a fairly healthy state. Shareholders are getting a good return on their investment when compared with commercial borrowing rates. Is this a fair reflection? Perhaps not, since the fixed assets of the company may still be stated at historic cost. This will have had a positive impact on ROCE and ROSC. Further investigation is required on this point.

Profitability is strong and looks to be improving. The company has only a small amount of long-term debt, so interest payments are not a problem. However, the increase in profitability has led to a relative fall in asset turnover, indicating that the company is less efficient at generating sales. In addition to this, inventory turnover has fallen. This fall may be due to price increases. The ratios show that the movement in the numbers is small, but indicate that this needs to be monitored in the future.

Working capital is one area causing concern. Receivable days appear to be high and, given the level of payable days, the company is a net provider of funds, albeit only just. In general this is not good working capital management and this area requires further scrutiny since the proper management of working capital is fundamental to any organisation. Profits are good however, and the company would be able to cope with any bad debts that may arise.

In conclusion, profits, liquidity and gearing appear to be good, but the company needs to reassess its management of working capital.

Progress Point 12.1

Scamp Ltd had traded profitably for a number of years in the electronic component industry. Recently the bank overdraft has been steadily rising and Scamp is becoming concerned. The bank has contacted the company and has requested that the overdraft be reduced in the short term. The following summarised income statements and balance sheets have been give for the past three years.

Income statements			
For the year ending 31 March	2007	2008	2009
	£000	£000	£000
Sales	3,825	4,100	4,550
Cost of sales	2,563	2,788	3,185
Gross profit	1,262	1,312	1,365
Admin expenses	450	495	545
Distribution expenses	150	160	178
Interest payable	80	105	140
	680	760	863
Profit before taxation	582	552	502
Taxation	232	222	200
	350	330	302
Dividends	50	50	60
	300	280	242

Balance sheets			
As at 31 March	2007	2008	2009
	£000	£000	£000
Land and buildings	300	293	286
Plant and machinery	600	690	750
	900	983	1,036
Current assets			
Stock	700	850	1,100
Accounts receivable	740	920	1,105
Cash	20	30	35
	1,460	1,800	2,240
Creditors: amounts falling due within one year			
Accounts payable	400	415	425
Bank overdraft	720	828	1,019
Other creditors (including taxation)	220	230	250
	1,340	1,473	1,694
Net current assets	120	327	546
Deferred taxation	(110)	(120)	(150)
	910	1,190	1,432
Capital and reserves			
Share capital	300	300	300
Retained profit	610	890	1,132
	910	1,190	1,432

The following additional information is also available.

1. The current market value of the property is £800,000.
2. The bank overdraft is secured over the assets of the company.
3. To increase capacity a new machine will be required. This machine will cost £200,000.

Required

(a) Using appropriate accounting ratios, explain why the liquidity position has deteriorated.
(b) Outline what corrective action, if any, the company can take.
(c) What alternative sources of finance should be considered?

Solution

Ratio/trend	2007	2008	2009
Sales growth (2007 = 100)	100	107	119
Profit growth (2007 = 100)	100	93	81
ROCE	$\dfrac{(£582 + £80)}{£1,020} \times 100$ 65%	$\dfrac{(£552 + £105)}{£1,190} \times 100$ 50%	$\dfrac{(£502 + £140)}{£1,432} \times 100$ 41%
Gross profit/sales	$\dfrac{£1,262}{£3,825} \times 100$ 33%	$\dfrac{£1,312}{£4,100} \times 100$ 32%	$\dfrac{£1,365}{£4,550} \times 100$ 30%
Profit margin	$\dfrac{£300}{£3,825} \times 100$ 8%	$\dfrac{£280}{£4,100} \times 100$ 7%	$\dfrac{£242}{£4,550} \times 100$ 5%
Inventory turnover	$\dfrac{£2,563}{£700}$ 3.7 times	$\dfrac{£2,788}{£850}$ 3.3 times	$\dfrac{£3,185}{£1,100}$ 2.9 times
Receivables collection period	$\dfrac{£740}{£3,825} \times 365$ 71 days	$\dfrac{£920}{£4,100} \times 365$ 81 days	$\dfrac{£1,105}{£4,550} \times 365$ 89 days
Payable days	$\dfrac{£400}{£2,563} \times 365$ 57 days	$\dfrac{£415}{£2,788} \times 365$ 54 days	$\dfrac{£425}{£3,185} \times 365$ 48 days
Working capital	£1,460 : £1,340 1.09 : 1	£1,800 : £1,473 1.22 : 1	£2,240 : £1,694 1.32 : 1
Liquidity ratio	£760 : £1,340 0.57 : 1	£950 : £1,473 0.64 : 1	£1,140 : £1,694 0.67 : 1
Debt/equity	$\dfrac{£720}{£920} \times 100$ 78%	$\dfrac{£828}{£1,190} \times 100$ 70%	$\dfrac{£1,091}{£1,432} \times 100$ 71%

Summary of current situation (*based on the information given in the table above*)

Over the three-year period, sales have increased by 19%. Profitability has fallen over the same period. ROCE has dropped from 65% to 41%. Gross profit margin has fallen by 3%, from 33% to 30%, over the three-year period, while administration and distribution costs are running at around 16% of sales. Net profit margin has declined, also perhaps indicating that operating costs need to be more actively controlled.

Profit before taxation and the retained profit have been steadily declining over the period. Efficiency of operations, as measured by activity ratios, has also been deteriorating. This reinforces the reduction in profitability.

Inventory turnover has fallen from 3.7 times to 2.9 times, meaning that stock held at the end of March 2009 represented over four months' cost of sales. Given that the weekly cost of sales averages around £61,000, a reduction in stock turnover of 4 would release cash of around £300,000.

Control of trade receivables has also deteriorated from 71 days, sales outstanding to 89 days. This level is fairly high and therefore unacceptable. With sales at just under £90,000 a week, stricter control of receivables, reducing them to the 2007 level, would release £220,000, and a reduction to 70 days would release £230,000 for use elsewhere in the business.

Trade payables are currently being paid earlier: in 48 days rather than 57 days. This may be due in part to suppliers suspecting that the company has cash flow problems and therefore pushing to get paid. An alternative explanation could simply be lack of control in the company because the bank has not been limiting its funding.

The current liquidity position as indicated by the current and liquid ratios is static but showing a gradual improvement. It does, however, reflect increasing stocks and receivables being financed by an increasing overdraft.

The gearing of the company has decreased over the period and currently stands at a ratio of debt/equity of 71%. If the revaluation of the premises were to be incorporated in the books, then the gearing would be lowered to 52%.

Corrective action

Over the next few months it would be helpful if the company could:

- start an aggressive marketing policy to sell surplus inventory
- improve inventory control procedures and reduce stock turnover to four time a year (i.e. maintain three months' inventory levels)
- improve control of trade receivables and bring the average amount outstanding to 70 days over time, and in the longer term aim for a lower level
- enter into a discussion with the bank with a view to reducing the overdraft.

Other ratios

The ratios used up to now provide an overall picture of how the company is performing, and will be of use to a wide variety of interested parties. However, it may be that some groups – for example, shareholders and potential shareholders – will be more interested in other aspects of the business and will be concerned about their investment. The following additional investment ratios will be of use to a shareholder or potential shareholder.

Shareholder ratios

A potential shareholder in a company will be interested in both the security of any investment and in the return such an investment gives. In addition to the ratios previously mentioned, particularly those looking at profitability and risk, a potential shareholder will be interested in:

- earnings per share
- price/earnings ratio
- earnings yield
- dividend cover
- dividend yield.

Earnings per share (EPS)

This ratio shows how much of the profit left over is available to the ordinary shareholder. Earnings per share (EPS) is a measure of a company's profitability and of the company's ability to pay dividends. It is calculated as:

$$\frac{\text{Profit attributable to ordinary shareholders}}{\text{Number of ordinary shares in issue}}$$

The calculation of earnings per share can be more complicated if, for example, the company issues some new shares during the year, or when other financial instruments such as debentures can be converted into ordinary shares.

Price/earnings ratio (PER)

The price/earnings ratio (PER) is a measure of how the stock market rates the company. This ratio is calculated as:

$$\frac{\text{Market price per ordinary share}}{\text{Basic earnings per share}}$$

The ratio indicates how many times' the earnings an investor is prepared to pay to buy a share. The price/earnings ratio that can be expected generally depends on four things:

1.   overall level of the stock market
2.   the industry in which the company operates
3.   the company's record
4.   how the market views the company's prospects.

In general terms, the higher the PER the more valuable the earnings of the company.

Earnings yield

The earnings yield ratio is simply the inverse of the PER and shows earnings per unit of the company's share price. This is calculated as follows:

$$\text{Earnings yield} = \frac{1}{\text{PER}} = \frac{\text{Earnings per share}}{\text{Share prices}}$$

Dividend cover

The dividend cover is a measure of how many times the dividends actually paid are covered by the profits that were available for distribution to shareholders.

$$\text{Divided cover} = \frac{\text{Profits available for distribution or ordinary shareholders}}{\text{Dividends paid}}$$

Dividend cover is an important indicator for a potential investor. It indicates what size of dividend an investor might expect to receive given a specific level of company profits. Alternatively, it indicates how far earnings would have to fall before the dividend paid by the company would be reduced.

Dividend yield

The dividend yield measures the annual return received by way of a dividend as a percentage of the current share price. It must be remembered that this is not a measure of the total return of the shareholder because it does not take account of the growth in the value of shares. Also, it is based on the current share price, which may not be the same as the price paid by the shareholder to acquire the share. The ratio is calculated as follows:

$$\text{Dividend yield} = \frac{\text{Dividend per share}}{\text{Share price}} \times 100$$

The ratios given are some of the main ratios that are useful in the interpretation of the financial statements of a company. This list is neither definitive nor exhaustive. Other ratios may be used – for example, sales per employee or sales per square metre. What is important is that ratios are not calculated just for the sake of calculating them, so make sure there is a purpose behind the calculation of any ratio you use.

Limitations of ratio analysis

Having spent the bulk of the chapter explaining and defining ratios, it is important to remember that ratio analysis needs to be used with care. It does not provide all the answers. What ratio analysis does

is to highlight areas within an organisation that require further investigation. Ratios do have limitations and these need to be taken into consideration when using ratio analysis.

- Ratios use balance sheet information only applicable at the balance sheet date. Any seasonal factors may be missed altogether.
- The figures contained in financial statements themselves can contain certain assumptions and estimates, which can be very subjective.
- Sometimes organisations manipulate the year-end financial statements to improve the appearance of the ratios.
- Accounting policies may differ between organisations, which can make comparisons difficult – for example, the treatment of development costs.
- Accounting standards, when introduced for the first time, can make comparisons with previous periods difficult. The ratios may have to be recalculated.
- Care needs to be exercised in order to take all other relevant factors into account when interpreting the ratios. If the organisation, for example, has been the subject of a recent takeover then any cost reduction might be as a result of the takeover rather than an improvement in efficiency.

In addition to all this there are other sources of information contained within a company's financial statements that should always be taken into account. The sources of information available with which to assist in any analysis are numerous.

Internal sources of information

If the analysis is of a public limited company, there will be an annual report. This should be referred to, to provide information about the company's products, performance and capital investment strategy. A change in sales, for example, may be explained in the chairman's statement while the directors' report may give reasons for other significant changes that have been identified. The accounting policies notes may explain the reason for a change in results, while the notes to the financial statements can be used to provide greater detail on the summarised profit and loss account and balance sheet figures.

External sources of information

Benchmark information may be available from trade journals and published accounts of companies in the same industry sector. In addition, relevant information can be found in the finance sections of many newspapers and government statistics are also available. For more tailored information, it is possible to contact specialist agencies that sell industry-specific facts. There are numerous sources of inter-firm information but there are two main distinctions: there are those that gather their data from external published accounts and those that collect the data directly from surveyed companies on a strictly confidential basis.

Organisations that prepare inter-firm comparisons from external published accounts face all the limitations noted earlier associated with company accounts. There are, however, certain advantages of using such agencies: the scope of the comparison can be extremely wide and can include an analysis of any firm that produces published accounts. The quality of ratio analysis is improved because the survey organisations attempt to standardise the basis of every ratio in the survey, and the information can be accessed easily and at relatively low cost.

Data collected directly from member companies of the private inter-firm comparison scheme are usually available only to participating companies. The advantage of these schemes is that the data collected consist of a comprehensive analysis of every firm in the scheme and are more reliable due to there not being any statutory restrictions in place governing the content and presentation of the financial statement information. The disadvantages are that there are onerous requirements concerning the quality of information that companies contribute to private schemes, all information must comply with strict uniformity requirements, and it is relatively costly.

BASIC

INTERMEDIATE

ADVANCED

The information obtained from these internal and external sources would be used in conjunction with ratio analysis to explain further changes or results that the ratios themselves had identified.

12.4 Disclosure in practice

Logica gives the following five-year financial summary.

> The five-year financial summary below includes selected information on a calendar year basis, which has been extracted from audited Financial statements. The information for the years ended 31 December 2003 to 31 December 2006 was restated to show Telecoms Products as a discontinued operation.

	UK GAAP	Restated IFRS			IFRS
	2003	2004	2005	2006	2007
	£m	£m	£m	£m	£m
Revenue	1,428.1	1,421.1	1,579.4	2,420.7	3,073.2
Adjusted operating profit	102.6	99.8	107.8	203.4	207.6
Operating profit before goodwill amortisation/impairment and exceptional items	102.6	99.8	106.8	165.8	132.9
Goodwill amortisation/impairment and exceptional items	(130.4)	(17.8)	0.5	(23.9)	(23.2)
Share of post-tax profits from associates	0.4	0.4	1.4	0.3	1.2
Net finance costs payable	(11.7)	(15.2)	(16.2)	(25.6)	(26.8)
Profit/(loss) on ordinary activities before tax	(39.1)	67.2	92.5	116.6	84.1
Tax on profit/(loss) on ordinary activities	(6.0)	(26.1)	(28.2)	(31.2)	(5.4)
Profit/(loss) on ordinary activities after tax	(45.1)	41.1	64.3	85.4	78.7
Result from discontinued operation	1.4	(15.9)	4.5	3.7	89.4
Minority interests	(2.4)	(0.6)	(3.0)	(7.1)	1.8
Profit/(loss) for the year attributable to ordinary shareholders	(46.1)	24.6	65.8	82.0	169.9
Closing number of employees from continuing operations	17,825	17,914	19,734	38,789	38,740
Turnover growth from continuing operations	(14%)	–	11%	53%	27%
Adjusted operating margin from continuing operations	7.2%	7.0%	6.8%	8.4%	6.8%
Adjusted basic earnings per share from continuing operations	8.0p	7.1p	7.0p	10.4p	10.2p
Dividends per share	5.01p	5.10p	5.31p	5.60p	5.80p

Figure 12.1 Logica: five-year summary

The main pieces of information in the five-year summary are clearly the revenue and profit items. Note that basic earnings per share is given as is the dividend per share. Also, the number of employees over the five-year period this has increased from nearly 18,000 to 39,000, clearly an indication of growth from the point of view of the company, and one that it would wish to highlight.

Section 3: Advanced Aspects

In Chapter 9, statements of cash flow were shown to provide additional information showing cash inflows and outflows. In addition, such statements can be incorporated within ratio analysis to provide additional insights into the company's financial position.

12.5 Cash flow statements: some further aspects

The cash flow statement can also be used to derive accounting ratios. As before, the analysis should begin with a general overview and once the figures have been put in context, then ratios may be calculated to focus the user's attention on areas requiring further analysis. Such questions may be in relation to, for example, identifying future cash requirements.

A general concern may relate to when any existing borrowing will require to be repaid. On a more detailed level, the analysis may consider, for example, working capital requirements and the desire of a company to expand. This may involve the use of ratios to assist in analysing the cash requirements, and whether these can be met internally or from external sources.

A ratio that is calculated from the cash flow statement is the cash flow ratio. It is calculated as follows:

$$\frac{\text{Total cash inflows}}{\text{Total cash outflows}}$$

A ratio greater than 1 indicates a net inflow of cash, while a ratio of less than 1 indicates a net outflow of cash.

Working capital requirements

In general, when a business expands, working capital will rise in line with the increase in turnover. In order to see the relationship between working capital and sales, it makes sense to use the working capital ratio, which is calculated as follows:

$$\frac{\text{Stock + trade receivables − trade payables}}{\text{Sales}} \times 100$$

The answer is usually expressed as a percentage.

A company with a low working capital ratio will find it easier to expand than one with a high working capital ratio. In general terms, any business that can sell its goods before it has to pay for them will not need any additional working capital for expansion. Conversely, companies that have to carry large amounts of inventory will need additional working capital if they want to expand.

In addition, expenditure on fixed assets will be difficult to determine with any degree of accuracy unless the company discloses the information.

Increasing cash: possible solutions

What can a company do if the cash flow looks certain to be less than that required to meet these commitments? The following are some suggestions.

- Use its overdraft, but there would be problems if the overdraft was at its limit. As indicated above, there is no way of knowing this.
- Borrow more on a longer-term basis. Again the borrowing limits would need to be adhered to.
- If the company has investments it could sell these; or it may be able to sell some of the business activities. Care needs to be taken with this not to damage the business.
- Sell and lease back some of the properties of the business.

BASIC

INTERMEDIATE

ADVANCED

- Reduce capital expenditure.
- Tighten credit and stock controls.
- Cut dividend payments.
- Sell more shares.

If a company has a cash shortfall and doesn't take action, then it will inevitably go into an overtrading situation, which will cause a cash crisis, unless as a last resort, the company reduces it level of trading.

An important number derived from the cash flow statement is what is known as free cash flow (FCF). This is the cash that is left over to spend once all the fixed commitments have been made. Fixed commitments include those items that must be paid, such as taxation and interest, and, to an extent, dividends. Although there is no legal requirement to pay a dividend, any company that cuts its dividend or does not pay a dividend without a very good reason is asking for trouble!

Working capital and overtrading

Working capital is defined as current assets less current liabilities. It is that part of the financing of a firm used to generate profits. Working capital is the life-blood of any business. The faster the working capital cycle can be made to operate, the faster profits will accumulate.

Problems can arise, however, where a business has too little working capital. Working capital may become depleted for several reasons, the most common of these being excessive dividends or drawings, or the purchase of fixed assets.

An expanding business may need to buy new equipment or premises to meet increased demand for its product or services. Unless a business has adequate reserves, it may have little working capital left if it has financed the purchase of fixed assets using working capital. Such an investment in fixed assets will remove some of the current assets into fixed assets and so have an impact on working capital.

As a result of this, the company may have to rely on extended trade credit in order to purchase goods for resale. If creditors demand payment, the only way to settle the debts may be to sell some of its fixed assets. The next step is likely to be bankruptcy as a business will not be able to function without its full complement of fixed assets. A business that tries to manage with inadequate working capital is said to be *overtrading*.

How, then, does the company expand?

Clearly, not every business will end up bankrupt if it tries to expand. If the fall in working capital caused by the purchase of fixed assets is quickly replaced by extra profits from increased trade then no problems ought to arise. Where a business grows steadily, this should not be problematic either. The danger comes when the expansion is too rapid and the working capital is inadequate to meet this rapid expansion.

The following example will help illustrate this point.

Example

Oakwood has the following balance sheet at 31 December:

		£
Fixed assets		70,000
Current assets		
Stock	£20,000	
Debtors	£40,000	
Bank	£20,000	
	£80,000	
Creditors	£30,000	
Net current assets		£50,000
		£120,000
Issued share capital		£100,000
Retained profit		£20,000
		£120,000

The working capital is £50,000 and the company makes profits of £15,000 per annum.

A competitor company has announced that it is to leave the market, which will enable Oakwood to double its profits – however, this will involve the purchase of a new storage facility costing £160,000. Oakwood requires an overdraft facility from the bank of £140,000 to supplement the cash it already has.

The balance sheet would now be as follows:

	£	£
Fixed assets		230,000
Current assets		
Stock	£20,000	
Debtors	£40,000	
Bank	0	
	£60,000	
Creditors	£30,000	
Bank overdraft	£140,000	
	£170,000	
Net current liabilities		£(110,000)
		£120,000
Issued share capital		£100,000
Retained profit		£20,000
		£120,000

The working capital is now minus £110,000. Current liabilities exceed current assets.

Oakwood now faces three potential problems.

1. Unless the bank overdraft can be increased further, the company will have to rely on extended trade credit to purchase additional stocks.
2. The working capital, which has been depleted, will be replaced only gradually as profits are earned and this is likely to take at least four years (i.e. 4 × £30,000 profits).

3.   If stock is not turned over quickly and cash generated to pay creditors, then the company could be forced into liquidation.

This is of course an extreme example. It is unlikely that a bank would allow a company to use an overdraft to facilitate such an expansion. However, rapid expansion on a smaller scale is quite common and, unfortunately, so are the related problems when it is not financed correctly.

Expansion on such a scale is better financed by the use of long-term loans, the term length matched as far as possible with the length of time the company is likely to benefit from the use of the asset. Alternatively, the company could issue new shares.

Financed in this way, the working capital remains intact. Remember that working capital consists of current assets less current liabilities. Fixed assets, long-term loans and share capital do not form part of working capital. They are long-term assets and long-term sources of finance.

Indicators of financial distress

A number of methods have been devised to give some indication of when a company is likely to become insolvent. Ratio analysis is one such method, and has been described in detail in this chapter. The other methods are referred to as the Z-score and the A-score.

Ratio analysis

As has been seen earlier in this chapter, ratio analysis is often used to determine the financial health of a company. However, it can also be used to indicate any potential financial distress. If profitability and liquidity ratios are falling and management ratios show a reduction in efficiency, while at the same time the gearing ratios are increasing, then this may show early signs of trouble ahead. The company may not have long to survive. Ratio analysis, then, is a good first step in gauging the health of a company.

It is unlikely that the directors of a company will admit that the company is in trouble. Forecast information provided by directors will be of limited use in that they will be designed to show an improving position. The financial statements themselves will provide more robust information. By making good use of accounting ratios financial statement will show the trends in profitability and in liquidity. However, when calculating ratios it is important to keep the following points in mind.

- Have there been any significant changes in management recently? If the company has not been successful in the recent past, then it is unlikely that improvement will happen unless there is a change in management.

- Has anything happened to the auditors? Have they been changed recently? If so, this may indicate a disagreement over some issue of reporting.
- Is staff morale good? Employees will be concerned about their jobs if they sense that there a problems within the business.
- As far as borrowing is concerned, does the management of the company match borrowings to assets acquired?
- The creation of intangible assets or of a revaluation reserve may indicate that management is desperate to improve the appearance of the financial position of the business.

- Is directors' remuneration realistic in terms of the company's performance?

Z-score

This was developed back in 1968 as a way of overcoming some of the basic difficulties in using accounting ratios to predict the financial health of a company. The Z-score is calculated by adding together a number of ratios, with each ratio being weighted according to its usefulness as a predictor of financial failure.

The Z-score is calculated as follows:

$$
\begin{aligned}
Z \quad = \quad & 1.2 \ (\text{working capital/total assets}) \\
+ \quad & 1.4 \ (\text{retained earnings/total assets}) \\
+ \quad & 3.3 \ (\text{profit before interest and tax/total assets}) \\
+ \quad & 0.6 \ (\text{market capitalisation/book value of debts}) \\
+ \quad & 1.0 \ (\text{sales/total assets})
\end{aligned}
$$

A score of 3.0 and above is considered to be a sign of a healthy company, whereas a score of less than 1.8 may mean that a company is heading for bankruptcy. The Z-score is used in practice by banks and other institutions for assessing the risk of their customers. There are some limitations of this model that need to be recognised:

- There is no scientific proof of the model.
- The information used in the model is historic.
- Different companies may classify similar items in a different way.
- There is no specified time-frame within which the company being assessed is deemed to be 'safe'.

A-score

A third method of predicting corporate failure is completely different from the above ratio-based methods. As such it avoids the problems inherent in these methods.

The A-score uses a list of questions that have a specific score associated with them. A company could score up to 100 points, depending on the answers to the questions. A score of more than 25 is deemed to be bad, and may indicate that a company is heading for failure. The A-score questions are divided into three sections, concerned with defects, mistakes and symptoms. Defects deal with issues relating to reaction to change, management and accounting; mistakes deal with gearing and trading levels, while symptoms deal with the results of ratio analysis.

It is important to note that the use of the Z- and A-scores is not commonplace. The results of ratio analysis are more likely to guide accountants, together with general observations about the company – for example, the company not being able to pay its debts, not replacing equipment, staff leaving. The A-score is more like a 'scorecard' approach: in certain industries these are used to analyse company performance.

Chapter summary

Ratio analysis

- Ratio analysis is a very important tool that can be used by the stakeholders of a company to analyse the profitability, liquidity, management and risk of a company by using the information contained in its annual statements.
- It is possible to get a broad indication of the health of a company by doing a trend analysis and by using common size statements. Using accounting ratios is also a good technique of analysis and there are a number of ratios that can be computed. These are described fully in the chapter.
- When computing ratios it is important to be consistent, to calculate those ratios that are relevant in the analysis, and to be aware of the limitations inherent in ratio analysis. In terms of specific ratios, bear in mind the following information.

ROCE

- Beware of revaluation of fixed assets, which has an adverse effect on ROCE. A revaluation will increase the denominator of the ratio, so the ratio itself will decrease. Note the use of the bank overdraft as a long-term source of finance and take care to include this in capital employed. It is important to analyse the movements in this ratio in terms of net profit margin and asset turnover.

Current ratio

- If the ratio is increasing then this may suggest poor working capital management, while if the ratio is deteriorating this may suggest liquidity problems.
- Trade receivable and payable days: these can be compared to establish whether the company is a net provider or recipient of funds.

Overall interpretation

- There is no ideal ratio. A better comparison is with the industry average and with the trend in ratios over time. It is not helpful to analyse each ratio in isolation, it is better to consider the ratios collectively to give a more complete picture.
- Ratios are generally useful as a guide in attempting to identify financial distress. They can be used in conjunction with the Z-score and the A-score, together with general observations about the company, in order to get a proper understanding of the future financial health of the company.

Key terms for review

Definitions can be found in the glossary at the end of the book.

Horizontal analysis   *Collection period for receivables*
Vertical analysis   *Payment period for payables*
Ratio analysis   *Gearing ratio*
Return on capital employed (ROCE)   *Interest cover*
Return on shareholders' capital (ROSC)   *Earnings per share (EPS)*
Net profit margin   *Price/earnings ratio (PER)*
Asset turnover   *Earnings yield*
Gross margin   *Dividend cover*
Current ratio   *Dividend yield*
Liquidity ratio   *Z-score*
Inventory turnover   *A-score*

Review questions

1. Explain what is meant by the term *horizontal analysis*.
2. Explain what is meant by the term *vertical analysis*.
3. Explain whether the advantages of ratio analysis outweigh the disadvantages.
4. Explain the uses and limitations of ratio analysis when used to interpret the published financial statements of a company.
5. Identify and explain the ratios that provide information on performance for investors.
6. Explain why liquidity is important to a company.
7. Identify and explain the ratios that provide information on liquidity.
8. Identify and explain the ratios that provide information on profitability.
9. What methods have been devised to give indications of financial distress?
10. What sources of information outside the business are available to assist in the interpretation process?

Exercises

1. Level II

Fastbru plc is a listed company. The principal business of the company is the manufacture and distribution of soft drinks. The company has been in operation for ten years but the major shareholders have become particularly concerned about the performance of the company over the last two years. At a recent meeting the board of directors of Quickbru adopted a short-term plan for recovery. The key elements of this plan were:

(i) to restructure the finances of the company by issuing more shares and reducing bank borrowing
(ii) to change the operating practices of the distribution network, which has relied on local depots holding stocks for distribution by local carriers to retailers.

The financial statements of the company for the three years ended 31 December 2006–2008 are given below:

Profit and loss account for the year ended 31 December

	2006 £000	2007 £000	2008 £000
Turnover	5,210	5,295	5,380
Cost of sales	3,768	3,836	3,904
Gross profit	1,442	1,459	1,476
Distribution and administration costs	1,117	1,176	1,208
Operating profit	325	283	268
Interest paid	55	67	100
Profit before tax	270	216	168
Taxation	85	65	44
Profit after tax	185	159	124
Dividends	120	120	120
Retained profit	65	39	4

Balance sheets as at 31 December

	2006 £000	2007 £000	2008 £000
Tangible fixed assets:			
Land and buildings	1,093	1,053	1,013
Plant, machinery, and motor vans	898	1,242	1,420
	1,991	2,295	2,433
Current assets:			
Stocks	355	525	789
Debtors	204	231	323
Cash	52	25	17
	611	781	1,129
Creditors: amounts falling due within one year			
Bank overdraft	–	115	458
Trade creditors	182	249	375
Other creditors	41	48	65
	223	412	898
Net current assets	388	369	231
Total assets less current liabilities	2,379	2,664	2,664
Creditors: amounts falling due after more than one year			
Long-term loan (secured)	544	540	536
	1,835	2,124	2,128
Capital and reserves:			
Issued ordinary share capital (£1 each)	1,000	1,250	1,250
Retained profit	835	874	878
	1,835	2,124	2,128

The following are average industry ratios for the sector in which Fastbru plc operates. These ratios have been consistent over the year period 2006–2008.

Return on capital employed	13%
Gross margin	25%
Sales to net assets	300%
Gearing	40%
Stock turnover (based on year-end figures)	12 times
Interest cover	3 times

(a)   Calculate from the financial statements of Fastbru plc, for each of the three years given, the same ratios as given for the industry sector.

(b)   Compare the ratios calculated in (a) above with the industry average and comment on this comparison.

(c)   Based on your answers to (a) and (b) above, discuss the merits of the key elements of the recovery plan to be adopted by the directors.

2. Level II

CFC International, Inc., a US-based company headquartered in Chicago, is a worldwide holography and speciality coated film company. It designs, manufactures and markets chemically complex, multi-layer, transferable coatings and sophisticated holographic technologies. It's coatings provide superior performance for a wide variety of consumer and industrial products (both for product authentication and eye-catching packaging), under a wide range of operating solutions. The company does this by coating rolls of plastic film and selling them to its customers, who transfer the coatings to their products for protective or informative purposes. CFC International makes its coatings by mixing pigments, solvents and resins into formulations, which come in many colours, patterns and surface finishes designed to resist chemical and physical abuse.

CFC International manufactures it own coatings, which provide the company with the flexibility to customise and meet its customers' specific needs. For a relatively small cost compared to the cost of the finished products, CFC's technology adds to the functionality and increases the customer value of a variety of everyday products (e.g. toothpaste packaging and credit cards).

Below are provided:

■   the consolidated income statements for the financial years ended 31 December 1997–1999 (source: Annual Report, 1999).

■   the common-size income statements for the same period.

Income statement			
In US$	1999	1998	1997
Net sales	66,147,299	51,047,399	42,319,147
Cost of goods sold	44,714,285	31,914,511	26,063,431
Gross profit	21,433,014	19,132,888	16,255,716
Marketing and selling expenses	7,048,868	5,544,129	4,813,880
General and administrative expenses	7,689,424	4,871,277	4,032,066
Research and development expenses	2,021,555	1,585,458	1,343,678
	16,759,847	12,000,864	10,189,624
Operating income	4,673,167	7,132,024	6,066,092
Other expenses/(income):			
interest	1,029,755	569,573	412,920
miscellaneous	475,881	311,823	(65,183)
	1,505,636	881,396	347,737
Income before income taxes and minority interest	3,167,531	6,250,628	5,718,355
Provision for income taxes	922,219	2,259,607	2,207,021
	2,245,312	3,991,021	3,511,334
Minority interest	0	-343,029	-290,131
Net income	2,245,312	3,647,992	3,221,203

Common size income statement			
	1999	1998	1997
Net sales	100.0%	100.0%	100.0%
Cost of goods sold	67.6%	62.5%	61.6%
Gross profit	32.4%	37.5%	38.4%
Marketing and selling expenses	10.7%	10.9%	11.4%
General and administrative expenses	11.6%	9.5%	9.5%
Research and development expenses	3.1%	3.1%	3.2%
	25.3%	23.5%	24.1%
Operating income	7.1%	14.0%	14.3%
Other expenses (income):			
interest	1.6%	1.1%	1.0%
miscellaneous	0.7%	0.6%	-0.2%
	2.3%	1.7%	0.8%
Income before income taxes and minority interest	4.8%	12.2%	13.5%
Provision for income taxes	1.4%	4.4%	5.2%
	3.4%	7.8%	8.3%
Minority interest	0.0%	-0.7%	-0.7%
Net income	3.4%	7.1%	7.6%

Analyse and comment on these different statements. What can you infer happened during these three years? What are the significant evolutions an analyst or investor might be interested in?

3. Level II

The Audi Group is a multinational manufacturer and retailer of motor vehicles. Summary financial statements are given below for the years ended 31 December 2005 and 2004.

Income statements for the year ended		
	31 Dec 2005	31 Dec 2004
	Euro '000	Euro '000
Revenue	26,590,603	24,505,864
Cost of sales	23,428,829	21,989,159
Gross profit	3,161,774	2,516,705
Distribution costs	1,876,600	1,754,315
Administrative expenses	240,062	241,914
Operating profit	1,045,112	520,486
Other income	515,244	819,054
Interest payable	250,355	196,190
Profit before tax	1,310,001	1,143,350
Tax	485,868	272,229
Profit after tax	824,133	871,121
Earnings per share:		
Basic	19.17	20.21

Balance sheets as at	31 Dec 2005	31 Dec 2004
	Euro '000	Euro '000
Fixed assets	8,596,613	8,970,805
Current assets:		
Stock	2,041,837	1,831,613
Debtors	1,497,703	1,393,050
Investments	870,957	949,726
Cash in bank	3,104,976	1,759,211
	7,515,473	5,933,600
Current liabilities:		
Loans and finance leases	3,143,189	2,435,314
Trade creditors	2,149,818	2,074,061
Accruals	348,047	127,923
	5,805,949	4,785,537
Net current assets	1,709,524	1,148,063
Long-term liabilities	4,201,887	4,291,056
Net assets	6,104,250	5,827,812
Called-up share capital	110,080	110,080
Other reserves	251,730	56,730
Profit & loss account	5,742,440	5,656,945
Minority interests	–	4,057
	6,104,250	5,827,812

Required

Prepare a report on the financial performance of Audi for the year ended 31 December 2005, using the 2004 information for comparative purposes. In analysing the group's performance, you should use ratio analysis to measure its profitability, liquidity and gearing.

4. Level II

ABCD Ltd is a company engaged in building construction and renovation for private-sector customers. The company has a healthy order book but, despite this, is experiencing considerable cash flow problems. In view of this the company has approached it bankers and had requested an extension of overdraft facilities. This request has been refused until the company can explain the reasons for the cash flow problems and establish a recovery plan.

   Extracts from the management accounting information provide the following summarised information.

Balance sheets	2007	2008	2009
	£000	£000	£000
Fixed assets	84	96	128
Current assets:			
Inventory	28	24	30
Work in progress	620	740	640
Payments on account	(500)	(530)	(300)
Trade receivables	250	190	260
	398	424	630
Current liabilities			
Trade payables	298	274	396
Bank overdraft	140	60	158
	438	334	554
Net current assets (liabilities)	(40)	90	76
Total net assets	44	186	204

Income statements	2007	2008	2009
	£000	£000	£000
Sales:			
New houses	1,150	796	604
Commercial developments	400	856	1,146
	1,550	1,652	1,750
Cost of sales:			
Materials	656	690	740
Labour	486	540	716
Overheads	154	166	190
	1,296	1,396	1,646
Gross profit	254	256	104
Administration overheads	90	98	88
	164	158	16
Interest payable	21	10	23
Profit (loss) before tax	143	148	(7)

The following information has been provided by the directors.

1.   Fixed assets are made up of:
   - old building, which has been converted to offices and stores
   - a house that is currently rented to a tenant
   - plant
   - machinery
   - motor vehicles.

The property was recently valued at £40,000 more than its book value, but this has not been incorporated into the accounts.
2.   Some land suitable for a private housing development is owned by the company.
3.   The overdraft limit is £130,000, which was agreed in 2006.

Required

Identify and discuss the possible reasons for the cash flow problems of the company. List the points that should be included in the action plan for recovery.

5. Level II

Gold Ltd is a metal manufacturing company. The managing director is concerned that sales cannot continue at their current level without increased borrowing. The management accounts for the period 2007 to 2009 are as follows:

Gold Ltd			
Income statements for the year ending 31 March			
	2007	2008	2009
	£	£	£
Net sales	3,315,000	3,442,500	3,570,000
Cost of goods sold	(2,652,000)	(2,754,000)	(2,856,000)
Gross profit	663,000	688,500	714,000
Administration and selling expenses	(255,000)	(280,500)	(306,000)
Depreciation	(102,000)	(127,500)	(153,000)
Miscellaneous expenses	(51,000)	(107,100)	(153,000)
Net profit before tax	255,000	173,400	102,000
Taxation	(76,500)	(52,020)	(30,600)
Net profit after tax	178,500	121,380	71,400
Balance sheet			
As at 31 March	2007	2008	2009
	£	£	£
Fixed assets:			
Land and buildings	61,200	163,200	153,000
Machinery	188,700	147,900	127,500
Other fixed assets	35,700	10,200	7,600
	285,600	321,300	288,100
Current assets:			
Stock	382,500	637,500	1,032,800
Accounts receivable	306,000	346,800	484,500
Cash	76,500	35,700	25,500
	765,000	1,020,000	1,542,800
Total assets	1,050,600	1,341,300	1,830,900
Share capital			
Ordinary shares	459,000	459,000	459,000
Retained profits	351,900	438,600	489,600
	810,900	897,600	948,600
Long-term loan	56,100	51,000	45,900
Current liabilities			
Accruals	61,200	71,400	96,900
Accounts payable	122,400	193,800	382,500
Bank overdraft	0	127,500	357,000
	1,050,600	1,341,300	1,830,900

The following are the industry ratios for the metal manufacturing industry. These ratios are based on year-end balance sheet figures.

Metal manufacturing industry ratios:

Quick ratio	1.0 : 1
Current ratio	27 : 1
Inventory turnover	7 times
Average collection period	32 days
Fixed asset turnover	13 times
Return on total assets	19%
Return on capital employed	36%
Debt/equity ratio	50%
Profit margin	7%

Required

Write a report to the managing director analysing the financial position of Gold in light of the industrial average ratios. Your report should include an analysis of the firm's strengths and weaknesses.

Further reading

Altman, E. (1968) Financial ratios, discriminant analysis and the prediction of corporate bankruptcy. *Journal of Finance*, 23, 4, 589–609.

Company REFS – Really Essential Financial Statistics: Tables Volume, devised by Jim Slater, Hemmington Scott.

Dun & Bradstreet: *Key Business Ratios: The Guide to British Business Performance*. Dun & Bradstreet Ltd.

Extel (1992) *Handbook of Market Leaders*. Extel Financial Ltd.

Holmes, G., Sugden, A. and Gee, P. (2008) *Interpreting Company Reports and Accounts*. FT/PrenticeHall,

HS Financial Publishing: *The Company Guide*. HS Financial Publishing.

Taffler, R. (1982) Forecasting company failure in the UK using discriminant analysis and financial ratio data. *Journal of the Royal Statistical Society*, Series A, 145, 3, 342–58.

Glossary

Accounting profit	Accounting profit is profit or loss for a period before deducting tax expense.
Accounting profits and taxable profits	Accounting profits and taxable profits are seldom the same because the tax rules for allowing expenses to be charged against profit differ from the accounting rules.
Acquisition accounting	This is sometimes called the purchase method and is the method required to account for an interest in a subsidiary company.
Amortisation	Amortisation is the systematic allocation of the depreciable amount of an intangible asset over its useful life.
A-score	The A-score uses a list of questions that have a specific score associated with them. A company could score up to 100 points, depending on the responses to the questions. The result of such a score is used to predict the likelihood of a company failing.
Asset	An asset is a resource controlled by the enterprise as a result of past events, and from which future economic benefits are expected to flow to the enterprise.
Asset turnover	A ratio that provides useful information about the efficiency of the company at generating sales from its capital.
Associate company	This is where one company has a substantial stake in another company such that it gives some degree of influence, but not total control, over the operating and financial policies. This is a 'significant' degree of influence.
Borrowing costs	Borrowing costs are interest or other costs incurred by an entity in connection with the borrowing of funds.
Carrying amount	Carrying amount is the amount at which an asset is recognised after deducting any accumulated depreciation and accumulated impairment losses.
Cash	Cash comprises cash on hand and demand deposits.
Cash equivalents	Cash equivalents are short-term highly liquid investments that are readily convertible to known amounts of cash and subject to an insignificant risk of changes in value.
Cash flows	Cash flows are inflows and outflows of cash and cash equivalents.

Cash generating unit	A cash generating unit is the smallest identifiable group of assets that generates cash inflows that are largely independent of the cash inflows from other assets or groups of assets.
Closing rate method	This is sometimes referred to as the net investment method. It is the method that is dealt with explicitly in IAS 21 for translating into the presentation currency, and is used as the method of translation when the subsidiary company is an independent entity. All balance sheet items are translated at the rate of exchange ruling at that time (i.e. the closing rate); all income statement items are (mainly) translated at the average rate. Any exchange differences are shown as a movement on reserves.
Collection period for receivables	A ratio that measures how effective the business is in collecting its debts. The ratio is a measure of how many days' credit customers are taking to pay.
Compound financial instruments	A compound financial instrument is a financial instrument containing both a liability component and an equity component.
Construction contract	A construction contract is a contract specifically negotiated for the construction of an asset, or a combination of assets that are closely interrelated or interdependent in terms of their design, technology and function, or their ultimate purpose or use.
Contingent liability	A contingent liability is an obligation that is not recognised in the balance sheet because it depends upon some future event happening.
Cost	The cost of a non-current asset is the cost of making it ready for use.
Cost plus contract	A cost plus contract is a construction contract in which the contractor is reimbursed for allowable or otherwise defined costs, plus a percentage of these costs or a fixed fee.
Costs of disposal	Costs of disposal are incremental costs directly attributable to the disposal of an asset or cash generating unit, excluding finance costs and income tax expense.
Credit risk	The risk that one party to a financial instrument will cause a financial loss for the other party by failing to discharge an obligation.
Current asset	An asset that is reasonably expected to be realised in cash, or sold, or otherwise consumed during the normal operating cycle of the business, or within one accounting year if longer.
Current liability	A current liability is a liability that satisfies any of the following criteria: (a) it is expected to be settled in the entity's normal operating cycle; (b) it is held primarily for the purpose of being traded; (c) it is due to be settled within 12 months after the balance sheet date.
Current ratio	A ratio that focuses on the working capital of a business. It assesses the ability of the company to meet its short-term debt.
Current tax	Current tax is the amount of income taxes payable (recoverable) in respect of the taxable profit (tax loss) for a period.
Date of acquisition	This is the date at which a parent company acquires its stake in the subsidiary company.
Date of consolidation	This is the date at which the financial statements are being prepared.
Deductible temporary differences	Deductible temporary differences are temporary differences that will result in amounts that are deductible in determining taxable profit (tax loss) of future periods when the carrying amount of the asset or liability is recovered or settled.

Depreciable amount	Depreciable amount is the cost of an asset, or other amount substituted for cost, less its residual value.
Depreciation	Depreciation is the systematic allocation of the depreciable amount of an asset over its useful life.
Derivative	A derivative is a financial instrument that changes in value with an underlying item, requires no or relatively little investment, and is settled at a future date.
Development	Development is the application of research findings or other knowledge to a plan or design for the production of new or substantially improved materials, devices, products, processes, systems or services before the start of commercial production or use.
Distributable reserves	Distributable reserves are reserves that can be distributed to shareholders by way of dividends and other distributions (e.g. revenue reserves).
Dividend	This is the return paid to shareholders as a reward for holding shares in a company. Dividends are payable only when the directors of the company declare them. There are usually two dividends declared during the year: one part way through the year (i.e. an interim dividend) and one at the end of the financial year (a final dividend).
Dividend cover	The dividend cover is a measure of how many times the dividends actually paid are covered by the profits that were available for distribution to shareholders.
Dividend yield	The dividend yield measures the annual return received by way of a dividend as a percentage of the current share price.
Earnings per share (EPS)	A ratio that shows how much of the profit remaining is available to the ordinary shareholder. Earnings per share is a measure of a company's profitability and of the company's ability to pay dividends.
Earnings yield	This ratio is simply the inverse of the *price/earnings ratio*, and shows earnings per unit of the company's share price.
Equity accounting	This method of accounting is required to account for an interest in an associate or joint venture.
Equity instrument	An equity instrument is any contract that evidences a residual interest in the assets of an entity after deducting all of its liabilities. Ordinary shares are the most common example of an equity instrument.
Exchange difference	This refers to any gain or loss arising from a movement in the exchange rate.
Fair value	Fair value is the amount for which an asset could be exchanged between knowledgeable, willing parties in an arm's length transaction.
Fair value less costs to sell	Fair value less costs to sell is the amount obtainable from the sale of an asset or cash generating unit in an arm's length transaction between knowledgeable willing parties, less the costs of disposal.
Finance lease	A finance lease is a lease that transfers substantially all the risks and rewards incidental to ownership of an asset to the lessee. The underlying substance of the transaction is a financing arrangement.
Finance lease (initial recognition)	Lessees shall recognise, at the commencement of the lease term, finance leases as assets and liabilities in their balance sheets at amounts equal to the fair value of the leased property or, if, lower, the present value of the minimum lease payments.

Financial asset	A financial asset is any asset that is: (a) cash; (b) an equity instrument of another entity; (c) a contractual right to receive cash or another financial asset from another entity.
Financial instrument	Any contract that gives rise to a financial asset for one party and a financial liability or equity instrument for another.
Financial liability	A financial liability is any liability that is a contractual obligation to deliver cash or another financial asset to another entity.
Financing activities	Financing activities are activities that result in changes in the size and composition of the contributed equity and borrowings of the entity.
Fixed price contract	A fixed price contract is a construction contract in which the contractor agrees to a fixed contract price, or a fixed rate per unit of output, which in some cases is subject to cost escalation clauses.
Functional currency	The currency of the primary economic environment in which a company operates.
Gearing ratio	Gearing is concerned with the capital structure of the company. This ratio shows what proportion of the assets of the company have been financed by borrowing.
Goodwill	Sometimes referred to as 'cost of control' or 'premium on acquisition', goodwill is calculated as the excess of the cost of an investment in a subsidiary over the 'value' of the proportion of net assets acquired.
Grants related to assets	Grants related to assets are government grants whose primary condition is that an entity qualifying for them should purchase, construct or otherwise acquire long-term assets.
Gross investment in the lease	Gross investment in the lease is the aggregate of the minimum lease payments receivable by the lessor under a finance lease and any unguaranteed residual value accruing to the lessor.
Gross margin	A ratio that measures the ability of a business to sell goods for more than they cost to make.
Hedge	A finance technique to minimise the risk of exchange rate movements by entering into an agreement to buy currency ahead of time and so fix the exchange rate.
Horizontal analysis	Used to examine trends over a number of accounting periods. Horizontal analysis is useful where comparisons are for periods greater than two years.
Impairment loss	An impairment loss is the amount by which the carrying amount of an asset exceeds its recoverable amount.
Initial recognition	See *Finance lease (initial recognition)*.
Intangible asset	An intangible asset is an identifiable non-monetary asset without physical substance.
Interest cover	A ratio that shows how much the profits of the company can fall before the interest payments are threatened.
Interest rate implicit in the lease	The interest rate implicit in the lease is the discount rate that, at the inception of the lease, causes the aggregate present value of (a) the minimum lease payments and (b) the unguaranteed residual value to be equal to the fair value of the leased asset.

Inventories	Inventories are assets: (a) held for sale in the ordinary course of business; (b) in the process of production for such sale; or (c) in the form of materials or supplies to be consumed in the production process or in the rendering of services.
Inventory turnover	A ratio that shows how quickly the company is turning over its stock during the year. This can give an indication of slow-moving stocks, or how efficient the stock control policy of the company is.
Investing activities	Investing activities are the acquisition and disposal of long-term assets and other investments not included in cash equivalents.
Investment property	Investment property is property (land or a building or part of a building, or both) held (by the owner or by the lessee under a finance lease) to earn rentals or for capital appreciation, or both.
Joint venture	This is where one company has a stake in another company and shares control jointly with others (venturers), through some contractual arrangement.
Lease	A lease is an agreement whereby the lessor conveys to the lessee in return for a payment, or series of payments, the right to use an asset for an agreed period of time.
Lease payments	See *Operating leases (lease payments)*.
Lease term	The lease term is the non-cancellable period for which the lessee has contracted to lease the asset, together with any further terms for which the lessee has the option to continue to lease the asset when at the inception of the lease it is reasonably certain that the lessee will exercise the option.
Liability	A liability is a present obligation of the enterprise arising from past events, the settlement of which is expected to result in an outflow from the enterprise of resources embodying economic benefits.
Limited liability company	A limited liability company is a company where the liability of the owners is limited to the amount of share capital subscribed for.
Liquidity ratio	The liquidity ratio, sometimes called the 'acid test' or 'quick ratio', is a refinement of the current ratio. It measures the extent to which a company can meet its short-term obligations.
Liquidity risk	The risk that an entity will encounter difficulty in meeting obligations associated with financial liabilities.
Local currency	The currency in which the foreign company measures and records its transactions.
Market risk	The risk that the fair value or future cash flows of a financial instrument will fluctuate due to changes in market prices.
Minimum lease payments	Minimum lease payments are the payments over the lease term that the lessee is required to make.
Minority interest	The proportion of a subsidiary not owned by the parent company. This minority interest is accounted for and shown separately in the group balance sheet.
Monetary items	These are usually items such as cash, accounts payable and receivable, bank overdrafts and loans.
Net investment in the lease	Net investment in the lease is the gross investment in the lease discounted at the interest rate implicit in the lease.

Net profit margin	A ratio that expresses profit before interest and tax (PBIT) as a percentage of sales. It shows how much profit is generated from sales.
Net realisable value	Net realisable value is the estimated selling price in the ordinary course of business less the estimated costs of completion and the estimated costs necessary to make the sale.
Nominal value	The nominal value is the amount stated on the face of a share certificate as the named value of the share when issued.
Non-current asset (fixed asset)	Any asset that does not meet the definition of a current asset. Also described as a fixed asset.
Non-current (long-term) liability	A non-current or long-term liability is a liability that does not meet the definition of a current liability.
Non-distributable reserves	Non-distributable reserves are reserves that cannot be distributed to shareholders (e.g. revaluation reserve, share premium account, capital redemption reserve).
Non-monetary items	These usually comprise long- and short-term assets such as inventory, property, plant and equipment.
Operating activities	Operating activities are the principal revenue-producing activities of the entity and other activities that are not investing or financing activities.
Operating lease	An operating lease is a lease other than a finance lease. The underlying substance of the transaction is a rental arrangement.
Operating leases (lease payments)	Lease payments under an operating lease shall be recognised as an expense on a straight line basis over the lease term unless another systematic basis is more representative of the time pattern of the user's benefit.
Ordinary shares	Ordinary shares are shares in a company that entitle the holder to a share of the dividend declared and a share in the net assets on a winding-up of the business.
Payment period for payables (period taken)	This ratio calculates how many days' credit the business is taking from suppliers.
Permanent capital	Permanent capital comprises share capital plus non-distributable reserves.
Pre-acquisition profits and reserves	These are profits and reserves that were in existence at the time the subsidiary was acquired. Such profits and reserves cannot be shown as part of the group reserves, and are capitalised as part of the cost of control.
Preference shares	Preference shares entitle to the holders to preferential treatment in that they are entitled to a dividend before the ordinary shareholders. In general terms, the preference dividend is usually a fixed percentage.
Presentation currency	The currency in which the financial statements of a company are presented.
Price/earnings ratio (PER)	This ratio is a measure of how the stock market rates the company. It indicates how many times' the earnings an investor is prepared to pay to buy a share.
Private and public companies	A private company ends its name with 'Limited' or 'Ltd'. Private companies will have a few shareholders and cannot offer their shares for sale on the stock exchange. A public company has 'plc' after its name. Such a company can offer shares for sale to the general public.

Profit vs cash flow	The making of a profit does not necessarily result in an increased bank balance. Profit deals with revenues earned and expenses incurred, while cash flow is concerned with cash received and cash paid.
Property, plant and equipment	Property, plant and equipment are tangible assets that are held for use rather than realisation, and are intended to provide services or generate revenues over future accounting periods.
Provision	A provision is a liability of uncertain timing or amount.
Qualifying asset	A qualifying asset is an asset that necessarily takes a substantial period of time to get ready for its intended use or sale.
Ratio analysis	Describes the relationship between two different accounting numbers taken from the financial statements.
Recognised	An item is recognised when it is included by means of words and amount within the main financial statements of an entity.
Recognition of asset	Items of property, plant and equipment should be recognised as assets when it is probable that: (a) the future economic benefits associated with the asset will flow to the enterprise; and (b) the cost of the asset can be measured reliably.
Recognition of liability	A liability is recognised in the balance sheet when: (a) it is probable that an outflow of resources embodying economic benefits will result from the settlement of a present obligation; and (b) the amount at which the settlement will take place can be measured reliably.
Recoverable amount	Recoverable amount is the higher of an asset's net selling price and its value in use.
Research	Research is original and planned investigation undertaken with the prospect of gaining new specific or technical knowledge and understanding.
Reserves	Reserves represent the claims that the owners have on the assets of a company because the company has created new wealth for them over the period since it began.
Residual value	The estimated amount that an entity would currently obtain from disposal of the asset, after deducting the estimated cost of disposal, if the asset were already of the age and in the condition expected at the end of its useful life.
Restructurings	A restructuring is a programme that is planned and controlled by management and materially changes either: (a) the scope of a business undertaken by an entity; or (b) the manner in which that business is conducted.
Retained earnings	These are the profits after tax (less any losses), which the company keeps within the business. These profits have not been paid out by way of dividend nor transferred to any other reserve. A company can choose to use some of these retained earnings to pay any future dividends.
Return on capital employed (ROCE)	A ratio that measures the return made by the organisation from using its capital resources. This is sometimes referred to as the primary ratio and gives an indication of how efficient the organisation is at generating profits from its capital.
Return on shareholders' capital (ROSC)	A ratio that is similar in nature to ROCE, but considers the profit made by the company in relation to the capital contributed by shareholders.

Revaluation reserve	Some non-current (fixed) assets may have been purchased several years ago and have risen in value over time. When this increase in value is recorded, it is put into the revaluation reserve.
Share capital	Share capital is the nominal value of shares either authorised by a company or actually issued to the members.
Share premium	The share premium is the excess of issue price over nominal value.
Shareholders	These are the owners of the shares and are entitled to receive a share of the profit of the company.
Statement of changes in equity	IAS 1 requires a company to present a statement of changes in equity as a separate component of the financial statement. The statement reconciles the capital and reserves at the beginning of the period with those at the end.
Statement of comprehensive income	IAS 1 sets out the minimum information to be presented on the face of the income statement. The statement will include all items of income and expense recognised in a period. The information may be presented in: (a) a single statement; (b) two statements – displaying the components of profit or loss.
Subsidiary company	This is where one company has a substantial stake in another company, such that total control over the operating and financial policies can be exerted thus giving 'dominant influence' over the other company.
Tax base	The tax base of an asset or liability is the amount attributed to that asset or liability for tax purposes.
Taxable profit	Taxable profit (tax loss) is the profit (loss) for a period, determined in accordance with the rules established by the taxation authorities, upon which income taxes are payable (recoverable).
Taxable temporary differences	Taxable temporary differences are temporary differences that will result in taxable amounts in determining taxable profit (tax loss) of future periods when the carrying amount of the asset or liability is recovered or settled.
Temporal method	This is the method used to translate into the *functional currency*. It is used when the subsidiary company is seen as an extension of the parent company. All monetary items are translated at the rate of exchange ruling at the balance sheet date. All non-monetary assets are translated at the rate ruling when the transaction was undertaken. All income statement items are translated at the average rate. Any exchange gain or loss is taken to the income statement.
Temporary differences	Temporary differences are differences between the carrying amount of an asset or liability in the balance sheet and its tax base.
Transaction	A transaction is an agreement to purchase or sell goods or services on credit or for cash. A transaction results in a decrease in the finances of the purchaser and an increase in the benefits of the sellers. In terms of foreign currency transactions, the buyer and the seller will usually be in different countries, using different currencies.
Translation	The process of converting an amount from one currency to another. For example, US$15 translates (converts) to £10 when the exchange rate is £1 = US$1.5.
Translation reserve	The specific reserve to which any exchange difference is put.

Treasury shares	Treasury shares are an entity's own shares that have been purchased by the entity and held for sale at some future date.
Useful life	Useful life is the period over which an asset is expected to be available for use by an entity, or the number of production or similar units expected to be obtained from the asset by an entity.
Value in use	Value in use is the present value of the future cash flows expected to be derived from an asset or cash generating unit.
Vertical analysis	This is done by equating the totals in a financial statement to 100 and then expressing the other figures as a percentage of the total and so produce a 'common size' statement.
Z-score	A score developed by applying a specific weight to a number of accounting ratios. The resulting figure is called the Z-score and is used to predict the health of a company.

Index